STUDENT TESTED, FACU

MW01226740

THE ACCT SOLUTION

Every 4LTR Press solution includes:

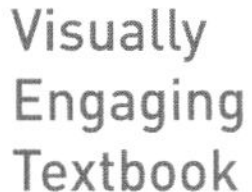

Visually Engaging Textbook

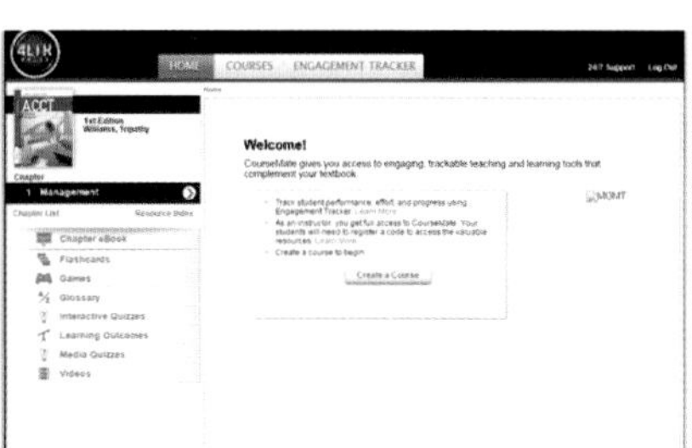

Online Study Tools

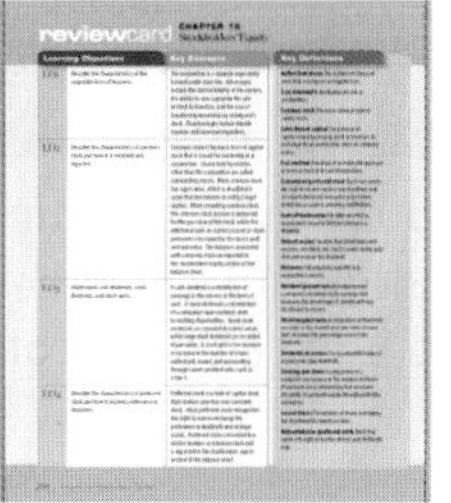

Review Pages

Stock Dividends

While cash dividends are by far the most common type of dividend, some companies distribute stock dividends. A **stock dividend** is a distribution of a company's common stock to existing stockholders. Stock dividends are declared by a company's board of directors and are usually stated in percentage terms. For example, a 10% stock dividend means that the company will issue additional shares equal to 10% of the current out-

Heading Numbers Connect Print & eBook

Interactive eBook

STUDENT RESOURCES:

- Interactive eBook
- Interactive Quizzes
- Flashcards
- Games
- Videos

INSTRUCTOR RESOURCES:

- All Student Resources
- Engagement Tracker
- LMS Integration
- Solutions Manual
- PowerPoint® Slides

Students sign in at www.cengagebrain.com

Instructors sign in at www.cengage.com/login

THE  PROCESS

Like all 4LTR Press solutions, FINANCIAL ACCT, 2e begins and ends with student and faculty feedback. For the Financial Accounting course, here's the process we used:

CONTINUOUSLY IMPROVING

Conduct research with students on their challenges and learning preferences.

With the average introductory accounting textbook having more than 800 pages, students expressed it was challenging to quickly manage and prioritize the important information. They understood the need to find relevant content, fast.

SHOW

Develop the ideal product mix with students to address each course's needs.

With an average of 20 pages per chapter, Financial ACCT, 2e's efficient presentation and crisp writing style makes need-to-know content accessible. Key formulas are highlighted and Revie sections are included for quick studying. Digital tools provide a wealth of learning aids, such a eBook, games, quizzes and more.

TEST

Share student feedback and validate product mix with faculty.

Financial ACCT, 2e with accompanying online resources is a unified print and digital solution validated by thousands of instructors. Further, the text's infusion of real world examples from companies like Asian Paints and Maruti Suzuki give students realistic picture of accounting's role in business today.

Publish, a Student-Tested, Faculty-Approved solution.

By making accounting accessible and relevent to students both print and online. Financial ACCT, 2e efficiently addresses student and faculty needs in one, price conscious package.

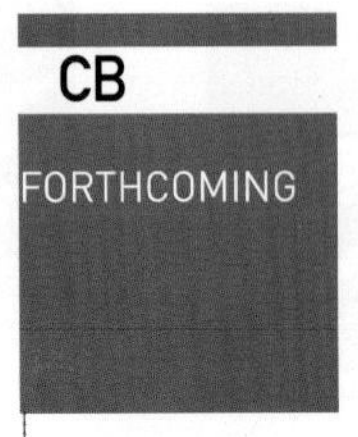

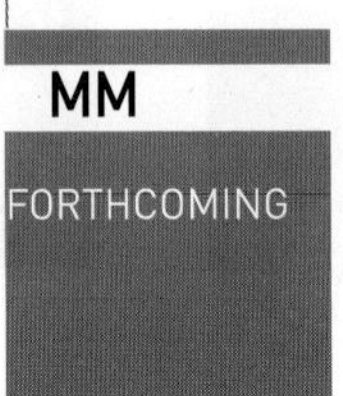

SELL

FORTHCOMING

GLOBAL

FORTHCOMING

2e

FINANCIAL ACCT

A South-Asian Perspective

Norman H. Godwin
Auburn University

C. Wayne Alderman
Auburn University

Debashis Sanyal
School of Business Management,
Narsee Monjee Institute of Management Studies,
Mumbai

Andover • Melbourne • Mexico City • Stamford, CT • Toronto • Hong Kong • New Delhi • Seoul • Singapore • Tokyo

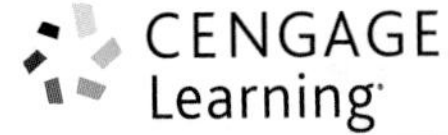

Financial ACCT
2e

Norman H. Godwin
C. Wayne Alderman
Debashis Sanyal

Cover Image: ©iStock/Thinkstock

Financial ACCT, SE Package

This edition is adapted by license from South-Western Cengage Learning, for sale in India, Pakistan, Bangladesh, Nepal and Sri Lanka only.

ISBN-13: 978-81-315-2024-6
ISBN-10: 81-315-2024-2

Cengage Learning Pvt. Ltd
418, F.I.E., Patparganj
Delhi 110092

Cengage Learning is a leading provider of customized learning solutions with office locations around the globe, including Andover, Melbourne, Mexico City, Stamford (CT), Toronto, Hong Kong, New Delhi, Seoul, Singapore, Tokyo. Locate your local office at: **www.cengage.com/global**

Cengage Learning products are represented in Canada by Nelson Education, Ltd.

For product information, visit **www.cengage.co.in**

Printed in India

Preface

4LTR Press, a Cengage Learning product, is a widely acclaimed concept of learning with a simple approach—creating an innovative teaching and learning solution built around today's learners and teachers. The idea behind bringing out this series of books is to introduce students and teachers in South Asia to an innovative concept in management studies. Since the launch, 4LTR Press has helped more than 1,800,000 college students at over 2,000 schools succeed worldwide. Every book in the series is built on the findings based on the inputs from discipline-specific focus groups, conversations, and surveys.

The books in this series present visually engaging page layouts and succinct yet thorough topical coverage and are designed from the ground up to meet the needs of teachers and students. These books help increase students' classroom engagement and improve learning outcomes.

The books address a number of concerns, including the reality of the reading habits of the majority of today's students. 4LTR Press offers information in the formats students find engaging, while still providing the high-quality content instructors need. The chapters in these books are short and understandable. The text is easier to pay attention to, and the books are actually enjoyable to read. Everything is much more inviting than a regular textbook. The review cards at the end of each chapter serve a unique purpose: Students first go through the review card to preview the new concepts, then they read the chapter to understand the material, and finally they go through the review card again to make sure they have registered the key concepts.

We are sure that this series, a first of its kind in the South Asian market, will revolutionize the way students approach and become familiar with the concepts of management.

© HAMERA/THINKSTOCK

ACCT

Brief Contents

Contents

© ISTOCKPHOTO.COM/SEAN LOCKE

SALES GROWTH

© ISTOCKPHOTO.COM/ANDREW RICH

©HEMERA/THINKSTOCK

7 Inventory 166

8 Fixed Assets and Intangible Assets 198

© STOCKBYTE/THINKSTOCK

comprehensive chart of accounts

Assets

- Cash
- Petty cash
- Accounts receivable
- Allowance for bad debts
- Fuel
- Interest receivable
- Inventories/Inventory
- Supplies
- Office supplies
- Prepaid insurance
- Prepaid rent
- Notes receivable
- Other current assets
- Short-term investments
- Long-term investments
- Property, plant and equipment
- Land
- Buildings
- Accumulated depreciation—buildings
- Equipment
- Accumulated depreciation—equipment
- Studio equipment
- Accumulated depreciation—studio equipment
- Automobiles
- Accumulated depreciation—automobiles
- Truck
- Accumulated depreciation—truck
- Delivery Van
- Accumulated depreciation—delivery van
- Boat
- Computers
- Gas can
- Lawn mower
- Patents
- Other assets

Liabilities

- Accounts payable
- Bond interest payable
- Dividends payable
- Dividends payable—common stock
- Dividends payable—preferred stock
- Federal income tax payable
- FICA taxes payable
- Interest payable
- Income tax payable
- Notes payable-short-term
- Salaries payable
- Sales tax payable
- State income tax payable
- Utilities Payable
- Unearned revenue
- Unearned service revenue
- Bonds payable
- Discount on bonds payable
- Premium on bonds payable
- Mortgage payable
- Notes payable—long-term

Equity

- Capital stock
- Common stock
- Common Stock to be Distributed
- Additional paid in capital
- Additional paid in capital—Treasury stock
- Preferred stock
- Retained earnings
- Dividends
- Treasury stock

Revenues

- Sales
- Sales discounts
- Sales returns and allowances
- Revenue
- Service revenue
- Interest revenue
- Bowling revenue
- Gain on disposal

Expenses

- Cost of sales
- Cost of goods sold
- Administrative expenses
- Advertising expense
- Bad debt expense
- Cash over and short
- Commission expense
- Depreciation expense
- Depreciation expense—building
- Depreciation expense—truck
- Freight-in/transportation-in
- Fuel expense
- Gain on redemption of bonds
- General and administrative expenses
- Income tax expense
- Insurance expense
- Interest expense
- Loss on disposal
- Loss on redemption of bonds
- Miscellaneous expense
- Operating expenses
- Operating permit expense
- Payroll tax expense
- Permit expense
- Postage expense
- Purchases
- Rent expense
- Salaries expense
- Selling expenses
- Service charge expense
- Supplies expense
- Utilities expense

*Note: Cost of sales and cost of goods sold are listed first since they are used to compute gross profit.

ACCT

Financial Accounting

Introduction

Imagine for a moment that you were at home for the summer and decided to start a business with your mother, a housewife, to sew ladies garments and sell them in the neighborhood. With mother's contribution of ₹9,000 and a bank loan of ₹20,000 you purchased a peddle sewing machine for ₹21,000, cloth lengths and the material for ₹8,000. During May and June, you were able to sell finished goods amounting to ₹16,000. At the end of June, you had raw material ₹1,500 in stock, cash balance ₹14,000, interest due ₹500 and ₹2,000 to be received for garments sold on credit.

Given this information, can you tell what happened to your business in May and June? Were you profitable? What do you have to show for your efforts? How can you tell? Getting answers to such questions requires accounting.

Accounting is the process of identifying, measuring, and communicating economic information to permit informed judgments and decisions. Put more simply, accounting is the "language of business." When you want to know about the financial results of a business, you must understand and speak accounting. The purpose of this book is to teach you this language.

With this overall purpose in mind, the current chapter introduces the basic terms, principles and rules that comprise the grammar of the accounting language. It does so by creating the June financial statements of the garment business for the first two months described above. At the end of the chapter, you should be familiar with the four main financial statements of accounting. You should also have a working accounting vocabulary that can be built upon in the following chapters.

Learning Objectives

After studying the material in this chapter, you should be able to:

LO1 Describe the four assumptions made when communicating accounting information.

LO2 Describe the purpose and structure of an income statement and the terms and principles used to create it.

LO3 Describe the purpose and structure of a balance sheet and the terms and principles used to create it.

LO4 Describe the purpose and structure of a statement of retained earnings and how it links the income statement and the balance sheet.

LO5 Describe the purpose and structure of a statement of cash flows and the terms and principles used to create it.

LO6 Describe the qualitative characteristics that make accounting information useful.

LO7 Describe the conceptual framework of accounting.

LO1 Beginning Assumptions

The purpose of accounting is to identify, measure, and communicate economic information about a particular entity to interested users. As a foundation for accomplishing this purpose, accountants make the following four assumptions: economic entity, time period, monetary unit, and going concern.

Accounting The process of identifying, measuring, and communicating economic information to permit informed judgments and decisions.

Accounting, the "language of business," would describe this picture as a lady using an asset (the sewing machine) to generate a revenue (the money she will be paid).

Economic Entity Assumption

The **economic entity assumption** states that the financial activities of a business can be separated from the financial activities of the business's owner(s). This assumption allows a user to examine a company's accounting information without concern that the information includes the personal affairs of the owner(s). For the garment business example in the introduction, this means that personal activities such as buying material for your personal use should not be included with business activities such as buying

Economic entity assumption Accountants assume that the financial activities of a business can be separated from the financial activities of the business's owner(s).

MAKING IT REAL

After conducting its 2008 audit of General Motors Corporation, the public accounting firm Deloitte & Touche LLP wrote the following in its auditor's report:

© AP IMAGES/DAVID ZALUBOWSKI

"[General Motors'] recurring losses from operations, stockholders' deficit, and inability to generate sufficient cash flow to meet its obligations and sustain its operations raise substantial doubt about its ability to continue as a going concern."

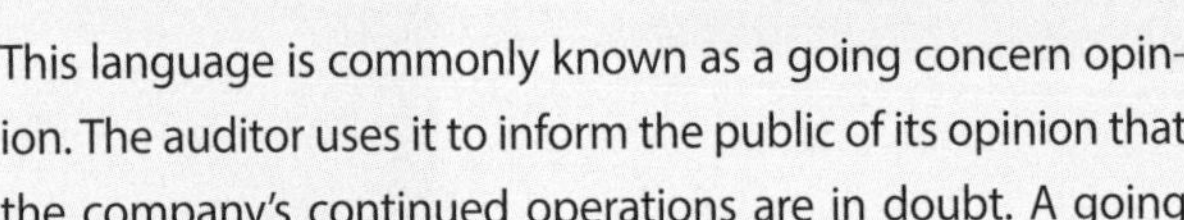

This language is commonly known as a going concern opinion. The auditor uses it to inform the public of its opinion that the company's continued operations are in doubt. A going concern opinion does not always mean that the company will cease operations. But it does mean that there is significant doubt that the company will continue without significant changes. In the case of General Motors, those significant changes came on June 1, 2009, when the company filed for Chapter 11 bankruptcy protection.

Going concern opinions are designed to protect a company's stakeholders and allow them to make decisions with the most accurate information available. In General Motors' situation, the going concern opinion accurately predicted the future and gave external users an early warning of the likely bankruptcy.

materials for the garment business. These activities can and should be accounted for separately.

Time Period Assumption

Business owners and other interested parties usually do not want to wait long before they receive information about how a business is doing. They want periodic measurements of the business's success or failure. Accountants therefore assume that economic information can be meaningfully captured and communicated over short periods of time, even if those time periods are somewhat artificial, such as one month or one quarter. This is known as the **time period assumption**.

Most companies communicate to users on both a quarterly and annual basis. In fact, publicly traded companies such as Maruti Suzuki India Limited are required by law to file quarterly and annual financial statements with the Securities and Exchange Board of India (SEBI). For the garment business example, the time period for preparing the financial statements are two months, May and June.

Time period assumption Accountants assume that economic information can be meaningfully captured and communicated over short periods of time.

Monetary unit assumption Accountants assume that the dollar is the most effective means to communicate economic activity.

Going concern assumption Accountants assume that a company will continue to operate into the foreseeable future.

Monetary Unit Assumption

The **monetary unit assumption** assumes that the rupee is the most effective means to communicate economic activity. If an economic activity cannot be expressed in rupees, then it is not recorded in the accounting system. It assumes further that the rupee is reasonably stable with respect to inflation and deflation. As a result, accountants do not adjust economic values based on inflation or deflation. A rupee earned in 1980 is the same as a rupee earned in 2014.

Going Concern Assumption

The **going concern assumption** states that a company will continue to operate into the foreseeable future. This assumption enables accountants to use certain techniques that will be described later in the chapter. Unless there is evidence to the contrary, most companies are assumed to be going concerns. Those that are not going

MARUTI SUZUKI ANALYSIS

On Maruti Suzuki's income statement, in Appendix C, you can find the following four descriptions: 1) Maruti Suzuki India Limited, 2) amounts in millions, 3) Fiscal Year Ended March 31, 2013. Which assumption does each description best relate?

1) economic entity, 2) monetary unit, 3) time period

concerns are often in the process of liquidation (that is, selling their resources and paying off their obligations). Because the garment business will continue through the summer, it is a going concern at the end of June.

LO2 Reporting Profitability: The Income Statement

One of the first questions asked of any business is whether it makes money. Stated differently in "accounting" words, is the business profitable? Does it generate more resources than it uses? Accounting provides answers to these questions with a financial statement called an *income statement*. An income statement reports a company's *revenues* and *expenses*.

Revenues

A **revenue** is an increase in resources resulting from the sale of goods or the provision of services. Receiving ₹500 from selling a garment is an example of a revenue. You have ₹500 more than you did previously because you have sold a garment. Other revenue common to businesses is investment income.

Revenues are recorded according to the revenue recognition principle. The **revenue recognition principle** states that a revenue should be recorded when a resource has been earned. A resource is earned when either the sale of the good or the provision of the service is substantially complete and collection is reasonably assured.

Given these definitions, total May and June revenues for the business are as follows. You have only one source of revenue—receipt from sale of garments. Assuming that your customers will pay, for the garments you sell creates a revenue each time a piece of garment is sold. So, if you sold 32 pieces of garments at ₹500 each, revenue total ₹16,000 for the two months. Of those revenues, you have received payment for all except ₹2,000.

Expenses

An **expense** is a decrease in resources resulting from the sale of goods or provision of services. The materials consumed for making garments is an example of an expense. Other expenses common to businesses are wages, taxes, advertising, and utilities.

Expenses are recorded according to the matching principle. The **matching principle** states that expenses should be recorded in the period resources are used to generate revenues. For example, interest on loan used for the business in May and June, will be included as interest cost for the months of May–June.

Given these definitions, total May-June expenses for the garment business are as follows. Unlike the revenue side, the garment business has three sources of expenses. The first is fairly clear—material. The amount of material used during May–June can be calculated as follows from the given information:

+ Amount purchased during May–June	₹8,000
− Amount on hand on June 30	1,500
Amount used during June	₹6,500

Therefore, expenses on materials for the period May–June is ₹6,500.

Revenue An increase in resources resulting from the sale of goods or the provision of services.

Revenue recognition principle The principle that a revenue should be recorded when a resource has been earned.

Expense A decrease in resources resulting from the sale of goods or provision of services.

Matching principle The principle that expenses should be recorded in the period resources are used to generate revenues.

The second expense relates to your borrowing. You have ₹500 due to pay to the bank at the end of June to compensate for loaning ₹20,000 from bank. Paying for the use of someone else's money is called interest. Therefore, interest expense is ₹500.

The third expense relates to your equipment—the sewing machine. Because this equipment was used in May–June to generate revenues, the matching principle requires that some portion of the equipment's cost be expensed in June. This is called depreciation expense. Chapter 8 will discuss the various methods for calculating depreciation expense, but for now we will keep things simple. Assuming that the equipment will be used for 24 months, it is reasonable to expense the equipment's cost each month. This equals ₹1,750 for the sewing machine (₹21,000/24 months × 2). Therefore, depreciation expense for the period May–June is ₹1,750.

The Income Statement

Once a company's revenues and expenses are calculated, they are reported on an income statement. An **income statement** is a financial statement that shows a company's revenues and expenses over a specific period of time. Its purpose is to demonstrate the financial success or failure of the company over that specific period of time. When revenues exceed expenses, a company generates net income. When expenses exceed revenues, a company generates a net loss. The basic structure of the statement is as follows:

Revenues − Expenses = Net Income or Net Loss

Given the revenues and expenses determined previously, the garment business's May–June income statement would appear as Exhibit 1-1. It contains the company name, the statement name, and the time reference, which for this example is the months of May–June. It also shows that the garment business generated ₹7,250 of net income during May–June.

Income statement A financial statement that reports a company's revenues and expenses over a specific period of time.

The income statement's purpose is to demonstrate the financial success or failure of the company over a specific period of time.

Exhibit 1-1 Income Statement for Garment Business, Inc.

Garment Business, Inc
Income Statement
For the Two Months Period Ending June 30

Revenues		₹16,000
Expenses:		
Material	₹6,500	
Interest	500	
Depreciation	1,750	
Total expenses		8,750
Net income		₹7,250

MARUTI SUZUKI ANALYSIS

Look at Maruti Suzuki's income statement in Appendix C. The statement contains three revenues and list of expenses. Can you identify them? What was the company's net income for the most current year?

Revenues: net sales from product, other operating revenue (note 25), other income (note 26)

Expenses: Cost of material consumed, purchase of stock-in-trade, change in inventories, employees benefit expenses, finance costs, depreciation and amortization expenses, other costs

Net income (called net earnings): ₹23,921 million

LO3 Reporting Financial Position: The Balance Sheet

Another important issue for any business is its current financial position. What does the business own? What does it owe? Accounting provides answers to these questions with a financial statement called a *balance sheet*. A balance sheet reports a company's *assets*, *liabilities*, and *equity*.

Assets

An asset is a resource of a business. More formally, an **asset** is an economic resource that is objectively measurable, that results from a prior transaction, and that will provide future economic benefit. Cash is a good example of an asset. It can be counted, it is received through a transaction with someone else, and it can be used to buy things in the future. Other common assets include merchandise inventory, equipment, supplies, and investments.

Assets are recorded and reported according to the historical cost principle, which is often shortened to the cost principle. The **cost principle** states that assets should be recorded and reported at the cost paid to acquire them.

Given these definitions, the garment business has several assets at the end of June—₹14,000 of cash, ₹1,500 of remaining raw material, and ₹2,000 of receivables from customers. It also has a sewing machine, but the value of those assets are calculated a little differently because they will be used over several periods. The sewing machine originally cost ₹21,000, but the matching principle required the expensing of ₹1,750 of that cost in May–June. As a result, the sewing machine's remaining cost is ₹19,250 (₹21,000 – 1,750). Again, Chapter 8 will discuss in much more detail the accounting for equipment.

Liabilities

A liability is an obligation of a business. More formally, a **liability** is an obligation of a business that results from a past transaction and will require the sacrifice of economic resources at some future date. Examples of liabilities common to businesses include notes payable to creditors, accounts payable to vendors, salaries payable to employees, and taxes payable to governments. The liabilities of garment business at the end of June are ₹21,000 borrowed from bank and ₹500 interest outstanding to the bank, who is considered a creditor. As will be explained below, the business does not have a liability for the ₹9,000 of your own money that was contributed to the company. You are an owner, not a creditor.

Equity

Equity is the difference between a company's assets and liabilities and represents the share of assets that are claimed by the company's owners. An example of equity with which you may be familiar is home equity. A homeowner's equity refers to the difference between the value of the home and the amount owed to the bank. Equity in accounting is the same principle except that it refers to the difference between the cost of the business's assets and its liabilities.

A company can generate equity in two ways. The first is through contributed capital. **Contributed capital** is defined as the resources that investors contribute to a business in exchange for an ownership interest. The ₹9000 that you, the owner, put into the garment business is contributed capital. Note here that contributed capital is not a revenue. The increase of ₹9,000 did not result from the garment business providing a service or selling a product. It came by selling an ownership interest. The most common method that companies use to generate contributed capital is the sale of common stock to investors.

The second way a company generates equity is through profitable operations. When a company generates net income, it can either distribute those profits to owners or retain them in the business to grow the business further. Profits that are distributed to owners

Asset An economic resource that is objectively measurable, results from a prior transaction, and will provide future economic benefit.

Cost principle The principle that assets should be recorded and reported at the cost paid to acquire them.

Liability An obligation of a business that results from a past transaction and will require the sacrifice of economic resources at some future date.

Equity The difference between a company's assets and liabilities, representing the share of assets that is claimed by the company's owners.

Contributed capital The resources that investors contribute to a business in exchange for ownership interest.

Because a balance sheet is reported at a specific point in time, it is often referred to as a snapshot of a business.

are called **dividends**. Note here that dividends are not an expense of a company. They are simply a distribution of company assets to owners. Profits that are retained in the business are called **retained earnings.** A company's retained earnings therefore represent the equity generated and retained from profitable operations. Since the garment business did not distribute any assets to you, the owner, it retained the entire ₹7,250 of June earnings.

The Balance Sheet

A company's assets, liabilities, and equity are reported on a balance sheet. A **balance sheet** is a financial statement that shows a company's assets, liabilities, and equity at a specific point in time. Its purpose is to show, at a given point in time, a company's resources and its claims against those resources. Because a balance sheet is reported at a specific point in time, it is often referred to as a snapshot of a business. The basic structure of the statement is as follows:

Assets = Liabilities + Equity

Given the assets, liabilities, and equity determined previously, the garment business balance sheet would appear as Exhibit 1-2. It contains the company name, the statement name, and the time reference, which for this example is June 30.

Notice that total assets equal total liabilities plus total equity. This will always be the case for any business. An entity's assets are always claimed by someone. Either they are owed to someone (in this case, your bank) or claimed by an owner (in this case, you). No asset of any business is ever unclaimed. This relationship between assets, liabilities, and equity is represented by the following equation, known as the fundamental accounting equation: **Assets = Liabilities + Equity**. This fundamental accounting equation is what the balance sheet reports. That is why it is called a *balance* sheet.

Dividends Profits that are distributed to owners.

Retained earnings Profits that are retained in the business.

Balance sheet A financial statement that reports a company's assets, liabilities, and equity at a specific point in time.

Exhibit 1-2 Balance Sheet for Garment Business, Inc.

Garment Business, Inc.
Balance Sheet
June 30

Cash	₹14,000	
Accounts receivable	2,000	
Raw material stock	1,500	
Sewing machine	19,250	
Total assets		36,750
Bank loan and interest due	₹20,500	
Total liabilities		₹20,500
Contributed capital	₹9,000	
Retained earnings	7,250	
Total equity		₹16,250
Total liabilities and equity		₹36,750

MARUTI SUZUKI ANALYSIS

Look at Maruti Suzuki balance sheet in Appendix C. Write out in numbers the company's accounting equation (A = L + E) for the most current year. How many different assets does the company disclose?

1) A = L + E: ₹266,880 million = ₹81,091 million + ₹185,789 million

2) Twelve different assets are listed on Maruti Suzuki's balance sheet.

LO4 Reporting Equity: The Statement of Retained Earnings

Owners of a business are usually interested in how their equity is growing as a result of profitable operations. They are also interested in how that equity is distributed in the form of dividends. Such information is reported on the statement of retained earnings. A **statement of retained earnings** shows the change in a company's retained earnings over a specific period of time. The basic structure of the statement is as follows:

Retained Earnings, Beginning Balance
+/− Net Income/Loss
− Dividends
= Retained Earnings, Ending Balance

The Garment Business's statement of retained earnings would appear as Exhibit 1-3. It contains the company name, the statement name, and the time reference, which for this example is the month of June.

Your business started with no retained earnings but generated net income of ₹7,250 during the period May–June. Since none of that income was distributed through dividends, the business retained all of those net assets. Therefore, retained earnings increased from ₹0 to ₹7,250.

Exhibit 1-3 Statement of Retained Earnings for Garment Business, Inc.

Garment Business, Inc.
Statement of Retained Earnings
For the Two Months Period Ending June 30

Retained earnings, May 1	₹0
+ Net income	7,250
- Dividends	0
Retained earnings, June 30	₹7,250

Linking the Income Statement and the Balance Sheet

In addition to showing the change in retained earnings, the statement of retained earnings links the income statement and the balance sheet. A company cannot calculate its retained earnings balance at the end of the period without factoring in the income earned during the period. The statement of retained earnings provides this link by including net income in the calculation of retained earnings, which is then reported on the balance sheet. This means that when preparing financial statements for any business, the income statement must be prepared first, followed by the statement of retained earnings and then the balance sheet. A graphical depiction of these links is included in Exhibit 1-4.

When preparing financial statements, the income statement must be prepared first, followed by the statement of retained earnings and then the balance sheet.

Exhibit 1-4 Relationship Among Financial Statements

Income Statement

Revenues	₹16,000
- Expenses	8,750
Net income	₹7,250

Statement of Retained Earnings

Retained earnings, May 1	₹0
+ Net income	7,250
- Dividends	0
Retained earnings, June 30	₹7,250

Balance Sheet

Total assets	₹36,750
Liabilities	₹20,500
Contributed capital	9,000
Retained earnings	7,250
Total liabilities and equity	₹36,750

Statement of retained earnings A financial statement that reports the change in a company's retained earnings over a specific period of time.

MARUTI SUZUKI ANALYSIS

Look at Maruti Suzuki's Balance Sheet equity in Appendix C. Which Note To The Financial Statements of the Annual Accounts contains the statement of retained earnings? For the most recent year presented, is the amount for net income the same as net income on the income statement? Is the balance in retained earnings the same as the balance on the balance sheet?

Note 3 – Reserve and Surplus contains the retained earning. The opening balance of retained earning is indicated in row 12. In the most recent year presented, the amount for net income is ₹23,921 million, which is the number shown on the income statement, (Profit and Loss Account) as Profit for the year and the balance in retained earnings is ₹1,84,279, which is the same balance shown on the balance sheet under Reserve and Surplus.

LO5 Reporting Cash Flows: The Statement of Cash Flows

Another important issue for any business is its management of cash. Where does a company get its cash? Where does its cash go? Will there be enough cash to pay bills? Accounting provides answers to these questions with a financial statement called a *statement of cash flows*. A statement of cash flows reports a company's cash inflows and outflows from its *operating*, *investing*, and *financing activities*.

Financing Activities

Most businesses must raise funds to begin. Borrowing money from creditors and receiving contributions from investors are both ways to finance a business's operations. Therefore, generating and repaying cash from creditors and investors are considered *financing activities*. In the garment business example, you contributed ₹9,000 of your own money and borrowed ₹20,000 from the bank. Both of these inflows are from financing activities. Therefore, the cash inflow in May from financing activities is ₹29,000.

Investing Activities

Once a company has raised sufficient capital from creditors and investors, it usually acquires the revenue-generating assets that it needs for operations. The buying and selling of such assets are considered *investing activities*. In the garment business example, you paid ₹21,000 for the sewing machine. Therefore, the cash flows from investing activities were –₹21,000. In other words, the garment business experienced a cash outflow of ₹21,000 in May from investing activities.

Statement of cash flows A financial statement that reports a company's sources and uses of cash over a specific period of time.

Operating Activities

After the proper equipment is acquired, a business can begin operations. Operating a business includes the purchase of supplies, the payment of employees, and the sale of products. These transactions are considered *operating activities*. In the garment business example, cash flows from operations in the months of May–June included ₹14,000 received from customers from sale of garments, ₹8,000 paid for materials. As a result, the net cash inflow from operating activities for the month was ₹6,000 (₹14,000 – ₹8,000). Since interest of ₹500 is due, but not paid it is not a cash flow item. Similarly, the amount of ₹2,000 yet to received from customers for sale of garments is not a cash inflow.

The Statement of Cash Flows

The details of cash inflows and outflows for a business are reported on a *statement of cash flows*. The **statement of cash flows** is a financial statement that shows a company's sources and uses of cash over a specific period of time. Its purpose is to inform users about how and why a company's cash changed during the period. The basic structure of the statement is as follows:

An important issue for any business is its management of cash. Where does a company get its cash? Where does its cash go? Will there be enough cash to pay bills?

Cash Flows Provided (Used) by Operating Activities
+/− Cash Flows Provided (Used) by Investing Activities
+/− Cash Flows Provided (Used) by Financing Activities
= Net Increase (Decrease) in Cash

Exhibit 1-5 Statement of Cash Flows for Garment Business, Inc

Garment Business, Inc.
Statement of Cash Flows
For the two Months period Ending June 30

Operating activities		
Cash received from customers	₹14,000	
Cash paid for materials	(8,000)	
Net cash provided by operating activities		₹6,000
Investing activities		
Cash paid for sewing machine	₹(21,000)	
Net cash used by investing activities		₹(21,000)
Financing activities		
Cash received from borrowing	₹20,000	
Cash received from contributions	9,000	
Net cash provided by financing activities		29,000
Net increase in cash		₹14,000
Cash balance, May 1		0
Cash balance, June 30		₹14,000

Given the cash inflows and outflows described previously, the garment business's June statement of cash flows would appear as Exhibit 1-5. It contains the company name, the statement name, and the time reference, which for this example is the months of May–June. It also shows a net change in cash from May 1 to June 30 of ₹14,000.

Note that the ending cash balance on the statement agrees with the cash balance shown on the balance sheet in Exhibit 1-2. Since ₹21,000 of the ₹29,000 of cash generated from financing activities was invested into the sewing machine, the majority of the ₹14,000 of cash on hand was generated through operations. This, of course, is a good sign and bodes well for your ability to generate enough cash in the future both to pay your banker and to keep for yourself.

LO6 Qualitative Characteristics of Accounting Information

Even though accounting is a very quantitative process and the financial statements introduced thus far are full of numbers, accounting information must possess certain qualitative characteristics to be considered useful. The following qualitative characteristics help ensure that accounting information is indeed useful.

Understandability

Accounting information should first and foremost be understandable. **Understandability** refers to the ability of accounting information to "be comprehensible to those who have a reasonable understanding of business...

Understandability The ability of accounting information to "be comprehensible to those who have a reasonable understanding of business...and are willing to study the information with reasonable diligence."

MARUTI SUZUKI ANALYSIS

Look at Maruti Suzuki's statement of cash flows in Appendix C. How much cash did Maruti Suzuki generate or use for operating, investing, and financing activities during the most recent year?

Operating Activities: Generated ₹43,842 million
Investing Activities: Used ₹(35,741) million
Financing Activities: Used ₹(9,663) million

and are willing to study the information with reasonable diligence" (SFAC No. 2, par. 40). Notice that this definition puts much of the responsibility on the user of accounting information. Users must be willing to spend a "reasonable" amount of time studying the information. No specifics are given on what is a "reasonable" amount of time, but it is obvious that the more time you spend studying accounting information, the more you will understand.

Relevance

Relevance refers to the capacity of accounting information to make a difference in decisions. Accounting information has this capacity when it possesses feedback value or predictive value. *Feedback value* refers to the ability to assess past performance, while *predictive value* refers to the ability to form expectations of future performance. In the garment business example, four financial statements were created to demonstrate the financial activities for May–June. The statements provided feedback on the success of the business, but they also provided the data to generate expectations about future. As a result, the financial statements are relevant to our decision making, which makes them useful.

In addition to having feedback or predictive value, accounting information must be *timely* to be relevant. Information that helps you forecast August revenues is relevant when it is received in July, not when it is received in September. Information is relevant only if it is generated on a timely basis.

Reliability

Reliability refers to the extent to which accounting information can be depended upon to represent what it purports to represent, both in description and in number. To be considered reliable, accounting information should be verifiable, should have representational faithfulness, and should be neutral.

Information is *verifiable* if it can be proven to be free from error. One can often prove that accounting information is free from error by comparing the information to an original source document such as an invoice or a contract. For example, the original cost of the sewing machine in your garment business is verifiable because you could check the cost against the amount included on the sales receipt. If the two agree, the information is free from error and you can depend on it.

Information has *representational faithfulness* when the description corresponds to the underlying phenomenon. For example, in your garment business, the sewing machine purchased can be reported as an asset in the balance sheet. This reporting was a faithful representation of what the item truly was—a resource.

Information is *neutral* if it is presented in a way that is unbiased toward or against the reporting entity. In other words, neutral information does not portray an entity in a more or less favorable light than the information requires. In the garment business example, income was reported to be ₹7,250, not more or less. The ₹7,250 figure was a neutral measure of the activities of the service.

Relevance The capacity of accounting information to make a difference in decisions.

Reliability The extent to which accounting information can be depended upon to represent what it purports to represent, both in description and in number.

Comparability The ability to use accounting information to compare or contrast the financial activities of different companies.

Consistency The ability to use accounting information to compare or contrast the financial activities of the same entity over time.

Comparability

Comparability refers to the ability to use accounting information to compare or contrast the financial activities of different companies. Being able to compare information across companies allows an entity to assess its market position within an industry, to gauge its success against a competitor, and/or to set future goals based on industry standards.

Comparability does not imply uniformity. Accounting rules allow for some discretion in the manner in which accounting is applied to economic phenomenon. As a result, two businesses with the same economic phenomenon could have different accounting information because they use different acceptable accounting methods. Because such differences in accounting methods are a challenge to comparability, accounting rules require that entities disclose the accounting methods that they use so that information can be more easily compared across entities. Usually, such methods are disclosed in the notes to the financial statements, which are discussed in Chapter 2.

Consistency

Consistency refers to the ability to use accounting information to compare or contrast the financial activities

Materiality thresholds vary across different companies and different settings.

© STOCKBYTE/THINKSTOCK

of the same entity over time. Consistency is obviously highest when an entity uses the same accounting methods year after year. In such a case, year-to-year comparisons can be very useful because they can reveal trends that help in generating expectations about future performance. However, entities sometimes change the manner in which they account for a particular economic event. Because such changes hinder consistency, accounting rules require that changes be disclosed by the company so that interested parties can assess the effect of the change. Such disclosures are usually found in the notes to the financial statements.

Materiality

Materiality is a concept that is closely related to relevance in that it refers to the threshold at which an item begins to affect decision making. Items meeting or exceeding the threshold are said to be material—that is, they are large enough to possibly affect decision making. Items below the threshold are said to be immaterial—that is, they are small enough that they will not affect decision making. The threshold varies across different companies and across different settings. As a company gets larger, its materiality threshold usually gets larger as well. Often, the materiality threshold is set at some percentage of assets or sales.

To see how materiality is applied, consider the following example from the garment business. When you purchased the sewing machine for ₹21,000, the matching principle required that its cost be spread out over its useful life of twenty four months. Suppose that instead of spreading out the cost, you expensed it entirely in the month it was purchased. Doing so would violate the matching principle and would result in ₹21,000 expense instead if ₹1,750 and would lower income by ₹19,250. Would such a violation affect your decision making about the service? Probably not. In other words, violation of the matching principle is immaterial because at times the amount may too small to affect your decision making.

While materiality is largely quantitative in nature, the materiality threshold is not always solely a function of rupee amounts. For example, an error of ₹1,000 in a routine transaction may be considered immaterial while a ₹1,000 error in a nonroutine transaction may be considered material. In addition, transactions that a company may consider immaterial may be considered material by users of the information. Materiality judgments are just that—judgments—and should be made with caution. Furthermore, just because something is immaterial does not mean that errors in accounting should be accepted and condoned. Accounting information must be reliable, so it should be free from error as much as possible.

Conservatism

Conservatism refers to the manner in which accountants deal with uncertainty regarding economic situations. When accountants are faced with uncertainty about how to account for or report a particular transaction or situation, conservatism dictates that they use the accounting that is least likely to overstate the company's assets and revenues or to understate the company's liabilities and expenses. A common example of conservatism in action is the lower-of-cost-or-market rule for inventory. According to this rule, inventory must be recorded and reported at the lower of its cost or its current market value. This ensures that the value of inventory is not overstated. Other applications of conservatism will be discussed in subsequent chapters.

Materiality The threshold at which a financial item begins to affect decision making.

Conservatism The manner in which accountants deal with uncertainty regarding economic situations.

LO7 The Conceptual Framework

This chapter introduced many of the terms, principles, assumptions, and qualitative characteristics that are necessary to communicate the financial activities and position of a business. While they were initially described as the grammar of the financial accounting language, they are more formally known as components of the conceptual framework of accounting. The **conceptual framework of accounting** is the collection of concepts that guide the manner in which accounting is practiced.

Conceptual framework of accounting The collection of concepts that guide the manner in which accounting is practiced.

The following tables summarize the elements of this conceptual framework. They will provide a good reference for you as you proceed through the remaining

Terms Used to Identify and Describe Economic Information

Term	Definition	Reported on the
Asset	A resource of a business	Balance sheet
Liability	An obligation of a business	Balance sheet
Equity	The difference between assets and liabilities	Balance sheet
Contributed capital	Equity resulting from contributions from owners	Balance sheet
Retained earnings	Equity resulting from profitable operations	Balance sheet and statement of retained earnings
Revenue	An increase in assets resulting from selling a good or providing a service	Income statement
Expense	A decrease in assets resulting from selling a good or providing a service	Income statement
Dividend	A distribution of profits to owners	Statement of retained earnings

Principles Used to Measure Economic Information

Principle	Definition	Ramification
Revenue recognition	Revenues are recorded when they are earned.	The receipt of cash is not required to record a revenue.
Matching	Expenses are recorded in the time period when they are incurred to generate revenues.	For many assets, the cost of the asset must be spread over the periods that it is used.
Cost	Assets are recorded and maintained at their historical costs.	Except in a few cases, market values are not used for reporting asset values.

Assumptions Made When Communicating Economic Information

Assumption	Definition	Ramification
Economic entity	The financial activities of a business can be accounted for separately from the business's owners.	We do not have to worry that the financial information of the owner is mixed with the financial information of the business.
Monetary unit	The rupee, unadjusted for inflation, is the best means of communicating accounting information in India.	All transactions in foreign currencies are converted to rupees.
Time period	Accounting information can be communicated effectively over short periods of time.	Most businesses prepare quarterly and annual financial statements.
Going concern	The company for which we are accounting will continue its operations indefinitely.	If an entity is not selling its assets, then the cost principle is appropriate.

chapters. As you tackle more complex accounting methods and procedures, keep in mind that they are simply extensions of the basic grammar presented in the tables. So, with a good understanding of the conceptual framework, you have the grammar necessary to begin your study of accounting.

Qualitative Characteristics that Make Accounting Information Useful

Term	Definition	Ramification
Understandability	Accounting information should be comprehensible by those willing to spend a reasonable amount of time studying it.	Users must spend a reasonable amount of time studying accounting information for it to be understandable.
Relevance	Accounting information should have the capacity to affect decisions.	Information should have predictive or feedback value and should be timely.
Reliability	Accounting information should be dependable to represent what it purports to represent.	Information should be free from error, a faithful representation, and neutral.
Comparability	Accounting information should be comparable across different companies.	Entities must disclose the accounting methods that they use so that comparisons across companies can be made.
Consistency	Accounting information should be comparable across different time periods within a company.	An entity should use the same accounting methods year to year and disclose when they change methods.
Materiality	The threshold over which an item could begin to affect decisions.	When an amount is small enough, normal accounting procedures are not always followed.
Conservatism	When uncertainty exists, accounting information should present the least optimistic alternative.	An entity should choose accounting techniques that guard against overstating revenues or assets.

Financial Statements Used to Communicate Economic Information

Statement	Purpose	Structure	Links to Other Statements
Balance sheet	Shows a company's assets, liabilities, and equity at a specific point in time	Assets = Liabilities + Equity	The balance in retained earnings comes from the statement of retained earnings. The balance in cash should agree with the ending cash balance on the statement of cash flows.
Income statement	Shows a company's revenues and expenses over a specific period of time	Revenue − Expenses = Net Income/Loss	Net income goes to the statement of retained earnings to compute retained earnings.
Statement of retained earnings	Shows the changes in a company's retained earnings over a specific period of time	Beginning Retained Earnings +/− Net Income/Loss − Dividends = Ending Retained Earnings	Ending retained earnings goes to the balance sheet.
Statement of cash flows	Shows a company's inflows and outflows of cash over a specific period of time	Operating Cash Flows +/− Investing Cash Flows +/− Financing Cash Flows = Net change in cash	The ending cash balance on the statement of cash flows should agree with the balance in cash on the balance sheet.

CONCEPT QUESTIONS

1. What is the definition of accounting?
2. What is the going concern assumption of accounting and why is it necessary for accounting?
3. What is the economic entity assumption of accounting and why is it important?
4. What two terms are used to determine and describe the profitability of an entity?
5. When are revenues recognized?
6. What does the matching principle state about the recording of revenues and expenses?
7. How are revenues different from assets?
8. What five terms are used to describe the financial position of an entity?
9. How are liabilities different from expenses?
10. Explain the difference between contributed capital and equity.
11. What are the three principles used in recording revenues, expenses, and assets?
12. How are assets recorded?
13. How are the balance sheet and income statement linked?
14. Explain why the different financial statements are used in accounting, and what purpose each statement serves.
15. What are the qualitative characteristics of accounting and why are they necessary to accounting information?
16. How are relevance and materiality related?
17. What is the conceptual framework of accounting and what purpose does it serve?

MULTIPLE CHOICE

1. Which of the following is not included in the definition of accounting?
   a. Identifying economic information
   b. Measuring economic information
   c. Developing economic information
   d. Communicating economic information
2. Which assumption states that an economic entity will continue its operations indefinitely?
   a. Monetary unit
   b. Time period
   c. Going concern
   d. Economic entity
3. Net income is created in a time period when:
   a. assets exceed liabilities.
   b. revenues exceed expenses.
   c. revenues are less than expenses.
   d. liabilities are greater than assets.
4. Which financial statement reports revenues and expenses?
   a. Statement of retained earnings
   b. Balance sheet
   c. Statement of cash flows
   d. Income statement
5. The revenue recognition principle states that:
   a. assets are recorded and maintained at their historical costs.
   b. revenues are recorded when they are earned.
   c. the dollar, unadjusted for inflation, is the best means of accounting in the U.S.
   d. revenues are recorded when cash is received.
6. During the year, Callie's Bagel Shop had revenues of ₹1,25,000. Rent expense was ₹12,000. Salaries expense was ₹25,000. Short-term investments were ₹35,000. Other expenses totaled ₹40,000. What was Callie's net income?
   a. ₹85,000
   b. ₹13,000
   c. ₹48,000
   d. ₹60,000
7. Which of the following accurately describes the matching principle?
   a. Matches assets and liabilities
   b. Matches income and dividends
   c. Matches retained earnings and income
   d. Matches revenues and expenses
8. The basic accounting equation states:
   a. assets and liabilities equal equity.
   b. assets equal liabilities plus equity.
   c. liabilities equal equity plus assets.
   d. revenues minus expenses equals net income.
9. Which financial statement reports assets, liabilities, and equity?
   a. Statement of cash flows
   b. Balance sheet
   c. Income statement
   d. Statement of retained earnings
10. Retained earnings is defined as:
    a. the difference between assets and liabilities.
    b. equity generated from profitable operations and retained in the business.
    c. a decrease in assets resulting from selling a good or providing a service.
    d. equity resulting from contributions from owners.
11. As of December 31, Lurie Company has assets of ₹18,400 and equity of ₹6,500. What are the liabilities for Lurie Company as of December 31?
    a. ₹24,900
    b. ₹11,900
    c. ₹14,200
    d. ₹8,600
12. Maker's Company had the following account totals: cash ₹25,000; inventory ₹15,000; accounts payable ₹15,000; retained earnings ₹25,000; equipment ₹80,000; investments ₹10,000; and other assets ₹40,000. What is Maker's total assets?
    a. ₹1,70,000
    b. ₹1,90,000
    c. ₹85,000
    d. ₹2,10,000

13. The statement of retained earnings links which two financial statements?
    a. The income statement and the balance sheet
    b. The balance sheet and the statement of cash flows
    c. The income statement and the statement of cash flows
    d. The statement of retained earnings does not link any statements
14. A company begins a period with a ₹5,000 retained earnings balance. The company generates ₹12,000 of revenues and ₹10,000 of expenses during the period and pays ₹1,000 of dividends. What is the retained earnings balance at the end of the period?
    a. ₹7,000
    b. ₹5,000
    c. ₹6,000
    d. ₹1,000
15. Which of the following is not one of the sections on the statement of cash flows?
    a. Investing activities
    b. Financing activities
    c. Operating activities
    d. Income activities
16. Which of the following is not a qualitative characteristic of accounting?
    a. Understandability
    b. Relevance
    c. Pertinence
    d. Consistency

BRIEF EXERCISES

1. Calculate Net Income

Ted's Typing Service generated ₹4,000 in revenue in the month of January. Salaries were ₹1,500 for the month, and supplies used were ₹200. Additionally, Ted's incurred ₹50 for advertising during the month.

Required
Calculate Ted's net income for the month of January.

2. Calculate Net Income

A manager of a small company has a goal of generating ₹13,000 in net income. He is confident that his expenses will be approximately ₹82,500.

Required
Calculate the amount of revenue the manager must generate to reach his goal.

3. Calculate Equity

A company reports assets of ₹10,000 and liabilities of ₹6,000.

Required
Calculate the company's equity.
Identify which principle relates to each statement.

4. Identify Accounting Principles

Each of the following statements is an application of the revenue recognition principle, the matching principle, or the cost principle.

1. A company records Equipment for the purchase price of ₹10,000 although the "suggested retail price" was ₹13,000.
2. A company receives ₹2,000 for a service to be performed but records only ₹1,000 as Service Revenue because it earned only half in the current period.
3. A company pays ₹6,000 for insurance but uses only ₹4,000 during the period. Therefore, it records only ₹4,000 as Insurance Expense.

5. Calculate Retained Earnings

At the beginning of the year, a company has retained earnings of ₹1,75,000. During the year, the company generates ₹1,10,000 of net income and distributes ₹10,000 in dividends.

Required
Calculate the company's retained earnings at year end.

6. Calculate Cash Flows

A company starts the year with ₹1,75,000 in cash. During the year, the company generates ₹6,80,000 from operations, uses ₹5,16,000 in investing activities, and uses ₹98,000 in financing activities.

Required
Calculate the company's cash at year end.

7. Identify Accounting Assumptions and Qualitative Characteristics

Consider the following independent scenarios:

1. Luigi's Pizza has been in business for 25 years. All of its operations are profitable, and the accountants believe that the company will operate into the foreseeable future.
2. A bank used the information presented in Tiger Auto's financial statements to determine if it should extend a ₹300,000 loan to Tiger. The information in the financial statements made a difference in the bank's lending decision.
3. Jim Furio, manager of Martha's Antiques, does not like to change accounting procedures because it hinders his ability to make year-to-year comparisons.
4. Lynn Hagood, owner of Jonesboro Animal Hospital, informs his accountant that he does not want to review any accounting issue that is smaller than 1% of net income.

Required
Identify the accounting assumption or qualitative characteristic that relates to each scenario.

EXERCISES

8. Principles and Assumptions

The following basic accounting principles and assumptions were discussed in the chapter:

- Economic entity
- Going concern
- Monetary unit
- Cost principle
- Time period

________ 1. Lester Company has a division in Germany. Before preparing the financial statements for the company and the foreign division, Lester translates the financial statements of its Germany division from the euro to Indian rupee.

________ 2. Matt enters into a partnership to start a bike shop with a friend. Each partner makes an initial cash investment of ₹8 lakh. Matt opens a checking account in the name of the company and transfers ₹8 lakh from his personal account into the new account.

________ 3. Dreamland Inc. has always prepared financial statements with a year-end of March 31. However, the company is going to sell stock to the public for the first time and is required by the SEC to give quarterly financial reports.

________ 4. Platt Corp. purchases a fifty acre plot of land to build the world's largest factory. The company recorded the property at the amount of cash given to acquire it.

________ 5. Lockbox Corp. is in its ninetieth year of business. The owner of the company is going to retire in two months and turn the company over to his son.

Required

Fill in the blank with the appropriate principle or assumption.

9. Identify Income Statement Accounts

The following accounts are taken from a company's financial statements:

1. Rent expense
2. Service revenue
3. Dividends
4. Interest revenue
5. Interest expense
6. Accounts receivable

Required

Indicate whether each account is a revenue (R), expense (E), or neither (N).

10. Accounting Terms

Consider the following information:

a. Accounts receivable
b. Salaries payable
c. Office supplies
d. Land
e. Contributed capital
f. Notes payable

Required

Indicate whether each of the above items is an asset (A), a liability (L), or part of equity (E).

11. Accounting Terms

Consider the following information:

Item	Appears On	Classified As
1. Salaries expense	________	________
2. Equipment	________	________
3. Cash	________	________
4. Accounts payable	________	________
5. Buildings	________	________
6. Contributed capital	________	________
7. Retained earnings	________	________
8. Interest revenue	________	________
9. Advertising expense	________	________

Required

Classify each of the items above according to (1) whether it appears on the income statement or balance sheet and (2) whether it is classified as a revenue, expense, asset, liability, or equity.

12. Accounting Terms

The following items were taken from the financial statements of Tiger Inc.:

a. Income tax expense
b. Interest expense
c. Service revenue
d. Accounts receivable
e. Retained earnings
f. Inventory
g. Accounts payable
h. Contributed capital
i. Dividends

Required

Identify whether each item would appear on the balance sheet, the income statement, or the statement of retained earnings.

13. Classify Cash Flows

A company entered into the following cash transactions:

1. Cash paid to suppliers
2. Cash received from issuing new common stock
3. Cash paid to purchase new office furniture
4. Cash paid in dividends to owners
5. Cash received from customers

Required

Indicate the section of the statement of cash flows in which each item would appear: operating activities (O), investing activities (I), or financing activities (F).

14. Accounting Terms

Consider the following information:

a. Revenues during the period
b. Supplies on hand at the end of the year
c. Cash received from borrowings during the year
d. Total liabilities at the end of the period
e. Dividends paid during the year
f. Cash paid for a building
g. Cost of buildings owned at year end

Required
Indicate whether you would find each of the above items on the income statement (IS), the balance sheet (BS), the statement of retained earnings (SRE), or the statement of cash flows (SCF).

15. Financial Statements

Listed below are questions posed by various users of a company's financial statements.

User	Questions	Financial Statement
Stockholder	How did this year's sales figures compare with last year's sales figures?	________
Banker	How much in borrowings does the company currently owe?	________
Supplier	How much does the company owe its suppliers in total?	________
Stockholder	Did the company have any dividends in the prior year?	________
Advertising agent	How much advertising did the company incur in order to generate sales?	________
Banker	What was the company's total interest cost last year?	________

Required
Fill in the blank with the financial statement(s) (income statement, balance sheet, statement of retained earnings, and/or statement of cash flows) the user would most likely use to find this information.

16. Net Income and Retained Earnings

Nova Corporation reports the following as of December 31:

Revenues	₹1,00,000
Beginning retained earnings	₹2,00,000
Expenses	₹8,00,000
Dividends	₹1,00,000

Required
Calculate net income and ending retained earnings for the year ending December 31.

17. Balance Sheet Equation

Consider the following information:

Assets	Liabilities	Equity
50,000	25,000	?
30,000	?	17,000
?	45,000	15,000
68,000	?	13,000
?	14,000	6,000

Required
Use the accounting equation to fill in the missing amounts.

18. Balance Sheet Equation

Consider the following information:

a. Jenkins Company starts the year with ₹5,00,000 in assets and ₹4,00,000 in liabilities. Net income for the year is ₹1,25,000, and no dividends are paid. How much is Jenkins' equity at the end of the year?
b. McCay Inc. doubles the amount of its assets from the beginning to the end of the year. At the end of the year, liabilities are ₹5,00,000, and equity is ₹3,00,000. What is the amount of McCay's assets at the beginning of the year?
c. During the year the liabilities of Hudson Corp. triple. At the beginning of the year, assets were ₹4,00,000, and equity was ₹2,00,000. What is the amount of liabilities at the end of the year?

Required
Use the accounting equation to answer each of the independent questions above.

19. Statement of Retained Earnings

War Eagle Company's retained earnings on January 1 is ₹2,45,800. The following information is available for the first two months of the year:

	January	February
Revenues	₹80,000	₹1,02,000
Expenses	85,000	80,000
Dividends	0	7,000

Required
Prepare a statement of retained earnings for the month ending February 28.

20. Statement of Cash Flows

The following information is for Pasture Corp.:

Cash received from customers	₹65,000
Cash received from lenders	20,000
Cash paid to suppliers	20,000
Cash paid for new equipment	50,000
Cash paid for dividends	4,000

Required
Indicate on what section of the statement of cash flows each item would appear and calculate Pasture's net change in cash.

21. Statement of Cash Flows

Dividend received
Dividend paid
Sale proceed from Fixed Assets
Profit from sale of Fixed Assets
Short Term Borrowing
Interest received

Required
Indicate on what section of the cash flow will the above appear.

22. Links Between Financial Statements

Below are incomplete financial statements for Sterling Inc.:

Balance Sheet	
Assets	
Cash	₹ 8,000
Inventory	22,000
Building	40,000
Total assets	₹70,000
Liabilities	
Accounts payable	₹7,000
Equity	
Contributed capital	(a)
Retained earnings	(b)
Total liabilities & equity	₹70,000

Income Statement	
Service revenue	₹90,000
Salaries expense	(c)
Utilities expense	20,000
Net income	₹ (d)

Statement of Retained Earnings	
Retained earnings, beginning balance	₹20,000
Net income	(e)
Dividends	10,000
Retained earnings, ending balance	₹60,000

Required

Calculate the missing amounts.

23. Complete Financial Statements

The following are incomplete financial statements for Mackabee Inc.:

Balance Sheet	
Assets	
Cash	₹ 60,000
Inventory	2,00,000
Building	(a)
Total assets	₹6,40,000
Liabilities	
Accounts payable	₹ 70,000
Equity	
Contributed capital	(b)
Retained earnings	(c)
Total liabilities and equity	₹6,40,000

Income Statement	
Service revenue	₹12,00,000
Salaries expense	7,00,000
Administrative expense	3,00,000
Net income	₹ (d)

Statement of Retained Earnings	
Beginning retained earnings	₹2,00,000
Net income	(e)
Dividends	(f)
Ending retained earnings	₹4,00,000

Required

Calculate the missing amounts.

24. Qualitative Characteristics

The following qualitative characteristics of accounting were discussed in the chapter:

- Consistency
- Relevance
- Understandability
- Comparability
- Conservatism
- Materiality
- Reliability

________ 1. The ability of accounting information to be comprehensible to those who have a reasonable understanding of business and are willing to study the information with reasonable diligence.

________ 2. The capacity to affect business decisions.

________ 3. The dependability of accounting information.

________ 4. The ability to compare and contrast the financial activities of the same company over a period of time.

________ 5. The threshold over which an item begins to affect decision making.

________ 6. The way in which accountants deal with uncertainty.

________ 7. The ability to compare and contrast the financial activities of different companies.

Required

Fill in the blank with the appropriate characteristic.

25. Assumptions and Principles

Harbor Corp. had the following situations during the year:

a. Inventory with a cost of ₹1,86,400 is reported at its market value of ₹2,35,600.

b. Harbor added four additional weeks to its fiscal year so that it could make its income look stronger. Past years were 52 weeks.

c. Harbor's CEO purchased a yacht for personal use and charged it to the company.

d. Revenues of ₹25,000 earned in the prior year were recorded in the current year.

Required

In each situation, identify the assumption or principle that has been violated and discuss how Harbor should have handled the situation.

PROBLEMS

26. Prepare Financial Statements

This information relates to York Inc. for the year:

Advertising expense	₹ 24,000
Dividends paid	70,000
Rent expense	1,04,000
Retained earnings, January 1	5,70,000
Salaries expense	2,80,000
Service revenue	6,10,000
Utilities expense	18,000

Required
Prepare an income statement and a statement of retained earnings for the year.

27. Prepare Financial Statements

The following items are available from the records of Honky Tonk Records Inc. at the end of the year:

Accounts payable	₹2,70,000
Accounts receivable	2,10,000
Advertising expense	60,000
Buildings	7,60,000
Contributed capital	3,00,000
Cash	63,200
Notes payable	7,00,000
Salaries expense	95,000
Service revenue	1,68,200
Equipment	2,50,000

Required
Prepare Honky Tonk's income statement and statement of retained earnings for the year and its balance sheet at the end of the year.

28. Identify and Correct Income Statement Errors

Muncie Group was organized on January 1. At the end of the year, the company used a first-year accounting student to prepare the following income statement:

Muncie Group
Income Statement
December 31

Income from services		₹17,00,000
Accounts receivable		4,00,000
Total income		₹21,00,000
Less: Expenses		
Salaries	₹ 5,70,000	
Advertising	(1,40,000)	
Dividends	1,00,000	
Utilities	2,20,000	
Total expenses		₹ 7,50,000
Net income		₹13,50,000

Required
List all of the deficiencies that you can identify in this income statement and prepare a proper income statement.

29. Identify and Correct Balance Sheet Errors

Bizilia's Inc. was organized on January 1. At the end of the year, an employee with a mathematics degree prepared the following balance sheet:

Bizilia's Inc.
Balance Sheet
For the Year Ending December 31

Resources:	
Cash	₹ 3,00,000
Stuff we can sell	4,00,000
Land	5,30,000
Retained earnings	1,70,000
Grand total	₹14,60,000
Debts:	
Money we owe to vendors	₹ 4,30,000
Contributed capital	6,30,000
Grand total	₹10,60,000

Required
List all of the deficiencies that you can identify in this balance sheet and prepare a proper balance sheet.

30. Errors in Accounting

The Mock Corporation was formed on January 1. At December 31, William Mock, CEO and sole owner, prepared the company's balance sheet as follows:

Mock Corporation
Balance Sheet
December 31

Assets	
Cash	₹2,50,000
Accounts receivable	4,00,000
Inventory	3,50,000
Building	2,00,000
Liabilities and Equity	
Accounts payable	₹4,00,000
Building loan	1,50,000
Retained earnings	3,70,000

William is not an accountant by trade, and he believes there may be some mistakes in his balance sheet. He has provided you with the following additional information:

1. The building is William's personal beach house. However, he plans on using it for company retreats and for hosting some large clients. He decided to list the asset and the corresponding liability for this reason.
2. The inventory was originally purchased at ₹1,20,000, but due to a recent increase in demand, he believes he could sell it for at least ₹3,50,000.

He thought that ₹3,50,000 would best portray the economic reality of his inventory.

3. William included ₹50,000 in accounts receivable and retained earnings for a service that he will provide next year. Since he is an honest man and will provide the service, he decided to record the amount in this year's balance sheet.

Required
Comment on what accounting assumptions or principles are violated, briefly describe how each item should be accounted for, and prepare a correct balance sheet.

31. Preparing Financial Statements

On June 1 you begin an ocean tour business for the summer by contributing ₹60,000 of contributed capital and borrowing ₹60,000 from your parents. With your money, you pay ₹48,000 in June to rent a boat and supplies consisting of snorkels, fins, masks, and life-jackets. You also purchase advertising in a local paper for ₹2,500 and gasoline for ₹13,500. You decide to charge ₹2,500 per passenger. At the end of the month of June, you have serviced 240 customers and purchased and used an additional ₹20,000 in gasoline. Included in those 240 customers were two neighbors who promised future payment which you have not received (totaling ₹22,500). You also pay your parents ₹500 for monthly interest.

Required
Prepare an income statement and a statement of retained earnings for the month ending June 30 and a balance sheet at June 30.

32. Preparing Financial Statements

During the month of April, you conduct art seminars for children. On April 1, you borrow ₹50,000 from your parents, buy ₹40,000 of supplies, and pay ₹5,000 for advertising on the radio and ₹2,500 to rent a room in a local recreation center. You charge ₹2,000 per child per seminar. At the end of the month, you have held seminars for 80 children, of which you have received payment for 76. You have ₹3,000 of supplies remaining, and you pay your parents ₹500 for the use of their money during the month.

Required
Prepare an income statement and a statement of retained earnings for the month ending April 30 and a balance sheet at April 30.

33. Preparing Cash Flow Statements

	₹ lakhs
Net profit before tax	30,000
Sale of fixed asset	450
Profit on sale of fixed assets	100
Depreciation	9,600
Dividend received	400
Dividend paid	1,500
Purchase of fixed asset	1,000
Loss of foreign exchange	600
Short term borrowing	8,400
Repayment of borrowings	10,000
Cash and cash equivalents (opening)	1,700
Tax paid	4,750
Provision for doubtful debt	50

Required
Prepare a cash flow statement from the above information.

CASES

34. Read, Locate, and Compare Financial Statements

Access the financial statements in the 2013 annual report for **Hindustan Unilever Limited** by clicking on the *Investors* and *Annual Reports* links at www.hul.co.in.

Required

a. For Hindustan Unilever Limited current year, identify the amounts reported for net revenues, net earnings, total assets, and cash flows from operating activities. Also, identify the date on which the financial statements are prepared.
b. Locate **P&G India** financial statements for the same year. Identify the same information as in the previous requirement.
c. Compare P&G and HUL. Identify which company is (1) the largest, (2) the most profitable, and (3) the best able to generate cash from its operations.

35. Ethics in Accounting

As the top accountant at Blaire's Costume Jewelry Company, you discover that net income in each of the previous five years has been overstated due to an error in accounting. After much thought, you decide to approach the company president. His response is, "What the public doesn't know won't hurt them. We'll just adjust this year's income to make up for the mistakes. We had a pretty good year, and I think our income for this year can absorb the errors."

Required
Identify the ethical dilemma of this situation, identify the ways that you could respond, and explain the possible consequences of your responses.

36. Written Communication Skills

Your Uncle Ted just won the lottery. He is trying to find companies in which to invest his winnings. However, he is having trouble reading the financial statements because he has no idea what they are saying. Knowing you are in an accounting class, Uncle Ted asks for your advice.

Required

Prepare a written response to your Uncle Ted explaining what information is contained in each financial statement and how it is relevant to investors.

reviewcard CHAPTER 1 Financial Accounting

Learning Objectives		Key Concepts
LO1	Describe the four assumptions made when communicating accounting information.	When communicating accounting information, accountants assume that the activities of a company can be separated from those of the owners, that economic information can be effectively communicated in rupees over short periods of time, and that the business will continue into the foreseeable future.
LO2	Describe the purpose and structure of an income statement and the terms and principles used to create it.	An income statement reports a company's revenues and expenses over a period of time. A revenue is an inflow of resources from providing services, while an expense is an outflow of resources from providing services. Revenues are recorded when they are earned (revenue recognition principle), and expenses are recorded when they are incurred (matching principle). When revenues exceed expenses, a company generates net income.
LO3	Describe the purpose and structure of a balance sheet and the terms and principles used to create it.	A balance sheet reports a company's assets, liabilities, and equity accounts at a point in time. An asset is a resource of a business. A liability is an obligation of a business. Equity is the difference between assets and liabilities. Assets are recorded at their costs (cost principle). Assets are always equal to liabilities plus equity.
LO4	Describe the purpose and structure of a statement of retained earnings and how it links the income statement and the balance sheet.	A statement of retained earnings reports the change in a company's retained earnings balance over a period of time. The statement links the income statement and the balance sheet. Net income reported on the income statement is used to calculate the retained earnings balance reported on the balance sheet.
LO5	Describe the purpose and structure of a statement of cash flows and the terms and principles used to create it.	A statement of cash flows reports a company's sources and uses of cash over a period of time. Cash inflows and outflows are categorized into operating, investing, or financing activities.
LO6	Describe the qualitative characteristics that make accounting information useful.	Accounting information is useful only if it possesses several qualitative characteristics. It should be understandable, relevant, reliable, easily comparable, and consistent across time.
LO7	Describe the conceptual framework of accounting.	The conceptual framework is the collection of concepts that guide the practice of accounting. It includes the principles followed, the assumptions made, and the terms and statements used to communicate accounting information. It also includes the qualitative characteristics that make the information useful.

Key Definitions

Accounting The process of identifying, measuring, and communicating economic information to permit informed judgments and decisions.

Asset An economic resource that is objectively measurable, results from a prior transaction, and will provide future economic benefit.

Balance sheet A financial statement that reports a company's assets, liabilities, and equity at a specific point in time

Comparability The ability to use accounting information to compare or contrast the financial activities of different companies.

Conceptual framework of accounting The collection of concepts that guide the manner in which accounting is practiced.

Conservatism The manner in which accountants deal with uncertainty regarding economic situations.

Consistency The ability to use accounting information to compare or contrast the financial activities of the same entity over time.

Contributed capital The resources that investors contribute to a business in exchange for ownership interest

Cost principle The principle that assets should be recorded and reported at the cost paid to acquire them.

Dividends Profits that are distributed to owners.

Economic entity assumption Accountants assume that the financial activities of a business can be separated from the financial activities of the business's owner(s).

Equity The difference between a company's assets and liabilities, representing the share of assets that is claimed by the company's owners.

Expense A decrease in resources resulting from the sale of goods or provision of services.

Going concern assumption Accountants assume that a company will continue to operate into the foreseeable future.

Income statement A financial statement that reports a company's revenues and expenses over a specific period of time.

Liability An obligation of a business that results from a past transaction and will require the sacrifice of economic resources at some future date.

Key Definitions (continued)

Matching principle The principle that expenses should be recorded in the period resources are used to generate revenues.

Materiality The threshold at which a financial item begins to affect decision making.

Monetary unit assumption Accountants assume that the dollar is the most effective means to communicate economic activity.

Relevance The capacity of accounting information to make a difference in decisions.

Reliability The extent to which accounting information can be depended upon to represent what it purports to represent, both in description and in number.

Retained earnings Profits that are retained in the business.

Revenue An increase in resources resulting from the sale of goods or the provision of services.

Revenue recognition principle The principle that a revenue should be recorded when a resource has been earned.

Statement of cash flows A financial statement that reports a company's sources and uses of cash over a specific period of time.

Statement of retained earnings A financial statement that reports the change in a company's retained earnings over a specific period of time.

Time period assumption Accountants assume that economic information can be meaningfully captured and communicated over short periods of time.

Understandability The ability of accounting information to "be comprehensible to those who have a reasonable understanding of business. . . and are willing to study the information with reasonable diligence."

Demonstration Problem

On August 1, Sarah begins a tutoring service that she will operate for four months. With ₹400 borrowed from a friend and ₹1,000 of her own money, she purchases a ₹1,200 accounting textbook and ₹80 of school supplies. Sarah promises to pay her friend ₹10 at the end of each month and to pay back the full ₹400 at the end of December.

Sarah charges ₹200 per tutoring session. During August, she conducted ten sessions and bought ₹100 of additional school supplies. At the end of the month, Sarah has not collected on four of the ten sessions, and she has ₹50 of school supplies left over. Prepare Sarah's income statement and statement of retained earnings for the month ending August 31 and her balance sheet on August 31.

Key Formulas

Income Statement	Revenues − Expenses = Net Income or Net Loss
Balance Sheet	Assets = Liabilities + Equity
Statement of Retained Earnings	Retained Earnings, Beginning Balance +/− Net Income/Loss − Dividends = Retained Earnings, Ending Balance
Statement of Cash Flows	Cash Flows Provided (Used) by Operating Activities +/− Cash Flows Provided (Used) by Investing Activities +/− Cash Flows Provided (Used) by Financing Activities = Net Increase (Decrease) in Cash

Demonstration Problem Solution

Sarah's Tutoring Service
Income Statement
For One Month Ending August 31

Revenues:		₹2,000
Expenses:		
Depreciation (textbook)	₹ 300	
Supplies	130	
Interest	10	
Total expenses		440
Net income		₹1,560

Sarah's Tutoring Service
Statement of Retained Earnings
For One Month Ending August 31

Retained earnings, August 1	₹ 0
Add: Net income	1,560
Less: Dividends	0
Retained earnings, August 31	₹1,560

Sarah's Tutoring Service
Balance Sheet
August 31

Cash	₹1,210	
Accounts receivable	800	
Textbook	900	
Supplies	50	
Total assets		₹2,960
Note payable	₹ 400	
Total liabilities		₹ 400
Contributed capital	₹1,000	
Retained earnings	1,560	
Total equity		2,560
Total liabilities and equity		₹2,960

Corporate Financial Statements

Learning Objectives

After studying the material in this chapter, you should be able to:

LO1 Describe the three major forms of business.

LO2 Define generally accepted accounting principles and their origins.

LO3 Describe the main classifications of assets, liabilities, and equity in a classified balance sheet.

LO4 Describe the main subtotals of income on a multi-step income statement.

LO5 Analyze the balance sheet and the income statement using horizontal and vertical analyses.

LO6 Describe the purpose of a statement of stockholders' equity.

LO7 Describe the types of information usually disclosed along with financial statements.

Introduction

Chapter 1 introduced the terms, assumptions, principles, and statements that accounting uses to capture and communicate a company's economic activities. This chapter takes a more detailed look at the accounting information provided by companies, particularly public corporations such as Asian Paints. Specifically, the chapter introduces the classified balance sheet, the multi-step income statement, and the statement of stockholders' equity. Each of these three financial statements represents a more detailed version of the balance sheet, the income statement, and the statement of retained earnings covered in Chapter 1. The chapter also introduces two analysis techniques, horizontal and vertical analyses, that are simple but powerful tools for generating a more thorough understanding of a company's balance sheet and income statement. At the end of this chapter, you should be comfortable reading through and using the financial statements of most any company.

LO1 Business Forms

One of the first decisions that any new business faces is the form that it will take. Businesses have the following three basic options:

- **Sole proprietorship**
- **Partnership**
- **Corporation**

A **sole proprietorship** is a business owned by one person and is the most common type of business in India. In a sole proprietorship, the owner maintains complete control of the business, bears all the risk of failure, and reaps all the rewards of success. For accounting pur-

Sole proprietorship A business owned by one person.

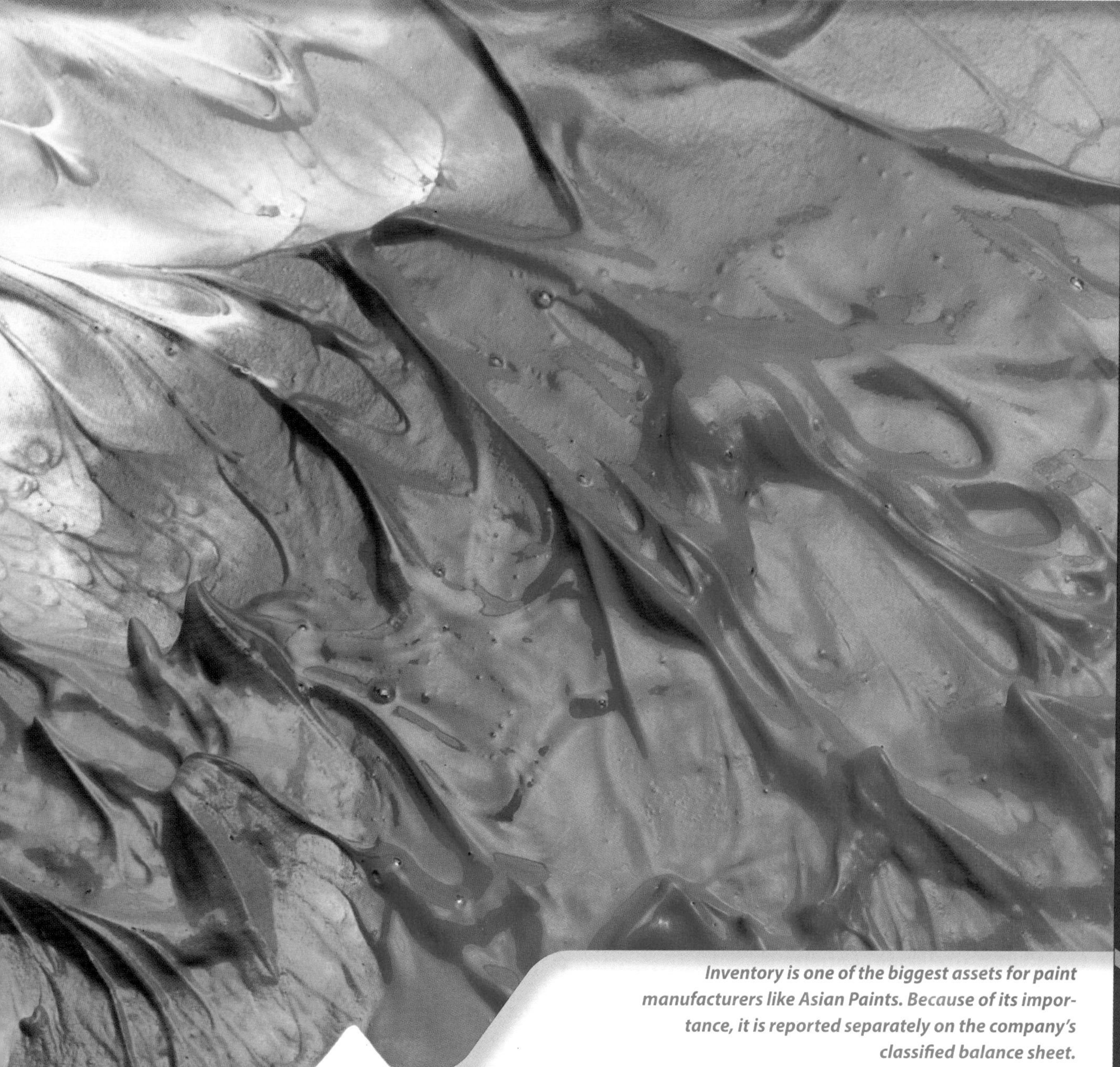

Inventory is one of the biggest assets for paint manufacturers like Asian Paints. Because of its importance, it is reported separately on the company's classified balance sheet.

ACCT

poses, a sole proprietorship is accounted for separately from the proprietor's personal affairs. This is an application of the economic entity assumption. For tax purposes, though, a sole proprietor's business is not separated from the proprietor. The income from the business is reported as owner's personal tax return.

A **partnership** is a business that is formed when two or more proprietors join together to own a business. Partnerships can be established by either a written or oral agreement and can include any number of partners. Partnerships are formed for various reasons, such as joining proprietors with different skills, combining

Partnership A business that is formed when two or more proprietors join together to own a business.

One of the first decisions that any new business faces is the form that it will take.

resources, and spreading the financial risk of the business among several people. Like sole proprietorships, a partnership is considered a separate accounting entity from the individual partners. However, also like sole proprietorships, a partner's share of partnership income is reported on the partner's individual tax return.

A **corporation** is a separate legal entity that is established by filing articles of incorporation in a state, usually with the secretary of state's office. Once a corporation is formed, it sells shares to individuals who want to own part of the corporation. This is one of the main reasons that corporations are formed—the ability to raise capital through the sale of ownership interests. It is also why corporation owners are called stockholders. Like a sole proprietorship and a partnership, a corporation is accounted for separately from its owners. However, it is also taxed separately. Income generated by a corporation is taxed on a corporate tax return, not on the stockholders' individual tax returns.

Corporations can take several forms, one of which is a public corporation. A **public corporation** is one in which ownership is available to the public at large. The stock of a public corporation is usually bought and sold on an open exchange such as the Bombay Stock Exchange (BSE) or the National Stock Exchange of India Ltd. (NSE). Such corporations are said to be *publicly traded*. Examples of publicly traded corporations are Wipro, ITC, and Asian Paints. From this point forward, this text will focus on the accounting for publicly traded corporations. This will allow you to see accounting issues in companies with which you may be familiar.

Corporation A separate legal entity that is established by filing articles of incorporation in a state.

Public corporation A separate legal entity in which ownership is available to the public at large.

Generally accepted accounting principles The accounting standards, rules, principles, and procedures that comprise authoritative practice for financial accounting.

The **Securities and Exchange Board of India (SEBI)** The Government of India's regulator for the security market in India. It is charged to protect investors and maintain the integrity of securities markets.

LO2 Generally Accepted Accounting Principles

When accounting for their economic activities, public corporations must follow *generally accepted accounting principles*. **Generally accepted accounting principles (GAAP)** are the accounting standards, rules, principles, and procedures that comprise authoritative practice for financial accounting. These principles have been developed over time by several regulatory bodies, the most significant of which are listed as follows.

- Securities and Exchange Board of India
- Financial Accounting Standards Board
- The Institute of Chartered Accountants of India

The **Securities and Exchange Board of India (SEBI)** is the Government of India regulatory body charged to protect investors and maintain the integrity of securities markets. SEBI was established in April 12, 1992 in accordance with the provisions of the Securities and Exchange Board of India Act, 1992. It was given the

MARUTI SUZUKI ANALYSIS

Look at the full company name at the top of any of Maruti Suzuki's financial statements in Appendix C. Can you tell from the name what form of business Maruti Suzuki uses?

The full company name is "Maruti Suzuki India Limited". Limited stands for limited liabilities. Thus, Maruti Suzuki is a limited liability company.

authority to protect the interests of investors in securities and to promote the development of, and to regulate the securities market and for matters connected therewith or incidental thereto. However, instead of writing all of the rules itself, the SEBI delegated much of its accounting rule-making authority to the accounting profession. Today, the accounting organization that sets major accounting standards is the Financial Accounting Standards Board and The Institute of Chartered Accountants of India.

The **Financial Accounting Standards Board (FASB)** is a standard setting body whose mission is "to establish and improve standards of financial accounting and reporting for the guidance and education of the public, including issuers, auditors, and users of financial information." The FASB usually tackles large issues, such as the accounting for pensions, leases, stock options, and derivatives. It also maintains the conceptual framework discussed in Chapter 1. The Board consists of seven full-time voting members who oversee a standard-setting process of research, deliberation, public input, and board approval.

While the FASB is accounting's main standard-setting body, the **Institute of Chartered Accountants of India (ICAI)** also plays a role in establishing accounting rules. The ICAI, which is the professional organization of certified public accountants of India, maintains a board that establishes rules that are often more technical and more specific to certain industries. For example, the ICAI has issued rules for determining profits in the film industry. The rules set by the ICAI are also enforced by the SEC.

The organizations mentioned above are based in India and in the United States. However, accounting is practiced throughout the world, and there is a movement to develop one set of international accounting standards to be used by all countries. The **International Accounting Standards Board (IASB)** is a board, similar to the FASB, whose mission is to develop a single set of high quality standards requiring transparent and comparable information. Those standards, which have

IFRS

The accounting organization that **sets major accounting standards** in India is the Institute of Chartered Accountants of India. International Standards are set by the International Accounting Standards Board(IASB).

International Financial Reporting Standards (IFRS) foundation developed a single set of globally accepted International Financial Reporting Standards.

Financial Accounting Standards Board The standard setting body whose mission is "to establish and improve standards of financial accounting and reporting for the guidance and education of the public, including issuers, auditors, and users of financial information."

The Institute of Chartered Accountants of India (ICAI) The professional organization of certified public accountants whose board establishes rules that are often more technical and more specific to certain industries.

International Accounting Standards Board A board, similar to the FASB, whose mission is to develop a single set of high quality standards requiring transparent and comparable information.

International Financial Reporting Standards Standards issued by the International Accounting Standards Board.

MARUTI SUZUKI ANALYSIS

Look at the sixth paragraph in Maruti Suzuki's Independent Auditor's Report in Appendix C. According to the auditor, are Maruti Suzuki's financial statements prepared in accordance with GAAP?

Yes. As the Independent Auditor's Report states, "In our opinion, and to the best of our information and according to the explanations given to us, the accompanying financial statements give the information required by the Act in the manner so required and give a true and fair view in conformity with the accounting principles generally accepted in India."

both similarities to and differences from GAAP, are called **International Financial Reporting Standards (IFRS)**. Because adoption of IFRS is voluntary, the effectiveness of the IASB at accomplishing its mission has been somewhat limited. However, the IASB and the FASB have both agreed to a commitment to the convergence of U.S. and international standards. At some time in the future, the world may very well use one set of global accounting standards set by a global board. In India, starting April 1, 2011, a road map for convergence of Indian Accounting Standards with IFRS in three phases has been designed.

LO3 The Classified Balance Sheet

Chapter 1 introduced the balance sheet. A balance sheet is a financial statement that summarizes a company's assets, liabilities, and equity at a given point in time. The balance sheet shown in Chapter 1 reported every account of the company. However, most public corporations are much too large to report every account, so they prepare a classified balance sheet instead. A **classified balance sheet** groups together accounts of similar nature and reports them in a few major classifications.

The following sections discuss the various asset, liability, and equity classifications commonly used on classified balance sheets. The March 31, 2013, classified balance sheet of Asian Paints in Exhibit 2-1 will be used as an illustration. As you review the statement, note that all numbers except per share data are in crores, meaning that each reported number has seven 0's missing. Note also that two years of data are presented, with the most recent year listed first. This is the normal format for most corporate balance sheets. It is also why such statements are often called *comparative* balance sheets.

Classified balance sheet A type of balance sheet that groups together accounts of similar nature and reports them in a few major classifications.

Current asset Any asset that is reasonably expected to be converted to cash or consumed within one year of the balance sheet date.

Long-term investments The investments in the common stock or debt of another entity that will not be sold within a year.

Fixed assets The tangible resources that are used in a company's operations for more than one year and are not intended for resale.

Assets

An asset is a resource of a business. Assets are generally grouped into five main categories on a classified balance sheet. However, in a company balance sheet it is grouped as fixed assets, investments, and current assets:

- current assets
- long-term investments
- fixed assets
- intangible assets
- other assets

Current Assets A **current asset** is any asset that is reasonably expected to be converted to cash or consumed within one year of the balance sheet date. Common examples include cash, investments that will mature or be sold within a year, accounts receivable from customers, inventories, and other assets such as prepaid insurance. Current assets are listed in order of their liquidity, which refers to the speed with which a resource can be converted to cash. Inventory is listed first, followed by receivables, cash, other assets and then short-term investments.

Asian Paints reports six current assets totaling ₹3,041.26 crore on its March 31, 2013, balance sheet. Vast majority of those assets (₹1,480.79 crore) is in *inventories,* with a substantial amount also in *sundry debtors.* The company also reports some *Short Term Loans* and *Advances* and *Other current assets.*

Noncurrent Investments **Noncurrent investments** are a company's investments in the common stock or debt of another entity that will not be sold within a year. Companies typically list any noncurrent investments as their noncurrent asset. Asian Paints reports ₹359.70 crore in *noncurrent investment securities.*

Fixed Assets **Fixed assets** are the tangible resources that are used in a company's operations for more than one year and are not intended for resale. Examples include land, buildings, equipment, furniture, and fixtures.

Asian Paints reports over ₹2,154.44 crore of fixed assets on its March 31, 2013, balance sheet, making them the largest asset, which makes sense for a manufacturer. Note, however, that the company in Notes 11 to Financial Statements uses the term *Gross Block and Net Block* rather than fixed assets. Gross Block is a common name for aggregate fixed assets. Note also the word "net" in the description. Most fixed assets are

Exhibit 2-1 Asian Paints Classified Balance Sheet

ASIAN PAINTS LIMITED
Balance Sheet as at March 31, 2013

(₹ in crores)

	As at 31.03.2013 Current Year	As at 31.03.2012 Previous Year
EQUITY AND LIABILITIES		
Share holder's Funds		
Share Capital	95.92	95.92
Reserves and Surplus	2,926.34	2,391.86
	3,022.26	2,487.78
NONCURRENT LIABILITIES		
Long-Term Borrowings	46.76	52.11
Deferred Tax Liability (Net)	143.33	80.75
Other Long-Term Liabilities	0.50	3.62
Long-Term Provisions	76.77	65.16
	267.36	201.64
CURRENT LIABILITIES		
Short-Term Borrowings	—	110.51
Trade Payables	1,214.12	1,034.68
Other Current Liabilities	720.99	606.33
Short-Term Provisions	423.55	355.07
	2,358.66	2,106.59
Total	5,648.28	4,796.01
ASSETS		
NONCURRENT ASSETS		
Fixed Assets		
Tangible Assets	2,074.91	987.79
Intangible Assets	26.98	21.25
Capital work-in-progress	52.55	602.84
	2,154.44	1,611.88
Non-Current Investments	359.70	279.22
Long Term Loans and Advances	92.88	180.52
CURRENT ASSETS		
Current Investments	90	263
Inventories	1,480.79	1,264.42
Trade Receivables	633.88	500.24
Cash and Bank Balances	566.86	500.97
Short-Term Loans and Advances	164.08	100.5
Other Current Assets	105.65	95.26
	3,041.26	2,724.39
Total	5,648.28	4,796.01

subject to depreciation, which is the process of expensing the cost of an asset over its useful life. Therefore, fixed assets are reported "net" of any depreciation to date. Chapter 8 will discuss depreciation in much more detail.

Intangible Assets An **intangible asset** is a resource that is used in operations for more than one year, is not intended for resale, and has no physical substance. Examples include trademarks, patents, fran-

Intangible asset A resource that is used in operation for more than one year, is not intended for resale, and has no physical substance.

chise rights, copyrights, and goodwill. Like fixed assets, intangible assets are subject to depreciation (although it is actually called amortization instead of depreciation) and are reported net of amortization to date. Notes 11 to Financial Statements to Asian Paints Balance Sheet reports two Intangible Assets—"Trademark" and "Software".

Other Assets **Other assets** are those resources that do not fit well into one of the other classifications. The classification can also include those assets that are small enough that they do not warrant separate reporting. Asian Paints does not report any amount as "other assets".

Liabilities

A liability is an obligation of a business. Liabilities are generally classified into two main categories on a classified balance sheet:

- Current liabilities
- Long-term liabilities

Current Liabilities A **current liability** is an obligation that is reasonably expected to be satisfied within one year. Examples include accounts payable to vendors, salaries payable to employees, and taxes payable to taxing authorities. Even long-term debt, if maturing within one year, is classified as a current liability.

Asian Paints reports current liabilities and short-term provision totaling almost ₹2,358.66 crore on its March 31, 2013, balance sheet. Note 9 to the Balance Sheet reports that the largest is ₹1,214.12 crore in *Trade Payables (including Acceptances):* which is the amount owed to suppliers. Also, ₹5.86 crore is reported in *Unpaid/Unclaimed dividend.* Finally, the company reports ₹423.55 as short-term provision which includes ₹350.10 (Note 7) crore proposed Dividend. Provision for tax (including provision for Income tax on Proposed Dividend) is reported as 59.68.

Other assets Resources that do not fit well into one of the other asset classifications or are small enough that they do not warrant separate reporting.

Current liability An obligation that is reasonably expected to be satisfied within one year.

Long-term liability An obligation that is not expected to be satisfied within one year.

Retained earnings The amount of equity a company generates by being profitable and retaining those profits in the business.

Contributed capital The amount of equity a company generates through the sale of stock to investors.

Long-Term Liabilities A **long-term liability** is an obligation that is not expected to be satisfied within one year. Examples include secured and unsecured loans and bonds/debentures payable. Asian Paints has both secured and unsecured long-term liabilities at March 31, 2013. It reports ₹9.28 crore in *Secured Loan and ₹37.48 crore as Unsecured Loan.*

Asian Paints also reports ₹143.33 crore as Deferred Tax Liabilities (net). Deferred tax represents liability for tax owned by a company that is postponed to future periods.

Equity

Equity is the difference between a company's assets and its liabilities. It is generated from the following two sources:

- Retained earnings
- Contributed capital

Retained earnings is the amount of equity a company generates by being profitable and retaining those profits in the business. **Contributed capital** is the amount of equity a company generates through the sale of stock to investors. Such equity is often referred to as capital stock. Examples of capital stock include common stock and preferred stock.

Like most publicly traded companies, Asian Paints reports its equity accounts in one general section called Shareholders' Funds. The largest balance in the section is the ₹2,926.34 crore of Reserve and Surplus or *Retained earnings*. This balance indicates a very strong record of profits in previous years. Asian Pains reports ₹95.92 Share Capital that represents the Contributed Capital of the shareholders.

LO4 The Multi-Step Income Statement

Chapter 1 also introduced the income statement. The income statement is a financial statement that summarizes a company's revenues and expenses over a period of time. Companies generally use one of two forms for their incomè statements—a single-step statement or a multi-step statement.

A **single-step income statement** calculates total revenues and total expenses and then determines net income in one step by subtracting total expenses from total revenues. The income statement prepared in Chapter 1 was a single-step income statement. The major advantage of a single-step statement is its simplicity. However, the disadvantage is that it does not present the information in a manner that is very useful. As a result, most companies prepare multi-step income statements.

A **multi-step income statement** calculates income by grouping certain revenues and expenses together and calculating several subtotals of income. These subtotals provide information on the profitability of various aspects of the company's operations. While most companies prepare multi-step statements, there is some slight variation in how they are prepared. However, most include either some or all of the following four subtotals of income.

- Gross profit
- Operating profit
- Income before taxes
- Net income

Indian companies in most cases do not calculate gross profit. They calculate "Profit before Interest and Tax", "Profit before Taxes," and "Profit after Tax". The following sections discuss these subtotals that are commonly used by companies. For illustration purposes, Exhibit 2-2 contains Asian Paint's income statement for the fiscal year ended March 31, 2013. Note also that like the balance sheet, the numbers are in crores. The presentation of multiple years of data therefore yields comparative income statements.

Gross Profit

In a multi-step statement, sales revenue is listed first. **Sales revenue,** which is often labeled net sales, is the resources that a company generates during a period from selling its inventory. Listed next is cost of sales. **Cost of sales,** which is sometimes called cost of goods sold, represents the cost of the inventory that was sold during a period. Subtracting cost of sales from net sales then yields the first subtotal of income, gross profit. **Gross profit,** which is sometimes called gross margin, represents the profit that a company generates when considering only the sales price and the cost of the product sold. It therefore represents the gross rupee markup that a company is able to achieve when selling its inventory.

Asian Paints does not report Gross profit separately.

Operating Profit

After gross profit is reported, operating expenses are listed. **Operating expenses** are the expenses that a company incurs during normal operations. Such expenses are recurring, meaning that they are incurred year after year as the company runs its business. Examples include advertising, salaries, utilities, depreciation, and insurance.

In most multi-step statements, operating expenses are summed together and subtracted from gross profit to yield the second subtotal of income, operating profit. **Operating profit** represents the profit that a company generates when considering both the cost of the in-

Single-step income statement Calculates total revenues and total expenses and then determines net income in one step by subtracting total expenses from total revenues.

Multi-step income statement Calculates income by grouping certain revenues and expenses together and calculating several subtotals of income.

Sales revenue The resources that a company generates during a period from selling its inventory.

Cost of sales The cost of the inventory sold during a period.

Gross profit The profit that a company generates when considering only the sales price and the cost of the product sold.

Operating expenses Recurring expenses that a company incurs during normal operations.

Operating profit The profit that a company generates when considering both the cost of the inventory and the normal expenses incurred to operate the business.

Exhibit 2-2 Asian Paints Limited Multi-step Income Statement

Statement of Profit and Loss
for the year ended March 31, 2013
Asian Paints Limited

(₹ in crores)

	Year 2012–13	Year 2011–12
(I) INCOME		
Revenue from sales of goods and services (Net of discounts)	9,990.04	8,708.30
Less: Excise Duty	1,068.91	783.60
Revenue from sales of goods and services (Net of discounts and excise duty)	8,921.13	7,924.70
Other Operating Revenue	50.57	39.46
Other Income	126.15	141.49
Total Revenue (I)	**9,097.85**	**8,105.65**
(II) Expenses		
Cost of Materials Consumed	5,125.48	4,722.74
Purchases of Stock-in-Trade	199.56	138.67
Changes in inventories of finished goods, work in progress and stock-in-trade	(136.17)	(115.07)
Employee Benefits Expense	404.59	341.63
Other Expenses	1,830.97	1,524.44
Total (II)	**7,424.43**	**6,612.41**
EARNINGS BEFORE INTEREST, TAX, DEPRECIATION AND AMORTISATION (EBITDA) (I) - (II)	1,673.42	1,493.24
Depreciation and Amortisation Expense	126.98	99.49
Finance Costs	30.56	30.82
PROFIT BEFORE TAX	**1,515.88**	**1,362.93**
less: **Tax Expenses**		
Current Tax	406.03	402.76
Deferred Tax	62.59	4.16
(Excess) Tax provision for earlier years	(2.74)	(2.38)
Total Tax Expenses	465.88	404.54
PROFIT AFTER TAX	**1,050.00**	**958.39**
Earnings per share (₹) Basic and diluted	109.47	99.92
(Face value of ₹10 each)		
Significant Accounting Policies		
Notes are an integral part of the financial statements		

ventory and the normal expenses incurred to operate the business. Other names for operating profit include income from operations or operating income. Asian Paints reports. "Profit before Interest, Depreciation Taxes, and Exceptionally Items."

Asian Paints reports ₹7,424.43 crore of operating expenses which includes materials cost, employee cost, manufacturing, administrative, selling, and distribution expenses. Subtracting these operating expenses from total income yields an *Operating profit or Profit before interest, Depreciation, Tax, and Exceptional items* of about ₹1,673.42 crore. So, after considering its major expenses—Asian Paints's ₹9,097.85 crore income yielded about ₹1,673.42 crore in profits.

Income Before Taxes

In addition to cost of sales and operating expenses, companies sometimes generate revenues and expenses that are outside of their normal operations. Common

Just like individuals do, corporations must pay taxes on their incomes.

examples include interest revenue and interest expense. Such items are listed separately as **other revenues and expenses** and are netted against operating profit to yield the third subtotal of income, income before taxes. **Income before taxes,** also called earnings before income taxes and other similar titles, represents the profit that a company generates when considering all revenues and expenses except for income taxes.

After reporting its operating profit, Asian Paints reports *Interest* cost as ₹30.56 crore and depreciation as ₹126.98 crore. With no exceptional items in 2012–13, the Profit before Tax after adjusting the interest and depreciation, is reported to be ₹1,515.88 crore.

Net Income

Like individuals, corporations must pay taxes on their incomes. Usually, the amount of tax in a given period is listed separately on a multi-step statement as tax expenses. **Tax expenses** is the amount of income tax expense for a given period. When tax expenses is subtracted from income before taxes, the final income mea-

Other revenue and expenses Revenues and expenses generated outside of normal operations.

Income before taxes The profit that a company generates when considering all revenues and expenses except for income taxes.

Provision for income taxes The amount of income tax expense for a given period.

MARUTI SUZUKI ANALYSIS

Look at Maruti Suzuki's Income Statement in Appendix C. What form of income statement does the company use?

Maruti Suzuki uses a multi-step income statement. It shows several subtotals of income, including Profit before Interest, Depreciation, Tax and Amortization; Profit before Tax and Profit after Tax.

sure, **net income,** is determined. Asian Paints reports a ₹465.88 crore *tax expenses*, ₹406.03 crore as current tax, deferred tax ₹62.59 and ₹(2.74) crore excess tax provision for the previous year. After subtracting that from income before taxes yields *Profit after Taxes* or *Net earnings* of approximately ₹1,050.00 crore.

In summary, Asian Paints' multi-step income statement provides a picture of how the company generated its profits in the last period. It generated ₹9,097.85 as Total Income. Once it subtracted its operating expenses, it had profit before interest, Depreciation, and Tax of ₹1,673.42 crore. After considering interest, depreciation and taxes, ₹1,050.00 crore of Profit after Tax was arrived at.

LO5 Horizontal and Vertical Analyses

The previous sections demonstrate that financial statements communicate economic information about a company to interested parties. For example, investors and creditors learn from Asian Paints' income statement that the company earned ₹1,050.00 crore of income in the most recent year. This is useful information because it demonstrates that the company was profitable during the year. However, the information can be even more useful if it is compared to something else. For example, is ₹1,050.00 crore better or worse than last year? Is it high enough given sales for the period? How does it compare to competitors? Such comparisons provide the necessary context for a more thorough understanding of a company's financial activities. Such context can be easily generated through two techniques called horizontal and vertical analyses.

Horizontal Analysis

Horizontal analysis is a method of analyzing a company's account balances over time. It is normally conducted on both the balance sheet and the income statement. The analysis calculates both the absolute and percentage change in each account balance on a financial statement. As a result, it is very useful in identifying promising or troubling trends in a company. The analysis is called "horizontal" because the calculation compares an account's balance across the columns of yearly data—that is, horizontally across the financial statement.

Horizontal analysis is calculated as follows. First, the rupee change in an account is determined. This is defined as the current year balance less the prior year balance. The rupee change is then divided by the prior year balance to yield a percentage change. These two calculations are shown below.

$$\text{Rupee change in account balance} = \text{Current year balance} - \text{Prior year balance}$$

$$\text{Percentage change in account balance} = \frac{\text{Rupee change}}{\text{Prior year balance}}$$

To illustrate, consider the *Inventories* balance from Asian Paints' balance sheet in Exhibit 2-1:

(in ₹ crores)	March 31, 2013	March 31, 2012
Inventories	₹1,480.79	₹1,264.42

The company's inventory increased ₹216.37 crore from March 31, 2012, to March 31, 2013. Dividing that increase by the March 31, 2012, balance yields a percentage change of 17.11%. These calculations are shown in the following table. Also shown are similar calculations for a horizontal analysis of *Net earnings* from the company's income statement in Exhibit 2-2. Note that the *Net earnings* calculations result in a 9.56 percentage change.

IFRS

Under Indian/US GAAP, unusual and infrequent expense can be reported on the income statement as an extraordinary item. Under IFRS, extraordinary items are prohibited from the income statement.

Net Income or Profit After Tax The final income measure after the provision for income taxes is subtracted from income before taxes.

Horizontal analysis A method of analyzing a company's account balances over time by calculating absolute and percentage changes in each account.

(in ₹ crores)	*Inventories*	*Net earnings*
Current Year Balance	₹ 1,480.79	₹ 1,050.00
− Prior Year Balance	− ₹ 1,264.42	− ₹ 958.39
Rupee Change	₹ 216.37	₹ 91.61
Rupee change / Prior year balance	₹ 216.37 / ₹ 1,264.42	₹ 91.61 / ₹ 958.39
= Percentage change	= 17.11%	= 9.56%

For a full horizontal analysis, both rupee and percentage changes are calculated for each account on both the balance sheet and the income statement. Exhibit 2-3 contains a horizontal analysis of Asian Paints' balance sheet and income statement. The column headings show the general calculations, with CY and PY representing current year and prior year, respectively.

Exhibit 2-3A Horizontal Analysis of Asian Paints' Balance Sheet

Asian Paints Limited

Balance Sheet as at March 31, 2013

(₹ in crores)

	As at 31.03.2013 Current Year (CY)		As at 31.03.2012 Previous Year (PY)	CY-PY	CY-PY/PY % Change
EQUITY AND LIABILITIES					
Share holder's Funds					
Share Capital	95.92		95.92	0	0
Reserves and Surplus	2,926.34		2,391.86	534.48	22.35
		3,022.26	2,487.78	534.48	21.48
NON-CURRENT LIABILITIES					
Long Term Borrowings	46.76		52.11	−5.35	−10.27
Deferred Tax Liability (Net)	143.33		80.75	62.58	77.50
Other Long Term Liabilities	0.5		3.62	−3.12	−86.19
Long Term Provisions	76.77		65.16	11.61	17.82
		267.36	201.64	65.72	32.59
CURRENT LIA BILITIES					
Short Term Borrowings	0		110.51	−110.51	−100.00
Trade Payables	1,214.12		1,034.68	179.44	17.34
Other Current Liabilities	720.99		606.33	114.66	18.91
Short Term Provisions	423.55		355.07	68.48	19.29
		2,358.66	2,106.59	252.07	11.97
Total		**5,648.28**	**4,796.01**	**852.27**	**17.77**
ASSETS					
NON-CURRENT ASSETS					
Fixed Assets					
Tangible Assets	2,074.91		987.79	1,087.12	110.06
Intangible Assets	26.98		21.25	5.73	26.96
Capital work-in-progress	52.55		602.84	−550.29	−91.28
		2,154.44	1,611.88	542.56	33.66
Non-Current Investments	359.7		279.22	80.48	28.82
Lon g Term Loans and Advances	92.88		180.52	−87.64	−48.55
CURRENT ASSETS					
Current Investments	90		263	−173.00	−65.78
Inventories	1,480.79		1,264.42	216.37	17.11
Trade Receivables	633.88		500.24	133.64	26.72
Cash and Bank Balances	566.86		500.97	65.89	13.15
Short Term Loans and Advances	164.08		100.5	63.58	63.26
Other Current Assets	105.65		95.26	10.39	10.91
		3,041.26	2,724.39	316.87	11.63
Total		**5,648.28**	**4,796.01**	**852.27**	**17.77**

Exhibit 2-3B Horizontal Analysis of Asian Paints Income statement

Statement of Profit and Loss for the year ended March 31, 2013
Asian Paints Limited

(₹ in crores)

	Year 2012–13		Year 2011–12		
	CY		PY	CY-PY	CY-PY/PY % change
(I) INCOME					
Revenue from sales of goods and services (Net of discounts)	9,990.04		8,708.30	1,281.74	14.72
Less: Excise Duty	1,068.91		783.6	285.31	36.41
Revenue from sales of goods and services		8,921.13	7,924.70	996.43	12.57
(Net of discounts and excise duty)					
Other Operating Revenue	50.57		39.46	11.11	28.16
Other Income	126.15		141.49	−15.34	−10.84
Total Revenue (I)		**9,097.85**	**8,105.65**	**992.20**	**12.24**
(II) Expenses					
Cost of Materials Consumed	5,125.48		4,722.74	402.74	8.53
Purchases of Stock-in-Trade	199.56		138.67	60.89	43.91
Changes in inventories of finished goods, work in progress and stock-in-trade	−136.17		−115.07	−21.10	18.34
Employee Benefits Expense	404.59		341.63	62.96	18.43
Other Expenses	1,830.97		1,524.44	306.53	20.11
Total (II)		**7,424.43**	**6,612.41**	**812.02**	**12.28**
EARNINGS BEFORE INTEREST, TAX, DEPRECIATION AND AMORTISATION (EBITDA) (I) - (II)		1,673.42	1,493.24	180.18	12.07
Depreciation and Amortisation Expense	126.98		99.49	27.49	27.63
Finance Costs	30.56		30.82	−0.26	−0.84
PROFIT BEFORE TAX		1,515.88	1,362.93	152.95	11.22
less: Tax Expenses					
Current Tax	406.03		402.76	3.27	0.81
Deferred Tax	62.59		4.16	58.43	1404.57
(Excess) Tax provision for earlier years	−2.74		−2.38	−0.36	15.13
Total Tax Expenses		465.88	404.54	61.34	15.16
PROFIT AFTER TAX		1,050.00	958.39	91.61	9.56
Earnings per share (₹) Basic and diluted		109.47	99.92		
(Face value of ₹ 10 each)					
Significant Accounting Policies					
Notes are an integral part of the financial statements					

An examination of the balance sheet shows overall growth. Total asset 2011 was ₹3,861.66 (2,115.68 + 1,745.98) crore as compared to ₹3,134.15 (1,673.71 + 1,460.44) crore in 2010 and was thus ₹727.51 crore (23.21%) higher than the previous year. All assets except *Capital work in Progress and Cash and Bank balance* increased from the prior year, with *Fixed Assets* having the largest increase by far. Since *Total liabilities*, Long term Loan plus Current Liabilities, increased by 20.23% though the long term liabilities decreased by 3.73% indicating that the company's asset growth was generated by borrowing from creditors. *Total shareholders' equity* was up 26.85% from the prior year, with the majority of that increase caused by a substantial increase in *Retained earnings*.

An examination of the income statement also shows growth. *Net sales* were 23.36% higher than the prior year. However, *operating expenses went up by 25.82%*. When a company's expenses grow faster than its sales revenues, its profitability will decline. Thus the profit after tax went up by a marginal amount of ₹0.65 crore.

In summary, horizontal analysis of the balance sheet and income statement shows that Asian Paints is growing and is profitable overall. That is the good news. The bad news is that the company profit has not grown. Horizontal analysis has provided the context for a much more thorough understanding of the financial statements.

Vertical Analysis

Vertical analysis is a method of comparing a company's account balances within one year. It also is normally conducted on both the balance sheet and the income statement. The analysis is calculated by dividing each account balance by a base account, yielding a percentage. The base account is total assets for balance sheet accounts and net sales or revenues for income statement accounts. These two calculations are shown below.

	For the Balance Sheet	For the Income Statement
Percentage	Account balance / Total Assets	Account balance / Net Sales or Revenue

The product of a vertical analysis is sometimes called a common-size financial statement. A **common-size financial statement** is a statement in which all accounts have been standardized by the overall size of the company. Common-size statements are very useful because they allow investors and creditors to determine the importance of each account to the overall company and to compare that importance to other companies, even those of vastly different sizes.

Common-size statements allow investors and creditors to compare companies of vastly different sizes.

To illustrate, consider again the *inventories* balance from Asian Paints' balance sheet in Exhibit 2-1. Also shown are the company's *Total assets*.

(in ₹ crores)	March 31, 2013	March 31, 2012
Inventories	₹1,480.79	₹1,264.42
Total assets	5,648.28	4,796.01

A vertical analysis divides each inventory balance by total assets for that year. These calculations are shown in the following table. Also shown are similar calculations that would be made for a vertical analysis of *Net earnings* from the company's income statement in Exhibit 2-2. The only difference is that *Net earnings* is divided by *Net sales*, not *Total assets*.

(in ₹ crores)	*Current Year*	*Prior Year*
Inventory Balance	₹ 1,480.79	₹ 1,264.42
Total Assets	₹ 5,648.28	₹ 4,796.01
= Percentage of Total Assets	= 26.22%	= 26.36%
Net Earnings	₹1,050.00	₹ 958.39
Net Sales	₹ 8,921.13	₹7,924.70
= Percentage of Net Sales	= 11.77%	= 12.09%

For a full vertical analysis, percentages are calculated for every account on each financial statement. Exhibit 2-4 contains a vertical analysis of Asian Paints' balance sheet and income statement. The column headings show the general calculations, with CY and PY representing current year and prior year, respectively.

An examination of the balance sheet shows that the bulk of Asian Paints' assets are held in *Fixed Assets*,

Vertical analysis A method of comparing a company's account balances within one year by dividing each account balance by a base amount to yield a percentage.

Common-size financial statement A statement in which all accounts have been standardized by the overall size of the company.

Exhibit 2-4A Vertical Analysis of Asian Paints Classified Balance Sheet

Asian Paints Limited
Balance Sheet as at March 31, 2013

(₹ in crores)

	As at 31.03.2013 Current Year (CY)	CY/Total Assets %	As at 31.03.2012 Previous Year (PY)	PY/Total Assets %
EQUITY AND LIABILITIES				
Share holder's Funds				
Share Capital	95.92	1.70	95.92	2.00
Reserves and Surplus	2,926.34	51.81	2,391.86	49.87
	3,022.26	53.51	**2,487.78**	51.87
NON-CURRENT LIABILITIES				
Long Term Borrowings	46.76	0.83	52.11	1.09
Deferred Tax Liability (Net)	143.33	2.54	80.75	1.68
Other Long Term Liabilities	0.50	0.01	3.62	0.08
Long Term Provisions	76.77	1.36	65.16	1.36
	267.36		**201.64**	4.20
CURRENT LIA BILITIES				
Short Term Borrowings	–		110.51	2.30
Trade Payables	1,214.12	21.50	1,034.68	21.57
Other Current Liabilities	720.99	12.76	606.33	12.64
Short Term Provisions	423.55	7.50	355.07	7.40
	2,358.66	41.76	2,106.59	43.92
Total	**5,648.28**	100.00	**4,796.01**	100.00
ASSETS				
NON-CURRENT ASSETS				
Fixed Assets				
Tangible Assets	2,074.91	36.74	987.79	20.60
Intangible Assets	26.98	0.48	21.25	0.44
Capital work-in-progress	52.55	0.93	602.84	12.57
	2,154.44	38.14	1,611.88	33.61
Non-Current Investments	359.70	6.37	279.22	5.82
Lon g Term Loans and Advances	92.88	1.64	180.52	3.76
CURRENT ASSETS				
Current Investments	90	1.59	263	5.48
Inventories	1,480.79	26.22	1,264.42	26.36
Trade Receivables	633.88	11.22	500.24	10.43
Cash and Bank Balances	566.86	10.04	500.97	10.45
Short Term Loans and Advances	164.08	2.90	100.5	2.10
Other Current Assets	105.65	1.87	95.26	1.99
	3,041.26	53.84	2,724.39	56.81
Total	**5,648.28**	100.00	**4,796.01**	100.00

Exhibit 2-4B Vertical Analysis of Asian Paints Income Statement

Asian Paints Limited Multi-step Income Statement
Statement of Profit and Loss for the year ended March 31, 2013

(₹ in crores)

	Asian Paints Limited Year 2012–13 (CY)	CY/Net Sales	Year 2011–12 (PY)	PY/Net Sales
(I) INCOME				
Revenue from sales of goods and services (Net of discounts)	9,990.04	111.9817781	8,708.30	109.89
Less: Exicse Duty	1,068.91	11.98177809	783.6	9.89
Revenue from sales of goods and services (Net of discounts and excise duty)	8,921.13	100	7,924.70	100.00
Other Operating Revenue	50.57	0.566856441	39.46	0.50
Other Income	126.15	1.414058533	141.49	1.79
Total Revenue (I)	**9,097.85**	**101.980915**	**8,105.65**	**102.28**
(II) Expenses				
Cost of Materials Consumed	5,125.48	57.45325984	4,722.74	59.60
Purchases of Stock-in-Trade	199.56	2.236936352	138.67	1.75
Changes in inventories of finished goods, work in progress and stock-in-trade	−136.17	−1.526376143	−115.07	−1.45
Employee Benefits Expense	404.59	4.535187807	341.63	4.31
Other Expenses	1,830.97	20.5239695	1,524.44	19.24
Total (II)	**7,424.43**	**83.22297736**	**6,612.41**	**83.44**
EARNINGS BEFORE INTEREST, TAX, DEPRECIATION AND AMORTISATION (EBITDA) (I) - (II)	1,673.42	18.75793762	1,493.24	18.84
Depreciation and Amortisation Expense	126.98	1.423362287	99.49	1.26
Finance Costs	30.56	0.342557501	30.82	0.39
PROFIT BEFORE TAX	1,515.88	16.99201783	1,362.93	17.20
less: Tax Expenses				
Current Tax	406.03	4.55132926	402.76	5.08
Deferred Tax	62.59	0.701592735	4.16	0.05
(Excess) Tax provision for earlier years	−2.74	−0.030713598	−2.38	−0.03
Total Tax Expenses	465.88	5.222208397	404.54	5.10
PROFIT AFTER TAX	**1,050.00**	**11.76980943**	**958.39**	**12.09**

Investments, and Inventory. Note, however, that all three have registered growth compared to previous year. Note also that the percentage in *Cash and cash equivalents* decreased significantly from 0.91 to 0.5% of assets. This shows that as Asian Paints grew its assets during the year, it chose to keep more in the form of Fixed Assets, Long Term Investments, and Inventory which are not very liquid.

Regarding liabilities and equity, the largest liability are the Current Liabilities, while the largest equity account is *Retained earnings*. It is most common for such type of manufacturer. The analysis also reveals Asian Paints' capital structure. Capital structure refers to the degree to which a company's assets are generated from liabilities versus equity. In general, a capital structure more heavily weighted towards liabilities is riskier. According to the vertical analysis, Asian Paints generated around 38% of assets from *Total liabilities* and 51% from *Total shareholders' equity* in the most recent year. This is a relatively low-risk capital structure.

An examination of the income statement shows that *Material Cost* was 57.68%, Employee cost 4.75% and Manufacturing, Administrative, Selling and Distribution Expenses was 19.46% of *Net sales*. Taken together, these three major expense categories consumed over 81% of the company's sales revenues. The

MAKING IT REAL

A company's balance sheet often reflects its business model, and a vertical analysis can help you identify one model from another. For example, take the following vertical analyses of selected assets from the 2010 balance sheets of two well-known retailers—Amazon and Wal-Mart. Can you tell which company is which?

	Company A	Company B
Cash and cash equivalents	20.0%	4.6%
Accounts receivable	8.4%	2.4%
Inventories	17.0%	19.4%
Fixed assets, net	12.8%	58.3%

Both Amazon and Wal-Mart are in the business of selling inventory, but their models are different. Wal-Mart is a traditional "bricks and mortar" company that sells its inventory in stores, while Amazon is a dot com company that sells its inventory online. Therefore, Wal-Mart should have a greater percentage of its total assets in fixed assets. Company B has 58.3% of its assets in fixed assets. Therefore, Company B is Wal-Mart.

© AP IMAGES/PAUL SAKUMA

result was that *Net earnings* were 12.26% of *Net sales*. This means that the company earned around 12 paise of profit for every rupee of sales. Note that this percentage is much lower than the 15% achieved in the prior year. As seen in the horizontal analysis, Asian Paints is profitable, but its profits are declining.

MARUTI SUZUKI ANALYSIS

Conduct and interpret horizontal and vertical analyses of Maruti Suzuki's inventory and operation cost found in Appendix C.

<u>Inventory</u>

H/A: (₹18,407 – ₹17,965) / ₹17,965 = 2.46%

V/A: ₹18,407 / ₹2,66,880 = 6.89%

<u>Operating cost</u>

H/A: (₹3,36,284 – ₹2,89,096) / ₹2,89,096 = 16.32%

V/A: ₹3,36,284 / ₹4,26,126 = 78.9%

The horizontal analyses indicate that both inventory and operating cost increased during the year. This reveals that the company is keeping more inventory. However, the vertical analyses indicate that inventory makes up around 7% of Maruti Suzuki's assets. Moreover, for every rupee of sales, Maruti Suzuki spends around 79 paise on the car sold. This leaves only 20 paise to cover all other expenses and generate a profit.

©HEMERA/THINKSTOCK

The statement of retained earnings links a company's income statement and balance sheet.

LO6 The Statement of Stockholders' Equity

Chapter 1 introduced the statement of retained earnings. The statement of retained earnings links a company's income statement and balance sheet by showing how net income and dividends change the company's retained earnings balance. All corporations prepare a statement of retained earnings, but most show it as a component of a more comprehensive statement of stockholders' equity.

A **statement of stockholders' equity** is a financial statement that shows how and why each equity account in the company's balance sheet changed from one year to the next. It therefore focuses not only on retained earnings, but also on other equity accounts relating to a company's contributed capital.

For illustration purposes, Exhibit 2-5 contains Asian Paints' statement of shareholders' equity for the fiscal year ended March 31, 2013. This statement reports two years of data. However, unlike the income statement, each column reflects the activity in a specific equity account rather than a period of time. The four columns of the statement refer to the five equity accounts from the classified balance sheet. That is, the balances at the bottom of the statement are the same balances from the most recent balance sheet. Note that the numbers are in crores. Note also that Asian Paints uses the word *shareholders'* in the title rather than stockholders'.

The first two accounts, *Common Stock* and *Additional Paid-In Capital*, represent the capital that

Statement of stockholders' equity A financial statement that shows how and why each equity account in the company's balance sheet changed from one year to the next.

Exhibit 2-5 Asian Paints' Statement of Shareholders' Equity

Consolidated Statements of Shareholders' Equity
Asian Paints

(in ₹ crores)	Common Stock		Additional Paid-in Capital	Retained Earnings	Accumulated Other Comprehensive Income (Loss)	Total
(in crores)	Shares	Amount				
Balance at April 1, 2012	9,59,19,779	95.92	Nil	₹2,391.86	₹ —	2,487.78
Net earnings						958.39
Balance at March 31, 2013	**9,59,19,779**	**95.92**	**Nil**	**2,926.34**	**—**	**3,022.26**
Net earnings						1,050.00

has been contributed to the company through the issuance of stock. Chapter 10 will discuss in more detail why contributed capital is divided into two accounts. For now, you simply need to add the balances together to yield the total amount received to date.

The account, *Retained Earnings,* represents the equity that has been generated through profitable operations and retained in the business. The retained earnings column is in fact Asian Paints' statement of retained earnings. In each year presented, net income is added to the beginning retained earnings balance, after dividends are subtracted.

The last account, *Accumulated Other Comprehensive Income (Loss),* is beyond the scope of this chapter.

LO7 Information Beyond the Financial Statements

A company's financial statements contain a significant amount of information about the financial activities and position of the company. However, they are not exhaustive, and much information that is useful to creditors and investors is not included on the statements. As a result, companies like Asian Paints prepare and report additional information beyond the financial statements. These items are normally included in a company's annual report that is distributed to all shareholders annually. Three items of significance are the following:

- **Notes to the financial statements**
- **Auditor's report**
- **Management's discussion and analysis**

Notes to the Financial Statements

After each of Asian Paints' financial statements is the following quote: *Notes to Financial Statements.* A company's financial statements cannot communicate or disclose to users all the information necessary to adequately understand the financial activities and condition of an entity. Additional information, both quantitative and qualitative, is necessary and can be found in the notes to the financial statements.

Notes to the financial statements The additional textual and numerical information immediately following the financial statements.

The **notes to the financial statements** are the textual and numerical information immediately following the financial statements that (1) disclose the accounting methods used to prepare the financial statements, (2) disclose additional detail and explanation of account balances, and (3) provide information not recognized in the financial statements. Financial statements should not be examined without considering the notes to the financial statements.

The content of the notes to the financial statements varies by company, but there are some similarities across companies. Note 1 to Notes to Financial Statements summarize the significant accounting policies used to prepare the financial statements. For example, you can find how a company accounted for its inventory, how the company uses estimates, and how the company recognizes its revenue. This note is especially useful in maintaining the comparability of financial statements across companies. Second, most companies include a note for each of their significant accounts. These notes can vary depending on the type of business, but most companies have notes for significant items such as property and equipment, income taxes, and employee benefit plans, among other things. Exhibit 2-6 contains

Exhibit 2-6 Asian Paints' Significant Accounting Policies and Notes to Financial Statements

1. Significant Accounting Policies and Notes

1.1 Basis of preparation of financial statement- Basis of Accounting and Use of Estimates
1.2 Tangible and Intangible Assets
1.3 Revenue Recognition
1.4 Lease Accounting—Assets taken on operating lease and Assets given on operating lease
1.5 Inventory
1.6 Investments
1.7 Transactions in Foreign Currency
1.8 Trade Receivables
1.9 Employee Benefits
1.10 Research and Development
1.11 Provision for Taxation
1.12 Provisions and Contingencies
1.13 Earnings Per Share
1.14 Proposed Dividend
1.15 Borrowing Cost
1.16 Cash and Cash Equivalents
1.17 Government Grants and Subsidies
1.18 Measurement of EBITDA

the titles of the notes to Asian Paints' most recent financial statements.

Auditor's Report

How do you know if Asian Paints' financial statements and notes can be depended upon to be a fair depiction of its financial condition? Since you don't have the ability to determine whether the reported numbers are reliable, you must rely on a third party to provide assurance that the information is reliable. This is why all annual reports contain an *independent auditor's report*.

An **independent auditor's report** is a report, prepared by a certified public accountant for the public shareholder, stating an opinion on whether the financial statements present fairly, in conformity with GAAP, the

IFRS

Since you don't have the ability to determine whether a company's reported numbers are reliable, you must rely on a third party to provide assurance that the information is reliable.

Independent auditor's report A report, prepared by a certified public accountant for the public shareholder, stating an opinion on whether the financial statements present fairly, in conformity with GAAP, the company's financial condition and results of operations and cash flows.

Exhibit 2-7 Asian Paints' Auditor's Report

REPORT OF INDEPENDENT REGISTERED PUBLIC ACCOUNTING FIRM

Auditors' Report to the Members of Asian Paints Limited

We have audited the accompanying financial statements of Asian Paints Limited ('the Company') which comprise the Balance Sheet as at 31st March, 2013, the Statement of Profit and Loss and the Cash Flow Statement for the year then ended and a summary of significant accounting policies and other explanatory information.

Our responsibility is to express an opinion on these financial results based on our audit. We conducted our audit in accordance with Standards on Auditing issued by the Institute of Chartered Accountants of India. Those standards require that we comply with ethical requirements and plan and perform the audit to obtain reasonable assurance about whether the financial statements are free of material misstatement. We believe that the audit evidence we have obtained is sufficient and appropriate to provide a basis for our audit opinion.

In our opinion and to the best of our information and according to the explanations given to us, the financial statements give the information required by the Act in the manner so required and give a true and fair view in conformity with the accounting principles generally accepted in India:

(i) in the case of the Balance Sheet, of the State of Affairs of the Company as at 31st March, 2013;

(ii) in the case of Statement of Profit and Loss, of the profit of the Company for the year ended on that date; and

(iii) in the case of cash flow statement, of the cash flows for the year ended on that date.

As required by the Companies (Auditor's Report) Order, 2003 ("the Order"), as amended, issued by the Central Government of India in terms of sub-section (4A) of section 227 of the Act, we give in the Annexure a statement on the matters specified in paragraphs 4 and 5 of the Order.

Further to our comments in the Annexure referred to above, we report that:

(a) we have obtained all the information and explanations, which to the best of our knowledge and belief were necessary for the purpose of our audit;
(b) in our opinion, proper books of account as required by law have been kept by the Company so far as appears from our examination of those books;
(c) the Balance Sheet, Profit and Loss Account, and Cash Flow Statement referred to in this report are in agreement with the books of account;
(d) in our opinion, the Balance Sheet, Profit and Loss Account, and Cash Flow Statement dealt with by this report comply with the Accounting Standards referred to in Section 211(3C) of the Act of Section 211 of the Act; and
(e) on the basis of written representations received from the Directors as at 31st March, 2013, and taken on record by the Board of Directors, we report that none of the directors of the Company is disqualified as on 31st March, 2013, from being appointed as a director in terms of clause (g) of sub-section (1) of Section 274 of the Act.

For B S R & Associates
Chartered Accountants
Firm Registration No: 116231W
Natrajh Ramakrishna
Partner
Membership No: 032815
Bengaluru
9th May, 2013

For Shah & Co.
Chartered Accountants
Firm Registration No: 109430W
Ashish Shah
Partner
Membership No: 103750
Mumbai
9th May, 2013

company's financial condition and results of operations and cash flows. Exhibit 2-7 contains Asian Paints' most recent auditor's report.

As you can see in the above report, Shah & Co and B S R & Associates are the two, public accounting firms, performed the audit. Auditors' opinion is stated under the heading 'Opinion' in the Auditor's Report: In our opinion and to the best of our information and according to the explanations given to us, the financial statements give the information required by the Act in the manner so required and give a true and fair view in conformity with the accounting principles generally accepted in India:

(i) in the case of the Balance Sheet, of the State of Affairs of the Company as at 31st March, 2013;
(ii) in the case of Statement of Profit and Loss, of the profit of the Company for the year ended on that date; and
(iii) in the case of cash flow statement, of the cash flows for the year ended on that date.

With this assurance from auditors, users can consider the financial statements reliable.

Management's Discussion and Analysis A discussion and analysis of the financial activities of the company by the company's management.

Management's Discussion and Analysis

In addition to financial statements, notes, and the auditor's report, all annual reports contain a section called Management's Discussion and Analysis. **Management's Discussion and Analysis (MD&A)** is a discussion and analysis of the financial activities of the company by the company's management. The MD&A normally precedes the financial statements in the annual report and contains, among other things, comments on the company's results of operations, its ability to satisfy its current obligations, and its expansion plans.

In some areas, the MD&A is useful in understanding past performance. For example, management usually compares the current year's operating results to the prior year's and explains the reasons for any differences. In other areas, the MD&A is useful in generating expectations for the future. For example, management often discloses how many stores it plans to open or how much in new property and equipment it plans to purchase in the coming year.

Given that the MD&A provides feedback value and predictive value, it is therefore relevant information and should be read along with the financial statements. Exhibit 2-8 contains two excerpts from Asian Paints' most recent MD&A.

Exhibit 2-8 Excerpts from Asian Paints' Management's Discussion and Analysis

Human Resources (HR)

People are central to your Company. The HR function of your Company has been structured and aligned in line with the business needs and requirements. The development of people in your Company has many facets. At a basic level, focus has been to ensure all employees at different managerial grades are aware of what is expected of them from a people management angle, through an initiative titled 'Learnscape'.

Also, digitisation of HR processes have been initiated to provide efficient and effective HR process management. A variety of learning methodologies have been deployed to ensure that development requirements are addressed appropriately and effectively. These include online business simulation, classroom sessions, e-learning tools, on the job learning, coaching, etc. These have been offered both as independent units of learning and blended solutions. In your Company, employee engagement is also actively driven through an inclusive process of dialogue and articulation of collective dreams. This was facilitated in the Sales and Research & Technology (R&T) functions. There is also a strong emphasis on building employee ownership at the shop floor level through effort in the direction of ensuring 'inclusive growth and participation'. Building people development capabilities in line managers is also another initiative by which internal trainers, coaches and facilitators have been developed. The international units of your Company also saw an increased focus on Learning and Development. Development and training for improving functional capabilities in the areas of Technology, Marketing, Finance and IT were completed with action plans for implementation.

Environment Health and Safety

Environment, Health and Safety (EHS) is one of the primary focus areas for your Company. Your Company's EHS policy is to consider compliance to statutory EHS requirements as the minimum performance standard and is committed to go beyond and adopt stricter standards wherever appropriate. Your Company's seven paint manufacturing facilities and the two chemical factories have the ISO 14001 environmental certification. All the seven paint manufacturing facilities (including the recently commissioned Khandala factory) and one chemical factory are 'Zero Discharge outside the factory' and also have rainwater harvesting capabilities. Minimisation of hazardous waste through reduction at source has been a key focus area in all the factories of your Company. This has resulted in reduction in specific generation of effluents and hazardous waste.

CONCEPT QUESTIONS

1. What are the three main forms of business?
2. What are the advantages and disadvantages to each form of business?
3. To what does the term GAAP refer?
4. Who has the authority to determine GAAP?
5. How are accounts classified in a classified balance sheet?
6. What is the difference between a fixed asset and an intangible asset?
7. What are the differences and similarities between the categories of liabilities in the classified balance sheet?
8. How is equity classified in a classified balance sheet, and what are the differences in each category?
9. Why is a multi-step income statement divided into multiple sections?
10. What are the characteristics of each subtotal of income on a multi-step income statement?
11. How is horizontal analysis used?
12. How is vertical analysis used?
13. How is horizontal analysis different from vertical analysis?
14. What is shown on the statement of stockholders' equity?
15. How is retained earnings calculated? How are retained earnings and stockholders' equity related?
16. What information do companies disclose in addition to the financial statements?

MULTIPLE CHOICE

1. The form of business in which one individual bears all risk is a:
   a. partnership.
   b. sole proprietorship.
   c. corporation.
   d. none of the above.
2. Which form of business issues shares of ownership to the public?
   a. Partnership
   b. Sole proprietorship
   c. Corporation
   d. None of the above
3. Which of the following institutions does not play a role in determining GAAP?
   a. Securities Exchange Board of India
   b. Financial Accounting Standards Board
   c. The Institute of Chartered Accountant of India
   d. All of the above play a role in determining GAAP
4. GAAP stands for:
   a. Generally Accepted Auditing Procedures.
   b. Governmental Auditing and Accounting Procedures.
   c. Generally Accepted Accounting Principles.
   d. Guidelines for All Accounting Professionals.
5. In a classified balance sheet, assets are usually classified as:
   a. current assets, long-term investments, fixed assets, intangible assets, other assets.
   b. current assets, property and equipment, long-term investments, short-term investments, other assets.
   c. short-term assets, long-term assets, tangible assets, intangible assets.
   d. fixed assets, noncurrent Investments, long-term loans and advances, other noncurrent assets, current assets.
6. Which of the following would not be a current asset?
   a. Inventory
   b. Accounts receivable
   c. Equipment
   d. Supplies
7. Which of the following is not included in a calculation of net income?
   a. Operating expenses
   b. Cost of sales
   c. Sales
   d. Goodwill
8. Mayer Corporation had sales of ₹2,40,000, cost of sales of ₹1,00,000, advertising expense of ₹85,000, and income tax expense of ₹15,000. What is *gross profit*?
   a. ₹40,000
   b. ₹1,40,000
   c. ₹55,000
   d. ₹1,25,000
9. Mayer Corporation had sales of ₹2,40,000, cost of goods sales of ₹1,00,000, advertising expenses of ₹85,000, and income tax expense of ₹15,000. What is *operating profit*?
   a. ₹40,000
   b. ₹1,40,000
   c. ₹55,000
   d. ₹1,25,000
10. Horizontal analysis:
    a. states each account balance as a percentage of a base account.
    b. compares account balances within a year.
    c. does not show trends over time.
    d. compares account balances over time.
11. The base account for a vertical analysis of the income statement is:
    a. net income.
    b. income before taxes.
    c. net sales.
    d. operating profit.
12. A horizontal analysis of inventory yields 5.5%. This means that:
    a. inventory was 5.5% of total assets.
    b. inventory was 5.5% of net sales.
    c. inventory increased 5.5% from the prior year to the current year.
    d. inventory decreased 5.5% from the prior year to the current year.

13. A vertical analysis of depreciation expense yields 5.5%. This means that:
   a. depreciation expense was 5.5% of total assets.
   b. depreciation expense was 5.5% of net sales.
   c. depreciation expense increased 5.5% from the prior year to the current year.
   d. depreciation expense decreased 5.5% from the prior year to the current year.
14. Last year J&M had assets of ₹1,00,000. This year assets are ₹1,20,000. A horizontal analysis of assets would yield:
   a. (20.0%).
   b. 16.7%.
   c. 20.0%.
   d. 16.7%.
15. Miller Corporation has current assets of ₹1,50,000, total assets of ₹8,50,000, and net sales of ₹1,32,000. A vertical analysis of current assets would yield:
   a. 17.6%.
   b. 11.4%.
   c. 64.4%.
   d. 21.8%.
16. McGee Inc. has administrative expenses of ₹1,20,000, total assets of ₹7,60,000, and net sales of ₹9,00,000. A vertical analysis of administrative expenses would yield:
   a. 10.6%.
   b. 15.8%.
   c. 25.1%.
   d. 13.3%.
17. Jones Services generated ₹12,30,000 in net income in its first year and ₹11,50,000 in its second year. A horizontal analysis of net income would yield:
   a. 7.0%.
   b. (6.5%).
   c. 8.7%.
   d. (7.0%).
18. Which of the following would not be included on a statement of stockholders' equity?
   a. Common stock
   b. Treasury stock
   c. Retained earnings
   d. Investments in common stock
19. Notes to the financial statements do not include:
   a. additional detail and explanation of financial statement account balances.
   b. accounting methods used in the preparation of the financial statements.
   c. information such as contingencies and future commitments.
   d. discussion and analysis of the company's financial activities by the company's management.
20. The auditor's report states an opinion on whether a company's financial statements are:
   a. completely error free.
   b. presented fairly in accordance with GAAP.
   c. better than competitor financial statements.
   d. none of the above.

BRIEF EXERCISES

1. Miscellaneous Terms

The following definitions were discussed in the chapter:

1. A form of business in which multiple entities join together.
2. Information following the financial statements that provides additional information and disclosures.
3. A form of business that is established by filing proper forms in a state.
4. A report that attests to the fair presentation of a company's financial statements.
5. The most common form of business.
6. Analysis of a company's financial activities that focuses on results of operations, ability to pay debts, and expansion plans.

Required
Match each definition with one of the following terms: Sole proprietorship; Management's Discussion and Analysis; Notes to the financial statements; Partnership; Auditor's Report; Corporation.

2. Generally Accepted Accounting Principles

The following definitions were discussed in the chapter:

1. The accounting rules followed by Indian corporations.
2. The governmental entity whose mission is to protect investors.
3. The accounting organization that establish and improve standards of financial accounting and reporting.
4. The major accounting rule-making body in India.
5. The international accounting rule-making body.

Required
Match each definition with one of the following terms: FASB; ICAI; SEBI; IASB; GAAP.

3. Classified Balance Sheet

The following accounts were taken from a company's balance sheet:

Supplies	Interest payable
Retained earnings	Equipment
Prepaid insurance	Salaries payable

Required
For each account, indicate whether the account is an asset, a liability, or an equity account. Also indicate the specific asset, liability, or equity classification the account would be reported under on the balance sheet. For example, cash is an asset that would be reported as a current asset.

4. Classified Balance Sheet

The following is a list of accounts taken from Jim's Uniforms:

Accounts receivable	₹1,20,000
Sales	18,00,000
Inventory	3,15,000
Accounts payable	4,62,000
Cash	7,33,000
Prepaid insurance	2,80,000
Equipment	13,50,000
Short-term investments	80,000

Required

Prepare the current asset section of Jim's balance sheet. Make sure to list the accounts in the proper sequence.

5. Calculating Gross Profit

During the month, a retailer generates ₹1,50,000 of sales, ₹25,000 of operating expenses, and ₹1,15,000 in cost of sales. At the end of the month, the company had ₹70,000 of merchandise inventory on hand.

Required

Calculate the company's gross profit for the month.

6. Calculating Operating Profit

Johnson Clothing Supercenter generated a gross profit of $7,750,000 during the year. Also during the year, Johnson incurred advertising expense of $1,500,000, salaries expense of $2,100,000, and income tax expense of $2,000,000.

Required

Calculate the company's operating profit and net income for the year.

7. Horizontal and Vertical Analyses

A company reports the following information from its financial statements:

	Current Year	Prior Year
Inventory	₹ 66,54,000	₹ 63,18,000
Sales	19,040,500	20,145,000
Total assets	27,045,000	24,068,000

Required

Conduct horizontal and vertical analyses of inventory for the current year. Round percentages to one decimal point (i.e., 10.1%).

8. Horizontal and Vertical Analyses

The following information (in millions) was taken from a recent income statement of **The J.M. Smucker Company**:

	Current Year	Prior Year
Net sales	₹4,605	₹3,758
Cost of sales	2,818	2,506
Gross profit	₹1,787	₹1,252

Required

Conduct horizontal and vertical analyses of gross profit. Was the company more or less profitable in the current year? Do both horizontal and vertical analyses indicate that? For your calculations, round percentages to one decimal point (i.e., 10.1%).

9. Horizontal Analysis

A horizontal analysis of a company's sales resulted in a ₹1.5 million increase, which equaled a percentage change of 22.8%.

Required

Interpret the rupee change and percentage change and identify which item(s) from the following list would potentially explain the results of the analysis.

a. A sales promotion was highly successful.
b. A manufacturing plant was offline for much of the year due to maintenance.
c. The company opened several new stores.
d. The company lost market share to a new competitor.
e. The company issued ₹1.5 million of shares during the year.

10. Statement of Stockholders' Equity

A company provides the following account balances for the current year:

Common stock	₹ 20,60,000
Retained earnings, beginning of year	62,49,600
Additional paid-in capital	10,000,000
Dividends	9,50,000
Treasury stock	(22,00,000)
Net income	22,13,300

Required

Prepare a statement of stockholders' equity at year-end.

EXERCISES

11. Classified Balance Sheet

The following is a list of accounts:

- Mortgage payable, due in 15 years
- Short-term investments
- Cash
- Prepaid rent
- Patents
- Common stock
- Accounts payable
- Buildings
- Notes payable, due in 6 months

Required

Identify each account as a Current asset, Long-term investment, Fixed asset, Intangible asset, Other asset, Current liability, Long-term liability, Contributed capital, or Retained earnings.

12. Classified Balance Sheet

A company reports the following accounts on its classified balance sheet:

Additional paid-in capital	Accounts receivable
Land	Bonds payable, due in 10 years
Treasury stock	Copyrights
Income taxes payable	Dividends payable
Long-term investments	Notes payable, due in 20 months

Required
Identify each account as a Current asset, Long-term investment, Fixed asset, Intangible asset, Other asset, Current liability, Long-term liability, Contributed capital, or Retained earnings.

13. Classified Balance Sheet Terms

The following is a list of balance sheet classifications and descriptions:

a. Current asset
b. Long-term investment
c. Fixed asset
d. Intangible asset
e. Other asset
f. Current liability
g. Long-term liability
h. Capital stock
i. Retained earnings

1. An obligation that is reasonably expected to be satisfied within the normal operations of business.
2. An investment in the common stock or bonds of another entity that the company does not intend to sell within one year.
3. Assets that do not fit into a particular classification of assets (for example, deferred tax liability).
4. An obligation that is not expected to be satisfied within one year.
5. The portion of equity contributed by stockholders through the purchase of stock, which includes common stock and preferred stock.
6. Resources that are reasonably expected to be converted to cash or consumed during the normal operations of business.
7. Tangible resources that are used in the company's operations for more than one year and are not intended for resale.
8. The profits that a company earns over time and retains in the business.
9. Resources to be used in the company's operations for more than one year that have no physical substance.

Required
Match each classification with the appropriate description.

14. Classified Balance Sheet

The following are independent cases:

	Sally's Fish & Chips	Brina's Bar & Grill	Ely's Tanning Salon
ASSETS (in millions)			
Current assets	3,000	2,500	4,500
Long-term investments	45,500	______	60,000
Fixed assets	125,750	100,000	150,000
Intangible assets	32,250	55,250	15,000
Other assets	______	35,500	6,500
Total assets	**220,000**	**225,750**	______
LIABILITIES (in millions)			
Current liabilities	15,500	7,000	______
Long-term liabilities	45,000	______	65,500
Total liabilities	______	**75,000**	**69,000**
STOCKHOLDERS' EQUITY (in millions)			
Capital stock	55,000	______	67,500
Retained earnings	______	105,000	______
Total liabilities and stockholders' equity	**220,000**	______	______

Required
Fill in each blank with the appropriate rupee amount.

15. Classified Balance Sheet

The following items were taken from the December 31 balance sheet of Auburn Bowling Lanes:

Buildings, net	₹6,02,000
Accounts receivable	1,45,200
Prepaid insurance	46,800
Cash	2,08,400
Equipment, net	6,36,800
Land	6,12,000
Mortgage payable	10,30,400
Common stock	6,60,000
Retained earnings	4,00,000
Interest payable	36,000
Accounts payable	1,24,800

Required
Recreate the company's classified balance sheet, assuming that ₹1,36,000 of the mortgage payable balance will be paid within three months of the balance sheet date.

16. Prepare a Classified Balance Sheet

The following information was taken from the February 26, 2011, balance sheet of **Best Buy**:

(in millions)	
Accounts payable	₹ 48,940
Accounts receivable	23,480
Additional paid-in capital	180
Cash	11,030
Short-term investments	220
Common stock	390
Intangible assets	25,870
Long-term liabilities	18,940
Other current assets	11,030
Other current liabilities	37,690
Other equity	8,630
Other assets	9,660
Fixed assets	38,230
Retained earnings	63,720
Inventory	58,970

Required

Prepare Best Buy's classified balance sheet at February 26, 2011.

17. Balance Sheet and Income Statement Classifications

A company uses the following pairs of accounts for its financial statements:

- Sales and Accounts receivable
- Interest payable and Interest expense
- Supplies expense and Supplies
- Inventory and Cost of sales
- Salaries payable and Salaries expense
- Income tax expense and Income tax payable

Required

For each pair of accounts, identify which account would be reported on the balance sheet and which would be reported on the income statement. For each balance sheet account, identify its classification. For each income statement account, identify which subtotal(s) of income would be affected by the account.

18. Multi-Step Income Statement

The following are all independent cases:

	The Bike Shop	The Rental Center	The Uniform Center
Sales	₹ ____	₹ 78,000	₹ 35,000
Cost of sales	45,000	____	____
Gross profit	18,000	____	7,000
Selling expenses	____	9,000	3,000
Administrative expenses	2,800	____	____
Total operating expenses	8,800	13,600	____
Operating profit	9,200	25,400	____
Income tax expense	____	11,000	1,000
Net income	7,700	____	1,500

Required

Fill in each blank with the appropriate rupee amount.

19. Multi-Step Income Statement

These items were taken from the financial records of Brown's Used Cars:

Utilities expense	₹ 1,76,500
Interest expense	500
Selling expense	1,46,000
Administrative expense	1,52,300
Interest revenue	5,000
Cost of sales	7,56,200
Net sales	15,49,000

Required

Prepare a multi-step income statement assuming Brown's falls into the 30% tax bracket and has a December 31 year end.

20. Multi-Step Income Statement

The following income statement items are taken from the records of Matthews Music Group for the year ending December 31:

Advertising expense	₹ 62,100
Cost of sales	8,39,100
Income tax expense	22,500
Insurance expense	39,600
Interest expense	41,150
Interest revenue	60,550
Rent expense	1,14,100
Salaries expense	2,85,250
Sales	15,30,100
Supplies expense	56,000

Required

Prepare a multi-step income statement for the year ending December 31.

21. Completing a Multi-Step Income Statement

The following multi-step income statement was provided by Reece Corp.:

Reece Corp.
Income Statement
For the Year Ending December 31

Net sales	₹ (a)
(b)	9,60,000
(c)	₹9,20,000
Insurance expense	(d)
Salaries expense	1,15,000
(e)	₹5,25,000
Interest revenue	92,000
Interest expense	(f)
(g)	₹ (h)
(i)	1,49,900
Net income	₹2,83,100

Required
Identify the missing amounts and descriptions.

22. Financial Statement Accounts

The following is a list of accounts:

Treasury stock	Interest payable
Interest revenue	Common stock
Buildings	Cost of sales
Dividends	Administrative expense
Accounts payable	Additional paid-in capital
Retained earnings	Cash

Required
Identify if each account would appear on the balance sheet, income statement, and/or statement of stockholders' equity.

23. Horizontal and Vertical Analyses

Comparative income statements are available for Johanna's Fine Furs:

	2012	2011
Sales	₹850,000	₹800,000
Cost of sales	325,000	275,000
Gross profit	525,000	525,000
Operating expenses	175,000	120,000
Operating profit	350,000	405,000
Income tax expense	105,000	121,500
Net income	₹245,000	₹283,500

Required
Perform horizontal and vertical analyses on each of the items in the above comparative income statements. Round percentages to one decimal point (i.e., 10.1%).

24. Horizontal and Vertical Analyses

The following condensed balance sheets are available for Delta Electronics:

	2012	2011 (₹ million)
Cash	₹ 142	₹ 160
Accounts receivable	35	30
Inventory	428	382
Current assets	605	572
Equipment, net	880	790
Total assets	₹1,485	₹1,362
Accounts payable	₹ 201	₹ 220
Salaries payable	169	162
Current liabilities	370	382
Bonds payable	350	300
Total liabilities	720	682
Retained Earnings	382	300
Common Stock	383	380
Total equity	765	680
Total liabilities and equity	₹1,485	₹1,362

Required
Perform horizontal and vertical analyses on each of the items in the above comparative balance sheets. Round percentages to one decimal point (i.e., 10.1%).

25. Horizontal and Vertical Analyses

Comparative balance sheet data is available for Ellis Enterprises:

	2012	2011 (₹ million)
Total assets	₹850,000	₹700,000
Total liabilities	₹240,000	₹280,000
Total equity	₹610,000	₹420,000

Required
Perform horizontal and vertical analyses on each of the items above. Round percentages to one decimal point (i.e., 10.1%). If generating assets through debt is considered more risky than generating assets through equity, is Ellis more or less risky in 2012?

26. Horizontal and Vertical Analyses

A company provides the following information:

	Current Year	Prior Year (₹ million)
Net sales	₹121,345	₹119,872
Accounts receivable	₹ 30,192	₹ 12,676
Total assets	₹246,933	₹250,361

Required
Should the company be concerned about its performance? Use horizontal and vertical analyses to "prove" why or why not. Round percentages to one decimal point (i.e., 10.1%).

27. Financial Accounting Terms

The following are various terms and definitions from financial accounting:

a. Common-size financial statement	1. A technique that compares account balances within one year by stating each account balance as a percentage of a base amount.
b. Notes to the financial statements	2. Textual and numerical information immediately following the financial statement's disclosing information such as accounting methods used, detail and explanation of account balances, and information not recognized in the financial statements.
c. Management's Discussion and Analysis	3. A statement in which all accounts have been standardized by the overall size of the company.
d. Auditor's Report	4. A discussion and analysis of the financial activities of the company by the company's management.

e. Vertical analysis	5. A report, prepared by a certified public accountant for the public shareholder, stating an opinion on whether the financial statements present fairly in conformity with GAAP the company's financial condition and results of operations and cash flows.
f. Horizontal analysis	6. A technique that calculates the change in an account balance from one period to the next and expresses that change in both dollar and percentage terms.

Required
Match each term with the appropriate definition.

PROBLEMS

28. Prepare a Classified Balance Sheet

Bay Company thinks there may be a problem with its balance sheet:

Bay Company Classified Balance Sheet For the Year Ending December 31	
Assets (₹ lakhs)	
Current assets	
Buildings	₹ 70,000
Interest revenue	11,000
Equipment	41,000
Cash	8,000
Other current assets	4,000
Total current assets	134,000
Accounts receivable	12,000
Land	20,000
Interest payable	14,000
Total noncurrent assets	46,000
Total assets	₹180,000
Liabilities and Stockholders' Equity (in lakhs)	
Current liabilities	
Accounts payable	₹ 16,000
Interest expense	39,000
Total current liabilities	55,000
Stockholders' equity	
Retained earnings	50,000
Common stock	35,000
Bonds payable	40,000
Total stockholders' equity	125,000
Total liabilities and stockholders' equity	₹180,000

Required
Prepare a corrected classified balance sheet.

29. Prepare a Multi-Step Income Statement

The auditor for Foshee Corporation noticed that its income statement was incorrect:

Foshee Corporation Income Statement December 31 (in lakhs)		
Sales		₹130,000
Cost of sales		80,000
Accounts receivable		19,500
Gross profit		30,500
Interest expense	₹15,000	
Selling expense	13,000	
Total operating expenses		28,000
Operating profit		2,500
Interest revenue	16,500	
Interest payable	4,000	8,500
Income before taxes		11,000
Income tax expense		12,850
Net income (loss)		₹ (1,850)

Required
Prepare a corrected multi-step income statement.

30. Multi-Step Income Statement and Classified Balance Sheet

The following items were taken from the financial statements of Wilson Inc. for 2012: (in lakhs)

Accounts payable	₹15,780
Accounts receivable	8,470
Advertising expense	4,200
Cash	16,080
Common stock	15,400
Cost of sales	41,250
Dividends	2,310
Equipment, net	45,420
Income tax expense	3,260
Insurance expense	4,680
Long-term liabilities	9,920
Prepaid insurance	5,970
Retained earnings, Jan. 1	28,450
Salaries expense	17,420
Salaries payable	5,210
Sales	78,420
Utilities expense	4,180

Required
Prepare a multi-step income statement for the year ending December 31, 2012, and a classified balance sheet at December 31, 2012. Hint: You must calculate ending retained earnings.

31. Prepare and Analyze the Classified Balance Sheet

The following balance sheet items are available from Carnell Inc. as of December 31, 2012:

	2012	2011 (in millions)
Accounts payable	₹ 75,500	₹ 35,035
Accounts receivable	50,000	85,065
Bonds payable, due 12/31/2016	125,000	25,000
Buildings, net	240,000	300,000
Capital stock, ₹5 par	100,000	80,000
Cash	15,000	25,635
Equipment, net	24,000	24,000
Income taxes payable	12,250	16,465
Interest payable	13,755	7,550
Inventory	25,650	27,270
Land	300,000	200,000
Long-term investments	125,000	100,000
Notes payable, due 6/30/2013	100,000	100,000
Supplies	12,500	13,500
Additional paid-in capital	200,000	190,000
Patents	6,000	6,000
Prepaid rent	10,150	12,275
Retained earnings	146,295	306,135
Salaries payable	35,500	33,560

Required

a. Prepare a comparative, classified balance sheet for Carnell Inc.

b. Perform horizontal and vertical analyses and interpret the results. Round percentages to one decimal point (i.e., 10.1%).

c. Assume the same information above except that in 2012, Bonds payable is ₹0 while Retained earnings is ₹271,295. Does this new information change any interpretations previously made?

32. Prepare and Analyze the Multi-Step Income Statement

The following income statement items are available from Dansby Inc. for the years ending December 31:

	2012	2011 (₹ in millions)
Advertising expense	₹ 7,765	₹ 9,789
Commissions expense	4,879	6,010
Cost of sales	48,596	58,896
Income tax expense	2,217	2,684
Insurance expense	4,897	5,236
Interest expense	2,584	2,695
Interest revenue	4,287	4,189
Sales	95,950	106,569
Supplies expense	1,654	2,106
Salaries expense	19,320	21,012
Rent expense	7,634	7,856

Required

a. Prepare a comparative, multi-step income statement for Dansby Inc.

b. Perform horizontal and vertical analyses and interpret the results. Round percentages to one decimal point (i.e., 10.1%).

c. Assume the following change in information: Cost of sales in 2012, ₹62,470 and in 2011, ₹45,670. Does this new information change any interpretations previously made?

33. Horizontal Analysis of the Income Statement

The following items were taken from a recent income statement of **Pep.Co**:

	Current Year	Prior Year (in ₹ milions)
Net sales	₹43,251	₹39,474
Cost of sales	20,351	18,038
Selling and administrative expenses	15,965	14,266
Operating income	6,935	7,170
Other income	86	461
Income before taxes	7,021	7,631
Provision for income taxes	1,879	1,973
Net income	5,142	5,658

Required

Perform a horizontal analysis on each account. Round percentages to one decimal point (i.e., 10.1%). What conclusions can you make about Pep.Co?

34. Using Horizontal and Vertical Analyses

The president of ABC Inc. is disappointed that the company was less profitable this year than last year. Comparative income statements for ABC Inc. are as follows:

	Current Year	Prior Year
Sales	₹800,000	₹500,000
Cost of sales	300,000	200,000
Gross profit	₹500,000	₹300,000
Operating expenses	167,000	130,000
Operating income	₹333,000	₹170,000
One-time gain		180,000
Net income	₹333,000	₹350,000

Required

Why was ABC's net income lower in the current year? Use horizontal and vertical analyses to show the ways in which ABC was more profitable in the current year. Round percentages to one decimal point (i.e., 10.1%).

CASES

35. Reading and Analyzing Financial Statements

Refer to **Maruti Co's** Annual Report contained in Appendix C of the textbook.

Required

a. Identify the company's current-year and prior-year balances in total current assets, net property and equipment, total assets, total current liabilities, total liabilities, and total stockholders' equity.
b. Conduct horizontal analysis on each account balance in part a. What broad trend is indicated by the calculations? Round percentages to one decimal point (i.e., 10.1%).
c. Identify the company's current-year and prior-year gross profit, operating income, earnings before income taxes, and net earnings.
d. Conduct horizontal analysis on each account balance in part c. What broad trend is indicated by the calculations? Round percentages to one decimal point (i.e., 10.1%).

36. Understanding Financial Statements

Refer to Maruti Udyog classified balance sheet and notes to the financial statement contained in Appendix C of the textbook.

Required

a. State the head under which current maturities of long-term debt will be reported. Explain what this account represents and why it is included in current liabilities if it relates to long-term debt.
b. The liability section contains an account entitled "Deferred Tax Liabilities". Explain what this account represents and how it is different from Deferred Tax Assets.
c. Under the account entitled 'Cash and Bank Balances' 'there is a term' 'Cash Equivalents'. Explain the term 'Cash Equivalents' and give examples of 'Cash Equivalents'.

37. Understanding Financial Statements

Refer to Maruti Udyog's income statement contained in Appendix C of the textbook.

Required

a. Identify the line item "Depreciation and Amortisation Expense." Explain in your own words what you think this line item represents.
b. Look at the note to the financial statements and explain what 'Impairment of Assets' represents.
c. Do you think 'Impairment of Assets' item should be reported separately on the income statement? Why or why not?

38. Research and Analysis

Access the 2012–13 annual report for **Ashok Leyland** by clicking on the *Investors* and *Annual Reports* links at www.ashokleyland.com.

Required

Conduct horizontal analysis of the company's net sales, cost of sales, and gross profit for the current year and vertical analysis for the same accounts for both the current and prior year. Round percentages to one decimal point (i.e., 10.1%). What conclusions can you draw about the company's ability to earn a profit from its sales?

39. Communication in Accounting

You and some friends have decided to start an investment club. Several of the new members of the club, however, have no knowledge of financial statements, particularly the income statement. They understand that a company must "make money," but they get confused when they read a multi-step income statement.

Required

Prepare a short memo for current and future members that describes the subtotals of income on a multi-step income statement.

reviewcard CHAPTER 2 Corporate Financial Statements

Learning Objectives		Key Concepts
LO1	Describe the three major forms of business.	The three major forms of business are sole proprietorship, partnership, and corporation. A sole proprietorship is owned by one person. A partnership is owned by multiple partners. A corporation is established in a state and is owned by investors who purchase the corporation's stock. Corporations whose stock is available to the public at large are called public corporations.
LO2	Define generally accepted accounting principles and their origins.	Generally accepted accounting principles are the accounting standards, rules, principles, and procedures that comprise authoritative practice for financial accounting. They have been developed over time by several regulatory bodies, including the Securities and Exchange Board of India, the Financial Accounting Standards Board, and the The Institute of Chartered Accountants of India.
LO3	Describe the main classifications of assets, liabilities, and equity in a classified balance sheet.	A classified balance sheet summarizes an entity's financial position at a point in time by grouping similar asset, liability, and equity accounts together and reporting them in several major classifications. Assets are classified into current assets, long term investments, fixed assets, intangible assets, and other assets. Liabilities are classified into current liabilities and long term liabilities. Equity is classified into contributed capital and retained earnings.
LO4	Describe the main subtotals of income on a multi-step income statement.	A multi-step income statement calculates income in multiple steps by grouping certain revenues and expenses together and calculating several subtotals of income. These subtotals include gross profit, operating profit, income before taxes, and net income.

Key Definitions

The Institute of Chartered Accountants of India (ICAI) The professional organization of certified public accountants whose board establishes rules that are often more technical and more specific to certain industries.

Classified balance sheet A type of balance sheet that groups together accounts of similar nature and reports them in a few major classifications.

Common-size financial statement A statement in which all accounts have been standardized by the overall size of the company.

Contributed capital The amount of equity a company generates through the sale of stock to investors.

Corporation A separate legal entity that is established by filing articles of incorporation in a state.

Cost of sales The cost of the inventory sold during a period.

Current asset Any asset that is reasonably expected to be converted to cash or consumed within one year of the balance sheet date.

Current liability An obligation that is reasonably expected to be satisfied within one year.

Financial Accounting Standards Board The standard setting body whose mission is "to establish and improve standards of financial accounting and reporting for the guidance and education of the public, including issuers, auditors, and users of financial information."

Fixed assets The tangible resources that are used in a company's operations for more than one year and are not intended for resale.

Generally accepted accounting principles The accounting standards, rules, principles, and procedures that comprise authoritative practice for financial accounting.

Learning Objectives		Key Concepts
LO5	Analyze the balance sheet and the income statement using horizontal and vertical analyses.	Horizontal analysis calculates the change in an account balance from one period to the next and expresses that change in both absolute and percentage terms. Because a horizontal analysis shows the growth or decline in each account, it is useful for identifying trends. Vertical analysis states each account balance as a percentage of some base account—sales on the income statement and total assets on the balance sheet. Because a vertical analysis standardizes each account by a measure of company size, it is useful in comparing different companies. The product of a vertical analysis is called a common-size statement.
LO6	Describe the purpose of a statement of stockholders' equity.	The statement of stockholders' equity shows the changes in all equity accounts, including retained earnings and contributed capital, over a period of time.
LO7	Describe the types of information usually disclosed along with financial statements.	In addition to its financial statements, a company will include the following in its annual report distributed to stockholders: notes to the financial statements, the auditor's report, and management's discussion and analysis.

Key Definitions (continued)

Gross profit The profit that a company generates when considering only the sales price and the cost of the product sold.

Horizontal analysis A method of analyzing a company's account balances over time by calculating absolute and percentage changes in each account.

Income before taxes The profit that a company generates when considering all revenues and expenses except for income taxes.

Independent auditor's report A report, prepared by a certified public accountant for the public shareholder, stating an opinion on whether the financial statements present fairly, in conformity with GAAP, the company's financial condition and results of operations and cash flows.

Intangible asset A resource that is used in operation for more than one year, is not intended for resale, and has no physical substance.

International Accounting Standards Board A board, similar to the FASB, whose mission is to develop a single set of high quality standards requiring transparent and comparable information.

International Financial Reporting Standards Standards issued by the International Accounting Standards Board.

Long-term investments The investments in the common stock or debt of another entity that will not be sold within a year.

Long-term liability An obligation that is not expected to be satisfied within one year.

Management's Discussion and Analysis A discussion and analysis of the financial activities of the company by the company's management.

Multi-step income statement Calculates income by grouping certain revenues and expenses together and calculating several subtotals of income.

Net income or Profit after tax The final income measure after the provision for income taxes is subtracted from income before taxes.

Notes to the financial statements The additional textual and numerical information immediately following the financial statements.

Key Definitions (continued)

Operating expenses Recurring expenses that a company incurs during normal operations.

Operating profit The profit that a company generates when considering both the cost of the inventory and the normal expenses incurred to operate the business.

Other assets Resources that do not fit well into one of the other asset classifications or are small enough that they do not warrant separate reporting.

Other revenue and expenses Revenues and expenses generated outside of normal operations.

Partnership A business that is formed when two or more proprietors join together to own a business.

Provision for income taxes The amount of income tax expense for a given period.

Public corporation A separate legal entity in which ownership is available to the public at large.

Retained earnings The amount of equity a company generates by being profitable and retaining those profits in the business.

Sales revenue The resources that a company generates during a period from selling its inventory.

Securities and Exchange Commission The federal agency charged to protect investors and maintain the integrity of securities markets.

Single-step income statement Calculates total revenues and total expenses and then determines net income in one step by subtracting total expenses from total revenues.

Sole proprietorship A business owned by one person.

Statement of stockholders' equity A financial statement that shows how and why each equity account in the company's balance sheet changed from one year to the next.

Vertical analysis A method of comparing a company's account balances within one year by dividing each account balance by a base amount to yield a percentage.

Key Formulas

Classified balance sheet

Assets
- Fixed Assets (including intangible assets)
- Long-term investment
- Current assets
- Other assets
- Total assets

Equity and Liabilities
- Contributed capital
- Retained earnings
- (A) Total equity
- Long-term liabilities
- Current liabilities
- (B) Total liabilities
- (A) + (B) Total equity and liability

Multi-step income statement

Net sales or revenues
− Cost of goods sold
Gross profit
− Operating expenses
Operating profit
+/− Other revenues and expenses
Income before taxes
− Income tax expense
Net income

Horizontal Analysis

Rupee change in account balance = Current year balance – Prior year balance

$$\text{Percentage change in account balance} = \frac{\text{Rupee change}}{\text{Prior year balance}}$$

Vertical Analysis

	For the Balance Sheet	For the Income Statement
Percentage	$\frac{\text{Account balance}}{\text{Total Assets}}$	$\frac{\text{Account balance}}{\text{Net Sales or Revenue}}$

Demonstration Problem

The following items were taken from the financial statements of a US Company Columbia Sportswear Company. Use the items to prepare a multi-step income statement for the year ending December 31 and a classified balance sheet at December 31. For each statement, prepare a vertical analysis. All dollar amounts are in thousands of dollars.

Accounts payable	$ 62,432
Accounts receivable	206,024
Accrued liabilities	43,789
Cash and cash equivalents	264,585
Common stock	205,465
Cost of sales	511,101
Current portion of long-term debt	4,596
Deferred tax asset, current	17,442
Deferred tax liability, long-term	7,716
Goodwill	12,157
Income tax expense	70,548
Income taxes payable	8,069
Intangibles and other assets	24,475
Interest expense	1,627
Interest revenue	2,107
Inventories	126,808
Long-term debt	16,335
Net sales	951,786
Prepaid expenses and other current assets	6,028
Property, plant, and equipment	126,247
Retained earnings	435,364
Selling, general and administrative expenses	250,496

Demonstration Problem Solution

Columbia Sportswear Company
Income Statement
For the Year Ending December 31

Net sales	$951,786	100.0%
Cost of sales	511,101	53.7%
Gross profit	$440,685	46.3%
Selling, general, and administrative expenses	250,496	26.3%
Operating profit	$190,189	20.0%
Other revenues and expenses:		
Interest revenue	2,107	0.2%
Interest expense	(1,627)	0.2%
Income before income tax	$190,669	20.0%
Income tax expense	70,548	7.4%
Net income	$120,121	12.6%

Columbia Sportswear Company
Balance Sheet
December 31

Assets

Current assets:		
Cash and cash equivalents	$264,585	33.8%
Accounts receivable, net	206,024	26.3%
Inventories, net	126,808	16.2%
Deferred tax asset	17,442	2.2%
Prepaid expenses and other current assets	6,028	0.8%
Total current assets	$620,887	79.2%
Property, plant, and equipment, net	126,247	16.1%
Intangibles and other assets	24,475	3.1%
Goodwill	12,157	1.6%
Total assets	$783,766	100.0%

Liabilities and Shareholders' Equity

Current liabilities:		
Accounts payable	$ 62,432	8.0%
Accrued liabilities	43,789	5.6%
Income taxes payable	8,069	1.0%
Current portion of long-term debt	4,596	0.6%
Total current liabilities	$118,886	15.2%
Long-term debt	16,335	2.1%
Deferred tax liability	7,716	1.0%
Total liabilities	$142,937	18.2%
Shareholders' equity:		
Common stock	$205,465	26.2%
Retained earnings	435,364	55.6%
Total shareholders' equity	$640,829	81.8%
Total liabilities and shareholders' equity	$783,766	100.0%

ACCT

Recording
Accounting Transactions

Learning Objectives

After studying the material in this chapter, you should be able to:

LO1 Describe the purpose of an accounting information system.

LO2 Analyze the effect of accounting transactions on the accounting equation.

LO3 Understand how T-accounts and debits and credits are used in a double-entry accounting system.

LO4 Describe the purpose of the journal, ledger, and trial balance.

LO5 Record and post accounting transactions and prepare a trial balance and financial statements.

Introduction

The first two chapters of this book focused on how economic information is communicated to users through financial statements: the balance sheet, the income statement, the statement of stockholders' equity, and the statement of cash flows. This chapter and Chapter 4 focus on how the activities of a business are captured by the accounting system so that these financial statements can be prepared. More specifically, Chapters 3 and 4 describe the accounting cycle. Because financial statements must be prepared periodically, the process of capturing and reporting information is a repetitive process, or cycle. This chapter explores the first three steps in the accounting cycle. The next chapter explores the remaining steps.

LO1 The Accounting Information System

A company's **accounting information system** is the system that identifies, records, summarizes, and communicates the various transactions of a company. Accounting information systems vary widely, ranging from manual, pencil-and-paper systems in some organizations to highly complex electronic systems in other organizations. However different their forms, though, all accounting systems are built to capture and report the effects of a company's *accounting transactions.*

An **accounting transaction** is any economic event that affects a company's assets, liabilities, or equity at the time of the event. Examples include the purchase of equipment, the consumption of supplies in operations, and the issuance of debt or stock. In each example, the event increases or decreases a specific asset, liability, or equity account of the company. Accounting transactions between a company and an external party (for example, an equipment purchase or the issuance of stock) are *external* transactions, while transactions within a company (the consumption of supplies) are *internal* transactions.

Accounting information system The system that identifies, records, summarizes, and communicates the various transactions of a company.

Accounting transaction Any economic event that affects a company's assets, liabilities or equity at the time of the event.

CHAPTER 

Much like a video camera, an accounting information system captures business activity so that others can view it.

© JEFF GREENBERG/ALAMY

To record accounting transactions and summarize the resulting information, companies use accounts. An **account** is an accounting record that accumulates the activity of a specific item and yields the item's balance. For example, a company's cash account is increased and decreased as cash is received and paid, and it shows the amount of cash held at any point in time. The various accounts that a company uses to capture its business activities are often listed in a **chart of accounts**. An example, complete with numerical references for each account, is found in Exhibit 3-1.

Charts of accounts will vary across companies. For example, a bank will have accounts relating to customer deposits while a biotech company will have accounts relating to research and development.

Account An accounting record that accumulates the activity of a specific item and yields the item's balance.

Chart of accounts The list of accounts that a company uses to capture its business activities.

Accounting information systems are built to capture and report the effects of a company's accounting transactions.

Exhibit 3-1 Chart of Accounts

100–199	ASSETS
100	Cash
101	Accounts Receivable
110	Supplies
120	Equipment
200–299	LIABILITIES
210	Accounts Payable
211	Unearned Revenues
230	Notes Payable
300–399	EQUITY
300	Common Stock
350	Retained Earnings
400–499	REVENUES
400	Service Revenue
500–599	EXPENSES
501	Administrative Expense
502	Advertising Expense
600–699	DIVIDENDS

Of course, there certainly will be many commonalities across charts of accounts—for example, practically every company will have an account for cash—but there will be differences depending on the company's activities. As a result, you can tell a lot about what a company does if you have its chart of accounts.

Dual nature of accounting Every accounting transaction must affect at least two accounts.

LO2 Accounting Transactions and the Accounting Equation

All accounting transactions must be recorded in the accounting information system. To understand the nature of recording transactions, it is best to start with the fundamental accounting equation:

$$\text{Assets} = \text{Liabilities} + \text{Equity}$$

The equation states that a company's assets must always equal the sum of its liabilities and equity. This means that any change to one part of the equation must be accompanied by a second change to another part. For example, suppose that a transaction increases an asset account. For the equation to stay in balance, the transaction must also either decrease another asset account or increase a liability or equity account. This means that every accounting transaction must affect at least two accounts. This is known as the **dual nature of accounting**.

Transaction Analysis

To illustrate how accounting transactions affect the accounting equation, consider the following ten transactions in the first month of operations of Circle Films, a company that documents weddings, birthdays, and other significant life events. Although the example is a small hypothetical company, the transactions would be treated in the same way by all companies, large or small.

MARUTI SUZUKI ANALYSIS

Look at Maruti Suzuki's Balance Sheet in Appendix C and determine how many accounts it uses to report its assets, liabilities, and equity. Also, consider the scenario when one stockholder of Maruti Suzuki sells his or her stock to another stockholder. Is this an economic event relating to Maruti Suzuki? Is it an accounting transaction?

Maruti Suzuki's Balance Sheet reports 22 different accounts, comprised of 12 asset accounts, 8 liability accounts, and 2 equity accounts.

When Maruti Suzuki's stock is sold on the Bombay Stock Exchange, the sale is an economic event of interest to Maruti Suzuki. However, because Maruti Suzuki is not involved in the transaction, it is not an accounting transaction.

Transaction Analysis

TRANSACTION #1: After incorporating, Circle Films issues 3,000 shares of common stock to investors for ₹15,000 cash. Because Circle Films receives cash of ₹15,000, assets increase. Its equity also increases because investors have contributed cash for an ownership interest in the company. More specifically, Circle Films' common stock increases.

	Assets	=	Liabilities	+	Equity
	Cash	=		+	Common Stock
Prior Bal.	₹ 0				₹ 0
#1	+₹15,000				+₹15,000
New Bal.	₹15,000				₹15,000
	₹15,000	=	₹0	+	₹15,000

TRANSACTION #2: Circle Films purchases a video camera for ₹9,000 and memory cards for ₹1,000. In this transaction, the company is exchanging one asset (cash) for other assets (equipment and supplies). Therefore, assets both increase and decrease by ₹10,000. The net effect is no change in total assets.

	Assets			=	Liabilities	+	Equity
	Cash	Supplies	Equipment	=		+	Common Stock
Prior Bal.	₹15,000	₹ 0	₹ 0				₹15,000
#2	−₹10,000	+₹1,000	+₹9,000				
New Bal.	₹ 5,000	₹1,000	₹9,000				₹15,000
	₹15,000			=	₹0	+	₹15,000

TRANSACTION #3: Circle Films receives a ₹1,500 payment immediately after filming a customer's wedding. Since Circle Films is receiving cash, assets increase. But unlike the previous transaction in which assets were exchanged, the increase in assets in this transaction results from filming the wedding. Note an inflow of assets from providing a service is a revenue. Revenues increase net income and therefore retained earnings. As a result, Circle Films' equity increases.

	Assets			=	Liabilities	+	Equity	
	Cash	Supplies	Equipment	=		+	Common Stock	Retained Earnings
Prior Bal.	₹5,000	₹1,000	₹9,000				₹15,000	₹ 0
#3	+₹1,500							+₹1,500
New Bal.	₹6,500	₹1,000	₹9,000				₹15,000	₹1,500
	₹16,500			=	₹0	+	₹16,500	

TRANSACTION #4: Circle Films receives a ₹2,000 deposit from a customer to film her parents' fiftieth wedding anniversary. In this transaction, Circle Films again receives cash from a customer, so assets increase. However, it has not yet provided the service, so it has an obligation to the customer. As a result, Circle Films' liabilities increase for the amount of cash received.

	Assets			=	Liabilities	+	Equity	
	Cash	Supplies	Equipment	=	Unearned Revenue	+	Common Stock	Retained Earnings
Prior Bal.	₹6,500	₹1,000	₹9,000		₹ 0		₹15,000	₹1,500
#4	+₹2,000				+₹2,000			
New Bal.	₹8,500	₹1,000	₹9,000		₹2,000		₹15,000	₹1,500
	₹18,500			=	₹2,000	+	₹16,500	

TRANSACTION #5: Circle Films paid ₹250 cash to run an ad in the local paper. Because Circle Films paid cash, assets decrease. The decrease in assets results from advertising its business. Recall from Chapter 1 that a decrease in assets from operating a business is an expense. Expenses decrease net income and therefore retained earnings. As a result, Circle Films' equity decreases.

	Assets			=	Liabilities	+	Equity	
	Cash	Supplies	Equipment	=	Unearned Revenue	+	Common Stock	Retained Earnings
Prior Bal.	₹8,500	₹1,000	₹9,000		₹2,000		₹15,000	₹1,500
#5	−₹ 250							−₹ 250
New Bal.	₹8,250	₹1,000	₹9,000		₹2,000		₹15,000	₹1,250
	₹18,250			=	₹2,000	+	₹16,250	

TRANSACTION #6: Circle Films films a dance competition, leaving a ₹3,500 invoice with the customer. Because Circle Films receives no cash at the time of the competition, it is tempting to conclude that there is no accounting transaction and therefore no effect on the accounting equation. However, not all accounting transactions affect cash. By completing the job and leaving an invoice with the customer, Circle Films now has a receivable from the customer. Therefore, assets increase. And because the receivable is generated by providing a service, the firm has additional revenues and therefore more equity. So, equity increases as well. Note that this transaction is very similar to transaction #3, with the only difference being the type of asset that increases.

	Assets				=	Liabilities	+	Equity	
	Cash	Accounts Receivable	Supplies	Equipment	=	Unearned Revenue	+	Common Stock	Retained Earnings
Prior Bal.	₹8,250	₹ 0	₹1,000	₹9,000		₹2,000		₹15,000	₹1,250
#6		+₹3,500							+₹3,500
New Bal.	₹8,250	₹3,500	₹1,000	₹9,000		₹2,000		₹15,000	₹4,750
	₹21,750				=	₹2,000	+	₹19,750	

TRANSACTION #7: Circle Films purchases another ₹9,000 video camera by signing a nine-month promissory note requiring the payment of principal and interest at maturity. Interest is charged at a 6% annual rate. Like transaction #2, Circle Films receives equipment, so assets increase. Unlike transaction #2, though, Circle Films promises to pay cash and interest in nine months instead of paying cash. Therefore, its liabilities increase.

	Assets				=	Liabilities		+	Equity	
	Cash	Accounts Receivable	Supplies	Equipment	=	Unearned Revenue	Notes Payable	+	Common Stock	Retained Earnings
Prior Bal.	₹8,250	₹3,500	₹1,000	₹ 9,000		₹2,000	₹ 0		₹15,000	₹4,750
#7				+₹ 9,000			+₹9,000			
New Bal.	₹8,250	₹3,500	₹1,000	₹18,000		₹2,000	₹9,000		₹15,000	₹4,750
	₹30,750				=	₹11,000		+	₹19,750	

TRANSACTION #8: Circle Films receives ₹3,500 from the customer in payment of the open invoice from transaction #6. In this transaction, Circle Films exchanges one asset for another. It receives cash in satisfaction of the receivable that was created when the service was performed. As a result, cash increases while receivables decrease. There is no change in total assets.

	Assets				=	Liabilities		+	Equity	
	Cash	Accounts Receivable	Supplies	Equipment	=	Unearned Revenue	Notes Payable	+	Common Stock	Retained Earnings
Prior Bal.	₹ 8,250	₹3,500	₹1,000	₹18,000		₹2,000	₹9,000		₹15,000	₹4,750
#8	+₹ 3,500	−₹3,500								
New Bal.	₹11,750	₹ 0	₹1,000	₹18,000		₹2,000	₹9,000		₹15,000	₹4,750
	₹30,750				=	₹11,000		+	₹19,750	

TRANSACTION #9: Circle Films pays wages of ₹2,000 to its employees. In this case, its cash decreases by ₹2,000, so its assets decrease. Since the payments are an outflow of assets from operating the business, the payments are an expense, which is a reduction to equity. Therefore, equity decreases.

	Assets				=	Liabilities		+	Equity	
	Cash	Accounts Receivable	Supplies	Equipment	=	Unearned Revenue	Notes Payable	+	Common Stock	Retained Earnings
Prior Bal.	₹11,750	₹0	₹1,000	₹18,000		₹2,000	₹9,000		₹15,000	₹4,750
#9	−₹ 2,000									−₹2,000
New Bal.	₹ 9,750	₹0	₹1,000	₹18,000		₹2,000	₹9,000		₹15,000	₹2,750
	₹28,750				=	₹11,000		+	₹17,750	

TRANSACTION #10: At the end of the month, Circle Films pays its owners a ₹1,500 cash dividend. In this transaction, cash and therefore assets decrease. Payments to a company's owners are dividends. Recall from Chapter 1 that dividends decrease retained earnings, so equity decreases as well.

	Assets				=	Liabilities		+	Equity	
	Cash	Accounts Receivable	Supplies	Equipment	=	Unearned Revenue	Notes Payable	+	Common Stock	Retained Earnings
Prior Bal.	₹9,750	₹0	₹1,000	₹18,000		₹2,000	₹9,000		₹15,000	₹2,750
#10	−₹1,500									−₹1,500
New Bal.	₹8,250	₹0	₹1,000	₹18,000		₹2,000	₹9,000		₹15,000	₹1,250
		₹27,250			=	₹11,000		+	₹16,250	

Summary of Transactions

The ten transactions of Circle Films are summarized in Exhibit 3-2. Circle Films started the month with nothing but an idea and ended the month with ₹27,250 in assets, ₹11,000 in liabilities, and ₹16,250 in equity. As you review the exhibit, note that changes to the left side of the equation equaled changes to the right side of the equation for all transactions. As a result, the accounting equation was always in balance. Note also that every transaction affected at least two specific accounts. Sometimes the transaction affected two asset accounts (#2 and #8), sometimes an asset and a liability account (#4 and #7), and sometimes an asset and an equity account (#1, #3, #5, #6, #9, and #10). Any combination affecting assets, liabilities, and equity can occur, as long as the equation stays in balance.

Exhibit 3-2 Transaction Summary for Circle Films

	Assets				=	Liabilities		+	Equity	
	Cash	Accounts Receivable	Supplies	Equipment	=	Unearned Revenue	Notes Payable	+	Common Stock	Retained Earnings
#1	+15,000				=			+	+15,000	
#2	−10,000		+1,000	+9,000	=			+		
#3	+1,500				=			+		+1,500
#4	+2,000				=	+2,000		+		
#5	−250				=			+		−250
#6		+3,500			=			+		+3,500
#7				+9,000	=		+9,000	+		
#8	+3,500	−3,500			=			+		
#9	−2,000				=			+		−2,000
#10	−1,500				=			+		−1,500
	₹8,250	₹0	₹1,000	₹18,000	=	₹2,000	₹9,000	+	₹15,000	₹1,250
		₹27,250			=	₹11,000		+	₹16,250	

LO3 The Double-Entry Accounting System

While the preceding analysis is an excellent way to understand and visualize the effect of accounting transactions, accounting information systems do not record transactions using plusses and minuses in a tabular format since such an approach, while accurate, would be very cumbersome. Rather, they use a *double-entry system* that traces its origins back to a mathematical treatise written in the fifteenth century by a Franciscan monk, Luca Pacioli. The double-entry system is based on the dual nature of accounting demonstrated in the preceding transaction analyses. That is, every accounting transaction affects at least two accounts, so accounting systems record those transactions with a "double" or "two-fold" entry. The following sections explain the mechanics of this double-entry system, starting with the T-account.

The T-Account

All accounts can be characterized or represented in the following form known as a T-account due to its resemblance to a capital T.

Account Name	
Debit Side	Credit Side

The name of the account is listed at the top with two columns appearing below. The left column is the *debit* side while the right column is the *credit* side. The term **debit** simply means left side of an account while the term **credit** simply means right side of an account.

T-accounts work as follows. When a transaction affects an account balance, the amount of the transaction is entered on the account's debit side or credit side, depending on the transaction. You will see how transactions are recorded shortly. An entry on the debit side is called a "debit," while an entry on the credit side is called a "credit." Once all entries are made, the balance in an account is determined by separately adding up all debits and all credits and subtracting the smaller total from the larger, leaving the difference as the account balance. The following three examples illustrate this process.

You can tell a lot about what a company does if you have its chart of accounts.

Examples of T-Account Mechanics

Asset		Liability		Equity	
1,000	5,000	2,000	6,000	7,000	2,000
4,000	3,000	1,000	4,000		3,000
8,000		3,000			3,000
5,000			4,000		1,000

The areas between the horizontal lines contain the activity in each account, with the account balance below. The asset account has three debit entries totaling ₹13,000 and two credit entries totaling ₹8,000, leaving a debit balance of ₹5,000. The liability account has debit entries totaling ₹6,000 and credit entries totaling ₹10,000, resulting in a ₹4,000 credit balance. The equity account has a ₹1,000 credit balance after having ₹7,000 of debit entries and ₹8,000 of credit entries.

It is no coincidence that in this example the asset account has a debit balance while the liability and equity accounts have credit balances. In a double-entry system, asset accounts should normally have debit balances while liability and equity accounts should normally have credit balances. Such "normal" balances mirror the accounting equation, where assets are on the left side of the equal sign and liabilities and equity are on the right side.

Normal Account Balances

Asset Accounts		Liability Accounts		Equity Accounts	
Normal Balance			Normal Balance		Normal Balance

Accounting Equation

Assets = Liabilities + Equity

Debit The left side of an account.

Credit The right side of an account.

Any change to the accounting equation must be accompanied by a second change.

This arrangement of normal balances is the key to a how a double-entry system works. To keep the accounting equation balanced, a double-entry system must keep debit balances equal to credit balances. This means that every accounting transaction must be recorded with equal changes to debit and credit balances. That, again, is why the system is "double-entry." How debits and credits are used to change account balances is discussed next.

Debit and Credit Rules

In a double-entry system, changes in account balances are recorded according to the following basic rules.

To *increase* an account balance	Record transaction on the same side as the normal balance.
To *decrease* an account balance	Record transaction on the opposite side as the normal balance.

These two rules seem simple enough, but their application can be confusing at first because different accounts have different normal balances. The following sections demonstrate how these rules are applied to asset, liability, and equity accounts. Also demonstrated is how these rules are applied to the three types of accounts that affect equity: revenues, expenses, and dividends. Once you have mastered the mechanics of these six types of accounts, you should be able to record most any accounting transaction correctly.

Asset Accounts Asset accounts have normal debit balances. Therefore, increases to assets are recorded on the debit side while decreases are recorded on the credit side.

Asset Accounts

Record increases on debit side	Record decreases on credit side
Balance	

To illustrate, suppose that a company starts the day with ₹5,000 in cash, receives ₹300 from a customer, and pays ₹250 to a vendor. The beginning balance of ₹5,000 is recorded on the debit side of the cash T-account. The increase of ₹300 is also recorded on the debit side, but the ₹250 decrease in cash is recorded on the side opposite of the normal balance—the credit side. Netting the debit and credit sides yields a debit balance of ₹5,050.

Cash

5,000	250
300	
5,050	

Liability and Equity Accounts Liability and equity accounts have normal credit balances. Therefore, increases are recorded on the credit side, while decreases are recorded on the debit side.

Liability and Equity Accounts

Record decreases on debit side	Record increases on credit side
	Balance

To illustrate a liability account, suppose that a company owing ₹2,500 to a vendor buys an additional ₹150 of product on account and then pays ₹850 of its obligation. The beginning balance of ₹2,500 is recorded on the credit side of the Accounts Payable T-account. The additional payable of ₹150 is also recorded on the credit side. In contrast, the ₹850 payment, which is a reduction to the payable, is recorded on the debit side. Netting the debit and credit sides yields a credit balance of ₹1,800.

Accounts Payable

850	2,500
	150
	1,800

To illustrate an equity account, suppose that a company has ₹34,000 of common stock outstanding. The company then issues additional common stock for ₹10,000 and later buys back and retires ₹6,000 of stock. The original ₹34,000 balance appears on the credit side of the Common Stock T-account. Since the Common Stock account has a normal credit balance, the ₹10,000 increase is recorded on the credit side while the ₹6,000 decrease is recorded on the opposite or debit side of the account. Netting the debit and credit sides yields a credit balance of ₹38,000.

Common Stock	
6,000	34,000
	10,000
	38,000

> Any combination affecting assets, liabilities and equity can occur in a transaction, as long as the accounting equation stays in balance.

Revenue Accounts When a company generates a revenue, it is increasing its equity. As demonstrated previously, increasing an equity account requires a credit entry. Therefore, revenue accounts are set up so that they also are increased with a credit entry. That is, revenue accounts have normal credit balances and are increased with credit entries and decreased with debit entries.

Revenue Accounts	
Record decreases on debit side	Record increases on credit side
	Balance

To illustrate, suppose that a company has ₹1,15,000 in existing service revenue. The company then earns an additional ₹13,000 in revenue. Since the Service Revenue account has a normal credit balance, both the existing ₹1,15,000 balance and the ₹13,000 increase are shown on the credit side, resulting in a balance of ₹1,28,000.

Service Revenue	
	115,000
	13,000
	128,000

Expense and Dividend Accounts When a company incurs expenses or pays dividends, it is decreasing its equity. As demonstrated previously, decreasing equity requires a debit entry. Therefore, for expense and dividend accounts to effectively reduce equity, they have normal debit balances. Expense and dividend accounts are therefore increased with debit entries and decreased with credit entries.

Expense and Dividend Accounts	
Record increases on debit side	Record decreases on credit side
Balance	

To illustrate an expense, suppose that a company has ₹66,000 in salaries expense when it incurs an additional ₹6,000 in salaries expense. Since the Salaries Expense account has a normal debit balance, both the ₹66,000 in existing expense and the ₹6,000 increase should be recorded on the debit side of the account, yielding a balance of ₹72,000.

Salaries Expense	
66,000	
6,000	
72,000	

Summary of Debit and Credit Rules

You have now seen each major type of account and how the debit and credit columns are used to increase or decrease those accounts. For asset, expense, and dividend accounts, increases are recorded in the debit column and decreases are recorded in the credit column. For liability, equity, and revenue accounts, increases are recorded in the credit column and decreases are recorded in the debit column. A summary of these rules is presented in Exhibit 3-3.

Exhibit 3-3 Summary of Debit and Credit Rules

Type of Account	Normal Balance	Increase with a	Decrease with a
Asset	Debit	Debit	Credit
Liability	Credit	Credit	Debit
Equity	Credit	Credit	Debit
Revenue	Credit	Credit	Debit
Expense	Debit	Debit	Credit
Dividend	Debit	Debit	Credit

In a double-entry system, asset accounts have debit balances while liability and equity accounts have credit balances.

LO4 Recording Transactions in the Accounting System

This section examines the actual process of recording accounting transactions in a double-entry system. Accounting transactions are not recorded directly in T-accounts. Instead, accounting transactions are first recorded in a journal. Once recorded, the information is transferred or posted to a ledger. Information in the ledger is then summarized in a worksheet known as a trial balance. Financial statements are then prepared from the information in the trial balance.

The Journal

A **journal** is a chronological record of transactions. Because the journal is where transactions are first recorded into the accounting system, it is often called the book of original entry. Entries recorded in the journal are called *journal entries*. Companies can have various types of journals in which they record transactions, but since the mechanics of all journals are the same, we will focus on the most basic of journals, the general journal.

Journal A chronological record of transactions.

The general journal and an example journal entry take the form shown in Exhibit 3-4.

Exhibit 3-4 General Journal Form

General Journal

Date	Account and Explanation	Debit	Credit
Date of transaction	Account(s) Debited	Amount	
	Account(s) Credited		Amount
	(Explanation of transaction)		

At the far left of the journal is a column for the transaction date. To the right of the date is a column to record the names of the accounts affected by the transaction and an explanation. The account(s) receiving debit entries are listed first followed by the account(s) receiving credit entries, which are slightly indented. To the right of the account names are debit and credit columns to record the monetary amounts of the transaction. As explained previously, the totals in the debit and credit columns should be the same for each transaction. When an accounting transaction is recorded in the general journal, we often say that the transaction has been *journalized*.

The general journal is useful in that it contains in one place a chronological record of all the accounting transactions of a company. Thus, a company can examine its journal if it has a question about whether a transaction was recorded or whether it was recorded correctly. However, the general journal is not very useful if a company is trying to determine the balance in a particular account. To get an account balance, one would have to find all journal entries affecting that account and then compute a balance. To avoid such a time-consuming task, the information recorded in the general journal is transferred to a *ledger*.

MARUTI SUZUKI ANALYSIS

Look at Maruti Suzuki's Income Statement in Appendix C. Which of the accounts would be increased with a credit entry? Would the remaining accounts be increased with a debit entry?

Maruti Suzuki's income statement (Profit and Loss Account) lists around fourteen different accounts. Of those accounts, Net Sales, Other Operating Revenue, other income (by and large Investment Income) would be increased with a credit entry. All of these accounts are revenue accounts. The other eleven accounts are expense accounts and are increased with a debit entry.

When an accounting transaction is recorded in the general journal, we often say that the transaction has been *journalized.*

The Ledger

A **ledger** is a collection of accounts and their balances. While most companies have various types of ledgers containing different accounts, we will focus on the most basic type of ledger, the general ledger. The general ledger is nothing more than a collection of T-accounts for a company, which means that the general ledger contains both the activity and balances of all company accounts.

Account balances in the general ledger are updated as follows. When an accounting transaction is recorded in the general journal, the amounts recorded in the debit and credit columns are transferred to the debit and credit columns of the respective T-accounts in the ledger. This process of copying or transferring the information from the journal to the ledger is called *posting* and results in up-to-date account balances. Thus, companies look to the ledger for balances in their accounts.

The Trial Balance

After accounting transactions are recorded in the journal and posted to the ledger, companies prepare a trial balance. A **trial balance** is a listing of accounts and their balances at a specific point in time. In a trial balance, all accounts in a company's ledger are listed in a column on the left. Asset accounts are listed first, followed by liability accounts, equity accounts, and then revenue, expense, and dividend accounts. Each account's balance from the ledger is listed in the appropriate debit or credit column. At the bottom of each column, a total is calculated. The form of the trial balance is shown in Exhibit 3-5.

Ledger A collection of accounts and their balances.

Trial balance A listing of accounts and their balances at a specific point in time.

MAKING IT REAL

Although the text primarily discusses a manual accounting system, there are several popular computerized accounting information systems utilized by small businesses. One of the most popular is Tally Accounting Software.

Tally Accounting Software is favored largely for its simplicity and ease of use for individuals with little to no accounting experience.

The accounting software provides banking, general ledger, accounts payable, accounts receivable, payroll, and inventory features and can keep track of income and expenses by customer, job, and department. Many reports can be created by the system to analyze business performance. The system also provides security features to ensure only authorized users are accessing the businesses' accounting information.

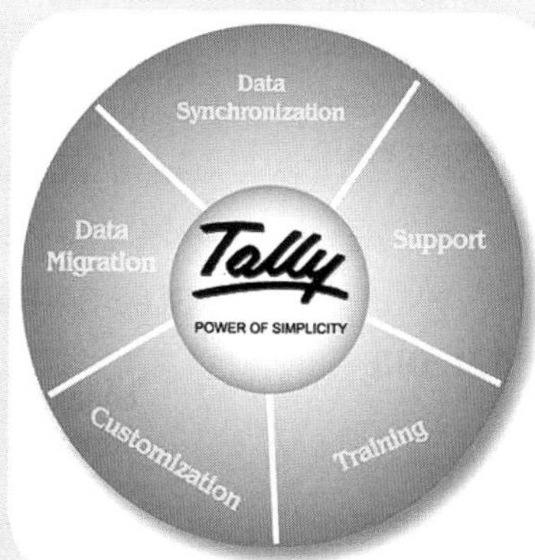

Overall, such computerized software system is a great tool for businesses because it helps ensure that a company's accounting information is captured and communicated effectively and efficiently.

Exhibit 3-5 Trial Balance Form

	Debit	Credit
Asset Account(s)	Amount	
Liability Account(s)		Amount
Equity Account(s)		Amount
Revenue Account(s)		Amount
Expense Account(s)	Amount	
Dividends	Amount	
Totals	Total Debits	Total Credits

A trial balance serves several functions. First and foremost, a trial balance proves that total debit balances equal total credit balances. If they are unequal, then the accounting equation is out of balance and a correction is warranted. Second, a trial balance summarizes in one place all accounts of an entity and their respective balances. Financial statements are then prepared from those balances. Finally, a trial balance is helpful in making any necessary adjustments to account balances at the end of an accounting period. We will see this function in Chapter 4.

LO5 Comprehensive Example: Journal Entries to Financial Statements

The following section uses the Circle Films transactions to demonstrate the recording of transactions in the journal, the posting of information to the ledger, the preparation of a trial balance, and the preparation of financial statements.

Recording Transactions in the Journal and Posting to the Ledger

Circle Films entered into ten transactions. A four-step process will be used to demonstrate how to properly record each transaction and post it to the ledger. First, the accounts affected by the transaction will be identified. Second, the relevant debit/credit rules for those accounts will be identified. Third, the transaction will be recorded in the journal. Fourth, the transaction will be posted to the ledger. This four-step process can be followed when recording and posting any accounting transaction.

Transaction #1 Circle Films issued 3,000 shares of common stock for ₹15,000.

Step 1—What accounts are affected and how? Circle Films receives cash, so cash increases. Circle Films issues common stock, so common stock increases.

Step 2—What debit and credit entries are required? Cash is an asset, so debit the Cash account to increase it. Common Stock is an equity account, so credit the Common Stock account to increase it.

Step 3—Record the journal entry.

#1	Cash	15,000	
	Common Stock		15,000
	(Owners invest cash in business)		

Assets	=	Liabilities	+	Equity
+15,000				+15,000

Step 4—Post the information to the ledger.

Cash	
15,000	
15,000	

Common Stock	
	15,000
	15,000

Transaction #2 Circle Films buys a ₹9,000 video camera and ₹1,000 of memory cards for ₹10,000 cash.

Step 1—What accounts are affected and how? Circle Films receives a camera and some tapes, so both equipment and supplies increase. Circle Films pays with cash, so cash decreases.

Step 2—What debit and credit entries are required? Equipment and supplies are assets, so debit the Equipment and Supplies accounts to increase them. Cash is also an asset, so credit the Cash account to decrease it.

Step 3—Record the journal entry.

#2	Equipment	9,000	
	Supplies	1,000	
	Cash		10,000
	(Purchase video camera and tapes)		

Assets	=	Liabilities	+	Equity
+9,000				
+1,000				
−10,000				

Step 4—Post the information to the ledger.

Cash		Supplies		Equipment	
15,000	10,000	1,000		9,000	
5,000		1,000		9,000	

Transaction #3 Circle Films films a wedding for ₹1,500 cash.

Step 1—What accounts are affected and how? Circle Films receives cash, so cash increases. The increase in cash results from Circle Films providing its service, so service revenue increases.

Step 2—What debit and credit entries are required? Cash is an asset, so debit the Cash account to increase it. Revenues increase equity, so credit the Service Revenue account to increase it.

Step 3—Record the journal entry.

		Debit	Credit
#3	Cash	1,500	
	Service Revenue		1,500
	(Provide service to customer)		

Assets	=	Liabilities	+	Equity
+1,500				+1,500

Step 4—Post the information to the ledger.

Cash		Service Revenue	
15,000	10,000		1,500
1,500			
6,500			1,500

Transaction #4 Circle Films receives ₹2,000 to film a future reception.

Step 1—What accounts are affected and how? Circle Films receives cash, so cash increases. Because Circle Films has not yet performed the required service, it has a new liability to the customer called unearned revenue.

Step 2—What debit and credit entries are required? Cash is an asset, so debit the Cash account to increase it. Unearned Revenue is a liability, so credit the Unearned Revenue account to increase it.

Step 3—Record the journal entry.

		Debit	Credit
#4	Cash	2,000	
	Unearned Revenue		2,000
	(Cash received in advance of providing service to customer)		

Assets	=	Liabilities	+	Equity
+2,000		+2,000		

Step 4—Post the information to the ledger.

Cash		Unearned Revenue	
15,000	10,000		2,000
1,500			
2,000			
8,500			2,000

Transaction #5 Circle Films pays ₹250 cash for advertising.

Step 1—What accounts are affected and how? Circle Films pays cash, so cash decreases. The decrease in cash results from Circle Films' advertising its service, so advertising expense increases.

Step 2—What debit and credit entries are required? Cash is an asset, so credit the Cash account to decrease it. Expenses decrease equity, so debit the Advertising Expense account to increase it.

Step 3—Record the journal entry.

		Debit	Credit
#5	Advertising Expense	250	
	Cash		250
	(Pay for advertising)		

Assets	=	Liabilities	+	Equity
−250				−250

Step 4—Post the information to the ledger.

Cash		Advertising Expense	
15,000	10,000	250	
1,500	250		
2,000			
8,250		250	

Transaction #6 Circle Films films an event for ₹3,500 and leaves an invoice with the customer.

Step 1—What accounts are affected and how? Circle Films performed a service for a customer, so its service revenue increases. Circle Films has not yet received any payment from the customer, so its accounts receivable also increases.

Step 2—What debit and credit entries are required? Accounts Receivable is an asset, so debit the Accounts Receivable account to increase it. Revenues increase equity, so credit the Service Revenue account to increase it.

Step 3—Record the journal entry.

#6	Accounts Receivable	3,500	
	Service Revenue		3,500
	(Provide service to customer on account)		

Assets	=	Liabilities	+	Equity
+3,500				+3,500

Step 4—Post the information to the ledger.

Accounts Receivable	
3,500	
3,500	

Service Revenue	
	1,500
	3,500
	5,000

Transaction #7 Circle Films buys another camera by signing a ₹9,000 note payable.

Step 1—What accounts are affected and how? Circle Films receives a camera, so equipment increases. It signs a note for payment, so notes payable increases.

Step 2—What debit and credit entries are required? Equipment is an asset, so debit the Equipment account to increase it. Notes Payable is a liability, so credit the Notes Payable account to increase it.

Step 3—Record the journal entry.

#7	Equipment	9,000	
	Notes Payable		9,000
	(Purchase of a video camera with a promissory note)		

Assets	=	Liabilities	+	Equity
+9,000		+9,000		

Step 4—Post the information to the ledger.

Equipment	
9,000	
9,000	
18,000	

Notes Payable	
	9,000
	9,000

Transaction #8 Circle Films receives ₹3,500 from a customer in payment of services provided.

Step 1—What accounts are affected and how? Circle Films receives cash, so cash increases. Circle Films collects a receivable from a customer, so its accounts receivable decreases.

Step 2—What debit and credit entries are required? Cash is an asset, so debit the Cash account to increase it. Accounts Receivable is also an asset account, so credit the Accounts Receivable account to decrease it.

Step 3—Record the journal entry.

#8	Cash	3,500	
	Accounts Receivable		3,500
	(Receive payment from customer)		

Assets	=	Liabilities	+	Equity
+3,500				
−3,500				

Step 4—Post the information to the ledger.

Cash	
15,000	10,000
1,500	250
2,000	
3,500	
11,750	

Accounts Receivable	
3,500	3,500
0	

Transaction #9 Circle Films pays ₹2,000 in salaries to employees.

Step 1—What accounts are affected and how? Circle Films pays cash, so cash decreases. This reduction in cash results from salaries paid to employees, so salaries expense increases.

Step 2—What debit and credit entries are required? Cash is an asset, so credit the Cash account to decrease it. Expenses decrease equity, so debit the Salaries Expense account to increase it.

Step 3—Record the journal entry.

#9	Salaries Expense	2,000	
	Cash		2,000
	(Pay salaries to employees)		

Assets	=	Liabilities	+	Equity
−2,000				−2,000

Step 4—Post the information to the ledger.

Cash	
15,000	10,000
1,500	250
2,000	2,000
3,500	
9,750	

Salaries Expense	
2,000	
2,000	

Transaction #10 Circle Films pays ₹1,500 in dividends to the owners.

Step 1—What accounts are affected and how? Circle Films pays cash, so cash decreases. The cash payment is a distribution of company assets to the owners, so dividends increase.

Step 2—What debit and credit entries are required? Cash is an asset, so credit the Cash account to decrease it. Dividends decrease equity, so debit the Dividends account to increase it.

Step 3—Record the journal entry.

#10	Dividends	1,500	
	Cash		1,500
	(Pay dividends to owners)		

Assets	=	Liabilities	+	Equity
−1,500				−1,500

Step 4—Post the information to the ledger.

Cash	
15,000	10,000
1,500	250
2,000	2,000
3,500	1,500
8,250	

Dividends	
1,500	
1,500	

Summary After recording and posting the ten transactions, Circle Films' complete Journal and Ledger would appear as follows:

General Journal

Transaction	Account	Debit	Credit
#1	Cash	15,000	
	Common Stock		15,000
#2	Equipment	9,000	
	Supplies	1,000	
	Cash		10,000
#3	Cash	1,500	
	Service Revenue		1,500
#4	Cash	2,000	
	Unearned Revenue		2,000
#5	Advertising Expense	250	
	Cash		250
#6	Accounts Receivable	3,500	
	Service Revenue		3,500
#7	Equipment	9,000	
	Notes Payable		9,000
#8	Cash	3,500	
	Accounts Receivable		3,500
#9	Salaries Expense	2,000	
	Cash		2,000
#10	Dividends	1,500	
	Cash		1,500

General Ledger

Cash	
15,000	10,000
1,500	250
2,000	2,000
3,500	1,500
8,250	

Accounts Receivable	
3,500	3,500
0	

Supplies	
1,000	
1,000	

Equipment	
9,000	
9,000	
18,000	

Unearned Revenue	
	2,000
	2,000

Notes Payable	
	9,000
	9,000

Common Stock	
	15,000
	15,000

Service Revenue	
	1,500
	3,500
	5,000

Advertising Expense	
250	
250	

Salaries Expense	
2,000	
2,000	

Dividends	
1,500	
1,500	

Preparing a Trial Balance

Once all transactions are recorded in the journal and posted to the ledger, a trial balance can be prepared.

Circle Films Trial Balance May 31		
	Debit	Credit
Cash	₹ 8,250	
Supplies	1,000	
Equipment	18,000	
Unearned Revenue		₹ 2,000
Notes Payable		9,000
Common Stock		15,000
Service Revenue		5,000
Advertising Expense	250	
Salaries Expense	2,000	
Dividends	15,000	
Total	₹31,000	₹31,000

Recall that a trial balance is a listing of all accounts and their balances at a specific point in time, starting with assets and followed by liabilities, equity, revenues, expenses, and dividends. Therefore, it is a summary of the balances in the ledger. You can confirm that the trial balance includes only the balances from the general ledger by reviewing again Circle Films' ledger on the previous page. As expected, total debit balances of ₹31,000 equal total credit balances of ₹31,000 in the trial balance.

Preparation of Financial Statements

Once the trial balance is finished, the final product of the accounting system can be prepared—the financial statements. As demonstrated in Chapter 1, the income statement must be prepared first, followed by the statement of retained earnings, and then the balance sheet.

The income statement shows a company's revenues and expenses. Circle Films' May 31 trial balance contains only one revenue account and two expense accounts. Therefore, its income statement for the month of May would appear as follows.

Circle Films Income Statement For the Month Ending May 31		
Service revenue		₹5,000
Advertising expense	₹ 250	
Salaries expense	2,000	
Total expenses		2,250
Net income		₹2,750

With net income calculated, Circle Films' statement of retained earnings can be prepared. Recall from Chapter 1 that the statement of retained earnings takes the beginning balance in retained earnings, adds net income, and subtracts dividends to yield the current balance in retained earnings. Its May 31 trial balance shows no balance in beginning retained earnings because it just started its business. It also shows a ₹1,500 balance in dividends. Combining these two balances with net income yields the following statement of retained earnings for the month of May:

Circle Films Statement of Retained Earnings For the Month Ending May 31	
Retained earnings, May 1	₹ 0
+ Net income	2,750
− Dividends	1,500
Retained earnings, May 31	₹1,250

With retained earnings calculated, the company's balance sheet can be prepared. A balance sheet shows a company's assets, liabilities, and equity at a point in time. Circle Films' May 31 trial balance shows four asset accounts, two liability accounts, and one equity account (Common Stock). These seven accounts, along with the amount of retained earnings from the May statement of retained earnings, should be included on the balance sheet. Therefore, its May 31 balance sheet would appear as follows:

© ISTOCKPHOTO.COM/SCOTT KOCHSIEK

Circle Films Balance Sheet May 31	
Cash	₹ 8,250
Supplies	1,000
Equipment	18,000
Total assets	₹27,250
Unearned revenue	₹ 2,000
Notes payable	9,000
Common stock	15,000
Retained earnings	1,250
Total liabilities and stockholders' equity	₹27,250

CONCEPT QUESTIONS

1. What is an accounting information system?
2. What is an accounting transaction?
3. What is the main function of an account?
4. What does a chart of accounts contain?
5. What is the fundamental accounting equation?
6. Do accounting transactions have to affect both sides of the fundamental accounting equation? Explain.
7. Does the double entry system mean that each transaction is recorded twice? Explain.
8. True or false: debit means "increase" and credit means "decrease." Why?
9. What are the normal account balances for the following accounts: a) Equipment; b) Unearned Revenue; c) Supplies Expense; d) Accounts Payable; e) Retained Earnings?
10. What is used to decrease an asset account, a liability account, a revenue account, and an expense account?
11. Where are transactions first recorded?
12. What is a ledger, and from where does the input for a ledger come?
13. In what order are accounts listed in a trial balance?
14. To what does the term "posting" refer?
15. What are the three main purposes of a trial balance?

MULTIPLE CHOICE

1. When considering accounting information systems, which of the following is false?
   a. Accounting information systems vary in size across companies
   b. An accounting information system records and summarizes economic events
   c. All accounting information systems use the same basic procedures to identify, record, and communicate the effects of economic events
   d. Accounting information systems record all economic events
2. Which of the following would be considered an accounting transaction?
   a. Hiring a new CEO
   b. Selling an in-house developed patent
   c. Establishing a new company dress code
   d. Posting journal entries to the general ledger
3. Which of the following would not be an account found in the financial statements?
   a. Equipment
   b. Salaries Payable
   c. Employees' Personal Data
   d. Dividends
4. Which of the following is false regarding a chart of accounts?
   a. The total number of asset accounts must equal the total number of liability accounts
   b. A chart of accounts is a listing of all the accounts that a company uses to record accounting information
   c. Each account listing contains an account name and a numerical reference
   d. Charts of accounts will vary across companies
5. Which of the following is false?
   a. A company can have a transaction that affects only the left side of the fundamental accounting equation
   b. In each accounting transaction, total debits to assets must equal total credits to liabilities
   c. The fundamental accounting equation will always balance after each correctly recorded accounting transaction
   d. All of the above are true
6. Which of the following is true?
   i. In the double-entry system, each accounting transaction is recorded twice
   ii. Each journal entry will at least affect two accounts.
   a. i. only
   b. ii. only
   c. Both i. and ii.
   d. Neither i. nor ii.
7. Which of the following groups of accounts shows only accounts that are increased with a debit?
   a. Assets, Liabilities, Dividends
   b. Assets, Equity, Dividends
   c. Assets, Expenses, Dividends
   d. Assets, Equity, Expenses
8. Which of the following is true?
   i. Paying out a dividend of ₹1,00,000 would result in a debit to the Dividends account.
   ii. In the general ledger, this ₹1,00,000 would be entered on the right side of the Dividends T-account.
   a. i. only
   b. ii. only
   c. Both i. and ii.
   b. Neither i. nor ii.
9. What would be the result of a credit to these accounts?

	Cash	Service Revenue	Common Stock
a.	Increase	Increase	Decrease
b.	Decrease	Increase	Increase
c.	Decrease	Increase	Decrease
d.	Increase	Decrease	Increase

10. The general journal:
    a. pulls all information from the general ledger.
    b. only contains revenue and expense accounts.
    c. is where transactions are recorded.
    d. is a collection of all of the accounts maintained by a company.

11. The general ledger:
    a. is the first place a transaction is recorded.
    b. records economic events as well as accounting transactions.
    c. shows the activity in, and balances for, all of the company's accounts.
    d. requires adjusting entries in order for total debit balances to equal total credit balances.
12. Which of the following is false?
    a. A trial balance is considered to be a financial statement
    b. In a trial balance, total debit balances must equal total credit balances
    c. A trial balance summarizes in one place all accounts of an entity and their respective balances
    d. Preparation of a trial balance is part of the accounting cycle
13. Which of the following would cause a trial balance not to balance?
    a. Recording a ₹3,500 purchase of supplies on account as a debit to Supplies and a credit to Cash
    b. A ₹4,250 payment on account is unrecorded
    c. A ₹4,000 purchase on account is debited to Supplies for ₹4,000 and credited to Accounts Payable for ₹40,000
    d. A ₹5,000 purchase of supplies on account is credited to Supplies and debited to Accounts Payable
14. Which of the following is not a purpose of the trial balance?
    a. To summarize in one place all accounts of an entity and their respective balances
    b. To provide a chronological order of a company's transactions
    c. To serve as a helpful tool in preparing financial statements
    d. To prove that total debit balances equal total credit balances
15. A journal entry does not contain:
    a. the date of the transaction.
    b. the balance of the accounts involved.
    c. an explanation of the transaction.
    d. at least two accounts.
16. Incurring ₹50,000 in salaries while earning ₹1,50,000 of revenue would result in a:
    a. ₹1,50,000 net increase in net income.
    b. ₹1,00,000 net increase in net income.
    c. ₹2,00,000 net increase in net income.
    d. none of the above.
17. Which of the following properly demonstrates the flow of information through the accounting system?
    a. Journal ⇒ Ledger ⇒ Trial Balance ⇒ Financial Statements
    b. Ledger ⇒ Journal ⇒ Trial Balance ⇒ Financial Statements
    c. Journal ⇒ Trial Balance ⇒ Ledger ⇒ Financial Statements
    d. Trial Balance ⇒ Ledger ⇒ Journal ⇒ Financial Statements

BRIEF EXERCISES

1. Chart of Accounts

The following accounts were taken from the charts of accounts of a retailer, a bank, and/or a chemical company:

Cash	Property and Equipment
Research and Development Expense	Dividends Payable
Retained Earnings	Salaries Expense
Mortgage Receivable	Sales Returns

Required

Indicate whether each account would likely appear in the chart of accounts of the retailer (R), the bank (B), the chemical company (C), or all three (A).

2. Accounting Transactions

A company enters into the following economic events:

1. Hired a new receptionist.
2. Billed customers for services performed.
3. Announced the signing of a contract that should produce ₹100,000 of new revenue.
4. Paid for insurance that will not be used until next year.

Required

Indicate whether each economic event would be considered an accounting transaction.

3. Analyze Transactions

EA Systems entered into the following transactions during the month of August:

1. Received ₹6,35,000 for services performed during August.
2. Purchased ₹1,20,000 of supplies on account.
3. Paid employee salaries of ₹3,28,000 for the first week of August.
4. Paid ₹90,000 towards the previous purchase of supplies.

Required

Indicate whether each transaction increases, decreases, or has no effect on assets, liabilities, and equity. If a transaction affects equity, indicate whether the transaction affects revenues or expenses.

4. Journalize Transactions

Review the EA Systems information in the preceding Brief Exercise.

Required

Prepare journal entries for each transaction (omitting explanations).

5. T-Accounts

A company reports the following asset and liability T-accounts:

Account #1 (in lakhs)		Account #2		Account #3	
1,000	6,000	8,400	3,250	4,280	3,600
4,000	3,000		2,120	1,660	1,120

Required
Determine the balance in each account and identify whether each account would most likely be an asset account or a liability account.

6. Normal Balances

The following is a list of possible accounts found in a trial balance:

1. Equipment
2. Notes Payable
3. Dividends
4. Supplies
5. Rent Expense
6. Service Revenue
7. Unearned Revenue

Required
Indicate each account's normal balance and the effect of a debit and credit to the account.

7. Posting Transactions

A company records the following transactions during November:

Date	Account Title	Debit	Credit
Nov. 1	Accounts Receivable	3,20,000	
	Service Revenue		3,20,000
Nov. 6	Cash	1,00,000	
	Accounts Receivable		1,00,000
Nov. 15	Utilities Expense	25,000	
	Cash		25,000
Nov. 26	Inventory	2,36,000	
	Accounts Payable		2,36,000

Required
Post the transactions to appropriate T-accounts and prepare a Trial Balance.

8. Recording Transactions

Barrett Fisher, a clerk for Naval Supplies, received a payment from a customer and recorded the following journal entry:

Date	Account Title	Debit	Credit
Mar. 1	Cash	1,00,000	
	Accounts Payable		1,00,000

Required
Is this entry correct or not? Explain why it is or is not correct.

9. Trial Balance

Harris Consulting provides the following incomplete trial balance:

Harris Consulting Trial Balance (in millions) September 30		
	Debit	**Credit**
(a)	₹8,850	
Accounts Receivable	(b)	
Supplies	1,625	
Notes Payable		₹3,000
Common Stock		10,000
Retained Earnings		(c)
Service Revenue		15,630
Salaries Expense	10,560	
Utilities Expense	2,350	
Totals	₹33,765	₹ (d)

Required
Determine the missing values.

10. Prepare Financial Statements

Review the Harris Consulting information in the preceding Brief Exercise.

Required
Using the given information and your answers for a-d, prepare Harris' income statement and statement of retained earnings for September and its balance sheet at September 30.

EXERCISES

11. Transaction Analysis

The following is a list of independent economic events:

1. Purchased inventory on account.
2. Paid dividends at the end of the year.
3. Received cash in payment for services.
4. Issued common stock for cash.
5. Paid rent in cash.
6. Received a bill for utilities incurred.
7. Bought equipment for cash.
8. Billed customers for services.

Required
Indicate a) the accounts that would be affected by each transaction and b) whether each transaction increases, decreases, or has no effect on assets, liabilities, and stockholders' equity.

12. Transaction Analysis

The following are a few possible ways in which the accounting equation can be affected by a transaction:

Assets	= Liabilities	+	Stockholders' Equity
1. Increase	Increase		
2. Decrease			Decrease
3. Increase			Increase
4. Increase/Decrease			
5. Decrease	Decrease		

Required
Describe at least two situations that could result in each of the five scenarios listed.

13. Transaction Analysis

Handyman Services was founded on January 1 and entered into the following transactions during January:
(in lakhs)

1. Issued common stock of ₹30,000 in exchange for cash.
2. Purchased an old warehouse for ₹50,000 by issuing notes payable.
3. Purchased a truck for ₹15,000 cash.
4. Purchased shop supplies for ₹5,000 on account.
5. Provided services of ₹15,325, receiving ₹12,200 in cash.
6. Paid ₹1,000 for local advertising for January.
7. Received payment of ₹3,125 from customers in #5.
8. Paid ₹4,000 on open account from #4.
9. Paid dividends of ₹1,000 to stockholders.
10. Paid employee salaries of ₹4,000 for January.
11. Billed customers ₹3,500 for services provided during January.
12. Paid ₹100 interest on notes payable.

Required
a. Show the effects of each transaction on the accounting equation by preparing a tabular analysis using the following column headings: Cash, Accounts Receivable, Supplies, Property and Equipment, Accounts Payable, Notes Payable, Common Stock, Retained Earnings.
b. Calculate Handyman's net income for the month of January.

14. Normal Balances

The following is a list of possible accounts found in a trial balance:

1. Accounts Receivable
2. Common Stock
3. Cash
4. Retained Earnings
5. Accounts Payable
6. Salaries Expense
7. Long-term Investments
8. Service Revenue
9. Dividends

Required
Indicate each account's normal balance and the effect of a debit and a credit to the account.

15. T-account Mechanics

The general ledger for TPC Company contains the following accounts:

Cash

Debit	Credit
2,000	3,000
8,000	(a)
4,000	

Notes Payable

Debit	Credit
10,000	5,500
	18,100
	(b)

Salaries Expense

Debit	Credit
13,500	
(c)	
15,900	

Accounts Payable

Debit	Credit
23,850	45,300
(d)	12,775
	17,300

Service Revenue

Debit	Credit
	(e)
	33,210
	88,690

Accounts Receivable

Debit	Credit
(f)	3,500
2,500	9,570
7,660	

Required
Determine the missing values.

16. Transaction Analysis

Tsunami, Inc., entered into the following transactions during one month of operations:

1. Purchased ₹3,00,000 of computer equipment on account.
2. Issued ₹7,50,000 of common stock to investors in exchange for cash.
3. Purchased supplies for ₹30,000 in cash.
4. Billed customers ₹2,50,000 for services rendered.
5. Paid salaries of ₹3,50,000 to employees.
6. Paid dividends to stockholders in the amount of ₹1,00,000.
7. Received ₹50,000 cash in payment of services earned and billed in the previous month.
8. Paid cash for the purchase in #1.
9. Borrowed ₹50,00,000 from the bank.

Required
a. Indicate the specific accounts affected by each transaction.
b. Indicate whether those accounts were increased or decreased.
c. Designate the normal balances for each of the specific accounts.

17. Recording Transactions

Prepare journal entries for the transactions listed in the preceding exercise (omitting explanations).

18. Recording Transactions

The following information pertains to York Rafting Company:

Jan. 2 Issued common stock to investors for ₹25,00,000.
3 Bought ₹3,50,000 of supplies on account.
4 Paid rent for January in the amount of ₹1,20,000.
9 Billed a customer ₹7,00,000 for services provided.
16 Paid ₹1,50,000 cash to vendor for the January 3 purchase.

24 Borrowed ₹10,00,000 from local bank.
26 Received payment for billing made on January 9.

Required
Prepare journal entries for each transaction (omitting explanations).

19. Posting Transactions

Post the journal entries prepared in the preceding exercise to their appropriate T-accounts and prepare a trial balance at January 31.

20. Recording Transactions

In the month of March, C. D. Goose, Inc. entered into the following transactions:

Mar. 2 Bought a new building for ₹1,35,00,000.
3 Paid February utility bill of ₹86,000.
11 Issued common stock to investors in return for ₹5,00,000.
13 Hired a new administrative assistant for a ₹35,00,000 salary.
19 Received payment in the amount of ₹75,000 for service billed in February.
31 Paid dividends of ₹1,00,000.

Required
Prepare all necessary journal entries for March (omitting the explanations).

21. Recreate Journal Entries

The general ledger for King Consulting contains the following accounts:

Cash	
23,500	7,200
13,000	10,500
15,000	1,000
32,800	

Accounts Receivable	
14,200	13,000
19,300	15,000
5,500	

Salaries Expense	
10,500	
10,500	

Accounts Payable	
7,200	8,100
	900

Service Revenue	
	14,200
	19,300
	33,500

Supplies	
8,100	
8,100	

Dividends	
1,000	
1,000	

Common Stock	
	23,500
	23,500

Required
Recreate the nine journal entries that resulted in King's ledger balances.

22. Transaction Analysis

The following is a tabular analysis of transactions in the month of September for the Fresh Company:

	Cash	+	Accounts Receivable	+	Supplies	+	Equipment	=	Accounts Payable	+	Stockholders' Equity	Additional Information
1.	+2,000		+7,000								+9,000	Service Revenue
2.					+1,000				+1,000			
3.	−500								−500			
4.	−1,500										−1,500	Dividends
5.	−750										−750	Advertising
6.	+10,000										+10,000	Common Stock
7.	+5,000		−5,000									
8.	−2,000										−2,000	Rent
9.									+2,500		−2,500	Utilities
10.							+5,000		+5,000			

Required

a. Provide a probable explanation for each individual event.
b. Recreate the appropriate journal entries.
c. Prepare an income statement for the month of September.
d. Prepare a statement of retained earnings for the month of September. Assume beginning Retained Earnings is ₹1,000.

23. Accounting Terms

The following is a list of various terms and definitions associated with accounting information systems:

a. Accounting information system
b. Accounting transaction
c. Account
d. Double-entry accounting
e. Chart of accounts
f. Debit
g. Credit
h. Journal
i. Ledger
j. Trial balance

1. A listing containing a name and a numerical reference for all the accounts that a company uses to record accounting information.
2. A recording system in which at least two accounts will be affected when recording every accounting transaction.
3. The system that identifies economic events to be recorded, measures and records those events, and then processes the resulting information so that financial statements can be prepared.
4. An accumulation of the activity and balance for a specific item.
5. Any economic event that affects specific asset, liability, or equity accounts at the time of the event.
6. The right side of an account.
7. The left side of an account.
8. A collection of accounts and their balances.
9. A listing of all accounts and their balances at a specific point in time.
10. A chronological record in which transactions are first recorded.

Required
Match terms a–j with their appropriate definitions.

24. Errors in Recording Transactions

Chappy's Chapstick, Inc. recently hired a new accountant, who made the following errors:

1. Recorded a ₹20,000 cash purchase of inventory as a debit to inventory and a credit to accounts payable.
2. Failed to record the payment of ₹30,000 for advertising for the period.
3. Debited supplies for ₹15,000 and credited cash for invoice amount of ₹51,000.
4. Recorded ₹10,000 cash received for services but forgot to record the service revenue.

Required
a. Recreate each entry that was made and prepare each entry that should have been made.
b. Which of the four errors would result in the trial balance being out of balance?

25. Posting Information

The following is the general journal of Dee's Fur Company for the month of November (in ₹ lakhs):

Date	Account Titles	Debit	Credit
Nov. 1	Cash	15,000	
	Common Stock		15,000
8	Equipment	5,000	
	Accounts Payable		
	Cash		2,000
11	Accounts Receivable	7,500	
	Service Revenue		7,500
18	Accounts Payable	1,700	
	Cash		1,700
21	Cash	5,000	
	Notes Payable		5,000
24	Dividends	1,500	
	Cash		1,500
25	Cash	3,500	
	Accounts Receivable		3,500

Required
a. Post the journal entries to the appropriate T-accounts assuming Dee's Fur starts its business in November.
b. Prepare a trial balance for the month ending November 30.

26. Trial Balance

Saxon Company provides the following account balances as of July 31:

Accounts Payable	₹12,44,500
Accounts Receivable	12,30,000
Buildings	99,84,000
Cash	33,20,000
Common Stock	15,00,000
Dividends	4,00,000
Notes Payable	33,00,000
Salaries Expense	45,20,500
Retained Earnings	45,70,000
Service Revenue	49,70,000
Supplies	6,98,000

Required
Prepare a trial balance as of July 31.

27. Trial Balance

During the audit of Hines Brewery, the auditor discovered the following errors:

1. A purchase of equipment in the amount of ₹3,50,000 was recorded as a debit to Equipment for ₹35,000 and a credit to Accounts Payable for ₹35,000.
2. A credit of ₹5,60,000 to Service Revenue in the general journal was posted to the general ledger at ₹6,50,000.
3. ₹1,00,000 cash paid for salaries incurred in previous months was recorded as a debit to Salaries Expense and a credit to Cash.

4. A journal entry recording a purchase of ₹1,20,000 of supplies on account was posted twice to the general ledger.
5. A credit posting to Service Revenue of $4,000 was omitted.

Required
For each error, indicate whether or not the trial balance will still balance after the error is made. Also, indicate the manner in which the trial balance will be incorrect (for example, Service Revenue will be overstated by ₹50,000).

PROBLEMS

28. Transaction Analysis

Gels and Shells, Inc., was established on January 1 and entered into the following transactions during its first month of business (in lakhs):

1. Issued common stock of ₹50,000 in exchange for cash.
2. Purchased equipment for ₹24,000 cash.
3. Purchased supplies of ₹6,000 on account.
4. Received ₹235 bill for January advertising in the newspaper.
5. Billed customers ₹14,680 for services.
6. Paid salaries of ₹2,015.
7. Received payment of ₹6,023 from customers for bills in #5.
8. Received ₹5,000 cash for services to be performed in March.
9. Paid ₹4,500 to suppliers for purchase in #3.
10. Received bill for January utilities in the amount of ₹175.
11. Paid dividends of ₹300 to stockholders.
12. Borrowed ₹10,000 from bank on a long-term basis.
13. Paid ₹100 interest on the bank loan.

Required
a. Show the effects of each transaction on the accounting equation by preparing a tabular analysis using the following column headings: Cash, Accounts Receivable, Supplies, Property and Equipment, Accounts Payable, Unearned Revenue, Notes Payable, Common Stock, Retained Earnings.
b. Prepare an income statement for the month of January.
c. Prepare a statement of retained earnings for the month of January.
d. Prepare a balance sheet at January 31.

29. Recording Transactions

Darby Consulting, Inc., was established on March 1, and during March, Darby entered into the following transactions (in lakhs):

Mar. 1 Issued ₹10,000 common stock in exchange for cash.
3 Purchased ₹300 of supplies on account.
7 Prepaid ₹1,500 total for April, May, and June rent.
8 Paid ₹175 towards the March 3 purchase of supplies.
11 Billed customers ₹5,780 for services rendered.
12 Paid ₹700 for March advertising.
25 Received ₹4,500 from customers billed on March 11.
28 Paid ₹200 in dividends to stockholders.
29 Paid ₹1,200 for March salaries.
29 Paid ₹760 for March utilities.

Required
a. Prepare journal entries for each transaction (omitting explanations).
b. Post journal entries to appropriate T-accounts.
c. Prepare a trial balance at March 31.
d. Prepare an income statement and a statement of retained earnings for the month of March. Prepare a balance sheet at the end of March.

30. Recording Transactions

The trial balance for ShirtCraft, Inc., at January 31 is shown as follows:

ShirtCraft, Inc.
Trial Balance (in lakhs)
January 31

	Debit	Credit
Cash	₹5,600	
Accounts Receivable	12,890	
Supplies	9,235	
Prepaid Rent	1,500	
Equipment	30,500	
Accounts Payable		₹7,625
Unearned Revenue		6,400
Notes Payable		15,000
Common Stock		25,000
Service Revenue		9,650
Salaries Expense	2,300	
Utilities Expense	650	
Dividends	1,000	
Totals	₹63,675	₹63,675

During February the following transactions occurred:

Feb. 1 Billed customers ₹2,500 for services rendered.
1 Paid ₹150 interest on note from bank.
4 Received ₹4,500 from customers billed in January.
8 Bought ₹560 of office supplies on account.
12 Completed a ₹3,500 service for which payment was received in January.

18 Paid ₹1,895 towards a January purchase of supplies on account.
26 Paid ₹1,000 in dividends to stockholders.
27 Paid ₹2,100 for February salaries and ₹775 for February utilities.

Required

a. Prepare opening T-accounts for the month of February.
b. Prepare journal entries for transactions in the month of February.
c. Post journal entries to appropriate T-accounts.
d. Prepare a trial balance at February 28.

31. Recording Transactions

On November 1, Josh White started an amusement park. The park experienced the following transactions during the first month of operations:

Nov. 1 Stockholders contributed ₹50,00,000 in exchange for common stock.
2 Hired six employees to staff the park.
3 Purchased go-carts for ₹12,50,000 on account.
3 Borrowed ₹10,00,000 from bank.
3 Purchased arcade games for ₹4,00,000.
4 Paid ₹1,00,000 to advertise the park's opening.
7 Purchased bumper boats for ₹11,75,000 on account.
10 Billed Mr. Jones ₹1,10,000 for his son's birthday party.
11 Received cash of ₹2,20,000 for entry fees into the park.
15 Paid ₹5,00,000 cash towards go-cart bill.
20 Received ₹3,40,000 for entry fees into the park.
25 Received full payment from Mr. Jones.
28 Paid utilities in the amount of ₹56,000.
30 Paid ₹10,000 interest on loan.

Required

Prepare journal entries for each transaction, including explanations.

32. Recording and Posting Journal Entries

Carbon Company entered into the following transactions during November:

Nov. 1 Issued common stock in exchange for ₹15,00,000 cash.
4 Purchased ₹6,50,000 of equipment, paying ₹4,00,000 in cash and the remainder on account.
8 Paid ₹5,00,000 for investments, which will mature in six months.
12 Billed customers ₹12,55,000 for services rendered.
16 Hired office assistant at a salary equal to being paid ₹1,00,000 every two weeks.
21 Received ₹8,95,000 from customers billed on November 12.
22 Purchased ₹1,50,000 of supplies on account.
24 Paid ₹1,00,000 towards the remaining balance on the equipment purchase.
29 Paid ₹50,000 in dividends to stockholders.
30 Paid ₹3,40,000 for November salaries.

After journalizing these transactions, Carbon Company's general ledger appeared as follows:

Cash

Debit		Credit	
1st	15,000	4th	4,000
21st	8,950	8th	5,000
		24th	1,000
		30th	3,400

Accounts Payable

Debit		Credit	
24th	1,000	4th	2,500
		16th	1,000
		22th	1,500

Accounts Receivable

Debit		Credit	
12th	12,550		

Common Stock

Debit		Credit	
29th	500	1st	15,000

Supplies

Debit		Credit	
22th	1,500		

Service Revenue

Debit		Credit	
		12th	12,550
		21th	8,950

Short-Term Investments

Debit		Credit	
8th	5,000		

Salaries Expense

Debit		Credit	
16th	1,000		
30th	4,300		

Equipment

Debit		Credit	
4th	6,500		

Dividends

Debit		Credit	
		29th	500

Required

a. Reproduce Carbon Company's journal entries for November.
b. Post the journal entries to the appropriate T-accounts.
c. Compare your postings to those of Carbon Company and identify Carbon's recording errors.
d. Prepare a trial balance at November 30.

CASES

33. Read and Interpret Financial Statements

Access **Hindustan Unilever Ltd.** balance sheet in its 2012-13 annual report by clicking on the *Investor Relations* and *Annual Report/Proxies* links at www.hul.co.in.

Required

a. Identify the dollar change in the following subtotals: total current assets; total noncurrent assets; total current liabilities; total noncurrent liabilities; and total shareholders' equity.

b. Identify whether the accounting system would debit or credit each subtotal to achieve the change. Treat each subtotal description as if it were an account.
c. Prepare one journal entry that records the changes in all subtotals. Again, use the subtotal descriptions as if they were actual accounts.
d. Does the entry in part of the balance? Should it? Explain why or why not.

34. Ethics in Accounting

You are a staff accountant at a large service provider. Your company is under tremendous pressure to meet earnings targets so that the company stock price can continue to grow and the company can continue to acquire other companies. For the current year, it appears that the company will miss its earnings targets. Your boss, who has been a mentor to you, asks you to prepare a journal entry to record ₹1,00,00,000 of revenue for a fictitious job. He provides a fabricated invoice as documentation. He states that as soon as the new year begins, he will make a reversing entry that removes the receivable from the books. He asks you to do this as a personal favor to him.

Required

a. Identify the ethical issues associated with this scenario.
b. What factors other than accounting are at play here?
c. What are your alternatives?

35. Written Communication

Since you are enrolled in an introductory accounting class, a friend asks you the following: "I've never understood debits and credits. All I know is that debit means bad and credit means good."

Required

Write a brief explanation of the terms *debit* and *credit* and how they are used in an accounting information system. Explain why debit and credit cannot mean good and/or bad.

reviewcard CHAPTER 3 Recording Accounting Transactions

Learning Objectives		Key Concepts
LO1	Describe the purpose of an accounting information system.	The purpose of an accounting information system is to identify economic events to be recorded, to measure and record those events, and to process the resulting information so that financial statements can be prepared.
LO2	Analyze the effect of accounting transactions on the accounting equation.	All accounting transactions must affect at least two accounts so that the fundamental accounting equation remains in balance. This is known as the dual nature of accounting.
LO3	Understand how T-accounts and debits and credits are used in a double-entry accounting system.	The double entry accounting system uses debits and credits to record accounting transactions. For every transaction, total debit entries must equal total credit entries. Asset, and expense accounts have debit balances, so they are increased with debit entries and decreased with credit entries. Liability, equity, and revenue accounts have credit balances, so they are increased with credit entries and decreased with debit entries.
LO4	Describe the purpose of the journal, ledger, and trial balance.	Accounting transactions are recorded in the general journal, which captures information chronologically. Information in the general journal is posted to the general ledger, which summarizes information by account. Balances from the general ledger are listed on a trial balance, which contains all account balances and proves that debit balances equal credit balances.
LO5	Record and post accounting transactions and prepare a trial balance and financial statements.	After determining which accounts are affected by an accounting transaction, the transaction is recorded and posted. Once all transactions are posted, a trial balance is prepared, from which financial statements are prepared.

Key Definitions

Account An accounting record that accumulates the activity of a specific item and yields the item's balance.

Accounting information system The system that identifies, records, summarizes, and communicates the various transactions of a company.

Accounting transaction Any economic event that affects a company's assets, liabilities or equity at the time of the event.

Chart of accounts The list of accounts that a company uses to capture its business activities.

Credit The right side of an account.

Debit The left side of an account.

Dual nature of accounting Every accounting transaction affects at least two accounts.

Journal A chronological record of transactions.

Ledger A collection of accounts and their balances.

Trial balance A listing of accounts and their balances at a specific point in time.

Key Exhibit

Debit and Credit Rules

Type of Account	Normal Balance	Increase with a	Decrease with a
Asset	Debit	Debit	Credit
Liability	Credit	Credit	Debit
Equity	Credit	Credit	Debit
Revenue	Credit	Credit	Debit
Expense	Debit	Debit	Credit
Cash dividend	Debit	Debit	Credit

Demonstration Problem

The following transactions occurred during the first month of operations for Auburn Windows, Inc. Prepare all necessary journal entries, post the information to the ledger, and prepare a trial balance at March 31.

Mar.	1	Issued 15,000 shares of common stock for ₹20,00,000 cash.
	1	Purchase a used truck for ₹7,20,000 cash.
	3	Purchased cleaning supplies for ₹5,00,000 cash.
	5	Paid ₹2,40,000 cash on a one-year insurance policy effective March 1.
	12	Billed customers ₹4,80,000 for cleaning services.
Mar.	20	Paid ₹2,30,000 cash for employee salaries.
	21	Collected ₹4,00,000 cash from customers billed on March 12.
	25	Billed customers ₹5,20,000 for cleaning services.
	31	For the month, paid for and used ₹60,000 of fuel.
	31	Declared and paid ₹20,000 cash dividend.

Demonstration Problem Solution

Date	Account	Debit	Credit
Mar. 1	Cash	20,00,000	
	Common Stock		20,00,000
	(Initial investment by owner)		
Mar. 1	Equipment	7,20,000	
	Cash		7,20,000
	(Purchase of equipment)		
Mar. 3	Supplies	5,00,000	
	Cash		5,00,000
	(Purchase of supplies)		
Mar. 5	Prepaid Insurance	2,40,000	
	Cash		2,40,000
	(Purchase of insurance policy)		
Mar. 12	Accounts Receivable	4,80,000	
	Service Revenue		4,80,000
	(Provide services on account)		
Mar. 20	Salaries Expense	2,30,000	
	Cash		2,30,000
	(Pay employees)		
Mar. 21	Cash	4,00,000	
	Accounts Receivable		4,00,000
	(Collect receivables from customers)		
Mar. 25	Accounts Receivable	5,20,000	
	Service Revenue		5,20,000
	(Provide services on account)		
Mar. 31	Fuel Expense	60,000	
	Cash		60,000
	(Pay for fuel consumed)		
Mar. 31	Dividends	20,000	
	Cash		20,000
	(Pay for dividends)		

Cash

Debit	Credit
20,00,000	7,20,000
4,00,000	5,00,000
	2,40,000
	2,30,000
	60,000
	20,000
6,30,000	

Accounts Receivable

Debit	Credit
4,80,000	4,00,000
5,20,000	
6,00,000	

Equipment

Debit	Credit
7,20,000	
7,20,000	

Prepaid Insurance

Debit	Credit
2,40,000	
2,40,000	

Supplies

Debit	Credit
5,00,000	
5,00,000	

Common Stock

Debit	Credit
	20,00,000
	20,00,000

Service Revenue

Debit	Credit
	4,80,000
	5,20,000
	10,00,000

Salaries Expense

Debit	Credit
2,30,000	
2,30,000	

Fuel Expense

Debit	Credit
60,000	
60,000	

Dividends

Debit	Credit
20,000	
20,000	

Trial Balance
March 31

Account	Debit	Credit
Cash	₹ 6,30,000	
Accounts Receivable	6,00,000	
Prepaid Insurance	2,40,000	
Supplies	5,00,000	
Equipment	7,20,000	
Common Stock		₹20,00,000
Service Revenue		10,00,000
Fuel Expense	60,000	
Salaries Expense	2,30,000	
Dividends	20,000	
Totals	₹30,00,000	₹30,00,000

Accrual Accounting and Adjusting Entries

Learning Objectives

After studying the material in this chapter, you should be able to:

LO1 Describe how income is measured and reported under the accrual and cash bases of accounting.

LO2 Identify the four major circumstances in which adjusting journal entries are necessary.

LO3 Record and post adjusting journal entries, and prepare an adjusted trial balance and financial statements.

LO4 Describe the purpose of the closing process and prepare closing entries.

LO5 Describe the steps of the accounting cycle.

Introduction

Chapter 3 introduced the first three steps in the accounting cycle—recording transactions, posting information to the ledger, and preparing a trial balance from which financial statements are prepared. This chapter explores the remaining steps in the cycle. This includes the adjusting process that leads to accrual-based financial statements and the closing process that prepares the accounting system for the next period. Both the adjusting and closing processes occur at the end of each accounting period.

LO1 Accrual and Cash Bases of Accounting

One of the main functions of the accounting information system is to record the revenues and expenses that a business generates. In accounting, there are two possible bases for recording revenues and expenses—the cash basis and the accrual basis. The main difference between the two is the timing of when revenues and expenses are recorded.

The **cash basis of accounting** records revenues when cash is received and records expenses when cash is paid. The best example of a cash basis accounting system is your personal checking account. Revenues such as job wages are recorded only when you are paid. Expenses such as utilities are recorded only when you write the check.

In contrast, the **accrual basis of accounting** records revenues when they are earned and records expenses when they are incurred. This is an application of the revenue recognition and matching principles, respectively, discussed in Chapter 1. In an accrual accounting system, revenues such as job wages are recorded when earned, regardless of when payment is received. Likewise, expenses such as utilities are recorded when used, regardless of when payment is made. A summary of each basis is as follows.

Cash basis of accounting Records revenues when cash is received and records expenses when cash is paid.

Accrual basis of accounting Records revenues when they are earned and records expenses when they are incurred.

When a retailer like Shoppers Stop sells a gift voucher, it records a liability. It records a revenue when the customer redeems the voucher.

	Cash Basis	**Accrual Basis**
Record revenues when:	Cash is received	Revenue is earned
Record expenses when:	Cash is paid	Expense is incurred

To illustrate the difference between the cash and accrual bases, suppose that a neighbor leaves town for the months of June and July and asks you to collect his mail and newspapers. Before he leaves, he pays you ₹100. Suppose further that you agree to pay a friend ₹40 to do the work, but you pay him at the end of July after the work is completed. Income for June and July under each basis would be calculated as follows.

The best example of a cash basis accounting system is your personal checking account.

Under the cash basis, June revenues are ₹100 because you received ₹100 during the month. Likewise, June expenses are ₹0 because you paid nothing during the month. As a result, June income is ₹100. For July, you received no money but paid your friend ₹40, so revenues are ₹0 and expenses are ₹40. Therefore, July income is –₹40.

	Cash Basis			Accrual Basis		
	June	July	Total	June	July	Total
Revenues	₹100	₹ 0	₹100	₹50	₹50	₹100
– Expense	0	40	40	20	20	40
Net Income	₹100	₹(40)	₹ 60	₹30	₹30	₹ 60

Under the accrual basis, revenues for June are ₹50 because you earned half of the ₹100 during June. And, even though you don't pay your friend until July, he provided half of the agreed labor in June, so June expenses are ₹20. As a result, June income is ₹30. Because the exact same circumstances occur in July, income for July is also ₹30.

The comparative income statements show that although each basis results in the same ₹60 of cumulative income, monthly income varies considerably. The cash-based statement reports that you generated a ₹100 profit one month and a ₹40 loss the next, while the accrual-based statement reports that you generated ₹30 in profits each month. Given that your activities were exactly the same each month, accrual-based income of ₹30 each month makes more sense than a ₹100 profit and a ₹40 loss. Even though both bases result in the same ₹60 income over the long term, the accrual basis provides a better representation of income over the two shorter periods of time. As a result, the accrual basis is required by Generally Accepted Accounting Principles.

Reporting Accrual- and Cash-Based Income

Because Generally Accepted Accounting Principles require the accrual basis, income statements report accrual-based income. However, cash basis information is also useful in understanding the financial condition of a company. A company that generates accrual income but never generates cash is a company that will soon fail. As a result, cash-based income is reported on the statement of cash flows. Recall from Chapter 1 that the operating activities section of a company's statement of cash flows calculates and reports the cash generated from operating the business. Cash generated from operations is the same as cash-based income.

To illustrate, consider the following condensed version of the operating activities section of Maruti Suzuki's statement of cash flows shown in Exhibit 4-1.

Maruti Suzuki India Limited (see Appendix C) uses the indirect method of reporting operating cash flows, which means that it calculates cash-based income by adjusting accrual-based income. The top line shows income on an accrual basis. For the current year, Maruti Suzuki generated over ₹29,910 million of profit before tax under the accrual basis. This number would also be found on Maruti Suzuki's income statement. After ₹5,333 million of tax adjustments, cash basis income is determined to be over ₹43,842 million. Cash basis income is lower than accrual basis income. In all two years presented, income on a cash basis is lower than income on an accrual basis.

Exhibit 4-1 Maruti Suzuki's Condensed Statement of Cash Flows—Operating Activities

(in million) **For the Years Ended**	**03/31/13**	**03/31/12**
Operating activities:		
Net income	₹29,910	₹21,462
Adjustments to reconcile net income to cash provided:		
Depreciation and amortization	18,612	11384
⋮	⋮	⋮
Adjustments for change in working capital		
Tax paid	₹(5,333)	₹(2509)
Net cash provided by operating activities	₹43,842	₹25,599

MARUTI SUZUKI ANALYSIS

In Appendix C, look at the Revenues paragraph in Maruti Suzuki's notes 1.3: Summary of Significant Accounting Policies. How can you tell from that paragraph that Maruti Suzuki uses the accrual basis of accounting?

Also, look at Maruti Suzuki's statement of cash flows in Appendix C. Over the two years presented, what was the total net income on a cash basis and how does that compare to total net income on an accrual basis?

The Revenues paragraph states that the company recognizes revenues from domestics and export sales on transfer of significant risk and rewards to the customers which takes place on dispatch of good from the factory and port respectively. The company recognizes income from services on rendering of services.

As mentioned in the previous paragraph, the company's statement of cash flows shows that cash basis income was lower than accrual basis income in both the years presented.

	2013	2012
Net income (cash basis):	₹43,842	₹25,599
Net income (accrual basis):	₹29,910	₹21,462

LO2 Adjusting Journal Entries

To ensure that revenues and expenses are properly recorded under an accrual basis, accounting information systems use adjusting journal entries. **Adjusting journal entries** are entries made in the general journal to record revenues that have been earned but not recorded and expenses that have been incurred but not recorded. The process of recording and posting adjusting entries is the fourth step in the accounting cycle and occurs at the end of each accounting period after the trial balance is prepared. After adjusting entries are journalized and posted, an "adjusted" trial balance is then prepared, from which financial statements are generated.

While adjusting entries can vary significantly across companies, they all arise because the exchange of cash does not always coincide with the earning of a revenue or incurrence of an expense. For example, sometimes cash is received *before* a revenue is earned while at other times cash is received *after* a revenue is earned. Likewise, sometimes cash is paid *before* an expense is incurred while at other times cash is paid *after* an expense is incurred. These four basic scenarios are the reasons that adjusting journal entries are necessary. Each scenario is listed in the following table and is discussed in the following sections.

Scenario	Classification of Adjusting Entry
1. Cash is received before revenue is earned	Deferred Revenue
2. Cash is received after revenue is earned	Accrued Revenue
3. Cash is paid before expense is incurred	Deferred Expense
4. Cash is paid after expense is incurred	Accrued Expense

Scenario 1: Deferred Revenue

Companies sometimes receive cash before they earn the revenue. For example, airlines get your money before you fly. When a company receives cash before it provides the service, it has a *deferred revenue*. The term *deferred* is used because at the time of cash receipt, the company has not yet provided the promised service and therefore cannot record a revenue in its accounting system. Instead, it must record a liability. Recording of the revenue must be *deferred* until the revenue is earned.

Adjusting journal entries Entries made in the general journal to record revenues that have been earned but not recorded and expenses that have been incurred but not recorded.

MARUTI SUZUKI ANALYSIS

Look at the Trade receivables (sundry Debtors), Trade Payables (Sundry creditors) and Advanced from customer/Dealers in Maruti Suzuki's Note 9,10 and 20, found in Appendix C. Do these items represent examples of deferred revenues, accrued revenues, deferred expenses, or accrued expenses?

The Trade receivables (sundry Debtors) explains the example of receiving payment after providing the good or service (accrued revenue). The Trade Payables (Sundry creditors) explains the example of making payment after consuming the goods or service (accrued expense). Advanced from customer/dealer explains the example of receiving payment before goods or services are delivered (deferred revenues).

Subscription Revenue To illustrate a deferred revenue adjustment, suppose that a company sells 12-month subscriptions to its monthly magazine. On October 1, the company receives a total of ₹1,200 for 12 subscriptions. To record this transaction, the company would record the following entry in its general journal:

Oct. 1	Cash	1,200	
	Unearned Subscription Revenue		1,200
	(To record cash received for future magazines)		

Assets	=	Liabilities	+	Equity
+1,200		+1,200		

This entry first increases the Cash account by the amount received. And, because the company now has an obligation to its customers to deliver the magazines, the entry also increases a liability account called Unearned Subscription Revenue. As a result, both assets and liabilities are increasing. The entry would then be posted to the relevant T-accounts as follows:

Cash (Dr)	Cash (Cr)	Unearned Subscription Revenue (Dr)	Unearned Subscription Revenue (Cr)	Subscription Revenue (Dr)	Subscription Revenue (Cr)
1,200			1,200		0
1,200			1,200		0

Suppose further that the company prepares financial statements at the end of each month. As of October 31, the company has provided one month of magazines and has therefore earned one month of revenue, or ₹100 (₹1,200 ÷ 12 months). Because the accounting system does not yet reflect this earned revenue, the following adjusting journal entry should be made on October 31:

Oct. 31	Unearned Subscription Revenue	100	
	Subscription Revenue		100
	(To record revenue earned during October)		

Assets	=	Liabilities	+	Equity
		−100		+100

This entry increases the Subscription Revenue account by the amount earned during the month and decreases the liability account Unearned Subscription Revenue by the same amount. As a result, liabilities are decreasing and equity is increasing. The entry would be posted to the relevant T-accounts as follows:

Cash (Dr)	Cash (Cr)	Unearned Subscription Revenue (Dr)	Unearned Subscription Revenue (Cr)	Subscription Revenue (Dr)	Subscription Revenue (Cr)
1,200			1,200		0
		100			100
1,200			1,100		100

After posting, the Subscription Revenue T-account reflects the ₹100 earned in the current period while the Unearned Subscription Revenue T-account reflects the remaining ₹1,100 to be earned over the next 11 months. These two accounts have been *adjusted* so that they properly reflect revenues earned during October and liabilities owed on October 31. The Cash account is not affected by the adjusting journal entry. Cash was exchanged and recorded on October 1.

General Rule When a company receives cash before it provides a service, the company should always increase a liability account for the amount received. As the company provides the service, the liability account is adjusted down (decreased) and the related revenue account is adjusted up (increased). So, the adjusting journal entry for this scenario will always be a reduction to a liability account and an increase to a revenue account, as shown in Exhibit 4-2.

Scenario 2: Accrued Revenue

Companies often provide a service and then collect the cash. When a company earns a revenue before it receives cash, it has an *accrued revenue*. The term *accrue* means to accumulate or increase. An accrued revenue is another name for a receivable.

The **process of recording and posting adjusting entries** is the fourth step in the accounting cycle and occurs at the end of each accounting period after the trial balance is prepared.

Service Revenue To illustrate an accrued revenue adjustment, suppose that an accounting firm agrees to provide a service to a client for a ₹1,000 fee. The firm completes its work on September 23, bills the client

Exhibit 4-2 Entries in a Deferred Revenue Scenario

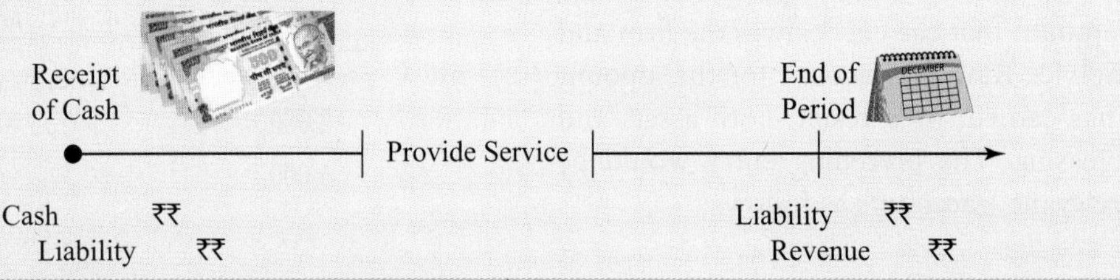

MAKING IT REAL

Although gift vouchers have existed for many years, their ever-growing popularity in recent times is causing some accounting issues for retailers.

Many people would assume that retailers record revenue with each gift voucher purchased. However, the transfer of merchandise is required for revenue to be recognized. Therefore, gift voucher sales represent a deferred revenue, which is a liability. Revenue is not generated until the gift vouchers is redeemed. For companies like Shoppers Stop, this liability is significant.

Gift vouchers create another accounting challenge because of "breakage"—gift vouchers that are never redeemed. When a retailer determines that a voucher will not be redeemed, it can reduce its liability and increase its revenue for the breakage estimate. In the notes to its financial statements, Shoppers Stop states, "In respect to gift vouchers and point reward schemes operated by the company, sales are recognized when the gift vouchers or points are redeemed and the merchandise is sold to the customers".

on October 10, and receives payment on October 21. Suppose further that the accounting firm prepares its own financial statements at the end of each month, which in this case is September 30.

Because the accrual basis requires that revenues be recorded in the period in which they are earned, the accounting firm must record the ₹1,000 of revenue on September 30 with the following adjusting journal entry:

Sept. 30	Accounts Receivable	1,000	
	Service Revenue		1,000
	(To record revenue earned during September)		

Assets	=	Liabilities	+	Equity
+1,000				+1,000

The entry increases the Accounts Receivable account for the amount that the client owes the firm and increases the Service Revenue account for the amount that the firm has earned. As a result, both assets and equity are increasing. The preceding entry would be posted to the relevant T-accounts as follows:

Cash		Accounts Receivable		Service Revenue	
0		1,000			1,000
0		1,000			1,000

After posting, the Service Revenue T-account reflects the ₹1,000 earned in the current period while the Accounts Receivable T-account reflects the ₹1,000 of expected cash receipts from the client. These two accounts have been *adjusted* so that they properly reflect revenues earned during September and receivables held on September 30.

When the customer pays cash on October 21, the following entry is made:

Oct. 21	Cash	1,000	
	Accounts Receivable		1,000
	(To record receipt of cash)		

Assets	=	Liabilities	+	Equity
+1,000				
−1,000				

This entry increases the Cash account and decreases the Accounts Receivable account for the amount collected. As a result, although specific asset accounts are changing, total assets remain unchanged. No revenue is recorded because it was recorded in the prior period when it was earned. The entry would be posted to the relevant T-accounts as follows:

Cash		Accounts Receivable	
0		1,000	
1,000			1,000
1,000		0	

General Rule When a company earns a revenue before it receives cash, the company should always increase a receivable account and a revenue account for the amount earned. In other words, the receivable account should be adjusted up (increased) and the revenue account should also be adjusted up (increased). When the company collects the receivable, the receivable account is decreased and the cash account is increased. So, the adjusting journal entry for this scenario will always be an increase to an asset account and an increase to a revenue account, as shown in Exhibit 4-3.

Exhibit 4-3 Entries in an Accrued Revenue Scenario

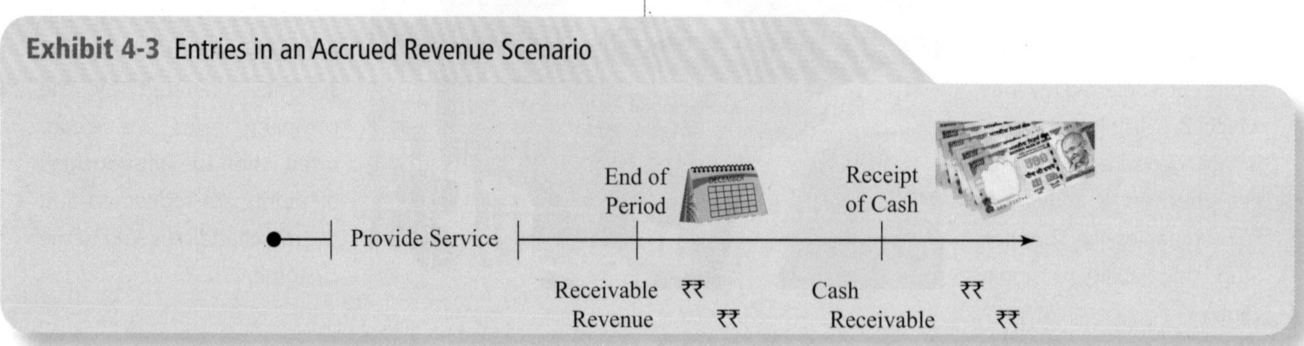

Scenario 3: Deferred Expense

Companies often pay cash before they incur an expense. You need look no further than your own personal expenses to find numerous examples of payments made before you use the service. One example is insurance. You pay for insurance for several months in advance and are then covered.

When a company pays for a resource before it uses or consumes it, the company has a *deferred expense*. We use the term *deferred* because at the time of cash payment for the resource, the company has yet to use or consume the resource it is acquiring and therefore cannot record an expense in the accounting system. Instead, it records an asset. Recording of the expense must be *deferred* until the expense is incurred. You should note that a *deferred expense* is nothing more than an asset—a resource to be used.

Insurance Expense To illustrate a deferred expense adjustment, suppose that on March 1, a company purchases a 12-month general liability insurance policy for ₹36,000. To record this transaction, the company would record the following entry in its general journal:

		Debit	Credit
Mar. 1	Prepaid Insurance	36,000	
	Cash		36,000
	(To record purchase of insurance)		

Assets	=	Liabilities	+	Equity
−36,000				
+36,000				

This entry increases the asset account Prepaid Insurance to reflect the amount of insurance bought and decreases the Cash account for the same. Since both of these accounts are assets, this entry does not change total assets. The entry would then be posted to the relevant T-accounts as follows. For illustration purposes, assume that the cash account has a ₹1,00,000 balance prior to the entry.

Cash		Prepaid Insurance		Insurance Expense	
100,000	36,000	36,000		0	
64,000		36,000		0	

Suppose further that the company prepares financial statements at the end of March. As of March 31, the company has been covered for one month and has therefore consumed one month of insurance, or ₹3,000 (₹36,000 ÷ 12 months). Because the accounting system does not yet reflect this expense, the following adjusting journal entry should be made on March 31:

		Debit	Credit
Mar. 31	Insurance Expense	3,000	
	Prepaid Insurance		3,000
	(To record expense incurred during March)		

Assets	=	Liabilities	+	Equity
−3,000				−3,000

This entry increases the Insurance Expense account by the amount consumed during the month and decreases the asset account Prepaid Insurance by the same amount. As a result, both assets and equity are decreasing. The entry would be posted to the relevant T-accounts as follows:

Cash		Prepaid Insurance		Insurance Expense	
100,000	36,000	36,000		0	
			3,000	3,000	
64,000		33,000		3,000	

After posting, the Insurance Expense T-account reflects the ₹3,000 of insurance that was consumed in the current period while the Prepaid Insurance T-account reflects the remaining ₹33,000 of insurance to be consumed over the next eleven months. These two accounts have been *adjusted* so that they properly reflect expenses incurred during March and unexpired assets on March 31. The Cash account is not affected by the adjusting journal entry. Cash was exchanged and recorded on March 1.

Depreciation Expense Another example of an expense where cash is paid before the expense is incurred is depreciation. Depreciation is the process of spreading out over their useful lives the cost of noncurrent assets such as equipment and buildings. For example, suppose that on August 1, a company purchases a delivery truck for ₹2,00,000. This transaction would be recorded into the accounting system as follows:

Aug. 1	Vehicles	2,00,000	
	Cash		2,00,000
	(To record purchase of truck)		

Assets	=	Liabilities	+	Equity
−2,00,000				
+2,00,000				

This entry increases the asset account Vehicles to reflect the cost of the truck and decreases the Cash account for the same. Since both of these accounts are assets, this entry does not change total assets. The entry would then be posted to the relevant T-accounts as follows. We will assume that the cash account has a ₹7,00,000 balance prior to the entry.

Cash (Dr)	Cash (Cr)	Vehicles (Dr)	Vehicles (Cr)	Depreciation Expense (Dr)	Depreciation Expense (Cr)
7,00,000	2,00,000	2,00,000		0	
5,00,000		2,00,000		0	

Suppose further that the company prepares financial statements at the end of August. As of August 30, the company has used the truck for one month and should therefore record some amount of expense associated with the use of the truck. If we assume for simplicity that the amount of expense to be recognized in the current month is ₹4,000, the following adjusting journal entry should be made on August 31:

Aug. 31	Depreciation Expense	4,000	
	Accumulated Depreciation		4,000
	(To record expense incurred during August)		

Assets	=	Liabilities	+	Equity
−4,000				−4,000

This entry increases the Depreciation Expense account by the amount of expense allocated to the current month. However, instead of decreasing the Equipment account directly, the entry increases Accumulated Depreciation. We discuss accumulated depreciation in detail in Chapter 8, but for now you should know that the account is a contra-asset account that accumulates depreciation expense to date and is subtracted from the Equipment account to yield the net balance of the asset. As a result of the entry, both assets and equity are decreasing. Equity is decreasing because the company recorded an expense. Assets are decreasing because the net balance of Vehicles and Accumulated Depreciation at the end of August is now ₹1,96,000 (₹2,00,000 – ₹4,000). The entry would be posted to the relevant T-accounts as follows:

Vehicles (Dr)	Vehicles (Cr)	Accumulated Depreciation (Dr)	Accumulated Depreciation (Cr)	Depreciation Expense (Dr)	Depreciation Expense (Cr)
2,00,000			0	0	
			4,000	4,000	
2,00,000			4,000	4,000	

The Depreciation Expense and Accumulated Depreciation accounts have been *adjusted* so that they properly reflect the ₹4,000 of expenses incurred during August and the ₹1,96,000 of net unexpired balance of Vehicles on August 31.

General Rule When a company pays cash before it incurs an expense, the company should always increase an asset account for the amount paid. As the company consumes the asset, the asset account is adjusted down (decreased) and the related expense account is adjusted up (increased). Depending on the type of asset, either the actual asset account will be decreased or a related contra-asset account will be increased. So, the adjusting journal entry for this scenario will always be a reduction to an asset account and an increase to an expense account, as shown in Exhibit 4-4.

Exhibit 4-4 Entries for a Deferred Expense Scenario

Payment of Cash — Use Resource — End of Period

Payment of Cash			End of Period		
Asset	₹₹		Expense	₹₹	
Cash		₹₹	Asset		₹₹

Scenario 4: Accrued Expense

Companies often incur expenses and pay for them later. A good example is employee salaries. Practically all companies pay their employees after the employees have provided labor for the company. When this occurs, the company has an *accrued expense*. An accrued expense is another name for a liability.

Salaries Expense To illustrate an accrued expense adjustment, suppose that a company's daily payroll is ₹1,00,000. The company pays its employees via direct deposit every Saturday for the work the employees have provided through Friday. Suppose further that the company prepares its financial statements on April 30, which is a Friday.

Because the accrual basis requires that expenses be recorded in the period in which they are incurred, the company must record the ₹5,00,000 of expense on April 30 with the following adjusting journal entry:

Apr. 30	Salaries Expense	5,00,000	
	Salaries Payable		5,00,000
	(To record salaries incurred during April)		

Assets	=	Liabilities	+	Equity
		+5,00,000		−5,00,000

The preceding entry increases the Salaries Expense account for the ₹5,00,000 of salaries incurred for the week and increases the Salaries Payable account for the same since it owes the employees those salaries. As a result, liabilities are increasing and equity is decreasing. The preceding entry would be posted to the relevant T-accounts as follows:

Cash (Dr)	Cash (Cr)	Salaries Payable (Dr)	Salaries Payable (Cr)	Salaries Expense (Dr)	Salaries Expense (Cr)
8,00,000			5,00,000	5,00,000	
8,00,000			5,00,000	5,00,000	

After posting, the Salaries Expense T-account reflects the ₹5,00,000 incurred in the current period while the Salaries Payable T-account reflects the ₹5,00,000 owed to employees on April 30. These two accounts have been *adjusted* so that they properly reflect expenses incurred during April and the payable owed on April 30.

The Cash account is not affected by the adjusting journal entry. Cash, which has an ₹8,00,000 balance for illustrative purposes, will be paid on Saturday, May 1. When the company pays its employees, the following entry would be made:

May 1	Salaries Payable	5,00,000	
	Cash		5,00,000
	(To record payment of cash)		

Assets	=	Liabilities	+	Equity
−5,00,000		−5,00,000		

The entry decreases the Cash account for the ₹5,00,000 paid to employees and decreases the Salaries Payable account by the same ₹5,00,000. No expense is recorded because it was recorded in the prior period when the expense was incurred. As a result, both assets and liabilities are decreasing. The entry would be posted to the relevant T-accounts as follows:

Cash (Dr)	Cash (Cr)	Salaries Payable (Dr)	Salaries Payable (Cr)
8,00,000			5,00,000
	5,00,000	5,00,000	
3,00,000			0

Interest Expense Interest is another example of incurring an expense before cash is paid. For example, suppose that a company borrows ₹1,00,000 on November 1. The annual interest rate on the loan is 6%, and interest is payable on the first day of each month. Suppose further that the company prepares its financial statements on November 30.

As of November 30, the company has used the borrowed money for one month, so it has incurred one month's worth of interest. To calculate the amount of interest, we simply multiply the principal amount (₹1,00,000) by the annual interest rate (6%) and by the relevant number of periods (1 month out of 12, or 1/12). So, interest for the month of November is:

Principal × annual rate × time = ₹1,00,000 × 0.06 × 1/12 = ₹5,000

Therefore, the following adjusting journal entry should be made on November 30:

Nov. 30	Interest Expense	5,000	
	Interest Payable		5,000
	(To record interest incurred during November)		

Assets	=	Liabilities	+	Equity
		+5,000		−5,000

The preceding entry increases the Interest Expense account for the ₹5,000 of interest for November and increases the Interest Payable account for the same. As a result, liabilities are increasing and equity is decreasing. The preceding entry would be posted to the relevant T-accounts as follows:

Cash		Interest Payable		Interest Expense	
1,00,000			5,000	5,000	
1,00,000			5,000	5,000	

After posting, the Interest Expense T-account reflects the ₹5,000 incurred in the current period and the Interest Payable T-account reflects the ₹5,000 owed to the bank on November 30. These two accounts have been *adjusted* so that they properly reflect expenses incurred during November and the payable owed on November 30.

The Cash account is not affected by the adjusting journal entry. Cash, which has a ₹1,00,000 balance for illustrative purposes, will be paid on December 1. On that date, the following entry would be made:

Dec. 1	Interest Payable	5,000	
	Cash		5,000
	(To record payment of cash)		

Assets	=	Liabilities	+	Equity
−5,000		−5,000		

The preceding entry decreases the Cash account for the ₹5,000 paid to the bank and decreases the Interest Payable account by the same ₹5,000. As a result, both assets and liabilities are decreasing. The entry would be posted to the relevant T-accounts as follows:

Cash		Interest Payable	
1,00,000			5,000
	5,000	5,000	
95,000			0

General Rule When a company incurs an expense before it pays cash, the company should always increase a payable account and an expense account for the amount incurred. In other words, the payable account should be adjusted up (increased) and the expense account should also be adjusted up (increased). When the company pays the liability, the liability account is reduced and the cash account is decreased. So, the adjusting journal entry for this scenario will always be an increase to a liability account and an increase to an expense account, as shown in Exhibit 4-5.

Summary of Adjusting Journal Entries

Exhibit 4-6 summarizes the four scenarios that give rise to adjusting journal entries and the characteristics of the relevant entries.

As you review this exhibit, consider the following generalizations of all adjusting entries:

1. The purpose of adjusting entries is to record revenues that have been earned but not recorded and expenses that have been incurred but not recorded.

Exhibit 4-5 Entries in an Accrued Expense Scenario

Use Resource

End of Period

Payment of Cash

Expense ₹₹
Liability ₹₹

Liability ₹₹
Cash ₹₹

Exhibit 4-6 Summary of Adjusting Journal Entry Scenarios

Scenario	Classification	Entry Before End of Period	Adjusting Entry at End of Period	Entry After End of Period
Cash is received *before* revenue is earned	Deferred Revenue	Cash ₹₹ Liability ₹₹	Liability ₹₹ Revenue ₹₹	
Cash is received *after* revenue is earned	Accrued Revenue		Receivable ₹₹ Revenue ₹₹	Cash ₹₹ Receivable ₹₹
Cash is paid *before* expense is incurred	Deferred Expense	Prepaid Asset ₹₹ Cash ₹₹	Expense ₹₹ Prepaid Asset ₹₹	
Cash is paid *after* expense is incurred	Accrued Expense		Expense ₹₹ Payable ₹₹	Payable ₹₹ Cash ₹₹

2. Every adjusting journal entry will affect at least one revenue or one expense account. In addition, every adjusting journal entry will affect at least one asset or liability account. This means that every adjusting entry will affect at least one account from the income statement and one account from the balance sheet.

3. Adjusting journal entries arise because the timing of revenue and expense recognition differs from the exchange of cash. Therefore, cash will never be increased or decreased in an adjusting entry.

LO3 Comprehensive Example: Adjusting Journal Entries

To illustrate the process of making adjusting journal entries from a trial balance and then preparing an adjusted trial balance, the Circle Films example from Chapter 3 will be continued. As a result of the transactions entered into by Circle Films during its first month of operations, the following unadjusted trial balance was prepared at May 31. Notice that it is an unadjusted trial balance because adjusting entries have not yet been made.

Circle Films
Unadjusted Trial Balance
May 31

	Debit	Credit
Cash	₹ 8,250	
Supplies	1,000	
Equipment	18,000	
Unearned Revenue		₹ 2000
Notes Payable		9,000
Common Stock		15,000
Service Revenue		5,000
Advertising Expense	250	
Salaries Expense	2,000	
Dividends	1,500	
Totals	₹31,000	₹31,000

In addition to these accounts and balances, the following information was available on May 31:

1. On May 31, Circle Films filmed the retirement reception for the customer who paid ₹2,000 on May 10 (see transaction #4 in Chapter 3 on page 48).

2. On May 31, Circle Films filmed the first night of a two-night local play. The second night will be filmed on June 1, at which time Circle Films will bill the customer. The customer has agreed to pay Circle Films ₹1,500 for each night.

3. After a physical count, Circle Films determined that it had ₹650 of supplies remaining.
4. The interest rate for the promissory note is 6%.
5. Circle Films estimates that depreciation for May on its two cameras totals ₹600.

Given this information, the following adjusting entries can be prepared.

Journalizing and Posting Adjusting Entries

Adjustment #1 (Deferred Revenue) Circle Films has now filmed the retirement reception, so it no longer has a liability to the customer. It has a revenue instead. However, the trial balance still shows the ₹2,000 liability. Thus, the adjusting entry to adjust the liability down and the revenue up is as follows:

Date	Account	Debit	Credit
May 31	Unearned Revenue	2,000	
	Service Revenue		2,000
	(To record revenue earned)		

Assets	=	Liabilities	+	Equity
		−2,000		+2,000

The entry would be posted to the relevant T-accounts as follows:

Unearned Revenue

Debit	Credit
	2,000
2,000	
	0

Service Revenue

Debit	Credit
	5,000
	2,000
	7,000

Adjustment #2 (Accrued Revenue) Circle Films filmed one night of a local play. Therefore, it has earned revenue for one night, or ₹1,500. The trial balance does not reflect this because Circle Films has not issued a bill, so the adjusting journal entry to adjust receivables and revenues up is as follows:

Date	Account	Debit	Credit
May 31	Accounts Receivable	1,500	
	Service Revenue		1,500
	(To record revenue earned)		

Assets	=	Liabilities	+	Equity
+1,500				+1,500

The entry would be posted to the relevant T-accounts as follows:

Accounts Receivable

Debit	Credit
0	
1,500	
1,500	

Service Revenue

Debit	Credit
	5,000
	2,000
	1,500
	8,500

Adjustment #3 (Deferred Expense) Circle Films has ₹650 in supplies on hand. However, the trial balance shows ₹1,000 in the Supplies account, which is the amount that Circle Films originally purchased. Therefore, Circle Films must have used ₹350 of supplies (₹1,000 – ₹650). To adjust the Supplies account down from ₹1,000 to ₹650 and to record the ₹350 in expense, the following adjusting journal is required.

Date	Account	Debit	Credit
May 31	Supplies Expense	350	
	Supplies		350
	(To record expense incurred)		

Assets	=	Liabilities	+	Equity
−350				−350

The entry would be posted to the relevant T-accounts as follows:

Supplies

Debit	Credit
1,000	
	350
650	

Supplies Expense

Debit	Credit
0	
350	
350	

Adjustment #4 (Accrued Expense) Circle Films must pay interest on the promissory note at a 6% annual rate. Therefore, after one month, Circle Films has incurred ₹45 of interest expense (₹9,000 × 6% × 1/12). This expense and the related obligation are not reflected in the trial balance because they have not yet been recorded. To record them, the following adjusting entry is required:

Date	Account	Debit	Credit
May 31	Interest Expense	45	
	Interest Payable		45
	(To record expense incurred)		

Assets	=	Liabilities	+	Equity
		+45		−45

Once an adjusted trial balance is prepared, financial statements can be generated.

The entry would be posted to the relevant T-accounts as follows:

Interest Payable		Interest Expense	
	0	0	
	45	45	
	45	45	

Adjustment #5 (Deferred Expense) Circle determines that depreciation on its cameras should be ₹600 for the month of May. To record this depreciation, the following adjusting entry is required.

May 31	Depreciation Expense	600	
	Accumulated Depreciation		600
	(To record expense incurred)		

Assets	=	Liabilities	+	Equity
−600				−600

The entry would be posted to the relevant T-accounts as follows:

Equipment		Depreciation Expense		Accumulated Depreciation	
18,000		0			0
		600			600
18,000		600			600

Preparing an Adjusted Trial Balance

Once all of the preceding adjusting entries are journalized and posted to the ledger, an adjusted trial balance can be prepared. Like the previous trial balance, the adjusted trial balance simply lists all balances from the ledger. Since the ledger now reflects several adjustments, so does the adjusted trial balance.

© ISTOCKPHOTO.COM/ZEFFSS1

The following is Circle Films' May 31 adjusted trial balance. The accounts that were either created or adjusted by the adjusting entries are highlighted.

Circle Films
Adjusted Trial Balance
May 31

	Debit	Credit
Cash	₹ 8,250	
Accounts Receivable	1,500	
Supplies	650	
Equipment	18,000	
Accumulated Depreciation		₹ 600
Unearned Revenue		0
Interest Payable		45
Notes Payable		9,000
Common Stock		15,000
Service Revenue		8,500
Supplies Expense	350	
Interest Expense	45	
Depreciation Expense	600	
Advertising Expense	250	
Salaries Expense	2,000	
Dividends	1,500	
Totals	₹33,145	₹33,145

Preparing Financial Statements

Once all revenues and expenses are recorded and an adjusted trial balance is prepared, financial statements can be generated. Recall from Chapter 1 that the income statement should be prepared first. Using the adjusted revenue and expense account balances from the adjusted trial balance, Circle Films' income statement for the month of May would appear as follows:

Circle Films
Income Statement
For the Month Ending May 31

Revenues		₹ 8,500
Expenses		
Supplies expense	₹ 350	
Interest expense	45	
Depreciation expense	600	
Advertising expense	250	
Salaries expense	2,000	
Total expenses		3,245
Net income		₹ 5,255

After a period ends and financial statements are prepared, all temporary accounts must be reset to zero for the start of the next period.

© PHOTOS.COM/THINKSTOCK

With net income calculated, Circle Films' statement of retained earnings can be prepared. Recall that the statement of retained earnings takes the beginning balance in Retained Earnings, adds net income, and subtracts dividends to yield the current balance in Retained Earnings. Circle Films' May 31 adjusted trial balance shows no balance in beginning Retained Earnings and a ₹1,500 balance in dividends. Therefore, Circle Films' statement of retained earnings for the month of May would appear as follows.

Circle Films
Statement of Retained Earnings
For the Month Ending May 31

Retained earnings, May 1	₹ 0
Add: Net income	5,255
Less: Dividends	(1,500)
Retained earnings, May 31	₹ 3,755

With Retained Earnings calculated, Circle Films' balance sheet can be prepared. Circle Films' May 31 adjusted trial balance shows several balance sheet accounts, starting with Cash and continuing through Common Stock. These accounts, along with the amount of Retained Earnings from the May statement of retained earnings, should be included on the balance sheet. Therefore, Circle Films' May 31 balance sheet would appear as follows.

Circle Films
Balance Sheet
May 31

Cash		₹ 8,250
Accounts receivable		1,500
Supplies		650
Equipment	₹18,000	
Less: Accumulated depreciation	600	17,400
Total assets		₹27,800
Interest payable	₹ 45	
Notes payable	9,000	
Total liabilities		₹ 9,045
Common stock	₹15,000	
Retained earnings	3,755	
Total stockholders' equity		18,755
Total liabilities and stockholders' equity		₹27,800

Closing process The process of transferring all revenue, expense, and dividend account balances to the Retained Earnings account.

Temporary accounts Accounts that accumulate balances only for the current period.

LO4 Closing Process

After financial statements are prepared, companies conduct the closing process. The **closing process** is the process of transferring all revenue, expense, and dividend account balances to the Retained Earnings account. This transfer is necessary for two reasons.

First, revenue, expense, and dividend accounts are **temporary accounts**, meaning that they accumulate balances only for the current period. After the period ends and financial statements are prepared, all temporary accounts must be reset to zero for the start of the next period.

Second, the transfer updates the Retained Earnings account to its proper end-of-period balance. In the preceding example, the balance in Retained Earnings is generated from the statement of retained earnings, not the adjusted trial balance. The closing process is the mechanism that updates the actual Retained Earnings account balance in the ledger.

The closing process is accomplished with several entries. **Closing entries**, which are made in the journal and posted to the ledger, eliminate the balances in all temporary accounts and transfer those balances to the Retained Earnings account. Usually, one entry is made for revenues, one for expenses, and a final entry for dividends. To illustrate, the temporary accounts from Circle Films' adjusted trial balance are shown in the following partial adjusted trial balance:

Circle Films
Partial Adjusted Trial Balance
May 31

	Debit	Credit
Service Revenue		₹8,500
Supplies Expense	₹ 350	
Interest Expense	45	
Depreciation Expense	600	
Advertising Expense	250	
Salaries Expense	2,000	
Dividends	1,500	

Circle Films has one revenue account with an ₹8,500 credit balance. To eliminate that balance and transfer it to the Retained Earnings account, the following closing entry is required.

May 31	Service Revenue	8,500	
	Retained Earnings		8,500
	(To close revenue account)		

In this entry, the revenue balance is eliminated while the Retained Earnings account is increased.

Expense and dividend accounts are closed in a similar fashion. To eliminate those balances and transfer them to Retained Earnings, the following closing entries are required.

May 31	Retained Earnings	3,245	
	Supplies Expense		350
	Interest Expense		45
	Depreciation Expense		600
	Advertising Expense		250
	Salaries Expense		2,000
	(To close expense accounts)		

May 31	Retained Earnings	1,500	
	Dividends		1,500
	(To close dividend account)		

In the first entry, all expense accounts are eliminated, and the Retained Earnings account is decreased for the same. In the second entry, the dividend account is eliminated, and the Retained Earnings account is decreased for the same.

All three closing entries would be posted to the appropriate T-accounts as follows.

Retained Earnings

Debit	Credit
	8,500
3,245	
1,500	
	3,755

Supplies Expense

Debit	Credit
350	
	350
0	

Interest Expense

Debit	Credit
45	
	45
0	

Depreciation Exp.

Debit	Credit
600	
	600
0	

Advertising Expense

Debit	Credit
250	
	250
0	

Salaries Expense

Debit	Credit
2,000	
	2,000
0	

Service Revenue

Debit	Credit
	8,500
8,500	
	0

Dividends

Debit	Credit
1,500	
	1,500
0	

Notice that after the closing entries are posted, all revenue, expense, and dividend accounts have zero balances as desired. They are now ready to begin the next reporting period. Also, Retained Earnings has a ₹3,755

Closing entries Entries made in the journal and posted to the ledger that eliminate the balances in all temporary accounts and transfer those balances to the Retained Earnings account.

credit balance. This is the balance reported on Circle Films' statement of retained earnings and balance sheet. In other words, the Retained Earnings account now has the proper balance at the end of the period.

As a final check that all accounts have been properly closed, a new trial balance is prepared. Appropriately called a post-closing trial balance, it contains all account balances for the beginning of the next accounting period. Circle Films' post-closing trial balance is as follows.

Circle Films
Post-Closing Trial Balance
May 31

	Debit	Credit
Cash	₹ 8,250	
Accounts Receivable	1,500	
Supplies	650	
Equipment	18,000	
Accumulated Depreciation		₹ 600
Interest Payable		45
Notes Payable		9,000
Common Stock		15,000
Retained Earnings		3,755
Totals	₹28,400	₹28,400

Accounting cycle The sequence of steps in which an accounting information system captures, processes, and reports a company's accounting transactions during a period.

LO5 The Accounting Cycle—A Summary

This and the previous chapter covered the accounting cycle. The **accounting cycle** is the sequence of steps in which an accounting information system captures, processes, and reports a company's accounting transactions during a period. Chapter 3 demonstrated the first three steps—how to record journal entries in the journal, post the information to the ledger, and prepare a trial balance. This chapter demonstrated the two major processes that occur at the end of the period—adjusting and closing. The adjusting process includes the recording and posting of adjusting entries and the preparation of an adjusted trial balance, from which financial statements are prepared. The closing process includes the recording and posting of closing entries and the preparation of a post-closing trial balance. Once closing is completed, the accounting information system is prepared to begin the next period. Exhibit 4-7 summarizes these steps.

Exhibit 4-7 The Accounting Cycle

1. Journalize and post accounting transactions.
2. Prepare a trial balance.
3. Journalize and post adjusting entries.
4. Prepare an adjusted trial balance.
5. Prepare financial statements.
6. Journalize and post closing entries.
7. Prepare a post-closing trial balance.

CONCEPT QUESTIONS

1. When are revenues and expenses recognized under the cash basis of accounting?
2. When are revenues and expenses recognized under the accrual basis of accounting?
3. Which basic accounting principle(s) does the cash basis of accounting violate?
4. Income under the cash basis of accounting is not reported at all under Generally Accepted Accounting Principles. Do you agree or disagree? Explain.
5. Why will income under the cash basis and the accrual basis be the same in the long run?
6. What is the purpose of adjusting journal entries, and when are they made?
7. What circumstances give rise to a deferred revenue? a deferred expense?
8. What circumstances give rise to an accrued revenue? an accrued expense?
9. List the four basic classifications of adjusting entries and describe the nature of each adjusting entry.
10. Deferred expense and accrued expense are interchangeable terms. Explain why this statement is false.
11. Is it possible for adjusting entries to affect only the balance sheet? Why or why not?
12. How is the adjusted trial balance used to prepare financial statements?
13. What does the term "temporary accounts" mean? List the general types of accounts that fall under this classification.
14. At the beginning of an accounting period, a company's revenue, expense, and dividend accounts will always have zero balances. Do you agree or disagree? Explain.
15. Describe the three possible closing entries.

MULTIPLE CHOICE

1. The cash basis of accounting:
   a. is a basis for when to record revenues and expenses.
   b. is required by Generally Accepted Accounting Principles.
   c. records expenses when they are incurred.
   d. records revenues only when they have been earned.
2. On December 31, a company receives a ₹5,00,000 payment for services not yet rendered and a ₹50,000 electric bill for the month of December. Under the cash basis of accounting, this company would recognize:
   a. ₹4,50,000 of revenue and ₹50,000 of expense.
   b. ₹5,00,000 of revenue and ₹0 of expense.
   c. ₹5,00,000 of revenue and ₹50,000 of expense.
   d. ₹0 of revenue and ₹50,000 of expense.
3. On December 31, a company receives a ₹5,00,000 payment for services not yet rendered and a ₹50,000 electric bill for the month of December. Under the accrual basis of accounting, this company would recognize:
   a. ₹4,50,000 of revenue and ₹50,000 of expense.
   b. ₹5,00,000 of revenue and ₹0 of expense.
   c. ₹5,00,000 of revenue and ₹50,000 of expense.
   d. ₹0 of revenue and ₹50,000 of expense.
4. Which of the following situations would likely not require an adjusting entry?
   a. Revenue is earned before cash is received
   b. Expense is incurred before cash is paid
   c. Cash is received before revenue is earned
   d. Cash is paid before equipment is received
5. Which of the following accounts is most likely associated with a deferred revenue?
   a. Depreciation Expense
   b. Salaries Payable
   c. Unearned Revenue
   d. Accounts Receivable
6. Which of the following accounts is most likely associated with an accrued expense?
   a. Depreciation Expense
   b. Salaries Payable
   c. Unearned Revenue
   d. Accounts Receivable
7. Which of the following is false?
   a. Adjusting entries are made at the end of an accounting period
   b. Adjusting entries are not necessary under the cash basis of accounting
   c. The cash account will always be affected by adjusting journal entries
   d. Adjusting journal entries always affect at least one revenue or expense account and at least one asset or liability account
8. A company prepays rent of ₹50,000 and receives a ₹3,00,000 payment for services not yet rendered. Under the accrual basis of accounting, these two transactions will:
   a. increase net income ₹2,50,000.
   b. increase net income ₹3,00,000.
   c. decrease net income ₹50,000.
   d. have no effect on net income.
9. A company has ₹3,00,000 of supplies on hand at the beginning of the year. During the year, the company buys ₹7,50,000 of supplies. At the end of the year, supplies on hand total ₹4,00,000. What is the amount of Supplies Expense reported on the company's income statement?
   a. ₹4,00,000
   b. ₹7,50,000
   c. ₹6,50,000
   d. ₹10,50,000
10. On December 1, Smiles, Inc. prepays ₹2,40,000 for three months of rent. On December 31, Smiles prepares financial statements. After the appropriate adjusting entry for rent, Smiles' balance sheet would show:
    a. prepaid Rent of ₹2,40,000.
    b. rent Expense of ₹80,000.
    c. prepaid Rent of ₹1,60,000.
    d. prepaid Rent of ₹80,000.

11. A company has a ₹4,00,000 balance in Unearned Revenue on its unadjusted trial balance. At the end of the year, the company has earned all but one-fourth of the revenue. The adjusting journal entry necessary at year-end would include:
    a. a debit to Service Revenue of ₹4,00,000.
    b. a credit to Unearned Revenue for ₹3,00,000.
    c. a debit to Unearned Revenue for ₹3,00,000.
    d. a credit to Service Revenue of ₹1,00,000.
12. A company fails to record the expiration of insurance that it purchased previously. Because of this error, the company's assets and equity are:
    a. overstated.
    b. understated.
    c. unaffected.
    d. cannot tell from the given information.
13. A company's unadjusted trial balance shows a ₹12,00,000 balance in Salaries Expense while the adjusted trial balance shows a balance of ₹13,00,000. Which of the following best describes the reason for the difference?
    a. An adjusting entry to reduce Salaries Expense by ₹1,00,000 was prepared
    b. An adjusting entry to reduce Salaries Payable by ₹1,00,000 was prepared
    c. An adjusting entry to record the payment of ₹1,00,000 of salaries was prepared
    d. An adjusting entry to increase Salaries Expense by ₹1,00,000 was prepared
14. Tom and Judy's Bed and Breakfast received the following bills for December utilities:
    i. Electricity - ₹50,000 on December 31, 2011
    ii. Water - ₹75,000 on December 29, 2011
    iii. Telephone - ₹37,500 on January 1, 2012
    On the December 31, 2011, financial statements, Tom and Judy's should show accrued expenses of:
    a. ₹1,62,500.
    b. ₹1,25,000.
    c. ₹50,000.
    d. None of the above.
15. The closing process:
    a. updates the retained earnings account.
    b. prepares all revenue and expense accounts for the next period.
    c. puts any dividend account to zero.
    d. all of the above.
16. Claw's Irrigation, Inc. paid ₹2,00,000 of dividends in the prior year and ₹4,50,000 of dividends in the current year. The closing entry for the current year would include:
    a. a debit to Retained Earnings for ₹6,50,000.
    b. a credit to Dividends for ₹6,50,000.
    c. a credit to Dividends for ₹4,50,000.
    d. a credit to Retained Earnings for ₹4,50,000.
17. Collins Construction Co. uses the accrual basis of accounting. During the year, Collins reported ₹45,00,000 of revenue, ₹12,50,000 of expenses, and ₹1,20,000 of dividends. On December 31, Collins prepares all closing entries. The net effect on Retained Earnings is a:
    a. decrease of ₹1,20,000.
    b. increase of ₹42,50,000.
    c. increase of ₹31,30,000.
    d. decrease of ₹13,70,000.
18. Which of the following is not a possible closing entry?
    a. A debit to Retained Earnings and a credit to Dividends
    b. A debit to Revenue and a credit to Retained Earnings
    c. A debit to Retained Earnings and a credit to Expense
    d. A debit to Expense and a credit to Retained Earnings
19. Which of the following is not a step in the accounting cycle?
    a. Prepare an adjusted trial balance
    b. Prepare and post closing entries
    c. Prepare financial statements
    d. Each of the above is a step in the accounting cycle
20. Which of the following best summarizes the order of the accounting cycle?
    a. Journalize, post, adjust, close
    b. Journalize, adjust, post, close
    c. Journalize, close, adjust, post
    d. Journalize, post, close, adjust

BRIEF EXERCISES

1. Cash and Accrual Basis

During the year, Black Diamond Company earned ₹86,50,000 in revenue. At year-end, only ₹65,00,000 of that revenue had been collected. Also, Black Diamond incurred ₹44,00,000 of expenses of which only ₹35,00,000 had been paid.

Required

Determine net income for the year under (a) the cash basis of accounting and (b) the accrual basis of accounting.

2. Adjusting Journal Entries

Consider the following incomplete adjusting journal entries:

1. Utilities Expense	2,900	
(a)		2,900
2. (b)	19,500	
Service Revenue		19,500
3. (c)	7,000	
Prepaid Insurance		7,000
4. Unearned Revenue	4,650	
(d)		4,650

Required
Identify the likely account(s) that would complete each adjusting journal entry.

3. Adjusting Journal Entries

Consider the four entries in the preceding brief exercise.

Required
Identify each entry as an accrued expense, an accrued revenue, a deferred expense, or a deferred revenue.

4. Adjusting Journal Entry—Revenue

On March 1, Global Airlines received ₹3,50,000 cash from customers who bought tickets. Only half of the tickets were used by the end of March, and the remaining tickets were expected to be used in April. Global prepares adjusting entries monthly.

Required

a. Determine whether the revenue is a deferred or accrued revenue and explain why.
b. Prepare the journal entries that Global would make on March 1 and March 31.

5. Adjusting Journal Entry—Expense

White Star Enterprises records salaries expense each Friday when employees are paid. The company is preparing its financial statements on June 30, which is a Wednesday. Salaries are ₹50,000 a week.

Required

a. Prepare any adjusting journal entry necessary on June 30.
b. Explain if this situation is a deferred or accrued expense.
c. Show the T-accounts with the adjusting journal entry posted to them.

6. Adjusting Journal Entry—Expense

On January 1, PGD Corporation bought equipment for ₹20,00,000 cash. For the year, PGD calculates a total of ₹1,25,000 of depreciation on the equipment. PGD records depreciation annually on December 31.

Required

a. Prepare all journal entries relating to the purchase and depreciation of the equipment.
b. Post the December 31 journal entry to the relevant T-accounts.

7. Adjusting Journal Entry Errors

Suppose that a company fails to make the proper adjusting journal entries associated with the following expenses and revenues:

1. Prepaid insurance that has expired
2. Interest that has accrued on notes payable
3. Unearned revenue that has now been earned

Required
Determine the likely accounts that are affected by each error and whether those accounts are understated or overstated as a result of the error.

8. Calculate Expenses and Revenues

The current- and prior-year balance sheets of Banter Company show the following account balances: (in lakhs)

	Current Year	Prior Year
Supplies	₹3,000	₹4,500
Unearned Revenue	7,200	7,000

During the current year, Banter purchased ₹11,300 of supplies and received ₹9,200 of cash for services to be performed later.

Required
Using T-accounts, determine Banter Company's supplies expense and service revenue for the current year.

9. Adjusting Journal Entries

Big E Services provides the following selected information from its trial balance and adjusted trial balance at August 31:

Big E Services
Trial Balance (in lakhs)
August 31

	Unadjusted		Adjusted	
	Debit	Credit	Debit	Credit
Accounts Receivable	₹8,910		₹9,240	
Supplies	3,400		2,200	
Service Revenue		₹17,480		₹17,810
Supplies Expense	5,320		6,520	

Required
Prepare the adjusting journal entries that Big E must have made at August 31.

10. Prepare Financial Statements from Trial Balance

The adjusted trial balance for Handle Coffee is as follows:

Handle Coffee
Adjusted Trial Balance (in lakhs)
November 30

	Debit	Credit
Cash	₹2,500	
Accounts Receivable	350	
Supplies	1,800	
Accounts Payable		₹ 750
Salaries Payable		2,000
Retained Earnings		1,000
Service Revenue		4,400
Salaries Expense	2,900	
Supplies Expense	600	
Total	₹8,150	₹8,150

Required
Prepare Handle's income statement and statement of retained earnings for the month of November and its balance sheet at November 30.

11. Closing Entries

Ivey Publishing generates and records ₹15,000 of revenues and ₹12,000 of expenses during the month. It also pays and records ₹500 in dividends for the month.

Required
Prepare Ivey's closing entries for the month and determine the net change in Retained Earnings as a result of those entries.

12. Adjusting and Closing Process

Consider the following accounts:

Cash
Accounts Receivable
Interest Payable
Common Stock
Service Revenue
Salaries Expense

Required
Determine which accounts fall into the following categories: A) Accounts that can be adjusted and closed; B) Accounts that can be adjusted but not closed; C) Accounts that are not normally adjusted nor closed.

EXERCISES

13. Cash and Accrual Income

During 2012, Stacker Enterprises earned ₹55,00,000 from services provided and incurred ₹15,50,000 of expenses. At the end of the year, Stacker had received cash for ₹35,75,000 of the revenues and had paid ₹11,60,000 of the expenses. Also during 2012, Stacker received ₹3,50,000 cash for services to be performed in 2013 and paid ₹4,50,000 for rent for the first six months of 2013.

Required
Determine 2012 net income under (a) the cash basis and (b) the accrual basis of accounting.

14. Adjusting Journal Entries

Following are several independent accounting situations:

1. Interest of ₹1,50,000 on a loan outstanding during 2012 is due on January 1, 2013.
2. Received ₹100,00,000 in 2012 for a service project that is 45% complete at year-end.
3. Received a ₹45,000 utility bill for the month of December on January 3, 2013.
4. ₹75000 of prepaid rent for the month of December has expired.
5. ₹5,00,000 of revenue for services performed on December 14, 2012, is uncollected.
6. Prepay ₹6,50,000 of insurance on December 31, 2012, for the entire year of 2013.
7. Intend to buy a warehouse on January 1, 2013, for ₹1,25,00,000.
8. Equipment depreciation is ₹5,00,000 for the year.

Required
For each independent situation, determine the basic type of adjustment, if any, that is needed on December 31, 2012 (deferred revenue, deferred expense, accrued revenue, accrued expense). What would be the cumulative effect on 2012 net income of all adjustments made in situations 1–8?

15. Adjusting Journal Entries

The following selected accounts were taken from the general ledger of the Cone Corporation on September 30 before adjusting entries have been made. Cone makes adjusting entries *quarterly*.

	Debit	Credit
Supplies	4,000	
Prepaid Rent	5,400	
Building	100,000	
Notes Receivable	25,000	
Accumulated Depreciation		20,000
Unearned Revenue		8,500

Additional Information:

1. Rent expires at a rate of ₹900 per month.
2. Supplies on hand total ₹2,000.
3. Utilities incurred in September but not yet recorded or paid are ₹500.
4. The building depreciates at a rate of ₹2,700 per quarter.
5. ₹5,000 of the ₹8,500 unearned revenue has been earned during the quarter.
6. Interest of ₹250 on the notes receivable has been earned but not yet recorded.

Required
Prepare the necessary adjusting journal entries at September 30.

16. Adjusting Journal Entries

For each of the transactions for Cone Corporation in Exercise 15, indicate the amount of the increase or decrease on the appropriate element of the balance sheet or income statement. The first transaction has been completed as an example.

	Balance Sheet			Income Statement		
Transaction	Assets	Liability	Equity	Revenues	Expenses	Net Income
1.	−2,700	NE	−2,700	NE	+2,700	−2,700
2.						
3.						
4.						
5.						
6.						

17. Adjusting Journal Entries

In its first year of operations, Lien Corporation entered into the following transactions, among others:

1. January 1: Bought equipment, ₹10,50,000.
2. March 31: Prepaid one year's rent, ₹24,00,000.
3. July 1: Took out a one year loan from the bank at an annual interest rate of 8%, ₹20,00,000.
4. August 1: Received payment for services not yet rendered, ₹12,00,000.

On December 31, Lien has earned ₹8,00,000 of the ₹12,00,000 in transaction 4 and has incurred but not recorded ₹45,000 of utilities. Lien prepares adjusting entries on an annual basis.

Required

Prepare journal entries for transactions 1–4. Prepare any adjusting journal entries needed at December 31. Assume that the equipment depreciates ₹15,00,000 annually.

18. Adjusting Journal Entries

Mikato Company's annual accounting period ends on June 30, 2012. Mikato makes adjusting journal entries semiannually, and the following information applies to all necessary adjusting journal entries at June 30, 2012:

1. Mikato carries the following two insurance policies:

Policy	Purchase Date	Policy Length	Cost at Purchase Date
A	July 1, 2010	5 years	₹48,00,000
B	July 1, 2011	2 years	16,00,000

2. At January 1, 2012, office supplies totaled ₹1,80000. In the past six months, additional supplies of ₹2,70,000 were purchased, and a count revealed ₹2,15,000 available supplies at June 30, 2012.
3. Mikato owns one building:

Cost	Useful Life	Annual Depreciation
₹150,00000	25	₹6,00000

4. Mikato decides to rent out a portion of its building. On June 1, 2012, Mikato received a prepayment of ₹5,70,000 for rent for the months of June, July, and August.
5. The Mikato staff consists of seven employees. Each employee earns a total of ₹1,20,000 a week and is paid each Monday for the previous week's work. June 30, 2012, falls on Thursday.

Required

Prepare all necessary adjusting entries at June 30, 2012, and indicate whether each entry relates to a deferred revenue, deferred expense, accrued revenue, or accrued expense.

19. Errors in Adjusting Journal Entries

Consider the following independent situations.

1. A company provides a service but has not yet received payment. Therefore, the company does not record any revenue for the service.
2. A company receives cash in advance of providing a service and properly records a liability to the customer. At year-end, the company has not provided any of the service. The company does not adjust the liability at year-end.
3. Half of a company's prepaid insurance expires during the year, but the company does not adjust the prepaid insurance account to reflect the expiration.
4. A company incurs legal expenses associated with defending a lawsuit. No bill has been received at year-end, so the company does not record any expenses associated with the lawsuit.

Required

For each independent scenario, determine whether the company's accounting was correct or incorrect. If it was incorrect, determine whether the error resulted in the company's assets, liabilities, equity, revenues, and expenses being correct, understated, or overstated.

20. Adjusting Journal Entries

Coy Williams, a first-year accountant at Protein Plus, has asked you to review the following items for potential errors. Protein Plus has a December 31 year-end.

1. Did not adjust the Prepaid Insurance account for the ₹6,60,000 of insurance that expired during the year.
2. Recorded a full year of accrued interest on a ₹20,00,000, 10% note payable that was entered into on July 1. Interest is payable each July 1.
3. Did not record ₹8,50,000 of depreciation on an office building.
4. Recorded revenues of ₹12,00,000 when payment was received for a job that will be completed next year.
5. Recorded ₹60,000 of utilities expense for December utilities even though Protein Plus will not pay the bill until January of next year.

Required

Determine if Coy made any errors in the five items. For those in which an error was made, prepare the entry that Coy should have made. What was the net effect of Coy's errors on the net income of Protein Plus?

21. Closing Entries

Ivey Publishing provides the following trial balance at March 31:

Ivey Publishing Trial Balance March 31		
	Debit	**Credit**
Cash	₹4,280	
Prepaid Insurance	3,500	
Unearned Revenue		₹3,000
Retained Earnings		2,380
Service Revenue		14,820
Insurance Expense	2,300	
Salaries Expense	8,920	
Dividends	1,200	
Totals	₹20,200	₹20,200

Required
Prepare Ivey's closing entries at March 31 and its Post-Closing Trial Balance.

22. Closing Process

A partial adjusted trial balance is shown as follows for Sparks Electricity:

Sparks Electricity Partial Adjusted Trial Balance June 30		
	Debit	**Credit**
Retained Earnings		₹17,150
Service Revenue		30,500
Advertising Expense	₹ 1,200	
Depreciation Expense	10,750	
Interest Expense	560	
Salaries Expense	5,000	
Supplies Expense	2,500	
Utilities Expense	2,080	
Dividends	1,000	

Required

a. Prepare Sparks' income statement and statement of retained earnings for the month of June.
b. Prepare the appropriate closing entries at June 30.
c. What is the purpose of "closing the books" at the end of an accounting period?

23. Closing Process

The following T-accounts contain the December postings to the general ledger of Swoops, Inc. The December 1 postings are beginning balances, while the December 31 postings are closing entries.

Service Revenue

12/31	75,000	12/1	64,000
		12/8	4,000
		12/24	3,000
		12/30	4,000

Salaries Expense

12/1	15,000	12/31	17,000
12/15	1,000		
12/30	1,000		

Supplies Expense

12/1	1,800	12/31	2,500
12/30	700		

Depreciation Expense

12/1	4,400	12/31	4,800
12/30	400		

Interest Expense

12/1	1,500	12/31	1,800
12/24	300		

Retained Earnings

12/31	2,500	12/1	51,550
12/31	26,100	12/31	75,000

Dividends

12/1	2,000	12/31	2,500
12/15	500		

Required
Recreate the closing journal entries made by Swoops on December 31.

24. Errors in Closing Entries

Landers Manufacturing prepares the following three closing entries at the end of the year:

#1 Retained Earnings	45,550	
Service Revenue		45,550
#2 Retained Earnings	39,200	
Advertising Expense		10,400
Rent Expense		4,500
Salaries Expense		18,800
Supplies Expense		4,500
#3 Retained Earnings	2,000	
Dividends Payable		2,000

Required
Identify the potential error(s) in Landers' closing entries.

25. Match Terms and Definitions

The following is a list of various accounting terms and definitions:

1. Accrual basis of accounting
2. Cash basis of accounting
3. Adjusting journal entries

a. The final step in the accounting cycle whereby all revenue, expense, and dividend account balances are transferred to the Retained Earnings account.
b. Cash is received before revenue is earned.
c. Entries made into the general journal at the end of an accounting period that record previously unrecorded revenues or expenses.

4. Deferred revenue	d. Expense is incurred before cash is paid.
5. Accrued revenue	e. Revenues are recorded only when cash is received, and expenses are recorded only when cash is paid.
6. Deferred expense	f. Cash is paid before expense is incurred.
7. Accrued expense	g. Revenues are recorded only when they are earned, and expenses are recorded only when they are incurred.
8. Closing process	h. Revenue is earned before cash is received.

Required
Match each accounting term with the appropriate definition.

PROBLEMS

26. Cash and Accrual Income

Olga Industries keeps records under the cash basis of accounting rather than the accrual basis. Olga's 2012 income statement and additional data from 2011 and 2012 are as follows:

Olga Industries
Cash-Basis Income Statement (in lakhs)
For the Year Ending December 31, 2012

Revenues		₹54,000
Expenses		35,000
Net income		₹19,000
Additional Information:		
	12/31/11	**12/31/12**
Accrued Revenues	6,000	8,000
Deferred Revenues	13,000	4,500
Accrued Expenses	5,000	4,000
Deferred Expenses	10,000	9,500

All accrued revenues and expenses as of 12/31/11 were collected and paid, respectively, in 2012. All deferred revenues and expenses as of 12/31/11 were earned and used, respectively, in 2012.

Required
Convert revenues and expenses from the cash basis to the accrual basis and recalculate income. Briefly explain why each adjustment is made.

27. Adjusting Entries and Trial Balance

The unadjusted trial balance of Sweet Cheeks Facial Spa is shown as follows:

Sweet Cheeks Facial Spa
Unadjusted Trial Balance (in lakhs)
September 30

	Debit	Credit
Cash	₹ 4,300	
Supplies	2,250	
Equipment	18,000	
Accumulated Depreciation		₹ 2,400
Unearned Revenue		1,500
Notes Payable		10,000
Common Stock		10,000
Service Revenue		4,000
Advertising Expense	650	
Depreciation Expense	1,200	
Interest Expense	400	
Salaries Expense	600	
Dividends	500	
Totals	₹27,900	₹27,900

Additional Information:

1. On September 30, Sweet Cheeks completed a service for which it had received payment in August, ₹1,500.
2. On September 30, Sweet Cheeks determined that it had earned but not yet billed revenues of ₹500.
3. Monthly depreciation on Sweet Cheeks' equipment is ₹150.
4. The interest rate on the promissory note is 6%.
5. A count of the supplies revealed ₹500 of supplies remaining on September 30.
6. Assume the trial balance was last adjusted on August 31.

Required
Prepare all necessary adjusting entries for the month of September and prepare an adjusted trial balance as of September 30.

28. Adjusting Entries and Closing Entries

The unadjusted and adjusted trial balances of HD Rizzle, Inc. are as follows:

HD Rizzle, Inc.
Trial Balance (in lakhs)
December 31

	Unadjusted		Adjusted	
	Debit	**Credit**	**Debit**	**Credit**
Cash	₹ 3,500		₹ 3,500	
Accounts Receivable	8,250		10,750	
Prepaid Insurance	4,600		3,400	
Supplies	600		200	
Buildings	165,000		165,000	
Land	75,000		75,000	

(Continued)

Accumulated Depreciation		₹ 15,000		₹ 31,500
Accounts Payable		9,950		11,000
Salaries Payable		0		1,800
Unearned Revenue		12,050		10,050
Notes Payable		50,000		50,000
Common Stock		100,000		100,000
Retained Earnings		34,600		34,600
Service Revenue		48,550		53,050
Advertising Expense	5,600		5,600	
Depreciation Expense			16,500	
Insurance Expense			1,200	
Salaries Expense	7,600		9,400	
Supplies Expense			400	
Utilities Expense			1,050	
Totals	₹270,150	₹270,150	₹292,000	₹292,000

Required

a. Compare the two trial balances and recreate all adjusting journal entries that were made at December 31.
b. What is the net effect of the adjusting journal entries on net income?

29. Adjusting Entries and Financial Statements

The June 30 unadjusted trial balance of Prime Realty appears as follows:

Prime Realty Unadjusted Trial Balance (in lakhs) June 30		
	Debit	**Credit**
Cash	₹ 6,900	
Accounts Receivable	4,500	
Prepaid Rent	6,300	
Supplies	2,250	
Equipment	18,000	
Accumulated Depreciation		₹ 900
Unearned Revenue		1,500
Notes Payable		10,000
Common Stock		8,000
Retained Earnings, Jan. 1		12,200
Service Revenue		11,200
Advertising Expense	650	
Depreciation Expense	900	
Interest Expense	150	
Rent Expense	2,100	
Salaries Expense	1,700	
Dividends	350	
Totals	₹43,800	₹43,800

Additional Information:

1. Rent expires at a rate of ₹700 per month.
2. Monthly depreciation on equipment is ₹300.
3. Interest on the 6% promissory note is paid quarterly on April 1, July 1, October 1, and January 1.
4. Performed services for which payment was received in April, ₹800.
5. Received utility bill to be paid next month, ₹500.
6. Services to customers earned during June but unrecorded at June 30, ₹2,500.
7. Supplies on hand totaled ₹1,500 at June 30.
8. Owed employees for salaries for the last week of June to be paid in July, ₹800.
9. Prime Realty prepares adjusting entries each quarter. Adjustments were last made on March 31.

Required

a. Prepare all adjusting journal entries for the quarter ending June 30.
b. Post journal entries to T-accounts using totals on the unadjusted trial balance as the opening balances.
c. Prepare an adjusted trial balance as of June 30.
d. Prepare an income statement and a statement of retained earnings for the six months ending June 30.
e. Prepare a classified balance sheet as of June 30.

30. Adjusting Entries and Closing Entries

The unadjusted and adjusted trial balances of Wang, Inc. are shown as follows:

Wang, Inc. Trial Balance (in lakhs) December 31				
	Unadjusted Trial Balance		**Adjusted Trial Balance**	
	Debit	**Credit**	**Debit**	**Credit**
Cash	₹ 8,000		₹ 8,000	
Accounts Receivable	12,250		16,250	
Prepaid Insurance	6,400		5,600	
Supplies	2,400		1,200	
Buildings	250,000		250,000	
Land	75,000		75,000	
Accumulated Depreciation		₹ 25,000		₹ 50,000
Salaries Payable				2,000
Unearned Revenue		9,500		7,000
Utilities Payable		15,450		20,950
Notes Payable		75,000		75,000
Common Stock		150,000		150,000
Retained Earnings		22,100		22,100
Service Revenue		75,500		82,000
Advertising Expense	8,500		8,500	
Depreciation Expense			25,000	
Insurance Expense			800	
Salaries Expense	8,000		10,000	
Supplies Expense			1,200	
Utilities Expense			5,500	
Dividends	2,000		2,000	
Totals	₹372,550	₹372,550	₹409,050	₹409,050

Required

a. Compare the unadjusted trial balance and the adjusted trial balance and recreate all adjusting journal entries that were made at December 31.
b. Prepare the income statement and a statement of retained earnings for the year. Also prepare a classified balance sheet at December 31.
c. Prepare necessary closing entries.

31. The Accounting Cycle

Ruberstein, Inc. was founded on April 1 and entered into the following transactions:

Apr. 1 Issued common stock to shareholders in exchange for cash, ₹20,00000.
1 Purchased a delivery van (equipment), ₹13,00000.
1 Purchased a one-year insurance policy to be consumed evenly over the next 12 months, ₹4,80000.
1 Took out a loan from First Bank, ₹20,00,000.
6 Hired two new employees on salary of ₹1,00,000 a month each.
6 Received prepayment for a contracted job to be performed in May, ₹4,50,000.
7 Purchased office supplies on credit, ₹1,20,000.
8 Billed customers for services provided, ₹7,50,000.
12 Paid to have an ad placed on a billboard during April, ₹1,30,000.
18 Billed customers for services provided, ₹8,60,000.
24 Paid dividends to stockholders, ₹1,00,000.
30 Received utility bills for the month of April to be paid next month, ₹74,000.
30 Prepaid the next six months of rent starting with May, ₹3,60,000.

Additional Information:

1. April depreciation for the delivery van is ₹21,700.
2. Interest on the loan from the bank is paid annually at a rate of 6%.
3. An inventory count of office supplies at April 30 showed ₹50,000 of supplies on hand.
4. Prepaid insurance has expired.
5. Employees' salaries earned during April but to be paid in May, ₹2,00,000.

Required

a. Journalize the transactions for the month of April.
b. Post the journal entries to the general ledger using T-accounts.
c. Prepare a trial balance as of April 30.
d. Prepare all necessary adjusting journal entries and post the entries to the appropriate T-accounts.
e. Prepare an adjusted trial balance as of April 30.
f. Prepare an income statement and a statement of retained earnings for the month of April. Also prepare a classified balance sheet as of April 30.
g. Prepare all closing entries for the temporary accounts and post the entries to the appropriate T-accounts.
h. Prepare a post-closing trial balance as of April 30.

CASES

32. Locate and Understand Accounting Information

Access the latest annual report for **Tata Global Beverages Ltd.** by clicking on the *Investor Relations* and *Annual Reports* links at www.tataglobalbeverages.com.

Required

Review the note to the financial statements and answer the following questions.

a. When does Tata Global Beverages Ltd. recognize revenue? Where does it report outstanding customer balances? Is this an example of a deferred or accrued revenue?
b. When does Tata Global Beverages Ltd. recognize fees and income from services revenues?
c. When does Tata Global Beverages Ltd. recognize interest and dividend income?
d. Does Tata Global Beverages Ltd. recognize all advertising costs as they are incurred? If not, does it treat those advertising costs as a deferred or accrued expense?

33. Communication Activity

You are the chief financial officer of a small corporation, and the date is December 31. You recently asked the new accountant to prepare the initial draft of the financial statements for your review. However, when you receive the draft, you quickly notice that no adjusting journal entries were made.

Required

Write a short memo explaining the importance of adjusting entries and the potential misstatements that can result from their exclusion.

34. Ethics and Adjusting Entries

Traction Tires is a large producer of automobile tires. During the current year, Traction was on pace to have record revenues and profits. However, towards the end of the current year, a string of accidents linked to Traction's tires resulted in numerous lawsuits and a product recall of Traction's Premiere line. Traction's President, Hal Marker, recently approached chief accountant Ronnie Williams about the inevitable losses next year and asked Ronnie to defer all possible revenue until next year and to accrue all possible expenses to the current year. "We have so much revenue to spare this year," Hal said, "but next year, we will need all the help we can get."

Required

a. What ethical issues are involved in this scenario?
b. If Hal gets his way, what accounting principles would be violated?
c. Some may say that Hal is simply managing his earnings like he manages all other aspects of his business. What is your opinion of "earnings management"?

35. Ethics and Adjusting Entries

You are a service associate with a major company. When you sell a service, the customer pays cash and you provide the service. At the end of each year, you are required to estimate how much of each outstanding service contract has been earned. At year-end, you have ₹100,00,000 of outstanding contracts. You estimate that you have earned somewhere between 40% and 60% of those contracts.

Required

Under the following independent conditions, identify the amount of outstanding contracts that you would report earned. Explain why you would report those amounts.

a. Your compensation is based on performance, and you are ₹80,00,000 short of your quota before your estimate.
b. Your compensation is based on performance, and you are ₹50,00,000 short of your quota before your estimate.
c. Your compensation is based on your group's performance, and while you have met your quota before your estimate, the group needs ₹60,00,000 to meet the group quota.

reviewcard

CHAPTER 4

Accrual Accounting and Adjusting Entries

	Learning Objectives	Key Concepts
LO1	Describe how income is measured and reported under the accrual and cash bases of accounting.	The cash basis records revenues when cash is received and expenses when cash is paid. The accrual basis records revenues when they are earned and expenses when they are incurred. Although both bases result in the same income over the long term, the accrual basis best reflects income over short periods of time, so it is required by GAAP.
LO2	Identify the four major circumstances in which adjusting journal entries are necessary.	Adjusting journal entries are necessary to record revenues that have been earned and expenses that have been incurred. The four scenarios in which adjusting entries arise are (1) a deferred revenue—revenue is earned after cash is received, (2) an accrued revenue—revenue is earned before cash is received, (3) a deferred expense—an expense is incurred after cash is paid, and (4) an accrued expense—an expense is incurred before cash is paid.
LO3	Record and post adjusting journal entries, and prepare an adjusted trial balance and financial statements.	At the end of an accounting period, adjusting journal entries are prepared to properly record revenues and expenses. Once these entries are posted to the ledger, an adjusted trial balance is prepared, from which financial statements are created.
LO4	Describe the purpose of the closing process and prepare closing entries.	The purpose of the closing process is to (1) update the Retained Earnings account to reflect all revenues, expenses, and dividends from the period and (2) prepare all revenue, expense, and dividend accounts for the next period by setting their balances to zero. The closing process is accomplished through "closing entries" recorded in the journal after financial statements are prepared.
LO5	Describe the steps of the accounting cycle.	The steps in accounting cycle are as follows: (1) journalize and post transactions, (2) prepare a trial balance, (3) journalize and post adjusting entries, (4) prepare an adjusted trial balance, (5) prepare financial statements, (6) journalize and post closing entries, (7) prepare a post-closing trial balance.

Key Definitions

Accounting cycle The sequence of steps in which an accounting information system captures, processes and reports a company's accounting transactions during a period.

Accrual basis of accounting Records revenues when they are earned and records expenses when they are incurred.

Adjusting journal entries Entries made in the general journal to record revenues that have been earned but not recorded and expenses that have been incurred but not recorded.

Cash basis of accounting Records revenues when cash is received and records expenses when cash is paid.

Closing entries Entries made in the journal and posted to the ledger that eliminate the balances in all temporary accounts and transfer those balances to the Retained Earnings account.

Closing process The process of transferring all revenue, expense, and dividend account balances to the Retained Earnings account.

Temporary accounts Accounts that accumulate balances only for the current period.

Demonstration Problem

Given the following March 31 Unadjusted Trial Balance and the additional information at the end of the month, prepare all necessary adjusting journal entries and prepare an Adjusted Trial Balance as of March 31.

Unadjusted Trial Balance
March 31

(in ₹ hundreds)	Debit	Credit
Cash	₹ 6,300	
Accounts Receivable	6,000	
Equipment	7,200	
Prepaid Insurance	2,400	
Supplies	5,000	
Common Stock		₹20,000
Service Revenue		10,000
Fuel Expense	600	
Salaries Expense	2,300	
Dividends	200	
Totals	₹30,000	₹30,000

Additional Information:

1. Depreciation on truck is ₹15,000 monthly.
2. One-twelfth of the insurance expired during the month.
3. An inventory count shows ₹1,00,000 of cleaning supplies on hand at March 31.
4. Earned but unpaid employee salaries were ₹25,000 on March 31.

Demonstration Problem Solution

Adjusting Journal Entries on March 31

		Debit	Credit
1	Depreciation Expense	15,000	
	Accumulated Depreciation		15,000
	(To record depreciation on the truck: ₹15,000 is given)		
2	Insurance Expense	20,000	
	Prepaid Insurance		20,000
	(To record expired insurance: ₹2,40,000 × 1/12)		
3	Supplies Expense	4,00,000	
	Supplies		4,00,000
	(To record supplies used: ₹5,00,000 – ₹1,00,000)		
4	Salaries Expense	25,000	
	Salaries Payable		25,000
	(To record salaries earned but not paid: ₹25,000 is given)		

Adjusted Trial Balance
March 31

(₹ hundreds)	Debit	Credit
Cash	₹ 6,300	
Accounts Receivable	6,000	
Equipment	7,200	
Prepaid Insurance	2,200	
Supplies	1,000	
Accumulated Depreciation		₹ 150
Salaries Payable		250
Common Stock		20,000
Service Revenue		10,000
Depreciation Expense	150	
Fuel Expense	600	
Insurance Expense	200	
Salaries Expense	2,550	
Supplies Expense	4,000	
Dividends	200	
Totals	₹30,400	₹30,400

ACCT

Internal Control and Cash

Learning Objectives

After studying the material in this chapter, you should be able to:

LO1 Describe the role of internal control in a business.

LO2 Describe the five components of internal control.

LO3 Understand two methods of internal control over cash—bank reconciliations and petty cash funds.

LO4 Describe the reporting of cash.

LO5 Evaluate cash through the calculation and interpretation of horizontal, vertical, and ratio analyses.

Introduction

This chapter examines the concepts of internal control and how those concepts affect the accounting for cash. Internal control is a company-wide process that seeks to improve a company's operations and its financial reporting. Among other things, internal control helps a company protect its assets. There are few assets that are more prone to theft than cash, so internal control is quite relevant and important to the accounting for cash.

This chapter begins with the role and overall concepts of internal control and then examines two control activities relating to cash—bank reconciliations and petty cash funds. The chapter concludes with how cash is reported and how a company's cash position can be analyzed.

LO1 Internal Control

In recent years, there have been numerous widely publicized accounting frauds. Major corporations such as Enron, WorldCom, and HealthSouth failed as a result of fraudulent activity. Many began to question the reliability and integrity of financial reporting of publicly traded companies.

Faced with this crisis, the United States Congress passed the Sarbanes-Oxley Act (SOX) in July 2002. The act sought to restore public confidence in financial reporting by enacting major changes in the manner in which accounting is practiced in the United States. Several of those changes focused on *internal control.*

Internal control The system of policies and procedures used in a company to promote efficient and effective operations, reliable financial reporting, and compliance with laws and regulations.

In its broadest sense, internal control is the process that a company's management uses to help the company meet its operational and financial reporting objectives. More specifically, **internal control** is the system of policies and procedures that a company puts in place to provide reasonable assurances that:

- the company's operations are effective and efficient,

Manufacturing bikes is probably the most prominent process at a Hero MotoCorp's manufacturing units, but equally important are internal control processes.

- the company's financial reporting is reliable, and
- the company is complying with applicable laws and regulations.

All companies have systems of internal control. The only question is how strong or weak those systems are.

Recognizing that internal control affects a company's success or failure, Section 404 of SOX contained several new requirements for publicly traded companies regarding internal control. One of the most important requirements is that corporations include in their annual reports

Internal control report Annual report in which management states its responsibility for internal control and provides an assessment of its internal control.

to shareholders an **internal control report** containing the following two items:

- A statement that it is management's responsibility to establish and maintain an adequate internal control structure and procedures for financial reporting.
- An assessment of the effectiveness of the internal control structure and procedures for financial reporting for the most recent year.

These requirements publicly place the burden of internal controls squarely on management. Management must take responsibility for, as well as provide an assessment of, internal control. This forces management to be engaged with respect to its internal control.

In addition to requiring an internal control report, SOX also requires management to obtain an annual audit of its internal control structure and its assessment. In other words, SOX requires an independent, third-party evaluation of management's assessment. This evaluation is performed by the public accounting firm performing the company's financial audit.

To illustrate these requirements, Exhibit 5-1 contains the comments of the Director of Hero MotoCorp Ltd. on internal control and also Auditor's comments on internal control. The highlighted sections of the internal control report show that Hero MotoCorp's management (1) takes responsibility for its internal control, (2) states that it has conducted an evaluation of the effectiveness of its internal control, and (3) concludes that its internal control is effective. The highlighted portion of the audit report shows that the audit firm agrees. Based on its audit of Hero MotoCorp's internal controls, A. F. Ferguson & Co. Chartered Accountant's opinion is Hero MotoCorp maintained effective internal control over financial reporting during the most recent period. This is the opinion that management wants to receive.

All companies have systems of **internal control**. The only question is how strong or weak those systems are.

Exhibit 5-1 Internal Control Reporting by Hero MotoCorp Ltd.

Excerpt of Director's Report on Internal Controls

The Company has a proper and adequate system of internal controls. This ensures that all assets are safeguarded and protected against loss from unauthorized use or disposition and those transactions are authorized, recorded, and reported correctly.

An extensive program of internal audits and management reviews supplements the process of internal control. Properly documented policies, guidelines, and procedures are laid down for this purpose. The internal control system has been designed to ensure that the financial and other records are reliable for preparing financial and other statements and for maintaining accountability of assets.

Excerpt from Report of Independent Auditor

In our opinion and according to information and explanations given to us, having regard to the explanations that some of the items purchased are of special nature and suitable alternative sources are not readily available for obtaining comparable quotations, there is an adequate internal control system commensurate with the size of the Company and the nature of its business with regard to the purchases of inventories and fixed assets and for the sale of goods and services. During the course of our audit, we have not observed any major weakness in such internal control system.

DELOITTE HASKINS & SELLS
Chartered Accountants
(Firm Registration No. 015125N)
Vijay Agarwal
New Delhi (Partner)
(Membership No. 094468)
April 26, 2013

The *COSO Framework* is the standard for understanding what good internal control looks like in an organization.

In 1992 an influential report was released by the Committee of Sponsoring Organizations (COSO) of the Treadway Commission. The report was the culmination of the committee's exhaustive research and deliberation on the elements of sound internal control. The committee's objective was to provide a common understanding of internal control—a framework for implementing good internal control practices. Its success is clear. The *Framework* has become the standard for understanding what good internal control looks like in an organization, and it is the basis for the discussion in this chapter.

LO2 Components of Internal Control

The broad purpose of internal control is to help management achieve effective and efficient operations, reliable financial reporting, and compliance with laws and regulations. *Internal Control—Integrated Framework* states that good internal control consists of the following five interrelated components:

- Control Environment
- Risk Assessment
- Control Activities
- Information and Communication
- Monitoring

Control Environment

The **control environment** is the foundation for all other components of internal control. It is the atmosphere in which the members of an organization conduct their activities and carry out their responsibilities. The control environment is often called the "tone at the top" because it reflects the overall control consciousness of an organization.

Many factors affect an organization's control environment. One of the most important is the overall integrity and ethical values of personnel. These attributes translate into standards of behavior that can permeate throughout an organization's operations. Other factors include management's philosophy and operating style, the assignment of authority and responsibility, and the general structure of an organization. Each of these factors contributes to the overall corporate culture within which internal control operates. Without a sound control environment, the remaining elements of internal control suffer.

Control environment The atmosphere in which the members of an organization conduct their activities and carry out their responsibilities.

MARUTI SUZUKI ANALYSIS

Look at the Report of Independent Registered Public Accounting Firm accompanying Maruti Suzuki's financial statements in Appendix C. What was the auditor's opinion regarding the effectiveness of Maruti Suzuki's internal control?

In the auditor's opinion of Maruti Suzuki Ltd. "In our opinion, and according to the information and explanations given to us, having regard to the explanation that for certain items of inventory purchased which are of special nature for which suitable alternative sources do not exist for obtaining comparative quotations, there is an adequate internal control system commensurate with the size of the Company and the nature of its business for the purchase of inventory, fixed assets and for the sale of goods and services. Further, on the basis of our examination of the books and records of the Company, and according to the information and explanations given to us, we have neither come across, nor have we been informed of any continuing failure to correct major weaknesses in the aforesaid internal control system."

The control environment is often called the "tone at the top" because it reflects the overall control consciousness of an organization.

Risk Assessment

All organizations face a variety of risks that threaten the achievement of organizational objectives. **Risk assessment** refers to the identification and analysis of these risks, with the goal of effectively managing them. Because business conditions change throughout time, risk assessment is an ongoing organizational activity.

Organizational risks can arise from both external and internal sources. External sources might include new competitors, changing customer expectations, or even natural catastrophes. Internal sources might include inadequate workforce training, errors in financial reporting of activities, or theft of assets by employees.

Once an organization identifies its risks, the risks can be analyzed with the following general process:

- Estimate the significance of a risk
- Assess the likelihood of the risk occurring
- Consider what actions should be taken to manage the risk

Risks of minor significance or those with a lower likelihood of occurrence generally do not warrant serious concern. For example, the risk of a meteorite destroying a company's warehouse can likely be ignored. In contrast, significant risks with higher likelihood demand considerable attention. For example, the risk of an employee stealing cash from customer collections likely requires some attention. That attention comes in the form of control activities.

Control Activities

Control activities are the policies and procedures management establishes to address the risks that might prevent the organization from achieving its objectives. Although specific control activities vary widely across organizations, they generally fall into one of several categories.

Establishing Responsibility A critical factor in good internal control is establishing responsibility for the performance of a given task. When responsibility is clear, two benefits arise. First, the employee knows that he or she will be held accountable for completion of the task. Second, management knows who to consult if the task is not completed satisfactorily.

A good example is a retailer's cashiers. Each cashier is assigned sole responsibility over a specific cash drawer. No other cashier has access to or responsibility for that drawer. If a drawer is returned to the company short of cash, management knows exactly who to speak to. As a result, cashiers are motivated to perform their tasks well, and the risk of theft or error is reduced.

Maintaining Adequate Documentation Accounting information is useful only when it is reliable, which means that it must be free from error. Control activities are necessary in all organizations to promote error-free accounting records. Consider the sale of a company's inventory as an example. Good control practices would require that the sale be documented on a sales invoice, preferably a sequentially numbered one so that the sale will neither be lost nor recorded twice. The invoice might also require the employee's initials to establish responsibility for the sale, and it will have multiple copies to be sent throughout the organization for proper fulfillment and recording of the sale. Such invoices and processes are increasingly computerized, which brings additional controls that further reduce the introduction of errors into the accounting system.

Segregation of Duties Segregation of duties is a technique that limits one person's control over a particular task or area of a company. Often called separation of duties, it is accomplished by spreading responsibility among multiple employees so that one employee's work can serve as a check against another's work. For example, consider the process of ordering, receiving, and paying for merchandise. If one employee handles all three tasks, there is greater risk of error and possibly theft of assets. However, if these three tasks are handled by different employees, errors by one employee can be caught by another employee. Moreover,

Risk assessment The identification and analysis of the risks that threaten the achievement of organizational objectives.

Control activities The policies and procedures established to address the risks that threaten the achievement of organizational objectives.

unless the employees work unethically together, company assets are more protected against theft.

Physical Security Good internal control includes an effort to safeguard company assets and records. Most of these safeguarding controls are meant to prevent the loss of assets. Examples include secured facilities, fire and alarm systems, computer passwords and encryption, video monitors, and door sensors that signal when product is inappropriately taken from a store. Other controls are meant to detect the loss of assets. An example is the periodic counting of inventory for comparison to accounting records. Significant discrepancies can then be investigated.

Independent Verification Independent verification is the process of reviewing and reconciling information within an organization. This is particularly useful when reconciling an asset balance with the accounting records for that asset. An example would be a bank reconciliation, where the bank's balance and the company's balance are reconciled. Often, the most effective verifications are conducted on a surprise basis and are conducted by individuals who have no connection to the process or the employee being verified. Internal audit divisions of organizations commonly perform such verifications.

Information and Communication

Information and communication is another element of sound internal control. **Information and communication** refers to the need for the open flow of relevant information throughout an organization. Information must be captured and communicated in a form and a timeframe that enables employees to complete their responsibilities. This requires information systems that produce relevant and reliable reports. It also requires both upward and downward lines of communication. Management must communicate with employees, and employees must communicate with management.

Monitoring

Monitoring refers to the assessment of the quality of an organization's internal control. Monitoring can be accomplished in two ways. The first is through ongoing activities. For example, in his recurring daily responsibilities, a supervisor can check for evidence that a control activity is functioning properly. He or she can also ask employees if they understand the controls in place and if those controls are being completed. The second is through a separate evaluation. The audit of internal controls required by SOX is an example of a separate evaluation. In both ways, the purpose of monitoring is to continuously improve internal control.

Control activities are necessary in all organizations to promote error-free accounting records.

Limitations of Internal Control

Regardless of how well internal control is designed within an organization, it can provide only reasonable assurances that a company is meeting its objectives. Internal control systems are limited in their effectiveness because of (1) the human element and (2) cost-benefit analysis.

The *human element* refers to the fact that internal controls are often based on human judgment and action. Despite our best efforts, we all make mistakes at times, and internal control cannot eliminate them all. Furthermore, employees can purposefully circumvent controls for personal gain. Sometimes this will be a manager who overrides the control activities in place. Other times this will be multiple employees working together to circumvent existing controls. Such collusion among employees can be very effective at defeating a company's internal controls.

Cost-benefit analysis refers to the cost of implementing a control activity versus the benefit that the control provides. For example, a company could install retina-scanning security systems for its warehouses to decrease the risk of theft. However, the cost of the installation may far outweigh the marginal advantage that retina-scanning security provides over normal lock-and-key security. In such a case, security would be limited to lock-and-key because the cost of the extra security would far outweigh its benefit.

Information and communication Required for the open flow of relevant information throughout an organization.

Monitoring The assessment of the quality of an organization's internal control.

Collusion among employees can be very effective at defeating a company's internal controls.

LO3 Cash Controls

The best asset to use in demonstrating internal control is cash. Cash is a highly desired asset. It is easily concealed, taken, and converted into other assets with only a small chance of detection. As a result, companies normally institute many controls to safeguard their cash and to report it properly. Two of these controls are bank reconciliations and petty cash funds. Each is discussed in the following sections.

Bank Reconciliations

Most companies keep the majority of their cash in a bank. This in itself is a good control procedure because it limits opportunities for theft. It is difficult to steal cash when it is locked up in the bank. The use of a bank also provides two sources of independent record keeping. That is, both the company and the bank keep a record of all cash transactions between them. As a result, a company can compare these records to verify its cash balance. This comparison is called a bank reconciliation.

A **bank reconciliation** is the process of reconciling the differences between the cash balance on a bank statement and the cash balance in a company's records. The purpose of a bank reconciliation is twofold. First, it confirms the accuracy of both the bank's and the company's cash records. Second, it determines the actual cash balance to be reported on the company's balance sheet. A bank reconciliation is prepared as follows:

- Reconcile the bank balance to the actual cash balance
- Reconcile the company's book balance to the actual cash balance
- Adjust the company's book balance to the actual cash balance

Bank reconciliation The process of reconciling the differences between the cash balance on a bank statement and the cash balance in a company's records.

Deposit in transit A deposit that has been made by the company but has not cleared the bank as of the statement date.

Outstanding check A check that has been distributed by the company but has not cleared the bank as of the statement date.

© GOODSHOOT/THINKSTOCK

Reconciling the Bank Balance The first step in a bank reconciliation is to adjust the cash balance reported on the bank statement to the company's actual cash balance. The bank balance will differ from the actual cash balance and will therefore need adjustment for two main reasons.

The first reason relates to deposits and payments made by the company that are not reflected on the bank statement. For example, a **deposit in transit** is a deposit that has been made by the company but does not appear on the bank statement because it had not cleared the bank as of the statement date. Because the cash is now in the bank, deposits in transit should be added to the bank's cash balance. An **outstanding check** is a check that has been distributed by the company but does not appear on the bank statement because it had not cleared the bank as of the statement date. Because the cash is no longer in the bank, outstanding checks should be subtracted from the bank cash balance.

The second reason relates to errors made by the bank. Although bank errors are rare, they do occur and must also be reconciled. An error can result in the need to add to or subtract from the bank balance. For example, suppose that the bank erroneously records a ₹1,450 deposit as ₹1,540. The bank balance is overstated by ₹90 and should therefore be reduced by ₹90. In contrast, suppose that the bank records a ₹100 check as ₹100. In that case, the bank balance is understated by ₹900 and should be increased ₹900.

Once all adjustments to the bank balance are made, the adjusted bank balance should equal the actual cash balance to be reported on the balance sheet.

A bank reconciliation confirms the accuracy of a company's cash records and determines the actual balance to be reported on the balance sheet.

Reconciling the Company Book Balance The second step in a bank reconciliation is to adjust the cash balance reported on the company's books to the actual cash balance. The company book balance may differ from the actual cash balance, and therefore need adjustment, for two main reasons.

The first reason relates to bank activities that change a company's cash balance but have not been recorded by the company. Usually, companies are notified of these changes through bank memoranda notes. More specifically, a **credit memorandum** (credit note) is notification of an addition to the cash balance on the bank statement. Credit memoranda arise when the bank collects cash on behalf of the company—often through the collection of a company receivable or interest on a note. Credit memoranda should be added to the company's book balance. A **debit memorandum** is notification of a subtraction from the cash balance on the bank statement. Common examples are fees charged for banking services and customer checks returned for insufficient funds. Both of these examples reflect cash that the company no longer has, so they should be subtracted from the company's book balance.

The second reason relates to errors made in the company's cash records. For example, suppose that during the reconciliation a company discovers that it erroneously recorded for ₹100 a check written as ₹1,000. The company's balance is overstated by ₹900 and should be reduced by ₹900.

Adjusting the Cash Balance Once the bank balance and the company's book balance are reconciled, the company's cash balance must be adjusted to the actual cash balance determined by the reconciliations. Therefore, the third step in a bank reconciliation is to record the journal entries necessary to adjust the company's book balance to the actual cash balance. The journal entries are based on the credit and debit memoranda and errors identified during the reconciliation of the company's balance.

Bank Reconciliation Example

To illustrate a bank reconciliation, suppose that Chapman Enterprises maintains an account with State Bank. At the end of March, Chapman shows a cash balance of ₹54,567 while State Bank shows a balance of ₹49,880. The differences result from the following:

1. Deposits of ₹6,450 on March 30 and ₹1,236 on March 31 do not appear on the March 31 bank statement since they had not cleared the bank as of March 31.

   Resolution: These are deposits in transit. Add them to the bank balance.

2. Checks written in late March for ₹589 (#1987), ₹900 (#1990), and ₹1,180 (#1991) do not appear on the March 31 bank statement since they had not cleared the bank as of March 31.

   Resolution: These are outstanding checks. Subtract them from the bank balance.

3. The March 31 bank statement shows the collection of a ₹550 receivable from one of Chapman's customers and a ₹50 monthly service fee. Chapman had not recorded either of these two items.

   Resolution: The collection is a credit memorandum. Add it to Chapman's cash balance. The fee is a debit memorandum. Subtract it from Chapman's cash balance.

4. The March 31 bank statement shows that a ₹220 customer check was returned to the bank for nonsufficient funds (NSF). Chapman had not recorded this item.

   Resolution: The NSF check is a debit memorandum because no cash was received from the customer's check that Chapman deposited earlier. Subtract it from Chapman's cash balance.

5. A check clearing the bank for ₹400 was erroneously recorded in Chapman's records at ₹450. The check was written to pay off an open account payable.

   Resolution: Chapman recorded ₹50 too much for the check. Therefore, Chapman's cash is understated by ₹50. Add the ₹50 to Chapman's cash balance.

Credit memorandum An addition to the cash balance on the bank statement for items such as the collection of interest.

Debit memorandum A subtraction from the cash balance on the bank statement for items such as service charges.

Chapman's resulting bank reconciliation is shown as follows. The top half shows the reconciliation of the bank balance while the bottom half shows the reconciliation of the company's book balance.

Chapman Bank Reconciliation
March 31

Balance per bank statement		₹49,880
Add deposits in transit:		
March 30	₹6,450	
March 31	1,236	7,686
Deduct outstanding checks:		
No. 1987	₹ 589	
No. 1990	900	
No. 1991	1,180	2,669
Actual cash balance		₹54,897
Balance per company records		₹54,567
Add:		
Collection of receivable	₹ 550	
Error by Chapman	50	600
Deduct:		
Monthly service charge	₹ 50	
NSF check	220	270
Actual cash balance		₹54,897

Both reconciliations correctly show an actual cash balance of ₹54,897. To adjust the company's cash balance to that actual balance, the following entries must be made. Note that each of the four entries comes from the four adjustments made in the reconciliation of the book balance to the actual balance.

Entry 1—Collection of the Receivable Chapman updates its cash balance to reflect the bank's collection of the receivable.

Mar. 31	Cash	550	
	Accounts Receivable		550
	(To record the collection of a receivable by the bank)		

Assets	=	Liabilities	+	Equity
+550				
−550				

Entry 2—Correction of Error Chapman corrects the error made when the ₹400 check was recorded for ₹450. This requires Chapman to add back to both cash and accounts payable.

Mar. 31	Cash	50	
	Accounts Payable		50
	(To correct error)		

Assets	=	Liabilities	+	Equity
+50		+50		

Entry 3—Monthly Service Charge Chapman records the monthly service charge as an expense. As a result, both assets and equity decrease.

Mar. 31	Service Charge Expense	50	
	Cash		50
	(To record monthly expense for bank account)		

Assets	=	Liabilities	+	Equity
−50				−50

Entry 4—NSF Check Chapman records the effect of a check returned for non-sufficient funds by reinstating the receivable and reducing its cash balance. Since the check was no good, the receivable has not yet been collected. Chapman must now try to collect again.

Mar. 31	Accounts Receivable	220	
	Cash		220
	(To reinstate customer receivable)		

Assets	=	Liabilities	+	Equity
+220				
−220				

After these four entries are recorded, the company's cash balance is updated to the actual cash balance.

Petty Cash Funds

Most companies require that all disbursements of cash be made with a check. This is a basic control activity that allows a company to better monitor its cash outflows. However, there are many instances when only a minor amount of cash is needed and the process of writing a check is burdensome. Examples would in-

© ISTOCKPHOTO/THINKSTOCK

clude postage for small mailings and the purchase of miscellaneous office supplies. To handle such cases, companies often establish a petty cash fund.

A **petty cash fund** is an amount of cash kept on hand to pay for minor expenditures. While the size and scope of a petty cash fund will vary across companies, its operation will involve the following three activities:

- Establishing the fund
- Making payments from the fund
- Replenishing the fund

Establishing the Fund A petty cash fund is established by writing a check for the amount of the fund, cashing the check, and placing the cash under the care of an employee designated as custodian. A journal entry is then made to record the establishment of the fund.

To illustrate, suppose that on May 1, Barnett Design Group cashes a ₹1,000 check to establish a petty cash fund and gives the cash to John Stephens, the custodian. On this date, Barnett would record the following entry.

May 1	Petty Cash	1,000	
	Cash		1,000
	(To establish ₹1,000 petty cash fund)		

Assets	=	Liabilities	+	Equity
+1000				
−1000				

The entry increases Petty Cash and decreases Cash. Notice that there is no change in total assets. Barnett has simply designated ₹1,000 to be used in a petty cash fund. Barnett still has its cash. It has not yet disbursed any cash outside of the company.

Making Payments from the Fund After the fund is established, the cash is used to pay for qualifying expenditures. Payments are usually made in one of two ways. Cash can be taken from the fund to make payment, or employees can seek reimbursement from the fund for payments they have personally made. In either case, the custodian should collect receipts for the use of any cash. As payments are made from petty cash, no journal entries are made. Journal entries are recorded only when the fund is replenished.

Replenishing the Fund As the cash in the fund decreases, the fund must be replenished. To do so, the remaining cash in the fund is counted, and the company cashes a check for the amount that brings the total cash in the fund back to the original balance. The receipts in the fund are then used as documentation for recording expenses.

To illustrate, suppose that on May 31, Stephens examines the petty cash fund and prepares the following report.

Petty Cash Fund Replenishment Report

Petty cash fund	₹1,000
Less: cash remaining in the fund	150
Cash requested to replenish fund	₹ 850
Receipts in the fund:	
Postage	₹ 250
Office supplies	470
Miscellaneous	130
Total receipts	₹ 850

The report shows that the fund needs ₹850 to be fully replenished. It also shows that there are receipts totaling ₹850. As a result, Barnett would cash a check for ₹850 to replenish the fund and record expenses as follows.

May 31	Postage Expense	250	
	Supplies Expense	470	
	Miscellaneous Expense	130	
	Cash		850
	(To replenish petty cash fund and record various expenses)		

Assets	=	Liabilities	+	Equity
−850				−250
				−470
				−130

The entry increases the three expense accounts related to the expenditures and decreases the Cash account for the amount of the check. Because Barnett is recording the expenses resulting from fund use, the entry reduces both assets and equity. This same type of entry would be repeated each time the fund is replenished.

Cash Over and Short When a petty cash fund is replenished, the amount of cash needed for replenishment should equal the total amount of receipts. However, this will not always be the case. Sometimes, the custodian will not obtain all receipts or will give incorrect change, resulting in a discrepancy between the cash needed for replenishment and the amount of receipts. In such cases, the discrepancy is charged to an account called Cash Over and Short. Cash Over and Short is a temporary account that can have either a debit

Petty cash fund An amount of cash kept on hand to pay for minor expenditures.

or credit balance, depending on the situation. A debit balance increases expenses while a credit balance decreases expenses.

To illustrate, assume the same facts as previously except that Stephens counts only ₹130 of cash in the fund before replenishment.

Petty Cash Fund Replenishment Report

Petty cash fund	₹1,000
Less: Cash remaining in the fund	130
Cash requested to replenish fund	₹ 870
Receipts in the fund:	
Postage	₹ 250
Office supplies	470
Miscellaneous	130
Total receipts	₹ 850

In this case, a check must be written for ₹870 to fully replenish the fund. However, there is only ₹850 of receipts. The ₹20 difference is charged to the Cash Over and Short account as follows.

May 31	Postage Expense	250	
	Supplies Expense	470	
	Miscellaneous Expense	130	
	Cash Over and Short	20	
	Cash		870
	(To replenish petty cash fund and record various expenses)		

Assets	=	Liabilities	+	Equity
−870				−250
				−470
				−130
				− 20

In this entry, the Cash Over and Short account is debited, which indicates an increase to expenses. Most likely, the balance would be reported as a miscellaneous expense.

Cash A medium of exchange.

Cash equivalent Any investment that is readily convertible into cash and has an original maturity of three months or less.

Restricted cash Cash a company has restricted for a specific purpose.

Cash takes many forms—the coins and dollar bills in your pocket, your checking and savings accounts, even a check from a friend that has not yet been deposited.

LO4 Reporting Cash and Cash Equivalents

At its most basic level, **cash** is a medium of exchange. A general rule is that something is cash if you can deposit it into a bank and readily use it to pay someone. Cash takes many forms—the coins and bank notes in your pocket, your checking and savings accounts, even a check from a friend that has not yet been deposited. Money orders and travelers checks are other examples of cash.

In addition to these forms of cash, companies often hold investments that are so much like cash that they are deemed to be *equivalent to cash*. A **cash equivalent** is any investment that (1) is readily convertible into a known amount of cash and (2) has an original maturity of three months or less. Examples of cash equivalents can include Treasury bills, certificates of deposit, money market accounts, and commercial paper, as long as they mature in three months or less. Cash equivalents are so much like cash that they are combined with cash for reporting purposes.

Cash and cash equivalents are reported on the balance sheet as a current asset. Most companies report their balances in the first line under the "Current Account" reading in the balance sheet. In some countries (like in USA), though, a company will restrict some of its cash for a specific purpose. For example, a company may designate a certain amount of cash for the payment of interest. To inform investors and creditors of such restrictions, companies will report such **restricted cash** separately from cash and cash equivalents.

An example of such a company is Domino's Pizza of USA Exhibit 5-2 contains the first two accounts of Domino's 2010 balance sheet as well as the notes to the financial statements addressing the company's cash balances.

Exhibit 5-2 Cash Information from Domino's (USA) 2010 Annual Report

Balance Sheet

(in thousands)	2010	2009
Cash and cash equivalents	$47,945	$42,392
Restricted cash	85,530	91,141

Notes to the financial statements

Cash and Cash Equivalents

Cash equivalents consist of highly liquid investments with original maturities of three months or less at the date of purchase. These investments are carried at cost, which approximates fair value.

Restricted Cash

Restricted cash includes $37.2 million of cash held for future interest payments, $35.4 million cash held in interest reserves, $10.0 million cash held for capitalization of entities and $0.5 million of other restricted cash.

As you can see, Domino's has over $48 million in cash and cash equivalents at the end of 2010. It reports even more in restricted cash—over $85 million. Domino's notes disclose the purpose of this restriction. The majority of restricted cash is intended for interest payments.

LO5 Analyzing Cash

A company's management of cash is critical to its success. If a company can't keep enough cash, it can quickly run into major problems. The following sections examine the cash position of Hero MotoCorp Ltd. The examination will require the cash balance from the company's balance sheet and various items from its statement of cash flows. The required information is found in Exhibit 5-3, excerpted from Hero MotoCorp Ltd. 2012–13 Annual Report.

Exhibit 5-3 Account Balances from Hero MotoCorp's Annual Report

(₹ Crore)

Source	Accounts	2013	2012	2011
Balance Sheet	Cash and cash equivalents	181.04	76.82	39.32
	Total assets	₹9,641.65	₹9,888.92	10,844.69
Statement of Cash Flows	Net cash provided by operating activities	1,890.43	2,359.78	2,288.11
	Net cash used in investing activities	(732.94)	92.79	(1,322.31)
	Net cash used in financing activities	(1,056.27)	(2,458.16)	(981.98)

MARUTI SUZUKI ANALYSIS

Maruti Suzuki's balance sheet in Appendix C reports Cash and Cash Equivalents of ₹1,250 million. Looking at the Cash Equivalents paragraph in Maruti Suzuki's first note, what types of investments does the company include in cash equivalents?

Maruti Suzuki's Cash Equivalents note states that its cash equivalents include items like cash & cheques in hand, balance in bank and other short-term highly liquid investment with original maturities of six months or less.

Horizontal and Vertical Analyses

A good place to start the analysis of any asset account is horizontal and vertical analyses. Recall from Chapter 2 that horizontal analysis calculates the rupee change in an account balance, defined as the current year balance less the prior year balance, and divides that change by the prior year balance to yield the percentage change. Vertical analysis divides each account balance by a base account, yielding a percentage. The base account for an analysis of cash is total assets. These calculations are summarized as follows:

Horizontal Analysis

Rupee change in account balance = Current year balance − Prior year balance

$$\text{Percentage change in account balance} = \frac{\text{Rupee change}}{\text{Prior year balance}}$$

Vertical Analysis

$$\text{Percentage} = \frac{\text{Cash}}{\text{Total Assets}}$$

Given Hero MotoCorp Ltd information in Exhibit 5-3, horizontal and vertical analyses of cash result in the following:

Horizontal Analysis

	Change	Percentage Change
Cash and cash equivalents	181.04 − 76.82 104.22	$\frac{104.22}{76.82} = 135.67\%$

Vertical Analysis

	2013	2012
Cash and cash equivalents	$\frac{181.04}{9{,}641.65} = 1.88\%$	$\frac{76.82}{9{,}888.92} = 0.78\%$

The horizontal analysis shows that Hero MotoCorp's cash balance increased by ₹104.22 crore in 2012–13, which equals to 135.67% increase over the prior year. The vertical analysis shows that cash made up about 1.88% of the total assets in 2013. This was an increase

MAKING IT REAL

Cash on hand is critical to any successful business. Without available cash, a company cannot pay its bills and obligations.

Recently, companies have begun holding onto their cash as long as possible due to stricter limits related to bank loans. These companies need their cash to finance their day-to-day operations and many are less focused on paying their obligations in a timely manner.

© HAMERA/THINKSTOCK

Large companies are in the prime position to take advantage of smaller companies in order to maximize their cash on hand. Large corporations often represent a large percentage of sales for smaller businesses. Therefore, these small businesses are forced to accept delayed payment in order to maintain a supplier relationship with their large customers. At the same time, these large corporations require payment from their customers in a timely manner or the customers will quickly be faced with collection litigation. This double standard is possible because of the wide-reaching power and resources many large corporations possess.

Until credit requirements are again loosened, companies will continue to hoard their available cash for daily operations and will push the limits of making good on their obligations.

© STEPHEN COBURN/SHUTTERSTOCK.COM

from the prior year, when cash made up 0.78% of total assets.

While the preceding analysis shows that Hero MotoCorp's cash increased during 2013, it does not indicate why cash increased. To find out why, investors and creditors can look at the information on company's statement of cash flows. Recall from Chapter 1 that the statement of cash flows classifies a company's cash inflows and outflows into three main categories—operating activities, investing activities, and financing activities.

Operating activities include those transactions necessary to run the business. This would include selling a product, paying employees, and advertising. According to Exhibit 5-3, Hero MotoCorp Ltd. generated over ₹1,890.43 crore in cash from operations during 2013, which is less than that of 2012.

Investing activities include the buying and selling of revenue-generating assets such as buildings and equipment. Hero MotoCorp Ltd reports a net cash outflow of ₹(732.94) crore from investing activities in 2013.

Financing activities include the raising and repayment of capital through debt and equity. During 2013, Hero MotoCorp Ltd. reports over ₹(1,056.27) crore in cash outflows from financing activities.

With this information, you can conclude that Hero MotoCorp's closing balance of cash increased by around ₹104 crore during 2013. This may be due to many reasons, such as decrease in financing cash outflow, increase in investing activities, etc.

Free Cash Flow

A company needs to generate enough cash to pay its bills. It also needs to generate enough to maintain its operational assets and to reward its shareholders with dividends. If a company can generate more cash than it needs for these commitments, it is generating free cash flow.

MARUTI SUZUKI ANALYSIS

Using Maruti Suzuki's financial statements in Appendix C, calculate and interpret (1) horizontal and vertical analyses of cash.

Horizontal Analysis

(₹7,750 – ₹24,361)/24,361 = (68.17%)

Vertical Analysis

₹7,750/(2,66,880) = 2.9%

The (68.17%) horizontal analysis indicates that cash decreased during the year by more than 68.17%. The 2.9% vertical analysis indicates that a very small portion of Maruti Suzuki's assets are in the form of cash.

Free cash flow is the excess cash a company generates beyond what it needs to invest in productive capacity and pay dividends to stockholders. That is, free cash flow is a measure of a company's ability to generate cash for expansion, for other forms of improved operations, or for increased returns to stockholders. While free cash flow can be defined in many ways, the most straightforward definition is as follows:

Free Cash Flow

Cash Flows from Operating Activities
Less: Capital Expenditures
Less: Dividends
Free Cash Flow

The ratio starts with cash flows from operating activities, which is a measure of a company's ability to generate cash from its current operations. Capital expenditures refers to the amount a company spends on fixed assets during the year. Dividends are payments to stockholders during the year. Each of these items is found on the statement of cash flows.

Free cash flow The excess cash a company generates beyond what it needs to invest in productive capacity and pay dividends to stockholders.

From the information in Appendix C, Maruti Suzuki's free cash flow for the most recent two years is calculated as follows:

Free Cash Flow	2013	2012
Cash Flows from Operating Activities	₹43,842	₹25,599
Less: Capital Expenditures	(38,549)	(29,697)
Less: Dividends	(2,167)	(2,167)
Free Cash Flow	₹3,126	₹(6,265)

In 2013, Maruti Suzuki produces positive free cash flow. And, from the statement of cash flow information in Appendix C, you can get an idea of how it has used that free cash flow. Notice the large cash outflows in the investing activity detail. In the two years reported, the company paid out ₹1,27,492 and ₹1,67,598 for "Purchase of Investments".

CONCEPT QUESTIONS

1. What did the Sarbanes-Oxley Act seek to do?
2. Internal control is supposed to provide reasonable assurance about what three things?
3. What two items should management's internal control report contain?
4. What are the five components of the *Internal Control—Integrated Framework*?
5. What phrase is often used to describe the control environment of a company?
6. What three general processes will an organization use to analyze risk?
7. What are two benefits that arise from establishing responsibility?
8. What are two limitations of internal control?
9. What is the purpose of a bank reconciliation?
10. What are the steps in preparing a bank reconciliation?
11. What are three ways in which the bank balance may need to be adjusted to reach the actual cash balance?
12. Why do credit and debit memorandums arise?
13. The operation of a petty cash fund involves what three activities?
14. Where are cash and cash equivalents reported?
15. When is a company generating free cash flow?

MULTIPLE CHOICE

1. Which of the following is not normally included in an internal control report?
   a. An assessment of the effectiveness of internal control
   b. A statement that it is management's responsibility to *establish* the internal control structure and procedures for financial reporting
   c. A statement that it is management's responsibility to *maintain* the internal control structure and procedures for financial reporting
   d. Suggestions on how the company can improve the internal control structure
2. Which of the following is not true of the Sarbanes-Oxley Act?
   a. It required an internal control report
   b. It was passed after many major corporations failed as a result of fraudulent activity
   c. It required that management obtain an audit of internal control
   d. It sought to restore management's confidence over financial reporting
3. "Tone at the top" is a phrase used to describe which component of internal control?
   a. Control Environment
   b. Monitoring
   c. Control Activities
   d. Information and Communication
4. Which of the following is not an example of a good control activity?
   a. Establishing responsibility for the performance of a given task
   b. Using computer passwords and encryption
   c. Having the same employee receive and pay for merchandise
   d. Using sequentially numbered sales invoices
5. Internal control systems are limited in their effectiveness by:
   a. the human element.
   b. cost-benefit analysis.
   c. both a and b.
   d. neither a nor b.
6. Which of the following would you see on a reconciliation of the bank balance to the actual cash balance?
   a. Outstanding check
   b. NSF check
   c. Bank service fee
   d. Collection of a receivable
7. Which of the following would you most likely see on a reconciliation of the book balance to the actual cash balance?
   a. Deposit in transit
   b. Collection of interest
   c. Outstanding check
   d. None of the above
8. Austin Corporation's ending cash book balance was ₹1,45,600. The bank statement showed the following reconciling items:

Bank service fee	₹1,500
NSF check from customer	₹1,800
Collection of receivable	₹5,000

   What is Austin's actual cash balance?
   a. ₹1,45,600
   b. ₹14,730
   c. ₹1,58,900
   d. ₹1,37,300
9. The month-end bank statement showed a ₹42,600 ending balance for Hurry Corporation's cash balance. Use the following items to calculate Hurry's actual ending cash balance:

Outstanding checks	₹4,240
Bank service fee	₹150
Deposit in transit	₹780

   a. ₹46,060
   b. ₹37,430
   c. ₹47,620
   d. ₹37,580
10. Which of the following represents an item that would likely be paid from petty cash?
    a. A manager's salary

b. Utilities for a warehouse
c. Miscellaneous office supplies
d. Insurance

11. Which of the following would least likely qualify as a cash equivalent?
    a. Treasury bills
    b. Commercial paper
    c. Certificate of deposit
    d. U.S. Savings Bond
12. Nickel Corporation's cash and cash equivalents balances for the current and prior year are presented below:

Current year	₹22,500
Prior year	₹19,350

Perform a horizontal analysis on Nickel's cash and cash equivalents.
    a. 16.3%
    b. 14.0%
    c. (14.0)%
    d. 13.9%
13. Using the following information taken from Reebals Incorporated's balance sheet, prepare a vertical analysis of Reebals' cash balance.

Cash and cash equivalents, current year	₹1,345
Cash and cash equivalents, prior year	₹1,267
Total assets, current year	₹38,500

    a. 3.5%
    b. 3.3%
    c. 6.2%
    d. 2.2%
14. Free cash flow is not affected by:
    a. dividends.
    b. purchase of an office building.
    c. purchase of a warehouse.
    d. purchase of raw materials.
15. Using the following information from Walker Enterprises, calculate free cash flow.

Cash flows from operating activities	₹75,200
Cash flows from investing activities	₹43,550
Dividends paid	₹7,500
Capital expenditures	₹25,320
Cost of goods sold	₹45,300

    a. ₹10,730
    b. ₹42,380
    c. (₹2,920)
    d. ₹49,880

BRIEF EXERCISES

1. Internal Control

The following items relate to internal control:
1. Sarbanes-Oxley Act of 2002
2. Management's Report on Internal Control
3. *Internal Control—Integrated Framework*
4. Five elements of internal control

Required
Provide a brief explanation of each of these items.

2. Internal Control

Consider the following independent scenarios:
1. A company's top management team promotes an atmosphere of ethical behavior within the organization.
2. A company discovers the need to increase measures taken to mitigate the risk of employee theft.

Required
Which element of internal control does each of the above scenarios best relate?

3. Internal Control Activities

Douglas Company has the following internal control procedures:
1. A pre-numbered shipping document is used for each shipment to customers.
2. The employee who writes checks cannot make entries in the general ledger.
3. An internal auditor reconciles the bank statement each month.
4. The company stores inventory in a room that is monitored by cameras.
5. The manager is required to authorize purchases before they are made by employees.

Required
For each item, identify the internal control principle that is being followed.

4. Bank Reconciliation Items

The following items may or may not be relevant to a company's bank reconciliation:
1. The company recorded a deposit as ₹540, but it correctly cleared the bank for ₹450.
2. A check recorded for ₹1,000 is shown on the bank statement as a ₹1,000 reduction to the cash balance.
3. The bank statement shows a ₹25 monthly service fee.
4. A ₹3,250 deposit made by the company is not reflected on the bank statement.
5. Payment received from a customer is reflected on the bank statement but not on the company's books.

Required
Identify whether each item is (a) an addition to or subtraction from the book balance, (b) an addition to or subtraction from the bank balance, or (c) not included on a bank reconciliation.

5. Petty Cash

On June 1, CWA Enterprises established a petty cash fund for ₹2,500. On June 30, the fund's custodian prepares a report showing ₹760.25 in cash remaining and receipts of ₹360.50 for postage, ₹760.45 for office supplies, and ₹600.80 for miscellaneous items. The custodian presents the report to the company accountant, who replenishes the fund.

Required
Prepare all necessary journal entries for the month of June.

6. Reporting Cash and Cash Equivalents

At the end of 2013 a company has a ₹1,00,000 certificate of deposit that matures in 120 days, ₹6,00,000 of cash in a checking account, and ₹10,00,000 of one-month T-bills.

Required
At what amount would the company report cash and cash equivalents on its 2013 balance sheet?

7. Calculate Free Cash Flow

During the year, a company had net income of ₹1,45,000 and cash flow from operations of ₹1,95,000. During the year the company also bought a new piece of equipment for ₹45,000, and ₹10,000 of dividends were paid.

Required
What is the company's free cash flow for the year?

8. Evaluate Cash

Howard Manufacturing strives to keep a "consistent" amount of cash on hand. Its latest balance sheet provides the following information:

Cash and cash equivalents, current year	₹ 5,959
Cash and cash equivalents, prior year	6,011
Total assets, current year	77,410
Total assets, prior year	68,744

Required
Using horizontal and vertical analyses, determine whether Howard is maintaining a "consistent" amount of cash. Round percentages to one decimal point (i.e., 9.4%).

EXERCISES

9. Internal Control Activities

Percy Printers uses the following control procedures:

1. Checks are not pre-numbered because the purchasing manager must approve payments before checks are signed.
2. The company's accountant records the receipt of cash and checks and makes deposits at the bank.
3. The employee who works the register reconciles cash to receipts at the end of the day.
4. Employees know that the internal auditor will perform a bank reconciliation at the end of each month.
5. Petty cash is kept in a back room but is not monitored during the day.
6. A cashier lets another employee work his assigned register while he helps a customer.

Required
Identify the problem with each internal control procedure.

10. Internal Control

Suppose that a company's president engages in the following independent behaviors:

1. Holds monthly meeting with staff during which the importance of internal control is stressed.
2. Signs documents without reading them.
3. Occasionally visits staff and reviews their work.
4. Requests contingency plans for every conceivable threat to the organization.

Required
For each behavior, identify the component of internal control that is affected and whether that component is strengthened or weakened by the behavior. Each behavior may affect multiple components.

11. Internal Control Activities

Lee County Medical Group is a medical practice that distributes several expensive and popular medications to patients. You are tasked with developing control procedures for distribution of the medications.

Required
For each of the following areas, provide one possible example control activity that could be implemented: Establishing responsibility, Maintaining adequate documentation, Segregation of duties, Physical security, and Independent verification.

12. Internal Control Activities

A company is considering implementing internal control procedures for the following processes:

1. The collection of significant amounts of cash from customers.
2. Employee use of small office supplies such as pens and paper clips.
3. The documentation of medical procedures performed to protect against malpractice claims and to ensure proper revenue collection.

Required
Using risk analysis and cost-benefit analysis, comment on the appropriateness of implementing control activities for the above scenarios.

13. Bank Reconciliation Items

Luther's Grille is preparing a bank reconciliation for the month of March and needs help with the following items:

1. A customer's ₹1,250 check was deposited on March 31 but does not appear on the bank statement.

2. A check clearing for ₹350 was recorded by Luther's Grille for ₹530.
3. The bank statement shows a ₹450 NSF check.
4. A service charge of ₹8,500 was reported on the bank statement.
5. The bank statement shows that the bank collected ₹800 of interest on Luther's Grille's behalf.
6. A charge of ₹300 for Internet banking was reported on the bank statement.
7. A ₹1,000 check written on March 31 does not appear on the bank statement.

Required
Identify whether each item is (1) an addition to the book balance, (2) a deduction from the book balance, (3) an addition to the bank balance, or (4) a deduction from the bank balance.

14. Bank Reconciliation Items

Consider the following two independent situations:

1. A company's January 31 bank reconciliation shows deposits in transit of ₹1,500. The company's books indicate deposits of ₹23,000 for the month of February, but the bank statement indicates deposits of ₹21,750 for February.
2. A company's January 31 bank reconciliation indicates outstanding checks of ₹2,500. The company's books indicate disbursements of ₹17,950 for the month of February, but the bank statement shows ₹18,900 of disbursements for February.

Required
For situation 1, determine deposits in transit at February 28. For situation 2, determine outstanding checks at February 28.

15. Prepare Bank Reconciliation

McKnight Company's June 30 bank statement shows a balance of ₹1,47,500. McKnight's books show a June 30 cash balance of ₹1,36,000. McKnight also has the following information:

1. Deposits in transit as of June 30, ₹10,000
2. Outstanding checks as of June 30, ₹25,000
3. ₹1,000 service charge reported on the bank statement
4. NSF check returned with bank statement, ₹15,000
5. Interest on note receivable collected by the bank, $12,500

Required
Prepare McKnight's bank reconciliation as of June 30 and prepare any necessary journal entries resulting from the reconciliation. What is the actual cash balance that should be reported on the June 30 balance sheet?

16. Prepare Bank Reconciliation

Hayley Company's September 30 bank statement shows a balance of ₹5,38,100. Hayley's September 30 cash balance is ₹4,58,000. Hayley also has the following information:

1. Deposits made but not appearing on the September bank statement, ₹55,000.
2. Check written but not appearing on the September bank statement, ₹1,22,000.
3. One check written for the purchase of Supplies was erroneously recorded for ₹890 but appears on the bank statement at ₹980.
4. Monthly service charges listed on the bank statement are ₹230. Hayley had already recorded the effect of ₹130 of those charges.
5. A customer payment for a ₹1,500 receivable was collected by the bank but not yet recorded by Hayley.

Required
Prepare Hayley's bank reconciliation as of September 30, and prepare any necessary journal entries resulting from the reconciliation.

17. Prepare Bank Reconciliation

The following bank statement for the month of May is for El Guapo Industries:

Bank Statement			
	Checks	Deposits	Balance
Balance, May 1			₹12,000
Deposits recorded during May			₹46,000
Checks cleared during May	₹34,000		
NSF checks—Hugo Company	2,500		
Interest collected on note receivable		5,600	
Bank service charge	35		
Service charge for new checks	65		
Balance, May 31			27,000

The following information was taken from the books at El Guapo:

Balance, May 1	₹12,000
Deposits during May	48,500
Checks written during May	36,500

Required
Prepare El Guapo's May bank reconciliation and prepare any necessary journal entries resulting from the reconciliation.

18. Bank Reconciliation Items

A company makes the following journal entries after preparing a bank reconciliation:

1. Accounts Receivable	₹34,000	
Cash		₹34,000
2. Service Charge Expense	4,500	
Cash		4,500
3. Cash	1,10,000	
Notes Receivable		1,00,000
Interest Revenue		10,000

Required
Explain the likely circumstance behind each of the entries.

19. Petty Cash

On September 1, Anders Properties establishes a petty cash fund for ₹2,000. On September 30, the fund's custodian prepares a report showing ₹1,300 in cash remaining and receipts of ₹120 for miscellaneous items, ₹200 for postage, and ₹350 for supplies. The custodian presents the report to the company accountant, who replenishes the fund.

Required
Prepare all necessary journal entries for the month of September.

20. Petty Cash

On January 1, Martin Co. establishes a petty cash fund in the amount of ₹500. On January 31, the fund is replenished. Before replenishment, there was ₹128.75 remaining in the petty cash drawer and the following receipts: parking fees, ₹103.50; postage, ₹50; office supplies, ₹198; and miscellaneous expenses, ₹22.

Required
Prepare all journal entries necessary to record the establishment and replenishment of the fund.

21. Petty Cash

Malone Gifts makes the following two entries to establish and replenish its petty cash fund.

Petty Cash	1,000	
Cash		1,000
Miscellaneous Expense	350	
Postage Expense	100	
Supplies Expense	300	
Cash Over and Short	20	
Cash		770

Required
Determine the effect on the accounting equation for each entry. Determine how much cash was in the petty cash fund when established, immediately before replenishment, and immediately after replenishment. Were receipts equal to the cash needed for replenishment?

22. Reporting Cash and Cash Equivalents

The following is a list of items that may or may not be included in the cash and cash equivalents total on the balance sheet:

1. Cash in checking account
2. Petty cash on hand
3. Shares of Coca-Cola common stock
4. Certificate of deposit maturing in 45 days
5. Certificate of deposit that matures in 120 days
6. One-month Treasury bills
7. Undeposited check from a customer
8. A customer's check returned by the bank and marked NSF

Required
For each of the stated items, indicate whether the item should be included or excluded from the Cash and Cash Equivalents total.

23. Reporting Cash and Cash Equivalents

The CPA Company invested in the following items during November and December of 2013:

November	
60-day Treasury bills	₹1,50,000
Preferred stock	2,55,000
Certificate of deposit, maturing 1/31/2015	3,40,000
Certificate of deposit, maturing 2/1/2014	5,00,000
December	
Common stock	₹6,00,000
Commercial paper, maturity date of 1/15/2014	9,00,000

Required
Determine the total of cash and cash equivalents that should be reported on the December 31, 2012, balance sheet, assuming that cash on hand was ₹55,000.

24. Evaluate Cash

In a recent annual report, **Good Foods** reported the following account balances (in millions):

Cash and cash equivalents, current year	₹1,244
Cash and cash equivalents, prior year	567
Total assets, current year	63,078
Cash flows from operating activities	4,141
Capital expenditures	1,367
Dividends	1,663

Required
a. Prepare horizontal and vertical analyses of Good's cash balance. Round percentages to one decimal point (i.e., 9.4%).
b. Calculate free cash flow.
c. Interpret the results of your calculations.

25. Free Cash Flow

A company provides the following information regarding cash flows (₹ in lakhs):

Cash flows provided by operating activities	₹67,505
Cash flows used in investing activities	30,599
Cash flows used by financing activities	22,700
Cash paid for fixed assets	13,686
Cash paid for dividends	5,118
Cash received from issuing notes payable	8,000
Cash paid to purchase treasury stock	10,500

Required
Calculate free cash flow. Given the company's free cash flow and the additional cash flow information provided, does it appear that the company is in a position to expand?

PROBLEMS

26. Prepare Bank Reconciliation

Helms Foundation's bank statement for the month of September and its general ledger cash account at September 30 are as follows (in ₹ lakhs):

Bank Statement			
Date	Disbursements	Deposits	Balance
Sept. 1			33,450
3	560		32,890
4		4,000	36,890
6	910		35,980
9	150		35,830
13		13,500	49,330
15	900		48,430
16	875		47,555
18	8,000		39,555
19	775		38,780
22	450		38,330
25		6,000	44,330
26	5,000		39,330
27	650		38,680
30		1,000	39,680
30	75		39,605
30	65		39,540

Cash			
Sept. 1	35,980	Sept. 5	150
12	13,500	8	875
24	6,000	9	900
30	9,000	10	8,000
		11	775
		17	5,000
		19	450
		22	650
		23	850
		25	900
		28	1,200

Additional information: At the end of August, Helms had two outstanding checks (₹560 and ₹910) and one ₹4,000 deposit in transit. On Helms' September bank statement, the two Sept. 30 disbursements were bank service charges. The Sept. 30 deposit of ₹1,000 was the result of the bank collecting a note receivable on behalf of Helms.

Required

Prepare a bank reconciliation for the month of September, and prepare any journal entries required at September 30.

27. Prepare Bank Reconciliation

Murphy Cotton Company's bank statement for the month of June and its general ledger cash account at the end of June are as follows (in millions):

Bank Statement					
Date	Disbursements		Deposits	Other	Balance
June 1					₹8,250
3	# 200	₹1,220			7,030
4			₹2,100		9,130
6	# 203	365			8,765
9	# 204	840			7,925
15	# 202	900			7,025
16	# 207	1,400			5,625
18	# 205	2,000			3,625
18			3,500		7,125
19	# 208	1,620			5,505
22	# 209	150			5,355
25			2,220		7,575
26	# 211	355			7,220
27	# 212	3,650			3,570
28			5,100		8,670
30				$100	8,770
30				130	8,640

Cash			
June 1	9,130	June 5 # 201	790
June 17	3,500	June 6 # 202	900
June 24	2,220	June 6 # 203	365
June 27	5,100	June 8 # 204	840
June 30	1,750	June 11 # 205	2,000
		June 15 # 206	1,180
		June 16 # 207	1,400
		June 18 # 208	1,260
		June 20 # 209	150
		June 22 # 210	560
		June 23 # 211	355
		June 26 # 212	3,650

Other information: Murphy had one deposit in transit of ₹2,100 and one outstanding check (#200) of ₹1,220 at May 31. All canceled check amounts agree with the bank statement.

Required

a. Identify all deposits in transit and outstanding checks at June 30.
b. Prepare a bank reconciliation for the month of June.
c. Prepare all journal entries required by Murphy at June 30. Assume any debit memorandum is a service charge, any credit memorandum is a collection of an account receivable, and any error relates to an account payable.

28. Evaluate Cash

In their recent annual reports, **Walgreens** and **CVS** reported the following account balances (in lakhs):

	Walgreens	CVS
Cash and cash equivalents, 12/31/10	₹1,880	1,427
Cash and cash equivalents, 12/31/09	2,087	1,086
Total assets	26,275	62,169
Cash flows from operating activities	3,744	4,779
Capital expenditures	1,014	2,005
Dividends	541	479

Required

For both companies, calculate and interpret (a) horizontal and vertical analyses of cash balance and (b) free cash flow. How do the cash positions compare? Round percentages to one decimal point (i.e., 9.4%).

CASES

29. Research and Analysis

Access the 2012–13 annual report for **Indian Oil Corporation Ltd. (IOCL)** by clicking on the *Investors* and *Financial Reports* links at www.iocl.com.

Required

a. Conduct horizontal and vertical analyses of IOCL's cash balance. Round percentages to one decimal point (i.e., 9.4%).
b. Examine the company's statement of cash flows and determine the major ways in which the company has been using its cash in the past three years.
c. Examine the report of the independent auditor and the local auditor's opinion on internal control over financial reporting.
d. Based on your answers above, write a paragraph explaining your opinion of IOCL's cash position. Use your answers as supporting facts.

30. Written Communication

You are the owner of Curry's, a small retail company in a college town. You have a store manager who supervises employees. Most employees are part-time college students, and your manager is having a difficult time getting the employees to follow internal control procedures. Most of the employees think that the procedures are "a waste of time" and that they don't relate to the main purpose of the company, which is to "sell stuff."

Required

Prepare a memo that can be given to incoming employees explaining to them the importance of the control environment in general and control activities specifically.

reviewcard CHAPTER 5 Internal Control and Cash

	Learning Objectives	Key Concepts
LO1	Describe the role of internal control in a business.	Internal control is management's system of policies and procedures that helps it operate efficiently and effectively, report financial information reliably, and comply with laws and regulations. The Sarbanes-Oxley Act of 2002 requires publicly traded companies to assess annually the effectiveness of their internal control. An auditor must also assess management's own assessment.
LO2	Describe the five components of internal control.	The report *Internal Control—Integrated Framework* provides guidance on good internal control practices. Internal control consists of five components—the control environment, risk assessment, control activities, information and communication, and monitoring. For internal control to be effective, each component must operate effectively.
LO3	Understand two methods of internal control over cash—bank reconciliations and petty cash funds.	Two methods of internal control over cash are bank reconciliations and petty cash funds. A bank reconciliation is the process of reconciling the cash balance shown on the bank statement with the cash balance shown in a company' records. Common items of reconciliation include deposits in transit, outstanding checks, credit memoranda, and debit memoranda. The purpose of a bank reconciliation is to confirm the accuracy of cash records and to determine the actual balance in cash. A petty cash fund is an amount of cash kept on hand for minor expenditures. Once established, a petty cash fund keeps receipts as expenditures are made. It is periodically replenished by bringing the total cash in the fund back to the original amount.
LO4	Describe the reporting of cash.	Cash is a medium of exchange that can take many forms. A cash equivalent is any investment that (1) is readily convertible into a specific amount of cash and (2) will mature in three months or less from the date it was acquired. Examples of cash equivalents can include Treasury Bills, certificates of deposit, etc. These cash equivalents are reported along with cash in current assets on the balance sheet.

Key Definitions

Bank reconciliation The process of reconciling the differences between the cash balance on a bank statement and the cash balance in a company's records.

Cash A medium of exchange.

Cash equivalent Any investment that is readily convertible into cash and has an original maturity of three months or less.

Control activities The policies and procedures established to address the risks that threaten the achievement of organizational objectives.

Control environment The atmosphere in which the members of an organization conduct their activities and carry out their responsibilities.

Credit memorandum An addition to the cash balance on the bank statement for items such as the collection of interest.

Debit memorandum A subtraction from the cash balance on the bank statement for items such as service charges.

Deposit in transit A deposit that has been made by the company but has not cleared the bank as of the statement date.

Free cash flow The excess cash a company generates beyond what it needs to invest in productive capacity and pay dividends to stockholders.

Information and communication Required for the open flow of relevant information throughout an organization.

Internal control The system of policies and procedures used in a company to promote efficient and effective operations, reliable financial reporting, and compliance with laws and regulations.

Internal control report Annual report in which management states its responsibility for internal control and provides an assessment of its internal control.

Monitoring The assessment of the quality of an organization's internal control.

Outstanding check A check that has been distributed by the company but has not cleared the bank as of the statement date.

Learning Objectives

	Learning Objectives	Key Concepts
LO5	Evaluate cash through the calculation and interpretation of horizontal, vertical, and ratio analyses.	Free cash flow shows the amount of cash that a company generates after it has paid for investments in property and equipment and for dividends to shareholders. More free cash flow gives a company more flexibility to expand or to provide greater returns to shareholders.

Key Definitions (continued)

Petty cash fund An amount of cash kept on hand to pay for minor expenditures.

Restricted cash Cash a company has restricted for a specific purpose.

Risk assessment The identification and analysis of the risks that threaten the achievement of organizational objectives.

Demonstration Problem

Bank Reconciliation

At the end of January, Estess shows a cash balance of ₹67,650. The January 31 bank statement shows a balance of ₹64,170. Estess discovers the following.

1. Deposits of ₹4,250 and ₹2,300 made on January 30 and January 31, respectively, do not appear on the January bank statement.
2. Checks written in late January for ₹620 (No. 1983), ₹950 (No.1986), and ₹1,200 (No. 1989) do not appear on the January bank statement.
3. The bank showed a ₹200 customer check deposited by Estess and returned to the bank for nonsufficient funds (NSF), charged a ₹50 service fee, and collected a ₹500 receivable from one of Estess' customers.
4. A check that Estess wrote cleared the bank at ₹300 but was erroneously recorded in Estess' books at ₹350.

Prepare a bank reconciliation for Estess.

Key Formulas

Horizontal Analysis

$$\text{Rupee change in account balance} = \text{Current year balance} - \text{Prior year balance}$$

$$\text{Percentage change} = \frac{\text{Rupee change}}{\text{Prior year balance}}$$

Vertical Analysis

$$\text{Percentage} = \frac{\text{Cash}}{\text{Total Assets}}$$

Free Cash Flow

Cash Flows from Operating Activities
Less: Capital Expenditures
Less: Dividends
Free Cash Flow

Demonstration Problem Solution

Estess Enterprises
Bank Reconciliation
January 31

Balance per bank statement		₹64,170
Add deposits in transit:		
January 30	₹4,250	
January 31	2,300	6,550
Deduct outstanding checks:		
No. 1983	₹ 620	
No. 1986	950	
No. 1989	1,200	2,770
Actual cash balance		₹67,950
Balance per company records		₹67,650
Add:		
Collection of receivable	₹ 500	
Error by Estess	50	550
Deduct:		
Service fee	₹ 50	
NSF check	200	250
Actual cash balance		₹67,950

ACCT

Receivables

Learning Objectives

After studying the material in this chapter, you should be able to:

LO1 Describe the recording and reporting of receivables.

LO2 Understand the methods used to account for uncollectible receivables.

LO3 Understand the methods for estimating bad debt expense.

LO4 Evaluate accounts receivable through the calculation and interpretation of horizontal, vertical, and ratio analyses.

LO5 Understand the accounting for notes receivable.

Introduction

This chapter examines the accounting for receivables. Specifically, the chapter focuses on how companies account for the recording, the collection, and the noncollection of accounts receivable. After a discussion of how to analyze a company's receivable position, the chapter concludes with the accounting for a second type of receivable, a note receivable.

LO1 Recording and Reporting Accounts Receivable

A receivable represents a company's claim on the assets of another entity. The most common type of receivable is an account receivable. An **account receivable** is an amount owed by a customer who has purchased the company's product or service. Sometimes these receivables are referred to as trade receivables because they arise from the trade of the company.

Recording Accounts Receivable

Receivables are recorded at the time of the sale. To illustrate, suppose that on June 4 Furio Company sells ₹1,000 of product to a customer on account. Furio would record the revenue and receivable arising from the sale with the following entry. Note that this example ignores the effects on Furio's inventory and cost of goods sold. These will be covered in Chapter 7.

June 4	Accounts Receivable	1,000	
	Sales		1,000
	(To record sale on account)		

Assets	=	Liabilities	+	Equity
+1,000				+1,000

Account receivable An amount owed by a customer who has purchased the company's product or service.

CHAPTER 6

Companies like Asian Paints commonly sell their products on account. Unfortunately, the receivables that are created are not always collected.

© PIXLAND/THINKSTOCK

Both assets and equity increase as a result of this sale. When Furio collects the receivable, it will increase its cash and eliminate the receivable.

In some cases, a customer will return a product instead of paying for it, and this affects the accounts receivable balance. To illustrate, suppose that on June 10, the customer returns a ₹150 product because it is not needed. Furio would record the return with the following entry. Again, the example focuses only on the effect on receivables and ignores the effects on inventory and cost of goods sold.

June 10	Sales Returns and Allowances	150	
	Accounts Receivable		150
	(To record sales return)		

Assets	=	Liabilities	+	Equity
−150				−150

The entry decreases Accounts Receivable for the sales price of the product. However, instead of decreasing the Sales account directly, the entry increases Sales Returns and Allowances. Sales Returns and Allowances is a contra-revenue account, meaning that its balance is subtracted from sales when calculating a company's net sales. Companies use this account to maintain a record of returns each period. Like the Sales account, Sales Returns and Allowances is a temporary account whose balance is zeroed-out at the end of each period.

In addition to returns, companies sometimes provide discounts to customers if they pay within a certain time period. For example, sales are commonly made with terms 2/10, n/30, meaning that customers can receive a 2% discount if they pay within 10 days of the invoice. To illustrate, suppose that Furio grants terms of 2/10, n/30. On June 12 the customer pays the remaining ₹850 bill. By qualifying for a 2% discount, the customer saves ₹17 (850 × 2%) and pays only ₹833. Furio would record the receipt of payment as follows:

June 12	Cash	833	
	Sales Discounts	17	
	Accounts Receivable		850
	(To record payment)		

Assets	=	Liabilities	+	Equity
+833				−17
−850				

The entry increases Cash for the ₹833 payment and decreases Accounts Receivable for the full ₹850 balance. The difference, which equals the discount of ₹17 for timely payment, goes into the Sales Discounts account. Like Sales Returns and Allowances, the Sales Discounts account is a contra-revenue account that is subtracted from sales when calculating net sales. Companies use this account to maintain a record of discounts each period. It is a temporary account whose balance is zeroed-out at the end of each period.

Reporting Accounts Receivable

Because accounts receivable are expected to be collected quickly, they are classified and reported as current assets. However, companies do not normally collect all of their receivables because customers do not always pay their bills. Among other reasons, customers have financial hardships, relocate without paying, or simply refuse to pay. As a result, companies must follow the principle of conservatism and report their accounts receivable at net realizable value.

Net realizable value The amount of cash that a company expects to collect from its total accounts receivable.

Companies must follow the principle of conservatism and report their accounts receivable at net realizable value.

Net realizable value is the amount of cash that a company expects to collect from its total or gross accounts receivable balance. It is calculated by subtracting from gross receivables the amount that a company does not expect to collect. For example, a company that has ₹1,000 of gross receivables but does not expect to collect ₹50 of them has receivables with a net realizable value of ₹950. The amount that a company does not expect to collect is usually called an allowance/provision. How companies estimate and record the allowance/provision will be examined later in the chapter.

To illustrate the reporting of receivables, consider the following receivables balances from Asian Paints' balance sheet.

Receivables Balances from Asian Paints' 2012–13 Balance Sheet

(in crores)	2013	2012
Receivables, net of provision of ₹5.73 and 4.75	₹633.88	₹500.24

Asian Paints reports a net realizable value of receivables of approximately ₹500.24 crore in 2012 and ₹633.88 crore in 2013. It also states textually that its receivables are *net of provisions of ₹5.73 crore and ₹4.75 crore*. Again, the term *provisions* refers to the amount of receivables that Asian Paints expects to be uncollectible. At the end of 2011–12 , the company was provisioning for ₹4.75 crore of uncollectible receivables. At the end of 2012–13, the provision had increased to ₹5.73 crore.

To demonstrate the relation among gross receivables, the provision, and net realizable value of receivables, Asian Paints' numbers are recast as follows.

(*in crores*)	2012–13	2011–12
Gross accounts receivable	₹639.61	₹504.99
Less: Allowance	5.73	4.75
Net realizable value	₹633.88	₹500.24

Note that gross accounts receivable is the one value that is not reported by the company.

While Asian Paints provides the provision balance on the face of the balance sheet or in the schedule to the annual accounts, many companies do not. Internationally many companies simply report their receivables at "net" and disclose the allowance for uncollectible accounts in their notes to the financial statements. An example is The Clorox Company, USA. The following shows both the company's receivables balances from its 2010 balance sheet and its Revenue Recognition note.

Receivables Balances and Revenue Recognition Note from The Clorox Company's 2010 Balance Sheet and Notes

(*amounts in millions*)	2010	2009
Receivables, net	$544	$486

Revenue Recognition
The Company provides for an allowance for doubtful accounts based on its historical experience and a periodic review of its accounts receivable. Receivables were presented net of an allowance for doubtful accounts $6 at June 30, 2010 and 2009.

As you can see, The Clorox Company provides the same information as Asian Paints. You just have to look in a different place to find it.

LO2 Uncollectible Receivables

As stated in the previous section, most companies are unable to collect all of their accounts receivable. Losses from the inability to collect accounts receivable are recorded in the accounting system as **bad debt expense.**

Because uncollectible accounts are a normal part of any business, bad debt expense is considered an operating expense. It is included in the calculation of net income but is usually combined with other operating expenses on the income statement. Thus, you will rarely find a company's bad debt expense listed separately on its income statement. If you do, it is likely bad news because the amount was large enough to warrant individual reporting.

There are two methods to account for bad debt expense:

- direct write-off method
- provision or allowance method

Each method is discussed in the following sections.

Direct Write-off Method

Under the **direct write-off method**, bad debt expense is recorded when a company determines that a receivable is uncollectible and removes it from its records. The receivable is eliminated or "written off" the company's accounting records, and bad debt expense is recorded for the amount of the receivable.

Direct write-off method Method in which bad debt expense is recorded when a company determines that a receivable is uncollectible and removes it from its records.

Bad debt expense The expense resulting from the inability to collect accounts receivable.

MARUTI SUZUKI ANALYSIS

Look at Maruti Suzuki's Balance Sheet in Appendix C. How can you tell whether the company's receivables are reported at net realizable value?

Maruti Suzuki reports the following for receivables: "Sundry Debtors ₹14,237 million." The "net" indicates that the reported balance is gross receivables less the provision for doubtful debt balance. Note 20 to the Financial Statements gives the details showing that a provision of ₹35 million has been made for bad and doubtful debt. The net balance of Sundry Debtors after all adjustments is ₹14,237 million.

To illustrate, suppose that Thompson Inc. makes a ₹4,000 credit sale to Brandon LLC during October 2012. In April 2013, Thompson determines that it will be unable to collect from Brandon. Thompson would make the following entries to reflect this activity:

Oct. 2012	Accounts Receivable	4,000	
	Sales		4,000
	(To record sale on account)		

Assets	=	Liabilities	+	Equity
+4,000				+4,000

April 2013	Bad Debt Expense	4,000	
	Accounts Receivable		4,000
	(To record bad debt expense and write off receivable)		

Assets	=	Liabilities	+	Equity
−4,000				−4,000

The first entry records the account receivable created from the sale. Both assets and equity increase as a result.

The second entry increases Bad Debt Expense to reflect the loss incurred from the inability to collect from Brandon. It also decreases Accounts Receivable to remove the receivable from Thompson's records. As a result of this write-off, both assets and equity decrease. All write-offs under the direct method will result in the same basic entry. The only difference will be the rupee amount.

The major advantage of the direct write-off method is its simplicity. When an account is deemed uncollectible, it is written off and an expense is recorded. The major disadvantage is that it can violate the matching principle. The matching principle requires that expenses be matched as closely as possible to the period in which the related revenues are recognized. In the preceding example, the revenue is recorded in 2012, but the expense is recorded in 2013. Assuming that Thompson prepares financial statements at the end of December, the expense is not matched to the year of the sale.

Because the direct method violates the matching principle, generally accepted accounting principles prohibit its use. The only exception to this prohibition is when bad debt expense is immaterial to the company. An expense is immaterial if it is small enough that failure to report it properly does not alter decision making. For example, if a company's bad debt expense totals ₹100 when it has ₹1 million in sales, failure to follow the matching principle will not likely affect decisions about the company. For most companies, though, bad debt expense is material, so they must use the provision/allowance method.

Provision or Allowance method Method in which companies use two entries to account for bad debt expense—one to estimate the expense and a second to write off receivables.

Provision for bad debts The rupee amount of receivables that a company believes will ultimately be uncollectible.

Because uncollectible accounts are a normal part of any business, **bad debt expense** is considered an operating expense.

Provision Method

While the direct write-off method accounts for uncollectible receivables with one entry, the **provision or allowance method** splits the accounting into two entries—one to record an estimate of bad debt expense and another to write off receivables when they become uncollectible. Both of these entries are described in the following sections.

Recording Bad Debt Expense The purpose of the provision method is to match the expense from uncollectible receivables to the period in which those receivables were created. To achieve this purpose, a company must record bad debt expense *at the end of each accounting period*. However, at the end of the period, the company does not yet know which receivables will be uncollectible.

Because of this inability to know which specific receivables will turn out to be uncollectible, the provision method requires a company to set up an " Provision for Bad Debt Account" when recording bad debt expense. That is, instead of writing off specific receivables at year end, a company increases a contra-asset account called Provision for Bad Debts. **Provision for bad debts** represents the rupee amount of receivables that a company believes will ultimately be uncollectible. As described earlier, its balance is subtracted from gross receivables to yield the receivables' net realizable value.

Because the direct method violates the matching principle, generally accepted accounting principles prohibit its use.

To illustrate, suppose that Duncan Sports makes credit sales of ₹8,00,000 during the financial year 2012–13. Based on past experience, Duncan estimates that ₹8,000 of these sales will not be collected. Duncan would therefore make the following entries to record this activity:

During 2012–13	Accounts Receivable	800,000	
	Sales		800,000
	(To record sales on account)		

Assets	=	Liabilities	+	Equity
+800,000				+800,000

End of 2012–13	Bad Debt Expense	8,000	
	Provision for Bad Debts		8,000
	(To record bad debt expense)		

Assets	=	Liabilities	+	Equity
−8,000				−8,000

The first entry increases Accounts Receivable and Sales for the credit sales during the year. This increases both assets and equity. The second entry increases both Bad Debt Expense and Provision for Bad Debts by ₹8,000. This effectively matches the expense of future uncollectible receivables to 2012–13 sales. It also reduces Duncan's net realizable value of receivables by ₹8,000 because it is now allowing for ₹8,000 of those receivables to be uncollectible. As a result, both assets and equity decrease.

The same basic entry will be recorded each time bad debt expense is estimated under the allowance method. The only difference will be the amount of the estimate, which will depend on circumstances and the estimation method a company uses. Methods of estimating bad debt expense are covered later in the chapter.

Recording a Write-Off Regardless of the method used to account for uncollectible receivables, a company must write off a receivable when it is deemed to be uncollectible. Under the direct write-off method, the company records bad debt expense at the time of the write-off. However, under the provision method, bad debt expense has already been estimated and recorded and a provision balance created for uncollectible receivables. Therefore, instead of increasing bad debt expense at the time of the write-off, the company reduces the balance in the provision account.

IFRS

GAAP and IFRS contain similar requirements that must be met to record a credit sale, but they are worded differently. GAAP states that collectibility should be reasonably assured while IFRS states that it must be probable that the economic benefits will flow to the company.

To illustrate, suppose that on February 8, 2013, Duncan Sports determines in 2012–13 that a ₹2,500 receivable from William Johnson is uncollectible and decides to write it off the books. Duncan would make the following entry:

Feb. 8 2013	Provision for Bad Debts	2,500	
	Accounts Receivable		2,500
	(To record write-off)		

Assets	=	Liabilities	+	Equity
−2,500				
+2,500				

The entry decreases Accounts Receivable and decreases an equal amount of Provision for Bad Debts. Note that the entry has no effect on total assets or net income. More specifically, the entry has no effect on Duncan's net realizable value of receivables. This is because both the asset account and the contra-asset account are decreasing by the same amount, thereby offsetting one another. Duncan now knows that Johnson will not pay, but Duncan had already allowed for that possibility. Therefore, Duncan's expected cash receipts are unchanged. This will be the case for all write-offs under the provision method.

Recording the Recovery of a Write-Off Occasionally, a company will collect a receivable that it had previously written off. For example, suppose that Johnson pays his bill in full later on March 22, 2013. When this payment occurs, the following two entries are made:

The provision method requires a company to estimate its bad debt expense and to set up an "provision" for uncollectible receivables.

March 22 2013	Accounts Receivable	2,500	
	Provision for Bad Debts		2,500
	(To reverse the original write-off)		

Assets	=	Liabilities	+	Equity
+2,500				
−2,500				

March 22 2013	Cash	2,500	
	Accounts Receivable		2,500
	(To collect the receivable)		

Assets	=	Liabilities	+	Equity
+2,500				
−2,500				

The first entry simply reverses the original entry writing off the receivable. The second entry records the collection of cash and the reduction of the receivable.

Percentage-of-sales approach Method that estimates bad debt expense as a percentage of sales.

Notice that once again there is no effect on total assets by either of these two entries.

LO3 Estimating Bad Debt Expense

The previous section demonstrated how to record bad debt expense under the provision method. This section demonstrates how to estimate the amount of bad debt expense to be recorded.

When estimating bad debt expense companies may use one of two different approaches.

- percentage-of-sales approach
- percentage-of-receivables approach

Both approaches use information such as past experience, industry norms or trends, and current customer credit ratings to make the estimate as accurate as possible. Each approach is discussed in the following sections.

Percentage-of-Sales Approach

Under the **percentage-of-sales approach**, bad debt expense is a function of a company's sales. It is calculated by multiplying sales for the period by some percentage

MAKING IT REAL

Most companies have a good idea of how long it takes them to collect their receivables. However, sometimes shocks to the economy can cause significant delays in collections. Take the recent recession and economic downturn. Customer payments have slowed significantly. The reduced cash flow is especially damaging to small businesses that might not have sufficient cash on hand to pay their own suppliers. This turns into a never-ending cycle where buyers and sellers are both past due on their bills and reduces the cash flow to the entire economy.

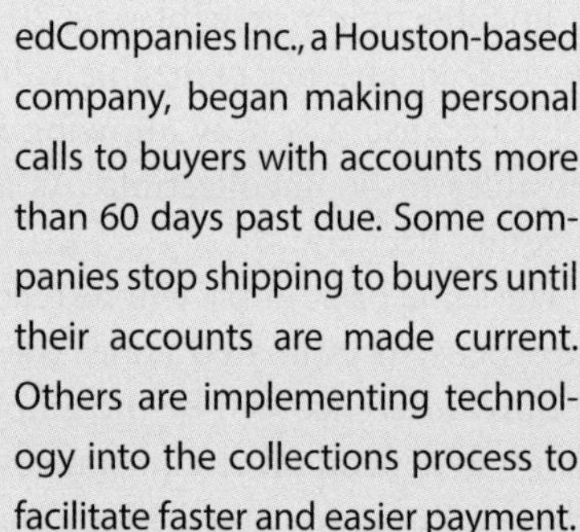

To combat this, companies are being forced to alter their collections policies. Traditionally, buyers with delinquent accounts would have their credit slashed or cancelled. Now, companies are considering alternative approaches which do not place undue pressure on the customer in the hopes of maintaining an agreeable relationship. The CEO of The UnitedCompanies Inc., a Houston-based company, began making personal calls to buyers with accounts more than 60 days past due. Some companies stop shipping to buyers until their accounts are made current. Others are implementing technology into the collections process to facilitate faster and easier payment.

The bottom line is that delayed collection of accounts receivable affects both the business and the customer. Longer collection cycles mean that businesses have a diminished cash flow and have to struggle to make do with less cash on hand. Without timely collections, many businesses are put in a situation where they might face delinquency with their own vendors or even bankruptcy from lack of liquidity.

set by the company. For example, suppose a company with ₹2,50,000 of sales in 2012–13 estimates that it will not collect 4% of those sales. The estimate for bad debt expense at the end of 2010 would be ₹10,000 (₹2,50,000 × 4%). The entry to record the estimate is shown below.

Mar. 31 2013	Bad Debt Expense	10,000	
	Provision for Bad Debts		10,000
	(To record bad debt expense)		

Assets	=	Liabilities	+	Equity
−10,000				−10,000

The advantages of this approach are its simplicity and the fact that it results in very good matching. Bad debt expense for a period is primarily a function of sales for that period. The main disadvantage is that no consideration is given to the resulting balance in the Provision for Bad Debts account. It is simply the existing balance plus the current estimate. Since the provision account is used to compute net realizable value, the percentage-of-sales approach results in a less meaningful net realizable value of receivables.

Percentage-of-Receivables Approach

Under the **percentage-of-receivables approach**, bad debt expense is a function of a company's receivables balance. It is calculated in two steps. The first step is to calculate what the balance in the Provision for Bad Debts account should be. This is accomplished by multiplying accounts receivable by a percentage set by the company. The second step is to adjust the provision account to that calculated balance. The amount of the adjustment is bad debt expense for the period.

To illustrate, suppose that a company has a receivables balance of ₹24,000 at the end of the financial year 2012–13. Based on past experience, the company expects that 2% of its receivables balance will be uncollectible. As a result, the balance in the provision account on March 31 should be 2% of receivables, or a ₹480 credit balance (₹24,000 × 2%). The next step is to make the adjustment.

Since the provision method for bad debts relies on estimates, a company's allowance balance prior to adjustment can have either a debit or credit balance. A debit balance means that the company has experienced greater write-offs during the year than expected. A credit balance indicates that write-offs have been less than expected. Whether the balance is a debit or credit does not require a company to correct its bad debt expense from the prior year. However, it does affect the adjustment for the current year.

To illustrate, assume that the provision account has a ₹100 credit balance prior to adjustment. To get the balance to a ₹480 credit requires a ₹380 credit entry. Therefore, bad debt expense for 2012–13 is ₹380. This is illustrated as follows.

Provision for Bad Debts (Dr)	Provision for Bad Debts (Cr)	
	100	Existing balance
	380	Adjustment required = Bad Debt Expense
	480	Desired balance (₹24,000 × 2%)

Mar. 31 2013	Bad Debt Expense	380	
	Provision for Bad Debts		380
	(To record bad debt expense)		

Assets	=	Liabilities	+	Equity
−380				−380

In contrast, assume that the provision account has a ₹50 debit balance prior to adjustment. In that case, the necessary adjustment is a ₹530 credit entry. Therefore, bad debt expense for 2012–13 is ₹530. This is illustrated as follows.

Provision for Bad Debts (Dr)	Provision for Bad Debts (Cr)	
50		Existing balance
	530	Adjustment required = Bad Debt Expense
	480	Desired balance (₹24,000 × 2%)

Mar. 31 2013	Bad Debt Expense	530	
	Provision for Bad Debts		530
	(To record bad debt expense)		

Assets	=	Liabilities	+	Equity
−530				−530

The major advantage of the percentage-of-receivables approach is that it results in a very meaningful net realizable value. This is because the provision account is determined as a set percentage of receivables. The disadvantage is that it does not match expenses as well as the percentage-of-sales approach. This is because the adjustment necessary is a function of both the set percentage and a company's prior experience with write-offs. As a result, current expenses are affected by prior year experiences.

Aging of Accounts Receivable Many companies use a more refined version of the percentage-of-receivables approach. Recognizing that receivables

Percentage-of-receivables approach
Method that estimates bad debt expense as a percentage of receivables.

become less collectible as they get older, companies often prepare aging schedules for their receivables. An **aging schedule** is a listing and summation of accounts receivable by their ages. Normally, receivables that are outstanding for 30 days or less are considered current and are grouped together. Receivables outstanding longer than 30 days are considered past due and are grouped together in 30-day increments. Companies then apply increasing uncollectible percentages to older receivables.

To illustrate, suppose that SC Works prepares an aging schedule at March 31, 2013, as shown in Exhibit 6-1. SC Works reports ₹66,600 of receivables and breaks them into Current and several categories of Past Due. Each category is assigned an expected percentage of uncollectable receivables that rises as the age of the receivables increases. The necessary allowance balance is then calculated by summing the totals from each category.

Recognizing that receivables become less collectible as they get older, companies often prepare **aging schedules** for their receivables.

an aging schedule provides a more accurate estimate of the allowance for bad debts and therefore a better estimate of bad debt expense. But an aging schedule has another benefit. It is a good internal control activity.

Recall from Chapter 5 that control activities are one of the five elements of a good internal control system. They are procedures put in place to assist companies in operating and reporting efficiently and effectively. Keeping track of receivables and their ages helps meet these objectives. For example, an aging schedule provides the information a company needs to pursue its receivables effectively. It also provides information for future credit decisions. A company may hesitate to provide credit to customers who have past due receivables.

Exhibit 6-1 Aging Schedule of Accounts Receivable—SC Works

		Number of Days Past Due				
Customer	**Current**	**1–30**	**31–60**	**61–90**	**Over 90**	**Total**
Ellis Manufacturing			₹4,100			₹ 4,100
Clayburn Company					₹2,400	₹ 2,400
MAG, Incorporated				₹2,750		₹ 2,750
Others	₹44,450	₹10,400	₹1,000	₹1,200	₹ 300	₹57,350
Totals	₹44,450	₹10,400	₹5,100	₹3,950	₹2,700	₹66,600
* % Uncollectible	1%	3%	15%	30%	50%	
Allowance Balance	₹ 4,450	₹ 312	₹ 765	₹1,185	₹1,350	₹ 8,062

Assuming that SC Works has a credit balance of ₹870 in the provision account prior to recording bad debt expense, the company would make the following entry to record bad debt expense.

Provision for Bad Debts		
	870	Existing balance
	7,192	Adjustment required = Bad Debt Expense
	8,062	Desired balance

Mar. 31 2013	Bad Debt Expense	7,192	
	Provision for Bad Debts		7,192
	(To record bad debt expense)		

Assets = Liabilities + Equity
−7,192 −7,192

As you can see, the entry to record bad debt expense is the same as previously described. The difference is that

Aging schedule A listing of accounts receivable by their ages.

LO4 Analyzing Accounts Receivable

Any investor, creditor, or manager of a company should be interested in how well a company manages its accounts receivable. Because a receivable is an uncollected sale, the main question that should be asked of a company is how well it collects its receivables. In general, better collection means better management of receivables.

The following sections examine how well Colgate-Palmolive, USA collects its receivables. The examination

An aging schedule provides a more accurate estimate of the allowance for bad debts and therefore a better estimate of bad debt expense.

will require information from the company's balance sheet and its income statement. The required information is found in Exhibit 6-2, excerpted from Colgate-Palmolive's (USA) 2010 Annual Report.

Exhibit 6-2 Account Balances from Colgate-Palmolive's (USA) 2010 Annual Report

Source	Accounts	2010	2009
Income Statement	Net Sales	\$15,564	\$15,327
	Net Accounts Receivable	\$ 1,610	\$ 1,626
Balance Sheet	Allowance for Bad Debts	53	52
	Total assets	11,172	11,134

Horizontal and Vertical Analyses

A good place to start the analysis of accounts receivable is with horizontal and vertical analyses. Recall from Chapter 2 that horizontal analysis calculates the rupee change in an account balance, defined as the current year balance less the prior year balance, and divides that change by the prior year balance to yield the percentage change. Vertical analysis divides each account balance by a base account, yielding a percentage. The base account is total assets for balance sheet accounts and net sales or total revenues for income statement accounts. These calculations are summarized as follows:

Horizontal Analysis

$$\text{Rupee change in account balance} = \text{Current year balance} - \text{Prior year balance}$$

$$\text{Percentage change in account balance} = \frac{\text{Rupee change}}{\text{Prior year balance}}$$

Vertical Analysis

		For the Balance Sheet	*For the Income Statement*
Percentage	=	$\frac{\text{Account Balance}}{\text{Total Assets}}$	$\frac{\text{Account Balance}}{\text{Net Sales or Revenue}}$

© MEDIABLITZIMAGES (UK) LIMITED / ALAMY

Given Colgate-Palmolive's financial information in Exhibit 6-2, horizontal and vertical analyses of accounts receivable and sales result in the calculations shown below. Note that the net realizable value of receivables, as reported on the balance sheet, is used in the calculations.

The calculations show slight improvement in Colgate-Palmolive's receivables position. Horizontal analysis shows that the company's receivables balance decreased \$16 million, or 1.0%, in 2010. Horizontal analysis of sales shows growth in sales of \$237 million, or 1.5%, during the year, so it does not appear that receivables are lower because sales have fallen. Vertical analysis shows that receivables as a percentage of assets were down slightly, from 14.6% in 2009 to 14.4% in 2010.

For comparison purposes, the 2010 horizontal and vertical analyses of The Clorox Company, USA are provided. The calculations show that The Clorox

Horizontal Analysis

	Change	*Percentage Change*
Accounts receivable	1,610 − 1,626 = (16)	$\frac{(16)}{1,626} = (1.0)\%$
Net sales	15,564 − 15,327 = 237	$\frac{237}{15,327} = 1.5\%$

Vertical Analysis

	2010	*2009*
Accounts receivable	$\frac{1,610}{11,172} = 14.4\%$	$\frac{1,626}{11,134} = 14.6\%$
Net sales	$\frac{15,564}{15,564} = 100\%$	$\frac{15,327}{15,327} = 100\%$

Because a receivable is an uncollected sale, the main question that should be asked of a company is how well it collects its receivables.

		Horizontal Analysis	Vertical Analysis
Accounts receivable	*Colgate*	(1.0)	14.4%
	Clorox	11.9%	11.9%
Net sales	*Colgate*	1.5%	100%
	Clorox	1.5%	100%

Company maintains less receivables as a percentage of assets than Colgate-Palmolive. They also show that while both companies generate the same percentage growth in sales, The Clorox Company experienced a much larger increase in receivables. This is a trend that the company may wish to monitor.

Receivables Turnover Ratio

The preceding analysis indicates that Colgate-Palmolive appears to be managing its receivables well. Another means to assess the management of receivables is to calculate a company's receivables turnover ratio. The **receivables turnover ratio** compares a company's credit sales during a period to its average receivables balance during that period. It is calculated as follows:

$$\text{Receivables Turnover Ratio} = \frac{\text{Credit Sales}}{\text{Average Receivables}}$$

Where average receivables is:

$$\frac{\text{Beginning Receivables} + \text{Ending Receivables}}{2}$$

Because the ratio divides credit sales during a period by the average receivables balance during the period, it indicates how many times during a period a company generates and collects receivables. In general, companies want this ratio to be higher rather than lower because a higher ratio indicates that the company collects, or turns over, its receivables faster.

Colgate-Palmolive's 2010 receivables turnover ratio is calculated as follows from the information in Exhibit 6-2. Note that net sales is used instead of net credit sales. While net credit sales would be preferable, it is infrequently reported by companies, so net sales is used as a substitute.

$$\frac{15{,}564}{(1{,}610 + 1{,}626)/2} = 9.6$$

The 9.6 ratio indicates that Colgate-Palmolive's 2010 sales were 9.6 times its average receivables balance. In other words, the company was able to generate and collect its receivables balance close to ten times in 2010.

Because the receivables turnover ratio is sometimes difficult to interpret, it is often converted into the days-in-receivables ratio. The **days-in-receivables ratio** divides the receivables turnover ratio into 365 days to express, in days, how long it takes a company to generate and collect its receivables. Thus, the days-in-receivables ratio is calculated as follows:

$$\text{Days-in-Receivables Ratio} = \frac{365}{\text{Receivables Turnover Ratio}}$$

$$\frac{365}{9.6} = 38.8$$

A ratio of 38.8 indicates that it takes Colgate-Palmolive, USA, about 39 days to generate and collect the average receivable. Whether this is good or bad requires some comparison. In the prior year, Colgate-Palmolive's ratio was 38.4. The Clorox Company's 2010 ratio was 34.0 days. So, you can conclude that Colgate-Palmolive's (USA), ability to collect receivables is fairly stable, it lags behind The Clorox Company's collection by about 4 days.

Allowance Ratio

One additional ratio that is useful in analyzing a company's management of receivables is the allowance ratio. The **provision/allowance ratio** compares the provision account to gross accounts receivable to determine the percentage of receivables that are expected to be uncollectible in the future. It is calculated as follows:

$$\text{Provision Ratio} = \frac{\text{Provision for Bad Debts}}{\text{Gross Accounts Receivable}}$$

Where gross accounts receivable is:

Net Accounts Receivable + Provision for Bad Debts

Receivables turnover ratio A comparison of credit sales to receivables that measures a company's ability to generate and collect receivables.

Days-in-receivables ratio A conversion of the receivables turnover ratio that expresses a company's ability to generate and collect receivables in days.

Allowance ratio A comparison of the allowance account to receivables that measures the percentage of receivables that are expected to be uncollectible in the future.

MARUTI SUZUKI ANALYSIS

Using Maruti Suzuki's financial statements in Appendix C, calculate and interpret (1) horizontal and vertical analyses of accounts receivable and sales, (2) receivables turnover and days-in-receivables ratios, and (3) the provision ratio.

(1) Horizontal Analysis

Accounts Receivable: (₹14237 – 9376)/9376 = 51.9%

Sales: (₹426126 – ₹347059)/347059 = 22.9%

Vertical Analysis

Accounts Receivable: ₹14237/(266,880) = 5.3%

Sales: ₹426126/₹426126 = 100%

The 51.9% horizontal analysis indicates that receivables increased during the year by almost 51.9%. With the company's increase in sales of 22.9%, an increase in receivables is not alarming. The 5.3% vertical analysis indicates that a very small portion of Maruti Suzuki's assets are in the form of receivables.

(2) Receivables Turnover Ratio:

₹426126/[(₹14237 + 9376)/2] = 36.1

Days-in-Receivables: 365/36.1 = 10.1

The 36.1 receivables turnover ratio indicates that Maruti Suzuki generates and collects its receivables quite quickly—about 36 times each year. The days-in-receivables ratio of 10.1 also indicates that receivables are collected rapidly.

(3) Provision Ratio:

₹35/₹(14237 + 35) = 14272 = 0.002

The 0.002 provision ratio of Maruti Suzuki clearly indicates that they have very good debtors and expects to collect virtually all of its outstanding accounts receivable.

A higher ratio indicates that a company expects more receivables to be uncollectible. In general, a company would want this ratio to be as low as possible. Colgate-Palmolive's, (USA) provision ratio for 2010 and 2009 is calculated as follows from the information in Exhibit 6-2.

2010		2009	
$\frac{47.4}{1{,}591.9 + 47.4}$	= 2.9%	$\frac{50.6}{1{,}680.7 + 50.6}$	= 2.9%

For 2009 and 2010, Colgate-Palmolive expected that it would not collect slightly over 3% of its receivables, or about 3 cents per dollar of receivables. For comparison purposes, The Clorox Company's 2010 ratio was 1.1%. Again, like the receivables turnover ratio, this shows that Colgate-Palmolive collects its receivables at a high rate, but not as high as The Clorox Company.

LO5 Notes Receivable

An account receivable is an amount owed by a customer who has purchased the company's product or service. Sometimes, because of a customer's poor credit rating or because of the size of the transaction, a company will enter into a more formal agreement with the customer beyond a normal account receivable. This is often accomplished through a promissory note.

A **promissory note** is a written promise to pay a specific sum of money on demand or at some specific date in the future. Promissory notes can be used to formalize

Promissory note A written promise to pay a specific sum of money on demand or at some specific date in the future.

Promissory notes can be used to formalize a receivable or to loan money to another entity.

© PHOTOS.COM/THINKSTOCK

a receivable or to loan money to another entity. In most cases, promissory notes require the payment of both principal and interest. The company that will receive the principal and interest is called the *payee*. The customer or borrower who will pay the interest and principal is called the *maker* of the note. This chapter focuses on the accounting of the payee.

When a company accepts a promissory note, it has a **note receivable**. Like other assets, a note receivable is reported on the balance sheet. However, its classification depends on its terms. If the note is due within a year, it is classified as a current asset. Otherwise, it is a non-current asset.

Accounting for a note receivable usually requires entries to record the following:

- Issuance of the note
- Interest earned on the note
- Collection of the note

To illustrate, suppose that on October 1, 2012, Bentonville Machine Works sells a lathe to Tilbury Designs for ₹12,000. Bentonville accepts a six-month, 8% promissory note from Tilbury for payment. The note stipulates that Bentonville will receive both principal and interest from Tilbury on March 31, 2013.

Recording the Note

A note receivable is recorded at its face value, which is ₹12,000 in this example. Therefore, Bentonville would record the sale of the lathe and the resulting note receivable as follows:

Oct. 1 2012	Note Receivable	12,000	
	Sales		12,000
	(To record sale in exchange for a promissory note)		

Assets	=	Liabilities	+	Equity
+12,000				+12,000

Note receivable An asset created when a company accepts a promissory note.

In this entry, Bentonville increases Note Receivable to reflect the receipt of the promissory note and increases Sales to reflect the inflow of assets resulting from the sale. As a result, both assets and equity increase. As in previous examples in this chapter, the effects on inventory and cost of goods sold are ignored.

Recording Interest

Most promissory notes require that the maker pay interest to the payee. The amount of interest is a function of (1) the principal or face value of the note, (2) the annual interest rate, and (3) the length of time the note is outstanding. The calculation is as follows:

$$\text{Interest} = \text{Principal} \times \text{Annual Rate of Interest} \times \text{Time Outstanding}$$

In this example, Bentonville's note receivable is outstanding for only six months. As a result, interest of 8% will be charged for six of the twelve months of the year. Therefore, interest over the life of the note is ₹480, calculated as follows.

$$\begin{aligned}\text{Interest} &= \text{Principal} \times \text{Annual Rate of Interest} \times \text{Time Outstanding}\\ &= ₹12{,}000 \times .08 \times 6/12 \text{ months}\\ &= ₹480\end{aligned}$$

According to the calculation, Bentonville will receive ₹480 of interest at the maturity of the note. However, the revenue recognition principle requires companies to record interest revenue when it is earned, even if cash will not be received until later. Assuming that Bentonville has a fiscal year-end prior to the maturity of the note, it must make an adjusting journal entry to record interest earned during the year. Recall from Chapter 4 that such an entry is an accrual adjusting entry.

To illustrate, suppose that Bentonville prepares financial statements on December 31. Bentonville has not yet received any interest payment from Tilbury because payment is not required until March 31, 2013. However, Bentonville has earned three months of interest, calculated as follows.

$$\text{Interest earned} = \text{Principal} \times \text{Annual Rate of Interest} \times \text{Time Outstanding}$$
$$= ₹12{,}000 \times .08 \times 3/12 \text{ months}$$
$$= ₹240$$

On December 31, Bentonville would record this interest revenue as follows.

Dec. 31 2012	Interest Receivable	240	
	Interest Revenue		240
	(To record interest earned on note)		

Assets	=	Liabilities	+	Equity
+240				+240

This entry increases Interest Receivable to reflect the additional receivable Bentonville now has from Tilbury. Bentonville will report this receivable on its balance sheet until the interest is paid in March 2013. The entry also increases Interest Revenue to reflect the inflow of assets attributable to the year 2012. As a result, both assets and equity increase.

Collecting the Note

The collection of a note receivable is much like the collection of an account receivable. When a note is collected, the note receivable is decreased and cash is increased. However, when a note receivable requires interest to be paid, the collection of the note often includes the collection of interest as well. This is the case for Bentonville.

On March 31, 2013, Bentonville collects cash and interest from Tilbury. The total interest over the six months Bentonville held the note is ₹480. The principal is ₹12,000. Therefore, Bentonville receives ₹12,480 in cash, recorded as follows:

Mar. 31 2013	Cash	12,480	
	Interest Receivable		240
	Note Receivable		12,000
	Interest Revenue		240
	(To record collection of note)		

Assets	=	Liabilities	+	Equity
+12,480				+240
−12,000				
−240				

This entry has four parts. First, the entry increases Cash for the amount of cash collected by Bentonville. Second, it decreases Interest Receivable to eliminate the asset that was created by the December 31 adjusting entry. Third, the entry decreases Note Receivable by its principal value because the note has been collected and is no longer outstanding. Finally, the entry increases Interest Revenue for the three months of interest (January, February, and March) earned in the current period (₹12,000 × 8% × 3/12). This interest revenue will be reported on Bentonville's 2013 income statement. The result of the entry is a net increase to assets of ₹240 and an increase to equity of ₹240. If this seems low to you, remember that equity was increased substantially when the sale was made and the note created. When Bentonville collects the note, it is simply exchanging one asset for another. The net ₹240 increase to assets and equity results from the interest earned during the three months of the current year.

CONCEPT QUESTIONS

1. When is an account receivable recorded?
2. Describe how accounts receivable are reported on the balance sheet.
3. What method of accounting for uncollectible receivables is recommended by GAAP?
4. When is bad debt expense recorded under the direct write-off method? Under the allowance method?
5. What happens when a receivable that previously had been written off is collected?
6. Identify the two ways to estimate bad debt expense under the allowance method.
7. What are the benefits of preparing an aging schedule?
8. Explain the logic of comparing the percentage increase in receivables to the percentage increase in sales.
9. State the formula for receivables turnover ratio and describe what this ratio tells an analyst.
10. State the formula for the allowance ratio and describe what this ratio tells an analyst.
11. Who is considered the *maker* of a promissory note?
12. How does one determine whether a note receivable will be classified as a current asset or a non-current asset?
13. The amount of interest earned on a note receivable is a function of what three factors?

MULTIPLE CHOICE

1. Which of the following statements is true?
    i. Accounts receivable may be reported as a current asset or a current liability.
    ii. Accounts receivable are reported at net realizable value on the balance sheet.
    a. i only
    b. ii only
    c. Both i and ii
    d. Neither i nor ii
2. Accounts receivable are:
    a. recorded at the time cash is received.
    b. netted with a liability account to be presented on the balance sheet at net worth.
    c. recorded when a revenue is earned but cash has not yet been received.
    d. reported as unearned revenue until payment is received.
3. Which of the following is not true of the Sales Returns and Allowances account?
    a. It is a contra-revenue account
    b. It is increased when sales are returned
    c. It is a contra-expense account
    d. It is a temporary account that is zeroed-out during the closing process
4. Under the direct write-off method:
    a. bad debt expense increases only when a receivable is deemed uncollectible.
    b. a contra-asset account is used to estimate the amount of receivables that will be uncollectible.
    c. the matching principle of accounting is not violated.
    d. the income statement approach is used to estimate Bad Debt Expense.
5. The allowance method:
    a. requires only one journal entry to write off uncollectible accounts and record bad debt expense.
    b. uses a contra-asset account to report accounts receivable at net realizable value.
    c. is not recommended by GAAP.
    d. is only used if the amount of accounts receivable is immaterial.
6. The percentage-of-sales approach to estimating bad debt expense:
    a. is considered a balance sheet approach.
    b. focuses on getting the allowance for bad debts account as accurate as possible.
    c. matches expenses and revenues better than the percentage-of-receivables approach.
    d. is calculated using gross margin.
7. Which is not true of the percentage-of-receivables approach to estimating bad debt expense?
    a. It is calculated in two steps
    b. It is a function of a company's receivables balance
    c. It results in a meaningful net realizable value
    d. It always results in less bad debt expense compared to the percentage-of-sales approach
8. Horizontal analysis of accounts receivable:
    a. calculates accounts receivable as a percentage of total assets.
    b. highlights the change in accounts receivable as a percentage of the prior year's receivables balance.
    c. calculates accounts receivable as a percentage of net sales.
    d. both "a" and "b" are correct.
9. Vertical analysis of accounts receivable:
    a. calculates accounts receivable as a percentage of total assets.
    b. highlights the change in accounts receivable as a percentage of the prior year's receivables balance.
    c. calculates accounts receivable as a percentage of net sales.
    d. both "a" and "b" are correct.

10. Which of the following statements is correct?
    i. The receivables turnover ratio is indicative of a company's ability to collect its receivables
    ii. Companies normally strive to maintain a high receivables turnover ratio.
    a. i only
    b. ii only
    c. Both i and ii
    d. Neither i nor ii
11. The allowance ratio:
    a. is calculated by dividing Bad Debt Expense by Gross Accounts Receivable.
    b. is normally a ratio that companies try to keep as high as possible.
    c. indicates how much of a company's receivables is estimated to be uncollectible.
    d. is calculated using income statement accounts.
12. Which of the following is not true of a note receivable:
    a. A note receivable can be reported as a current asset or a non-current asset depending on the maturity date of the receivable
    b. A note receivable is normally acquired through the acceptance of a promissory note in settlement of a debt
    c. When a note receivable is received for services rendered, the revenue is not reported until the maturity date of the note
    d. The entity borrowing the money is considered the maker of the note
13. When accounting for a note receivable:
    a. interest revenue is never recorded until payment is received.
    b. interest receivable is normally reported as a current asset.
    c. interest rates are normally stated at semi-annual rates.
    d. the note receivable is recorded at issuance with a credit entry.

BRIEF EXERCISES

1. Recording Sales Discounts

On July 1, Pam's Pizza Supply sold 100 pounds of pepperoni for ₹80,000 on account to a local pizza parlor. The terms of the sale were 2/10, n/30. The pizza parlor pays Pam's Pizza Supply in full on July 7.

Required
Prepare the entries that Pam would make to record the sale and the receipt of the payment.

2. Recording Sales Returns

On March 5, Monica's Cooking Company sells inventory to a customer for ₹2,00,000. On March 13, the customer returns ₹7,500 of merchandise. The accountant recorded the return with the following entry:

March 13	Sales	7,500	
	Accounts Receivable		7,500

Required
Prepare the entry the accountant should have made when the merchandise was returned on March 13 and explain why the accountant's entry was incorrect. Ignore any effect on cost of goods sold or inventory.

3. Compute Net Realizable Value

At the end of the year a company has gross accounts receivable of ₹65,500. The allowance for doubtful accounts has a balance of ₹7,600, and sales discounts for the year were ₹5,400.

Required
What is the net realizable value of accounts receivable that the company will report on its balance sheet?

4. Direct Write-off Method

Chandler Inc. sells ₹3,50,00 of goods to Tribbiani Company during January. In April, Chandler determines that it will be unable to collect the receivable from Tribbiani.

Required
Prepare the journal entries to record the sale and the bad debt expense if Chandler uses the direct write-off method. Ignore any effect on cost of goods sold or inventory.

5. Recording Bad Debt Expense

While reviewing outstanding accounts receivables, John's Tractor Supply Company determines that a receivable of ₹15,000 is now uncollectable.

Required
Journalize the entry to record bad debt expense assuming that John uses a) the direct write-off method or b) the allowance method. Is the use of the direct write-off method allowed under GAAP? If so, under what circumstances?

6. Estimating Bad Debt Expense

A company uses the percentage-of-sales approach to estimate bad debts. Sales for the year were ₹7,50,000, and gross profit was ₹4,50,000. The company estimates that 5% of sales are uncollectible.

Required
What is the company's estimated bad debt expense for the year? Would your answer change if the company was able to increase its gross profit from its sales?

7. Allowance Method

Phoebe's Massage Company uses the allowance method to account for bad debt expense. Phoebe makes credit sales of ₹7,00,000 during the year. At year end, Phoebe estimates that ₹70,000 of those sales will not be collected. The next year, Phoebe determines that a ₹15,000 receivable is uncollectible and should be written off.

Required

Prepare the journal entries to record the credit sales, bad debt expense, and the write-off of uncollectible accounts.

8. Estimating Bad Debt Expense

Rachel's Clothing Company has a receivables balance of ₹15,00,000 at the end of the year. Based on past history, Rachel estimates that it will not collect 2% of its receivables balance. Prior to any year-end adjustment, the balance in the allowance account is a ₹20,000 debit.

Required

a. Prepare the journal entry to record bad debt expense for the year. Show your calculation of bad debt expense in T-account form.
b. Assume that the balance in the allowance account was a ₹10,000 credit instead of the ₹20,000 debit. What is bad debt expense in this situation? Show your calculation in T-account form.

9. Horizontal and Vertical Analyses

The following information pertains to Moose Corporation:

(in lakhs)

	2013	2012
Net sales	₹3,50,000	₹3,42,000
Net accounts receivable	1,89,000	1,97,000
Bad debt expense	8,200	7,000
Total assets	4,10,000	4,25,000

Required

Prepare horizontal and vertical analyses of all four accounts. Round percentages to one decimal point (i.e., 23.9%).

10. Analyzing Receivables

The following information pertains to Skelton Resorts:

	(in lakhs)
Credit sales	₹4,50,000
Net accounts receivable, beginning	63,000
Net accounts receivable, ending	54,000
Allowance for bad debts, ending	5,000

Required

Compute Skelton's receivables turnover ratio, days-in-receivables ratio, and allowance ratio.

11. Effects of Recording Bad Debt Expense

You are the accountant for a company, and you are preparing the entry to record bad debt expense for the year under the allowance method. Your boss is not an accountant and provides you with the following grid to fill out so that he can understand the effect of the expense entry:

	Net Income	Amount in accounts receivable account	Amount of accounts receivables reported on the financial statements	Receivables turnover ratio
Effect of bad debt expense entry				

Required

Fill out the grid with Increase, Decrease, or No Effect.

12. Accounting for Notes Receivable

On March 1, Auburn Actuarial Services accepted from Meadows Inc. a six-month, 5%, ₹1,20,000 note receivable and ₹30,000 in cash in exchange for services. The note and interest were paid at maturity on September 1. Auburn has a December 31 year end.

Required

Prepare all journal entries Auburn would make to properly account for the sale and note.

13. Record Interest on Note Receivable

On July 1, West Tennessee Supply Group sold ₹1,50,000 of supplies to Russell Research Labs in exchange for a 7 month, 8% note receivable.

Required

Assuming that West Tennessee Supply Group prepares adjusting journal entries monthly, prepare all entries necessary in July to account for the note. Ignore any effects on inventory or cost of goods sold.

14. Calculating Interest on Notes Receivable

Bowers Technology is in the process of converting a customer's ₹10,00,000 account receivable into a note receivable. Bowers is considering the following three options in establishing the terms of the note:

1. 4% 9-month note
2. 6% 6-month note
3. 8% 3-month note

Required

Which option(s) should Bowers choose if it wants to maximize interest revenue? What reasons might Bowers have for choosing the options that results in the least amount of interest revenue?

EXERCISES

15. Recording Accounts Receivable

On February 4, Campbell Company sells inventory to a customer for ₹60,000. Terms of the sale are 1/15, net 30. On February 10, the customer returns ₹5,000 of merchandise. The customer pays on February 15.

Required

Prepare all journal entries to record the merchandise sale, its return, and the collection of the receivable. Ignore any effects on inventory or cost of goods sold.

16. Reporting Accounts Receivable

A company reports the following for accounts receivable:

(in thousands)	2013	2012
Accounts receivable, net of allowance of ₹234 and ₹267	₹5,432	₹4,905

Required

For each year, determine the company's total or gross accounts receivable, net realizable value of accounts receivable, and allowance for bad debts balance. What does net realizable value represent?

17. Uncollectible Receivables

Carnes Inc. reported the following information in its latest annual report:

	(in lakhs)
Allowance for bad debts, beginning balance	₹1,775
Bad debt expense for the year	325
Accounts receivable written off during the year	256

Required

Determine which method of accounting for bad debts Carnes uses, record all journal entries associated with the allowance account for the year, and determine the ending balance in the allowance account.

18. Accounting for Uncollectible Receivables

The following information pertains to Godwin Motors, which uses the allowance method for receivables:

	2013	2012
Gross receivables	₹ 6,48,750	₹ 5,80,498
Allowance for bad debts	33,560	24,650
Net sales	75,55,000	63,25,000

Required

a. Assuming that Godwin Motors recorded bad debt expense of ₹25,600 in 2013, what amount of accounts receivable were written off in 2013?
b. Prepare the journal entries to record the 2013 bad debt expense and the 2013 write-offs of uncollectible accounts.
c. Assuming that Godwin made all sales on credit, what amount of cash was collected in 2013?

19. Uncollectible Receivables

At December 31, Vicki's Designers had gross accounts receivable of ₹3,46,000. Historically, Vicki's Designers has estimated bad debt expense as 5% of gross receivables.

Required

a. Calculate bad debt expense for the year, assuming that the allowance account currently has (1) a credit balance of ₹5,000 and (2) a debit balance of ₹1,200.
b. Assume that on January 14, an account receivable of ₹2,000 is deemed uncollectible and written off. Prepare the journal entry to record this event. What effect does this have on (1) net income and (2) the net realizable value of receivables?

20. Estimating Bad Debt Expense

Buster's Furniture provides the following information for the year:

Net credit sales for the year	₹9,85,750
Accounts receivable at year end	4,50,000
Allowance for bad debts at year end	18,000 credit

Required

Estimate bad debt expense for the year as (a) 5% of accounts receivable and (b) 2% of net credit sales. Discuss why Buster's Furniture might choose one approach over the other.

21. Aging Schedule for Accounts Receivable

Outdoor Living has the following accounts receivable at year end, broken down by age:

Age	Amount (in lakhs)
Current	₹1,50,000
One month overdue	40,000
Two months overdue	18,000
Three months overdue	8,000

Prior experience has shown that the company will probably collect 95% of its current receivables. Furthermore, the collection percentage will fall by 15% for each additional month an account receivable remains outstanding past its due date.

Required

Develop an estimate of Outdoor Living's allowance account balance and prepare the journal entry for bad debt expense, assuming that the allowance has an existing (a) ₹4,000 credit balance and (b) ₹1,000 debit balance.

22. Analyzing Receivables

The following information was taken from the annual report of SC Enterprises: (in lakhs)

	2013	2012
Sales	₹2,40,000	₹2,50,000
Total assets	8,40,000	8,25,000
Accounts receivable	1,25,000	78,000

Required
Prepare and interpret horizontal and vertical analyses of all three accounts. Round percentages to one decimal point (i.e., 23.9%). Should the owners of the business be concerned?

23. Analyzing Receivables

The following information was taken from the annual report of Sparky Foundation:

	2013	2012
Gross receivables	₹ 7,84,560	₹6,85,000
Allowance for bad debts	56,895	45,600
Net sales	81,00,000	

Required
Compute and interpret Sparky's receivables turnover ratio and its days-in-receivables ratio.

24. Analyzing Receivables

The following information is from Canning Company:

(in lakhs)

2013	Allowance for bad debts	₹ 500
	Net accounts receivable	21,000
2012	Allowance for bad debts	350
	Net accounts receivable	19,500

Required
Calculate the allowance ratio for both years. Is Canning Company getting better or worse at collecting its receivables?

25. Recording Notes Receivable

On April 1, Fly Corporation accepted cash of ₹15,00,000 and a six-month, 6%, ₹75,00,000 interest-bearing note from Gonzo, Inc., as settlement of an account receivable. Fly has a fiscal year end of June 30, and Gonzo paid the principal and the interest at maturity.

Required
Identify the note's maker and payee and prepare all appropriate journal entries from the acceptance of the note to the maturity date.

26. Accounting for Notes Receivable

Brandon Enterprises makes the following entries regarding a note receivable:

Sep. 1	Notes receivable	60,000	
	Accounts receivable		60,000
Sep. 30	Interest receivable	400	
	Interest revenue		400
Dec. 1	Cash	61,200	
	Interest receivable		400
	Interest revenue		800
	Notes receivable		60,800

Required
Identify (a) whether Brandon is the maker or the payee, (b) the terms of the note (issuance date, maturity date, interest rate), and (c) Brandon's year end.

27. Interest on Notes Receivable

Consider the following independent scenarios.

1. On 9/1, a company accepts a ₹10,000, 5%, 8-month note receivable.
2. On 3/1, a company accepts a ₹20,000, 8%, 6-month note receivable.
3. On 6/15, a company accepts a ₹15,000, 10%, 4-month note receivable.

Required
Assuming a December 31 year end, calculate current-year interest revenue for each scenario.

28. Accounting Terms

The following is a list of terms and definitions associated with receivables:

1. Direct write-off method
2. Maker
3. Allowance method
4. Maturity value
5. Promissory note
6. Aging schedule
7. Payee
8. Maturity date
9. Notes receivable

a. An asset resulting from accepting a promissory note as payment for products sold or services rendered.
b. A schedule used to organize accounts receivable according to the length of time each has been outstanding.
c. The amount of cash the maker is to pay the payee on the maturity date of the note.
d. The date the promissory note is due.
e. Recognition of bad debts expense at the point in time at which the accounts receivable is deemed uncollectible and written off.
f. The party that will receive the money from a promissory note at some future date.
g. A method of estimating bad debts expense on the basis of either net credit sales or accounts receivable at the end of period.
h. A written promise to pay a specific sum of money on demand or at some specific date in the future.
i. The party that agrees to repay the money for a promissory note at some future date.

Required
Match each term with the appropriate definition.

PROBLEMS

29. Accounts Receivable Entries

During 2013, CE Electronics entered into the following transactions:

	(in lakhs)
Sales on account	₹14,00,000
Collections of credit sales	12,25,000
Wrote off accounts deemed uncollectible	20,000
Received payments on accounts previously written off	7,500

On its 2011 balance sheet, CE reported gross accounts receivable of ₹707,000 and an allowance account of ₹43,000.

Required

Prepare all journal entries to record each of the transactions that occurred in 2013 and the journal entry to record bad debt expense at the end of 2013, assuming that 7% of accounts receivable at the end of 2013 are uncollectible.

30. Comparing Methods for Uncollectible Receivables

The following data pertains to the operations of Knight Corporation for 2013:

Net credit sales	₹7,25,000
Net income (before bad debt expense)	1,35,000
Write-offs of uncollectible accounts	17,500
Estimated uncollectible percentage of net credit sales	3%

The controller is trying to decide which method of accounting for bad debts to use. The company is attempting to maximize its net income to meet projected figures. The bad debt expense is material to the company's financial statements.

Required

a. Calculate bad debt expense for 2013 under the direct write-off method and the allowance method.
b. Compute net income under both methods (assume a tax bracket of 30%).
c. Does Knight have the option of which method to use under GAAP?

31. Account Receivable Entries

The following financial information pertains to Sleepy Company:

	(in lakhs)
Accounts receivable, 12/31/11	₹ 2,75,000
Allowance for bad debts, 12/31/11	8,400
Net credit sales, 2012	19,80,000
Collections on credit sales during 2012	17,30,000
Accounts receivable written off in 2012	6,500

Required

a. Prepare all the necessary journal entries for 2013 sales, collections, and write-offs (using the direct write-off method).
b. Using the allowance method, prepare 2013 journal entries to record write-offs and to estimate bad debt expense assuming bad debt expense is estimated on a (i) percentage of net credit sales approach (2%) and (ii) percentage of accounts receivable approach (5%).
c. What is the net realizable value of accounts receivable in parts b(i) and b(ii)?
d. Explain the rationale for each of the approaches in part b.

32. Analyzing Receivables

The following information was taken from the annual reports of two high-end jewelry retailers:

(in lakhs)

	Company A	Company B
Net accounts receivable, 2012	₹ 5,84,000	₹ 4,60,000
Net accounts receivable, 2011	5,05,000	3,98,000
Net sales, 2012	24,25,000	21,95,000
Net sales, 2011	22,00,000	15,00,000

Required

a. Calculate the 2012 receivables turnover ratio for both companies.
b. Compare the two companies. Which one is more efficient with their receivables?
c. What other methods and factors would one consider when evaluating receivables? What one other comparison demonstrates one company's efficiency over the other?

33. Analyzing Receivables

The following information pertains to Rocky Foundation:

(in lakhs)

	2013	2012
Net sales	₹6,00,000	₹5,82,000
Net accounts receivable	4,65,000	4,50,000
Allowance for bad debts	14,000	13,200
Total assets	6,30,000	6,53,000

Required

a. Prepare and interpret horizontal and vertical analyses of all four accounts. Round percentages to one decimal point (i.e., 23.9%).
b. Calculate and interpret the receivables turnover ratio and days-in-receivables ratio.
c. Calculate and interpret the allowance ratio for both years.

34. Recording Notes Receivable

On February 15, Harpool Inc. sold equipment to Adams Corporation on account for ₹40,00,000. On November 1, Harpool deemed the account uncollectible and wrote it off. On December 31, Adams offered Harpool a six-month, 10%, ₹40,00,000 promissory note in payment of its obligation, which Harpool accepted. Adams paid the principal and the interest at the maturity date. Harpool uses the allowance method for bad debts.

Required

a. Prepare all of Harpool's necessary journal entries from the date of the equipment sale to the maturity date of the note. Ignore any effect on inventory or cost of goods sold.
b. What would be Adams' motives for offering a promissory note in settlement of such an old debt?

CASES

35. Research and Analysis

Access the 2012 annual report for **Nestlé India Limited** by clicking on the *Investor, Stock and Financials,* and *Annual Reports* links at www.nestle.in.

Required

a. Examine the company's income statement and balance sheet and conduct horizontal and vertical analyses of net revenues and accounts receivable. Round percentages to one decimal point (i.e., 23.9%).
b. Examine the company's Allowance for Doubtful Accounts paragraph in its Summary of Significant Accounting Policies (second note). What is the company's 2012 and 2011 balances in its provision for bad debts account? What factors are considered when estimating the balance? How often is the balance reviewed?
c. With the gathered information, calculate the company's receivables turnover and days-in-receivables ratios for 2012 and the company's provision ratio for 2012 and 2011.
d. Based on your answers above, write a paragraph explaining your opinion of Nestlé India Ltd. accounts receivable position. Use your answers as supporting facts.

36. Ethics in Accounting

The Hines Corporation is in the process of closing its books for the year. The company has been growing at an unexpected rate. The chief accountant at the Hines Corporation is currently determining the applicable percentage for the provision for bad debts and believes it should be based on 2% of net credit sales. The president of the company, Jay Hines, has expressed concerns about living up to the expectations established by the growth in the current year. The president approached the controller and has made a request to increase the provision for bad debts to 5% of net credit sales with the expectation that the lower net income will decrease the pressure to perform in future years.

Required

a. What factors should one consider when determining the applicable percentage to apply when using the income statement or balance sheet approach?
b. Should the controller be concerned with the company's growth rate when determining the allowance for bad debts? Explain.

37. Entrepreneurial Decision Making

Valley Clothing Shop is a small clothing retailer now in its fourth year of business. Through its first year of operations, Valley has operated on a pure cash or check basis. Currently, Valley has averaged ₹2,750,000 of annual cash sales with an average profit margin of 40%. Lately, many customers have expressed frustration over the fact that Valley does not accept credit sales, and Valley believes that this is beginning to have a substantial negative impact on the business. Valley is contemplating two plans of action, neither of which will impact the company's current cash sales.

Plan 1

Offer qualified customers the opportunity to purchase merchandise on account. Valley believes this will create new credit sales of 18% of current cash sales. Increased expenses would include 4% of net credit sales related to bad debts, 2% of net credit sales for billing, and 1% of net credit sales for increased recordkeeping.

Plan 2

Begin accepting credit cards. Valley believes this will create new credit sales of 23% of current cash sales. Increased expenses would include 5.5% of net credit sales-related credit card fees and 0.5% of net credit sales for increased recordkeeping.

Required

a. Compute net income under each plan assuming a tax rate of 30%.
b. Which plan would you recommend Valley accept?
c. What other factors should Valley consider when evaluating these options?

38. Written Communication

Assume you are the controller of a manufacturing plant that sells light machinery to businesses in the surrounding area. You are currently training new employees, and in a recent training session, you report that total credit sales for the year is ₹30,00,000, accounts receivable total ₹4,00,000 less a ₹20,000 allowance for bad debts, and bad debt expense is ₹35,000. After the session, a trainee approaches somewhat confused about why bad debt expense and the allowance balance differ.

Required

Prepare a written explanation to the trainee on the difference between bad debt expense and the allowance for bad debts.

39. Reading and Analyzing Financial Statements

Access the 2012–13 annual report for **Godrej Comsumer Product Limited** by clicking on the

Investor Services, Financial Information and *Annual Reports links* at www.godrej.com.

Required

a. Examine the company's current-year and prior-year balances in accounts receivable. Calculate the percentage change in the account. Round percentages to one decimal point (i.e., 23.9%).

b. Calculate the company's provision ratio for 2012 and 2011.

c. Do your calculations indicate a positive or negative trend in receivables?

d. Examine the fifth note to the financial statements. Would the company's accounts receivable balance increase due to the described activity?

reviewcard CHAPTER 6 Receivables

Learning Objectives		Key Concepts
LO1	Describe the recording and reporting of receivables.	Receivables are current assets reported at net realizable value, which is equal to the expected cash receipts from total receivables. Net realizable value is calculated as total receivables less the allowance for bad debts.
LO2	Understand the methods used to account for uncollectible receivables.	There are two methods to account for uncollectible receivables: the direct write-off method and the allowance/provision method. Under the direct write-off method, bad debt expense is recorded when a receivable is deemed to be uncollectible and is removed from the company's records. Because the method does not follow the matching principle, it is not allowable under generally accepted accounting principles unless the amount of bad debts is immaterial. Under the allowance/provison method, bad debt expense is estimated and recorded at the end of each accounting period and an allowance is set up for future write-offs. When a receivable is deemed uncollectible, both the specific receivable and the provision account are decreased for the value of the receivable.
LO3	Understand the methods for estimating bad debt expense.	Bad debt expense can be estimated with the percentage of sales approach or the percentage of receivables approach. Under percentage of sales, bad debt expense is a set percentage of sales for the period. This approach has the advantage of matching expenses to revenues well. Under percentage of receivables, bad debt expense is a function of receivables at the end of the period. This approach has the advantage of creating a very meaningful net realizable value. An aging schedule is a more refined version of the percentage of receivables approach.
LO4	Evaluate accounts receivable through the calculation and interpretation of horizontal, vertical, and ratio analyses.	The receivables turnover ratio shows how effective a company is at generating and collecting its accounts receivable during a period. The days-in-receivables ratio converts the turnover ratio into a number of days. The allowance ratio shows the percentage of receivables that a company expects will not be collected.
LO5	Understand the accounting for notes receivable.	A note receivable is created when a company accepts a promissory note. Accounting for a note requires the recording of the note, the accrual of any interest earned, and the recording of collection.

Key Definitions

Account receivable An amount owed by a customer who has purchased the company's product or service.

Aging schedule A listing of accounts receivable by their ages.

Allowance/Provision method Method in which companies use two entries to account for bad debt expense—one to estimate the expense and a second to write off receivables.

Bad debt expense The expense resulting from the inability to collect accounts receivable.

Days-in-receivables ratio A conversion of the receivables turnover ratio that expresses a company's ability to generate and collect receivables in days.

Direct write-off method Method in which bad debt expense is recorded when a company determines that a receivable is uncollectible and removes it from its records.

Net realizable value The amount of cash that a company expects to collect from its total accounts receivable.

Note receivable An asset created when a company accepts a promissory note.

Percentage-of-receivables approach Method that estimates bad debt expense as a percentage of receivables.

Percentage-of-sales approach Method that estimates bad debt expense as a percentage of sales.

Promissory note A written promise to pay a specific sum of money on demand or at some specific date in the future.

Provision for bad debts The rupee amount of receivables that a company believes will ultimately be uncollectible.

Provision ratio A comparison of the allowance account to receivables that measures the percentage of receivables that are expected to be uncollectible in the future.

Receivables turnover ratio A comparison of credit sales to receivables that measures a company's ability to generate and collect receivables.

Key Formulas

Percentage-of-Sales Approach	Bad debt expense 5 Sales 3 Percentage
Percentage-of-Receivables Approach	Bad debt expense 5 [Receivables 3 Percentage] 1 or 2 Provision for Bad Debts balance
Receivables Turnover Ratio	$\frac{\text{Credit Sales}}{\text{Average Receivables}}$
Average receivables	$\frac{\text{Beginning Receivables 1 Ending Receivables}}{2}$
Days-in-Receivables Ratio	$\frac{365}{\text{Receivables Turnover Ratio}}$
Provision Ratio	$\frac{\text{Provision for Bad Debts}}{\text{Gross Accounts Receivable}}$
Horizontal Analysis	Rupee change in account balance = Current year balance − Prior year balance $\text{Percentage change in account balance} = \frac{\text{Dollar change}}{\text{Prior year balance}}$
Vertical Analysis	*For the Balance Sheet*: $\text{Percentage} = \frac{\text{Account Balance}}{\text{Total Assets}}$ *For the Income Statement*: $\frac{\text{Account Balance}}{\text{Net Sales or Revenue}}$
Interest on Notes Payable	Principal × Annual Rate of Interest × Time Outstanding

Demonstration Problem

Bad debt estimation and write-off

Lambert Golf Supplies provides the following partial balance sheet and income statement information for 2013. Assume that Lambert uses the *provision method* for recording bad debts.

Gross accounts receivable at 12/31	₹11,760
Allowance for bad debts at 12/31	138 credit
Net sales for 2013	75,200
Receivables written off during 2010	800

Required:

1. Prepare the journal entry that Lambert made during 2013 to write off the ₹800 in receivables.
2. Prepare the journal entry to record bad debt expense for 2013 if Lambert estimates that 1% of net sales will be uncollectible. Calculate the resulting net realizable value of receivables.
3. Prepare the journal entry to record bad debt expense for 2013 if Lambert estimates that 5% of receivables will be uncollectible. Calculate the resulting net realizable value of receivables.
4. Assume that instead of the provision method, Lambert uses the direct write-off method. What would Lambert recognize as bad debt expense for 2013?

Demonstration Problem Solution

1.	Accounts Receivable	800	
	Provision for Bad Debts		800
2.	Bad Debt Expense (₹75,200 × 1%)	752	
	Provision for Bad Debts		752
	<u>Net Realizable Value:</u>		
	Gross accounts receivable		₹11,760
	Less: Provision (₹138 + ₹752)		890
	Net realizable value		₹10,870
3.	Bad Debt Expense [(₹11,760 × 5%) − ₹138]	450	
	Provision for Bad Debts		450
	<u>Net Realizable Value:</u>		
	Gross accounts receivable		₹11,760
	Less: Provision		450
	Net realizable value		₹11,310
4.	The ₹800 that was written off during the year.		

Inventory

Learning Objectives

After studying the material in this chapter, you should be able to:

LO1 Describe inventory and how it is recorded, expensed, and reported.

LO2 Calculate the cost of goods sold using different inventory costing methods.

LO3 Understand the income and tax effects of inventory cost flow assumptions.

LO4 Analyze the effects of inventory errors.

LO5 Demonstrate how inventory is estimated.

LO6 Apply the lower-of-cost-or-market rule to inventory.

LO7 Evaluate inventory through the calculation of horizontal, vertical, and ratio analyses.

LO8 Appendix: Record purchases and calculate the cost of goods sold under a periodic system.

Introduction

This chapter examines the accounting for inventory. In particular, it examines how companies record their inventory and how they determine the cost of the inventory that is sold. It also examines how errors in inventory can affect income for multiple periods, how inventory can be estimated if needed, and how inventory must be adjusted if its market value falls below its cost. The chapter concludes with how to analyze a company's inventory position. The appendix covers inventory accounting under a periodic system.

LO1 Recording, Expensing, and Reporting Inventory

Inventory is a tangible resource that is held for resale in the normal course of operations. For a retailer, inventory is the merchandise on the shelves or in the warehouse. For a manufacturer, inventory also includes the raw materials and work in process related to producing a finished product. This chapter focuses exclusively on the merchandise inventory of a retailer. You will study the issues concerning raw materials, work in process, and finished goods when you take a managerial accounting course.

As you consider the definition of inventory, note that the phrase "intended for resale" differentiates inventory from other operational assets. A tractor that Caterpillar Corp. intends to sell is inventory, while an identical tractor used in Caterpillar's operations is a fixed asset. Furthermore, the phrase "in the normal course of operations" means that some assets for sale are not classified as inventory. For example, Wal-Mart may vacate a store to relocate within a community. Although the vacated building is put up for sale, it is not classified as inventory because Wal-Mart is not in the business of selling buildings.

Inventory A tangible resource that is held for resale in the normal course of operations.

CHAPTER 7

For a retailer, inventory is an important asset, and accounting for it properly affects both the balance sheet and the income statement.

© INDIATODAYIMAGES.COM

ACCT

Recording Inventory

Following the cost principle, inventory is recorded at its acquisition cost. This includes all costs incurred to get the inventory delivered and, if necessary, prepared for resale. It also includes any reductions granted by the vendor or supplier after purchase. Examples of items affecting the cost of inventory would include, but not be limited to, the following.

- purchase price
- taxes paid
- costs for shipping the product
- insurance during transit
- labor required to assemble the product
- returns to and allowances from the vendor
- purchase discounts from the vendor

For a retailer, inventory is the merchandise on the shelves or in the warehouse. For a manufacturer, inventory also includes the raw materials and work in process related to producing a finished product.

While inventory is recorded at cost, how it is recorded into the accounting system depends on the inventory system that a company uses. A **perpetual inventory system** updates the inventory account each time inventory is bought or sold—that is, perpetually. Therefore, purchases of inventory are recorded directly into the Inventory account. In contrast, a **periodic inventory system** updates the inventory account only at the end of an accounting period—that is, periodically. Instead of recording purchases into the inventory account, they are recorded in an account called Purchases, which is a temporary account that is closed into Inventory at the end of the period. This chapter will demonstrate inventory accounting under a perpetual system. The periodic system is demonstrated in the appendix to the chapter.

To illustrate the recording of inventory, suppose that Devon Gifts purchases ₹20,000 of inventory on account on October 10. The purchase would be recorded as follows:

Oct. 10	Inventory	20,000	
	Accounts Payable		20,000
	(To record purchase of inventory)		

Assets	=	Liabilities	+	Equity
+20,000		+20,000		

Perpetual inventory system Updates the inventory account each time inventory is bought or sold.

Periodic inventory system Updates the inventory account only at the end of an accounting period.

Both assets and liabilities increase as a result of this transaction.

In some cases, a company must pay for the transportation necessary to obtain the inventory. Such additional costs are called *transportation-in* and are added to the overall cost of the inventory or carriage inward. To illustrate, suppose that Devon pays a third-party carrier ₹300 to transport the inventory to its warehouse. Devon would record the payment with the following entry:

Oct. 10	Inventory	300	
	Cash		300
	(To record transportation-in)		

Assets	=	Liabilities	+	Equity
+300				
−300				

Sometimes, a company will return inventory to the vendor or seek some reduction in the cost of the inventory due to defective merchandise. The former is called a *purchase return*, while the latter is a *purchase allowance*. Both reduce the cost of the inventory purchased.

To illustrate, suppose that on October 12 Devon is granted a ₹1,000 reduction in the cost of the merchandise due to blemishes on the inventory. Even though Devon keeps the inventory, its cost has decreased due to the purchase allowance. Therefore, Devon would reduce the cost of the inventory and its payable to the vendor with the following entry:

Oct. 12	Accounts Payable	1,000	
	Inventory		1,000
	(To record purchase allowance granted by vendor)		

Assets	=	Liabilities	+	Equity
−1,000		−1,000		

In addition to returns and allowances, companies sometimes receive discounts from vendors if payment is made within a certain time period. Such *purchase discounts* reduce the cost of the inventory. To illustrate, suppose that Devon pays its remaining ₹19,000 bill to the vendor on October 15, which qualifies Devon for a 1% discount. As a result, Devon would save ₹190 (₹19,000 × 1%) and pay only ₹18,810. The entry to record payment would be as follows:

Oct. 15	Accounts Payable	19,000	
	Inventory		190
	Cash		18,810
	(To record payment)		

Assets	=	Liabilities	+	Equity
−190		−19,000		
−18,810				

The entry decreases Accounts Payable for the full ₹19,000 (since the debt is paid in full) and decreases Cash for the ₹18,810 payment. The difference is a reduction to Inventory because the purchase discount of ₹190 has reduced the cost of the inventory. Both assets and liabilities decrease.

Given the preceding activity, Devon's *net purchases* of inventory can be calculated as follows:

Gross purchases	₹20,000
Add: Transportation-in	300
Less: Purchase returns and allowances	(1,000)
Purchase discounts	(190)
Net purchases	₹19,110

Expensing Inventory

Inventory becomes an expense when it is sold. The account Cost of Goods Sold or Cost of Sales is used to capture the amount of inventory expensed during a period. Like the recording of inventory purchases, the recording of cost of goods sold depends on a company's inventory system. Under a perpetual system, cost of goods sold is updated each time inventory is sold—that is, perpetually. Under a periodic system, cost of goods sold is calculated and recorded only at the end of the period—that is, periodically. Again, this chapter will demonstrate inventory accounting under a perpetual system, with the periodic system demonstrated in the appendix to the chapter.

To illustrate the recording of cost of goods sold, suppose that on November 2 Devon sells inventory costing ₹400 for ₹600 cash. Devon would record the sale with the following two entries:

Nov. 2	Cash	600	
	Sales		600
	(To record sale of inventory)		

Assets	=	Liabilities	+	Equity
+600				+600

Nov. 2	Cost of Goods Sold	400	
	Inventory		400
	(To record sale of inventory)		

Assets	=	Liabilities	+	Equity
−400				−400

The first entry records the effect of the sale on Devon's cash and revenues. Both Cash and Sales increase for the amount of the sale. As a result, both assets and equity increase by ₹600.

The second entry records the effect of the sale on Devon's inventory and expenses. Cost of Goods Sold increases for the cost of the inventory sold. Inventory decreases for the same amount. As a result, both assets and equity decrease by ₹400.

The net effect of both entries on assets and equity is a ₹200 increase, which is equal to the profit that Devon earned on the sale.

Reporting Inventory and Cost of Goods Sold

Inventory is expected to be sold within a year. Therefore, it is reported on the balance sheet as a current asset. Because cost of goods sold is usually a large and important expense for a retailer, it is normally reported as a separate line item on the income statement just below sales.

To illustrate, consider the following excerpts from Wal-Mart's 2010 balance sheet and income statement.

As you might expect from the world's largest retailer, inventory is an important asset. Wal-Mart reported Inventories of over $36 billion at the end of 2010—by far its largest current asset. It also reported over $315 billion in Cost of Sales for 2010, by far its largest expense. The same importance is seen in the 2010 financial statements of Wal-Mart's smaller but fierce rival, Target. Target reported $7.5 billion in inventory, and cost of sales of $45.7 billion is easily its largest expense.

Because cost of goods sold is usually a large expense for a retailer, it is normally reported separately on the income statement.

Excerpts from Wal-Mart's 2010 Financial Statements

amounts in millions	
Current Assets	
Cash and Cash Equivalents	$ 7,395
Receivables	5,089
Inventories	36,318
Prepaid Expenses and Other	2,960
Current Assets of Discontinued Operations	131
Total Current Assets	$ 51,893
Income Statement	
Revenues:	
Net Sales	$4,18,952
Membership and Other Income	2,897
Total Revenues	$4,21,849
Cost and expenses:	
Cost of Sales	$3,15,287
Operating, Selling, General and Admin. Expenses	81,020
Operating income	$ 25,542

LO2 Inventory Costing Methods

The previous section demonstrated the manner in which inventory and cost of goods sold are recorded under a perpetual system. When a sale is made, inventory is decreased and cost of goods sold is increased for the cost of the inventory that is sold. This

© ISTOCKPHOTO.COM/QUAVONDO

section demonstrates how companies determine the cost of the inventory sold.

To determine the cost of inventory sold, companies can use one of the following four inventory costing methods.

- specific identification
- first-in, first-out (FIFO)
- last-in, first-out (LIFO)
- moving average

To illustrate each method, the following example will be used. Suppose that Nell Farms sells a specialty maple syrup that it purchases from Waverly Manufacturing. During the month of September, Nell experiences the following inventory activity:

		Units	Unit Cost	Total
Sept. 1	Beginning Inventory	40	₹12	₹480
Sept. 4	Purchase	60	₹13	₹780
Sept. 10	Sale	(65)		
Sept. 15	Purchase	30	₹14	₹420
Sept. 23	Purchase	45	₹15	₹675
Sept. 30	Sale	(50)		

MARUTI SUZUKI ANALYSIS

Look at Maruti Suzuki's balance sheet and income statement in Appendix C. What name does the company use for its inventory and cost of goods sold? Is inventory the company's largest current asset? What is its cost? Is cost of goods sold the company's largest expense?

Maruti Suzuki uses the names Inventories and its cost of Goods Sold includes Consumption of Cost of Materials Consumed, Purchase of Stock-in-Trade and Change in Inventories of Finished Goods, Work-in-Progress, and Stock-in-Trade. Inventories are the company's second largest current asset and fourth largest asset only to Fixed Assets, Current Investments, Noncurrent Investments. Their cost is ₹18,407 million. Cost of Sales of ₹3,25,588 (₹3,05,741 + 19,613 + 234) is by far the largest expense of the company.

Specific Identification

The **specific identification method** determines cost of goods sold based on the actual cost of each inventory item sold. To use this method, a retailer must know which inventory item is sold and the exact cost of that particular item. As a result, the method is most likely to be used by companies whose inventory is unique. Examples might include an antiques store or a fine jeweler.

For illustration purposes, suppose that Nell specifically identifies each of its inventory items and provides the detailed inventory activity as shown in Exhibit 7-1.

Exhibit 7-1 shows that the September 10 sale consisted of thirty ₹12 units and thirty-five ₹13 units for a total cost of ₹815. The September 30 sale consisted of ten ₹12 units, twenty ₹13 units, ten ₹14 units, and ten ₹15 units, for a total cost of ₹670. Together, cost of goods sold for September is ₹1,485 (₹815 + ₹670). The 60 units remaining in ending inventory, as shown in the bottom right corner of Exhibit 7-1, have a cost of ₹870.

Because most companies cannot track the actual cost of every inventory item that is sold, they cannot use the specific identification method. Instead, they must make an *assumption* about the cost of inventory sold. They can assume that the cost of the inventory sold is the cost of the first unit purchased, the last unit purchased, or an average of all purchases. Each of these three assumptions is described as follows.

IFRS

International accounting standards do not allow the LIFO method in determining the cost of goods sold and inventory.

Specific identification method Determines cost of goods sold based on the actual cost of each inventory item sold.

Exhibit 7-1 Calculations for Specific Identification Method

	Transaction	Inventory Purchased			Inventory Sold			Inventory on Hand		
Sept. 1	Beginning Inventory							40	₹12	₹ 480
Sept. 4	Purchase #1	60	₹13	₹780				40	₹12	₹ 480
								60	₹13	780
								100		₹1,260
Sept. 10	Sell 65 units				30	₹12	₹360	10	₹12	₹ 120
					35	₹13	455	25	₹13	325
					65		₹815	35		₹ 445
Sept. 15	Purchase #2	30	₹14	₹420				10	₹12	₹ 120
								25	₹13	325
								30	₹14	420
								65		₹ 865
Sept. 23	Purchase #3	45	₹15	₹675				10	₹12	₹ 120
								25	₹13	325
								30	₹14	420
								45	₹15	675
								110		₹1,540
Sept. 30	Sell 50 units				10	₹12	₹120	0	₹12	₹ 0
					20	₹13	260	5	₹13	65
					10	₹14	140	20	₹14	280
					10	₹15	150	35	₹15	525
					50		₹670	60		₹ 870

First-In, First-Out (FIFO)

The **first-in, first-out (FIFO) method** calculates cost of goods sold based on the assumption that the first unit of inventory available for sale is the first unit sold. That is, inventory is assumed to be sold in the order that it is purchased. For most companies, the FIFO assumption matches the actual physical flow of their inventory. However, companies are not required to choose the assumption that matches their physical flow.

Exhibit 7-2 illustrates the calculation of cost of goods sold under the FIFO method.

At each sale, the FIFO method requires Nell to assign the costs of the first units purchased to cost of goods sold. On September 10, Nell sold 65 units. It therefore assumes that it sold all 40 units of beginning inventory and 25 of the units in Purchase #1. The total cost of those 65 units was ₹805.

For the September 30 sale, Nell assumes that it sold the 35 units remaining from Purchase #1 and 15 units of Purchase #2. The total cost of those 50 units was ₹665.

As a result of these two calculations, cost of goods sold for September is ₹1,470 (₹805 + ₹665). The 60 units remaining in ending inventory, as shown in the bottom right corner of Exhibit 7-2, have a cost of ₹885.

First-in, first-out method Calculates cost of goods sold based on the assumption that the first unit of inventory available for sale is the first unit sold.

Last-in, first-out method Calculates cost of goods sold based on the assumption that the last unit of inventory available for sale is the first unit sold.

Last-In, First-Out (LIFO)

The **last-in, first-out (LIFO) method** calculates cost of goods sold based on the assumption that the last unit of inventory available for sale is the first unit sold. That is, inventory is assumed to be sold in the opposite order of its purchase. Exhibit 7-3 illustrates the calculations under the LIFO method.

At each sale, the LIFO method requires Nell to assign the costs of the last or most recent units purchased to cost of goods sold. On September 10, Nell sold 65 units. It therefore assumes that it sold all 60 units of Purchase #1 and 5 of the units from

Exhibit 7-2 Calculations for FIFO Method

	Transaction	Inventory Purchased			Inventory Sold			Inventory on Hand		
Sept. 1	Beginning Inventory							40	₹12	₹ 480
Sept. 4	Purchase #1	60	₹13	₹780				40 60 100	₹12 ₹13	₹ 480 780 ₹1,260
Sept. 10	Sell 65 units				40 25 65	₹12 ₹13	₹480 325 ₹805	0 35 35	₹12 ₹13	₹ 0 455 ₹ 455
Sept. 15	Purchase #2	30	₹14	₹420				35 30 65	₹13 ₹14	₹ 455 420 ₹ 875
Sept. 23	Purchase #3	45	₹15	₹675				35 30 45 110	₹13 ₹14 ₹15	₹ 455 420 675 ₹1,550
Sept. 30	Sell 50 units				35 15 50	₹13 ₹14	₹455 210 ₹665	0 15 45 60	₹13 ₹14 ₹15	₹ 0 210 675 ₹ 885

Exhibit 7-3 Calculations for LIFO Method

	Transaction	Inventory Purchased			Inventory Sold			Inventory on Hand		
Sept. 1	Beginning Inventory							40	₹12	₹ 480
Sept. 4	Purchase #1	60	₹13	₹780				40	₹12	₹ 480
								60	₹13	780
								100		₹1,260
Sept. 10	Sell 65 units				5	₹12	₹ 60	35	₹12	₹ 420
					60	₹13	780	0	₹13	0
					65		₹840	35		₹ 420
Sept. 15	Purchase #2	30	₹14	₹420				35	₹12	₹ 420
								30	₹14	420
								65		₹ 840
Sept. 23	Purchase #3	45	₹15	₹675				35	₹12	₹ 420
								30	₹14	420
								45	₹15	675
								110		₹1,515
Sept. 30	Sell 50 units				5	₹14	₹ 70	35	₹12	₹ 420
								25	₹14	350
					45	₹15	675	0	₹15	0
					50		₹745	60		₹ 770

beginning inventory. The total cost of those 65 units was ₹840.

For the September 30 sale, Nell assumes that it sold all 45 units of Purchase #3 and 5 units of Purchase #2. The total cost of those 50 units was ₹745.

As a result, cost of goods sold for September is ₹1,585 (₹840 + ₹745). Ending inventory, as shown in the bottom right corner of Exhibit 7-3, has a cost of ₹770.

Moving Average

The **moving average method** calculates cost of goods sold based on the average unit cost of all inventory available for sale. That is, the cost of each inventory item sold is assumed to be the average cost of all inventory available for sale at that time.

To calculate cost of goods sold at each sale date, a retailer must calculate the average unit cost of the inventory available for sale on that date. This calculation is conducted as follows:

$$\text{Average Unit Cost} = \frac{\text{Cost of Goods Available for Sale}}{\text{Units Available for Sale}}$$

Once the average unit cost is known, it is multiplied by the units sold to determine cost of goods sold. Exhibit 7-4 contains Nell's calculations under the moving average method. Note that the average unit cost is rounded to the nearest paise, while inventory sold and inventory on hand is rounded to the nearest rupee.

At the September 10 sale, Nell has 100 units available for sale at a total cost of ₹1,260. Therefore, the average unit cost is ₹12.60 (₹1,260 ÷ 100). Nell uses that unit cost to determine the costs of the inventory sold and the inventory that remains. Having sold 65 units, Nell's cost of goods sold on September 10 is ₹819 (65 × ₹12.60). The cost of the 35 units on hand after the sale is therefore ₹441 (35 × ₹12.60).

For the September 30 sale, Nell must recalculate the average unit cost because it has purchased additional units of inventory. This is why the term "moving average" is used—because the average cost per unit can change during the period as new purchases are made.

Moving average method Calculates cost of goods sold based on the average unit cost of all inventory available for sale.

Exhibit 7-4 Calculations for Moving Average Method

	Transaction	Inventory Purchased			Inventory Sold			Inventory on Hand		
Sept. 1	Beginning Inventory							40	₹12.00	₹ 480
Sept. 4	Purchase #1	60	₹13	₹780				40	₹12.00	₹ 480
								60	₹13.00	780
								100		₹1,260
Sept. 10	Sell 65 units				65	₹12.60	₹819	35	₹12.60	₹ 441
Sept. 15	Purchase #2	30	₹14	₹420				35	₹12.60	₹ 441
								30	₹14.00	420
								65		₹ 861
Sept. 23	Purchase #3	45	₹15	₹675				35	₹12.60	₹ 441
								30	₹14.00	420
								45	₹15.00	675
								110		₹1,536
Sept. 30	Sell 50 units				50	₹13.96	₹698	60	₹13.96	₹ 838

At September 30, Nell has 110 units available for sale at a total cost of ₹1,536. Therefore, the new average unit cost, rounded to the nearest paise, is ₹13.96 (₹1,536 ÷ 110). Having sold 50 units, Nell's cost of goods sold on September 30 is ₹698 (50 × ₹13.96).

As a result of these two calculations, cost of goods sold for September is ₹1,517 (₹819 + ₹698). Ending inventory, as shown in the bottom right corner of Exhibit 7-4, has an average unit cost of ₹13.96, for a total cost of ₹838 (60 × ₹13.96).

LO3 Comparing Inventory Costing Methods

The previous sections show that a company's choice of inventory costing methods affects both its cost of goods sold and its ending inventory. To summarize these effects, Exhibit 7-5 puts Nell's inventory data in a form known as the cost of goods sold model and compares the results of each of the three cost flow assumptions. The specific identification method is omitted from the comparison because of its infrequent use.

MARUTI SUZUKI ANALYSIS

Look at the Inventories paragraph of Maruti Suzuki's first note in Appendix C. What cost flow assumption does the company use? As a result, which inventory units are represented by the `₹18,407 million balance on the company's balance sheet, and which units are represented by the ₹3,25,588 (₹3,05,741 + 19,613 + 234) million cost of sales on the company's income statement?

Note 1.7 indicates that the company uses the weighted average and net realizable value methods. Therefore, the ₹18,407 million balance in inventory represents the average inventory units that the company possesses. The ₹3,25,588 million balance in the cost of sales represents the weighted average cost of the inventory units purchased.

Exhibit 7-5 Comparison of Inventory Costing Methods

	Units	FIFO	Moving Average	LIFO
Beginning Inventory	40	₹ 480	₹ 480	₹ 480
Add: Net Purchases	135	1,875	1,875	1,875
Cost of Goods Available for Sale	175	₹2,355	₹2,355	₹2,355
Less: Ending Inventory	60	885	838	770
Cost of Goods Sold	115	₹1,470	₹1,517	₹1,585

Because inventory costing methods affect both income statement and balance sheet accounts, a company must disclose the method that it uses. It must also use the same method consistently.

The cost of goods sold model summarizes a company's inventory activity during a period by adding purchases to beginning inventory to yield cost of goods available for sale. This represents the total cost of the inventory that could have been sold during the period. That cost is then allocated to either what was sold (cost of goods sold) or what was not sold (ending inventory).

In Nell's case, it began the month of September with 40 units costing ₹480 and bought an additional 135 units costing ₹1,875 during the month. So, it could have sold up to 175 units with a total cost of ₹2,355. This is the case regardless of the inventory costing system chosen. However, the cost of the 115 units sold and the 60 units unsold depends on the cost flow assumption.

The FIFO method assigns the costs of the first and, in this case, less expensive units purchased to cost of goods sold, thereby yielding the lowest cost of goods sold. It also assigns the costs of the last and more expensive units to ending inventory, thereby yielding the highest ending inventory.

In contrast, the LIFO method assigns the costs of the last and, in this case, more expensive units to cost of goods sold, resulting in the highest cost of goods sold. The costs of the first and less expensive units are assigned to ending inventory, resulting in the lowest ending inventory.

The moving average assigns the average costs of all units purchased to cost of goods sold. Therefore, it yields cost of goods sold and ending inventory that fall in between the FIFO and LIFO extremes.

When a company experiences rising prices for its inventory, these relative differences will continue. These relationships are summarized as follows:

	Ending Inventory	Cost of Goods Sold
FIFO yields:	Highest	Lowest
Moving average yields:	Middle	Middle
LIFO yields:	Lowest	Highest

Because of these differences in both income statement accounts and balance sheet accounts, a company must disclose the inventory costing method that it uses. It must also use the same method consistently. These requirements allow for meaningful comparisons of inventory activity across different companies and across different periods within the same company.

While companies can use any of the four costing methods, some choose the LIFO method because of the resulting tax deferral. A **tax deferral** is a temporary delay in the payment of income taxes. Tax deferrals are beneficial because a company can keep and use its cash for a longer period of time.

To illustrate, suppose that Nell generated revenues of ₹5,240 from its sale of inventory during September. Suppose further that Nell incurred ₹1,850 in operating expenses during the month and that it is subject to a tax rate of 40%. Exhibit 7-6 contains comparative multi-step income statements prepared under each inventory costing method.

Exhibit 7-6 Comparative Income Statements

	FIFO	Moving Average	LIFO
Sales	₹5,240	₹ 5,240	₹5,240
Cost of goods sold	(1,470)	(1,517)	(1,585)
Gross margin	₹3,770	₹ 3,723	₹3,655
Operating expenses	(1,850)	(1,850)	(1,850)
Income before taxes	₹1,920	₹1,873	₹1,805
Income taxes (40%)	(768)	(749)	(722)
Net income	₹1,152	₹1,124	₹1,083

Tax deferral A temporary delay in the payment of income taxes.

Comparing the income tax obligations under the LIFO and FIFO assumptions (which are the two extremes), you can see that Nell can defer ₹46 in taxes (₹768 − ₹722) if it uses the LIFO method rather than the FIFO method. In other words, it can write a ₹722 check to the taxing authority instead of a ₹768 check. Keep in mind, though, that this deferral is only temporary. If Nell sold its entire inventory in the next period, the deferral would be eliminated.

The general amount of tax deferral a company generates from using LIFO can be determined from information found in the notes to the financial statements. Companies that use the LIFO method must disclose the LIFO reserve. The **LIFO reserve** is the difference between the inventory reported on the balance sheet and what inventory would be if reported on a FIFO basis. The reserve is cumulative, meaning that it represents the cumulative difference between LIFO and FIFO over the years. Thus, the amount of taxes deferred can be calculated by multiplying the reserve by the company's tax rate.

To illustrate, consider the following excerpt from Safeway's (USA) 2010 inventory note.

Excerpts from Safeway's 2010 Inventory Note

Merchandise inventory of $1,685 million at year-end 2010 and $1,629 million at year-end 2009 is valued . . . on a last-in, first-out ("LIFO") basis. . . . Such LIFO inventory had a replacement or current cost of $1,720 million at year-end 2010 and $1,692 million at year-end 2009. The FIFO cost of inventory approximates the replacement or current cost.

The note explains that while Safeway's inventory balance as determined under the LIFO method was $1,685 million at the end of 2010, the balance would have been $1,720 had the company used the FIFO method. Therefore, Safeway's 2010 LIFO reserve in millions is calculated as follows:

	2010
Inventories valued at FIFO	$1,720
Inventories valued at LIFO	1,685
LIFO reserve	$ 35

Assuming a tax rate of 30%, the taxes that Safeway has deferred as of the end of 2010 are $10.5 million ($35 × 30%).

LIFO reserve The difference between the LIFO inventory reported on the balance sheet and what inventory would be if reported on a FIFO basis.

LO4 Inventory Errors

Under a perpetual inventory system, the inventory account is updated each time inventory is bought or sold. However, most companies take a physical count of inventory at least once a year to confirm that the inventory balance from the accounting system matches the actual inventory on hand. Taking a physical inventory is an example of an internal control procedure discussed in Chapter 5. By counting inventory, a company can determine if it has lost inventory due to theft, damage, or errors in accounting.

Errors in the counting of inventory affect both the balance sheet (through inventory) and the income statement (through cost of goods sold). Moreover, because ending inventory in one period becomes beginning inventory in the next period, an error can affect not only the current period, but also the next period. To understand the effect of errors, consider the following scenario.

Suppose that Baggett Company has 3,000 units of inventory on January 1, 2012, and purchases an additional 34,000 units during the year. Included in those purchases are 1,000 units that ship on December 30. According to the shipping terms, Baggett owns the units while in transit, so they are properly included in its purchases. However, when Baggett counts its inventory on December 31, 2012, the 1,000 units are erroneously omitted from the count.

To demonstrate the effect of this error, the information is put into the cost of goods sold model. For simplicity purposes, each unit of inventory is assumed to cost Baggett ₹1.

In the year of the error (2012)

	Correct	As Counted	Effect
Beginning inventory	₹ 3,000	₹ 3,000	Not affected
Add: Net purchases	34,000	34,000	Not affected
Cost of goods available for sale	₹37,000	₹37,000	Not affected
Less: Ending inventory	4,000	5,000	Understated
Cost of goods sold	₹33,000	₹32,000	Overstated

The model shows that the counting error does not affect beginning inventory or purchases during 2012. These were recorded correctly. However, because 1,000 units were incorrectly omitted from the count, ending inventory of 4,000 units is understated by 1,000 units.

By counting inventory, a company can determine if it has lost inventory due to theft, damage, or errors in accounting.

This, in turn, results in the cost of goods sold being calculated at 33,000 units, which is an overstatement of 1,000 units. In the period of the error, assets are understated by ₹1,000 and cost of goods sold is overstated by ₹1,000. As a result, net income, and therefore equity, are also understated by ₹1,000.

The effect of the counting error is not limited to the year of the error. Because Baggett's ending inventory becomes beginning inventory in the next period, the effects of the 2012 counting error spill into 2013. To demonstrate, suppose that in 2013 Baggett purchases an additional 41,000 units of inventory and properly counts ending inventory at 6,000 units. The following cost of goods sold model shows how the error in 2012 affects 2013, even though no error is made in 2013.

In the period after the error (2013)

	Correct	As Counted	Effect
Beginning inventory	₹ 4,000	₹ 5,000	Understated
Add: Net purchases	41,000	41,000	Not affected
Cost of goods available for sale	₹45,000	₹46,000	Understated
Less: Ending inventory	6,000	6,000	Unaffected
Cost of goods sold	₹39,000	₹40,000	Understated

Beginning inventory of 4,000 units for 2013 is understated by 1,000 units. As a result, the 45,000 units of inventory available for sale is also understated by 1,000 units. If ending inventory for 2013 is properly counted, then the 39,000 units of inventory sold are understated by the same 1,000 units. If it is assumed that all units were purchased for ₹1 each, then the cost of goods sold model shows that the ending inventory account has the correct balance of ₹6,000, while the cost of goods sold balance is understated by ₹1,000 (₹39,000 versus the correct ₹40,000 balance). Thus, while the balance sheet in 2013 is not affected by the 2012 counting error (since inventory is now correctly counted), the 2013 income statement is affected since the beginning inventory value in the cost of goods sold model is understated.

The preceding scenario is an example of a counterbalancing inventory error. A counterbalancing error is an error whose effect on net income is corrected in the period after the error. Note that there was only one error in this scenario—the failure to include 1,000 units of inventory in the final inventory count of 2012. However, the error affected cost of goods sold in two years.

In 2012, cost of goods sold was overstated by ₹1,000 because *ending* inventory was incorrect. Cost of goods sold was reported as ₹33,000 when it should have been ₹32,000. In 2013, cost of goods sold was understated by ₹1,000 because *beginning* inventory was incorrect. Cost of goods sold was reported as ₹39,000 when it should have been ₹40,000. The overstatement in cost of goods sold in 2012 was followed by an equal understatement in 2013. In this way, the inventory error is counterbalancing.

The effects of such errors on inventory, cost of goods sold, and related financial measures are listed in in Exhibit 7-7.

Not all inventory errors are counterbalancing. For example, if a particular warehouse of inventory is not counted year after year, the error will not work itself out. However, a discussion of noncounterbalancing errors will be left to more advanced accounting courses.

Exhibit 7-7 Effect of Inventory Errors

	If inventory is understated		If inventory is overstated	
	Current period	Next period	Current period	Next period
Inventory	Understated	Correct	Overstated	Correct
Cost of goods sold	Overstated	Understated	Understated	Overstated
Net income	Understated	Overstated	Overstated	Understated
Total assets	Understated	Correct	Overstated	Correct

LO5 Estimating Ending Inventory

A company must sometimes estimate its inventory balance. One example is when inventory is destroyed by a natural catastrophe. Another example is when a company prepares interim financial statements. In such cases, a company can estimate its ending inventory with the gross profit method.

The **gross profit method** of estimating inventory uses a company's gross profit percentage to estimate cost of goods sold and then ending inventory. To apply the method, a company first subtracts its normal gross profit from its sales to yield an estimate of its cost of goods sold. That estimate is then put into the cost of goods sold model to estimate ending inventory.

To illustrate, assume that Alsup Hardware is preparing interim financial statements at the end of its first quarter and needs to estimate cost of goods sold and ending inventory. Alsup has generated quarterly sales of ₹4,00,000. In past quarters, Alsup's gross profit percentage has averaged 45%. Assuming that this quarter is similar to prior quarters, Alsup can estimate that gross profit on current-quarter sales is ₹1,80,000.

Current quarter sales (actual)	₹4,00,000
Historical gross profit percentage	× 45%
Gross profit (estimated)	₹1,80,000

Gross profit method A method of estimating inventory using a company's gross profit percentage to estimate cost of goods sold and then ending inventory.

A company must sometimes estimate its inventory balance. One example is when inventory is destroyed by a natural catastrophe. Another example is when a company prepares interim financial statements.

Alsup can then estimate cost of goods sold for the period as ₹2,20,000.

Current quarter sales (actual)	₹4,00,000
Gross profit (estimated)	(1,80,000)
Cost of goods sold (estimated)	₹2,20,000

Now that Alsup has estimated cost of goods sold, it can calculate its ending inventory by plugging the cost of goods sold estimate into the cost of goods sold model. Based on past financial reports and purchase records, Alsup knows that it started the quarter with ₹2,00,000 in inventory and bought ₹90,000 of inventory during the quarter. This means that Alsup had ₹2,90,000 in inventory available for sale during the period. With ₹2,20,000 in estimated cost of goods sold, the cost of goods sold model yields a ₹70,000 estimate for ending inventory.

Beginning inventory (actual)	₹2,00,000
Add: Net purchases (actual)	90,000
Cost of goods available for sale (actual)	₹2,90,000
Less: Cost of goods sold (estimated)	(2,20,000)
Ending inventory (estimated)	₹ 70,000

MAKING IT REAL

Inventory errors can originate from many different sources. Consider what happened at Winnebago Industries in its second quarter of 2005. During a review of its physical inventory counts, it was determined that a formula in an electronic worksheet was incorrect. The error in the formula resulted in an overstatement of quarter-ending inventory of approximately $2.8 million, which led to an equal understatement of cost of goods sold for the quarter. The error in cost of goods sold resulted in a $1.8 million after-tax overstatement of quarterly earnings. Since actual earnings were $12.6 million and reported earnings were $14.4 million, the mistake was a 14% overstatement of actual earnings. After finding the problem, the company corrected its financial statements and released them to the public with a statement that the previously released financial statements could not be relied upon due to the inventory counting error.

LO6 Lower-of-Cost-or-Market

The cost principle requires that inventory be recorded at its cost. However, because of the principle of conservatism, accounting rules require that inventory be reported on the balance sheet at its market value if the market value is lower than the inventory's cost. This is known as the **lower-of-cost-or-market (LCM) rule**.

The lower-of-cost-or-market rule is applied at the end of each accounting period by comparing inventory costs to market values. For purposes of our comparison, an inventory's market value is equal to the cost to replace the inventory. Companies have some discretion in how LCM is applied. For example, they can compare costs and market values of (1) inventories in total, (2) major groups of inventories, or (3) individual inventory items. When the cost is lower than the market value, nothing further is done. However, when the market value is lower than the cost, the company must adjust its inventory down to the lower market value.

To illustrate, suppose that Jeet Enterprise provides the March 31 inventory information shown in Exhibit 7-8.

IFRS

Under Indian and US GAAP, an LCM inventory adjustment cannot be reversed.
Under international standards, an LCM adjustment can be reversed if the reason(s) for the adjustment no longer exists.

Exhibit 7-8 LCM Calculation for Jeet Enterprise as of March 31

Item	Units	Unit Cost	Unit Market	Total Cost	Total Market	Total	Two Groups	Individual Items
A	5	₹ 40	₹ 80	₹ 200	₹ 400			₹ 200
B	8	₹ 65	₹ 50	520	400			400
Group 1				₹ 720	₹ 800		₹ 720	
C	4	₹100	₹160	₹ 400	₹ 640			400
D	10	₹ 30	₹ 50	300	500			300
Group 2				₹ 700	₹1,140		700	
Total				₹1,420	₹1,940	₹1,420	₹1,420	₹1,300

Jeet Enterprise has four types of inventory (A, B, C, and D) separated into two groups (1 and 2). Cost and market values are computed for each inventory type, each inventory group, and total inventory. The three right columns show the value that should be reported for inventory when applying LCM to total inventories, to the two groups of inventory, and to each individual inventory item.

When applied to total inventories, the total cost of ₹1,420 is lower than the total market value of ₹1,940. Therfore, the LCM value for the total inventory is the cost of ₹1,420, and no adjustment to the inventory is needed.

When applied to Groups 1 and 2, the ₹720 and ₹700 group costs are lower than the respective group market values of ₹800 and ₹1,140. Therefore, the LCM value of ₹1,420, and no adjustment to inventory is needed.

When applied to individual items, an adjustment is needed. The comparison of cost and market values of each item yields an LCM value of ₹1,300. Since this is lower than the inventory's cost of ₹1,420, the inventory must be adjusted down to ₹1,300. This is accomplished with the following entry:

Dec. 31	Cost of Goods Sold	120	
	Inventory		120
	(To adjust inventory to market)		

Assets	=	Liabilities	+	Equity
−120				−120

The journal entry increases Cost of Goods Sold to reflect the loss in value of the inventory and decreases Inventory to adjust the account down to the ₹1,300 market value. As a result, both assets and equity decrease. Jeet Enterprise's inventory is now ready to be reported on the balance sheet at its more conservative market value.

Lower-of-cost-or-market rule Requires inventory to be reported on the balance sheet at its market value if the market value is lower than the inventory's cost.

Any investor, creditor, or manager of a company should be interested in how well a company manages its inventory. A company manages its inventory by buying and selling efficiently and effectively.

LO7 Evaluating a Company's Management of Inventory

Any investor, creditor, or manager of a company should be interested in how well a company manages its inventory. A company manages its inventory by buying and selling efficiently and effectively.

The following sections examine the effectiveness of Target Corporation, USA in managing its inventory. The examination will require information from the company's balance sheet and income statement. The required information is found in Exhibit 7-9, excerpted from Target's 2010 annual report.

Exhibit 7-9 Account Balances from Target's 2010 Annual Report

Source	Accounts	2010	2009
Income Statement	Net sales	$65,786	$63,435
	Cost of sales	$45,725	$44,062
Balance Sheet	Inventory	$ 7,596	$ 7,179
	Total assets	$43,705	$44,533

Horizontal and Vertical Analyses

An easy and useful place to start an examination of inventory is with horizontal and vertical analyses. Recall from Chapter 2 that horizontal analysis calculates the rupee change in an account balance, defined as the current-year balance less the prior-year balance, and divides that change by the prior-year balance to yield the percentage change. Vertical analysis divides each account balance by a base account, yielding a percentage. The base account is total assets for balance sheet accounts and net sales or total revenues for income statement accounts. These calculations are summarized as follows:

Horizontal Analysis

$$\text{Dollar/Rupee change in account balance} = \text{Current-year balance} - \text{Prior-year balance}$$

$$\text{Percentage change in account balance} = \frac{\text{Dollar/Rupee change}}{\text{Prior-year balance}}$$

Vertical Analysis

Balance Sheet / *Income Statement*

$$\text{Percentage} = \frac{\text{Account Balance}}{\text{Total Assets}} \text{ or } \frac{\text{Account Balance}}{\text{Net Sales or Revenue}}$$

Given Target's financial information in Exhibit 7-9, horizontal and vertical analyses of inventory and cost of sales result in the following.

Horizontal Analysis

	Change	Percentage Change
Inventory	7,596 − 7,179 = 417	$\frac{417}{7,179} = 5.8\%$
Cost of sales	45,725 − 44,062 = 1,663	$\frac{1,663}{44,062} = 3.8\%$

Vertical Analysis

	2010	2009
Inventory	$\frac{7,596}{43,705} = 17.4\%$	$\frac{7,179}{44,533} = 16.1\%$
Cost of sales	$\frac{45,725}{65,786} = 69.5\%$	$\frac{44,062}{63,435} = 69.5\%$

MARUTI SUZUKI ANALYSIS

Look at Maruti Suzuki's inventory note in Appendix C. Does it follow the lower-of-cost-or-market rule?

Maruti Suzuki discloses that its inventory is reported at the lower-of-cost-or-market value. Cost is determined on a weighted average basis and net realizable value.

The calculations show a fairly stable inventory position. Horizontal analysis of inventory shows a \$417 million, or 5.8%, increase from 2009 to 2010. Vertical analysis indicates that inventories made up 16.1% of Target's total assets in 2009 and 17.4% of the total assets in 2010. So, inventory is growing both in total and as a percentage of assets.

The analysis of cost of goods sold shows an increase of \$1,663 million, which equals a 3.8% increase. Furthermore, vertical analysis indicates that cost of goods sold was 69.5% of sales in both 2009 and 2010. Thus, while the cost of goods sold increased during during the year, Target kept its cost of goods sold as a percentage of sales steady, which is a good sign.

For comparison purposes, the 2010 horizontal and vertical analyses of Wal-Mart are listed in Exhibit 7-10. While the horizontal analysis shows similar changes between the two companies, the vertical analysis shows a significant difference. The cost of goods sold as a percentage of sales is 69.5% for Target and 75.3% for Wal-Mart. Since a lower percentage means greater profits on sales, the comparison shows that Target outperformed Wal-Mart in 2010. This is a good sign.

Exhibit 7-10 Target versus Wal-Mart Comparison

	Account	Horizontal Analysis	Vertical Analysis
Target	*Inventory*	5.8%	16.1%
	Cost of goods sold	3.8%	69.5%
Wal-Mart	*Inventory*	11.0%	20.1%
	Cost of goods sold	3.6%	75.3%

Inventory Turnover Ratio

While horizontal and vertical analyses are useful for generating information about inventory, a more direct way to assess a company's ability to sell its inventory is to calculate the inventory turnover ratio. The **inventory turnover ratio** compares the cost of goods sold during a period to the average inventory balance during that period. It is calculated as follows:

$$\text{Inventory Turnover Ratio} = \frac{\text{Cost of Goods Sold}}{\text{Average Inventory}}$$

Where average inventory is:

$$\frac{\text{Beginning Inventory} + \text{Ending Inventory}}{2}$$

Because this ratio compares the cost of all inventory sold to the average cost of inventory on hand, it indicates how many times a company is able to sell its inventory balance in a period. All other things being equal, a higher ratio indicates that the company sold more inventory while maintaining less inventory on hand. This means that the company generated more sales revenue while reducing the costs of stocking inventory on the shelves.

Target's 2010 inventory turnover ratio is calculated as follows.

$$\frac{45{,}725}{(7{,}596 + 7{,}179) \div 2} = 6.2$$

The 6.2 ratio indicates that Target's cost of goods sold for 2010 was 6.2 times its average inventory balance. For every dollar of inventory on its shelves, on average, Target was able to sell over \$6.00 of inventory during the period.

Because the turnover ratio is sometimes difficult to interpret, it is often converted into the days-in-inventory ratio. The **days-in-inventory ratio** converts the inventory turnover ratio into a measure of days by dividing the

Inventory turnover ratio Compares cost of goods sold during a period to the average inventory balance during that period and measures the ability to sell inventory.

Days-in-inventory ratio Converts the inventory turnover ratio into a measure of days by dividing the turnover ratio into 365 days.

MARUTI SUZUKI ANALYSIS

Using Maruti Suzuki's information in Appendix C, calculate and interpret (1) horizontal and vertical analyses of inventory and cost of goods sold, (2) inventory turnover ratio, and (3) days-in-inventory ratio.

(1) *Horizontal Analysis*

Inventory: (₹18,407 – 17,965)/17,965 = 24.6%

Cost of Goods Sold: [(₹3,05,741 + 19,613 + 234) – (₹2,67,055 + 15,325 + (1,297))]/(₹2,67,055 + 15,325 + (1,297)) = 15.8%

Vertical Analysis

Inventory: ₹18,407/2,66,880 = 6.9%

Cost of Goods Sold: (3,05,741 + 19,613 + 234)/4,26,126 = 76.4%

The 24.6% and 15.8% horizontal analysis of inventory and cost of goods sold shows Maruti Suzuki's cost of sales and level of inventory during the year. The 6.9% vertical analysis of inventory shows that around 7% of the company's assets are tied up in inventory. This seems reasonable, given that Maruti Suzuki is the highest selling car manufacturer of India. The 76.4% vertical analysis of cost of goods sold indicates that inventory cost is a very large expense for the company. For the average rupee of sales, the cost of the inventory sold was about 76 paise.

(2) *Inventory Turnover Ratio*

(3,05,741 + 19,613 + 234)/((₹(18,407 + 17,965)/2 = 17.9

(3) *Days-in-Inventory*

365/17.9 = 20.4 days

The 17.9 inventory turnover ratio indicates that Maruti Suzuki inventory turns over about 18 times each year. The days in inventory ratio of 20 indicates that it takes the company almost three weeks to sell through its inventory.

turnover ratio into 365 days. Thus, the days-in-inventory ratio is calculated as follows:

$$\frac{365}{6.2} = 58.9$$

A ratio of 58.9 indicates that it takes Target about 59 days to sell as much inventory as it keeps on hand. Naturally, Target wants this ratio to be as low as possible. Its rival Wal-Mart generated a 40.1 ratio in 2010. This means it takes Target about 19 days longer than Wal-Mart to sell as much inventory as it has on hand.

Purchases An account used to accumulate the cost of all purchases.

Transportation-in An account that accumulates the transportation costs of obtaining the inventory.

Purchase Returns and Allowances An account that accumulates the cost of all inventory returned to vendors as well as the cost reductions from vendor allowances.

LO8 Appendix—Periodic Inventory System

A periodic inventory system does not update the inventory and cost of goods sold accounts during the period. When purchases are made, they are recorded in a temporary account called Purchases. When sales are made, the resulting revenue is recorded, but not the cost of goods sold. As a result, companies that use a periodic system must calculate and update the inventory and the cost of goods sold accounts at the end of the period. The following sections demonstrate the recording of purchases and the determination of ending inventory and cost of goods sold under a periodic system.

Recording Inventory

A periodic system uses the following four temporary accounts to capture the cost of inventory purchases during a period. The **Purchases** account accumulates the cost of all purchases. The **Transportation-in** (carriage inward) account accumulates the transportation costs of obtaining the inventory. Both of these increase the cost of inventory. The **Purchases Returns and Allowances**

When purchases are made in a periodic inventory system, they are recorded in a temporary account called Purchases. When sales are made, the resulting revenue is recorded, but not the cost of goods sold.

account accumulates the cost of all inventory returned to vendors as well as the cost reductions from vendor allowances. The **Purchase Discounts** account accumulates the cost reductions generated from vendor discounts granted for prompt payment. Both of these reduce the cost of inventory. Each of the four accounts is closed at the end of the period when the inventory and the cost of goods sold accounts are updated.

To illustrate the recording of inventory with these accounts, the example used in the chapter is repeated. Suppose that Devon Gifts purchases ₹20,000 of inventory on account on October 10. The purchase would be recorded as follows:

Oct. 10	Purchases	20,000	
	Accounts Payable		20,000
	(To record purchase of inventory)		

Assets	=	Liabilities	+	Equity
+20,000		+20,000		

Suppose further that Devon pays a third-party carrier ₹300 cash to transport the inventory to its warehouse. Devon would record the payment with the following entry:

Oct. 10	Transportation-in	300	
	Cash		300
	(To record transportation-in)		

Assets	=	Liabilities	+	Equity
+300		+300		

Suppose further that on October 12 Devon is granted a ₹1,000 reduction in the cost of the merchandise due to blemishes on the inventory. Devon would reduce its payable to the vendor and record the allowance as follows.

Oct. 12	Accounts Payable	1,000	
	Purchase Returns and Allowances		1,000
	(To record purchase allowance granted by vendor)		

Assets	=	Liabilities	+	Equity
−1,000		−1,000		

Finally, suppose that Devon pays its remaining ₹19,000 bill to the vendor on October 15, which qualifies Devon for a 1% discount. As a result, Devon would save ₹190 (₹19,000 × 1%) and pay only ₹18,810. The entry to record payment would be as follows:

Oct. 15	Accounts Payable	19,000	
	Purchase Discounts		190
	Cash		18,810
	(To record payment)		

Assets	=	Liabilities	+	Equity
−190		−19,000		
−18,810				

The entry decreases Accounts Payable for the full ₹19,000 and decreases Cash for the ₹18,810 payment. The difference is an addition to Purchase Discounts.

Given the preceding activity, Devon's **net purchases** of inventory can be calculated as follows:

Purchases	₹20,000
Add: Transportation-in	300
Less: Purchase returns and allowances	(1,000)
Purchase discounts	(190)
Net purchases	₹19,110

This is the same cost of net purchases as calculated under the perpetual system discussed in the chapter. Whether using a periodic or perpetual system, the cost of net purchases is the same. It is just captured in different accounts.

Inventory Costing Methods

A periodic system does not update the Inventory and the Cost of Goods Sold accounts during the period.

Purchase Discounts An account that accumulates the cost reductions generated from vendor discounts granted for prompt payments.

Net purchases The value of inventory purchased and transportation-in less purchase returns and allowances and purchase discounts.

Thus, the balances in these accounts must be calculated at the end of the period. This is accomplished in the following three steps:

1. Count the inventory on hand at the end of the period.
2. Use an inventory costing method to assign a cost to the ending inventory.
3. Calculate cost of goods sold using the cost of goods sold model.

To illustrate this process, the example used in the chapter is repeated. Suppose that during the month of September, Nell Farms experiences the following inventory purchases:

		Units	Unit Cost	Total
Sept. 1	Beginning inventory	40	₹12	₹480
Sept. 4	Purchase	60	₹13	₹780
Sept. 15	Purchase	30	₹14	₹420
Sept. 23	Purchase	45	₹15	₹675

At the end of the month, Nell counts 60 units on hand. Nell's cost of goods sold model for September is therefore as follows:

	Units	Cost
Beginning inventory	40	₹ 480
Add: Net purchases	135	1,875
Cost of goods available for sale	175	₹2,355
Less: Ending inventory	60	???
Cost of goods sold	115	???

To calculate the cost of the 60 units in ending inventory and therefore the cost of the 115 units sold, Nell must use one of the four inventory costing methods.

Specific Identification

Under the specific identification method, Nell determines the cost of ending inventory based on the actual cost of the units on hand. Suppose that Nell knows that the costs of the 60 units are five ₹13 units, twenty ₹14 units, and thirty-five ₹15 units. It can therefore calculate the cost of ending inventory as follows:

	Units	Unit Cost	Total Cost
Sept. 4 purchase	5	₹13	₹ 65
Sept. 15 purchase	20	₹14	₹280
Sept. 23 purchase	35	₹15	₹525
Ending inventory	60		₹870

Plugging this cost of ending inventory into the cost of goods sold model yields Nell's cost of goods sold of ₹1,485.

	Units	Cost
Cost of goods available for sale	175	₹2,355
− Ending inventory	60	870
= Cost of goods sold	115	₹1,485

First-In, First-Out (FIFO)

Under the FIFO method, Nell assumes that the first units of inventory purchased are the first units sold. As a result, the costs of the last (most recent) purchases are assigned to ending inventory. It can therefore calculate the cost of ending inventory as follows:

	Units	Unit Cost	Total Cost
Sept. 23 purchase	45	₹15	₹675
Sept. 15 purchase	15	₹14	210
Ending inventory	60		₹885

The cost of all 45 units purchased on September 23 and 15 of the units purchased on September 15 are assigned to ending inventory, yielding a cost of ₹885. Plugging this into the cost of goods sold model yields Nell's cost of goods sold of ₹1,470.

	Units	Cost
Cost of goods available for sale	175	₹2,355
− Ending inventory	60	885
= Cost of goods sold	115	₹1,470

Last-In, First-Out (LIFO)

Under the LIFO method, Nell assumes that the last units of inventory purchased are the first units sold. As a result, the costs of the first purchases are assigned to ending inventory. Nell can therefore calculate the cost of ending inventory as follows:

	Units	Unit Cost	Total Cost
Beginning inventory	40	₹12	₹480
Sept. 4 purchase	20	₹13	260
Ending inventory	60		₹740

The cost of all 40 units of beginning inventory and 20 of the units purchased on September 4 are assigned to ending inventory, yielding a cost of ₹740. Plugging this into the cost of goods sold model yields Nell's cost of goods sold of ₹1,615.

	Units	Cost
Cost of goods available for sale	175	₹2,355
− Ending inventory	60	740
= Cost of goods sold	115	₹1,615

Weighted Average

Under the weighted average method, Nell assumes that the cost of each unit in ending inventory is the average cost of all units available for sale during the period. The weighted average cost per unit is calculated as follows:

$$\text{Weighted Average Unit Cost} = \frac{\text{Cost of Goods Available for Sale}}{\text{Units Available for Sale}}$$

Note here that under a periodic system, the average unit cost is based on all the inventory available to be sold during the period. As a result, the average unit cost does not change during the period. Therefore, it is called a weighted average instead of a moving average (as under the perpetual system).

Nell's weighted average cost per unit, rounded to the nearest paise, is calculated as follows:

$$\frac{₹2{,}355}{175} = ₹13.46$$

Nell can therefore calculate the cost of ending inventory as follows, rounded to the nearest rupee:

	Units	Unit Cost	Total Cost
Ending inventory	60	₹13.46	₹808

Plugging this into the cost of goods sold model yields Nell's cost of goods sold of ₹1,547.

	Units	Cost
Cost of goods available for sale	175	₹2,355
− Ending inventory	60	808
= Cost of goods sold	115	₹1,547

CONCEPT QUESTIONS

1. On which financial statement would inventory be listed as a line item? How would it be classified on that financial statement?
2. When inventory is purchased, at what value is it recorded?
3. What accounts are used to record the purchase of inventory under perpetual and periodic inventory systems? Which method results in the inventory account being updated continually?
4. When inventory is sold, into what expense account is it transferred?
5. Which inventory costing method(s) is based on actual costs of the inventory sold and which method(s) is based on an assumption of which inventory is sold?
6. For each inventory costing method—LIFO, FIFO, and Moving Average—which costs are presumed to be in ending inventory? Which costs are presumed to be in cost of goods sold?
7. Why might a company choose to use the LIFO cost flow assumption? The FIFO assumption? The Moving Average assumption?
8. What is the LIFO reserve? What can be learned from it?
9. If ending inventory is incorrectly overstated, how will the current year's net income be affected? Current year retained earnings? Next year's net income?
10. Explain what is meant by a counterbalancing inventory error.
11. Explain how the gross profit method of estimating inventory works and why a company would use it.
12. Under what circumstances should a company adjust the carrying value of its inventory on its balance sheet to the inventory's market value?
13. List four common inventory analysis techniques (including ratios) that can be used to evaluate a company's inventory management.
14. Under a periodic inventory system, what four accounts are used to record the acquisition of inventory?
15. Under a periodic inventory system, what are the three steps in determining cost of goods sold for a period?

MULTIPLE CHOICE

1. The cost of inventory under a perpetual system does not include which of the following?
   a. Inventory price
   b. Freight charges
   c. Sales commissions
   d. Sales taxes on inventory purchase
2. The Cost of Goods Sold account represents the cost of inventory:
   a. remaining in a company's inventory account at year end and classified as ending inventory.
   b. purchased during the year plus inventory sold.
   c. sold during the year.
   d. available for sale at the beginning of the year.
3. When inventory is bought under a perpetual inventory system, what happens to the Inventory and Cost of Goods Sold accounts, respectively?
   a. No change, Increase
   b. Increase, No change
   c. Increase, Increase
   d. Decrease, No change
4. When an inventory item is sold under a perpetual inventory system:
   a. the Inventory account is not affected.
   b. inventory is decreased and Cost of Goods Sold is increased.
   c. inventory is increased and Cost of Goods Sold is increased.
   d. neither Inventory nor Cost of Goods Sold is affected until the end of the current period.
5. A company purchases a unit of inventory for ₹1.50 and then later purchases a second for ₹2.00. The company then sells one unit for ₹4.50. After the sale, the company purchases an additional unit for ₹2.50. The company uses a perpetual inventory system. Given these facts, which of the following is true?
   a. Cost of Goods Sold under FIFO is ₹1.50
   b. Ending Inventory under LIFO is ₹4.00
   c. Cost of Goods Sold under Moving Average is ₹1.75
   d. All of the above are true
6. A company purchases a unit of inventory for ₹1.50, another for ₹2.00 and then a third for ₹2.50. The company then sells one unit for ₹4.50. The company uses a perpetual inventory system. Given these facts, which of the following is true?
   a. Ending Inventory under FIFO is ₹1.50
   b. Cost of Goods Sold under LIFO is ₹2.50
   c. Cost of Goods Sold under Moving Average is ₹4.50
   d. Ending Inventory under LIFO is ₹4.50
7. Which of the following inventory costing methods is not based on an assumption about the cost of inventory sold?
   a. FIFO
   b. LIFO
   c. Specific Identification
   d. Moving Average
8. In a period of rising prices, under which inventory valuation method would ending inventory have the highest assigned value?
   a. FIFO
   b. LIFO
   c. Moving average
   d. All methods will result in the same value

9. Which inventory costing method generally results in less current taxes paid by the company?
   a. LIFO
   b. FIFO
   c. Moving Average
   d. All methods result in the same taxes paid
10. Which inventory costing method should a grocer use?
   a. LIFO
   b. FIFO
   c. Moving Average
   d. A grocer can use any of the inventory costing methods
11. A company that uses the FIFO costing method reports cost of goods sold for the year of ₹10,00,000. Had it used the LIFO method, cost of goods sold would have been ₹12,00,000. How much in taxes could the company have deferred in the current year if it had used the LIFO method? Assume a 30% tax rate.
   a. ₹2,00,000
   b. ₹60,000
   c. ₹1,40,000
   d. Cannot tell from the given information
12. A company overstates its ending inventory by ₹2,00,000. Which of the following is true concerning the effect of this error on cost of goods sold in the year of the error?
   a. Cost of goods sold will be unaffected
   b. Cost of goods sold will be understated
   c. Cost of goods sold will be overstated
   d. Cannot tell from given information
13. A company understates its ending inventory by ₹2,00,000. Which of the following is true concerning the effect of this error on cost of goods sold in the year after the error (assuming no other errors)?
   a. Cost of goods sold will be unaffected
   b. Cost of goods sold will be understated
   c. Cost of goods sold will be overstated
   d. Cannot tell from given information
14. A counterbalancing inventory error will result in:
   a. an overstatement of income.
   b. an understatement of income.
   c. both an overstatement and understatement of annual income that offset each other such that total net income over the two years is correct.
   d. cannot tell from given information.
15. Suppose that Lee Enterprises usually generates a 25% gross profit on sales. If Lee's annual sales are ₹1,00,000, what is Lee's estimated cost of goods sold using the gross profit method?
   a. ₹0
   b. ₹25,000
   c. ₹75,000
   d. ₹1,00,000
16. Suppose that Lee Enterprises usually generates a 40% gross profit on sales. If Lee's annual sales are ₹1,30,000 and cost of goods available for sale is ₹90,000, what is Lee's estimated ending inventory using the gross profit method?
   a. ₹38,000
   b. ₹90,000
   c. ₹78,000
   d. ₹12,000
17. What principle or assumption results in the use of lower-of-cost-or-market?
   a. Historical cost
   b. Conservatism
   c. Going concern
   d. Materiality
18. Under the lower-of-cost-or-market rule, an inventory item with a selling price of ₹6.00, a historical cost of ₹2.50, and a replacement cost of ₹3.50 would be reported at:
   a. ₹6.00.
   b. ₹3.50.
   c. ₹2.50.
   d. Cannot tell from given information.
19. A horizontal analysis of Cost of Goods Sold yields a percentage of 14.0%. Given that change, which of the following would cause the greatest concern for the company?
   a. Sales increased 20.1%
   b. Operating Expenses increased 14.2%
   c. Sales decreased 10.8%
   d. Inventory increased 12.4%
20. CG Films generates Cost of Goods Sold of ₹1,35,000 for the year. Inventory at the beginning and ending of the year was ₹40,000 and ₹46,000, respectively. Calculate CG's inventory turnover ratio.
   a. 3.1
   b. 3.4
   c. 116.2
   d. 0.3
21. Horizontal analysis of inventory:
   a. calculates inventory as a percentage of total assets.
   b. calculates cost of goods sold as a percentage of revenues.
   c. highlights the change in inventory as a percentage of the prior year's inventory balance.
   d. both "a" and "b" are correct.
22. Vertical analysis of inventory:
   a. calculates inventory as a percentage of total assets.
   b. calculates cost of goods sold as a percentage of revenues.
   c. highlights the change in inventory as a percentage of the prior year's inventory balance.
   d. both "a" and "b" are correct.
23. If a company uses a periodic inventory system and returns an inventory item to a vendor, the company would record the return as:
   a. a decrease to the Inventory account.
   b. an increase to the Cost of Goods Sold account.
   c. an increase to the Purchase Returns and Allowances account.
   d. an increase to the Purchase Discounts account.

24. Which of the following is not a part of the process to calculate costs of goods sold under a periodic inventory system?
   a. Count the ending inventory on hand at the end of the period
   b. Assign a cost to the ending inventory using an inventory costing method
   c. Use the cost of goods sold model to calculate cost of goods sold
   d. Each of the above is part of the process

BRIEF EXERCISES

1. Determining Inventory Costs

Matthews Electronics purchased 100 laptop computers from a vendor for ₹7,50,000. The vendor gave Mathews a ₹15,000 discount because of scratches on the screens of some of the laptops. The cost to ship the computers was ₹5,000.

Required
Determine Matthews' cost of inventory.

2. Recording Inventory Purchases

On March 20, Shelton Fireworks purchases on account ₹1,20,000 of fireworks with a list price of ₹1,30,000. Shelton pays the vendor on March 30, which qualifies Shelton for a 2% discount. Shelton uses a perpetual inventory system.

Required
Record all entries associated with Shelton's purchase of the inventory.

3. Reporting Inventory

Asheton Supplies Inc. purchases 1,000 fax machines from its main supplier for ₹10,00,000 cash. Asheton plans to resell 900 of them to customers for use in homes and offices. The additional fax machines will be used in Asheton's offices.

Required
Prepare the entry that Asheton would make to record the purchase. Explain your reasoning for the account(s) you use to record the new fax machines.

4. Inventory Costing Methods

A company with no inventory buys the following three inventory items:

Date	Item	Cost
January 7	A	₹600
January 9	B	₹700
January 12	C	₹800

On January 10, the company sells one item for ₹1,000. On January 15, the company sells a second item ₹1,000. The company uses a perpetual inventory system.

Required
Calculate the company's cost of goods sold under the a) FIFO, b) LIFO, and c) moving average inventory costing methods.

5. Effects of Inventory Methods

Assume that you are an accountant at a local retailer and your boss asks you to explain the financial statement impact of inventory costing methods. In particular, she is interested in whether the company should use the FIFO or LIFO method. She would like to use the method that results in the highest net income, the highest inventory balance, and the lowest taxes.

Required
Assuming that the company is experiencing rising prices, explain the effects of using the LIFO and FIFO methods on income, inventory, and taxes. Can your boss get all that she wants?

6. LIFO Reserve

A company's ending inventory balance is ₹1,40,000 using the LIFO method. If the company used the FIFO method, the balance would have been ₹1,72,000. If the company used the Moving Average method, the balance would have been ₹1,58,000. The company uses a perpetual inventory system and is subject to a 35% corporate tax rate.

Required
Calculate a) the company's LIFO Reserve and b) the total taxes deferred over time by using the LIFO method.

7. Inventory Errors

Suppose that a company's preliminary financial statements show net income of ₹2,30,000 and ending inventory of ₹39,500. Before finalizing the financial statements, management discovers that ending inventory should be ₹42,500.

Required
Describe the error in the inventory account (for example, inventory was overstated by ₹1,000) and calculate the company's correct net income for the year.

8. Estimating Inventory

Johnson Enterprises uses the gross profit method to estimate ending inventory. Current-year sales and cost of inventory available for sale were ₹7,00,000 and ₹5,40,000, respectively. Johnson's historical gross profit percentage is 40%.

Required
Estimate Johnson's ending inventory.

9. Applying Lower-of-Cost-or-Market

Alpaca Enterprises has an inventory balance of ₹1,56,000. At year end, the market value of Alpaca's inventory has fallen to ₹1,51,500.

Required
Prepare the journal entry that Alpaca should make at year end regarding its inventory balance and identify the accounting principle that makes the entry necessary.

10. Analyzing Inventory

A company's cost of goods sold for the year was ₹9,75,000. Ending inventory was ₹1,20,000 and ₹1,35,000 in the current and prior years, respectively.

Required
Calculate the company's inventory turnover ratio. If the company's ratio was 6.2 in the prior year, has the company become more or less efficient in selling its inventory?

11. Appendix—Recording Inventory Purchases

On March 20, Shelton Fireworks purchases on account ₹1,00,000 of fireworks. On March 25, Shelton returns ₹10,000 of the merchandise to the vendor. Shelton then pays the remaining bill, less a 3% discount for early payment, on March 30.

Required
Record all entries associated with the purchase of the inventory assuming that Shelton uses a periodic inventory system.

12. Appendix—Inventory Costing Methods

A company with no inventory purchases the following three inventory items:

Date	Item	Cost
January 7	A	₹600
January 9	B	₹700
January 12	C	₹800

On January 15, the company sells two items for ₹1,000 each. The company uses a periodic inventory system.

Required
Calculate the company's cost of goods sold under the a) FIFO, b) LIFO, and c) weighted average inventory costing methods. How would your answers change if one item was sold on January 10 while the second was sold on January 15?

EXERCISES

13. Determine Inventory Costs

Mary Cosmetics sells specialty lipstick for a retail price of ₹1,200.25 each. Mary purchases each tube for ₹500.00 and pays the following additional amounts: ₹100.50 per tube in freight charges, ₹40.00 per tube in taxes, and ₹200 per tube in commissions to employees for sales.

Required
Compute the cost of each tube of lipstick.

14. Record Inventory Purchases

Heston purchases inventory with a list price of ₹7,000 for ₹6,300 on account. Heston pays a transportation company ₹200 to deliver the inventory. Upon receipt, Heston notices some defects, contacts the vendor, and receives a ₹500 allowance. Heston pays the vendor three days later, which qualifies Heston for a 2% discount. Heston uses a perpetual inventory system.

Required
Prepare all journal entries Heston would make to record the preceding activity and calculate Heston's net purchases.

15. Recording Purchases and Sales of Inventory

Lowder Company purchased 275 units of inventory on account for ₹57,750. Due to early payment, Lowder received a discount and paid only ₹52,250. Lowder then sold 150 units for cash at ₹550 each, purchased an additional 65 units for cash at a cost of ₹14,300, and then sold 100 more units for cash at ₹550 each. Lowder uses a perpetual inventory system.

Required

a. Prepare all journal entries to record Lowder's purchases and sales assuming the FIFO inventory costing method.
b. Which journal entries would be different if Lowder used the LIFO inventory costing method? How would they be different?

16. Inventory Costing Methods

Avant Corporation's November inventory activity is as follows. Avant uses a perpetual inventory system.

Date	Transaction	Units	Unit Cost	Total Cost
11/1	Beginning inventory	32	₹55	₹1,760
11/7	Purchase	45	₹60	₹2,700
11/9	Sale	50		
11/14	Purchase	52	₹65	₹3,380
11/30	Sale	61		

Required
Compute the ending inventory and cost of goods sold under the FIFO, LIFO, and moving average costing methods. Round average unit costs to the nearest cent and cost of goods sold and inventory values to the nearest dollar.

17. Inventory Costing Methods

Hahn Hardware provides the following information relating to its June inventory activity. Hahn uses a perpetual inventory system.

Date	Transaction	Units	Unit Cost	Total Cost
June 1	Inventory	13	₹80.00	₹1040.00
June 7	Purchase	22	₹90.50	₹2090.00
June 12	Sale	20		
June 18	Purchase	10	₹100.25	₹1020.50
June 20	Sale	14		
June 26	Purchase	16	₹11.00	₹176.00
June 30	Sale	15		

Required

a. Put Hahn's given information into a cost of goods sold model. What is unknown?
b. Compute the ending inventory and cost of goods sold using the FIFO, LIFO, and moving average costing methods. Round dollar amounts to the nearest penny.
c. Calculate the sum of the ending inventory and cost of goods sold for each method. What do you notice about the answer for each method?

18. Inventory Costing Methods

Harrison, Charles & Company Inc. sells flower planters for ₹7 each. On its first day of business in January, the company purchased 2,000 planters for ₹3 each. The company sold 300 units during the first month of operations and sold an additional 1,300 units the next month. To prevent inventory stock-outs during summertime, the company bought an additional 700 units for ₹4.50 each in May. The company sold 850 units from May through December. The company uses a perpetual inventory system and the FIFO inventory costing method.

Required

a. Compute Harrison, Charles & Company's ending inventory balance at the end of the year and its cost of goods sold balance for the year.
b. Would those balances be different if the company had used the FIFO costing method under a periodic inventory system?

19. Choosing an Inventory Costing Method

LAN Corporation uses the LIFO inventory costing method to account for its inventory. In the most recent year, LAN had net sales of ₹40,000, cost of goods sold of ₹16,850, and operating expenses of ₹17,500. LAN is subject to a tax rate of 30%. Had LAN used the FIFO inventory costing method, its cost of goods sold for the year would have been ₹14,950.

Required

a. Prepare comparative income statements under LIFO and FIFO and identify the amount of taxes that LAN deferred in the current year by using LIFO rather than FIFO.
b. Explain why the term "tax deferral" is used in association with inventory costing methods rather than the term "tax savings."

20. Inventory Errors

Goodwin Grocery reported the following financial facts for 2012 and 2013:

	2012	2013
Beginning inventory	₹ 20,000	₹ 30,000
Cost of goods purchased	1,50,000	1,75,000
Cost of goods available for sale	₹1,70,000	₹2,05,000
Ending inventory	30,000	35,000
Cost of goods sold	₹1,40,000	₹1,70,000

Goodwin made two accounting errors during the years:

1. 2012 ending inventory was understated by ₹3,000.
2. 2013 ending inventory was overstated by ₹4,000.

Required

Compute Goodwin's correct cost of goods sold for each year.

21. Inventory Errors

Apollo Enterprise reported the following financial information for the years 2012 and 2013. At the end of 2012, ₹1,500 of inventory that was in transit and owned by Apollo was included in purchases but not counted in ending inventory. The inventory was received in 2013 and was ultimately sold during 2012.

	2012	2013
Beginning inventory	₹13,000	₹11,500
Purchases	16,000	17,000
Cost of goods available for sale	₹29,000	₹28,500
Ending inventory	11,500	12,500
Cost of goods sold	₹17,500	₹16,000

Required

a. Identify whether Apollo made an error in the accounting for its inventory. Specifically, was Apollo in error by including the inventory in transit in its 2011 purchases or by excluding it from its 2012 ending inventory?
b. If Apollo made an error, prepare corrected cost of goods sold models for 2012 and 2013. Use the models to demonstrate why some inventory errors are said to be counterbalancing.

22. Inventory Errors

FMA Enterprise reported the following income statement data:

	2012	2013
Sales	₹2,10,000	₹2,50,000
Beginning inventory	32,000	40,000
Cost of goods available for sale	2,05,000	2,42,000
Ending inventory	40,000	52,000
Cost of goods sold	1,65,000	1,90,000
Gross profit	45,000	60,000

Inventory balances at January 1, 2012, and December 31, 2013, are correct. However, the ending inventory at December 31, 2011, is overstated by ₹5,000.

Required
Prepare corrected data for 2012 and 2013, identify all accounts that were affected by the error and whether they were overstated or understated, and calculate the cumulative two-year effect of the inventory error on gross profit.

23. Estimating Inventory

Clayburn Enterprises reported the following information for the current year:

Sales	₹8,00,000
Beginning inventory	25,000
Purchases	5,02,000
Gross profit percentage	40%

Required
Using the gross profit method, estimate Clayburn's cost of goods sold for the year and the ending inventory at year end. Explain why a company might need to estimate its ending inventory.

24. Estimating Inventory and Cost of Goods Sold

Marshall Enterprise experiences a fire in its warehouse at the end of the year, which destroys its entire inventory. Marshall's records show that it started the year with ₹35,000 of inventory and purchased ₹1,50,000 during the year. It also shows sales of ₹3,10,000 for the year. Normally, Marshall's experiences a 55% gross profit percentage on sales.

Required
Use the gross profit method to estimate Marshall's cost of goods sold and ending inventory.

25. Applying Lower-of-Cost-or-Market

Kay Mart Company is preparing financial statements and provides the following information about several of its major inventory items at year end:

Item	Quantity on Hand	Unit Cost When Acquired	Replacement Cost (Market Value) as of December 31
R	25	₹15	₹19
S	60	₹22	₹20
T	34	₹30	₹33
U	50	₹10	₹11
V	13	₹50	₹55

Required
If Kay Mart uses the lower-of-cost-or-market rule (LCM), what should it report as the balance of inventory if (1) one market value is computed for all inventories or (2) a market value is computed for each inventory type?

26. Applying Lower-of-Cost-or-Market

Azalea Garden Center provides the following information about its inventory:

Group	Item	Units	Unit Cost	Unit Market
1	A	5	₹15	₹13
1	B	14	₹10	₹11
2	C	8	₹ 5	₹ 7
2	D	15	₹12	₹11

Required
a. If Azalea uses the lower-of-cost-or-market rule, what should it report as the balance of inventory if (1) one market value is computed for all inventories, (2) market value is computed by group, and (3) market value is computed for each inventory type?
b. Prepare any journal entries necessary based on your answers in part (a).

27. Accounting Terms

The following is a list of terms and definitions associated with inventory:

1. Perpetual inventory system
2. Periodic inventory system
3. LIFO costing method
4. FIFO costing method
5. Tax deferral
6. LIFO reserve
7. Counter-balancing error
8. Specific identification costing method
9. Lower-of-cost-or-market rule
10. Gross profit method

a. Updates the inventory account only at the end of an accounting period.
b. Calculates the cost of goods sold based on the assumption that the first unit of inventory available for sale is the first unit sold.
c. Determines the cost of goods sold based on the actual cost of each inventory item sold.
d. Updates the inventory account each time inventory is bought or sold.
e. A method of estimating inventory using a company's gross profit percentage.
f. Calculates the cost of goods sold based on the assumption that the last unit of inventory available for sale is the first one sold.
g. A temporary delay in the payment of income taxes.
h. The difference between the LIFO inventory reported on the balance sheet and what inventory would be if reported on a FIFO basis.
i. Requires inventory to be reported at its market value if market value is lower than the inventory's cost.
j. An error whose effect on net income is corrected in the period after the error.

Required
Match each term with the appropriate definition.

28. Analyzing Inventory

Available information from Panosian Company for the years 2013 and 2012 is as follows:

	2013	2012
Inventory	₹1,05,000	₹ 85,000
Other assets	3,85,000	3,15,000
Cost of goods sold	76,000	55,000
Sales	1,29,000	80,000
Retained earnings	1,35,000	1,00,000
Long term liabilities	1,20,000	1,35,000

Required

Prepare a horizontal analysis of Panosian Company's balances. Round percentages to one decimal point (i.e., 4.8%). Can you make a general conclusion about the direction of the company? How?

29. Analyzing Inventory

During the current year, Norlander Inc. implemented an inventory management system that it believes will result in greater efficiencies and profits. Norlander's CEO was therefore disappointed when he saw the following condensed income statement showing no increase in net income:

	2013	2012
Sales	₹6,50,000	₹7,75,000
Cost of goods sold	3,72,500	4,51,800
Operating expenses	2,32,500	2,78,200
Net income	45,000	45,000

Required

Using horizontal and vertical analyses, provide reasoning to the CEO that the inventory management system was effective. Round percentages to one decimal point (i.e., 4.8%).

30. Analyzing Inventory

The following information is provided for three different companies: A, B, and C:

in millions	A	B	C
Beginning inventory	₹ 569	₹ 774	₹ 989
Ending inventory	423	214	356
Cost of goods sold	1,376	1,232	1,771
Sales	2,232	1,836	3,025

Required

Calculate the inventory turnover ratio and days-in-inventory ratio for each company. How do the companies compare?

31. Analyzing Inventory

Comparative income statements for Berg Company are given as follows:

Berg Company
Comparative Income Statements
For the Years Ending March 31

	2013	2012
Net sales	₹8,12,000	₹8,12,000
Cost of goods sold	6,49,600	6,64,364
Gross profit	₹1,62,400	₹1,47,636
Operating expenses	84,448	79,724
Net income	₹ 77,952	₹ 67,912

Required

Prepare horizontal and vertical analyses of Berg's income statement data and comment on the current status of the company. Round percentages to one decimal point (i.e., 4.8%)

32. Appendix—Inventory Purchases

Consider the following separate situations:

	William's Widgets	Sarah's Sofas	Clay's Cars
Beginning inventory	₹4,000	₹2,350	₹ (e)
Purchases (gross)	4,230	(c)	7,340
Purchase returns	470	800	550
Purchase discounts	(a)	458	310
Transportation-in	150	500	420
Cost of goods available for sale	(b)	7,320	8,790
Ending inventory	1,890	1,750	(f)
Cost of goods sold	5,220	(d)	7,590

Required

Compute the missing amounts.

33. Appendix—Inventory Costing Methods (Periodic System)

Hahn Hardware provides the following information relating to its June inventory. Hahn uses a periodic inventory system and sold 49 units during the month.

Date	Transaction	Units	Unit Cost	Total Cost
June 1	Inventory	13	₹ 8.00	₹104.00
June 7	Purchase	22	₹ 9.50	₹209.00
June 18	Purchase	10	₹10.25	₹102.50
June 26	Purchase	16	₹11.00	₹176.00
	Totals	61		₹591.50

Required

a. Put Hahn's given information into a cost of goods sold model. What is unknown?

b. Compute the ending inventory and cost of goods sold using the FIFO, LIFO, and weighted average costing methods.

c. Calculate the sum of the ending inventory and cost of goods sold for each method. What do you notice about the answer for each method?

34. Appendix—Inventory Costing Methods

Avant Corporation's November inventory activity follows. Avant uses a periodic inventory system.

Date	Transaction	Units	Unit Cost	Total Cost
11/1	Beginning inventory	32	₹55	₹1,760
11/7	Purchase	45	₹60	₹2,700
11/14	Purchase	52	₹65	₹3,380
11/30	Ending inventory	18		

Required

a. Compute the ending inventory and cost of goods sold under the FIFO, LIFO, and weighted average costing assumptions. For the weighted average method, round the unit average to the nearest penny and the cost of goods sold and ending inventory values to the nearest rupees.
b. Which costing assumption gives the highest ending inventory? Highest cost of goods sold? Why?
c. Explain why the average item cost is not ₹60 under the weighted average costing assumption.

35. Appendix—Recording and Reporting Inventory

Lowder Company purchased 275 units of inventory on account for ₹57,750. Due to some defects in the merchandise, Lowder received a ₹20 per unit allowance and paid only ₹52,250. Lowder then sold 150 units for cash at ₹550 each, purchased an additional 65 units for cash at a cost of ₹14,300, and then sold 100 more units for cash at ₹550 each. Lowder uses a periodic inventory system.

Required

a. Prepare all journal entries to record Lowder's purchases of inventory.
b. Compute Lowder's cost of goods sold and ending inventory under the FIFO, LIFO, and weighted average inventory costing methods. For the weighted average method, round all values to the nearest cent.

PROBLEMS

36. Effects of Inventory Costing Methods on Income

Martin Merchandising has hired you to examine whether the company should use the LIFO or FIFO inventory costing method. The company uses a perpetual inventory system and has supplied the following information for the month:

Beginning inventory, 2,000 units at ₹40	₹ 80,000
Purchases on June 4, 12,000 units at ₹45	540,000
Sales on June 18, 10,500 units at ₹77	808,500
Operating expenses (excluding taxes)	148,000
Company tax rate	35%

Required

Prepare multi-step income statements under the LIFO and FIFO costing methods. Explain to Martin the advantages and disadvantages of using each inventory costing method. Use the income statements to support your explanation.

37. Analyzing Different Inventory Costing Methods

Farmville Tools sells shovels nationwide to farmers. For March, Farmville had beginning inventory of 270 shovels with a per-shovel cost of ₹15. During March, Farmville made the following purchases of additional shovels.

March 8	50 @ ₹16.25	March 22	115 @ ₹ 18.00
March 13	130 @ ₹17.50	March 29	60 @ ₹ 18.50

Farmville uses a perpetual inventory system. During March, 525 shovels were sold on the following dates:

March 10	100	March 21	175
March 17	120	March 30	130

Required

a. Determine the appropriate balance in ending inventory and cost of goods sold under each of the inventory cost flow assumptions (LIFO, FIFO, and moving average). Round all values to the nearest penny.
b. Compute the inventory turnover and days-in-inventory ratios under each inventory costing method.
c. Which method yields ratios that show the most effective turnover of inventory? Are the company's inventory sales different depending on the costing method chosen? If not, why are the ratios different?

38. Recording Inventory Activity

Campbell Candy Company starts the month of January with 40 boxes of Tiger Bars costing ₹20 each. The following transactions occurred during the month:

Jan. 2	Purchased 15 additional boxes for ₹22 each. Paid with cash.
Jan. 4	Paid freight costs of ₹30 on January 2 purchase.
Jan. 10	Sold 45 boxes for ₹40 each.
Jan. 27	Purchased 10 additional boxes on account for ₹23 each.

Campbell uses a perpetual inventory system and the FIFO inventory costing method.

Required

a. Prepare all necessary journal entries related to Campbell's inventory activity.
b. Suppose that the inventory has a replacement value of ₹375 at the end of the month. What entry, if any, is required?

39. Analyzing Inventory

The following is comparative financial data for JK Martin Company and Stratton Company (in thousands):

	JK Martin Company		Stratton Company	
	2013	2012	2013	2012
Net sales	₹20,00,000		₹5,50,000	
Cost of goods sold	11,00,000		2,40,000	
Operating expenses	3,05,000		75,000	
Income tax expense	52,000		6,500	
Cash	85,070	₹82,508	16,100	₹15,777
Inventory	2,50,000	2,25,000	70,000	65,600
Equipment	5,25,000	5,00,000	1,40,000	1,25,000
Current liabilities	65,000	75,000	35,000	30,000
Long-term liabilities	1,09,000	88,000	29,000	24,800
Common stock, ₹10 par	4,90,000	4,90,000	1,15,000	1,15,000
Retained earnings	1,73,000	1,47,520	40,756	30,289

Required

a. Prepare a vertical analysis of the 2013 income data. Round percentages to one decimal point (i.e., 4.8%). Is one company more profitable than the other?
b. Prepare a horizontal analysis of all accounts. Round percentages to one decimal point (i.e., 4.8%). What does this analysis show?
c. Compute the inventory turnover and days-in-inventory ratios for 2013. Do these ratios change your conclusions about these companies?

40. Appendix—Analyzing Different Inventory Costing Methods

Farmville Tools sells shovels nationwide to farmers. For March, Farmville had beginning inventory of 270 shovels with a per-shovel cost of ₹15. During March, Farmville made the following purchases of additional shovels.

March 8	50 @ ₹16.25	March 22	115 @ ₹18.00
March 13	130 @ ₹17.50	March 29	60 @ ₹18.50

Farmville uses a periodic inventory system. During March, 525 shovels were sold on the following dates:

March 10	100	March 21	175
March 17	120	March 30	130

Required

a. Determine ending inventory and cost of goods sold under each of the inventory cost flow assumptions (LIFO, FIFO, and weighted average).
b. Compute the inventory turnover and days-in-inventory ratios under each inventory costing method.
c. Which method yields ratios that show the most effective turnover of inventory? Are the company's inventory sales different depending on the costing method chosen? If not, why are the ratios different?

41. Appendix—Recording Inventory Activity

Campbell Candy Company starts the month of January with 40 boxes of Tiger Bars costing ₹20 each. The following transactions occurred during the month:

Jan. 2	Purchased 15 additional boxes for ₹22 each. Paid with cash.
Jan. 4	Paid freight costs of ₹30 on January 2 purchase.
Jan. 10	Sold 45 boxes for ₹40 each.
Jan. 27	Purchased 10 additional boxes on account for ₹23 each.

Campbell uses a periodic inventory system and the FIFO inventory costing method.

Required

Prepare all necessary journal entries related to Campbell's inventory activity. Calculate the cost of goods sold and the ending inventory under the FIFO, LIFO, and weighted average costing methods. Round all values to the nearest penny.

CASES

42. Research and Analysis

Access the 2010 annual report for **Shoppers Stop Ltd.** by clicking on the *Investors* and *Financial Reports* links at http://corporate.shoppersstop.com.

Required

a. Examine the company's income statement and balance sheet and conduct horizontal and vertical analyses of the company's cost of goods sold and inventory balances. Round percentages to one decimal point (i.e., 4.8%).
b. Examine the company's merchandise inventories note to its financial statements. What inventory costing method(s) does the company use to account for its inventory? How often does the company take a physical count of its inventory? Does the company follow the lower-of-cost-or-market rule?
c. Calculate the inventory turnover and days-in-inventory ratios for 2012–13.
d. Based on your answers above, write a paragraph explaining your opinion of Shoppers Stop's inventory position. Use your answers as supporting facts.

43. Research and Analysis

Access the 2012–13 annual report of **Bombay Dyeing and Manufacturing Company Ltd.** and annual report of **Raymond Ltd.** by clicking on the *Investors, Financial Information,* and *Annual Reports sections on their Web sites.*

Required

a. Conduct horizontal and vertical analyses of sales, cost of goods sold, gross profit, inventory, and total assets for each company.
b. Compute the inventory turnover and days-in-inventory ratios for each company.

c. Compare each company's management of inventory. Is one company better than the other?
d. Look in the notes to the financial statements. Do the companies use the same or different inventory costing methods? Do the methods used match the companies' actual physical flow of inventory?

44. Ethics in Accounting

As a newly hired staff accountant for Jordan Designs, you have been asked to conduct the year-end physical inventory count. During the process, you observe that much of the inventory is outdated and therefore could not be sold for the recorded cost. You recommend to your manager that the inventory be written down, based upon the lower-of-cost-or-market principle. However, the manager informs you that you should leave the inventory value at the cost value. She insists that the company frequently experiences inventory value changes and that the inventory will be marketable again in the future. Until that time, the company plans to leave the merchandise in its warehouse.

Required

a. Why would the manager want to keep the inventory at its current cost?
b. Who is affected by the decision to, or not to, write the inventory down to its market value?
c. What things should you consider when evaluating whether you should recommend an inventory write-down to your manager's boss?

reviewcard CHAPTER 7 Inventory

Learning Objectives		Key Concepts
LO1	Describe inventory and how it is recorded, expensed, and reported.	Inventory is a current asset that is recorded at its cost of acquisition, which can include purchase discounts, returns and allowance, and transportation-in. Inventory becomes an expense when it is sold.
LO2	Calculate the cost of goods sold using different inventory costing methods.	Companies can use one of four costing methods to determine cost of goods sold: specific identification, first-in, first-out (FIFO), last-in, first-out (LIFO), and moving average. Specific identification determines cost of goods sold from the costs of actual units sold. FIFO assumes that the first units available for sale are included in cost of goods sold. LIFO assumes that the last units available for sale are included in cost of goods sold. Moving average assumes that the cost of inventory sold is the average cost of all inventory available for sale.
LO3	Understand the income and tax effects of inventory cost flow assumptions.	When inventory costs are rising, the LIFO costing method will result in the highest cost of goods sold while the FIFO costing method will result in the smallest cost of goods sold. The LIFO method is often used because of the tax deferral resulting from the higher cost of goods sold. The amount of taxes a company has deferred can be approximated through examination of the LIFO reserve.
LO4	Analyze the effects of inventory errors.	An error in calculating ending inventory will result in a misstatement of cost of goods sold and thus, net income. In addition, since ending inventory becomes beginning inventory the following year, the error will also misstate cost of goods sold and net income the following year in the opposite direction.
LO5	Demonstrate how inventory is estimated.	Using the gross profit method, ending inventory can be estimated by first estimating cost of goods sold and subtracting it from cost of goods available for sale. Cost of goods sold is estimated by subtracting the usual gross profit on sales from actual sales.

Key Definitions

Days-in-inventory ratio Converts the inventory turnover ratio into a measure of days by dividing the turnover ratio into 365 days.

First-in, first-out method Calculates the cost of goods sold based on the assumption that the first unit of inventory available for sale is the first unit sold.

Gross profit method A method of estimating inventory using a company's gross profit percentage to estimate the cost of goods sold and then ending inventory.

Inventory A tangible resource that is held for resale in the normal course of operations.

Inventory turnover ratio Compares the cost of goods sold during a period to the average inventory balance during that period and measures the ability to sell inventory.

Last-in, first-out method Calculates the cost of goods sold based on the assumption that the last unit of inventory available for sale is the first unit sold.

LIFO reserve The difference between the LIFO inventory reported on the balance sheet and what inventory would be if reported on a FIFO basis.

Lower-of-cost-or-market rule Requires inventory to be reported on the balance sheet at its market value if the market value is lower than the inventory's cost.

Moving average method Calculates the cost of goods sold based on the average unit cost of all inventory available for sale.

Net purchases Gross purchases plus transportation-in less purchase returns and allowances and purchase discounts.

Periodic inventory system Updates the inventory account only at the end of an accounting period.

Perpetual inventory system Updates the inventory account each time inventory is bought or sold.

Purchases An account used to accumulate the cost of all purchases.

Purchase Discounts An account that accumulates the cost reductions generated from vendor discounts granted for prompt payments.

Learning Objectives		Key Concepts
LO6	Apply the lower-of-cost-or-market rule to inventory.	If the market value of inventory falls below its cost, the lower-of-cost-or-market rule requires a company to write down its inventory to the market value. This rule can be applied to individual inventory items or to groups of items.
LO7	Evaluate inventory through the calculation of horizontal, vertical, and ratio analyses.	The inventory turnover ratio indicates how fast a company sells its inventory. The days in inventory ratio shows how many days on average it takes a company to sell its inventory.
LO8	Appendix: Record purchases and calculate the cost of goods sold under a periodic system.	Companies can use one of four costing methods to determine cost of goods sold: specific identification, first-in, first-out (FIFO), last-in, first-out (LIFO), and weighted average. Specific identification determines cost of goods sold from the costs of actual units sold. FIFO assumes that the first units available for sale are included in cost of goods sold. LIFO assumes that the last units available for sale are included in cost of goods sold. Weighted average assumes that the cost of inventory sold is the average cost of all inventory available for sale.

Key Definitions

Purchase Returns and Allowances An account that accumulates the cost of all inventory returned to vendors as well as the cost reductions from vendor allowances.

Specific identification method Determines the cost of goods sold based on the actual cost of each inventory item sold.

Tax deferral A temporary delay in the payment of income taxes.

Transportation-in An account that accumulates the transportation costs of obtaining the inventory.

Key Formulas

Moving or Weighted Average Unit Cost

$$\frac{\text{Cost of Goods Available for Sale}}{\text{Units Available for Sale}}$$

Horizontal Analysis

Dollar change in account balance = Current-year balance − Prior-year balance

$$\text{Percentage change in account balance} = \frac{\text{Dollar change}}{\text{Prior-year balance}}$$

Vertical Analysis

For the Balance Sheet

$$\text{Percentage} = \frac{\text{Account Balance}}{\text{Total Assets}}$$

For the Income Statement

$$\text{Percentage} = \frac{\text{Account Balance}}{\text{Net Sales or Revenue}}$$

Inventory Turnover Ratio

$$\frac{\text{Cost of Goods Sold}}{\text{Average Inventory}}$$

Average Inventory

$$\frac{\text{Beginning Inventory} + \text{Ending Inventory}}{2}$$

Days-in-Inventory Ratio

$$\frac{365}{\text{Inventory Turnover Ratio}}$$

Cost of Goods Sold Model

Beginning Inventory
+ Purchases
Cost of Goods Available for Sale
− Ending Inventory
Cost of Goods Sold

Fixed Assets
and Intangible Assets

Learning Objectives

After studying the material in this chapter, you should be able to:

LO1 Describe fixed assets and how they are recorded, expensed, and reported.

LO2 Calculate and compare depreciation expense using straight-line, double-declining-balance, and units-of-activity methods.

LO3 Understand the effects of adjustments that may be made during a fixed asset's useful life.

LO4 Record the disposal of fixed assets.

LO5 Evaluate fixed assets through the calculation and interpretation of horizontal, vertical, and ratio analyses.

LO6 Describe the cash flow effect of acquiring fixed assets.

LO7 Describe intangible assets and how they are recorded, expensed, and reported.

Introduction

This chapter examines the accounting for property and equipment, or as it is sometimes called, "fixed assets." For most companies, the objectives associated with fixed assets are fairly simple. They want to acquire fixed assets, use them productively for some period of time, and then dispose of them. Thus, the chapter examines these three activities—the acquisition of fixed assets, the depreciation of fixed assets over their useful lives, and the disposal of fixed assets. It also examines a few issues that arise during the life of a fixed asset, such as additional expenditures and revisions of original estimates. The chapter then focuses on how to analyze a company's fixed asset position. It concludes with the accounting for intangible assets.

LO1 Recording, Expensing, and Reporting Fixed Assets

A **fixed asset** is any tangible resource that is expected to be used in the normal course of operations for more than one year and is not intended for resale. Examples include land, buildings, equipment, furniture, fixtures, etc. Fixed assets are reported on the balance sheet and are classified as noncurrent assets because they are used for more than one year.

As you consider the definition of a fixed asset, note that the phrase "not intended for resale" differentiates a fixed asset from inventory. A computer that Dell Corporation makes for sale is inventory, while an identical computer used by an employee in business operations is a fixed asset. Also, note that the phrase "used in the normal course of operations" differentiates a fixed asset from an investment. Land on which a company builds a manufacturing plant is a fixed asset, while land bought to be sold to a developer is an investment. The company's intended use of the asset dictates how the asset is classified.

Fixed asset A tangible resource that is expected to be used in operations for more than one year and is not intended for resale.

CHAPTER 8

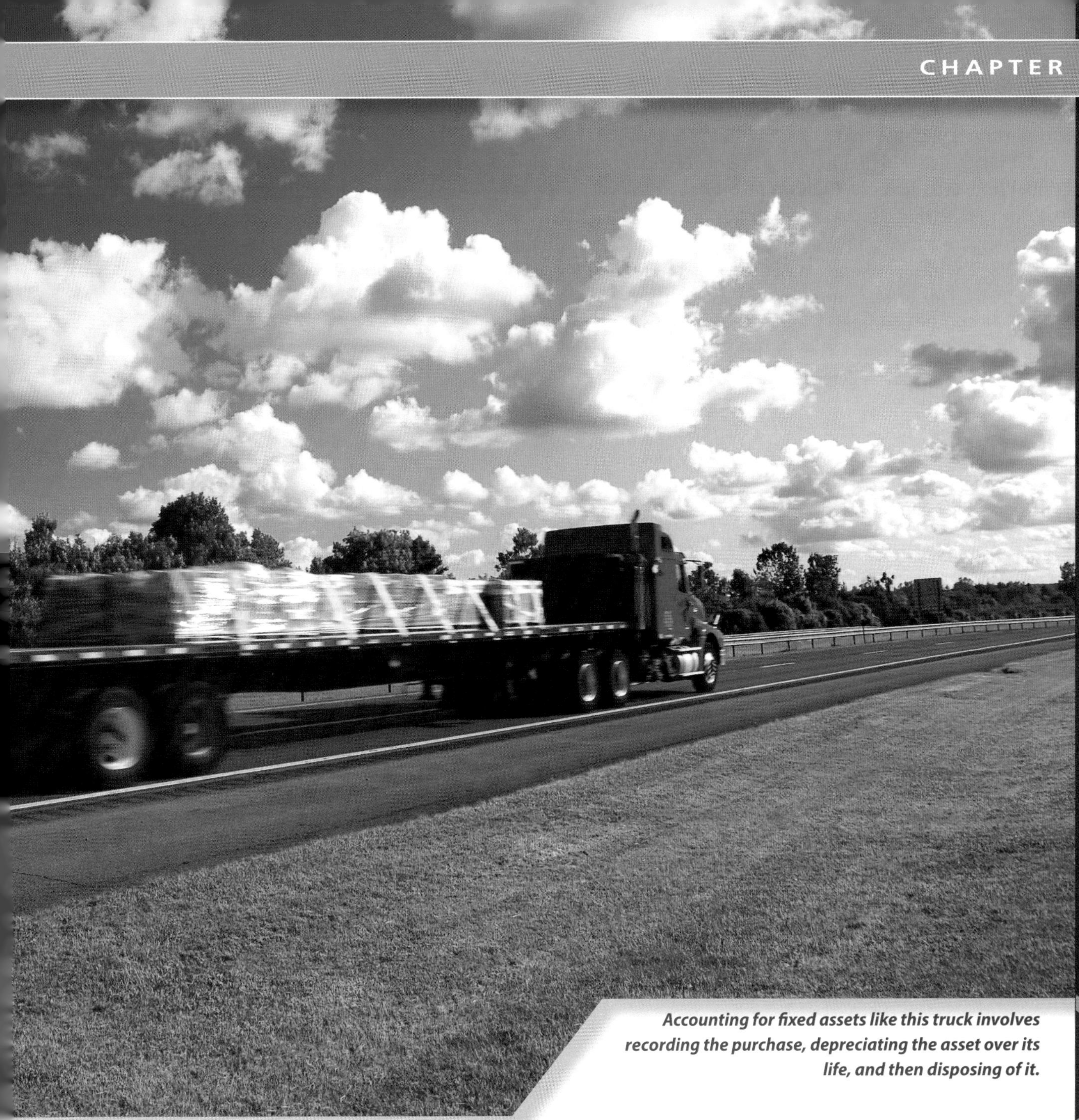

Accounting for fixed assets like this truck involves recording the purchase, depreciating the asset over its life, and then disposing of it.

© ISTOCKPHOTO.COM/ELENA ELISSEEVA

Recording Fixed Assets

Following the cost principle, fixed assets should be recorded at the cost of acquiring them. This includes all costs incurred to get the asset delivered, installed, and ready to use. Examples of expenditures to include in the cost of a fixed asset would therefore include, but not be limited to, the following:

- purchase price
- taxes paid on the purchase
- fees such as closing costs paid to attorneys
- delivery costs
- insurance costs during transit
- installation costs

To illustrate, suppose that Dozier Building Supply buys a delivery truck with a purchase price of ₹60,000, additional state sales taxes of ₹3,600, and a local tax of ₹400. Prior to receiving the truck, Dozier has the dealer paint the company's logo on the doors and install a specialized GPS. The dealer charges an additional ₹1,000 for this. Finally, Dozier pays an insurance company an additional ₹1,400 in premiums to add the truck to its coverage for the coming year. Given the preceding items, the cost of Dozier's truck is determined as follows:

Purchase price	₹60,000
Sales taxes	3,600
Local tax	400
Installation of logo and GPS	1,000
Total cost	₹65,000

All of the costs except for the insurance are necessary to get the asset into its condition and location for intended use and are therefore included in the cost of the truck. The insurance covers the truck during its operations and is therefore an operating expense during the year. Assuming that Dozier paid cash to the dealer, the entry to record the purchase of the truck would be as follows:

Delivery Truck	65,000	
Cash		65,000
(To record the purchase of truck)		

Assets	=	Liabilities	+	Equity
+65,000				
−65,000				

Consider another example. Suppose a company purchases a tract of land for a new building site. The purchase price is ₹5,00,000 plus ₹25,400 in taxes and fees paid to the realtor, the bank, and the attorneys. Included on the land are four small buildings that must be removed at a total cost of ₹12,000. Also, the land requires ₹1,00,000 in logging, grading, and filling before it can be used. The timber harvested from the logging is sold for ₹20,000. The total cost of the land is as follows:

Purchase price	₹5,00,000
Taxes and fees	25,400
Removal of buildings	12,000
Logging, grading, and filling	1,00,000
Less: Sales of timber	(20,000)
Total cost	₹6,17,400

In this case, each cost is included in the asset because the land is not in the condition for use until each of the activities is completed. Notice also that the proceeds from the sale of the timber reduce the cost of the land.

Expensing Fixed Assets

A fixed asset converts to an expense as it is used or consumed. The expensing of fixed assets is accomplished through *depreciation*. **Depreciation** is the process of allocating the cost of a fixed asset over its useful life. Depreciation is an application of the matching principle—because a fixed asset is used to generate revenues period after period, some of its cost should be expensed in, or matched to, those same periods. The amount of expense recognized each period is known as **depreciation expense**. The cumulative amount of depreciation expense recognized to date is known as **accumulated depreciation**.

Some students experience some confusion with depreciation because of its everyday use in our language. For example, it is often said that a new car "depreciates" in value once it is driven off the dealer's lot. When utilized in this way, the term depreciation implies a decline or loss in value because the car is used. For our purposes, depreciation is a process of allocating an asset's cost, not a method of determining an asset's market value.

While depreciation applies to fixed assets, not all fixed assets are depreciated. Depreciation applies only to those assets with limited useful lives. An asset has a limited useful life when its revenue generating potential

Depreciation The process of systematically and rationally allocating the cost of a fixed asset over its useful life.

Depreciation expense The portion of a fixed asset's cost that is recognized as an expense in the current period.

Accumulated depreciation The cumulative amount of depreciation expense recognized to date on a fixed asset.

For accounting purposes, depreciation is a process of allocating an asset's cost, not a method of determining an asset's market value.

is limited by wear and tear and/or obsolescence. Most fixed assets such as equipment and buildings have limited useful lives and are therefore subject to depreciation. The major exception to this is land, which has an unlimited useful life. As a result, land is not subject to depreciation.

Depreciation expense is normally calculated at the end of an accounting period and recorded with an adjusting journal entry. Regardless of the fixed asset being depreciated or the facts of the calculation, the general form of the entry is the same: Depreciation Expense and Accumulated Depreciation are increased.

To illustrate, suppose that Dozier calculates its truck's depreciation as ₹10,000 for the first year. At year-end, Dozier would make the following entry:

Year-end	Depreciation Expense	10,000	
	Accumulated Depreciation		10,000

Assets	=	Liabilities	+	Equity
−10,000				−10,000

This entry increases Depreciation Expense for the ₹10,000 of cost allocated to the current period. However, instead of decreasing Delivery Truck, the entry increases Accumulated Depreciation, which is a contra-asset account that accumulates all depreciation recorded to date. Its balance is subtracted from the fixed asset account to yield the net book value of the fixed asset. We will see an example of this later in the chapter. The result of this entry is a decrease to both equity and assets.

Like other expenses, depreciation expense is reported on the income statement. Most companies, such as the Power Grid Corporation of India Ltd, report it as a separate line item. A condensed version of Power Grid Corporation of India Ltd, 2011 operating expenses follows:

Power Grid Corporation of India Ltd
2012-13 Condensed Operating Expenses

in crores	
Costs and expenses	
Purchase of stock-in-trade	63.50
Employee benefit expenses	₹886.40
Transmission administration and other expenses	871.54
Depreciation and amortization expenses	3351.92
Finance costs	2535.52
Total	₹7708.58

Internationally there are other companies, such as McDonald's Corporation and Burger King Holdings of USA, do not separately disclose depreciation expense. Rather, they include it in a larger expense category, usually in Administrative Expenses. The operating expense portion of McDonald's 2010 income statement is shown as follows:

McDonald's 2010 Condensed Operating Expenses

in millions	
OPERATING COSTS AND EXPENSES	
Company-operated restaurant expenses:	
Food & paper	$ 5,300.1
Payroll & employee benefits	4,121.4
Occupancy & other operating expenses	3,638.0
Franchised restaurants—occupancy expenses	1,377.8
Selling, general & administrative expenses	2,333.3
Impairment and other charges, net	29.1
Other operating (income) expense, net	(198.2)
Total operating costs and expenses	$16,601.5

No reference is made to depreciation expense on the statement, but this does not mean that McDonald's had no depreciation expense. To find it, we must consult the notes to the financial statements. The following is an excerpt from McDonald's Property and Equipment note:

Excerpt from McDonald's
2010 Property and Equipment Note

Depreciation and amortization expense was (in millions): 2010—$1,200.4; 2009—$1,160.8; 2008—$1,161.6.

This note shows that over $1.2 billion in depreciation expense is included in one of the six operating expense subtotals in McDonald's 2010 income statement. Even though you don't see it on the income statement, it is there as a component of the reported expenses.

Reporting Fixed Assets

Fixed assets are reported on the balance sheet, usually as a separate line item under noncurrent assets. A condensed version of Power Grid Corporation 2013 balance sheet follows:

Power Grid Corporation India Ltd.
2012–13 Condensed Balance Sheet

in crores	
Fixed asset	₹ 80,515.56
Other noncurrent assets	24,352.55
Current assets	6,265.45
Total assets	₹1,11,133.56

Under the old Schedule VI of Indian Companies Act, some companies use "Property and Equipment" instead of "Fixed Assets." Because the bulk of fixed assets for most companies is property, buildings, and equipment, most companies use some variation of the term "property, plant and equipment" to describe their fixed assets. However, under the revised Schedule VI all companies report it under "Fixed Assets." Notice also that in the condensed Balance Sheet of Power Grid Ltd, the Fixed Assets figure is a "net" figure, net of depreciation. The term "net" is an abbreviation for the phrase *net book value*. **Net book value** represents the cost of a fixed asset that has been depreciated. It is calculated by subtracting the accumulated depreciation to date from the cost of the fixed asset. For example, an asset costing ₹5,000 with ₹1,000 of accumulated depreciation would have a net book value of ₹4,000.

Net book value The unexpired cost of a fixed asset, calculated by subtracting accumulated depreciation from the cost of the fixed asset.

IFRS

International accounting standards permit companies to revalue their fixed assets to current costs. Indian/US GAAP requires companies to maintain their fixed assets at historical cost.

Because condensed Balance Sheet of Power Grid only reports the net number on the balance sheet, those interested in how the net book value was calculated would need to consult the Schedule showing detail of Fixed Asset in the annual report. If one refers to Note 2.12 to 2.15 to the Financial Statements of Power Grid Corporation, one can get the detail of various asset held by Power Grid as on March 31, 2013, and also the detail regarding current years depreciation and accumulated depreciation.

MARUTI SUZUKI ANALYSIS

Look at Maruti Suzuki's Balance Sheet in Appendix C. What general name does the company use for its fixed assets and what specific fixed asset accounts does it list? What is the historical cost of its fixed assets, how much depreciation expense has been accumulated to date, and what is the net book value of those fixed assets? What does the company report for depreciation expense for the current year?

Maruti Suzuki uses the name Fixed Assets and goes on to calculate Net Block from Gross Block by subtracting accumulated depreciation. It also adds intangible assets (net) and Capital Work-in-Progress to arrive at total Fixed Assets Figure. Note 12 lists the following fixed assets: Freehold Land; Leasehold Land; Building; Plant and Machinery; Electronic Data Processing Equipment; Furniture, Fixtures and Office Appliances; Vehicles. Note 13 lists Intangible assets: Lump sum royalty. It states the Capital Work-in-Progress (Note 14) list Plant and Machinery and Civil Work in Progress. It reports ₹1,94,112 million (Note 12) and ₹3,895 (Note 13) million as Gross Block of Tangible and Intangible Fixed Assets, respectively, and Capital Work-in-Progress of ₹19,422 million. It also reports Accumulated Depreciation and Amortization to date of ₹98,347 million for tangible fixed assets and ₹1,668 million for intangible fixed assets. Together, these result in a net book value of ₹1,17,414 million.

While Power Grid Corporation reports "net" value of fixed assets internationally, there are companies, such as McDonald's, report both amounts directly on their balance sheets.

McDonald's
2010 Property and Equipment Note

in millions	
Property and equipment, at cost	$34,482.4
Accumulated depreciation and amortization	(12,421.8)
Net property and equipment	$22,060.6

McDonald's lists over $34 billion in cost of fixed assets and over $12 billion in accumulated depreciation of those assets. Thus, the net book value of its fixed assets is over $22 billion.

LO2 Calculating Depreciation Expense

When a company owns depreciable assets, it must calculate depreciation expense each period. Doing so requires the following information about the asset:

- Cost
- Salvage Value
- Useful Life
- Depreciation Method

Cost refers to the historical cost of the asset being depreciated. This is the amount that was recorded when the asset was purchased. **Salvage value** refers to the market value of the asset at the end of its useful life. It is the amount the company expects to receive when the asset is sold, traded-in, or scrapped. The difference between an asset's cost and its salvage value is the asset's net cost to the company, or its **depreciable cost**. The depreciable cost is the total amount that should be depreciated over time. **Useful life** refers to the length of time the asset will be used in operations.

Depreciation method refers to the method used to calculate depreciation expense. Generally accepted accounting principles allow the use of several different methods for calculating depreciation expense. This chapter focuses on the following three methods:

- Straight-line
- Double-declining-balance
- Units-of-activity

To illustrate how depreciation expense is calculated under each method, the Dozier Building Supply example will be continued. The following information about Dozier's delivery truck is available:

- Purchase Date: January 1, 2013
- Cost: ₹65,000
- Estimated Salvage Value: ₹15,000
- Estimated Useful Life: 5 years or 1,00,000 miles

Straight-Line Method

The **straight-line method** of depreciation spreads depreciation expense evenly over each year of the asset's useful life. It is a very simple calculation. The depreciable cost of the asset is divided by the useful life of the asset (in years) to yield the amount of depreciation expense per period. This calculation is shown below:

$$\text{Depreciation Expense} = \frac{\text{Cost} - \text{Salvage Value}}{\text{Useful Life}}$$

For Dozier's delivery truck, annual depreciation expense under the straight-line method would therefore be:

$$\text{Depreciation Expense} = \frac{₹65{,}000 - ₹15{,}000}{5} = ₹10{,}000$$

Cost The historical cost of a fixed asset being depreciated.

Salvage value An estimate of the value of a fixed asset at the end of its useful life.

Depreciable cost The difference between an asset's cost and its salvage value.

Useful life The length of time a fixed asset is expected to be used in operations.

Depreciation method The method used to calculate depreciation expense, such as the straight-line method, the double-declining-balance method, and the units-of-activity method.

Straight-line method A depreciation method that results in the same amount of depreciation expense each year of the asset's useful life.

Dozier would record the depreciation expense with the following adjusting journal entry at the end of the first year:

Dec. 31 2013	Depreciation Expense	10,000	
	Accumulated Depreciation		10,000

Assets	=	Liabilities	+	Equity
−10,000				−10,000

The same entry would be made at the end of each year through 2017. Exhibit 8-1 illustrates depreciation for the entire useful life of the asset.

Exhibit 8-1 Depreciation Schedule—Straight-Line Method

Year	Calculation	Depreciation Expense	Accumulated Depreciation	Net Book Value
			₹ 0	₹65,000
2013	(₹65,000 − ₹15,000) / 5	₹10,000	10,000	55,000
2014	(₹65,000 − ₹15,000) / 5	10,000	20,000	45,000
2015	(₹65,000 − ₹15,000) / 5	10,000	30,000	35,000
2016	(₹65,000 − ₹15,000) / 5	10,000	40,000	25,000
2017	(₹65,000 − ₹15,000) / 5	10,000	50,000	15,000

The depreciation schedule highlights several items. First, depreciation expense is the same each period. This will always be true under the straight-line method.

Second, the accumulated depreciation account grows each year by ₹10,000 until the balance equals the depreciable cost of the asset. This is no coincidence. The final balance in accumulated depreciation is the total of all depreciation expense recorded during the asset's life. Therefore, the balance should equal the asset's depreciable cost. This will be true regardless of the depreciation method used.

Finally, the net book value decreases each year by ₹10,000 until it equals the salvage value estimated for the asset. This is no coincidence either. Net book value represents the remaining unexpired cost of the asset. Therefore, an asset's final net book value should always equal the estimated salvage value at the end of the asset's useful life. This will be true regardless of the depreciation method used.

Double-Declining-Balance Method

The **double-declining-balance method** of depreciation is an accelerated method that results in more depreciation expense in the early years of an asset's life and less depreciation expense in the later years of an asset's life. As a result, the double-declining-balance method often matches expenses to revenues better than the straight-line method. More depreciation expense is recorded when the asset is more useful.

Double-declining-balance method A depreciation method that accelerates depreciation expense into the early years of an asset's life.

To calculate depreciation expense under the double-declining-balance method, the rate of depreciation is determined first by taking the straight-line rate of depreciation and doubling it (hence, the word *double* in the name). For example, if an asset has a four-year life, it has a straight-line rate of 25% (calculated by dividing 100% by four years). The straight-line rate is then doubled to 50%. An asset with a five-year life would have a 20% straight-line rate, which would be doubled to 40%. The doubled rate is then multiplied by the net book value of the asset to yield the amount of depreciation expense for the period. This calculation is shown as follows:

$$\begin{aligned}\text{Depreciation Expense} &= \text{Depreciation Rate} \times \text{Net Book Value}\\ &= (\text{Straight-Line Rate} \times 2)\\ &\quad \times (\text{Cost} - \text{Accumulated Depreciation})\end{aligned}$$

Before depreciation expense for Dozier is calculated, note again that the depreciation rate is applied to the net book value of the asset, not its depreciable cost. Because an asset's net book value declines as the asset is depreciated, the amount of depreciation expense will therefore differ each period. In fact, depreciation expense will become smaller and smaller each period as the depreciation rate is applied to a smaller net book value. This stands in contrast to the straight-line method and is why the name of this method contains the words *declining balance*.

Under the double-declining-balance method, Dozier's depreciation expense for the first year of the asset's life is calculated as follows:

Depreciation Expense for 2010 = (20% × 2) × (₹65,000 − ₹0) = ₹26,000

You can now see how the double-declining-balance method *accelerates* the depreciation. Instead of ₹10,000 of expense as under the straight-line method, depreciation expense in the first year is ₹26,000. In other words, ₹16,000 of depreciation expense is accelerated to the first year by using the double-declining-balance method instead of the straight-line method.

In the second year of the asset's life, the same formula is used. However, the resulting depreciation expense is lower because the depreciation rate is applied to a lower net book value. With ₹26,000 in depreciation to date, the accumulated depreciation balance is ₹26,000, yielding a net book value of ₹39,000 (₹65,000 – ₹26,000). Therefore, depreciation expense in the second year would be:

Depreciation Expense for 2011 = (20% × 2) × (₹65,000 − ₹26,000) = ₹15,600

As you can see, depreciation expense for the second year is lower than the first year, but it is still more than would be calculated under the straight-line method. In other words, depreciation expense is still being accelerated to the early years of the asset's life.

In the third year of the asset's life, the same formula is used again, but this time the net book value is ₹23,400 (cost of ₹65,000 less accumulated depreciation of ₹41,600). Therefore, the calculation of depreciation expense for the third year is as follows:

Depreciation Expense for 2012 = (20% × 2) × (₹65,000 − ₹41,600) = ₹9,360

Now, at this point we need to be careful. Over an asset's life, an entity cannot record more total depreciation than the asset's depreciable cost. Regardless of how much depreciation expense is calculated to be, an asset's accumulated depreciation balance should never exceed the asset's depreciable cost. In our example, Dozier's depreciable cost is ₹50,000. Accumulated depreciation after 2014 is ₹41,600. Therefore, depreciation expense in 2015 is limited to ₹8,400. This calculation is as follows:

Depreciable cost of asset (₹65,000 − ₹15,000)	₹50,000
Less: Accumulated depreciation at the end of 2014	41,600
Remaining depreciation to be taken	₹ 8,400

Even though the calculation yields ₹9,360, depreciation expense for 2015 is limited to ₹8,400. And, because Dozier's truck is fully depreciated after 2015, there is no depreciation expense for the remaining two years of the truck's life.

A schedule of depreciation for all five years is shown in Exhibit 8-2. The calculated amounts in 2015 are struck through and are replaced with the necessary amounts.

Exhibit 8-2 Depreciation Schedule—Double-Declining-Balance Method

Year	Calculation	Depreciation Expense	Accumulated Depreciation	Net Book Value
			₹ 0	₹65,000
2013	(20% × 2) × (₹65,000 − ₹0)	₹26,000	26,000	39,000
2014	(20% × 2) × (₹65,000 − ₹26,000)	15,600	41,600	23,400
2015	(20% × 2) × (₹65,000 − ₹41,600)	~~9,360~~	~~50,960~~	~~14,040~~
		8,400	50,000	15,000
2016		0	50,000	15,000
2017		0	50,000	15,000

Note that, as expected, depreciation expense is accelerated to the early years of the asset's life. Note also that, like the straight-line method, the double-declining-balance method results in a total of ₹50,000 of depreciation expense and a resulting net book value that is equal to the estimated salvage value of ₹15,000. The only difference between the methods is when depreciation expense is recognized.

Units-of-Activity Method

Both the straight-line and double-declining-balance methods are a function of the passage of time rather than the actual use of the asset. Each method assumes that the calculated depreciation is a reasonable representation of the actual usage of the asset. In contrast, the **units-of-activity method** of depreciation calculates depreciation based on actual asset activity. Because it relies on an estimate of an asset's lifetime activity, the method is limited to those assets whose units of activity can be determined with some degree of accuracy.

Calculating depreciation expense under the units-of-activity method starts by calculating depreciation per unit of expected activity. Depreciation per unit of expected activity is the depreciable cost of the asset divided by the estimated units of activity over the life of the asset.

$$\text{Depreciation Expense per Unit} = \frac{\text{Cost} - \text{Salvage Value}}{\text{Useful Life in Units}}$$

Note that this calculation is very similar to the straight-line calculation. Depreciable cost is divided by estimated life. But, instead of calculating depreciation expense per year, depreciation expense per unit is calculated. Once depreciation expense per unit is known, depreciation expense is determined by multiplying the per unit rate by the actual units of activity during the period. The calculation is as follows:

$$\text{Depreciation Expense} = \text{Depreciation Expense per Unit} \times \text{Actual Units of Activity}$$

For Dozier's truck, depreciation expense per unit will be a function of miles driven. Since Dozier estimates that the truck will be driven 1,00,000 miles, its estimated depreciation per mile would be ₹0.50 per mile.

$$\text{Depreciation Expense per Unit} = \frac{₹65{,}000 - ₹15{,}000}{1{,}00{,}000 \text{ miles}} = ₹0.50 \text{ per mile}$$

Units-of-activity method A depreciation method in which depreciation expense is a function of the actual usage of the asset.

With a ₹0.50 per mile rate, the actual miles driven in a given year is needed to calculate depreciation expense. Assume that Dozier drives the truck 24,000 miles in 2013. Its depreciation expense for 2013 would therefore be ₹12,000.

$$\text{Depreciation Expense} = ₹0.50 \times 24{,}000 = ₹12{,}000$$

Similar calculations would be made for the next four years of the asset's life. A depreciation schedule, complete with the actual miles driven in each of the five years, is shown in Exhibit 8-3.

As you review the schedule, note that depreciation expense fluctuates as the asset's activity fluctuates. As a result, depreciation expense is a function of usage. Second, note that the total number of miles driven over the five years equals 1,00,000 miles. This assumption is made for simplicity. However, had Dozier driven the truck more than 1,00,000 miles, total depreciation expense over the life of the asset would still be limited to ₹50,000, the asset's depreciable cost.

Exhibit 8-3 Depreciation Schedule—Units-of-Activity Method

Year	Calculation	Depreciation Expense	Accumulated Depreciation	Net Book Value
			₹ 0	₹65,000
2013	₹0.50 × 24,000 miles	₹12,000	12,000	53,000
2014	₹0.50 × 22,000 miles	11,000	23,000	42,000
2015	₹0.50 × 27,000 miles	13,500	36,500	28,500
2016	₹0.50 × 17,000 miles	8,500	45,000	20,000
2017	₹0.50 × 10,000 miles	5,000	50,000	15,000

Comparing Depreciation Methods

The calculations in the previous sections demonstrate that a company's depreciation expense in a given year will depend on the depreciation method chosen. For comparative purposes, Exhibit 8-4 summarizes the annual depreciation for Dozier's truck as well as the resulting net book values under the three methods.

The summary demonstrates that total depreciation expense over the life of the asset is ₹50,000 regardless of the method chosen. However, each method arrives at ₹50,000 differently. The straight-line method depreciates the same amount each year. The double-declining-balance method accelerates depreciation into the early years of the asset's life. The units-of-activity method depreciates different amounts each year depending on the asset's usage. No depreciation method is right. They are just different, and companies choose to use one over another for different reasons. One of the most common reasons is the effect on taxes.

One of the most common reasons that companies choose one depreciation method over another is the effect on taxes.

© STOCKBYTE/THINKSTOCK

Exhibit 8-4 Comparison of Three Depreciation Methods

Straight-Line			Double-Declining-Balance			Units-of-Activity		
Year	**Depr. Exp.**	**NBV**	**Year**	**Depr. Exp.**	**NBV**	**Year**	**Depr. Exp.**	**NBV**
2013	₹10,000	₹55,000	2013	₹26,000	₹39,000	2013	₹12,000	₹53,000
2014	10,000	45,000	2014	15,600	23,400	2014	11,000	42,000
2015	10,000	35,000	2015	8,400	15,000	2015	13,500	28,500
2016	10,000	25,000	2016	0	15,000	2016	8,500	20,000
2017	10,000	15,000	2017	0	15,000	2017	5,000	15,000
	₹50,000			₹50,000			₹50,000	

Like all expenses, depreciation expense reduces net income, which in turn reduces income taxes. Assuming a 40% tax rate in the example above, the ₹50,000 of depreciation on the truck will lower taxes by ₹20,000. The advantage of the double-declining-balance method is that all of the tax savings are realized in three years rather than five. This is beneficial to a company because the company can temporarily use the cash that would otherwise be paid to the government.

Many companies take advantage of this tax effect by using one method of depreciation for tax purposes and another for financial reporting purposes. The Internal Revenue Service (IRS) of USA allows companies to use a depreciation method known as the Modified Accelerated Cost Recovery System (MACRS). As its name implies, MACRS is an accelerated method much like the double-declining-balance method. However, the IRS does not require that a company use the same method on its tax return that it does for its financial statements. As a result, many companies that use MACRS for taxes use the straight-line method for financial reports. In India, however, reducing balance method of depreciation is allowed for Income Tax purpose.

Regardless of the method chosen, companies must disclose their choices in the notes to their financial statements so that comparisons can be made among different companies. This is an application of the qualitative characteristic of comparability. The disclosure is sometimes found in a note dedicated solely to fixed assets. However, most companies like Hindustan Unilever put it in the first note summarizing the significant accounting policies used to prepare financial statements.

Hindustan Unilever Disclosure of Depreciation Method (Note 2.4 to the Financial Statements)

Tangible assets are stated at acquisition cost, net of accumulated depreciation and accumulated impairment losses, if any. Subsequent expenditures related to an item of tangible asset are added to its book value only if they increase the future benefits from the existing asset beyond its previously assessed standard of performance.

Items of tangible assets that have been retired from active use and are held for disposal are stated at the lower of their net book value and net realisable value and are shown separately in the financial statements under "Other current assets." Any expected loss is recognized immediately in the statement of profit and loss.

Losses arising from the retirement of, and gains or losses arising from disposal of tangible assets which are carried at cost are recognized in the statement of profit and loss.

Depreciation is provided on a pro-rata basis on the straight line method over the estimated useful lives of the assets or at the rates prescribed under Schedule XIV to the Companies Act, 1956, whichever is higher. Accordingly,

- computers and related assets, included in office equipment are depreciated over four years;
- leasehold land is amortized over the primary period of the lease;
- certain assets of the cold chain, included in plant and equipment, are depreciated over four/ seven years; and
- vehicles are depreciated over six years

LO3 Adjustments Made During a Fixed Asset's Useful Life

> When actual experience shows that a past estimate was incorrect, accountants **change the estimate going forward** instead of correcting the past.

Since fixed assets are used for multiple years, companies sometimes must make adjustments as new information is available or as new activity occurs. These adjustments can arise from the following:

- Changes in estimates
- Additional expenditures to improve the fixed asset
- Significant declines in the asset's market value

Changes in Depreciation Estimates

Calculating depreciation expense requires that a company estimate the asset's useful life and its salvage value. These estimates are normally based on previous company experience with similar assets as well as factors such as the manufacturer's recommendations. As a result, they are usually fair and reasonable. However, estimates can differ from actual experience. When such errors are small and will not affect decision making, they are usually ignored. When the estimates are materially wrong, though, revisions can be made. We call this a change in estimate.

When an estimate is changed, the change is made prospectively, meaning that the change affects only the calculation of current and future depreciation expense. Depreciation expense for prior years is not retroactively corrected. Once an estimate is revised, current and future depreciation expense is calculated with the new estimate. This is done by (1) determining the remaining depreciable cost of the asset at the time of the revision and (2) depreciating that cost over the remaining useful life using the same depreciation method.

To illustrate, suppose that Thomas Supply purchases a machine for ₹90,000 on January 1, 2013. Thomas estimates that the machine will have a 10-year useful life and a ₹10,000 salvage value. Thomas uses the straight-line method of depreciation and records ₹8,000 of depreciation expense [(₹90,000 − ₹10,000) ÷ 10] each year as follows:

Dec. 31	Depreciation Expense	8,000	
	Accumulated Depreciation		8,000
	(To record depreciation expense)		

Assets	=	Liabilities	+	Equity
−8,000				−8,000

Now suppose that on January 1, 2017, Thomas decides that the machine will last only eight years rather than the ten years originally estimated and will have a salvage value of only ₹6,000 rather than ₹10,000. When these revisions are made, Thomas does not correct the four previous depreciation expense entries of ₹8,000 because they were based on reasonable estimates at the time. Instead, Thomas calculates the remaining depreciable cost of the asset and spreads it out over the remaining useful life.

To do this, Thomas must first calculate the net book value of the asset on the date of revision. This represents the unexpired cost of the asset.

Net book value at the time of estimate revision:	
Cost of the asset, January 1, 2013	₹90,000
Less: Accumulated depreciation for four years	32,000
Net book value on January 1, 2017	₹58,000

Next, Thomas subtracts from the net book value the asset's salvage value, which will result in the asset's remaining depreciable cost. Keep in mind that Thomas uses the revised salvage value. This is shown as follows:

Depreciable cost for future depreciation:	
Net book value on January 1, 2017	₹58,000
Less: Estimated salvage value	6,000
Remaining depreciable cost	₹52,000

Finally, under the straight-line method Thomas calculates depreciation expense by dividing the remaining depreciable cost by the remaining useful life. In this case, the total useful life is now estimated to be eight years instead of ten, which means that there are only four years remaining instead of six.

Depreciation expense under revised estimates:	
Remaining depreciable cost	₹52,000
Divided by remaining useful life	÷ 4
Annual depreciation expense	₹13,000

Under international standards, expenditures related to a major inspection of fixed assets should be capitalized. Under GAAP, such expenditure may be either capitalized or expensed as incurred.

Because classifying expenditures as **capital or revenue** is subjective, two accountants may classify the same expenditure differently.

With this new depreciation expense calculated, Thomas would make the following journal entry at the end of Years 5 through 8.

Dec. 31	Depreciation Expense	13,000	
	Accumulated Depreciation		13,000
	(To record depreciation expense)		

Assets	=	Liabilities	+	Equity
−13,000				−13,000

So, Thomas depreciates ₹8,000 per year in Years 1 through 4 and ₹13,000 per year in Years 5 through 8. This results in ₹84,000 of total depreciation over the life of the asset, which is equal to the original cost of the asset less its revised salvage value (₹90,000 − ₹6,000 = ₹84,000).

When a company has a material change in a fixed asset estimate, it will disclose the change in the notes to its financial statements. Exhibit 8-5 is an example from IBM, USA which in 1999 reduced income $404 million due to a change in useful life estimates on computers.

Exhibit 8-5 Change in Estimate—IBM

Change in Estimate
As a result of a change in the estimated useful life of personal computers from five years to three years, the company recognized a charge in the second quarter of 1999 of $404 million ($241 million after tax, $0.13 per diluted common share). In the second quarter of 1999, the company wrote off the net book value of personal computers that were three years old or older and, therefore, had no remaining useful life. The remaining book value of the assets will be depreciated over the remaining new useful life.

Expenditures After Acquisition

Most fixed assets require expenditures throughout their useful lives. You have to think no further than your personal automobile to see this. The purchasing price is only the first cost. Expenditures for oil changes, tune ups, minor repairs, and even major repairs come later. So, how are these additional expenditures treated from an accounting standpoint?

The accounting treatment for expenditures made during the useful life of a fixed asset depends on whether they are classified as *capital* or *revenue* expenditures. A **capital expenditure** increases the expected useful life or productivity of the asset. An example would be a new engine for an automobile. Capital expenditures are added to the cost of the asset and depreciated over the asset's remaining useful life. A **revenue expenditure** maintains the expected useful life or productivity of the asset. An example would be an oil change. Revenue expenditures are expensed in the period in which they are incurred. They are not added to the cost of the asset.

To illustrate, suppose that a company purchases a fixed asset for ₹50,000 on January 1, 2013. The company estimates the asset's useful life and salvage value at five years and ₹0, respectively. Using the straight-line depreciation method, the company records ₹10,000 of depreciation expense each year. Now suppose that on January 1, 2017, during the fifth and last year of the asset's life, the company incurs ₹1,000 in ordinary maintenance and ₹8,000 for upgrades. The upgrades allow the machine to be used productively in sixth and seventh year (2018 and 2019).

Given this information, the ₹1,000 is a revenue expenditure and should be expensed as follows:

Given this information, the ₹1,000 is a revenue expenditure and should be expensed as follows:

Jan. 1 2017	Maintenance Expense	1,000	
	Cash		1,000
	(To record normal maintenance)		

Assets	=	Liabilities	+	Equity
−1,000				−1,000

Capital expenditure An expenditure that increases the expected useful life or productivity of a fixed asset.

Revenue expenditure An expenditure that maintains the expected useful life or productivity of a fixed asset.

IFRS

Under international standards, expenditures related to a major inspection of fixed assets should be capitalized. Under GAAP, such expenditure may be either capitalized or expensed as incurred.

In contrast, the ₹8,000 for upgrades is a capital expenditure since the asset's useful life is extended two years. It should therefore be capitalized with the following entry:

Jan. 1 2017	Fixed Asset	8,000	
	Cash		8,000
	(To record upgrade to asset)		

Assets	=	Liabilities	+	Equity
+8,000				
−8,000				

Notice that this entry results in an increase and decrease to assets rather than a change in equity. This is because the company is capitalizing the expenditure rather than expensing it.

With this addition to the cost of the asset, depreciation expense for 2017 must be recalculated. To do so, the company follows the same general procedures used in the change of estimate scenario. It first calculates the net book value of the asset and then adds the calculate assets's remaining depreciable cost. This is accomplished by determining the asset's net book value at the time of expenditure, adding the new capital expenditure to yield an updated new book value. This is shown as follows:

Net book value after the capital expenditure:

Cost of the asset, January 1, 2014	₹50,000
Less: Accumulated depreciation for four years	(40,000)
Net book value on January 1, 2017	₹10,000
Add: Upgrades made in 2017	8,000
Updated net book value on January 1, 2017	₹18,000

Next, the company subtracts the asset's salvage value to get the remaining depreciable cost. Under the straight-line method of depreciation, the depreciable cost is then divided by the remaining useful life ,which

The classification of expenditures as capital expenditures rather than revenue expenditures was the source of one of the largest frauds in recent history.

is three years, to obtain depreciation expense. In 2017, 2018, and 2019, the company will record ₹6,000 of depreciation expense each year.

Depreciation expense after capital expenditure:

Updated net book value on January 1, 2014	₹18,000
Less: Estimated salvage value	0
Remaining depreciable cost on January 1, 2014	₹18,000
Divided by remaining useful life	÷ 3
Annual depreciation expense	₹ 6,000

While the classification of post-acquisition expenditures may seem rather unimportant, it is actually an area of great interest because of the potential for fraudulent behavior by companies. One of the largest corporate frauds in recent history centered on the treatment and reporting of revenue expenditures. In 2002, it was discovered that WorldCom was treating operating expenses associated with telecommunication lines as capital expenditures. Instead of appearing on the income statement as expenses, these costs were recorded as assets on the balance sheet. This resulted in a gross understatement of current expenses and overstatement of net income. Over the seven quarters that it committed this fraud, the company overstated its results by several billion dollars. After several years of investigation and prosecution, the chief executive officer of the company was found guilty of nine counts of securities fraud, conspiracy, and filing false documents.

Asset Impairment

Sometimes, a fixed asset's market value will fall substantially due to changing market conditions, technological improvements, or other factors. When a fixed asset's market value falls materially below its net book value and the decline in value is deemed to be *permanent*, the asset is considered *impaired*. Accounting rules require companies to write impaired assets down from their book values to their market values. This, like the lower-of-cost-or-market rule with inventory, is an application of the concept of conservatism.

MARUTI SUZUKI ANALYSIS

Look at Maruti Suzuki's Note 1.6 to the Financial Statements Depreciation/Amortization financial statements in Appendix C. State the methods followed for calculating depreciation/amortization.

Fixed assets are depreciated on the straight-line method at the rate prescribed in Schedule XIV of the Companies Act, 1956. Leasehold assets are amortized over the period of lease. Assets having written down value at the beginning of the year ₹ 5000 or less are depreciated at 100%. Lump sum royalty is amortized on straight-line basis over 4 years.

To illustrate, suppose a company has equipment that makes a unique toy that becomes extremely popular. The equipment has a net book value of ₹1,40,000 and a higher market value. Suppose further that the toy suddenly loses its popularity, and the company is unable to alter the machine to produce anything else. As a result, the market value of the machine plummets to ₹40,000. The company deems this decline in market value to be permanent and declares that the asset is impaired. The asset impairment would be recorded as follows:

Loss on Impairment	1,00,000	
Fixed Asset		1,00,000
(To record permanent impairment of asset)		

Assets	=	Liabilities	+	Equity
−100,000				−100,000

In the above entry, a Loss on Impairment is increased to reflect the decline in value of the asset. This reduces equity. In addition, the Equipment account is decreased to reflect the reduced value. This reduces assets. After the impairment entry, depreciation expense would be calculated based on the revised depreciable cost and remaining useful life.

Asset impairments are not uncommon. In fact, current accounting rules require companies to periodically assess whether any of their fixed assets are impaired. Consider the note to Ranbaxy Laboratories Limited financial statements as shown in Exhibit 8-6.

While the note speaks of issues that are beyond the scope of this book, you can at least see that asset impairments can be material to a company's financial results. Ranbaxy Laboratories Limited recorded ₹826.29 million in impairments in the year ending December 31, 2012.

LO4 Disposing of Fixed Assets

When a company decides that it no longer needs a fixed asset, it usually disposes of the asset in one of three ways. When the asset has no value, it will simply be discarded. When the asset still has value, it will either be sold or traded in for another asset, often a

Exhibit 8-6 Asset Impairment—Ranbaxy Laboratories Limited

Impairment of Assets

Fixed assets are reviewed at each reporting date to determine if there is any indication of impairment. For assets in respect of which any such indication exists and for intangible assets mandatorily tested annually for impairment, the asset's recoverable amount is estimated. For assets that are not yet available for use, the recoverable amount is estimated at each reporting date. An impairment loss is recognized if the carrying amount of an asset exceeds its recoverable amount. For the purpose of impairment testing, assets are grouped together into the smallest group of assets (Cash Generating Unit or CGU) that generates cash inflows from continuing use that are largely independent of the cash inflows of other assets or CGUs. The recoverable amount of an asset or CGU is the greater of its value in use and its net selling price. In assessing value in use, the estimated future cash flows are discounted to their present value using a pre-tax discount rate that reflects current market assessments of the time value of money and the risks specific to the asset or CGU. Impairment losses are recognized in the Statement of Profit and Loss.

MAKING IT REAL

The value of a company's equipment can be impaired or reduced for many reasons. One of those is a decrease in demand for the product that the equipment makes. Take Crocs, Inc., as an example.

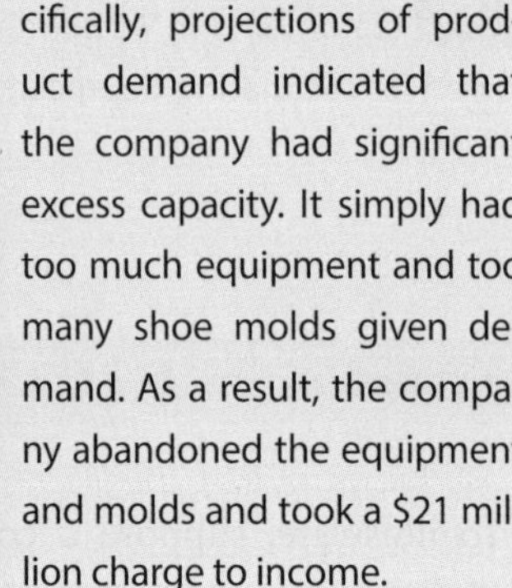

Crocs, Inc., is well known for its lightweight and colorful ventilated clogs. The company burst onto the scene in 2002 with the launch of its Beach™ model, and demand grew quickly. The company responded by rapidly diversifying into different styles and increasing production capacity and warehouse space. By 2007, the company was generating record profits of $168 million.

But things quickly changed. Demand for Crocs' products fell in 2008, resulting in a $185 million overall loss. Approximately 11% of that loss, or $21 million, was attributable to impairment charges on its manufacturing equipment. Specifically, projections of product demand indicated that the company had significant excess capacity. It simply had too much equipment and too many shoe molds given demand. As a result, the company abandoned the equipment and molds and took a $21 million charge to income.

And unfortunately for the company, the impairments continued into 2009. For the first six months of 2009, Crocs has recognized $17 million in asset impairment charges related to shoe molds and distribution facilities.

newer model. Since the accounting for trading an asset is beyond the scope of this book, we will focus on the first two cases—discarding or selling the asset.

The accounting for the disposal of a fixed asset consists of the following three steps:

1. Update depreciation on the asset.
2. Calculate gain or loss on the disposal.
3. Record the disposal.

The first step is to record any necessary depreciation expense to update the accumulated depreciation account. Usually, this means that depreciation expense must be recorded for a partial period. For example, a company that records annual depreciation expense on December 31 and sells equipment on the following February 15 must record depreciation expense for one and one-half months at the time of disposal.

The second step is to calculate any gain or loss on the disposal by comparing the asset's net book value to the proceeds from the asset's sale, if any. When the proceeds exceed the net book value, a gain on disposal is recognized. When the net book value exceeds the proceeds, a loss on disposal is recognized. This is summarized below:

> Gain on Disposal =
> Proceeds from Sale > Net Book Value
>
> Loss on Disposal =
> Proceeds from Sale < Net Book Value

The third and final step is to prepare a journal entry that decreases the asset account and its related accumulated depreciation account. If the asset is sold and cash is received, the entry must also record the increase in cash. Finally, any gain or loss on the disposal must be recorded.

To illustrate, suppose that a company purchases a machine on January 1, 2013, for ₹30,000. The company estimates the useful life and salvage value to be four years and ₹2,000, respectively. The company uses the straight-line method of depreciation and records depreciation expense annually on December 31. Given these facts, annual depreciation expense for the machine is ₹7,000 [(₹30,000 – ₹2,000) / 4].

Loss Example

Suppose further that the company sells the machine on June 30, 2015, for ₹12,000. To account for this sale, the company must first update the accumulated depreciation account. The asset has been used for six months since the last time depreciation was recorded (December 31), so the company must record six months of depreciation expense. Since annual depreciation expense is ₹7,000, six months of depreciation would be half of that, or ₹3,500. Therefore, the following entry would be made on June 30, 2015:

June 30 2015	Depreciation Expense	3,500	
	Accumulated Depreciation		3,500

Assets	=	Liabilities	+	Equity
−3,500				−3,500

As a result of this entry, the accumulated depreciation account is updated to a balance of ₹17,500 (₹7,000 in 2013, ₹7,000 in 2014, and ₹3,500 in 2015). With this balance, the gain/loss on disposal can be calculated as follows:

Proceeds from sale		₹12,000
Cost of machine	₹30,000	
Less: Accumulated depreciation	17,500	
Net book value at June 30, 2015		12,500
Loss on sale		₹ (500)

Because the asset's net book value of ₹12,500 exceeds the sale proceeds of ₹12,000, the company generates a ₹500 loss. With this information, the company can prepare the following journal entry to record the disposal:

June 30 2015	Cash	12,000	
	Accumulated Depreciation	17,500	
	Loss on Disposal	500	
	Machine		30,000

Assets	=	Liabilities	+	Equity
+12,000				−500
+17,500				
−30,000				

The entry first decreases the Machine account by ₹30,000 to eliminate the account. A common mistake is to think that the Machine account should be decreased by its net book value of ₹12,500. But remember that fixed assets are recorded and maintained at their costs, so the balance in the Machine account is ₹30,000 prior to disposal. Second, the entry decreases Accumulated Depreciation by ₹17,500. Because the company no longer has the asset, it should no longer maintain accumulated depreciation for the asset. Third, the entry increases the Cash account to reflect the asset received from selling the machine. Finally, the entry increases a Loss on Disposal account to reflect the loss on sale. This account is reported on the income statement among Other Revenues and Expenses. As a result of the entry, assets and equity decrease by ₹500, the amount of the loss.

A loss on the sale of a fixed asset is reported in other expenses so that operating expenses include only those expenses related to normal operations.

Gain Example

To illustrate a gain example, suppose that the company sells the machine on March 31, 2016, for ₹8,000. After updating depreciation, the Accumulated Depreciation account would have a balance of ₹22,750:

Three full years (2013, 2014, 2015)	₹21,000
One-fourth of 2016 (₹7,000 × ¼)	1,750
Accumulated depreciation at March 31, 2016	₹22,750

Therefore, the machine's net book value and the gain/loss on disposal at March 31, 2016, can be calculated as follows:

Proceeds from sale		₹8,000
Cost of machine	₹30,000	
Less: Accumulated depreciation	22,750	
Net book value at March 31, 2013		7,250
Gain on sale		₹ 750

Because the sale proceeds of ₹8,000 exceed the asset's net book value of ₹7,250, the company generates a

₹750 gain. With this information, the following journal entry can be prepared to record the disposal:

Mar. 31 2016	Cash	8,000	
	Accumulated Depreciation	22,750	
	Gain on Disposal		750
	Machine		30,000

Assets	=	Liabilities	+	Equity
+ 8,000				+750
+22,750				
−30,000				

Like the loss example, the entry decreases the Machine account by ₹30,000. It also decreases the machine's Accumulated Depreciation account by ₹22,750 to eliminate the account and increases the Cash account by ₹8,000 to reflect the asset received from selling the machine. Finally, the entry increases a Gain on Disposal account to reflect the gain on sale. Like the loss example, the net effect on the accounting equation is an equal change in assets and equity, with this example resulting in a ₹750 increase to both.

LO5 Evaluating a Company's Management of Fixed Assets

Because fixed assets comprise the largest category of assets for most companies, it is usually a good idea to evaluate a company's management of its fixed assets. A company manages fixed assets by acquiring them, using them productively, and then replacing them. Therefore, two issues of importance for any company with fixed assets would be as follows:

1. How productive are the company's fixed assets in generating revenues?
2. What is the condition of the company's fixed assets?

The following sections examine these issues for the fixed assets of McDonald's USA. The examination will require information from the company's balance sheet, income statement, and notes to the financial statements. The required information is found in Exhibit 8-7, excerpted from McDonald's 2010 Annual Report.

Horizontal and Vertical Analyses

A good place to start an analysis of fixed assets is with horizontal and vertical analyses. Recall from Chapter 2 that horizontal analysis calculates the dollar/rupee change in an account balance, defined as the current year balance less the prior year balance, and divides that change by the prior year balance to yield the percentage change. Vertical analysis divides each account balance by a base account, yielding a percentage. The base account is total assets for balance sheet accounts and net sales or total revenues for income statement accounts. These calculations are summarized as follows:

Horizontal Analysis

$$\text{Dollar/rupee change in account balance} = \text{Current year balance} - \text{Prior year balance}$$

$$\text{Percentage change in account balance} = \frac{\text{Dollar/rupee change}}{\text{Prior year balance}}$$

Vertical Analysis

Balance Sheet / *Income Statement*

$$\text{Percentage} = \frac{\text{Account Balance}}{\text{Total Assets}} \text{ or } \frac{\text{Account Balance}}{\text{Net Sales or Revenue}}$$

Exhibit 8-7 Account Balances from McDonald's 2010 Annual Report

Source	Accounts	2010	2009
Income Statement	Total revenues	\$ 24,074.6	\$ 22,744.7
Balance Sheet	Property and equipment, at cost	\$ 34,482.4	\$ 33,440.5
	Less: Accumulated depreciation	(12,421.8)	(11,909.0)
	Net property and equipment	\$ 22,060.6	\$ 21,531.5
	Total assets	\$ 31,975.2	\$ 30,224.9
Notes to Financial Statements	Depreciation expense	\$ 1,200.4	\$ 1,160.8

Given McDonald's financial information in Exhibit 8-7, horizontal and vertical analyses of fixed assets and depreciation expense result in the following. Note that the net book value of property and equipment is used in the calculations. Note also that vertical analysis is conducted on both years of data.

Horizontal Analysis

	Dollar Change	*Percentage Change*
Property and equipment	22,060.6 − 21,531.5 = 529.1	$\frac{529.1}{21,531.5} = 2.5\%$
Depreciation expense	1,200.4 − 1,160.8 = 39.6	$\frac{39.6}{1,160.8} = 3.4\%$

Vertical Analysis

	2010	*2009*
Property and equipment	$\frac{22,060.6}{31,975.2} = 69.0\%$	$\frac{21,531.5}{30,224.9} = 71.2\%$
Depreciation expense	$\frac{1,200.4}{24,074.6} = 5.0\%$	$\frac{1,160.8}{22,744.7} = 5.1\%$

The calculations show a fairly stable fixed asset position. Horizontal analysis shows a slight increase of 2.5% in fixed assets and an increase of 3.4% in depreciation expense from 2009 to 2010. Vertical analysis shows that fixed assets make up a large part of McDonald's asset base. In both years, around 70% of the company's assets are fixed assets. Furthermore, depreciation expense is shown to be about 5% in each year. This tells us that for every dollar in sales revenue, the company incurs about a nickel in depreciation expense. Overall, both of these analyses indicate fairly stable fixed assets over the two-year period.

For comparison purposes, the following table lists the 2010 horizontal and vertical analyses of Burger King Holdings, USA. The comparison shows that McDonald's has a larger percentage of its total assets in fixed. However, for both companies, depreciation expense consumes around 5% of total revenues, with Burger King's depreciation expenses increasing faster than McDonald's.

		Horizontal Analysis	Vertical Analysis
Fixed Assets	*McDonald's*	2.5%	69.0%
	Burger King	0.1%	37.0%
Depreciation Expense	*McDonald's*	3.4%	5.0%
	Burger King	13.9%	4.5%

Fixed Asset Turnover Ratio

The preceeding analyses indicate that McDonald's fixed assets were stable. But they do not indicate whether the company is using those fixed assets productively to generate revenues. One means to find out is to calculate the fixed asset turnover ratio. The **fixed asset turnover ratio** compares total revenues during a period to the average net book value of fixed assets during that period. It is calculated as follows:

$$\text{Fixed Asset Turnover Ratio} = \frac{\text{Total Revenues}}{\text{Average Net Book Value of Fixed Assets}}$$

where average net book value is:

$$\frac{\text{Beginning Net Book Value} + \text{Ending Net Book Value}}{2}$$

Because this ratio compares total revenues to fixed assets, it indicates the productivity of every dollar invested in fixed assets. In general, companies want this ratio to be higher rather than lower. All other things equal, a higher ratio indicates that the company is using its fixed assets more effectively to produce more revenue.

McDonald's 2010 fixed asset turnover ratio is calculated as follows.

$$\frac{24,074.6}{(22,060.6 + 21,531.5) \div 2} = 1.10$$

The 1.10 ratio shows that McDonald's total revenues for 2010 were 1.10 times the average net book value of its fixed assets. In other words, for every dollar of fixed assets, on average, McDonald's was able to generate $1.10 in revenue during the period. Whether this is good or bad requires some comparison. Burger King's fixed asset turnover ratio was 2.47. McDonald's trails its rival in generating revenues from its fixed assets.

Fixed asset turnover ratio A comparison of total revenues to the average net book value of fixed assets that measures the productivity of fixed assets.

MARUTI SUZUKI ANALYSIS

Using Maruti Suzuki's information in Appendix C, calculate and interpret (1) horizontal and vertical analyses of fixed assets and depreciation expense, (2) fixed asset turnover ratio, and (3) average life and average age of fixed assets.

(1) Horizontal Analysis

Fixed assets: (₹1,17,414 – ₹84,626)/₹84,626 = 38.7%

Depreciationexpense:(₹18,612–₹11,384)/₹11,384=63.5%

Vertical Analysis

Fixed assets: ₹1,17,414/₹2,66,880 = 44%

Depreciation expense: ₹18,612/₹4,26,126 = 4.37%

The horizontal analysis shows that while depreciation expense was up, overall fixed assets increased slightly during the year. The 44% vertical analysis of fixed assets shows how important fixed assets are to the company. The 4.3% vertical analysis of depreciation expense indicates that although the company has large fixed assets, depreciation expense consumes less than five cents per rupee of sales in the most recent year.

(2) Fixed Asset Turnover Ratio:

₹4,26,126/(₹1,17,414 + 84,626)/2 = 4.22

The 4.22 fixed asset turnover ratio indicates that Maruti Suzuki generates ₹4.22 in sales for every ₹1 of fixed assets that it owns. This could provide Maruti Suzuki with a benchmark expectation for Company. For example, a company in the same industry with ₹10 million of fixed assets could be expected to generate about ₹42 million in sales.

(3) Average Life Ratio: ₹1,17,414/₹18,612 = 6.3 years

Average Age Ratio: ₹1,00,015/18,612 = 5.37

The 6.3 average life ratio shows that Maruti Suzuki average fixed asset has about a 6-year life. The 5 average ratio indicates that the company's fixed assets have been used for about 5 years. Taken together, these two ratios indicate that Maruti Suzuki will need fixed asset replacement in the near term.

Average Life and Age of Fixed Assets

In addition to understanding the productivity of fixed assets, it is a good idea to understand the condition of a company's fixed assets. Fixed assets in poor condition are usually less productive and normally require significant expenditures either to repair or replace. While a user of McDonald's financial statements cannot physically examine the company's fixed assets, one way to get a rough idea of the general condition of a company's fixed assets is to look at the age of the assets in comparison to their useful lives. This can be accomplished by calculating the average useful life and average age of the assets.

The **average useful life of fixed assets** represents the number of years, on average, that a company expects to use its fixed assets. It is calculated as follows:

$$\text{Average Useful Life} = \frac{\text{Cost of Fixed Assets}}{\text{Depreciation Expense}}$$

The ratio divides the total cost of fixed assets by the amount of annual depreciation expense to approximate the number of years that it will take to fully depreciate the assets. A higher number represents a longer useful life. You may notice that this ratio is basically a rearrangement of the calculation of straight-line depreciation. Therefore, the ratio works best when the company uses the straight-line method.

The **average age of fixed assets** represents the number of years, on average, that the company has used its fixed assets. It is calculated as follows:

Average useful life of fixed assets A comparison of the cost of fixed assets to depreciation expense that estimates the number of years, on average, that a company expects to use its fixed assets.

Average age of fixed assets A comparison of accumulated depreciation to depreciation expense that estimates the number of years, on average, that the company has used its fixed assets.

$$\text{Average Age} = \frac{\text{Accumulated Depreciation}}{\text{Depreciation Expense}}$$

The ratio divides the accumulated depreciation balance by the amount of annual depreciation expense to approximate the number of years that the assets have already been depreciated. A higher number means that the assets are older. Like the average useful life ratio, the average age ratio works best when the company uses the straight-line method.

Calculating McDonald's 2010 ratios requires the cost of the fixed assets and their accumulated depreciation balances at the end of 2010. These are found on the balance sheet. It also requires depreciation expense for 2010. This is found in the company's Property and Equipment note to its financial statements. Each account balance is shown in Exhibit 8-7.

$$\text{Average Life} = \frac{34{,}482.4}{1{,}200.4} = 28.7$$

$$\text{Average Age} = \frac{12{,}421.8}{1{,}200.4} = 10.3$$

The ratios show that McDonald's fixed assets, on average, have about a 29-year expected life and are currently about 10 years old. Now, we have to be careful here not to read too much into these numbers. In its first note to its financial statements, McDonald's reports that it assumes lives of up to 40 years for buildings, up to 15 years for restaurant equipment, and up to 10 years for other equipment. Like many companies, McDonald's has various fixed assets with various useful lives. While this makes the average life and age ratios very general estimates, the calculations do allow us to draw the general conclusion that the company's fixed assets are relatively new. On average, the company has used its fixed assets for about one-third of their useful lives. Thus, we would not expect McDonald's to have abnormally high expenditures for repairing or replacing fixed assets in the near future.

LO6 Fixed Assets and Cash Flows

Another important aspect of fixed assets is their effect on a company's cash flows. Fixed assets affect cash flows the most when they are purchased. Because companies often purchase significant amounts of fixed assets each year, the cash paid for them is reported as a separate line item in the investing activities section of the statement of cash flows. The line item is often labeled as Capital Expenditures or something similar. McDonald's is a little more specific, reporting the following on the first line of its investing activities section:

A negative number for **capital expenditures** indicates that a company is investing in operating assets.

McDonald's 2010 Capital Expenditures from the Statement of Cash Flows

in millions	2010	2009	2008
Property and equipment expenditures	\$(2,135.5)	\$(1,952.1)	\$(2,135.7)

The negative number signifies a cash outflow. In 2010, McDonald's spent over \$2.1 billion in cash to purchase fixed assets. In the two previous years, the company spent about \$1.9 billion and \$2.1 billion. For the three years combined, this totals over \$6.1 billion in cash paid for fixed assets.

A natural question arising from this data is where the company got the \$6.1 billion it needed for these investments in fixed assets. Did it borrow the money or did it have it on hand? We can get an idea of where the money came from by looking one line above the capital expenditures. There we find the cash provided by operating activities, which is summarized as follows:

McDonald's 2010 Operating Cash Flows from the Statement of Cash Flows

in millions	2010	2009	2008
Cash provided by operations	\$6,341.6	\$5,751.0	\$5,917.2

In each year, McDonald's generated more cash from operating activities than it spent for fixed assets. For example, in 2010 the company generated \$6.3 billion in cash from operations while it paid out \$2.1 billion for fixed assets. This means that the company was able to finance its growth with money generated from profitable operations. When a company's capital expendi-

MARUTI SUZUKI ANALYSIS

Look at Maruti Suzuki's statement of cash flows in Appendix C. How much cash has the company spent to acquire fixed assets over the past two years in total? Compare Maruti Suzuki's capital expenditures in the most recent year to its cash from operations.

According to the investing activities section of its statement of cash flows, Maruti Suzuki spent a total of ₹68,246 million capital expenditures over the past two years (₹38,549 + ₹29,697 = 68,246 million).

Maruti Suzuki's capital expenditures in the most recent year were ₹38,549 million while its cash generated from operations was ₹43,842 million. Thus, it appears that Maruti Suzuki generated enough cash to pay for its growth in fixed assets without having to borrow the cash or dip into its reserves.

tures exceed its cash from operating activities, the company must get the needed cash from some other place. Either it must use its cash reserves or borrow the money from a creditor. Being able to generate enough cash to pay for new fixed assets is a good sign for McDonald's.

LO7 Intangible Assets

In addition to fixed assets, companies often possess other long-term assets known as intangible assets. An **intangible asset** is a resource that is used in operations for more than one year but has no physical substance. A patent is a good example. A **patent** is the right, granted by the Controller General of Patents, Designs & Trade Marks (CGPDTM) of India, for the holder of the patent to manufacture, sell, or use a particular product or process exclusively for a limited period of time. Although the right of exclusive use has no physical properties, it can be a very valuable resource to the holder. Consider the pharmaceutical industry. When a company develops a new drug that is approved by the Food and Drug Administration, which will be more valuable—the equipment that manufactures the drug or the patent that provides for exclusive manufacturing and selling of the drug? Pharmaceutical companies will likely tell you that the patent is most valuable to them.

You are probably familiar with other intangible assets. For example, a **trademark** or **trade name** is the right, granted by the Controller General of Patents, Designs & Trade Marks (CGPDTM), office of India, for a company to use exclusively a name, symbol, or phrase to identify the company. Often, you can tell if something is registered as a trademark if it has a small ™ or ® beside the name or symbol. Natural Ice Cream™ is an example. No other company, without permission from Natural Ice Cream's, can lawfully use this name in association with an ice cream drink. The Thumps Up™ is another example, as is the script Coca-Cola™.

Another recognizable intangible is a copyright. A **copyright** is the right, granted by the Copyright Registration Office in India, to reproduce or sell an artistic or published work. The publisher of this book owns the copyright to the material in the book and can reproduce and sell it as it pleases. The material cannot be reproduced by someone else lawfully without the permission of the publisher.

A third intangible with which you may be familiar is a franchise. A **franchise** is the right, granted by the franchisor, to operate a business under the trade name of the franchisor. Examples of franchises are all around you. For example, whenever you visit a McDonald's, you may be entering into a restaurant that is owned by an individual (the franchisee) who has purchased from

Intangible asset A resource that is used in operations for more than one year but that has no physical substance.

Patent The right to manufacture, sell, or use a particular product or process exclusively for a limited period of time.

Trademark (trade name) The right to use exclusively a name, symbol, or phrase to identify a company.

Copyright The right to reproduce or sell an artistic or published work.

Franchise The right to operate a business under the trade name of the franchisor.

McDonald's Corporation (the franchisor) the right to operate the restaurant.

Recording Intangible Assets

Like all other assets, intangible assets are recorded at their acquisition costs. However, what is included as an acquisition cost can vary given the type of intangible asset and how it is acquired.

Externally Acquired The easiest case is when an intangible asset is acquired through an external transaction. For example, suppose that a company purchases a product patent from another company for ₹1,00,000. Because the patent is purchased in an arm's length transaction with another company, the cost of the patent is the purchase price. In general, if an intangible asset is acquired through an external transaction, its cost is the purchase price.

A common example of an intangible that is created through an external transaction is goodwill. Goodwill is created when one company buys another company and pays more than the value of the net assets of the purchased company. **Goodwill** is equal to the excess of the purchase price over the value of the purchased net assets. For example, suppose that on December 8 Buyer Company purchases Seller Company for ₹8 million when the value of Seller Company's net assets is ₹6 million. In this transaction, Buyer Company pays ₹8 million and records ₹6 million of new assets and ₹2 million of goodwill. A condensed form of the entry Buyer Company would make to record this transaction would be as follows:

Dec. 8	Net Assets of Seller Company	60,00,000	
	Goodwill	20,00,000	
	Cash		80,00,000
	(To record the purchase of Seller)		

Assets	=	Liabilities	+	Equity
+60,00,000				
+20,00,000				
−80,00,000				

The above entry records the decrease in cash resulting from the purchase and the increase in net assets acquired through the purchase. The difference of ₹2 million is debited to Goodwill, which increases that asset account. The result of the entry is an increase and decrease to assets.

To understand what goodwill represents, think about why a company would pay a premium for another company. The purchasing company might want to acquire the other company's customers, its reputation, its employees, its market share, or its research. Whatever the reason, the purchasing company is paying for something intangible that the other company possesses. This intangible value is what goodwill represents. Note here that goodwill can be recorded by a company *only* when it purchases another company. Goodwill created internally by a company cannot be recorded as an asset because its cost cannot be reliably determined. Only through an independent purchase can the value of goodwill be objectively measured.

Goodwill can be a large asset on the balance sheets of companies that have acquired other companies. See Entertainment Enterprises Limited is a good example. On its March 31, 2011, the consolidated balance sheet of the company reports over ₹60,38,464 thousand in goodwill schedule 5. Most of this goodwill of Zee represents the difference between the group's shares in the net worth of the subsidiary or an associate, and the cost of acquisition at the time of making the investment in the subsidiary or the associate. McDonald's (USA) also has a large balance in goodwill. It reports over \$2.6 billion in goodwill on total assets of over \$32 billion. Goodwill makes up about 8% of McDonald's assets.

Internally Generated In the previous two examples, intangible assets were purchased externally and therefore recorded at their purchase prices. When an intangible asset is developed internally, the accounting is slightly different. The initial cost of an internally generated intangible asset is limited to the legal and administrative fees to establish the asset.

To illustrate, suppose that a company's researchers spend ₹1,50,000 creating a patentable product. To register the patent, the company spends ₹10,000. In this case, the cost of the patent is only ₹10,000. The ₹1,50,000 of research and development must be expensed in the period it is incurred, not added to the cost of the asset. While many disagree with this accounting treatment, it is another application of conservatism. It is very difficult to know whether particular research and development costs will result in productive assets and how long those assets might last. Given this uncertainty, excluding research and development costs from the cost

Goodwill An intangible asset equal to the excess that one company pays to acquire the net assets of another company.

of an internally developed intangible asset reduces the likelihood that the intangible asset is overstated.

Once an intangible asset is acquired and recorded, it is often challenged by other companies. For example, patent holders often must defend their rights against companies manufacturing similar products. When a company incurs costs to successfully defend the legality of its assets, such costs should be added to the cost of the asset. You can see this treatment in company disclosures. For example, eSpeed, Inc., USA a provider of business-to-business electronic solutions, discloses in its notes that "[i]ntangible assets consist of purchased patents, costs incurred in connection with the filing and registration of patents and *the costs to defend and enforce our rights under patents.*"

Amortizing Intangible Assets

Like fixed assets that are depreciated, intangible assets with limited useful lives are amortized. **Amortization** is the process of spreading out the cost of an intangible asset over its useful life. Two examples of intangible assets with limited lives are patents and copyrights. Patents are granted for up to 20 years, and copyrights are granted in India for the life of the creator plus 60 years. Companies usually use the straight-line method for amortization.

To illustrate, suppose that a company possesses a ₹60,000 patent that has the maximum legal life of 20 years. The company believes that the patent will be useful for only 12 years and will then be worthless. Amortization expense at the end of each year would be ₹5,000 (₹60,000 ÷ 12) and would be recorded as follows:

End of year	Amortization Expense	5,000	
	Patent		5,000

Assets	=	Liabilities	+	Equity
−5,000				−5,000

The result of this entry is an increase to expenses and a decrease to assets. Notice that the entry records amortization expense based on the 12-year useful life, not the 20-year legal life. Amortization should be based on the shorter of the legal life or useful life. Notice also that the entry directly reduces the patent account. Unlike fixed assets, the amortization of intangible assets need not require the use of an accumulated amortization contra-account. In India amortization is usually accumulated.

Amortization applies only to intangible assets with limited lives. Assets with indefinite lives such as trademarks and goodwill are instead examined periodically to check for impairment. This is similar to the impairment of fixed assets. In general, if the market value of the intangible asset permanently falls below its cost, then the asset is impaired. In such a case, the company records a loss on impairment and reduces the asset to its market value. As you can imagine, determining whether an intangible asset is impaired is a very subjective process and requires a great deal of judgment. In such cases, it is important for accountants to follow guiding principles such as conservatism, relevance, and reliability.

Amortization The process of spreading out the cost of an intangible asset over its useful life.

CONCEPT QUESTIONS

1. Define the term "fixed asset."
2. How and where are fixed assets recorded in the financial statements?
3. Define the term "depreciation."
4. List the three methods of depreciation and state the formula for each method.
5. Compare and contrast the three methods of depreciation.
6. A change in accounting estimate is said to be made "prospectively." What does this mean?
7. What is the effect of a change in estimate of the useful life of a fixed asset?
8. What are the two possible methods of accounting for expenditures made during the useful life of a fixed asset? How does one determine which method to apply?
9. What does it mean for an asset to be considered "impaired?"
10. What action is taken when an asset is considered impaired?
11. List the steps required to calculate the disposal of a fixed asset.
12. State the formula for fixed asset turnover ratio and describe what this ratio tells an analyst.
13. State the formula for the average age and average useful life of fixed assets and describe what they tell an analyst.
14. How is the cash paid for fixed assets reported on the statement of cash flows?
15. What is normally included in the cost of an internally developed intangible asset? How are research and development costs treated?

MULTIPLE CHOICE

1. A fixed asset is classified as a/an:
   a. current asset.
   b. non-current asset.
   c. intangible asset.
   d. fictitious asset.
2. Which of the following is not a characteristic of a fixed asset?
   a. Recorded at cost
   b. Used for less than one year
   c. Used in the normal course of operations
   d. Not intended for resale
3. Which of the following would not be included in the cost of purchased equipment?
   a. Taxes paid on the equipment
   b. Shipping costs to have equipment delivered
   c. Insurance premiums for the next month of use
   d. Installation costs of equipment
4. Teel, Inc., bought a new forklift and incurred the following costs in association with the purchase:

Purchase price	₹2,50,000
State sales tax	₹ 21,000
Delivery fees	₹ 3,500
Liability insurance for year 1	₹ 12,000

   At what value will the forklift be reported on Teel's balance sheet?
   a. ₹2,86,500
   b. ₹2,50,000
   c. ₹2,71,000
   d. ₹2,74,500
5. Which of the following is not an acceptable method of depreciation?
   a. Total cost
   b. Straight-line
   c. Double-declining-balance
   d. Units-of-activity
6. If Alcorn Industries purchases for ₹2,00,000 a new delivery truck with an estimated 5-year useful life and ₹2,50,000 salvage value, what is the depreciation expense for year one using the straight-line depreciation method?
   a. ₹3,50,000
   b. ₹4,00,000
   c. ₹4,50,000
   d. ₹5,00,000
7. Assume the same facts as the question above except that Alcorn Industries uses the double-declining-balance method of depreciation. What would Alcorn Industries record as depreciation expense for year one?
   a. ₹5,00,000
   b. ₹6,00,000
   c. ₹7,00,000
   d. ₹8,00,000
8. Which of the following statements about depreciation is false?
   a. Depreciation is necessary because of the matching principle
   b. Depreciation expense is reported as a reduction to income on the income statement
   c. All three methods of depreciation result in the same total depreciation over the life of an asset
   d. All of the above statements are true
9. Which of the following statements are true?
   i. All assets have a limited useful life
   ii. Net Book Value = Cost − Accumulated Depreciation
   a. i only
   b. ii only
   c. Both i and ii
   d. Neither i nor ii
10. A change in the estimate of the useful life of a fixed asset affects:
    a. depreciation expense of the prior years.

b. the current total in the accumulated depreciation account.
c. depreciation expense in the period of the change and all future periods.
d. depreciation expense in past, current, and future periods.

11. An expenditure that extends the useful life of a fixed asset should be:
a. expensed in the period in which it was incurred.
b. capitalized and depreciated over the remaining useful life of the asset.
c. recorded in the repairs and maintenance account.
d. ignored.

12. An expenditure that maintains the useful life of a fixed asset should be:
a. expensed in the period in which it was incurred.
b. capitalized and depreciated over the remaining useful life of the asset.
c. added to the historical cost of the asset.
d. ignored.

13. A fixed asset has a historical cost of ₹2,00,000, a net book value of ₹1,20,000, and a salvage value of ₹25,000. What is the gain (loss) on the disposal of the fixed asset if it is sold for ₹1,50,000?
a. ₹50,000 loss
b. ₹30,000 gain
c. ₹1,25,000 gain
d. ₹1,50,000 gain

14. Which of the following statements is false?
a. The impairment of a fixed asset is an application of conservatism
b. When an asset is considered impaired, its book value must be reduced to its fair market value
c. Impairment of a fixed asset results in a gain on the income statement
d. An asset is considered impaired if its market value is materially below its net book value and the difference is considered permanent

15. The following account totals appear in the general ledger of the Boston Company:

Equipment	₹1,20,000
Accumulated Depreciation	₹ 45,000

If the equipment is sold to an outside party for ₹55,000, what amount of gain (loss) will the Boston Company record on the disposal of the equipment?
a. ₹20,000 loss
b. ₹10,000 gain
c. ₹2,500 gain
d. ₹40,000 gain

16. Horizontal analysis of fixed assets:
a. calculates fixed assets as a percentage of total assets.
b. calculates depreciation expense as a percentage of revenues.
c. calculates the change in fixed assets as a percentage of the prior year's fixed assets balance.
d. both "a" and "b" are correct.

17. Vertical analysis of fixed assets and depreciation:
a. calculates fixed assets as a percentage of total assets.
b. calculates depreciation expense as a percentage of revenues.
c. calculates the change in fixed assets as a percentage of the prior year's fixed assets balance.
d. both "a" and "b" are correct.

18. The results of the fixed asset turnover ratio communicates to management:
a. how quickly a fixed asset is depreciated.
b. how many fixed assets were bought in the current period.
c. how much depreciation expense was recorded compared to total fixed assets.
d. how effectively a company is using its fixed assets to produce revenue.

19. The average useful life of a company's fixed assets is calculated by the formula:
a. Average Useful Life = Total Useful Lives of Assets/ Cost of Fixed Assets.
b. Average Useful Life = Depreciation Expense/ Cost of Fixed Assets.
c. Average Useful Life = Costs of Fixed Assets/ Accumulated Depreciation.
d. Average Useful Life = Costs of Fixed Assets/ Depreciation Expense.

20. Which of the following statements is true?
i. Cash paid for fixed assets is normally reported as a separate line item on the statement of cash flows
ii. Capital expenditures are normally reported as a cash outflow in the operating section of the statement of cash flows
a. i only
b. ii only
c. Both i and ii
d. Neither i nor ii

21. Which of the following is not an intangible asset?
a. Patent
b. Goodwill
c. Franchise
d. All of the above are intangible assets

22. Company A purchases Company B for a total of ₹2,800,000. Company B has total assets of ₹2,500,000, total liabilities of ₹400,000, and total equity of ₹2,100,000. How much Goodwill will Company A record as a result of the purchase of Company B?
a. ₹0
b. ₹300,000
c. ₹400,000
d. ₹700,000

23. Which of the following statements is true?
a. All intangible assets have an indefinite life
b. Spreading the cost of an intangible asset over its estimated useful life is called depreciation
c. The cost of an externally acquired intangible asset is its purchase price
d. Internally generated intangible assets cannot be recorded as an asset

BRIEF EXERCISES

1. Acquisition Cost

Orange & Blue, Inc., incurred the following expenditures when purchasing land: ₹4,70,000 purchase price; ₹45,000 in taxes; ₹20,000 of sales commissions; and ₹1,30,000 for clearing and grading, of which ₹80,000 was for removing an old building.

Required
Determine the acquisition cost of the land.

2. Reporting Fixed Assets

At the end of the year, The Puppy Emporium had property and equipment with a historical cost of ₹10,00,000. Collectively, these assets had been depreciated ₹2,50,000.

Required
Show two ways in which the property and equipment could be reported on The Puppy Emporium's balance sheet.

3. Depreciation Expense: Straight-Line

Garrett Deliveries purchases a car for ₹18,00,000. The car has an estimated salvage value of ₹40,000 and is expected to be driven for seven years. Garrett uses the straight-line method of depreciation.

Required
Calculate annual depreciation expense.

4. Determine Net Book Value

Suppose that an asset is purchased for ₹8,60,000. The asset has an estimated useful life of ten years and a salvage value of ₹40,000.

Required
Assuming straight-line depreciation, determine the net book value of the asset after two years.

5. Depreciation Expense: Double-Declining-Balance

Sanders Catering purchases a mini truck for ₹32,00,000. The mini truck has an estimated salvage value of ₹6,00,000 and is expected to be driven for four years. Garrett uses the double-declining-balance method of depreciation.

Required
Calculate depreciation expense for each of the four years of the asset's life.

6. Depreciation Expense: Units-of-Activity

City Taxi purchases a new taxi cab for ₹5,00,000. The cab has an estimated salvage value of ₹1,00,000 and is expected to be driven for approximately 1,20,000 miles over its useful life of five years.

Required

a. Calculate the depreciation expense per mile.
b. Prepare a deprecation schedule assuming that the actual miles driven for years one through five were as follows: 25,000; 27,000; 21,000; 28,000; and 19,000.

7. Change in Useful Life

A company purchases a fixed asset with an estimated useful life of 15 years and a salvage value of ₹1,00,000. When the asset has 7 years of life remaining, the company decides that the remaining useful life should be 5 years. The asset's net book value at the time of revision is ₹6,00,000.

Required
Using the straight-line method, calculate depreciation expense for the first year after the revision.

8. Expenditures After Acquisition

Tiger Logistics acquired a van for ₹7,50,000 in 2010. At the end of 2012, accumulated depreciation on the van was ₹2,50,000. On April 1, 2013, Tiger paid ₹20,000 for routine service on the van and ₹80,000 to overhaul the engine. The engine work is anticipated to extend the useful life of the truck by 5 years.

Required
Calculate the net book value of Tiger's van immediately after the service and overhaul.

9. Impairment Entry

Jenford Factories acquired equipment for ₹3,50,000. On March 15, 2013, Jenford determines that the equipment is impaired by ₹65,000.

Required
Prepare the entry to record the impairment of the equipment.

10. Calculating Gains and Losses on Disposal

Chris' Crispy Chicken sold one of its used deep fryers for ₹50,000. The original cost of the fryer was ₹1,50,000, and related accumulated depreciation at the time of the sale was ₹70,000.

Required
Calculate the gain or loss on the sale of the deep fryer. For what amount would Chris need to sell the equipment to generate no gain or loss?

11. Recording a Disposal

A company sells a building with a cost of ₹350,000 and accumulated depreciation of ₹270,000 and records the entry for the sale as follows:

Cash	70,000	
Loss on Disposal	10,000	
Building		80,000

Required

a. Did the company prepare the entry correctly? If not, prepare the correct entry.
b. What would the gain or loss on sale be if the sale price was ₹97,000?

12. Analyze Fixed Assets

In its annual report, Phono Corporation reported beginning total assets of ₹36,00,000, ending total assets of ₹40,60,000, beginning fixed assets of ₹30,00,000 (at cost), ending fixed assets of ₹31,10,000 (at cost), ending accumulated depreciation of ₹10,60,000, depreciation expense of ₹1,65,000, and net revenues of ₹120,000.

Required

Calculate Phono's fixed asset turnover ratio for the year and its average useful life and age of fixed assets at year-end.

13. Recording Intangible Assets

Gentry Software, Inc., incurred ₹40,00,000 in research costs and ₹50,00,000 in salaries to develop a new tablet application. Gentry paid ₹1,20,000 to register the patent protecting the application.

Required

Should Gentry record the patent as an asset, and if so, at what value?

14. Recording Amortization Expense

In 2012–13 Buckeye Research Labs patented a new polymer. The patent was capitalized at ₹55,00,000, but the market value is ₹80,000,000. Buckeye determines that the legal life of the patent is 8 years, although it knows that the useful life is only 5 years.

Required

Record the entry for amortization expense for 2012–13. Assume that Buckeye records a full year of expense.

EXERCISES

15. Acquisition Cost

Prince's Pipe Co. purchases equipment with a list price of ₹2,20,000. Regarding the purchase, Prince:

- Received a 2% discount off the list price
- Paid shipping costs of ₹8000
- Paid ₹17,500 to install the equipment, ₹12,000 of which was for a unique stand for the equipment
- Paid ₹28,000 to insure the equipment, ₹3,000 for delivery transit, and ₹25,000 for a two-year policy to cover operations
- Paid ₹6,000 to have the manufacturer train employees on safety features

Required

Determine the acquisition cost of the equipment.

16. Acquisition Costs

Knight Company acquired a new tract of land for ₹2,50,000. Knight also paid ₹20,000 in taxes and fees, ₹23,000 to remove an old building, and ₹75,000 for logging, grading, and filling the land prior to its use. Proceeds from the sale of timber as a result of logging were ₹40,000.

Required

Determine the amount that Knight would record as the cost of the land.

17. Depreciation Methods

Phigam Steel purchases a machine on January 1 for ₹3,00,000. The machine has an estimated useful life of seven years, during which time it is expected to produce 1,14,800 units. Salvage value is estimated at ₹13,000. The machine produces 15,500 and 16,200 units in its first and second years of operation, respectively.

Required

Calculate depreciation expense for the machine's first two years using the straight-line, double-declining-balance, and units-of-activity methods of depreciation. Round values to the nearest dollar.

18. Depreciation Methods

Xing, Inc., purchases a delivery truck on January 1 for ₹2,50,000. The truck has an estimated useful life of five years and an estimated salvage value of ₹25,000.

Required

For both the straight-line and double-declining-balance methods of depreciation, prepare a schedule of depreciation expense, accumulated depreciation, and net book value over the life of the asset. Advise Xing, Inc., of the advantages/disadvantages of the two depreciation methods.

19. Depreciation Methods and Taxes

On January 1, 2013, Scout Manufacturing purchased new equipment for ₹145,000. The equipment was estimated to have a five-year useful life and a salvage value of ₹15,000. Scout estimates that the equipment will produce 81,250 units over its useful life. However, it actually produces 18,000 units in 2013, 17,500 units in 2014, 17,750 units in 2015, 17,000 units in 2016, and 15,000 units in 2017.

Required

a. Prepare a depreciation schedule for Scout for each of the five years using the straight-line method, the double-declining-balance method, and the units-of-activity method.
b. Assuming a tax rate of 30%, how much more could Scout defer in taxes in the first year by using the double-declining-balance method versus the straight-line method?

20. Acquisition Costs and Depreciation

On January 1, Jones Company acquired a new delivery van for ₹4,00,000 cash. Additional cash payments during the year were as follows.

- Taxes and fees on delivery van, ₹32,000
- Installation of GPS system and painting of logo for truck, ₹30,000
- Auto and liability insurance premiums paid on truck, ₹15,000.

Required

a. Prepare all journal entries Jones would make regarding the delivery van.

b. Assume that the delivery van has an estimated useful life of five years and an estimated salvage value of ₹20,000. Calculate depreciation expense on the delivery van for the current year, assuming Jones uses the double-declining-balance method of depreciation.

c. Show how Jones would report the van on its current-year balance sheet.

21. Change in Estimates

On January 1, 2013, Roosters Co. purchases equipment for ₹3,00,000 and estimates a useful life of eight years and a salvage value of ₹20,000. On January 1, 2015, Roosters revises the equipment's useful life from eight years to five years. Roosters uses the straight-line method of depreciation and its financial year end on December 31 every year.

Required

a. Calculate depreciation expense for 2013, 2014, and 2015.

b. Recalculate 2015 depreciation expense assuming that Roosters leaves the useful life at eight years but reduces the salvage value to ₹0.

22. Capital/Revenue Expenditures

A company incurs the following expenditures related to currently owned fixed assets:

- Annual pressure washing of building, ₹50,000
- New engine in delivery truck, ₹4,50,000
- Repair of water damage caused by leaking roof, ₹35,000
- New tires on tractor, ₹2,00,000
- Addition of 1,000 square feet of office space, ₹22,00,000
- Modifications to machinery to improve efficiency, ₹7,20,000

Required

Identify each expenditure as a capital or revenue expenditure.

23. Adjustments to Fixed Assets

A company that uses the straight-line method of depreciation experiences the following independent items:

- Increases a useful life estimate from 5 years to 8 years
- Pays for maintenance of equipment
- Reduces a salvage value estimate by ₹10,000
- Pays ₹50,000 to significantly increase the productivity of an existing fixed asset
- Records an impairment on a fixed asset

Required

Identify whether each independent item would increase, decrease, or not affect depreciation expense for the underlying fixed asset.

24. Capital Expenditure

On January 1, 2013, Moran Manufacturing has a building with a net book value of ₹35,70,000, no salvage value, and a remaining useful life of 7 years. During January, major renovations in the amount of ₹7,30,000 are conducted and add five more years to the building's useful life and increase the salvage value to ₹40,000. Moran uses the straight-line method of depreciation.

Required

a. Determine the amount of depreciation that Moran recorded in 2013. Hint: think about how straight-line depreciation works.

b. Determine the net book value of the building immediately after the repairs were completed.

c. Calculate depreciation expense for the year 2013. Assume that the cost of the renovation is depreciated for a full year in 2013 and the financial year ends on December 31 every year.

25. Disposal

Ellis Industries sells a building that has an original cost of ₹200,000 and an accumulated depreciation balance of ₹100,000.

Required

Prepare the journal entry to record the sale assuming the sales price was (a) ₹100,000, (b) ₹95,000, and (c) ₹108,000.

26. Disposal

On January 1, 2013, A&G Company pays ₹4,00,000 for equipment with a 10-year estimated life and a ₹50,000 estimated salvage value. On January 1, 2016, A&G sells the equipment for ₹1,85,000.

Required

Calculate the gain or loss on the sale assuming A&G uses the straight-line method of depreciation. Where should the gain or loss on the sale be presented on the income statement?

27. Depreciation and Disposal

On January 1, 2013, the Von Schoppe Company purchased a delivery van for ₹2,00,000. The van had an estimated useful life of six years and a salvage value of ₹20,000. On September 30, 2015, Von Shoppe sold the van for ₹1,30,000. Von Shoppe uses the straight-line method of depreciation and records depreciation on December 31.

Required

a. Calculate the gain or loss on the disposal of the delivery van.

b. Prepare all entries necessary on September 30, 2015.

28. Evaluate Fixed Assets

In a recent annual report, **Nike** reported the following information (in millions): beginning total assets ₹6,821; ending total assets ₹7,891; beginning property, plant, and equipment ₹2,988 (at cost); ending property, plant, and equipment ₹3,132 (at cost); beginning accumulated depreciation ₹1,293; revenues ₹12,253; and depreciation expense of ₹252.

Required

Calculate the following ratios for Nike: fixed asset turnover, average useful life, and average age.

29. Evaluate Fixed Assets

The following data was taken from the annual financial statements of Grizzle Company:

	Revenues	Fixed Asset NBV
2007	4,889	150
2008	5,897	201
2009	6,583	245
2010	8,563	395
2011	10,589	524
2012	13,584	687
2013	14,555	793

Required

Calculate the fixed asset turnover ratio for the years presented. What does the trend in the ratio tell you about the company's performance?

30. Intangible Assets

Phoebe, Inc., incurred the following expenditures:

- Research and development costs of ₹6,00,000 were incurred to develop a new patentable product.
- Paid ₹10,000 in application fees for the patent.
- Paid ₹1,20,000 in legal fees to register the awarded patent.
- Incurred ₹50,000 in legal fees to successfully defend the patent against a competitor.

Required

Determine the total cost of the patent.

31. Amortization of Intangible Assets

Ramon Productions purchased the copyright to a film script for ₹26,40,000 on July 1. The copyright protects the owners' legal rights for the next 20 years, but producers at Ramon estimate they will only be able to use the copyright for the next 15 years. Ramon Productions uses the straight-line method of amortization and has a June 30 year-end.

Required

Prepare the journal entry to record amortization expense for the first year.

PROBLEMS

32. Depreciation Methods

Development Industries purchased a depreciable asset for ₹5,00,000 on January 1, 2013. The asset has a five-year useful life and a ₹1,00,000 estimated salvage value. The company will use the straight-line method of depreciation for book purposes. However, Development will use the double-declining-balance method for tax purposes. Assume a tax rate of 30%.

Required

a. Prepare depreciation schedules using the straight-line and double-declining-balance methods of depreciation for the useful life of the asset.

b. Calculate the 2013 tax savings from the use of the accelerated depreciation method for tax purposes.

c. Under the straight-line method of depreciation, what is the gain or loss if the equipment is sold (1) at the end of 2015 for ₹3,00,000 or (2) at the end of 2016 for ₹1,60,000?

d. How is the gain or loss on the disposal of the equipment presented in the financial statements? How does this differ from how depreciation expense is presented?

33. Various Transactions

On January 1, 2013, Ravioli, Inc., purchased a building for a cash price of ₹19,20,000 and accrued property taxes of ₹1,49,500. The building is estimated to have a useful life of 10 years and no salvage value. On the same day, Ravioli paid ₹2,54,500 in cash plus sales tax of ₹22,900 for a new delivery truck that is estimated to have a useful life of five years and a salvage value of ₹22,000. Another ₹11,000 was paid to paint the company logo on the truck. Over the next several years, the following events related to these fixed assets occurred:

1/1/2014	Uncovered new information which caused the estimated life of the truck to be reduced to three total years instead of five years.
6/30/2014	Repaired truck's air conditioning system which broke down for one week, ₹5000.
1/1/2015	Renovated bottom floor of the building for ₹1,50,000, adding three years of useful life to the building.
1/1/2015	Sold building for ₹16,30,000.
9/1/2016	Sold truck for ₹53,500.

Required

Prepare all entries for 2013 through 2016. Ravioli records annual depreciation expense on 12/31.

34. Recording and Expensing Fixed Assets

At the beginning of the year, Wiggins Co. purchased ten new computers in order to transform an existing café into an Internet café. The following expenditures were related to the purchase of the computers.

- Purchase price, ₹2,70,000
- Sales taxes, ₹24,000
- Freight costs, ₹18,000
- Installation, ₹4000

The accountant at Wiggins recorded ₹2,94,000 in the asset account Equipment and ₹22,000 in the expense account Delivery Expense. The computers have a three-year life and no salvage value. Wiggins depreciates all fixed assets using the straight-line method.

Required

a. How much depreciation expense will Wiggins record in year one of the computers? Do you agree with this amount? If not, what amount do you think should be recorded as depreciation expense for year one?

b. If income before any expense related to the purchase and depreciation of these computers is ₹8,00,000, what will Wiggins report as net income for year one? (Assume a tax rate of 40%.) What amount of income should Wiggins report?

c. Briefly explain to Wiggins' accountant why his net income is incorrect in year one.

35. Fixed Asset Transactions and Reporting

A partial portion of the balance sheet at December 31, 2012, for the Gusto Corporation is presented below:

Land		₹50,00,000
Buildings	₹63,000,000	
Less: Accumulated depreciation	25,00,000	38,00,000
Equipment	₹ 6,50,000	
Less: Accumulated depreciation	2,20,000	4,30,000
Total property and equipment		₹92,30,000

The following transactions occurred during 2013:

- On January 1, retired equipment with a net book value of ₹20,000. The equipment was purchased for ₹80,000. No value was received from the retirement.
- On January 1, Gusto sold a building with an original 30-year useful life and no estimated salvage value for ₹9,00,000 cash. The building was originally purchased on December 31, 2002 for ₹12,00,000.
- Purchased land for ₹9,00,000 on April 30.
- On July 1, Gusto purchased equipment for ₹3,00,000 by signing a long-term note payable.
- Prepared depreciation entries on December 31. Depreciation expense for the year was ₹4,00,000 for buildings and ₹45,000 for equipment.

Required

a. Prepare journal entries to record all of the above transactions.

b. Prepare the property and equipment portion of Gusto's balance sheet at December 31, 2013.

36. Evaluate Fixed Assets

The following information was available from recent financial statements of Papa John's Pizza:

	Current year	Prior year
Property and equipment, net	₹ 18,99,920	₹ 19,89,570
Total assets	38,64,680	40,18,170
Depreciation expense	3,18,000	3,06,000
Property and equipment, at cost	38,80,800	40,80,740
Accumulated depreciation	19,80,880	20,91,170
Total revenues	11,320,870	10,635,950

Required

Calculate and interpret (1) horizontal and vertical analyses of fixed assets and depreciation expense, (2) fixed asset turnover ratio, and (3) average life and average age of fixed assets. Round percentages to one decimal points (e.g., 45.2%).

37. Evaluate Fixed Assets

The following information comes from an analysis of two competitors, Claw Co. and the Smiles Company:

	Claw	Smiles
Net revenues	₹12,50,000	₹11,00,000
Net income	5,00,000	6,80,000
Average total assets	12,450,000	95,00,000
Average NBV of fixed assets	75,00,000	64,50,000
Accumulated depreciation	12,00,000	24,00,000
Depreciation expense	2,50,000	1,20,000

Required

a. For both competitors, compute the asset turnover ratio, average useful life of the assets, and the average age of the fixed assets.

b. After analysis, which of the two companies is better at using assets to generate revenues?
c. Are there factors that seem to contradict each other in these numbers? What could be some valid reasons for such circumstances?

38. Intangible Assets

During 2012–13, Haslem, Inc., invested ₹10,50,000 to successfully develop a new product, and a patent was granted on December 31, 2013. Haslem incurred ₹2,20,000 of legal fees and ₹12,000 of registration fees to secure the patent. Haslem estimates that the patent will have a useful life of 10 years and no salvage value. On January 1, 2015, Haslem's major competitor announced that it had developed a similar product, which reduced the value of Haslem's patent to ₹1,20,000. Haslem considers the loss in value permanent. Haslem has a December 31 year-end.

Required

a. What amount should be recorded as the cost of the patent? How are the remaining costs treated for financial reporting purposes?
b. Compute amortization expense for the patent for years 2012–13 and 2013–14 and prepare the appropriate journal entries.
c. What should Haslem do on January 1, 2015, if anything?

CASES

39. Research and Analysis

Access the 2012–13 annual report for **Britannia Industries Limited** by clicking on the *Investor Relations, Financial Information,* and *Annual Reports* links at www.britannia.co.in.

Required

a. Examine the company's balance sheet and conduct horizontal and vertical analyses of net property, plant, and equipment. Round percentages to one decimal points (e.g., 45.2%).
b. Calculate the company's 2012–13 fixed asset turnover ratio. Also, calculate the company's average age and useful life ratios at the end of FY 2013. Cost and accumulated depreciation data can be found in to the financial statements. Depreciation and amortization expense can also be found in Note to the Financial Statement.
c. Examine the company's statement of cash flows. How much cash did the company spend on property and equipment over the three years presented?
d. Based on your answers above, write a paragraph explaining your opinion of Columbia's fixed asset position. Use your answers as supporting facts.

40. Research and Analysis

Access the 2012–13 annual report for **Bata India Limited**, by clicking on the Investors and Annual Reports.

Required

a. Examine the balance sheet and identify the fixed assets. Are fixed assets reported at net book value?
b. Examine Note 7 and identify the original cost of Bata's fixed assets and the current balance in accumulated depreciation.
c. According to Note 1, what method of depreciation does Bata use?
d. According to the statement of cash flows, how much has Bata spent on fixed assets over the past three years? Does the company generate enough cash from operations to sustain that level of investment?
e. Calculate the average age and useful life of Bata's fixed assets. Use "Depreciation" on the statement of cash flows as depreciation expense for the year. What can you conclude from these calculations?

41. Written Communication

Play Hard Fitness Center is a chain of work-out facilities. Play Hard's financial analysts have forecasted sales to remain at a constant level for the next three years, but income taxes are forecasted to grow by 5% a year for the next five years. Play Hard is about to refurnish 50% of its centers with new equipment that will have an estimated useful life of five years. As a CPA, you know that companies can use one method of depreciation for tax purposes and another for book purposes. The two methods under consideration are the double-declining-balance method and straight-line method of depreciation.

Required

Write a short memo recommending the method you would use for tax purposes and the method you would use for book purposes. Be sure to discuss the advantages and disadvantages of both of the methods as well as the associated effects on income, depreciation over time, cash flows, etc.

42. Ethics in Accounting

A friend of yours claims that he likes accounting because there is always a right and wrong answer to a question and therefore there is no temptation for wrongdoing.

Required

Using capital and revenue expenditures as an example, explain how judgment can be involved in accounting decisions and how an individual's ethics can affect the manner in which he or she accounts for a particular item.

reviewcard CHAPTER 8 Fixed Assets and Intangible Assets

Learning Objectives		Key Concepts
LO1	Describe fixed assets and how they are recorded, expensed, and reported.	Fixed assets are recorded at cost, expensed over their useful lives by depreciation, and reported on the balance sheet at net book value, which is the asset's cost less its accumulated depreciation.
LO2	Calculate and compare depreciation expense using straight-line, double-declining-balance, and units-of-activity methods.	All depreciation methods depreciate an asset's net cost over its useful life, but they differ in the amount of depreciation expense recognized each year. Straight-line yields the same expense each year. Double-declining-balance accelerates the expense to early years. Units-of-activity bases the expense on asset usage.
LO3	Understand the effects of adjustments that may be made during a fixed asset's useful life.	When an estimate on an existing fixed asset is changed, depreciation expense from that point forward is based on the new estimate. Expenditures that significantly increase a fixed asset's useful life or productive capacity are added to the asset's cost. When a fixed asset's market value falls permanently below its net book value, the asset is impaired and must be written down to market value.
LO4	Record the disposal of fixed assets.	When disposing of fixed assets, companies record a gain on disposal when the asset is sold for more than its net book value. A loss is recorded when it is sold for less than net book value.
LO5	Evaluate fixed assets through the calculation and interpretation of horizontal, vertical, and ratio analyses.	The fixed asset turnover ratio shows how effective a company is at using its fixed assets to produce revenues. The average age and average useful life ratios provide an indication of the remaining life of a company's fixed assets.
LO6	Describe the cash flow effect of acquiring fixed assets.	Cash paid for fixed assets is reported as a separate line item in the investing activities section of the statement of cash flows. A negative number indicates that a company is buying fixed assets.
LO7	Describe intangible assets and how they are recorded, expensed, and reported.	Intangible assets are recorded at their cost and amortized over their useful lives. An internally developed intangible asset is recorded only for those costs necessary to register it.

Key Definitions

Accumulated depreciation The cumulative amount of depreciation expense recognized to date on a fixed asset.

Amortization The process of spreading out the cost of an intangible asset over its useful life.

Average age of fixed assets A comparison of accumulated depreciation to depreciation expense that estimates the number of years, on average, that the company has used its fixed assets.

Average useful life of fixed assets A comparison of the cost of fixed assets to depreciation expense that estimates the number of years, on average, that a company expects to use its fixed assets.

Capital expenditure An expenditure that increases the expected useful life or productivity of a fixed asset.

Copyright The right to reproduce or sell an artistic or published work.

Cost The historical cost of a fixed asset being depreciated.

Depreciable cost The difference between an asset's cost and its salvage value.

Depreciation The process of systematically and rationally allocating the cost of a fixed asset over its useful life.

Depreciation expense The portion of a fixed asset's cost that is recognized as an expense in the current period.

Depreciation method The method used to calculate depreciation expense, such as the straight-line method, the double-declining-balance method, and the units-of-activity method.

Double-declining-balance method A depreciation method that accelerates depreciation expense into the early years of an asset's life.

Fixed asset A tangible resource that is expected to be used in operations for more than one year and is not intended for resale.

Fixed asset turnover ratio A comparison of total revenues to the average net book value of fixed assets that measures the productivity of fixed assets.

Key Definitions (continued)

Franchise The right to operate a business under the trade name of the franchisor.

Goodwill An intangible asset equal to the excess that one company pays to acquire the net assets of another company.

Intangible asset A resource that is used in operations for more than one year but that has no physical substance.

Net book value The unexpired cost of a fixed asset, calculated by subtracting depreciation expense to date from the cost of the fixed asset.

Patent The right to manufacture, sell, or use a particular product or process exclusively for a limited period of time.

Revenue expenditure An expenditure that maintains the expected useful life or the productivity of a fixed asset.

Salvage value An estimate of the value of a fixed asset at the end of its useful life.

Straight-line method A depreciation method that results in the same amount of depreciation expense each year of the asset's useful life.

Trademark (trade name) The right to use exclusively a name, symbol, or phrase to identify a company.

Units-of-activity method A depreciation method in which depreciation expense is a function of the actual usage of the asset.

Useful life The length of time a fixed asset is expected to be used in operations.

Key Formulas

Straight-Line Method	$\text{Depreciation Expense} = \dfrac{\text{Cost} - \text{Salvage Value}}{\text{Useful Life}}$
Double-Declining-Balance Method	Depreciation Expense = Depreciation Rate × Net Book Value = (Straight-Line Rate × 2) × (Cost – Accumulated Depreciation)
Units-of-Activity Method	$\text{Depreciation Expense per Unit} = \dfrac{\text{Cost} - \text{Salvage Value}}{\text{Useful Life in Units}}$
	Depreciation Expense = Depreciation Expense per Unit × Actual Units of Activity
Net Book Value	Cost − Accumulated Depreciation

Disposals	Gain on Disposal: Proceeds from Sale > Net Book Value
	Loss on Disposal: Proceeds from Sale < Net Book Value

Fixed Asset Turnover Ratio	$\dfrac{\text{Total Revenues}}{\text{Average Net Book Value of Fixed Assets}}$ where average net book value is: $\dfrac{\text{Beginning Net Book Value} + \text{Ending Net Book Value}}{2}$
Average Useful Life Ratio	$\text{Average Useful Life} = \dfrac{\text{Cost of Fixed Assets}}{\text{Depreciation Expense}}$
Average Age Ratio	$\text{Average Age} = \dfrac{\text{Accumulated Depreciation}}{\text{Depreciation Expense}}$

Demonstration Problem

Rooney Inc. purchases a new machine for ₹37,750. The machine has a useful life of 10 years and a salvage value of ₹2,750. Rooney estimates that the machine will be used for 17,500 hours.

a. Calculate the machine's annual depreciation expense using the straight-line method.

b. Calculate depreciation expense for the first three years of the asset's life using the double-declining-balance method.

c. Assuming that the machine is used for 3,000 hours one year, calculate depreciation expense for that year using the units-of-activity method.

d. Suppose that after five years of straight-line depreciation, Rooney increases the machine's useful life an additional two years. Calculate depreciation expense for year six.

e. Suppose instead that after six years of straight-line depreciation, Rooney sells the machine for ₹16,300. Calculate the gain or loss on the sale.

Demonstration Problem Solution

a. (₹37,750 − ₹2,750) / 10 = ₹3,500 depreciation expense per year

b. Double-declining rate = (100% ÷ 10) × 2 = 20%
Year 1: 20% × ₹37,750 = ₹7,550 depreciation expense
Year 2: 20% × (₹37,750 − ₹7,550) = ₹6,040 depreciation expense
Year 3: 20% × (₹37,750 − ₹7,550 − ₹6,040) = ₹4,832 depreciation expense

c. (₹37,750 − ₹2,750) / ₹17,500 = ₹2 depreciation expense per hour
3,000 hours × 2 = ₹6,000 depreciation expense

d.

Cost of the asset	₹37,750
Less: Accumulated depreciation for five years (₹3,500 × 5)	17,500
Net book value at time of revision	₹20,250
Less: Salvage value	2,750
Remaining depreciable cost	₹17,500
Divided by remaining useful life (5 years + 2 more years)	÷ 7
Depreciation expense for year 6	₹ 2,500

e.

Cost of the asset	₹37,750
Less: Accumulated depreciation for six years (₹3,500 × 6)	21,000
Net book value at time of revision	₹16,750
Sales price	16,000
Loss on sale	₹ 750

ACCT

Liabilities

Learning Objectives

After studying the material in this chapter, you should be able to:

LO1 Describe the recording and reporting of various current liabilities.

LO2 Describe the reporting of long-term liabilities and the cash flows associated with those liabilities.

LO3 Understand the nature of bonds and record a bond's issuance, interest payments, and maturity.

LO4 Account for a bond that is redeemed prior to maturity.

LO5 Understand additional liabilities such as leases and contingent liabilities.

LO6 Evaluate liabilities through the calculation and interpretation of horizontal, vertical, and ratio analyses.

LO7 Appendix: Determine a bond's issuance price.

LO8 Appendix: Record bond interest payments under the effective interest method.

Introduction

The generation and payment of liabilities is common to every business. Some are generated daily and paid quickly. Others are paid over time and often require the payment of interest. Still others must be estimated, and some never come to fruition. This chapter examines the accounting for such liabilities. It focuses first on how some common current liabilities are generated and reported. It then examines long-term liabilities with a specific focus on the issuance of, interest on, and payment of bonds. It also discusses the obligations associated with leases and considers the treatment of potential obligations that may or may not become liabilities. As in previous chapters, the final section of the chapter focuses on the analysis of a company's position regarding its obligations. The appendix covers bond pricing and the effective interest method for bond amortization.

LO1 Current Liabilities

A **current liability** is an obligation of a business that is expected to be satisfied or paid within one year. Current liabilities can arise from regular business operations such as the purchase of inventory, the compensation of employees, the repayment of debt, and the incurrence of taxes. Most current liabilities, such as accounts payable and notes payable, will be satisfied through the payment of cash. Others, such as deferred revenues in which a customer prepays for a service to be performed later, will be satisfied through the performance of the service. The following sections present the accounting for some of the more common types of current liabilities.

Current liability An obligation of a business that is expected to be satisfied or paid within one year.

Taxes Payable

When conducting business, corporations generate a variety of tax obligations to central, state, and local taxing

A deposit in a bank is an asset to the customer, but it is a liability to the bank.

© LESTER LEFKOWITZ/STONE/GETTY IMAGES

authorities. One example is the income tax. Like individuals, corporations are subject to federal taxation of their income. And like individuals, they often wait until later to pay the bill, which creates a current liability. For example, suppose a company has ₹25,000 of annual income tax expense and plans to pay it in the next period. The company would make the following journal entry at year end to record the expense in the proper period:

Year-end	Income Tax Expense	25,000	
	Income Tax Payable		25,000
	(To record the income tax expense)		

Assets	=	Liabilities	+	Equity
		+25,000		−25,000

ACCT

Current liabilities arise from regular business operations such as the purchase of inventory, the compensation of employees, the repayment of debt, and the incurrence of taxes.

The entry increases both Income Tax Expense and Income Tax Payable. The result of the entry is a reduction to equity and an increase to liabilities.

Another example is sales taxes. Each time a company makes a retail sale, it collects sales tax according to state and/or local regulations. Because the company remits the taxes to the appropriate authority at some later date, the company must record a liability when the sale is made. To illustrate, suppose that a company sells a ₹1,000 item and collects an 8% sales tax. The following entry records the sale and the resulting liability:

Cash	1,080	
Sales		1,000
Sales Tax Payable		80
(To record sale of merchandise)		

Assets	=	Liabilities	+	Equity
+1,080		+80		+1,000

The entry increases Cash for the ₹1,080 received from the customer, increases Sales for the ₹1,000 earned from the sale, and increases Sales Tax Payable for the ₹80 of tax collected and now owed to the taxing authorities. Notice that the company does not incur any expense related to the sales tax. The sales tax liability is created only because the company has collected sales tax on behalf of the taxing authority.

Note payable A liability generated by the issuance of a promissory note to borrow money.

A third type of tax that generates a current liability is payroll taxes. When paying employee wages, employers must withhold income taxes (tax detected at source) owed by the employee. The employer then remits those taxes to the taxing authorities. To illustrate, suppose that an employee earns a monthly salary of ₹1,00,000. Based on the employee's filing status, the company must withhold 20% of the salary for central income taxes. On payday, the company would prepare the following entry:

Salaries Expense	1,00,000	
Income Tax Payable		20,000
Cash		80,000
(To record payment of salary)		

Assets	=	Liabilities	+	Equity
−80,000		+20,000		−1,00,000

The entry increases Salaries Expense for the ₹1,00,000 salary earned by the employee for the month. However, the employee is paid only ₹80,000. The difference is the amount that the employee owes in taxes. On behalf of the employee, the employer withholds those taxes and records the resulting liabilities. As a result of this entry, assets decrease, liabilities increase, and equity decreases for the amount of the total salaries expense.

Notes Payable

Chapter 6 introduced the concept of a promissory note, which is a written promise to pay a specific sum of money at some date in the future. That chapter focused on the party that accepted the note in exchange for cash. That is, the accounting for notes receivable was demonstrated. This chapter focuses on the party that accepts cash in exchange for the note. That is, the accounting for notes payable is demonstrated.

When a company issues a promissory note to borrow money, the company generates a **note payable**. Depending on the terms of the promissory note, a note payable can be classified as either a current liability or a long-term liability. If the note is payable within a year, it is a current liability. Otherwise, it is a long-term liability. The accounting for a note payable consists of recording the note, recording any interest that must be paid to the creditor, and recording the payment of the note.

To illustrate, suppose that on March 1 Brown Company borrows ₹30,000 by signing an 8%, 6-month note with State Bank of India. The note calls for interest to be paid when the note is repaid on August 31. On March 1, Brown would make the following entry to record the note:

Mar. 1	Cash	30,000	
	Note Payable		30,000
	(To record the note)		

Assets	=	Liabilities	+	Equity
+30,000		+30,000		

In this entry, Brown increases both Cash and Note Payable for ₹30,000. As a result, both assets and liabilities increase. Since this note matures within a year, the note payable would be reported as a current liability.

On August 31, Brown must pay State Bank of India the original ₹30,000 borrowed plus the interest on the note. Interest over the six months is calculated as follows:

Interest = Principal × Annual Rate of Interest × Time Outstanding

= ₹30,000 × 0.08 × 6/12 months
= ₹1,200

Therefore, Brown would pay ₹31,200 to the bank and make the following entry on August 31:

Aug. 31	Note Payable	30,000	
	Interest Expense	1,200	
	Cash		31,200
	(To record payment of note and interest)		

Assets	=	Liabilities	+	Equity
−31,200		−30,000		−1,200

In this entry, Brown increases Interest Expense to reflect the cost of borrowing the ₹30,000 over the six months. Brown also decreases the Note Payable account because the note is being paid. Finally, Brown decreases Cash for the payment of principal and interest. Because of the entry, Brown's assets, liabilities, and equity decrease.

Current Portion of Long-Term Debt

Companies that borrow money on a long-term basis often pay principal on a short-term basis. The **current portion of long-term debt** represents the portion of a long-term liability that will be paid within one year. To illustrate, suppose that a company borrows ₹5,00,000 from a bank. Because the loan is payable in 10 years, the company classifies it as a long-term liability. In year 10, the loan is reclassified as a current liability because it will be satisfied in a year.

Suppose instead that the bank requires the company to repay the principal in installments of ₹50,000 per year plus interest. In that case, when the loan is signed, the company has a long-term liability of ₹4,50,000 and a current liability of ₹50,000. Since the company must pay ₹50,000 each year until the note is repaid, the company will report ₹50,000 as Current Portion of Long-Term Debt each year.

As you consider these two examples, keep in mind that regardless of how the liability is classified on the balance sheet, the company is borrowing and repaying ₹5,00,000. The classification of the loan payable as current or long-term does not affect the borrowing or repayment of the loan. It only affects how the payable is reported on the balance sheet. However, this balance sheet reporting is important because it tells users of the financial statements what obligations will require payment in the short term.

In India, under the revised Schedule VI, current maturities of long-term borrowings is recorded under current liabilities. Note 11 to the Financial Statements of Ranbaxy Laboraties Ltd, 2012, states the amount outstanding in respect of current maturities of long-term borrowings.

Reporting Current Liabilities

Current liabilities are reported in a separate section on a classified balance sheet. The following is the current liabilities section of the 2012 balance sheet of Ranbaxy Laboratories:

Ranbaxy Laboratories Ltd. 2012 Current Liabilities

(in million)	
Short-term borrowings	₹28,067.95
Trade payables	8,588.11
Other current liabilities	13,320.78
Short-term provisions	27,831.11
Total	₹77,807.95

Current portion of long-term debt The portion of a long-term liability that will be paid within one year.

Ranbaxy Laboratories Ltd. reports ₹77,807.95 million in current liabilities. This total is made up mostly of short-term borrowings. Accounts payable normally represents what a company owes vendors for inventory that it stocks in its stores. Current account liability items like Income received in advance, overdraft,Interest accrued but not due on borrowings, etc., are reported under "Other current liabilities" in the Balance Sheet. Note 11 to the Financial Statements of Ranbaxy Laboraties Ltd., 2012, shows items of other current liabilities.

LO2 Long-Term Liabilities

A **long-term liability** is any obligation of a business that is expected to be satisfied or paid in more than one year. Like current liabilities, the type and size of long-term liabilities can vary across companies. However, the most common and largest long-term liabilities often arise from borrowing money. This is the case for Ranbaxy Ltd. The following shows the company's condensed liabilities from its 2012 balance sheet.

Ranbaxy Laboratories Ltd.'s 2012 Condensed Liabilities

(in Millions)	
Noncurrent liabilities	₹ 32,670.62
Current liabilities	77,807.95
Total liabilities	₹1,10,478.57

Ranbaxy Laboratories Ltd. reports three accounts under "Long-Term Liabilities". Note 6 to the Financial Statement states that unsecured loan is the largest. The balance sheet reports a total noncurrent liabilities of over ₹32,670 million, but it does not reveal why this long-term debt was generated or when it must be repaid. Such information is disclosed in the notes to the company's financial statements.

Long-term liability Any obligation of a business that is expected to be satisfied or paid in more than one year.

The most common and largest long-term liabilities often arise from borrowing money.

The note discloses that the company's total long-term debt is comprised primarily of two types of debt. The first is a revolving credit facility, which is a type of loan that does not require fixed principal payments during the term of the loan. (Your personal credit card is an example of revolving credit.) The second type of debt is a term loan. This is simply an interest-bearing loan with principal due at maturity.

While the balance sheet reports the balance in long-term liabilities, the statement of cash flows reports the cash flows associated with those liabilities in the financing activities section. The following are excerpts from Ranbaxy Laboratories Ltd.'s financing activities section of its 2012 statement of cash flows. These contain the significant cash flows resulting from the generation and repayment of the company's long-term liabilities.

Excerpts from Ranbaxy Laboratories Ltd.'s 2012 Statement of Cash Flows

(in millions)	2012	2011
Increase/decrease in short-term bank borrowings (net)	₹3,270.37	₹3,835.78
Proceeds from long-term bank borrowings	₹5,196.38	4,023.41
Re-payment of long-term bank borrowings	(₹3,241.67)	(₹27,506.56)

Cash flow statement of Ranbaxy Laboratories Ltd. reveals that Ranbaxy Laboratories Ltd. experienced significant debt-related cash inflows and cash outflows over the two-year period. However, while there was significant annual activity, the net effect was relatively small. In 2012 Ranbaxy Laboratories Ltd. borrowed short-term loan of ₹3,270.37 million and long-term loan ₹5,196.38 more than it repaid during the year. In 2011, it paid more than it borrowed, resulting in a ₹12,751.38 million cash outflow during the year.

©HEMERA/THINKSTOCK

A borrower "sells" or "issues" a bond and records a liability. A creditor "buys" a bond and records an investment.

LO3 Bonds

A tool that companies such as Ranbaxy Laboratories Ltd. often use to borrow money on a long-term basis is a bond. A **bond** is a financial instrument in which a borrower promises to pay future interest and principal to a creditor in exchange for the creditor's cash today. The borrower "sells" or "issues" the bond and records a liability. The creditor "buys" the bond and records an investment.

The terms and features of a bond are determined by the borrowing entity and can vary widely. However, all bonds have a face value, a stated interest rate, and a maturity date.

The **face value** is the amount that the borrowing company wants to borrow. It is also the amount that must be repaid to the creditor upon maturity of the bond. Another name for face value is principal value. The **stated interest rate** is the contractual rate at which interest is paid to the creditor. Other names for stated rate include face rate, nominal rate, contractual rate,

Bond A financial instrument in which a borrower promises to pay future interest and principal to a creditor in exchange for the creditor's cash today.

Face value The amount that is repaid at maturity of a bond.

Stated interest rate The contractual rate at which interest is paid to the creditor.

MARUTI SUZUKI ANALYSIS

Look at Maruti Suzuki's balance sheet and statement of cash flows in Appendix C. Using both statements, explain what happened to short-term debt during 2012–13.

Note 8 to the Financial Statements of Maruti Suzuki reveals that its short-term unsecured loan from bank has gone down from ₹10,783 million to ₹8,463 million. Note 10 reveals that the overdraft has also gone down from ₹594 million to ₹1,366 million. The statement of cash flows shows a ₹10,783 million cash outflow and cash inflow of ₹8,463 million for short-term borrowing during 2013. Although the numbers are not exactly the same, they demonstrate that the activity associated with the payments of short-term debt are shown on the financial statements.

Exhibit 9-1 Example Bond Certificate

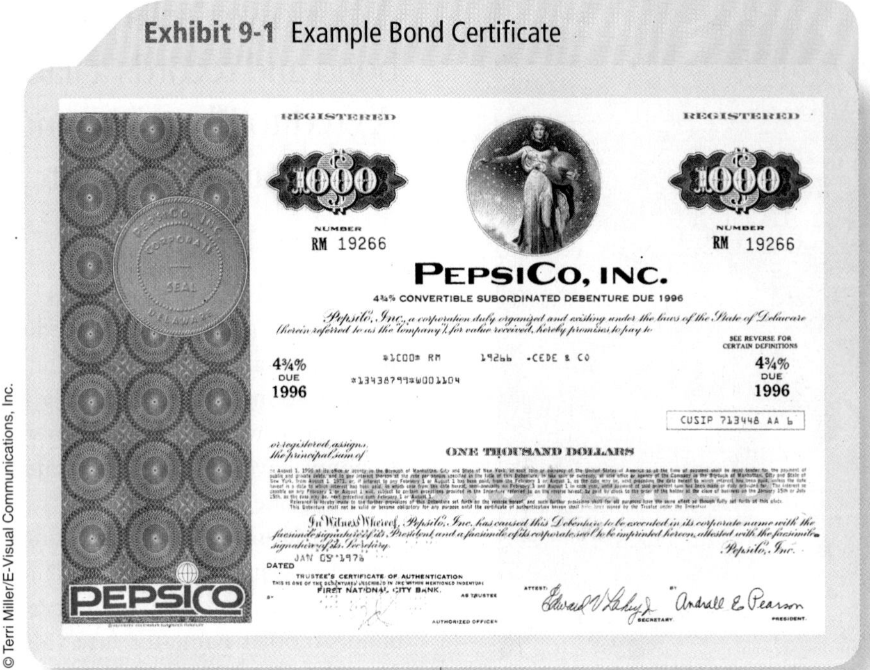

or coupon rate. Along with this stated rate, a bond will specify the timing of interest payments. These will usually be annually or semiannually. The **maturity date** is the date on which the face value must be repaid to the creditor. These three terms, which do not change over the life of the bond, are disclosed on the certificate that is given to the creditor or the creditor's trustee when the bond is purchased. An example certificate is shown in Exhibit 9-1.

Although these terms establish both the amount to be paid at maturity (the face value) and the amount of interest to be paid each period (the stated interest rate), they do not establish the issuance price of the bonds. A bond's issuance price is a function of these terms as well as a fourth item, the market rate of interest.

The **market (or effective) rate of interest** is the rate of return that investors in the bond markets demand on bonds of similar risk. The market rate is based on many complicated factors, including current and expected economic conditions. However, its relation to a bond's issuance price is relatively straightforward.

When a bond pays interest at a rate that is equal to what creditors demand in the market, the creditors will buy the bond at its face value. Creditors are getting the return that they demand, so no adjustment to price is needed. As a result, the borrower receives face value. We say that such bonds are issued at par value.

When a bond pays interest at a rate that is lower than what creditors demand, the creditors will purchase the bond only if the price is discounted. By discounting the price, the borrower is effectively increasing the rate of interest that the creditor earns. In fact, the bond will sell only when the price is reduced enough so that the effective interest rate that the creditor earns equals the market rate of interest. Bonds that are issued for less than face value are issued at a *discount*.

When a bond pays interest at a rate that is higher than what creditors demand, the borrower will sell the bond only if the price is raised. By raising the price, the borrower effectively lowers the rate of interest that the creditor earns. In fact, the bond will sell only when the price is raised enough so that the effective interest rate that the creditor earns equals the market rate of interest. Bonds that are issued for more than face value are issued at a *premium*.

Maturity date The date on which the face value must be repaid to the creditor.

Market (or effective) rate of interest The rate of return that investors in the bond markets demand for bonds of similar risk.

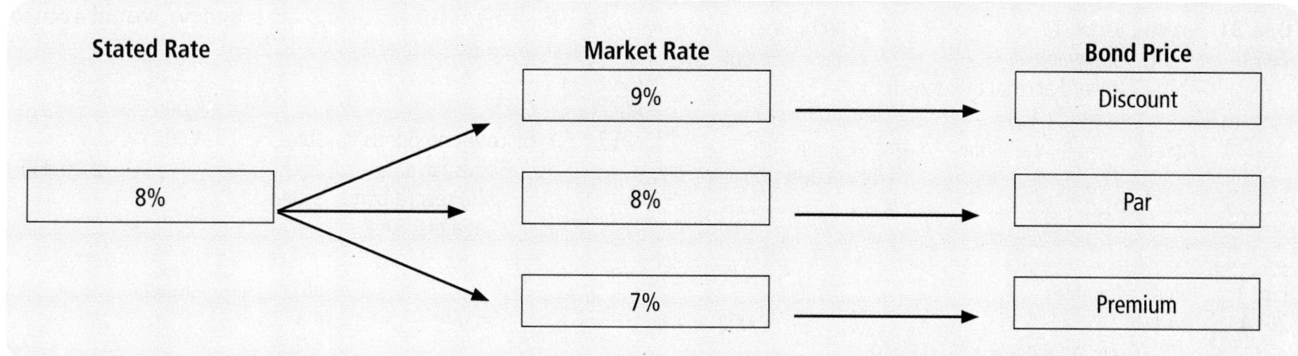

Actual issuance prices are calculated using present value computations. The chapter appendix illustrates these calculations. Here, you should simply understand that bonds sell for whatever price is necessary to make the effective rate of interest equal to the market rate of interest. Sometimes they sell for face value, sometimes at a discount, and sometimes for a premium. The following sections demonstrate how to account for a bond's issuance, the periodic interest payments, and the maturity of bonds under each scenario.

Bonds Issued at Face Value

To illustrate a bond issued at face value, suppose that on January 1, 2013, York Products sells bonds with a face value of ₹1,00,000. The bonds carry a 6% interest rate and a January 1, 2028, maturity date. Interest is to be paid semiannually on July 1 and January 1. Because the market rate of interest is also 6%, the bonds sell at face value.

Recording the Issuance In this example, York would record the bond issuance with a simple and straightforward entry to increase Cash and Bonds Payable:

		Debit	Credit
Jan. 1 2013	Cash	1,00,000	
	Bonds Payable		1,00,000
	(To record bonds issued at face value)		
	Assets = Liabilities + Equity		
	+1,00,000 = +1,00,000		

Note that this entry is practically the same as the entry recording the note payable earlier in the chapter. This should make sense since a bond is really just a more formalized note payable.

Recording Interest Payments Once the bond is issued, York must pay interest on July 1 and January 1 of each year. For any bond, the amount of interest paid each period is a product of the face value, the stated interest rate, and the length of the payment period. In this example, interest is paid every six months, or semiannually, so the amount paid is ₹3,000, calculated as follows:

Interest Paid = Face Value × Stated Interest Rate × Time Outstanding
= ₹1,00,000 × 0.06 × 6/12 months
= ₹3,000

Therefore, on July 1, York would record its interest payment with the following entry.

		Debit	Credit
July 1 2013	Interest Expense	3,000	
	Cash		3,000
	(To record payment of interest)		
	Assets = Liabilities + Equity		
	−3,000 = −3,000 (Equity)		

York increases Interest Expense to reflect the cost of borrowing over the six months and decreases Cash to reflect the payment made to the bondholders. The overall effect of the transaction is a decrease to York's assets and equity.

The next ₹3,000 interest payment is scheduled for January 1, 2014. However, assuming that York has a December 31 year-end, two entries are required. The first is a December 31 adjusting journal entry that accrues the interest expense and records the related payable so that the expense is properly matched to the period in which the money was used. The second entry records York's payment on January 1, 2014. These two entries are shown as follows:

Dec. 31 2013	Interest Expense	3,000	
	Interest Payable		3,000
	(To record accrual of interest)		

Assets	=	Liabilities	+	Equity
		+3,000		−3,000

Jan. 1 2014	Interest Payable	3,000	
	Cash		3,000
	(To record payment of interest)		

Assets	=	Liabilities	+	Equity
−3,000		−3,000		

Note that the interest expense is matched to 2013 and that the overall effect of the two entries is to decrease assets and equity by the amount of the interest paid. This is the same overall effect as the July 1 interest entry.

Interest is paid and recorded in the same manner every July 1 and December 31/January 1 for 15 years through the January 1, 2028, maturity date. Over time, York will make 30 payments of ₹3,000 for a total of ₹90,000 of interest paid. Thus, the total cost of borrowing the ₹1,00,000 over the 15 years is ₹90,000.

Recording the Maturity On the January 1, 2028, maturity date, York would record the repayment of the bonds in addition to the last interest payment.

Jan. 1 2028	Bonds Payable	1,00,000	
	Cash		1,00,000
	(To record repayment of the bonds)		

Assets	=	Liabilities	+	Equity
−1,00,000		−1,00,000		

Bonds Issued at a Discount

To illustrate a bond issued at a discount, suppose that on January 1, 2013, Agnew Company issues bonds with a face value of ₹2,00,000, a stated interest rate of 7%, and a maturity date of December 31, 2017. Interest is payable semiannually on June 30 and December 31. At the time of issuance, the market rate of interest is higher than the stated rate of 7%, and the bonds sell at a price of ₹1,96,000, or a ₹4,000 discount. At such a price, the bonds are said to have sold at 98, meaning that they were issued at 98% of face value (₹2,00,000 × 98% = ₹1,96,000).

Recording the Issuance Agnew would record the issuance as follows:

Jan. 1 2013	Cash	1,96,000	
	Discount on Bonds Payable	4,000	
	Bonds Payable		2,00,000
	(To record bonds issued at a discount)		

Assets	=	Liabilities	+	Equity
+1,96,000		+2,00,000		
		−4,000		

In this entry, Agnew increases Cash for the ₹1,96,000 received from the investors. Agnew also increases Bonds Payable to reflect the new obligation that it has. Notice that Bonds Payable is recorded at the bond's face value of ₹2,00,000. The Bonds Payable account is *always* recorded at the amount that will ultimately be repaid, which is face value. The difference of ₹4,000 is recorded in an account called Discount on Bonds Payable, which is a contra-liability account. Its balance is subtracted from the Bonds Payable account to yield the book value or carrying value of the bonds. As a result, both assets and liabilities increase by only ₹1,96,000.

After issuance, the bonds would be reported on the balance sheet as follows.

	Jan. 1, 2013
Bonds payable	₹2,00,000
Less: Discount on bonds payable	4,000
Carrying value	₹1,96,000

Notice that the carrying value of ₹1,96,000 at the time of issuance is equal to the cash received at issuance. This will always be the case at issuance, regardless of the price of the bond.

Recording Interest Payments Agnew's bonds call for semiannual interest payments over the life of the bonds. Each payment is calculated as follows:

$$\begin{aligned} \textbf{Interest Paid} &= \textbf{Face Value} \times \textbf{Stated Interest Rate} \\ &\quad \times \textbf{Time Outstanding} \\ &= ₹200{,}000 \times 0.07 \times 6/12 \text{ months} \\ &= ₹7{,}000 \end{aligned}$$

Note that this ₹7,000 interest payment is calculated the same way as the bond issued at face value. Whether a bond is issued at face value, at a discount, or at a premium, interest paid on a bond is always: face value × stated interest rate × time outstanding.

However, unlike the face value scenario, interest expense will be greater than interest paid. Recall that Agnew received only ₹1,96,000 at issuance but must repay ₹2,00,000 at maturity. That ₹4,000 discount is therefore an additional cost to Agnew that must be amortized over the life of the bond. To amortize the discount is to gradually reduce the discount balance and add the amount amortized to interest expense. Therefore, at each interest payment date, interest expense will be greater than interest paid.

There are two methods to amortize the discount on bonds payable—the straight-line method and the effective interest method. Because the straight-line method is easier to compute and is often close to the results from the effective interest method, the straight-line method is demonstrated here. However, the effective interest method is also demonstrated in the chapter appendix.

Under the **straight-line method of amortization**, an equal amount of the discount is amortized each time interest is paid. The amount amortized is calculated as follows:

$$\text{Discount Amortized} = \frac{\text{Discount at Issuance}}{\text{Number of Interest Payments}}$$

With a ₹4,000 discount and 10 semiannual interest payments, Agnew must amortize ₹400 (₹4,000 ÷ 10) each payment. As a result, Agnew's interest expense for each period is ₹7,400 (₹7,000 interest paid + ₹400 discount amortized). With this information, Agnew can make the following entry to record the first semiannual interest payment on June 30.

June 30 2013	Interest Expense	7,400	
	Discount on Bonds Payable		400
	Cash		7,000
	(To record the payment of interest)		

Assets	=	Liabilities	+	Equity
−7,000		+400		−7,400

The entry affects three accounts. First, Cash is decreased for the amount paid to the creditor. Second, the Discount on Bonds Payable account is decreased (or "amortized") by ₹400, resulting in a remaining balance of ₹3,600. Third, Interest Expense is increased by ₹7,400 to record the expense associated with the interest paid and the discount amortized. The effect of this entry is to decrease equity by ₹7,400 (the amount of expense), to decrease assets by ₹7,000 (the cash paid), and to increase liabilities by ₹400 (the discount amortized).

It may be counterintuitive to you that liabilities would *increase* as a result of the preceding interest entry. However, remember that the contra-liability Discount on Bonds Payable, which was first created for ₹4,000, is now only ₹3,600. Therefore, the carrying value of the bonds has increased by ₹400 because of the interest payment entry. This is illustrated as follows:

	Issuance	June 30, 2013
Bonds payable	₹2,00,000	₹2,00,000
Less: Discount on bonds payable	4,000	3,600
Carrying value	₹1,96,000	₹1,96,400

The carrying value will continue to increase by ₹400 each interest payment date as the discount is amortized. After ten total payments, the discount will be fully amortized (that is, it will have a zero balance), and the carrying value of the bonds will equal the face value of ₹2,00,000.

This movement of the carrying value from issuance price to face value is best illustrated in the schedule found in Exhibit 9-2. It is called an **amortization schedule** because it provides the details of the discount amortization and the resulting expense amounts and carrying values.

As you review the amortization schedule, note that it provides the rupee amounts for each semiannual interest entry. The first three columns provide the amounts of cash to be paid, discount to be amortized, and interest expense to be recognized each six months. Because the straight-line method of amortization is used, the amounts are the same each period. Thus, Agnew would make the same interest entry every six months until the bonds mature.

Note also that the schedule confirms that the total cost of borrowing is a combination of the interest paid and the original discount. Total interest expense over the life of the bonds is ₹74,000, which is the sum of interest paid (₹70,000) and the original discount

Straight-line method of amortization Method that amortizes an equal amount of the discount or premium each time interest is paid.

Amortization schedule A schedule that illustrates the amortization of a bond discount or premium over the life of a bond.

Exhibit 9-2 Amortization Schedule—Bonds Issued at a Discount

Interest Payment	Interest Paid	Discount Amortized	Interest Expense	Unamortized Discount	Carrying Value
				₹4,000	₹1,96,000
June 30, 2013	₹ 7,000	₹ 400	₹ 7,400	3,600	1,96,400
Dec. 31, 2013	7,000	400	7,400	3,200	1,96,800
June 30, 2014	7,000	400	7,400	2,800	1,97,200
Dec. 31, 2014	7,000	400	7,400	2,400	1,97,600
June 30, 2015	7,000	400	7,400	2,000	1,98,000
Dec. 31, 2015	7,000	400	7,400	1,600	1,98,400
June 30, 2016	7,000	400	7,400	1,200	1,98,800
Dec. 31, 2016	7,000	400	7,400	800	1,99,200
June 30, 2017	7,000	400	7,400	400	1,99,600
Dec. 31, 2017	7,000	400	7,400	0	2,00,000
	₹70,000	₹4,000	₹74,000		

(₹4,000). When bonds are issued at a discount, total interest expense will *always* exceed interest paid by the amount of the discount. An alternate calculation of the total cost of borrowing is as follows:

Interest payments (₹2,00,000 × 7% × 6/12)	₹ 7,000
× Number of payments	× 10
= Total interest paid	₹70,000
+ Discount	4,000
Total cost of borrowing	₹74,000

Recording the Maturity Agnew must repay ₹2,00,000 on December 31, 2017, to satisfy its obligation. The entry to repay the bonds requires a decrease to both Cash and the Bonds Payable account.

Dec. 31 2017	Bonds Payable	2,00,000	
	Cash		2,00,000
	(To record repayment of the bonds)		

Assets	=	Liabilities	+	Equity
−2,00,000		−2,00,000		

Bonds Issued at a Premium

To illustrate the accounting for a bond issued at a premium, suppose that on January 1, 2013, McCarthy Company issues bonds with a face value of ₹50,000, a stated interest rate of 8%, and a maturity date of December 31, 2015. Interest is payable semiannually on June 30 and December 31. At the time of issuance, the market rate of interest is lower than the stated rate of 8%, and the bonds sell at a price of ₹50,600, or a ₹600 premium. At such a price, the bonds are said to have sold at 101.2, meaning that they were issued at 101.2% of face value (₹50,000 × 101.2% = ₹50,600).

Recording the Issuance McCarthy would record the issuance as follows:

Jan. 1 2013	Cash	50,600	
	Premium on Bonds Payable		600
	Bonds Payable		50,000
	(To record bonds issued at a premium)		

Assets	=	Liabilities	+	Equity
+50,600		+50,000 +600		

In this entry, McCarthy increases Cash for the ₹50,600 received from creditors. McCarthy also increases Bonds Payable for the face value of ₹50,000. The ₹600 received in excess of the face value is recorded in an account called Premium on Bonds Payable. The balance in Premium on Bonds Payable is added to the Bonds Payable account to yield the bond's carrying value. The calculation of McCarthy's carrying value after issuance is shown as follows:

	Jan. 1, 2013
Bonds payable	₹50,000
Plus: Premium on bonds payable	600
Carrying value	₹50,600

As a result of this entry, McCarthy's assets and liabilities increase by ₹50,600.

In India, premium on bonds payable is disclosed under "Reserve and Surplus".

Recording Interest Payments McCarthy's bonds call for semiannual interest payments over the life of the bonds. Each payment is calculated as follows:

Interest Paid = Face Value × Stated Interest Rate × Time Outstanding

= ₹50,000 × 0.08 × 6/12 months

= ₹2,000

Like the discount example, McCarthy's interest payment will differ from its interest expense. McCarthy received ₹50,600 at issuance but must repay only ₹50,000 at maturity. The ₹600 premium is a reduction in McCarthy's cost. Like the discount example, the premium should be amortized over the life of the bond. As a result, at each interest payment date, interest expense will be less than interest paid.

The following is the amortization calculation using the straight-line method.

$$\text{Premium Amortized} = \frac{\text{Premium at Issuance}}{\text{Number of Interest Payments}}$$

With a ₹600 premium and 6 semiannual interest payments, McCarthy must amortize ₹100 (₹600/6) each payment. Therefore, interest expense for each period is ₹1,900 (₹2,000 interest paid − ₹100 premium amortized). This leads to the following entry to record the first semiannual interest payment on June 30.

June 30 2013	Interest Expense	1,900	
	Premium on Bonds Payable	100	
	Cash		2,000
	(To record the payment of interest)		

Assets	=	Liabilities	+	Equity
−2,000		−100		−1,900

The entry affects three accounts. First, Cash is decreased for the ₹2,000 payment. Second, the Premium on Bonds Payable account is amortized or decreased by ₹100, leaving a remaining balance of ₹500. Third, Interest Expense is increased by ₹1,900 to record the expense associated with the interest paid and the premium amortized. The effect of this entry is to decrease equity by ₹1,900 (the amount of expense), to decrease assets by ₹2,000 (the cash paid), and to decrease liabilities by ₹100 (the premium amortized).

After the entry, the carrying value of the bonds would be reported as follows:

	Issuance	June 30, 2013
Bonds payable	₹50,000	₹50,000
Plus: Premium on bonds payable	600	500
Carrying value	₹50,600	₹50,500

The bonds' carrying value is ₹100 smaller after the first interest payment. The carrying value will continue to decrease by ₹100 each interest payment date as the premium is amortized. After six total payments, the premium will be fully amortized and the carrying value of the bonds will equal the face value of ₹50,000. The amortization schedule in Exhibit 9-3 illustrates the change in the carrying value of the bonds over time.

Like the amortization schedule for bonds issued at a discount, the first three columns in the schedule provide the amounts of cash to be paid, premium to be amortized, and interest expense to be recognized each six months. Because of the straight-line method of amortization, the amounts are the same each period. Thus, McCarthy would make the same interest entry every six months until the bonds mature.

The schedule also illustrates that the total cost of borrowing is comprised of interest paid and the original premium. Total interest expense over the life of the bonds is ₹11,400, which is the amount of interest paid (₹12,000) less the original premium (₹600). When bonds are issued at a premium, total interest paid will *always* exceed interest expense by the amount of the premium. An alternate calculation of the total cost of borrowing is as follows.

Interest payments (₹50,000 × 8% × 6/12)	₹ 2,000
× Number of payments	× 6
= Total interest paid	12,000
− Premium	600
Total cost of borrowing	₹11,400

Recording the Maturity McCarthy must repay ₹50,000 on December 31, 2015, to satisfy its obligation. The entry to repay the bonds requires a decrease to both Cash and Bonds Payable:

Exhibit 9-3 Amortization Schedule—Bonds Issued at a Premium

Interest Payment	Interest Paid	Premium Amortized	Interest Expense	Unamortized Premium	Carrying Value
				₹600	₹50,600
Jun. 30, 2013	₹ 2,000	₹100	₹ 1,900	500	50,500
Dec. 31, 2013	2,000	100	1,900	400	50,400
Jun. 30, 2014	2,000	100	1,900	300	50,300
Dec. 31, 2014	2,000	100	1,900	200	50,200
Jun. 30, 2015	2,000	100	1,900	100	50,100
Dec. 31, 2015	2,000	100	1,900	0	50,000
	₹12,000	₹600	₹11,400		

Dec. 31 2015	Bonds Payable	50,000	
	Cash		50,000
	(To record repayment of the bonds)		

Assets	=	Liabilities	+	Equity
−50,000		−₹50,000		

LO4 Redeeming a Bond Before Maturity

Sometimes a bond is redeemed or retired before maturity. This can occur when the bond has a feature that allows the borrowing company to "call" or retire the bonds at a certain price. The call price is usually stated as a percentage of face value. For example, a call price of 105 means that the bonds can be retired by paying the creditor 105% of the face value of the bonds.

Bonds are retired early for various reasons. A company may simply want to reduce future interest expense or take advantage of falling interest rates by replacing existing bonds with less costly bonds. Whatever the reason, the accounting for the early retirement of a bond consists of the following three steps:

1. Update the carrying value of the bond.
2. Calculate gain or loss on the retirement.
3. Record the retirement.

The first step is to update the carrying value of the bond. Often this means that the bond must be amortized for a partial period. For example, if a bond is retired three months after the last interest payment date, the bond would be amortized for those three months to update the carrying value. Interest payable for the three months would also be recorded and would be paid in addition to the call price.

The second step is to calculate any gain or loss on retirement by comparing the carrying value to the call price. When the carrying value exceeds the call price, the company is paying less than the value of the liability. In that case, the company records a gain on the redemption. In contrast, when the call price exceeds the carrying value, the company is paying more than the value of the liability. In that case, the company records a loss on the redemption. This is summarized as follows:

Gain on Redemption =
Carrying value > Call price

Loss on Redemption =
Call price > Carrying value

To illustrate, suppose that Doyle Township issues a ₹20,000 eight-year bond on January 1, 2013, to fund the conversion of a warehouse to a youth activity center. The bond has a stated interest rate of 5% semianually and is callable at 103 any time after 2017. The bond pays interest semiannually on June 30 and December 31. The bond sells for ₹19,200, or an ₹800 discount. A condensed amortization schedule is presented in Exhibit 9-4.

Now suppose that Doyle decides to retire the bond a year early on December 31, 2019. The bond's call price of 103 means that Doyle can retire the bond by paying the bondholder 103% of face value, or ₹20,600 (₹20,000 × 103%). According to the amortization

A company may retire bonds early to reduce future interest expense or take advantage of falling interest rates by replacing existing bonds with less costly bonds.

the Discount on Bonds Payable. The entry then reduces Cash for the amount paid to retire the bond and records a ₹700 Loss on Redemption to reflect the loss on retiring the bond. This loss account is reported on the income statement, usually as an other or nonoperating expense. The overall effect of the entry is to decrease assets, liabilities, and equity.

Exhibit 9-4 Condensed Amortization Schedule—Bond Issued at a Discount

Interest Payment	Interest Paid	Discount Amortized	Interest Expense	Unamortized Discount	Carrying Value
				₹800	₹19,200
Jun. 30, 2013	₹1,000	₹50	₹1,050	750	19,250
Dec. 31, 2013	1,000	50	1,050	700	19,300
⋮	⋮	⋮	⋮	⋮	⋮
Jun. 30, 2018	1,000	50	1,050	250	19,750
Dec. 31, 2018	1,000	50	1,050	200	19,800
Jun. 30, 2019	1,000	50	1,050	150	19,850
Dec. 31, 2019	1,000	50	1,050	100	19,900
Jun. 30, 2020	1,000	50	1,050	50	19,950
Dec. 31, 2020	1,000	50	1,050	0	20,000

schedule, the December 31, 2019, carrying value of the bond is ₹19,900 (after the interest payment). Therefore, the gain or loss on redemption is calculated as follows:

Call price	₹20,600
Less: Carrying value on Dec. 31, 2019	19,900
Loss on redemption	₹ 700

Doyle would record the redemption with the following journal entry:

Date	Account	Debit	Credit
Dec. 31 2019	Bonds Payable	20,000	
	Loss on Redemption	700	
	Discount on Bonds Payable		100
	Cash		20,600
	(To record redemption of the bond)		

Assets	=	Liabilities	+	Equity
−20,600		−₹20,000 + 100		−700

This entry first decreases the Bonds Payable account by its face value of ₹20,000. Because Doyle no longer has the bond, it also decreases the remaining ₹100 balance in

LO5 Additional Liabilities

The next two sections examine two additional types of liabilities that are common to many organizations: lease liabilities and contingent liabilities.

Leases

When companies acquire fixed assets, they have a few ways to pay for them. One option is to pay with cash on hand. Another option is to issue notes or bonds to raise the necessary capital. A third option, which is the focus of this section of the text, is to use lease financing.

A **lease** is a contractual agreement in which the lessee obtains the right to use an asset by making periodic payments to the lessor. One of the major advantages of lease financing is its flexibility. Terms of usage, time

Lease A contractual agreement in which the lessee obtains the right to use an asset by making periodic payments to the lessor.

MAKING IT REAL

A financial crisis can often be an advantage to a company, and these current economic conditions are no exception. With interest rates at historic lows, many companies are issuing debt to lock in the rates. One example is Google, Inc.

In May of 2011, when its balance sheet showed a $37 billion cash balance, Google issued bonds for the first time in its history. Issuing three-year, five-year, and ten-year bonds, the company raised $3 billion. And it could have likely raised much more—orders from investors wanting to purchase the bonds exceeded $10 billion. Rates on the bonds were set very close to U.S. Treasury Notes, which were below 4% at issuance.

Why would a company with $37 billion borrow $3 billion more? The company says that it may use the funds to pay off short-term debt. Other analysts guess that it is just too good of a time to borrow to pass on the opportunity. The cash could be used to acquire another company or serve simply as a rather cheap way to maintain flexibility in a volatile economic climate. Regardless of the reason, Google joined many others in the technology industry such as Cisco Systems, Dell, and IBM who issued bonds in 2011.

Source: Cash-Rich Google Sells First Bonds, Wall Street Journal, May 2011.

limits, and payments are a few of the many aspects of lease contracts that can vary. As a result, one lease can look very different from another. However, from an accounting perspective, there are only two main types of leases—operating leases and capital leases.

An **operating lease** is a contract in which the lessee obtains the right to use an asset for a limited period of time but does not acquire ownership of the asset. Ownership remains with the lessor. As a result, the lessee does not record any asset or liability associated with the lease but simply records rent expense as lease payments are made. A common example of an operating lease is the leasing of an automobile from a dealership.

Operating leases can be very popular with companies because they are a form of off-balance-sheet financing. **Off-balance-sheet financing** occurs when a company's future obligations regarding an asset are not reported as a liability on the balance sheet. A common example is a noncancelable operating lease. Although such lease obligations are not reported on the balance sheet, accounting rules require that the future lease payments be disclosed in the notes to the financial statements.

Operating lease A contract in which the lessee obtains the right to use an asset for a limited period of time but does not acquire ownership of the asset.

Off-balance-sheet financing Occurs when a company's future obligations regarding an asset are not reported as a liability on the balance sheet.

The following is a portion of Ranbaxy Laboratories Ltd. note that covers the future minimum lease payments in respect of non-cancellable operating leases as at December 31, 2012:

Excerpt from Ranbaxy Laboratories Ltd. Lease Commitments Note

Future lease payment details as on 31.12.12 (₹ *in millions*):

	Total
Not later than one year	₹ 168.47
Later than one year but not later than five years	260.22
Later than five years	19.35

Again note to the financial statement of Hero MotoCorp reports the following regarding its lease rental commitment as contingent liability. The Company has entered into operating lease agreements for motor vehicles, dies, and data processing machines. These lease arrangements are cancelable in nature and range between two to four years. The aggregate lease rentals under these arrangements amounting to ₹12.40 crore (previous year ₹9.04 crore) have been charged under "Lease rentals"

One of the major advantages of lease financing is its flexibility. Terms of usage, time limits, and payments are a few of the many aspects of lease contracts that can vary.

IFRS

International Standards use the term "finance lease" instead of "capital lease."

In contrast to operating leases, a **capital lease** is a contract in which the lessee obtains enough rights to use and control an asset such that the lessee is in substance the owner of the asset. Because of this effective ownership, accounting rules require that the leased asset and the lease obligation be recorded by the lessee and reported on the balance sheet. This is why such contracts are called *capital* leases—because the asset is capitalized on the balance sheet. The actual entries associated with a capital lease and the criteria for determining whether a contract is a capital lease will be left to more advanced accounting courses.

Contingent Liabilities

A **contingent liability** is an obligation that arises from an existing condition whose outcome is uncertain and whose resolution depends on a future event. A good example of a contingent liability is a product warranty. The "existing condition" is the company's promise that it will replace the product or refund the price. The uncertain outcome is whether the product will be defective, and the resolution depends on both the product malfunctioning and the customer returning it. Another example is legal action against a company, which is an uncertain condition whose resolution depends on future events (e.g., a jury verdict).

Accounting rules state that a contingent liability should be recorded and reported on the balance sheet if it is *probable* that the liability will be incurred and it can be reasonably estimated. A warranty meets these two conditions. Most merchandisers or manufacturers will have defective products that customers return, and most

Capital lease A contract in which the lessee obtains enough rights to use and control an asset such that the lessee is in substance the owner of the asset.

Contingent liability An obligation that arises from an existing condition whose outcome is uncertain and whose resolution depends on a future event.

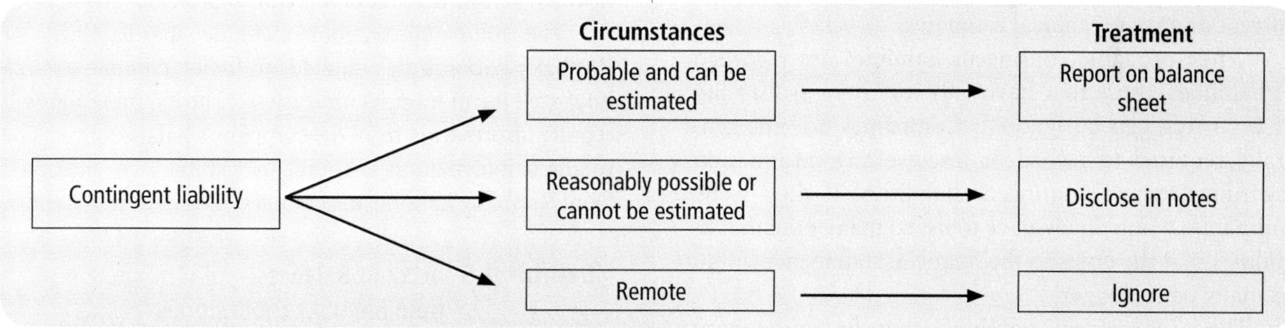

MARUTI SUZUKI ANALYSIS

Look at Maruti Suzuki's financial statement and notes in Appendix C and state whether the company have any obligation under capital lease or operating lease?

Maruti Suzuki's financial statement shows that the company does not have any obligation neither under capital lease. However, Note 51 to The Financial Statements states that the minimum lease payment outstanding on March 31, 2011 in respect of asset taken on non-cancellable operating lease are:

Within one year	**₹54 million**
Later than one year but less than five years	**₹227 million**
Later than five years	**₹682 million**

can reasonably estimate their future warranty claims by reviewing historical claims. As a result, most companies include warranty obligations among their liabilities.

For companies like Hero MotoCorp Ltd., warranty liabilities are shown as current liabilities. To illustrate, Hero MotoCorp Ltd.'s 2012–13 Note 10 to the financial statement show:

Hero MotoCorp Ltd. 2013 Note 10 to the financial statement

(in crores)	
Warranties March 31, 2013	₹ 5.66
Warranties March 31, 2012	5.70

Hero MotoCorp Ltd. shows that the 2013 balance in current liabilities as reported on the balance sheet includes over ₹5.66 crore of warranty obligations. Note 2(x) to the Financial Statements of Hero MotoCorp Ltd. states: The estimated liability for product warranties is recorded when products are sold. These estimates are established using historical information on the nature, frequency, and average cost of warranty claims and management estimates regarding possible future incidence based on corrective actions on product failures. The timing of outflows will vary as and when warranty claim will arise—being typically two to three years. The Company accounts for the post-contract support/provision for warranty on the basis of the information available with the Management duly taking into account the current and past technical estimates.

While probable contingent liabilities are recorded as liabilities, those that have only a *remote* probability of occurring can be ignored. Companies are not generally required to record or disclose any information regarding remote contingent liabilities. If they were, companies would likely have to list so many potential liabilities that the notes to the financial statements would be many pages longer!

Those contingent liabilities that lie in between probable and remote—that is, those that are *reasonably possible*—are disclosed in the notes to the financial statements. This same treatment is required of liabilities that are probable but cannot be reasonably estimated. Note that disclosing something in the notes brings it to the attention of investors, but it does not result in a change to a company's liabilities.

The following is an excerpt from Hero MotoCorp Ltd. contingencies note to its 2012–13 financial statements. It describes a contingency whose occurrence is at least reasonably possible but whose amount cannot be reasonably estimated:

IFRS

International standards permit reduced disclosures about a contingent liability if the disclosures seriously prejudice the company's position in a dispute about the related liability.

Excerpt from Hero MotoCorp Ltd.'s 2013 Contingencies Note

(in crores)	March 31, 2013	March 31, 2012
In respect of excise matters	47.09	39.99

The above matters are subject to legal proceedings in the ordinary course of business. The legal proceedings when ultimately concluded will not, in the opinion of management, have a material effect on the result of operations or the financial position of the Company.

LO6 Evaluating a Company's Management of Liabilities

As a company operates its business, it will generate liabilities. In fact, the generation of liabilities is usually the easy part of a business. It is the repayment of those liabilities that can create significant problems.

The following sections examine the liabilities of Ranbaxy Laboratories Limited, an Indian company, to see how well it can meet its obligations. The examination will require information from the company's balance sheet. The required information is found in Exhibit 9-5, excerpted from Ranbaxy Laboratories Limited' 2012 Annual Report.

Exhibit 9-5 Account Balances from Ranbaxy Laboratories Limited 2012 Annual Report

Source	Accounts	2012	2011
Balance Sheet	Current assets	₹66,563.91	₹78,953.37
	Total assets	1,29,699.34	1,43,209.25
	Current liabilities	77,807.95	96,161.74
	Total liabilities	1,10,478.57	1,23,960.95

Horizontal and Vertical Analyses

An easy and useful place to start an examination of liabilities is with horizontal and vertical analyses. Recall from Chapter 2 that horizontal analysis calculates the dollar/rupee change in an account balance, defined as the current year balance less the prior year balance, and divides that change by the prior year balance to yield the percentage change. Vertical analysis divides each account balance by a base account, yielding a percentage. The base account is total assets for balance sheet accounts and net sales or total revenues for income statement accounts. These calculations are summarized as follows:

Horizontal Analysis

$$\text{Dollar (Rupee) change in account balance} = \text{Current year balance} - \text{Prior year balance}$$

$$\text{Percentage change in account balance} = \frac{\text{Dollar (Rupee) change}}{\text{Prior year balance}}$$

Vertical Analysis

$$\text{Percentage} = \underset{\textit{Balance Sheet}}{\frac{\text{Account Balance}}{\text{Total Assets}}} \text{ or } \underset{\textit{Income Statement}}{\frac{\text{Account Balance}}{\text{Net Sales or Revenue}}}$$

Given Ranbaxy Laboratories' financial information in Exhibit 9-5, horizontal and vertical analyses of liabilities result in the following.

Horizontal Analysis

	Change	Percentage Change
Total Liabilities	1,10,478.57 −1,23,960.95 (13,482.38)	$\frac{(13,482.38)}{1,23,960.95} = (10.9)\%$

Vertical Analysis

	2012	2011
Total Liabilities	$\frac{1,10,478.57}{1,29,699.34} = 85.2\%$	$\frac{1,23,960.95}{1,43,209.25} = 86.6\%$

The calculations show a fairly stable position with regard to liabilities. Horizontal analysis shows a 10.9% decrease in liabilities. However, vertical analysis shows that total liabilities as a percentage of total assets has reduced from 86.6% to 85.2%. This means that liabilities grew slower than assets over the two years. In both years, around 0 .85 of every rupee of assets was generated through debt.

For comparison, the horizontal and vertical analyses of liabilities for Ranbaxy Laboratories Limited's, Novartis India Limited, and Cipla are shown as follows.

		Horizontal Analysis	Vertical Analysis
Liabilities	*Ranbaxy Laboratories Limited*	(10.9)%	85.2%
	Novartis India Limited	13.46%	20.88%
	Cipla	(7.37)%	16.05%

You can see that Ranbaxy Laboratories Limited and Cipla's liabilities witnessed a negative growth, Novartis India grew at 13.46%. Also, you can see that Ranbaxy Laboratories' has the highest of the two competitors when it comes to liabilities as a percentage of assets (vertical analysis).

In addition to an analysis of total liabilities, it is usually a good idea to conduct horizontal and vertical analyses on some of the larger individual liabilities to identify any potential areas of concern. For Ranbaxy Laboratories Limited, the two largest liabilities are short-term borrowings and long-term borrowings. (These balances are not reported in this text.) In 2012, short-term borrowings witnessed a negative growth (4.2%) while long-term borrowings increased by 108.4%. These changes need further investigation.

Current Ratio

Liquidity refers to a company's ability to pay off its obligations in the near future. Many parties are interested in a company's liquidity. For example, a loan officer would be interested in whether a company could pay monthly interest. A vendor would want to know if it could expect prompt payment. Employees are concerned with their employer's ability to satisfy payroll. One way to measure a company's liquidity is to calculate the current ratio.

The **current ratio** compares a company's current assets to its current liabilities as follows:

$$\text{Current Ratio} = \frac{\text{Current Assets}}{\text{Current Liabilities}}$$

By comparing what a company expects to turn into cash within a year to what it expects to pay within the year, this ratio suggests how well a company can pay its short-term liabilities. A higher current ratio indicates a greater ability to satisfy current obligations.

Ranbaxy Laboratories' 2012 current ratio is calculated as follows:

$$\frac{₹66,563.91}{₹77,807.95} = 0.86$$

Liquidity A company's ability to pay off its obligations in the near future.

Current ratio Compares a company's current assets to its current liabilities and measures its ability to pay current obligations.

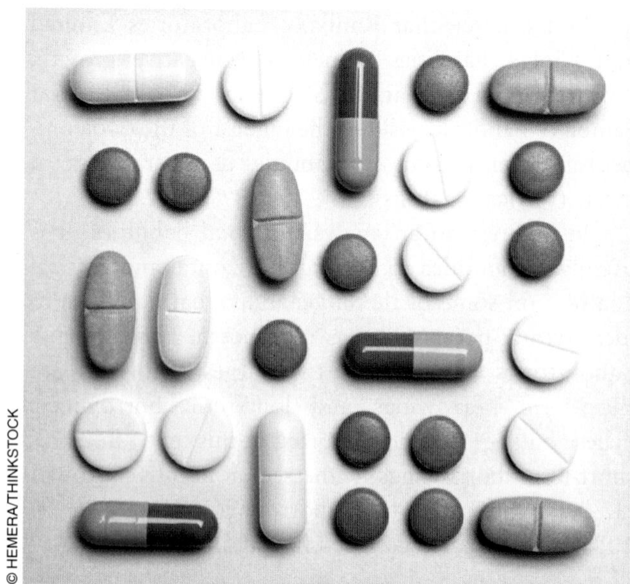
© HEMERA/THINKSTOCK

The 0.86 ratio shows that at the end of 2012, Ranbaxy Laboratories Limited had ₹0.85 in current assets for every rupee of current liabilities. That is, Ranbaxy Laboratories Limited have less current assets to satisfy its obligations coming due in the following year. The company's 2011 ratio was almost exactly the same (₹78,953.37/96,161.74 = 0.82). By way of comparison, Novartis India's 2012 current ratio was 4.8 and Cipla's was 0.45.

When interpreting the current ratio, it is a good idea to gauge whether a company can turn its current assets into cash. For example, a company that cannot sell its inventory cannot generate cash to pay its obligations. This could be a risk for Ranbaxy Laboratories Limited. Over ₹17,318.39 crore of its ₹66,563.91 crore of current assets is inventory. One way to gauge the impact of inventory is to calculate the inventory turnover ratio.

Recall from Chapter 7 that the inventory turnover ratio is calculated as follows: Cost of Goods Sold/Average Inventory. Ranbaxy Laboratories Limited inventory turnover ratio is 1.35, meaning that the company sells through its inventory 1.35 times during the year. This is similar to Cipla inventory turnover ratio of 1.54. Ranbaxy Laboratories Limited should not have a problem turning its inventory into cash and paying off its obligations.

Solvency A company's ability to continue in business in the long term by satisfying its long-term obligations.

Debt to assets ratio Compares a company's total liabilities to its total assets and measures its ability to satisfy its long-term obligations.

Capital structure The mix of debt and equity that a company uses to generate its assets.

When interpreting the current ratio, it is a good idea to gauge whether a company can turn its current assets into cash.

Debt to Assets Ratio

Solvency refers to a company's ability to continue in business in the long term by satisfying its long-term obligations. While predicting whether a company will survive in the long term is very difficult, we can get an idea of a company's prospects by calculating the debt to assets ratio. The **debt to assets ratio** compares a company's total liabilities to its total assets. It is calculated as follows:

$$\text{Debt to Assets Ratio} = \frac{\text{Total Liabilities}}{\text{Total Assets}}$$

This ratio takes all of the obligations a company reports and divides by all of the assets the company reports, yielding the percentage of assets that are provided by debt. Thus, the ratio is a good indicator of a company's capital structure. **Capital structure** refers to the mix of debt and equity that a company uses to generate its assets. Since debt must be repaid, a company that uses more debt has a riskier capital structure and therefore a greater risk of being unable to meet its obligations.

Ranbaxy Laboratories' 2012 debt to assets ratio is calculated as follows:

$$\frac{₹1,10,478.57}{₹1,29,699.34} = 0.85$$

The 0.85 ratio shows that at the end of 2012, 85% of Ranbaxy Laboratories' assets were generated through debt. In comparison, Novartis India Limited ratio was 0.209 in 2012 and Ciplas' was 0.161. Whether a ratio of 0.85, 0.209, or 0.161 is good or bad for a company depends on many factors. Some companies willingly expose themselves to liabilities and the risk that comes with them in order to provide a greater chance of significant profits. Others purposely reduce their risk by limiting the use of debt. Neither strategy is right or wrong. They are just different. This issue will be discussed in more detail in Chapter 12. At this point, you should simply recognize that Ranbaxy

Laboratories' appears to have more risk of insolvency than Novartis India Limited and Cipla.

As you consider the debt to assets ratios, you may recognize the numbers from earlier in the chapter. They are the same as those generated in the vertical analysis of total liabilities. In fact, the debt to assets ratio is equivalent to a vertical analysis of total liabilities. Both the debt to assets ratio and vertical analysis divide total liabilities by total assets and are interpreted the same. So, when you conduct a vertical analysis, you already have the debt to assets ratio.

A bond's issuance price will always be the present value of future cash flows discounted back at the current market rate of interest.

LO7 Appendix—Determining a Bond's Issuance Price

Calculating the issuance price of a bond requires the conversion of a bond's future cash flows into today's rupees. A conventional interest-paying bond has two types of future cash flows: the one-time principal payment made at maturity and the periodic interest payments made each year. The bond's issuance price will always be the present value of those future cash flows discounted back at the current market rate of interest.

To illustrate, suppose that the market rate of interest is 8% when Bowman Corporation issues a ₹1,00,000 4-year bond that pays interest annually at a rate of 10%. The future cash flows of this bond are represented graphically as follows:

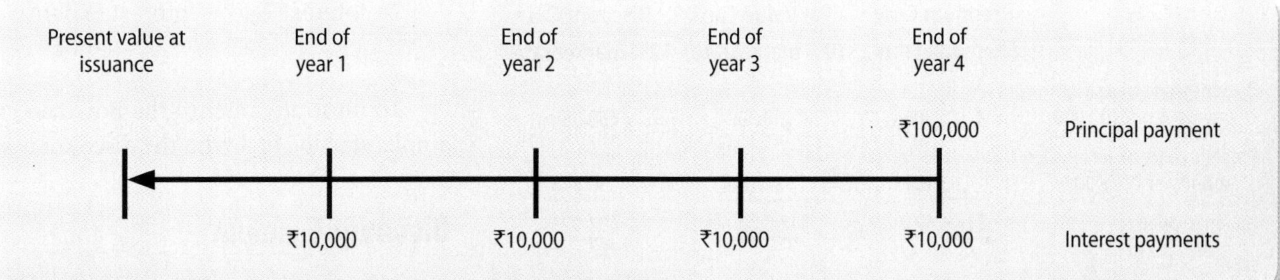

MARUTI SUZUKI ANALYSIS

Using Maruti Suzuki's information in Appendix C, calculate and interpret (1) horizontal and vertical analyses of liabilities, (2) the current ratio, and (3) the debt to assets ratio.

(1) *Horizontal Analysis*

(₹84,324 – ₹74,245)/₹74,245 = 13.6%

Vertical Analysis

₹84,324/₹2,74,708 = 30.69%

The 13.6% horizontal analysis reflects an increasing amount of obligations. The 30.69% vertical analysis of total liabilities shows that a nearly one-third of the company's assets are generated through liabilities, with the rest generated through equity.

(2) *Current Ratio*

₹1,11,541/₹69,719 = 1.60

The 1.60 Current Ratio indicates that Maruti Suzuki has ₹1.60 in current assets for every ₹1 of current liabilities. It appears that the company can pay off its current liabilities with its current assets.

(3) *Debt to Assets Ratio*

₹84,324/₹2,74,708 = 30.69%

The 30.69% Debt to Assets Ratio indicates that Maruti Suzuki has 30.69 paise in liabilities for every ₹1 of assets. This shows capital structure, comprise of almost two-third equity and nearly one-third debt.

The ₹1,00,000 principal payment is a single payment made at the end of year four. Therefore, it is discounted back four periods at an 8% rate using the appropriate factor found in Exhibit A-4, Present Value of ₹1. The factor for four periods (n = 4) and a rate of 8% (r = 8%) is 0.7350. Therefore, the present value of the ₹1,00,000 payment is ₹73,500 (₹1,00,000 × 0.7350).

The ₹10,000 interest payments are made at the end of each of the next four years. Therefore, they constitute an annuity that is discounted back four periods at an 8% rate using the appropriate factor found in Exhibit A-9: Present Value of an Ordinary Annuity. The factor for four periods (n = 4) and a rate of 8% (r = 8%) is 3.3121. Therefore, the present value of the ₹10,000 payments is ₹33,121 (₹10,000 × 3.3121).

Adding these two present values together yields ₹106,621. So, the bond sells for a premium. This calculation, along with similar calculations for 10% and 12% market rates are shown in Exhibit 9-6.

Exhibit 9-6 Calculations of Bond Issuance Prices

	Premium Case	Par Value Case	Discount Case
	8% market rate	10% market rate	12% market rate
Present value of a single payment of ₹100,000	₹ 73,500	₹ 68,300	₹63,550
Present value of an annuity of ₹10,000	33,121	31,700	30,373
Issuance price	₹1,06,621	₹1,00,000	₹93,923

Note that the prices calculated confirm that bonds are issued for (1) a premium when the stated interest rate exceeds the market rate, (2) face value when the two rates are equal, and (3) a discount when the market interest rate exceeds the stated rate.

LO8 Appendix—Effective Interest Method of Amortization

When a bond is issued at a discount or premium, the discount or premium must be amortized over the life of the bond. The following sections demonstrate the effective interest method of amortization.

Effective interest method of amortization Method that amortizes the bond discount or premium so that interest expense each period is a constant percentage of the bond's carrying value.

The **effective interest method of amortization** amortizes the bond discount or premium so that interest expense each period is a constant percentage of the bond's carrying value. Under this method, interest expense is calculated by multiplying the bond's carrying value by the market rate of interest at issuance by the time outstanding.

Interest Expense = Carrying Value × Market Rate of Interest at Issuance × Time Outstanding

Once interest expense is known, the amount of discount or premium amortized is the difference between interest expense and interest paid.

Discount Amount Amortized
= Interest Expense − Interest Paid

Premium Amount Amortized
= Interest Paid − Interest Expense

To illustrate, refer to the Bowman example, starting first with the discount case.

Discount Example

In the discount case for the Bowman bonds, the market rate of interest was 12% and the ₹1,00,000 bond was issued for ₹93,923, resulting in a discount of ₹6,077. The issuance would be recorded with the following entry:

Jan. 1	Cash	93,923	
	Discount on Bonds Payable	6,077	
	Bonds Payable		1,00,000
	(To record bonds issued at a discount)		

Assets	=	Liabilities	+	Equity
+93,923		+1,00,000		
		−6,077		

At the end of the first year, interest expense, interest paid, and the amount of the discount amortized would be calculated as follows. Note that "time outstanding" is omitted from the calculations because interest is paid annually.

When a bond is issued at a discount or premium, the discount or premium must be amortized over the life of the bond.

Interest Expense	Carrying value × Market rate	₹93,923 × 12%	₹11,271
Interest Paid	Face value × Stated rate	₹1,00,000 × 10%	₹10,000
Discount Amortized	Interest expense − Interest paid	₹11,271 − ₹10,000	₹1,271

With these values, Bowman would record the following entry on the first interest payment date:

Payment 1	Interest Expense	11,271	
	Discount on Bonds Payable		1,271
	Cash		10,000
	(To record the payment of interest)		

Assets	=	Liabilities	+	Equity
−10,000		+1,271		−11,271

Because the Discount on Bonds Payable account is reduced by this entry, the carrying value of the bonds will increase. As a result, the amount of interest expense for the second interest payment will increase as well. In fact, interest expense will continue to increase each period as the bond's carrying value increases toward the face value of ₹1,00,000. To illustrate this fact, a full amortization schedule for this bond is shown in Exhibit 9-7 (with the numbers rounded for presentation purposes):

Note that, like the straight-line method of amortization, the effective method amortizes the bond discount to zero, resulting in an ending carrying value equal to the face value. But, unlike the straight-line method, interest expense and the amount amortized under the effective interest method are different each period. Again, this is because the effective interest method makes sure that interest expense is a constant percentage (12%) of the current carrying value.

Premium Example

In the premium case, the market rate of interest was 8% and the ₹1,00,000 bond was issued for ₹1,06,621, resulting in a premium of ₹6,621. The issuance would be recorded with the following entry:

Jan. 1	Cash	1,06,621	
	Premium on Bonds Payable		6,621
	Bonds Payable		1,00,000
	(To record bonds issued at a premium)		

Assets	=	Liabilities	+	Equity
+1,06,621		+1,00,000		
		+6,621		

At the end of the first year, interest expense, interest paid, and the amount of the discount amortized would be calculated as follows:

Interest Paid	Face value × Stated rate	₹100,000 × 10%	₹10,000
Interest Expense	Carrying value × Market rate	₹106,621 × 8%	₹8,530
Premium Amortized	Interest paid − Interest expense	₹10,000 − ₹8,530	₹1,470

Exhibit 9-7 Amortization Schedule of Bond Discount Using Effective Interest Method

Interest Payment	Interest Paid	Discount Amortized	Interest Expense	Unamortized Discount	Carrying Value
				₹6,077	₹ 93,923
1	₹10,000	₹1,271	₹11,271	4,806	95,194
2	10,000	1,423	11,423	3,383	96,617
3	10,000	1,594	11,594	1,789	98,211
4	10,000	1,789	11,789	0	1,00,000
	₹40,000	₹6,077	₹46,077		

With these values, Bowman would record the following entry on the first interest payment date:

Payment 1	Interest Expense	8,530	
	Premium on Bonds Payable	1,470	
	Cash		10,000
	(To record the first bond payment)		

Assets	=	Liabilities	+	Equity
−10,000		−1,470		−8,530

Because the carrying value of the bonds decreases as a result of this entry, the amount of interest expense for the second interest payment will also decrease. Interest expense will continue to decrease each period as the bond's carrying value decreases toward the face value of ₹1,00,000. To illustrate, a full amortization schedule for this bond is shown in Exhibit 9-8 (with the numbers rounded for presentation purposes).

Note that like the straight-line method of amortization, the effective method amortizes the bond premium to zero, resulting in an ending carrying value equal to the face value. But, unlike the straight-line method, interest expense and the amount amortized are different each period under the effective method. Again, this is because the effective interest method makes sure that interest expense is a constant percentage (8%) of the current carrying value.

Exhibit 9-8 Amortization Schedule of Bond Premium Using Effective Interest Method

Interest Payment	Interest Paid	Discount Amortized	Interest Expense	Unamortized Discount	Carrying Value
				₹6,621	₹1,06,621
1	₹10,000	₹1,470	₹ 8,530	5,151	1,05,151
2	10,000	1,588	8,412	3,563	1,03,563
3	10,000	1,715	8,285	1,848	1,01,848
4	10,000	1,848	8,152	0	1,00,000
	₹40,000	₹6,621	₹33,379		

CONCEPT QUESTIONS

1. What is a current liability and where are current liabilities reported?
2. What are three examples of current liabilities?
3. What is a long-term liability?
4. Where are cash flows associated with long- term liabilities reported?
5. What are the main terms of a bond?
6. What is the difference between the stated and market interest rates associated with a bond?
7. When does a bond sell for face value, a premium, or a discount?
8. For a ₹1,00,000 bond, what amount is recorded in the Bonds Payable account? Does it matter whether the bond is issued at face value, a premium, or a discount?
9. What is the formula to calculate semiannual interest paid on a bond?
10. How will interest expense compare to interest paid if a bond is issued at a) face value, b) a discount or c) a premium?
11. What does a bond amortization schedule show?
12. What are the three steps in accounting for a bond that is redeemed before maturity?
13. What is the calculation for the gain or loss on redemption when a bond is redeemed before maturity?
14. What are the two main types of leases? Explain the differences in the two.
15. What is off-balance-sheet financing and what is a common example?
16. What are the three treatments of a contingent liability and when is each used?
17. How is the current ratio calculated and what does it measure?
18. How is the debt to assets ratio calculated and what does it measure?
19. To what is a bond's issuance price equal?
20. What is the effective interest method of amortization and how does it differ from the straight-line method?

MULTIPLE CHOICE

1. A current liability is any obligation of a business that:
   a. is expected to be satisfied or paid within six months.
   b. is expected to be satisfied or paid within two years.
   c. a business will not be able to pay off.
   d. is expected to be satisfied or paid within one year.
2. Floyd Corporation sells merchandise to a customer who pays ₹500 for the merchandise and ₹40 in sales tax. What amount will Floyd Corporation record as sales?
   a. ₹500
   b. ₹540
   c. ₹460
   d. ₹520
3. Which of the following is not a type of tax that is commonly withheld from an employee's paycheck?
   a. Income Tax
   b. Service Tax
   c. Professional Tax
   d. Sales Tax
4. Which of the following statements is true?
   i. A note payable can be classified as a current or long-term liability.
   ii. Taxes payable are never current liabilities.
   a. i only
   b. ii only
   c. Both i and ii
   d. Neither i nor ii
5. A company issues a ₹2,000 6% note payable due in 4 months. How much interest will the company pay for this note?
   a. ₹120
   b. ₹0
   c. ₹30
   d. ₹40
6. When will Long-Term Debt be considered a current liability?
   a. Never
   b. In the first year of its issuance
   c. Always
   d. Whatever portion of the debt is due within one year of the balance sheet date will be considered current
7. Cash flows associated with long-term liabilities are reported:
   a. in the operating activities section of the statement of cash flows.
   b. in the investing activities section of the statement of cash flows.
   c. in the financing activities section of the statement of cash flows.
   d. on the balance sheet.
8. Which of the following is a financial instrument used by an entity to borrow money?
   a. Bond
   b. Check
   c. Cash
   d. Note Receivable
9. Which of the following is used to determine the amount of interest a company issuing a bond must pay the investor?
   a. Stated Interest Rate

b. Face Value
c. Market Interest Rate
d. Both a and b

10. On January 1, Doroh Enterprises issues ₹2,00,000, 10-year, 6% bonds at par value with interest payable on July 1 and January 1. The entry on July 1 to record payment of bond interest will include a:
    a. debit to Interest Expense, ₹6,000.
    b. debit to Interest Expense, ₹12,000.
    c. credit to Cash, ₹12,000.
    d. credit to Interest Payable, ₹6,000.
11. Camp Corporation issues bonds with a stated interest rate of 8%. The current market rate of interest is 10%. These bonds likely sold at:
    a. par value.
    b. a discount.
    c. a premium.
    d. none of the above.
12. If bonds with a face value of ₹4,00,000 are issued at 102, how much cash is received by the borrowing company?
    a. ₹4,02,000
    b. ₹4,04,000
    c. ₹4,08,000
    d. ₹3,92,000
13. If bonds with a face value of ₹1,00,000 are sold for ₹96,000, how must this ₹4,000 difference be accounted for?
    a. It must be depreciated
    b. It must be amortized over the life of the bond
    c. It must be recorded as a loss on issuance
    d. It must be ignored
14. What does it mean when bonds are issued at a premium?
    a. The market interest rate exceeds the stated interest rate
    b. The market interest rate and the stated rate are the same
    c. The stated interest rate exceeds the market interest rate
    d. None of the above
15. Freeman Incorporated issues 5-year bonds with a face value of ₹3,00,000 for ₹2,88,000. Using the straight-line method of amortization, how much of this discount will be amortized each payment if interest is paid semiannually?
    a. ₹2,400
    b. ₹1,200
    c. ₹1,000
    d. ₹600
16. If bonds with a face value of ₹2,00,000 are issued at 102, what amount is recorded in the Bonds Payable account?
    a. ₹2,04,000
    b. ₹2,02,000
    c. ₹1,96,000
    d. ₹2,00,000
17. The carrying value of a bond issued at a discount is equal to:
    a. the face value less the unamortized discount.
    b. the face value plus the unamortized discount.
    c. the face value.
    d. None of the above.
18. A bond with a face value of ₹80,000 and an unamortized discount of ₹2,000 is redeemed at a price of ₹81,000. What is the gain or loss on redemption?
    a. ₹1,000 loss
    b. ₹3,000 loss
    c. ₹1,000 gain
    d. ₹3,000 gain
19. An operating lease:
    a. allows a company to finance an asset without reporting a liability on the balance sheet.
    b. can be disclosed in the notes to the financial statements.
    c. Both a and b
    d. Neither a nor b
20. Which of the following is necessary for a contingent liability to exist?
    a. There must be an existing condition
    b. The resolution of the condition must depend on some event in the future
    c. The outcome of the condition must be unknown
    d. All of the above
21. Which of the following is a common contingent liability that is often reported on the balance sheet as a liability because of its probable nature?
    a. Warranties
    b. Bonds
    c. Taxes
    d. Salaries
22. The debt to assets ratio is a measure of a company's:
    a. liquidity.
    b. solvency.
    c. capital structure.
    d. both b and c.
23. A company's current ratio increases. What does this mean?
    a. The company is less liquid.
    b. The company is more liquid.
    c. The company's liquidity is unchanged.
    d. None of the above.
24. A company issues bonds. The issuance price will be equal to:
    a. the present value of the interest payments.
    b. the present value of the principal payment.
    c. the present values of both the interest payments and the principal payment.
    d. the sum of the interest payments and the principal payment.
25. Under the effective interest method of amortization, interest expense is calculated as:
    a. face value times the stated interest rate.
    b. carrying value times the market interest rate.
    c. face value times the market interest rate.
    d. carrying value times the stated interest rate.

26. Under the effective interest method of amortization, the amount of discount or premium amortized each interest payment is equal to:
    a. the difference between interest expense and interest paid.
    b. the original discount or premium divided by the number of interest payments.
    c. the carrying value times the market rate of interest.
    d. None of the above.

BRIEF EXERCISES

1. Sales Tax Payable

A company makes a sale of ₹2,000. The sales tax rate is 9%.

Required

Prepare the entry to record the sale and related sales tax liability. Ignore any effects on inventory.

2. Current Liabilities

The following list represents liabilities on the December 31 balance sheet of Munday Motor Company.

1. Money owed to employees for work performed the last two weeks in December
2. Money owed to a supplier for goods purchased based on the terms net 30
3. Money owed to the government, based on the annual income of the company
4. Money owed to the bank on a note due in July

Required

Identify the liability account that would likely be used to report each item.

3. Unearned Revenues

Ivey Designs provides internet hosting services to customers who purchase annual maintenance contracts. Ivey charges ₹1,200 per year. On September 1, Durbin Farms signs a contract with Ivey and pays ₹1,200.

Required

Prepare a) the September 1 entry that Ivey makes to record the contract and b) the December 31 entry to recognize Ivey's revenues earned to date.

4. Reporting Liabilities

At the end of 2012–13, Brandon Corporation has total current liabilities of ₹17,55,000. Long-term debt is ₹8,50,000, and other long-term liabilities are ₹6,45,000.

Required

Prepare the liability section of Brandon Corporation's 2012–13 balance sheet.

5. Recording and Reporting Bonds

Johnson Galleries issued ₹5,00,000 of 10-year bonds on January 1, 2013. The bonds pay 8% interest semiannually on July 1 and January 1. The market rate of interest on the date of issuance was 8%.

Required

a. Prepare all journal entries necessary in 2013.
b. How would the issue price change if the market rate was lower than 8%? Higher than 8%?
c. What cash flows associated with the bond will be reported in the financing section of the 2013 statement of cash flows?

6. Recording and Reporting Bonds

On January 1, 2013, Mason Company issues ₹2 million of 5-year, 7% bonds at 98, with interest payable on June 30 and December 31. Mason uses the straight-line method of amortization.

Required

a. Prepare the journal entry to record the issuance of these bonds.
b. Prepare the journal entry to record interest expense and bond discount amortization on June 30, 2013.
c. Where will the issuance of the bond be reported on Mason's 2013 statement of cash flows?

7. Bond Interest and Amortization

Andrews Corporation issued ₹3,00,000 of 12%, 3-year bonds on January 1. Interest is payable semiannually on June 30 and December 31. Andrews uses the straight-line method of amortization.

Required

a. Prepare the journal entry to record the issuance of the bonds if they are issued at 101.
b. Prepare the journal entry to record the first payment of interest on June 30.
c. Will Andrews make the same interest payment entry on December 31?

8. Calculating Gain or Loss on Bond Redemption

Fly Corporation issued 10-year bonds on January 1, 2006. On July 1, 2012 Fly Corporation decides to retire the bonds early. The call price is ₹2,12,000 and the carrying value of the bonds on the date of redemption is ₹1,88,000.

Required

Calculate the gain or loss on redemption recognized by Fly.

9. Contingent Liabilities

Frank's Fireworks has a pending lawsuit because of an accident that a customer had with one of Frank's products. The suit has been filed, and based on similar suits against other fireworks companies,

Frank's believes that it is probable that it will lose the lawsuit. However, the cost of the suit to Frank's cannot be accurately estimated.

Required
Describe how Frank's should treat this contingent liability.

10. Analyzing Liabilities

A company has total assets of ₹1,85,00,000 and current assets of ₹97,50,000. Total liabilities are ₹1,22,25,000, and current liabilities are ₹68,50,000.

Required
Calculate the company's current and debt to assets ratios.

11. Appendix—Calculate Bond Issue Price

The market rate of interest was 7% when Greene Corporation issued a ₹1,00,000 5-year bond that pays interest annually at a rate of 10%. Present value of the principal is ₹71,300. The present value of the interest payments is ₹37,908.

Required
Calculate the amount of premium or discount at the time of issuance.

12. Appendix—Effective Interest Method

On January 1, 2013, a bond has a carrying value of ₹89,280 and a face value of ₹1,00,000. The market rate of interest is 9% and the stated rate of interest on the bond is 10%. Interest is paid on December 31 of each year.

Required
Calculate interest paid and interest expense for 2013 under the effective interest method.

EXERCISES

13. Current Liabilities

The following are accounts commonly used in accounting information systems:

1. Accounts payable
2. Salaries payable
3. Common stock
4. Current portion of long-term debt
5. Unearned revenue
6. Notes payable (due in 60 days)
7. Taxes payable
8. Allowance for doubtful accounts
9. Notes payable (due in 2 years)

Required
Identify whether each item would be classified on a balance sheet as a current liability, a long-term liability, or something else.

14. Current Liabilities

Jones Hardware Store has total receipts for the day of ₹12,550. This total includes 7% sales tax on all sales.

Required
Calculate sales tax payable and prepare the journal entry to record the sales. Ignore any effects on inventory and round numbers to the nearest dollar.

15. Current Liabilities

On March 1, Azalea Golf borrows ₹30,000 on a 6-month, 6% note from Augusta Bank. Assume interest is paid at the maturity of the note.

Required
Prepare (a) the journal entry to record the receipt of cash from the note, (b) the journal entry to record the accrual of interest if Azalea prepares financial statements on June 30, and (c) the journal entry to record the repayment of the note at maturity.

16. Current Liabilities

The employees of Pinehurst Company earned wages of ₹80,000 during the month of June. The following were withholdings related to these salaries: ₹5,000 for contribution to provident fund, ₹300 for professional tax, and ₹7,700 for income tax. Additional employer-contribution to provident tax was ₹5,450.

Required
Prepare (a) the journal entry to record the payment of these salaries assuming they are paid on June 30 and (b) the journal entry to record Pinehurst Company's additional payroll tax expense for June.

17. Recording and Reporting Notes Payable

On July 1, 2013, Williams Company borrows ₹8,00,000 from the bank by signing an ₹8,00,000, 8%, 2-year note payable. Annual interest is paid on June 30. Williams has a December 31 year-end.

Required

a. Prepare the journal entries to record the issuance of the note and accrued interest at December 31, 2013.
b. How would Williams report the note payable on its 2013 and 2014 balance sheets?

18. Bond Terms

The following is a list of terms and definitions associated with liabilities:

1. Face value	a. Amount paid when a bond matures.
2. Market interest rate	b. Rate of return investors who are buying similar bonds demand for their investments.

3. Stated interest rate — c. Rate used to determine the amount of interest the issuing company of a bond must pay to the investor.
4. Sold at a discount — d. The date on which the face value of the bond must be paid to the investor.
5. Maturity date — e. Document that contains the terms of the bond.
6. Bond certificate — f. This occurs when the stated rate of a bond is less than the market rate.
7. Amortization schedule — g. A schedule that illustrates the amortization of a bond discount or premium over time.
8. Sold at a premium — h. This occurs when the stated rate of a bond is greater than the market rate.

Required
Match each term with the appropriate definition.

19. Understanding Bonds

The following items are associated with bonds:

- Face value
- Interest expense
- Carrying value
- Interest paid
- Amortization of discount or premium
- Balance in unamortized discount or premium

Required
Assuming that bonds are issued at (a) a discount and (b) a premium, identify whether each item will increase, decrease, or remain the same as the bond approaches maturity. Assume straight-line amortization of any discount or premium.

20. Recording Bonds at a Premium and a Discount

On January 1, 2013, Hampton, Inc. issues ₹3 million of 5-year, 10% bonds with interest payable on July 1 and January 1. Hampton prepares financial statements on December 31 and amortizes any discount or premium using the straight-line method.

Required
Prepare all journal entries necessary in 2013 assuming the bonds were issued at (a) 96 and (b) 103.

21. Bond Amortization

On January 1, 2013, Thompson Company issues ₹4 million of 5-year, 8% bonds with interest payable on June 30 and December 31. Thompson amortizes any discount or premium using the straight-line method.

Required
Prepare a bond amortization schedule assuming the bonds were issued at (a) 101 and (b) 97.

22. Bond Amortization Schedule

Fred Corp. provides the following two lines of a bond amortization schedule:

(A)	Interest Paid	(B)	(C)	(D)	Carrying Value
6/30/2014	₹3,200	₹200	₹3,400	₹2,200	₹77,800
12/31/2014	₹3,200	₹200	₹3,400	₹2,000	₹78,000

Required
Answer the following:

a. Identify the column headings A–D.
b. Was the bond issued at a discount, a premium, or at face value?
c. What is the face value of the bonds?
d. What is the stated interest rate?
e. Is the market interest rate greater than, less than, or equal to the stated interest rate?

23. Bond Calculations

Consider the following two bonds:

- ₹1,00,000, 5-year, 7% bond issued for ₹1,03,000
- ₹2,50,000, 8-year, 8% bond issued for ₹2,40,000

Required
Calculate the total cost of borrowing for each bond. Assume that the bonds are outstanding through maturity.

24. Bond Errors

Consider the following independent situations. If necessary, assume the straight-line method of amortization.

1. A company issues a ₹1,00,000, 5-year, 4% bond for ₹1,02,000 and increases the Bond Payable account by ₹1,02,000.
2. A company issues a ₹2,50,000, 8-year, 8% bond for ₹2,40,000. On the first semiannual interest payment, the company amortizes ₹1,250 of the bond discount.
3. A company redeems an ₹85,000 bond with a carrying value of ₹86,000 for ₹85,000 and records a ₹1,000 gain on redemption.
4. A company issues ₹50,000 of bonds with a 6% stated interest rate when the market rate of interest is 7%. At the first semiannual interest payment date, the company pays ₹1,750.

Required
For each situation, identify whether the company made an error and if so, what the company should have done.

25. Bond Redemption

A company issues ₹80,000 of 10-year bonds for ₹86,000. Immediately after the thirteenth semiannual interest payment, the company redeems the bonds for ₹83,700. The company uses the straight-line method of amortization.

Required
Prepare the journal entry to record the bond redemption.

26. Bond Redemption

Immediately after making a semiannual interest payment, the carrying value of Woods Company's bonds were as follows:

Bonds payable	₹1,500,000
Less: Discount on bonds payable	80,000
Carrying value	₹1,420,000

Required

a. Calculate the gain or loss on redemption assuming Woods redeems the bonds at 101.
b. Prepare the journal entry to record the redemption.
c. Can a company redeem the bonds it issues at any time? Explain.
d. Why might a company want to redeem its bonds before maturity?

27. Leases

Glennon Incorporated needs a new piece of equipment for its factory. Instead of purchasing the asset, the company chooses to enter into a 5-year operating lease with annual payments of ₹50,000. Assume each lease payment is made on December 31.

Required

a. Prepare the journal entry to record the first annual lease payment.
b. What are the financial reporting advantages of an operating lease over a capital lease?
c. Why might Glennon have chosen to lease the equipment instead of buying it?

28. Contingent Liabilities

Tanner Toys had sales of ₹25,00,000 during 2013. In 2012, 5% of sales were returned for a refund, but Tanner believes that recent product changes will reduce warranty expense to about 3% of 2013 sales.

Required

a. What amount is Tanner expecting to refund customers for purchases made in 2013?
b. Should this amount be reported as a liability on the financial statements? Why or why not?
c. Is Tanner using a reasonable means to estimate warranty expense?

29. Contingent Liabilities

Harris Foods had the following independent situations.

1. A court recently found Harris liable for ₹4,00,000 in damages due to faulty coatings on paper plates it manufactures. Because Harris plans to appeal the decision and therefore currently accepts no blame, it ignores the ₹4,00,000 in its financial reports.
2. Harris buys discontinued utensils and repackages them for sale. Due to differing quality, each year Harris has average warranty returns of 25% of prior-year sales. Harris' policy is to provide full refunds for customers. Harris discloses the potential returns in the notes to its financial statements.
3. Harris prides itself on giving back to its community and considers it an obligation. In the coming year, Harris plans to give ₹50,000 to the local food bank. It therefore records a ₹50,000 contingent liability on its balance sheet.

Required

For each situation, identify whether Harris is using proper accounting and if not, how each situation should be handled.

30. Evaluate Liabilities

In a recent balance sheet, **Wal-Mart**, USA, reported the following information (in millions):

	Current year	Prior year
Current assets	$48,949	$48,020
Current liabilities	55,390	58,478

Required

Calculate Wal-Mart's current ratio for each year and answer the following questions:

a. Was the company more or less liquid in the current year?
b. Should an investor be concerned that the current ratio is less than 1.0? Why or why not?
c. What is likely to be the most important factor in Wal-Mart being able to pay its current liabilities in a timely manner? (Hint: Think about its largest current asset.)

31. Evaluate Liabilities

A company needs to raise ₹10 million to expand its operations. It is considering two options: (1) issuing bonds or (2) issuing common stock. Currently, the company's balance sheet shows the following (in millions):

Assets	Liabilities	Equity
₹53.8	₹37.9	₹15.9

Required

a. Calculate the company's debt to assets ratio prior to raising the ₹10 million and comment on the riskiness of the company's existing capital structure.
b. Recalculate the company's debt to assets ratio under the two options the company is considering and comment on how this changes the riskiness of the company's capital structure.
c. Can one of the options be considered the "correct" option?

32. Evaluate Liabilities

The following financial data were reported by **Speed Wireless** for two recent years (in millions):

Speed Wireless Balance Sheet (partial)		
	Current	Prior
Current assets	₹2,290	₹ 669
Current liabilities	2,257	2,172
Total liabilities	9,801	9,854
Total assets	5,131	6,200

Required
Calculate the current and debt to assets ratios for each year. How would the most recent ratios change if Verizon decided to pay off ₹1 billion of current liabilities with cash?

33. Appendix—Calculate Issuance Price

Suppose that a company issues the following bonds at different times. Interest on the bonds is paid annually.

1. ₹80,000 of 6%, 10-year bonds when the market rate of interest is 7%
2. ₹60,000 of 8%, 6-year bonds when the market rate of interest is 6%
3. ₹1,20,000 of 10%, 5-year bonds when the market rate of interest is 8%

Required
Calculate the issuance price for each bond.

34. Appendix—Bond Interest and Amortization

On January 1, 2013, Tallakson Company issues a ₹50,000, 5-year, 8% bond with interest payable annually on December 31. The market interest rate at issuance is 10%. Tallakson uses the effective interest method of amortization.

Required

a. Determine the issuance price of the bond by using the appropriate table(s) in Appendix A.
b. Prepare the entry for the first interest payment on December 31, 2013.
c. Prepare an amortization schedule for the bond.

35. Appendix—Effective Interest Amortization

On January 1, 2013, Big E Electronics issues a ₹1,00,000, 8-year, 8% bond for ₹1,05,970. The market rate of interest at the time of issuance was 7%. Interest is payable annually on December 31.

Required

a. Prepare entries for the bond issuance and the first three interest payments.
b. Prepare an amortization schedule for the bond.

PROBLEMS

36. Recording and Reporting Current Liabilities

The following is a list of liability accounts on the ledger of Chop House Incorporated on January 1:

Sales Tax Payable	₹ 75,000
Accounts Payable	95,000
Unearned Revenue	1,65,000

The following transactions occurred during the month of January:

Jan. 1 Borrowed ₹2,50,000 from Atlanta Bank on a 6-month, 6% note.
9 Provided service for customers who had paid ₹60,000 in advance.
15 Paid state treasurer for sales taxes collected in December, ₹75,000.
18 Bought inventory on credit for ₹1,20,000.
23 Sold goods on credit for ₹30,000, plus 7% sales tax.

The employees of the Chop House earned gross salaries of ₹4,50,000 during January. Withholdings were ₹25,000 for Social Security, ₹40,000 for income tax, and ₹1,900 for state income tax. The employer share of provident fund was also ₹25,000. Salaries earned in January will be paid during February.

Required

a. Prepare journal entries for the January transactions. Assume that purchases are recorded directly into the inventory account.
b. Prepare adjusting entries at January 31 related to salaries, payroll taxes, and notes payable.
c. Create the current liability section of the balance sheet at January 31.

37. Bond Presentation, Interest, and Redemption

The following is an excerpt taken from the December 31, 2012, balance sheet of the Wimbledon Company:

Current liabilities	
Bond interest payable	₹ 64,000
Long-term liabilities	
Bonds payable	16,00,000
Less: Discount on bonds payable	30,000
Carrying value	₹15,70,000

The bonds have a stated interest rate of 8% and mature on January 1, 2017. Interest is paid semiannually on July 1 and January 1. The bonds are callable at 105 on any semiannual interest date.

Required

a. Prepare the journal entry to record the payment of bond interest on January 1, 2013.
b. Prepare the journal entry to amortize the bond discount and pay the interest on July 1, 2013.
c. Prepare the journal entry to record the redemption of the bonds on July 1, 2013, after the interest has been paid.
d. Prepare the adjusting journal entry for December 31, 2013, assuming that the bonds were not redeemed.
e. Show how all liabilities related to the bonds would be reported on Wimbledon's balance sheet at December 31, 2013.

38. Bond Issuance, Interest, Redemption, and Reporting

Gateway Unlimited sold ₹20,00,000 of 6-year, 10% bonds on January 1, 2013. The bonds pay interest semiannually on July 1 and January 1. The bonds sell at 97. The straight-line method is used to amortize any bond premium or discount.

Required

a. Prepare all journal entries related to the bonds for 2013 and 2014 and show how the bonds would be reported on the December 31 balance sheets.
b. How would the 2013 statement of cash flows be affected by the bonds?
c. Prepare a bond amortization schedule.
d. On July 1, 2017, after the interest payment, Gateway redeems the bonds for 101. Prepare the entry to record the redemption.
e. How would the 2017 statement of cash flows be affected by the redemption?

39. Analyzing Liabilities

Explorer Corporation's board of directors is having its annual meeting to analyze the performance of the firm. One area the board is focusing on is total liabilities. The following are selected items from the December 31 balance sheet:

	2013	2012
Total assets	₹9,35,870	₹9,02,225
Total liabilities	5,75,430	5,62,855
Total equity	3,60,440	3,39,370

Required

Conduct horizontal and vertical analyses of total liabilities and interpret the results. Explain whether or not Explorer should be pleased with its financial position based on these calculations.

40. Appendix—Comparing Amortization Methods

On January 1, 2012, LED issues bonds with a face value of ₹3,00,000. These bonds have a stated interest rate of 4% and interest is paid annually on December 31. The bonds mature in four years. The market interest rate at the date the bonds are issued is 5%.

Required

a. Determine the amount of discount on the bonds at issuance.
b. How much of the discount will be amortized in the first year under (1) the straight-line method and (2) the effective interest method?
c. Does interest expense each year differ under the straight-line and effective interest methods of amortization?
d. Does total interest expense over the life of the bonds differ under the straight-line and effective interest methods of amortization?

CASES

41. Research and Analysis

Access the 2012 annual report for **Amazon** by clicking on the *Investor Relations* and *Annual Reports and Proxies* links at www.amazon.com.

Required

a. Examine the company's balance sheet and conduct horizontal and vertical analyses of all liability account balances, including total liabilities.
b. Examine the financing activities section of the company's statement of cash flows. Over the past three years, did the company receive or pay more cash related to debt and leases?
c. Calculate the company's current ratio and debt to assets ratios for 2012 and 2011.
d. Examine the company's long-term debt note. What was the weighted average interest rate on its long-term debt for 2012 and 2011?
e. Based on your answers above, write a paragraph explaining your opinion of Amazon's liability position. Use your answers as supporting facts.

42. Research and Analysis

Access the 2012–13 annual report for **UTV Software Communication Limited** by clicking on the link at www.utvgroup.com/investors.html.

Required

a. Perform horizontal and vertical analyses on the major subtotals from the company's balance sheet.
b. Calculate current and debt to assets ratios for the most recent two years.
c. Examine the amount of interest expense reported by the company on its income statement.
d. What conclusions can you make about the current health of the company? Would it surprise you that in the last ten years the company entered into and emerged from bankruptcy protection?

43. Written Communication

Bill Deere Tractors manufactures and sells all types of yard equipment. The company was recently sued by a plaintiff who claimed that a defective lawnmower caused a serious injury. The company was made aware of this at the end of its fiscal year but it is not sure how to report it in its financial statements.

Required

Write a brief memo explaining the possible treatments of this lawsuit for financial reporting purposes. Also, provide some ideas on how to estimate the potential liability if the company believes that liability is probable.

44. Ethics in Accounting

You are the accountant for a medium-size manufacturer. Your company has some existing debt that requires the company to maintain a current ratio of 1.50 or higher. If the ratio drops below that value, the lender can increase the interest rate from 6% to 9%. Recently, the company's current ratio has been hovering around 1.50, and the president believes that when some long-term debt maturing in the following year is reported as current, the ratio will fall below 1.50. The president asks you to keep the long-term debt as a long-term liability instead of reclassifying it as a current liability. "After all, "he says, "it is still reported as a liability."

Required

Is there an ethical issue with the president's request? How should you respond?

reviewcard CHAPTER 9 Liabilities

Learning Objectives		Key Concepts
LO1	Describe the recording and reporting of various current liabilities.	A current liability is an obligation that is reasonably expected to be satisfied or paid within one year. Current liabilities are reported on the balance sheet and include obligations relating to the purchase of inventory, the compensation of employees, the repayment of debt, and the incurrence of taxes.
LO2	Describe the reporting of long-term liabilities and the cash flows associated with those liabilities.	Long-term liabilities are reported on the balance sheet. The cash received from the issuance of long-term liabilities is reported in the financing activities section of the statement of cash flows.
LO3	Understand the nature of bonds and record a bond's issuance, interest payments, and maturity.	A bond payable is a long-term liability created when a company issues bonds. All bonds have a face value, a stated interest rate, and a maturity date. Interest is paid based on the stated rate and face value. Bonds are often issued at a discount or premium because the stated rate of interest differs from the market rate of interest at the time of issuance. The discount or premium is amortized over the life of the bond.
LO4	Account for a bond that is redeemed prior to maturity.	When a bond is paid prior to the maturity date, a gain is realized when the amount paid is greater than the bond's carrying value. A loss is realized when the amount paid is less than the bond's carrying value.
LO5	Understand additional liabilities such as leases and contingent liabilities.	A lease is an agreement in which the lessee obtains the right to use an asset by making periodic payments to the lessor. Operating leases are like rental contracts, and no liability is recorded by the lessee. Capital leases are like purchases, and the lease liability is recorded by the lessee. A contingent liability is an obligation arising from an existing condition whose outcome is uncertain and whose resolution depends on a future event. Whether a contingent liability is recorded, disclosed, or ignored depends on the likelihood that the liability will occur and the ability to estimate it.
LO6	Evaluate liabilities through the calculation and interpretation of horizontal, vertical, and ratio analyses.	The current ratio shows a company's liquidity, or its ability to pay its short term obligations. The debt to assets ratio shows a company's capital structure and therefore its risk of long-term solvency.

Key Definitions

Amortization schedule A schedule that illustrates the amortization of a bond discount or premium over the life of a bond.

Bond A financial instrument in which a borrower promises to pay future interest and principal to a creditor in exchange for the creditor's cash today.

Capital lease A contract in which the lessee obtains enough rights to use and control an asset such that the lessee is in substance the owner of the asset.

Capital structure The mix of debt and equity that a company uses to generate its assets.

Contingent liability An obligation that arises from an existing condition whose outcome is uncertain and whose resolution depends on a future event.

Current liability An obligation of a business that is expected to be satisfied or paid within one year.

Current portion of long-term debt The portion of a long-term liability that will be paid within one year.

Current ratio Compares a company's current assets to its current liabilities and measures its ability to pay current obligations.

Debt to assets ratio Compares a company's total liabilities to its total assets and measures its ability to satisfy its long-term obligations.

Effective interest method of amortization Method that amortizes the bond discount or premium so that interest expense each period is a constant percentage of the bond's carrying value.

Face value The amount that is repaid at maturity of a bond.

Lease A contractual agreement in which the lessee obtains the right to use an asset by making periodic payments to the lessor.

Liquidity A company's ability to pay off its obligations in the near future.

Long-term liability Any obligation of a business that is expected to be satisfied or paid in more than one year.

Learning Objectives / Key Concepts

	Learning Objectives	Key Concepts
LO7	Appendix: Determine a bond's issuance price.	A bond's issuance price is determined by converting the bond's future cash flows to present day values. The principal value is discounted back at the present value of a single sum. The interest payments are discounted back at the present value of an annuity.
LO8	Appendix: Record bond interest payments under the effective interest method.	The effective interest method amortizes any bond discount or premium so that interest expense is equal to the carrying value of the bond times the market rate of interest.

Key Formulas

Interest Payment on Notes Payable	Principal × Annual Interest Rate × Time Outstanding
Interest Payment on Bonds Payable	Face Value × Stated Interest Rate × Time Outstanding
Bond Discount or Premium Amortized Each Payment (Straight-Line Method)	$\frac{\text{Discount or Premium at Issuance}}{\text{Number of Interest Payments}}$
Bond Interest Expense (Straight-Line Method)	If Discount: Interest Payment + Discount Amortized If Premium: Interest Payment − Premium Amortized
Bond Carrying Value	If Discount: Face Value − Unamortized Discount If Premium: Face Value + Unamortized Premium
Bond Interest Expense (Effective Interest Method)	Carrying Value × Market Interest Rate × Time Outstanding
Bond Discount or Premium Amortized Each Payment (Effective Interest Method)	If Discount: Interest Expense − Interest Paid If Premium: Interest Paid − Interest Expense
Horizontal Analysis	$\text{Percentage change in account balance} = \frac{\text{Current year balance} - \text{Prior year balance}}{\text{Prior year balance}}$
Vertical Analysis	*For the Balance Sheet*: $\text{Percentage} = \frac{\text{Account Balance}}{\text{Total Assets}}$ or *For the Income Statement*: $\frac{\text{Account Balance}}{\text{Net Sales or Revenue}}$
Current Ratio	$\frac{\text{Current Assets}}{\text{Current Liabilities}}$
Debt to Assets Ratio	$\frac{\text{Total Liabilities}}{\text{Total Assets}}$

Key Definitions (continued)

Market (or effective) rate of interest The rate of return that investors in the bond markets demand for bonds of similar risk.

Maturity date The date on which the face value must be repaid to the creditor.

Note payable A liability generated by the issuance of a promissory note to borrow money.

Off-balance-sheet financing Occurs when a company's future obligations regarding an asset are not reported as a liability on the balance sheet.

Operating lease A contract in which the lessee obtains the right to use an asset for a limited period of time but does not acquire ownership of the asset.

Solvency A company's ability to continue in business in the long term by satisfying its long-term obligations.

Stated interest rate The contractual rate at which interest is paid to the creditor.

Straight-line method of amortization Method that amortizes an equal amount of the discount or premium each time interest is paid.

Stockholders' Equity

Learning Objectives

After studying the material in this chapter, you should be able to:

LO1 Describe the characteristics of the corporate form of business.

LO2 Describe the characteristics of common stock and how it is recorded and reported.

LO3 Understand cash dividends, stock dividends, and stock splits.

LO4 Describe the characteristics of preferred stock and how it receives preference in dividends.

LO5 Describe the characteristics of treasury stock and how it is recorded and reported.

LO6 Evaluate equity through the calculation and interpretation of horizontal, vertical, and ratio analyses.

Introduction

This chapter examines the accounting for stockholders' equity. It begins with a discussion of the corporate form of business. It then examines how companies account for common stock and any cash or stock dividends distributed on that stock. After discussing preferred stock, preferred stock dividends, and treasury stock, the chapter concludes with a discussion on how to analyze a company's equity position.

LO1 The Corporate Form of Business

Chapter 2 introduced the three major forms of business—the sole proprietorship, the partnership, and the corporation. The following sections describe some of the characteristics of the corporate form of business that distinguish it from sole proprietorships and partnerships. These corporate characteristics are as follows:

- Separate legal entity
- Ability to raise capital
- Limited liability of owners
- Transferability of ownership
- Double taxation
- Regulation

Separate Legal Entity

A corporation is a separate legal entity. It is formed under state law by submitting articles of incorporation to a state government and requesting the establishment of a corporate entity. The articles describe the business of the corporation and request authority to sell ownership interests (that is, shares) in the corporation. Once the articles are approved, the state grants a corporate charter that effectively creates a new legal entity. In most cases, this new legal entity can buy, own, and sell assets in its name and can also borrow money. It can sue and be sued. In other words, it has most of the rights and responsibilities of an individual in society.

CHAPTER 10

Google became a publicly traded corporation in 2004 when it sold stock to the public for the first time. It raised $1.6 billion in that initial public offering (IPO).

Ability to Raise Capital

Many sole proprietorships and partnerships have limited access to the capital needed to successfully operate or expand their businesses. In contrast, corporations can access capital through the sale of stock to investors, who then become stockholders. Most corporations begin by selling shares/stocks privately to a few owners. And while many corporations stay privately owned, others "go public" by offering shares/stocks to the public through an initial public offering (IPO). Such public offerings can generate substantial amounts of capital. For example, Google, Inc., raised over $1.6 billion in its 2004 IPO. If needed, a corporation can continue to raise capital in the future by selling additional stock. Google followed its IPO with a second stock offering in 2005, raising another $4.2 billion in capital. The ability to access capital through the sale of stock is certainly an advantage of the corporate form of business.

Stockholders normally have no personal liability for the corporation's obligations beyond their investment in the corporation's stock.

Limited Liability of Owners

Under a sole proprietorship and a general partnership, owners are personally liable for the actions and obligations of their businesses. However, stockholders normally have no personal liability for the corporation's obligations beyond their investment in the corporation's stock. If a corporation defaults and cannot meet its obligations, creditors cannot seek the assets of the stockholders as compensation for the corporate default. They can only pursue the assets of the corporation. As a result of this limited liability, stockholders stand to lose only the amount of their investments. This limited liability of owners is a significant advantage of the corporate form of business.

Transferability of Ownership

Another advantage of the corporate form of business is the ease with which ownership can be transferred. When a sole proprietor wants to transfer his or her ownership to another individual, the business itself must be sold. When a partner wants to transfer an ownership interest to another investor, usually all other partners must agree. Once the transfer occurs, a new partnership is formed. In both of these cases, the transfer of ownership can be burdensome.

In contrast, when stockholders of a publicly traded corporation want to transfer ownership to another investor, they need only to sell the stock to other investors. Such sales usually occur through an open stock exchange such as the Bombay Stock Exchange (BSC) or the National Stock Exchange (NSC). They can be accomplished by calling a broker or logging onto a online trading and executing a sell order. Hundreds of millions of shares of stock are bought and sold every day.

Double Taxation

While the corporate form has several advantages over sole proprietorships and partnerships, it does have some disadvantages. One is the double taxation of income.

A corporation's income is taxed at the Central. Dividends paid to stockholders are also taxed on the stockholders' personal tax returns. As a result, a corporation's income that is paid in dividends is taxed twice—once at the corporate level and a second time at the personal stockholder level. In contrast, the income of sole proprietorships and partnerships is reported only on personal tax returns and is therefore taxed only once—at the personal level.

To illustrate double taxation, suppose that a corporation earns ₹1.0 billion in pre-tax earnings and is subject to a 30% corporate tax rate. The corporation would pay ₹300 million in corporate taxes. Suppose further that the corporation distributed ₹200 million of its remaining profits to its stockholders, the company is liable to pay a Dividend Distribution Tax @15% on the amount declared, distributed or paid by such company by way of dividends. As a result, the corporation's pre-tax income of ₹1 billion is taxed twice.

Regulation

Another disadvantage of the corporation is the extent of regulation. Consider some of the reporting requirements

MARUTI SUZUKI ANALYSIS

Look at Maruti Suzuki's Balance Sheet in Appendix C. What tells you that Maruti Suzuki is a corporation?

You can tell in two ways. First, the balance sheet shows balances in Share Capital, which means that the company has shareholders and is therefore a corporation. Second, the company name refers to Maruti Suzuki India Limited. The "Limited" stands for Incorporated. Maruti Suzuki does not report where it is incorporated on its balance sheet, but it is incorporated in the NSC and BSC.

Common stock is sold in shares. That is, each unit of stock is called a "share" of stock.

of a publicly traded corporation such as Reliance Industries Limited (RIL). Reliance Industries Limited must file numerous reports with the Securities and Stock and Exchange Board of India. These include audited annual financial statements, unaudited quarterly financial statements, and any notifications of significant events, such as the hiring of a new chief executive officer or the announcement of a dividend or the closing of a factory. There are many other reporting and legal requirements arising from state laws, stock exchange regulations, the Internal Revenue Service, etc. Adherence to and compliance with laws and regulations consume significant amounts of the time, labor, and resources of corporations.

LO2 Common Stock

One of the distinguishing characteristics of the corporation is its ability to sell capital stock to investors to raise funds. The amount raised by issuing capital stock is called **contributed capital** because the funds are contributed by investors in exchange for an ownership claim on company assets. The most common type of capital stock is appropriately named **common stock** or equity capital. Investors who purchase common stock are called stockholders and are the owners of the corporation.

Authorized, Issued, and Outstanding Shares

Common stock is sold in shares. That is, each unit of stock is called a "share" of stock. There are three ways in which a company describes its shares of stock:

- Authorized shares
- Issued shares
- Outstanding shares

Authorized shares refers to the number of shares of stock that a company can legally issue. This capacity is set in the corporate charter filed with the state. Usually, corporations request authority to sell more shares than initially needed so that they do not have to amend the corporate charter to issue additional shares.

Issued shares refers to the number of shares a company has distributed to owners to date. Notice that the description "sold shares" is not used. Common stock is not always distributed via a sale. For example, some stock is issued to employees as part of their compensation. Thus, the description "issued shares" is used.

Outstanding shares refers to the number of shares that have been issued and are still held by someone other than the issuing company. When you hear news about a company's stock price rising or falling, the news is referring to a company's outstanding shares. The difference between a company's issued and outstanding shares is usually the number of shares the company has repurchased from investors, which is called treasury stock. Treasury stock is discussed later in this chapter.

Treasury shares are own shares acquired through a buyback arrangement and not issued by a company. In India, though the Companies Act allows buy back of shares, it does not allow a company to hold those shares. Bought back shares must be cancelled within seven days. Therefore, in India companies cannot hold treasury stock. However, under a court order, treasury stock may arise in some schemes of amalgamation.

Companies usually disclose the number of authorized, issued, and outstanding shares on their balance sheets or in the notes to their financial statements. You will see this in the section covering the reporting of common stock.

Contributed capital The amount of capital raised by issuing stock to investors in exchange for an ownership claim on company assets.

Common stock The most common type of capital stock.

Authorized shares The number of shares of stock that a company can legally issue.

Issued shares The number of shares a company has distributed to owners to date.

Outstanding shares The number of shares that have been issued and are still held by someone other than the issuing company.

Treasury shares Own shares acquired through a buyback arrangement and not issued by a company

Stockholder Rights

When a corporation issues common stock, it usually grants to stockholders the following four rights:

- the right to vote
- the right to participate proportionally in dividends
- the right to participate proportionally in residual assets
- the right of preemption

The *right to vote* ensures that a stockholder can participate in company governance by voting on issues and actions that require owner consent or approval. An example of such an action is the election of a corporation's board of directors.

The *right to participate proportionally in dividends* ensures that stockholders receive an appropriate amount of any dividends declared by the company. For example, if a stockholder owns 25% of a corporation's common stock, he or she has the right to receive 25% of any dividend the company distributes.

The *right to participate proportionally in residual assets* ensures that stockholders receive an appropriate amount of assets upon liquidation of the company. For example, if a stockholder owns 10% of a corporation's common stock when the company ceases operations and liquidates, he or she has the right to receive 10% of all residual assets.

The *right of preemption* ensures that stockholders can maintain their ownership percentage when new stock is issued. For example, if a company decides to issue additional shares of common stock, a stockholder who owns 15% of all shares of common stock has the right to purchase 15% of the new issuance. Because of the recordkeeping burden of this right and the ease with which an investor can purchase stock in the marketplace, this right may be withheld from stockholders. In India right of preemption is against the basic provision of Sec.111A of Companies Act which provides for free transferability of shares and hence it is void.

Par Value

A corporation normally assigns to its common stock a value known as a par value. **Par value** is an arbitrary value that determines an entity's legal capital. Legal capital is the amount of capital that a state requires a corporation to maintain in order to protect creditor claims. Most companies set par value very low. For example, Reliance Industries Limited has a ₹10 par value for its common stock, while Infosys has a ₹5 par value. Although most states still require corporations to set par values for their stock, the value has lost much of its legal significance over time. However, as the following section demonstrates, par value still affects both the recording and reporting of common stock.

Par value An arbitrary value that determines an entity's legal capital.

Recording Common Stock

Because a stock's par value is usually set very low, most common stock is issued for more than par value. When this occurs, a company uses two equity accounts to record the stock issuance—one account for the par value and a second account for the excess paid over par value.

To illustrate, suppose that a company issues 100 shares of ₹1 par value stock for ₹5 per share on April 5. The company would record this issuance as follows:

April 5	Cash	500	
	Common Stock		100
	Share Premium		400
	(To record sale of $1 par stock)		

Assets	=	Liabilities	+	Equity
+500				+100
				+400

This entry increases Cash for the amount received and divides the increase in equity into two accounts. The Common Stock account is increased for ₹100, which is the par value of the stock (₹1 par × 100 shares issued). The ₹400 excess paid over par value is recorded in Share Premium. Since both Common Stock and Share Premium Capital are equity accounts, this entry increases the company's assets and equity.

While most companies set a par value for their stock, some do not because their country of incorporation does not require it. Stock without a par value is called no-par stock. Countries like USA, Australia, Singapore, have abolished par value on shares and shifted to a no-par value regime. For no-par stock, the entire issuance is recorded directly into the common stock account. To illustrate, consider the previous example, except that the stock has no par value. The company would record the issuance as follows:

MARUTI SUZUKI ANALYSIS

Look at Maruti Suzuki's balance sheet in Appendix C. How many shares of common stock does Maruti Suzuki have authorized, and issued at the end of March 2013? What is the stock's par value? Has the company properly recorded the par value of common stock? Calculate the total capital contributed to the company through the issuance of stock.

Maruti Suzuki has 3,744 million equity shares authorized, but only 302 million issued at the end of March 2013. The par value of the common stock is ₹5 per share. The common stock account has a balance of ₹1,510 million million, which is equivalent to 30,20,80,060 issued shares times ₹5 par value per share (30,20,80,060 × ₹5 = ₹1,510 million). Adding the ₹1,510 million to the ₹4,241 million balance in Share Premium yields the total capital received from the issuance of common stock (₹1,510 million + ₹4,241 million = ₹5,751 million). Maruti Suzuki has received over ₹5,751 million from the issuance of common stock.

April 5	Cash	500	
	Common Stock		500
	(To record sale of no-par stock)		

Assets	=	Liabilities	+	Equity
+500				+500

Everything in the entry is the same as previously, except that Common Stock is increased for the entire issuance price rather than just the par value.

Reporting Common Stock

A company's balances in both common stock and share premium are reported in the stockholders' equity section of the balance sheet. Shown below is the stockholders' equity figures of Hindustan Unilever Limited balance sheet as of March 31, 2013.

Hindustan Unilever Limited (HUL) reports a ₹225 crore balance in Authorised Capital and a ₹216.25 crores balance in paid-in capital at the end of March 2013. In addition, it has built a reserve of ₹1,922.49 crore, including general reserve of ₹1,795.99 crore and Profit and Loss Account Balance of ₹535.28 crore. The total shareholdes' equity of HUL is ₹2709.35 crore as on March 31, 2013.

The textual description also provides information about HUL shares. It discloses that HUL stock has a par value of ₹1 each and that the company has the authority to issue 2,25,00,00,000 billion shares. Note that multiplying the number of shares issued by the par value yields the balance in the common stock account (2,16,24,72,310 × ₹1 = ₹2,16,24,72,310, which is rounded to ₹216.25 crore on the balance sheet).

Hindustan Unilever Limited 2012–13 Shareholders' Equity

	As at March 31, 2013
Shareholders' Equity	
Authorised Share Capital	
2,250,000,000 (March 31, 2012: 2,250,000,000) equity shares of ₹1 each	225.00
Issued, subscribed and fully paid up	
2,162,472,310 (March 31, 2012: 2,161,512,492) equity shares of ₹1 each	216.25
Capital Reserve	4.22
Capital Redemption Reserve	6.46
Securities Premium Reserve	55.69
Revaluation Reserve	0.67
Employee Stock Options Outstanding Account	38.27
Capital Subsidy	6.19
Export Profit Reserve (e)	12.22
Development Allowance Reserve (e)	0.27
General Reserve	1,795.99
Other Reserves	2.51
Surplus in statement of profit and loss	**535.28**

One additional reported item that relates to common stock is treasury stock. Treasury stock is common stock that has been repurchased by the company. Treasury stock will be covered later in the chapter, but notice here that HUL does not report possessing treasury stock. As in India, though the Companies Act allows buy back of shares, it does not allow a company to hold those shares. Bought back shares must be cancelled within seven days.

The goal of any corporation is to generate profits. Once generated, a company must decide whether or not to distribute those profits to its owners through dividends.

LO3 Dividends

The goal of any corporation is to generate profits. Once generated, a company must decide whether or not to distribute those profits to its owners through dividends. A **dividend** is a distribution of profits to owners. The decision to distribute any dividend rests with the company's board of directors, which is the group of individuals elected by stockholders to govern the company and represent the interests of all owners. The board will consider many factors in its decisions, including the financial condition of the company, the cash available for dividends, and the company's past history of dividends. When dividends are distributed, they are stated as a per share amount and are paid only on outstanding shares of stock.

When and how a company distributes dividends is called a company's dividend policy. In many countries a company's policy can often be found on its website. For example, Walgreens, US, reports it in its Frequently Asked Questions that "historically, dividend has been paid in March, June, September, and December" and that checks are "customarily mailed on approximately the 12th of each of these months." In other words, like many companies, Walgreens pays a dividend each quarter.

Dividend A distribution of profits to a corporation's owners.

Cash dividend A distribution of cash to stockholders.

Date of declaration The date on which a corporation's board of directors declares a dividend.

Payment date The date on which a dividend will be distributed.

Date of record The date that determines who receives the dividend; the stock's owner on the date of record receives the dividend.

Walgreens has over 938 million shares of common stock outstanding at the end of 2010.

Dividends are normally paid in cash, but they can also be paid in other forms such as stock. In India, however, no dividend shall be payable except in cash. The following sections discuss the practice of distributing dividends, starting with the most common type—the cash dividend.

Cash Dividends

As the name suggests, a **cash dividend** is a distribution of cash to stockholders. When a corporate board decides that a cash dividend is warranted, it will declare publicly that a dividend will be distributed. The date on which the board declares the dividend is called the **date of declaration**. On this date, the board legally obligates the company to pay the dividend, so a liability is created in many countries. The board's declaration will also include the payment date and the date of record. The **payment date** is the date on which the dividend will be distributed. The **date of record** determines who receives the dividend. The stock's owner on the date of record receives the dividend.

Exhibit 10-1 contains a press release from Walgreens, US announcing the declaration of a quarterly dividend of $0.1375 per share. Each of the three dates can be identified: declaration (April 12), record (May 20), and payment (June 12).

Exhibit 10-1 Walgreens' Press Release of Quarterly Dividend

Walgreens Declares Regular Quarterly Dividend

DEERFIELD, Ill., April 12, 2010 – The board of directors of Walgreens (NYSE, NASDAQ: WAG) today declared a regular quarterly dividend of 13.75 cents per share, a 22.2 percent increase over the year- ago dividend, payable June 12, 2010, to shareholder of records May 20, 2010.

Recording Cash Dividends The recording of cash dividends usually requires two entries. The first entry records the declaration of the dividend and the resulting liability. The second entry records the actual distribution on the payment date.

To illustrate, suppose that a company with 10,00,000 outstanding shares of stock declares a ₹0.50 per share dividend on November 3. The dividend is payable on November 30 to stockholders of record on November 21.

On the date of declaration, the company obligates itself to pay a ₹5,00,000 dividend (10,00,000 × ₹0.50). This obligation would be recorded as follows:

Nov. 3	Retained Earning or P/L Appropriation	5,00,000	
	Dividends Payable		5,00,000
	(To record declaration of dividend)		

Assets	=	Liabilities	+	Equity
		+50,000		−50,000

The entry decreases Retained Earnings /P/L Account because dividends reduce retained earnings. The entry also increases Dividends Payable, which is a current liability. The result of the entry is a reduction in equity and an increase in liabilities.

The distribution of cash on the payment date would be recorded as follows:

Nov. 30	Dividends Payable	5,00,000	
	Cash		5,00,000
	(To record payment of dividend)		

Assets	=	Liabilities	+	Equity
−50,000		−50,000		

This entry is simply a payment of an obligation. Both Dividends Payable and Cash are decreased for the amount of the payment. As a result, both assets and liabilities decrease.

Note that no entry is made on the date of record because no accounting transaction occurs on that date. The date of record only determines who will receive the dividend. Therefore, it is a date with administrative importance only.

Reporting Cash Dividends Companies usually report their dividends on two financial statements. Dividends *declared* during the year are reported on the statement of stockholders' equity. Recall that dividends reduce retained earnings/profit and loss appropriation balance, so they are reported in the retained earnings column or P/L appropriation balance of the statement of stockholders' equity or P/L Appropriation Account. The following is the profit/loss appropriation section of Hindustan Unilever Limited Annual Report 2012–13.

Profit/Loss Appropriation Section of Hindustan Unilever Limited Annual Report 2012–2013

(in crores)	
Earnings	
Balance brought forward	₹1,773.96
Net profit, March 31, 2013	3,796.67
Available for distribution	5,570.63
Interim dividend declared during the year (₹4.50 per share)	(972.98)
Special dividend on equity for the year (per share ₹8.00)	(1,729.53)
Proposed final dividend on equity shares (per share 6.00)	(1,297.48)
Tax on distributed profits	(655.69)
Transfer to General Reserve	(379.67)
Balance carried forward	₹ 535.28

The statement provides both the per share and total value of dividends declared during each year. Notice that the company declared the interim, special, and final dividends during the financial year 2012–13. Dividends are presented as negative numbers because they are subtracted from profit balance.

Dividends *paid* during the year are reported on the statement of cash flows. Because a cash dividend is a distribution of assets to an owner, dividends are considered to be a financing activity. Therefore, they are reported in the financing activities of the statement of cash flows. The following is the financing activities section of Hindustan Unilever Limited, 2012–13 statement of cash flows.

Because dividends are cash outflows, they are shown as negative numbers on the statement of cash flows. Note that the amount of dividends paid is not

Financing Activities Section of Hindustan Unilever Limited, 2012–13 statement of Cash Flows

(All amounts in ₹ crores)

	For the year ended 31st March, 2013	For the year ended 31st March, 2012
CASH FLOW FROM FINANCING ACTIVITIES:		
Dividends paid	(3550.31)	(1,509.31)
Dividend distribution tax paid	(575.51)	(245.32)
Addition to unpaid dividend accounts	(16.81)	(2.85)
Interest Paid	(25.15)	(1.24)
Proceeds from share allotment under employee stock options/ performance share schemes	7.34	33.55
Cash flow before exceptional items	(4,160.44)	(1,725.17)
Exceptional items	—	—
Net cash used in financing activities	**(4,160.44)**	**(1,725.17)**

the same as the amount of dividends declared. For example, the ₹3,550.31 crore of dividends paid in the most recent year is different than the ₹1,297.48 crore of dividends declared and reported on the P/L appropriation statement. In fact, dividends paid are different than dividends declared in each year of the two years presented. This occurs because HUL's last quarterly dividend of each fiscal year is paid in the next fiscal year, and dividends may be different each year.

Stock Dividends

While cash dividends are by far the most common type of dividend, some companies distribute stock dividends. A **stock dividend** is a distribution of a company's common stock to existing stockholders. Stock dividends are declared by a company's board of directors and are usually stated in percentage terms. For example, a 10% stock dividend means that the company will issue additional shares equal to 10% of the current outstanding shares. So, an investor owning 10,000 shares will receive 1,000 additional shares (10,000 × 10%). In India, as stated earlier, dividend can only be paid in cash. Stock dividend takes the form of bonus issue of shares in India.

Stock dividend A distribution of a company's common stock to existing stockholders.

At first glance, a stock dividend appears to be a great value to stockholders because they receive more shares. However, some argue that a stock dividend has very little value to stockholders because they are not receiving any assets—they are receiving only stock. Furthermore, because all stockholders receive the same percentage increase in shares, a stock dividend does not change a stockholder's ownership percentage. Finally, a stock dividend usually results in a reduction to the market price of individual shares such that the total market value of a stockholder's holdings remains unchanged. For example, a company distributing a 100% stock dividend will double the shares of stock outstanding, but this will usually result in the stock's market value being cut in half. As a result, each stockholder will have a higher number of shares but no additional monetary value.

So why do companies distribute stock dividends? There are a couple of potential reasons. First, a stock dividend can substitute for a cash dividend when a company does not have enough cash on hand. This

MARUTI SUZUKI ANALYSIS

Look at Maruti Suzuki's Statement of Stockholders' Equity and Statement of Cash Flows in Appendix C. What was the total and per share amount of dividends declared in the most recent year? What was the total amount of dividends paid during the year?

Maruti Suzuki declared ₹2,417, in dividends in the year 2012–13. It paid ₹2,167 million during 2012–13.

motivation can be especially strong when a company is trying to maintain a long and uninterrupted streak of declaring dividends. Second, a company may want to reduce the market price of its stock to keep its stock price in an "affordable" range for the average investor. Distributing more shares in the marketplace brings down the price of each individual share.

Like cash dividends, a stock dividend is paid out of retained earnings. However, unlike a cash dividend, a stock dividend is not a distribution of assets. It is a distribution of common stock. As a result, a stock dividend simply transfers an amount from retained earnings to contributed capital (that is, common stock and additional paid-in capital). The amount transferred depends on whether the dividend is considered small or large.

In USA a *small stock dividend* is a distribution of 25% or less of the existing outstanding shares. Small stock dividends are recorded at the market value of the stock on the date of declaration. A *large stock dividend* is a distribution of more than 25% of the existing outstanding shares. Large stock dividends are recorded at the par value of the stock. In India issue of bonus share is known as capitalization of reserve.

Recording Small Stock Dividends To illustrate a small dividend, suppose that Bethany Technologies, USA declares a 15% stock dividend on June 1 to be distributed on June 28 to stockholders of record on June 14. On June 1, Bethany has 1,00,000 shares of $1 par common stock outstanding, and the stock is trading at $10 per share. Because the dividend is small, it is recorded at the market value of the stock on the date of declaration. Thus, the amount of the dividend would be calculated as follows:

Outstanding shares	1,00,000
× Stock dividend	× 15%
Shares to be issued	15,000
× Market value per share	× $10
Value of stock dividend	$1,50,000

On the date of declaration, Bethany would make the following entry:

June 1	Retained Earnings	1,50,000	
	Common Stock to Be Distributed		15,000
	Additional Paid-In Capital		1,35,000
	(To record declaration of small stock dividend)		

Assets	=	Liabilities	+	Equity
				−1,50,000 +15,000 +1,35,000

This entry decreases Retained Earnings for the amount of the dividend and increases two contributed capital accounts. The first is Common Stock to Be Distributed. This account is exactly like Common Stock, except that the words "to Be Distributed" are added to indicate that the stock has yet to be issued. The account is recorded at the par value of the stock. The second is Additional Paid-In Capital, which is increased for the value of the dividend that exceeds par value—in this case, $1,35,000. The effect of the entry is a change in specific equity accounts, but no change in total equity. That again is the nature of a stock dividend. It is a transfer of equity between accounts, not a distribution of assets.

On the payment date, Bethany would make the following entry:

June 28	Common Stock to Be Distributed	15,000	
	Common Stock		15,000
	(To record payment of dividend)		

Assets	=	Liabilities	+	Equity
				−15,000 +15,000

This entry simply decreases Common Stock to Be Distributed and increases Common Stock to reflect that the stock has been issued. Like the first entry, there is no effect on total equity as a result of this second entry.

Recording Large Stock Dividends To illustrate a large dividend, suppose that Bethany Technologies declares a 50% dividend instead of 15%. Because the dividend is large, it is recorded at the par value of the stock. Thus, the amount of the dividend would be calculated as follows:

Outstanding shares	1,00,000
× Stock dividend	× 50%
Shares to be issued	50,000
× Par value per share	× $1
Value of stock dividend	$50,000

On the date of declaration, Bethany would make the following entry:

MARUTI SUZUKI ANALYSIS

Look at Maruti Suzuki's Statement of Stockholders Equity in Appendix C. Did the company issue any stock during the years presented? Was the issuance a stock dividend?

Maruti Suzuki issued 1,31,70,000 equity shares to the shareholders pursuant to a scheme of amalgamation. Maruti Suzuki being an Indian company cannot declare stock dividend. It can however, declare bonus share, but it did not do so during 2010-11.

June 1	Retained Earnings	50,000	
	Common Stock to Be Distributed		50,000
	(To record declaration of large stock dividend)		

Assets	=	Liabilities	+	Equity
				−50,000 +50,000

This entry decreases Retained Earnings and increases Common Stock to Be Distributed for the amount of the dividend. Because the dividend is recorded at par value, the entry does not affect Additional Paid-In Capital. As in the case of the small dividend, total equity is not affected by this entry.

On the payment date, Bethany would make the following entry to reflect that the stock has been distributed:

June 28	Common Stock to Be Distributed	50,000	
	Common Stock		50,000
	(To record payment of dividend)		

Assets	=	Liabilities	+	Equity
				−50,000 +50,000

Stock split An increase in a company's shares of stock according to some specified ratio.

Stock Splits

When a company wants to decrease the market price of its stock to make it more affordable, it can use a stock split instead of a stock dividend. A **stock split** is

MAKING IT REAL

While companies often split their stock to make the price more affordable to the average investor, one company takes the exact opposite approach. Berkshire Hathaway, the company made famous by its founder, Warren Buffett, has never split its stock. As a result, the value of each share of stock is quite high. During the month of February 2011, the value of one share of stock was approximately $125,000!

According to the company's website, the company does not split its stock so that it can attract high-quality investors who "think of themselves as business owners and invest in companies with the intention of staying a long time." The company continues that it wants owners who "keep their eyes focused on business results, not market prices." The company concludes that "(s)plitting the stock would . . . downgrade the quality of our shareholder population and encourage a market price less consistently related to intrinsic business value."

© AP IMAGES/NATI HARNIK

Source: FocusInvestor.com, http://www.focusinvestor.com/brkfaq.htm#Q8.

Usually, preferred stockholders relinquish the right to vote in exchange for preference to dividends and preference to assets upon liquidation of the company.

an increase in a company's shares of stock according to some specified ratio. For example, a company that declares a 2-for-1 split recalls all shares from existing stockholders and issues two shares in return, effectively doubling the shares outstanding. As result of this increased supply of shares, the market price of the stock usually falls proportionally. In a 2-for-1 split, the stock price would be cut in half.

Stock splits are very similar to stock dividends or bonus issue in that they both result in additional shares outstanding. In fact, a 2-for-1 stock split is the same as a 100% stock dividend. However, there are important differences. First, a stock split is not an accounting transaction, so no entry is recorded. Second, stock splits apply to all authorized shares, not just those shares outstanding. Whether a share is outstanding, is in treasury stock, or is authorized but unissued, it is split according to the ratio. Third, a stock split results in a proportional change in the par value of the stock. For example, a company declaring a 2-for-1 stock split on its ₹10 par value stock would reduce its par value in half to ₹5. The reduction in the per share par value then allows total par value to remain unchanged.

To illustrate, suppose that Sun Pharmaceutical Industries Limited declares a 5-for-1 stock split when it has 20,71,16,391 Equity Shares outstanding and 30,00,00,000 authorized. Before the stock splits, the share price is of ₹5 each. After the split, Sun Pharma would have 1,03,55,81,955 shares outstanding, 1,50,00,00,000 shares authorized, and a par value of ₹1. The stock would trade at around ₹555 per share.

LO4 Preferred Stock

While all corporations issue common stock, many also authorize the sale of preferred stock. **Preferred stock or preference share** is a form of capital stock that receives one or more priorities over common stock. Usually, preferred stockholders relinquish the right to vote in exchange for preference to dividends and preference to assets upon liquidation of the company. Preference to dividends means that preferred stockholders receive their dividends before common stockholders receive any dividends.

Recording Preferred Stock

Because it is a form of contributed capital, preferred stock is recorded in the same manner as common stock. To illustrate, suppose that a company issues 500 shares of ₹5 par value preferred stock for ₹15 per share on August 23. The company would record this issuance as follows:

Aug. 23	Cash	7,500	
	Preferred Stock		2,500
	Share Premium		5,000
	(To record sale of preferred stock)		

Assets	=	Liabilities	+	Equity
+7,500				+2,500
				+5,000

This entry increases Cash for ₹7,500, which is the amount paid by the investor. Preferred Stock is increased for ₹2,500, which is the par value of the stock (₹5 par × 500 shares issued). Share Premium Account is then increased for the excess paid over par value, which is ₹5,000 (₹7,500 − ₹2,500). As a result of this entry, both assets and equity increase.

Reporting Preferred Stock

A company's balances in both preferred stock and additional paid-in capital are reported in the stockholders' equity section of the balance sheet. In India Preference Share Capital is shown under 'Share Capital' where as Share premium is shown under "Reserve and Surplus". The following shows Walgreen's preferred stock balances from its 2010 balance sheet.

Walgreens' 2010 Preferred Stock

	2010	2009
Preferred stock, \$.0625 par value; authorized 32 million shares; none issued	\$ —	\$ —

Preferred stock A form of capital stock that receives one or more priorities over common stock.

Walgreens reports a zero balance in preferred stock for both years. Although the company is authorized to issue 32 million shares of $0.0625 par value preferred stock, it has not yet issued any.

Cash Dividends on Preferred Stock

When a company has both preferred and common stock outstanding, cash dividends must be allocated between the two. Because preferred stockholders have dividend preference, they are paid first, followed by common stockholders. The amount that is allocated to preferred stockholders depends on the dividend rate and whether the stock is cumulative or noncumulative.

The dividend rate refers to the annual dividend amount that preferred stockholders normally receive. The rate is usually set as a rupee amount per share or as a percentage of par value. For example, preferred stock may carry a dividend of ₹2 per share or a dividend of 6% of par value.

All preferred stock is either cumulative or noncumulative. **Cumulative preferred stock** carries the right to receive current-year dividends and all unpaid dividends from prior years before dividends are paid to common stockholders. This means that if a company fails to pay a dividend one year, the missed dividend will be paid the next time dividends are declared. The accumulated value of unpaid prior-year dividends is called **dividends in arrears**. Note that dividends in arrears is not a liability because dividends are declared at the discretion of the board of directors and become a legal obligation only when declared. Nonetheless, because dividends in arrears are informative, they are disclosed in the notes to the financial statements.

Noncumulative preferred stock carries the right to receive current-year dividends only. If a company does not declare a dividend in a particular year, noncumulative preferred stockholders lose the right to that annual dividend forever. As a result, a company with noncumulative preferred stock will not have dividends in arrears.

To illustrate the allocation of dividends to preferred and common stockholders, a company has the following two types of stock:

Common stock, ₹2 par, 1,00,000 shares outstanding

5% Preferred stock, ₹10 par, 20,000 shares outstanding

Suppose further that company does not pay dividends in 2010–11 or 2011–12 but declares ₹64,000 of dividends in 2012–13. The allocation of the 2012–13 dividend depends on whether the preferred stock is cumulative or noncumulative.

Cumulative Preferred Stock If the company stock is cumulative, the preferred stockholders receive not only the current-year annual dividend but also the two years of dividends in arrears. The annual dividend on preferred stock is ₹0.50 per share (₹10 par × 5%) and ₹10,000 in total (₹0.50 per share × 20,000 shares). Therefore, ₹30,000 is allocated to preferred stockholders, with the remainder going to common stockholders. These calculations are illustrated as follows:

Preferred stock is cumulative	Preferred	Common
Dividends in arrears—Year 2010–11	₹10,000	
Dividends in arrears—Year 2011–12	10,000	
Current-year preferred dividend	10,000	
Distribute remainder to common (₹64,000 − ₹30,000)		₹34,000
Total allocated in 2012–13	₹30,000	₹34,000

Once the allocation of dividends is calculated, the company would record the declaration and payment of the dividend as follows:

		Debit	Credit
Date of Declaration	Retained Earnings	64,000	
	Common Stock Dividend Payable		34,000
	Preferred Stock Dividend Payable		30,000
	(To record declaration of dividend)		

Assets	=	Liabilities	+	Equity
		+34,000		−64,000
		+30,000		

Cumulative preferred stock Stock that carries the right to receive current-year dividends and all unpaid dividends from prior years before dividends are paid to common stockholders.

Dividends in arrears The accumulated value of unpaid prior-year dividends.

Noncumulative preferred stock Stock that carries the right to receive current-year dividends only.

Payment Date	Common Stock Dividend Payable	34,000	
	Preferred Stock Dividend Payable	30,000	
	Cash		64,000
	(To record payment of dividend)		

Assets	=	Liabilities	+	Equity
−64,000		−34,000		
		−30,000		

As is the case with any cash dividend, the net overall result of the declaration and payment of the dividend is a decrease in the company's equity and its assets.

Noncumulative Preferred Stock If the company stock is noncumulative, the preferred stockholders receive only the current-year annual dividend. The missed dividends in 2010–11 and 2011–12 are irrelevant to the calculation for the current year. Therefore, only ₹10,000 is allocated to preferred stockholders, with the remainder going to common stockholders. These calculations are illustrated as follows.

Preferred stock is cumulative	**Preferred**	**Common**
Current-year preferred dividend	₹10,000	
Distribute remainder to common (₹64,000 − ₹10,000)		₹54,000
Total allocated in 2011	₹10,000	₹54,000

LO5 Treasury Stock

Like any investor, a corporation can purchase shares of its own common stock in the marketplace. The common stock that a company reacquires from stockholders is **treasury stock**. Because shares of treasury stock are no longer held by an external investor, they are no longer outstanding. However, they are still considered to be issued. In India, as stated earlier, though the Companies Act allows buy back of shares, it does not allow a company to hold those shares. Bought back shares must be cancelled within seven days. Therefore, in India companies cannot hold treasury stock.

© ISTOCKPHOTO.COM/JAMES C. PRUITT

One of the most common reasons that a company repurchases its common stock is to acquire shares that can be issued to employees under stock compensation plans.

The practice of purchasing treasury stock is commonplace in publicly traded companies today. One of the most common reasons is to acquire shares that can be issued to employees under the company's stock compensation plans. Walgreens , USA is an excellent example. The following shows the common stock column of Walgreens' statement of stockholders' equity. This column reports the number of shares of common stock outstanding.

Common Stock Column of Walgreens' 2010 Statement of Stockholders' Equity

	Common Stock Shares
Balance, August 31, 2007	991,141,357
Treasury stock purchases	(8,000,000)
Employees stock purchase and option plans	6,034,861
Balance, August 31, 2008	989,176,218
Treasury stock purchases	(10,270,000)
Employees stock purchase and option plans	9,655,172
Balance, August 31, 2009	988,561,390
Treasury stock purchases	(55,716,733)
Employees stock purchase and option plans	5,760,396
Balance, August 31, 2010	938,605,053

In each year presented, Walgreens reports significant purchases of treasury shares, which reduce the shares outstanding, and significant distributions to employees, which increase shares outstanding. Because Walgreens has purchased more shares than it has distributed during these three years, its total number of outstanding shares has decreased from over 991 million at the end of 2007 to over 938 million at the end of 2010.

Recording Treasury Stock

Companies record the purchase of treasury stock using either the cost method or the par value method. Because most companies use the cost method, it will be

Treasury stock Common stock that a company reacquires from its stockholders.

demonstrated. Under the **cost method**, treasury stock is recorded at its cost of acquisition.

To illustrate, suppose that Bahakel Inc. purchases 1,000 shares of its own common stock on May 3 when the stock is trading for $32 per share. Bahakel would record the purchase as follows:

		Debit	Credit
May 3	Treasury Stock	32,000	
	Cash		32,000
	(To record purchase of treasury stock)		

Assets	=	Liabilities	+	Equity
−32,000				−32,000

The entry increases Treasury Stock and decreases Cash for the $32,000 paid to acquire the stock. Notice that Treasury Stock is increased with a debit. Treasury Stock is a contra-equity account because it represents a reduction of capital. Its balance is therefore subtracted from Bahakel's total equity. As a result of this entry, both assets and equity decrease.

In many countries, the law permit treasury stock to be reissued at a later date. To illustrate how such a reissuance would be recorded, suppose that Bahakel reissued 100 shares of its treasury stock for $40 per share on July 22. Bahakel would record this transaction as follows:

		Debit	Credit
July 22	Cash	4,000	
	Treasury Stock		3,200
	Additional Paid-In Capital		800
	(To record issuance of treasury stock)		

Assets	=	Liabilities	+	Equity
+4,000				+3,200
				+ 800

Cost method A method of recording the purchase of treasury stock at its cost of acquisition.

This entry increases Cash for the $4,000 received from investors. It then decreases Treasury Stock for the cost of the shares that are reissued. The stock was originally repurchased for $32 per share, so Treasury Stock is decreased by $3,200 (100 shares × $32 cost per share). The difference between the cash received and the cost of the treasury stock represents additional contributed capital beyond the cost of the stock. Therefore, Additional Paid-In Capital that is the Share Premium Account is increased for the $800 difference. Note that although it appears that Bahakel has generated a gain on the sale of treasury stock, accounting rules prohibit the recording of a gain or loss on treasury stock transactions. As a result of this entry, both assets and equity increase.

Reporting Treasury Stock

A company's balance in treasury stock is reported in the stockholders' equity section of the balance sheet. The following shows Walgreen's treasury stock balances from its 2010 balance sheet.

Walgreens' 2010 Treasury Stock

	2010	2009
Treasury stock at cost, 86,794,947 shares in 2010 and 36,838,610 shares in 2009	$(3,101)	$(1,533)

Walgreens reports a little over $3.1 billion in treasury stock in 2010, which is roughly two times the balance of $1.5 billion in 2009. This is a large increase and is a result of the share repurchase program approved by Walgreens' board of directors and described in the company's notes to its financial statements. Because treasury stock is a contra-equity account, its balance is reported as a negative number. The textual description contains the words "at cost," which indicates that Walgreens uses the cost method to account for its treasury stock. It also discloses that at the end of 2010, Walgreens owned more than 86 million shares of treasury stock. This means that Walgreens has paid about $35.73 on average per share of treasury stock ($3,101,000,000 balance ÷ 86,794,947 shares).

MARUTI SUZUKI ANALYSIS

Look at Maruti Suzuki's Balance Sheet in Appendix C. How many shares of treasury stock does Maruti Suzuki have at the end of March 31, 2013?

Maruti Suzuki being an Indian company does not report possessing treasury stock. The Companies Act does not allow a company to hold those shares. Bought back shares must be cancelled within seven days.

Because a company's equity represents the owners' claim on corporate assets, stockholders are particularly interested in a company's ability to manage its equity.

LO6 Evaluating a Company's Management of Equity

Because a company's equity represents the owners' claim on corporate assets, stockholders are particularly interested in a company's ability to manage its equity. Some of the issues that are important to most stockholders are as follows:

1. How does the company generate equity for stockholders?
2. How does the company reward its stockholders through dividends?
3. How does the company's equity affect its cash flows?

The following sections examine these three issues for Hindustan Unilever Limited. The examination will require information from the company's balance sheet, income statement, and statement of cash flows. The required information is found in Exhibit 10-2, excerpted from Hindustan Unilever Limited's 2012–14 Annual Report. All amounts are in ₹ crores except the per share data.

Exhibit 10-2 Account Balances from Hindustan Unilever Limited 2012–13 Annual Report

(*₹ in crores*)

Source	Accounts	March 31, 2013	March 31, 2012
Balance Sheet	Total assets	₹ 11,512.47	₹ 10,958.27
	Total equity	2,674.02	3,512.93
Income Statement	Net income	₹ 3,796.67	₹ 2,691.40
	Earnings per share (basic)	17.56	12.46
Statement of Stockholders' Equity	Cash dividends declared	₹ 4,000	₹ 1,620.94
	Dividends per share	18.50	7.50
	Common shares outstanding	2,16,24,72,310	2,16,15,12,492

Horizontal and Vertical Analyses

A good place to start the analysis of accounts receivable is horizontal and vertical analyses. Recall from Chapter 2 that horizontal analysis calculates the rupee change in an account balance, defined as the current-year balance less the prior-year balance, and divides that change by the prior-year balance to yield the percentage change. Vertical analysis divides each account balance by a base account, yielding a percentage. The base account is total assets for balance sheet accounts and net sales or total revenues for income statement accounts. These calculations are summarized as follows:

Horizontal Analysis

$$\text{Rupee change in account balance} = \text{Current-year balance} - \text{Prior-year balance}$$

$$\text{Percentage change in account balance} = \frac{\text{Rupee change}}{\text{Prior-year balance}}$$

Vertical Analysis

For the Balance Sheet / *For the Income Statement*

$$\text{Percentage} = \frac{\text{Account Balance}}{\text{Total Assets}} \text{ or } \frac{\text{Account Balance}}{\text{Net Sales or Revenue}}$$

Given Hindustan Unilever Limited financial data in Exhibit 10-2, horizontal and vertical analyses result in the following.

Horizontal Analysis

	Change	Percentage Change
Stockholders' equity	2,674.02 − 3,512.93 = (838.91)	$\frac{(838.91)}{3,512.93} = (23.88)\%$

Vertical Analysis

	March 31, 2013	March 31, 2012
Stockholders' equity	$\frac{2,674.02}{11,512.47} = 23.23\%$	$\frac{3,512.93}{10,958.27} = 31.06\%$

The horizontal analysis reveals that total equity decreased by ₹838.91 crore during 2012–13, which is a decrease of 23.88% from the prior year. The vertical analysis shows that total equity as a percentage of total assets went down from 31.06% to 23.23%. Although not reported in this chapter, a closer look at specific equity accounts reveals that the majority of Hindustan Unilever Limited's increase in equity was due to an increase in retained earnings. This shows that Hindustan Unilever Limited's increased its equity through profitable operations.

For comparison purposes, the March 31, 2013 horizontal and vertical analyses of P&G India are listed below. HUL experienced decrease in growth in equity during the year, and also HUL's equity/total assets is lower than P&G's.

Total Equity	Horizontal Analysis	Vertical Analysis
HUL	(23.88)%	23.23%
P&G India	4.83%	64.49%

Earnings per Share

Note 4 to the Financial Statements shows that though HUL has earned more profit than in the previous year, it has also distributed much more dividend than in the previous year, resulting in a decrease in the total equity as compared to the previous year. All stockholders want—greater claims on assets resulting from profitable operations. Another measure of the ability to generate equity through profitable operations is earnings per share. **Earnings per share** compares a company's net income to the number of shares of common stock outstanding. It is calculated as follows:

$$\text{Earnings per Share} = \frac{\text{Net Income}}{\text{Average Number of Common Shares Outstanding}}$$

where average common shares outstanding is:

$$\frac{\text{Beginning shares outstanding} + \text{Ending shares outstanding}}{2}$$

Earnings per share is a useful ratio because it "standardizes" earnings by a company's size. The ratio can therefore be used to compare the profitability of companies of vastly different sizes.

Earnings per share A comparison of a company's net income to the number of shares of common stock outstanding that measures the ability to generate equity through profitable operations.

Return on equity A comparison of a company's net income to total stockholders' equity that measures the ability to use existing equity to generate additional equity.

HUL's earnings per share is calculated as follows using the information in Exhibit 10-2.

$$\frac{₹3{,}796.67 \text{ crore}}{2{,}16{,}04{,}92{,}230} = ₹17.57$$

2,160,492,230 shares are average number of shares outstanding.

The 17.57 ratio reveals that HUL earned ₹17.57 in profit for every share of common stock outstanding during the year. This is an improvement over the last year, when the company earned only ₹12.46 of earnings per share. However, it is less than the ₹26.75 earnings per share of its competitor, P&G.

Accounting standards require that companies disclose their annual earnings per share in their financial statements. Like most companies, HUL reports its ratio at the bottom of its income statement.

Return on Equity

Another measure of a company's ability to generate equity is return on equity. **Return on equity** compares a company's net income to its total stockholders' equity and provides an indication of how well a company uses its existing equity to generate additional equity. Stockholders naturally want this ratio to be as high as possible. It is calculated as follows:

$$\text{Return on Equity} = \frac{\text{Net Income}}{\text{Average Stockholders' Equity}}$$

where average stockholders' equity is:

$$\frac{\text{Beginning equity} + \text{Ending equity}}{2}$$

HUL's return on equity is calculated as follows from the information in Exhibit 10-2:

$$\frac{3{,}796.67}{(2{,}674.02 + 3{,}512.93) \div 2} = 122.7\%$$

The 122.7% ratio indicates that for every rupee of equity held during 2012–13, HUL generated almost 122.7% of additional equity through profitable operations. This compares favorably to P&G's return on equity of 13.27% over the same period. HUL's was successful in effectively using its existing equity to generate more equity for stockholders.

Dividend Payout Ratio

In addition to examining how well a company generates additional equity, stockholders often examine how a company pays out that equity through dividends. One ratio to do this is the dividend payout ratio.

The **dividend payout ratio** compares a company's dividends to its earnings. The ratio demonstrates the percentage of earnings a company has decided to distribute to owners through cash dividends. The ratio can be calculated in one of two ways, depending on how a company reports its dividend information. If a company reports only the rupee amount of annual dividends, the ratio is calculated by dividing total dividends by net income. If a company reports a dividend per share number, the ratio is calculated by dividing dividends per share by earnings per share. Either way, the result will be the same (except for small differences due to the rounding of per share values). Both calculations are as follows.

$$\text{Dividend Payout Ratio} = \frac{\text{Dividends}}{\text{Net Income}} \quad \text{or} \quad \frac{\text{Dividends per Share}}{\text{Earnings per Share}}$$

These amounts are included in Exhibit 10-2 and are used to calculate HUL's dividend payout ratio as follows:

Calculation based on totals:

$$\frac{4{,}000}{3{,}796.67} = 105.35\%$$

Calculation based on per share amounts:

$$\frac{18.50}{17.57} = 105.29\%$$

A ratio of 105.35% indicates that for every rupee of earnings during 2012–13, HUL declared about 105% in cash dividends. This is greater than P&G's ratio of 56.08%. However, a 105.35% ratio is not necessarily better than a 56.08% ratio. The ratios simply reflect each company's dividend policy. For 2012–13, HUL paid out more of its earnings than did P&G. Thus, stockholders who want to receive more of the profits in dividends would prefer HUL. However, stockholders who want the company to plow more earnings back into operations instead of paying more dividends would prefer P&G.

Dividend Yield

In addition to knowing what percentage of earnings is paid in dividends, stockholders want to know how much their investment in a company's stock returns to them. Stockholders generate a return on their investment in two ways—an increase in the stock price and a receipt of dividends. The return from receiving dividends can be calculated with the dividend yield ratio. The **dividend yield ratio** divides dividends per share by the market price per share of stock as follows:

$$\text{Dividend Yield} = \frac{\text{Dividends per share}}{\text{Market price per share}}$$

According to Exhibit 10-2, HUL reports dividends per share of ₹18.50 on its 2013 statement of stockholders' equity. Market price information can be found on most any financial website. We will use the stock price of ₹466.10, which is based on year-end closing prices quoted in the Bombay Stock Exchange. As a result, the dividend yield reveals the return to a stockholder who bought the stock at the beginning of the fiscal year ending March 31, 2013.

$$\frac{18.50}{466.10} = 3.96\%$$

The 3.96% ratio indicates that an investment in HUL stock on April 1, 2013, would yield a return from dividends equal to about 3.96% of each rupee invested. This compares to a dividend yield for P&G of 0.60%. Thus, the yield for HUL is higher.

Dividend payout ratio A comparison of a company's dividends to its earnings that measures the percentage of current earnings distributed to owners.

Dividend yield ratio A comparison of dividends per share to the market price per share of stock that measures the percentage return from dividends.

MARUTI SUZUKI ANALYSIS

Using Maruti Suzuki's information in Appendix C, calculate and interpret (1) horizontal and vertical analyses of total equity, (2) earnings per share, (3) return on equity, (4) dividend payout ratio, and (5) dividend yield, assuming a market price of ₹1,280.

(1) *Horizontal Analysis*

(₹1,85,789 – ₹1,51,874)/₹1,51,874 = 22.33%

Vertical Analysis

₹1,85,789/₹2,66,880 = 69.62%

The 22.33% horizontal analysis reflects good change in Maruti Suzuki's total equity. The 69.62% vertical analysis shows that 70% of the company's assets are generated through equity.

(2) *Earnings per share*

₹23,921 million/30,20,80,060 = ₹79.19

The ₹79.19 earnings per share indicates that Maruti Suzuki earned ₹79 in income for each share of stock outstanding. This ratio is higher than the previous year, which reveals that the company has been more profitable this year, given its size.

(3) *Return on Equity*

₹23,921/(1,85,789 + 1,51,874)/2 = 14.16%

The 14% return on equity ratio indicates that Maruti Suzuki earned almost 14 paise in income for every ₹1 of equity. Such a return gives the company many options. One option is to pay dividends to the owners, while another is to retain the profits and grow the company. Maruti Suzuki pays dividends, so it is doing both—rewarding its stockholders through dividends and growing the company.

(4) *Dividend Payout Ratio*

₹2,417/23,921 = 10.10% or ₹8.0/₹79.19 = 10.10%

The 10% dividend payout ratio indicates that Maruti Suzuki paid to owners approximately 10 paise for every rupee it earned during the year. In the preceding year, the company's ratio was 13.25%. The predominant reason for the decrease is that Maruti Suzuki's earning per share increased during that time, thereby increasing the payout ratio.

(5) *Dividend Yield*

₹8.0/₹1,280 = 0.62%

The 0.6% dividend yield indicates that Maruti Suzuki's dividend yield was 0.6% of the stock's value.

Stockholders' Equity and Cash Flows

When examining a company's equity, it is always important to analyze how equity has been used to generate or use cash. Equity can significantly affect a company's cash through the issuance of stock, the purchase of treasury stock, and the payment of cash dividends. Each of these activities is reported in the financing activities section of the statement of cash flows. The following is the financing activities of HUL's 2013 statement of cash flows.

Hindustan Unilever Limited activity affected cash flows in all two years presented. Over the two years, HUL has paid out ₹5,059.62 crore in cash dividends (3,550.31 + 1,509.31). This totals over ₹5,000 crore that has been paid out to stockholders over two years. This is a significant amount of cash.

Financing Activities Section of Hindustan Unilever Limited 2012–13 Statement of Cash Flows

(₹ in crores)	2012–13	20011–12
Cash Flows from Financing Activities		
Dividends paid	(3,550.31)	(1,509.31)
Tax on distributed profits	(575.51)	(245.32)
Addition to unpaid dividend accounts	(16.81)	(2.85)
Interest paid	(25.15)	(1.24)
Proceeds from share allotment under Employee Stock Option Scheme	7.34	33.55
Net cash used for financing activities	₹ (4,160.44)	₹ (1,725.17)

In addition to examining the statement of cash flows, it can be beneficial to examine the notes to the financial statements to find additional information provided as notes to the financial statement. For example, in 2010–11, HUL's note 2 (e) discloses the details of HUL's stock repurchase program.

Excerpts from Hindustan Unilever Limited 2010–11 Stockholders' Equity Note

Pursuant to the shareholders' approval for buy back of equity shares under section 77A of the Companies Act, 1956, the Company has bought back 22,883,204 equity shares through open market transactions for an aggregate amount of ₹625.30 crore, by utilizing Share Premium and General Reserve to the extent of ₹82.16 crore and 540.85 crore, respectively. Capital redemption reserve has been created out of general reserve for ₹2.29 crore being the nominal value of shares bought back in terms of section 77AA of the Companies Act, 1956.

MARUTI SUZUKI ANALYSIS

Look at Maruti Suzuki's Statement of Cash Flows in Appendix C. How much cash has the company paid in dividends and for the repurchase of stock over the past two years?

According to the financing activities section of its statement of cash flows, Maruti Suzuki has paid ₹4,334 (2,167 + 2,167) million over the past two years in dividends. No repurchase of shares took place during these two years.

CONCEPT QUESTIONS

1. What are the characteristics of a corporation that distinguish it from a sole proprietorship and a partnership?
2. What is the difference in the liability exposure of the owner of a corporation compared to the owner in a sole proprietorship or a partnership?
3. A corporation is subject to double taxation. In what ways is this true?
4. What is the difference between shares of common stock that are authorized, issued, and outstanding?
5. What are the four rights that an investor receives when purchasing common stock from a corporation?
6. What is par value of common stock, and how is it determined?
7. Where and how is common stock reported?
8. Who decides whether or not a company will issue a dividend?
9. What are the important dates associated with dividends?
10. How is the declaration of a cash dividend recorded?
11. Where and how are cash dividends reported?
12. What is a stock dividend, and why do some argue that a stock dividend has very little value to stockholders? Is a stock dividend allowed in India?
13. What are the differences between small and large stock dividends?
14. What is a stock split, and how does it compare to a stock dividend?
15. What is preferred stock?
16. What is the difference between cumulative and noncumulative preferred stock?
17. What is treasury stock, and how is it recorded and reported?
18. Are shares of treasury stock considered outstanding shares? Explain.
19. Describe four ratios used to evaluate a company's equity.
20. In what section of the statement of cash flows are equity activities reported?

MULTIPLE CHOICE

1. Which of the following is not a distinguishing characteristic of the corporation as a form of business?
   a. Separate legal entity
   b. Unlimited liability of owners
   c. Ability to raise capital
   d. Double taxation
2. The income of the corporation is taxed:
   a. at the personal level when dividends are paid.
   b. at the corporate level.
   c. both a and b.
   d. neither a nor b.
3. The number of shares that a company can issue according to its corporate charter is referred to as:
   a. issued shares.
   b. authorized shares.
   c. outstanding shares.
   d. none of the above.
4. Which of the following rights are received by investors when they purchase common stock?
   a. The right to participate proportionally in dividends
   b. The right to vote
   c. The right of preemption
   d. All of the above
5. What is the arbitrary value that determines an entity's legal capital?
   a. Issue value b. Face value
   c. Par value d. Stated value
6. A company issues 2,000 shares of ₹2 par value common stock for ₹10 per share. What amount will be credited to the Common Stock account when recording this transaction?
   a. ₹4,000 b. ₹20,000
   c. ₹16,000 d. None of the above
7. A company issues 2,000 shares of ₹2 par value common stock for ₹10 per share. What amount will be credited to the share premium account when recording this transaction?
   a. ₹4,000 b. ₹16,000
   c. ₹20,000 d. None of the above
8. A distribution of profits to owners by a corporation is known as:
   a. a gift. b. a settlement.
   c. a payment. d. a dividend.
9. Which of the following statements concerning dividends is true?
   a. The board of directors decides when to distribute dividends
   b. A corporation does not have to pay a dividend every year
   c. Dividends can be paid in methods other than cash
   d. All of the above are true
10. Relevant to the financial year ending 31 December, on February 1, a company declares a cash dividend, payable on March 1, to stockholders of record on February 20. March 1 is the:
    a. payment date. b. date of declaration.
    c. date of record. d. dividend date.
11. On the date that a dividend is declared, what account is debited for the total amount of the dividend?
    a. Cash b. Dividends Receivable
    c. Dividends Payable d. Retained Earnings
12. A company declares ₹1 per share dividend when it has 100,000 shares authorized and 40,000 issued

and outstanding. What is the amount of the dividend?

a. ₹1,00,000 b. ₹60,000
c. ₹40,000 d. ₹4,000

13. On June 4, a company declares a ₹3,20,000 dividend to be paid on June 15 to stockholders of record on June 10. On June 15, the company would record:
    a. no entry.
    b. an entry that debits Dividends Payable for ₹3,20,000.
    c. an entry that credits Dividends Payable for ₹3,20,000.
    d. an entry that debits Common Stock for ₹3,20,000.
14. If a company has 200,000 outstanding shares and issues 10% bonus shares, how many outstanding shares will there be following this dividend?
    a. 200,000 b. 180,000
    c. 202,000 d. 220,000
15. A company with 500,000 outstanding shares of ₹25 par common stock issues a 50% stock dividend when the stock is selling for ₹30 per share. What is the value of this stock dividend?
    a. ₹75,00,000 b. ₹1,25,000
    c. ₹62,500 d. ₹18,75,000
16. Which of the following is true concerning a stock dividend?
    a. A stock dividend is a distribution of assets
    b. A stock dividend does not change a stockholder's ownership percentage
    c. A stock dividend usually does not result in any change to the market price of individual shares
    d. A stock dividend is never stated in percentage terms
17. Which of the following describes the nature of a stock split?
    a. A stock split is not considered to be an accounting transaction
    b. Stock splits apply to all authorized shares
    c. A stock split results in a proportional change in the per share par value of the stock
    d. All of the above describe the nature of stock splits
18. Which of the following is true regarding preferred stock?
    a. Preferred stockholders are often given priority over common stockholders in the receipt of dividends
    b. When a company liquidates, preferred stockholders normally receive residual assets before common stockholders
    c. Both a and b
    d. Neither a nor b
19. When recording the issuance of preferred stock, what amount is credited to the Preferred Stock account if 100 shares of ₹3 par value preferred stock are issued for ₹6 per share?
    a. ₹600 b. ₹100
    c. ₹300 d. None of the above
20. A company with 4,000 shares of ₹1 par common stock and 3,000 shares of 10% ₹10 par preferred stock issues a ₹10,000 cash dividend. How is the dividend allocated to common and preferred stockholders if there was one year of dividends in arrears?
    a. ₹6,000 to common stockholders; ₹4,000 to preferred stockholders
    b. ₹4,000 to common stockholders; ₹6,000 to preferred stockholders
    c. ₹7,000 to common stockholders; ₹3,000 to preferred stockholders
    d. ₹3,000 to common stockholders; ₹7,000 to preferred stockholders
21. Corporations sometimes purchase treasury stock because:
    a. they want to increase the number of shares held by stockholders.
    b. management believes that the stock price is overvalued.
    c. they need shares that can be issued to employees under the company's stock compensation plans.
    d. none of the above.
22. What accounts are affected when recording the purchase of treasury stock?
    a. Debit Treasury Stock, Credit Cash
    b. Debit Cash, Credit Treasury Stock
    c. Debit Cash, Credit Common Stock
    d. Debit Treasury Stock, Credit Common Stock
23. How is treasury stock reported on the financial statements of a corporation in India?
    a. As a liability on the balance sheet
    b. As a positive amount in the stockholders' equity section of the balance sheet
    c. As a negative amount in the stockholders' equity section of the balance sheet
    d. None of the above
24. In performing a vertical analysis of total stockholders' equity, one would:
    a. divide current year equity by prior year equity.
    b. divide equity by liabilities.
    c. divide equity by total assets.
    d. divide common stock by total equity.
25. Which of the following is true regarding Earnings per share?
    a. This is a good measure of liquidity for a corporation
    b. It is calculated by dividing net income by average shares of common stock outstanding
    c. This calculation is not a required disclosure
    d. It is calculated by dividing net income by total equity
26. What ratio compares a company's dividends to its earnings to demonstrate the percentage of earnings a company has decided to distribute to owners through cash dividends?
    a. Earnings per share b. Dividend payout ratio
    c. Return on equity d. Dividend yield
27. Equity activities such as the issuance of stock and the payment of cash dividends are reported in which section of the statement of cash flows?
    a. Investing b. Financing
    c. Operating d. None of the above

BRIEF EXERCISES

1. Corporate Characteristics

Megan is a shareholder in Green Corporation. She mentions to you that any dividends that she receives from Green are taxed twice.

Required
Identify and describe the corporate characteristic to which Megan is referring.

2. Recording the Issuance of Common Stock

A company issued 200 shares of ₹2 par value stock for ₹10 per share on January 14.

Required
Prepare the entry that the company would make to record the issuance. How would the entry change if the par value was ₹1?

3. Calculating Cash Dividends

Jonathan owns 3% of the common stock of XYZ Corporation. On February 3, XYZ declares ₹30,00,000 in dividends, payable on February 22.

Required
What amount will Jonathan receive on February 22? What effect does the dividend have on XYZ's total stockholders' equity?

4. Recording Cash Dividends

A company with 2,000,000 outstanding shares of stock declared a ₹1 per share dividend on July 10. The dividend is payable on July 31 to stockholders of record on July 17.

Required
Prepare the entries that the company would make on the date of declaration and payment date. What is the total effect of both entries on total stockholders' equity?

5. Recording Large and Small Stock Dividends

Albertine Industries declared a 10% stock dividend on August 15 to be distributed on September 10 to stockholders of record on August 28. On August 15, Albertine had 3,000,000 shares of ₹1 par stock outstanding, and its stock was trading at ₹7 per share.

Required
Prepare the August 15 entry for Albertine. How would the entry change if the stock dividend was 50%?

6. Effect of a Stock Split

A company has 100,000 shares of ₹2.25 par common stock outstanding when it decides to split its stock 3-for-1.

Required
How many shares of stock are outstanding after the split. What is the new par value of each share of stock?

7. Recording the Issuance of Preferred Stock

A company issues 600 shares of ₹4 par value preferred stock for ₹12 per share on March 15.

Required
Prepare the entry that the company would make to record the issuance.

8. Cash Dividends

A company has common stock and cumulative preferred stock. The preferred stock is 4%, ₹10 par, and there are 25,000 shares outstanding. The company didn't pay dividends in the previous two years. In the current year, the company declares dividends of ₹37,000.

Required
Determine the amount of current year dividends allocated to common stockholders.

9. Recording the Purchase of Treasury Stock

Russell Corporation uses the cost method to account for treasury stock. On February 3, Russell purchases 3,000 shares of its own ₹2 par value common stock when it is trading for ₹15 per share.

Required
Prepare the entry that Russell Corporation would make to record the purchase.

10. Calculate Stockholders' Equity

Jet Prep Company, U.S.A., has a retained earnings balance of $150,000, a treasury stock balance of $30,000, and a common stock balance of $200,000. The market value of Jet Prep's common stock is $400,000.

Required
Calculate total stockholders' equity that would be reported on the balance sheet.

11. Effect of Equity Transactions

A company enters into the following independent transactions:

1. Issues common stock for cash
2. Declares and pays a cash dividend
3. Declares and distributes a stock dividend
4. Purchases treasury stock for cash
5. Declares a 2-for-1 stock split

Required
Describe whether each transaction would *increase, decrease,* or *not affect* total stockholders' equity, retained earnings, contributed capital, and cash flows from financing activities.

12. Reporting Stockholders' Equity

The following December 31 balances are provided by Ellen Corporation:

Treasury stock (20,000 shares)	₹ 1,00,000
Preferred stock (5%, ₹75 par, cumulative)	7,50,000
Additional paid-in capital	15,00,000
Retained earnings	22,24,000
Common stock (₹4 par value, 5,00,000 shares authorized)	14,00,000

Required
Prepare the stockholders' equity section of Ellen's balance sheet as per Indian GAAP. Will the treatment be different as per U.S. GAAP?

13. Calculate Return on Equity

During the year, a company generated ₹9,50,000 in net income. Also during the year, the company's stockholders' equity grew from ₹5,50,000 at the beginning of the year to ₹5,95,300 at the end of the year.

Required
Calculate the company's return on equity for the year. Round percentages to one decimal point (i.e., 9.4%).

14. Calculate the Dividend Payout Ratio

During the past year, Beems Company paid dividends of ₹3,50,000, earned net income of ₹16,50,000, and ended the year with earnings per share of ₹20.24.

Required
Calculate Beems' dividend payout ratio. Round percentages to one decimal point (i.e., 9.4%).

15. Reporting Cash Flows Associated with Equity

A company enters into the following transactions relating to its equity:

1. Issues preferred stock for cash
2. Converts preferred stock to common stock
3. Issues common stock for cash
4. Issues common stock for a building
5. Reissues for cash stock that was held as treasury stock
6. Purchases treasury stock for cash
7. Pays a cash dividend on common stock
8. Declares a 3-for-1 stock split
9. Distributes a 50% stock dividend

Required
Identify whether each transaction would be reported as a financing activity on the statement of cash flows or not reported on the statement of cash flows.

16. Evaluate Equity

A company provides the following information:

	2013	2012
Return on equity	33.4%	32.1%
Earnings per share	₹2.86	₹2.43
Dividend payout ratio	1.0%	1.0%
Dividend yield	0.0004%	0.0003%

Required
Comment on the profitability of the company and its dividend policy.

EXERCISES

17. Corporate Form of Business

The following characteristics were discussed in the text:

a. Separate legal entity
b. Liability of owners
c. Ability to raise capital
d. Transferability of ownership
e. Taxation
f. Regulation

Required
Describe how each characteristic relates to the corporate form of business.

18. Recording Stock Transactions

Irons Incorporated entered into the following stock transactions:

Apr. 5	Issued 30,000 shares of ₹3 par value common stock for ₹1,80,000.
May 31	Purchased 1,000 shares of treasury stock for ₹50,000.
Oct. 1	Issued 3,000 shares of ₹40 par value preferred stock for ₹65 per share.

Required
Prepare the journal entries to record the transactions. Use the cost method to account for the purchase of treasury stock.

19. Stock Terminology

The stockholders' equity section of Lester Company's balance sheet follows:

Stockholders' equity	
Common stock, 500,000 shares authorized, 450,000 shares issued	₹ 4,50,000
Additional paid-in capital	40,50,000
Retained earnings	14,25,000
Treasury stock, at cost, 16,000 shares	(4,80,000)
Total stockholders' equity	₹54,45,000

Required

a. How many shares of common stock are authorized, issued, and outstanding?
b. What is the par value per share of the common stock?
c. How much in total capital has Lester received from the issuance of stock?
d. What is the average cost of a share of treasury stock?

20. Cash Dividends

On December 15, Taylor Corporation declared a cash dividend of ₹77 per share to be paid on January 15 to stockholders of record on December 31. Taylor has 154 million shares of common stock outstanding.

Required
Identify the date of declaration, the date of record, and the payment date, and prepare all necessary journal entries on those dates.

21. Stock Dividends

Hudson High Rises declared a 10% stock dividend on July 1 to be distributed on August 1 to stockholders of record on July 15. On July 1, Hudson has 1,000,000 authorized shares and 250,000 outstanding shares. Hudson's ₹2 par stock is trading at ₹15 per share on July 1.

Required

a. Prepare all necessary journal entries to record the stock dividend.
b. Prepare all necessary journal entries to record the stock dividend, assuming the percentage was 30% instead of 10%.

22. Recording Cash and Stock Dividends

Kirk Corporation had the following amounts in equity before issuing its annual dividend:

Common stock (35,000 shares outstanding)	₹1,05,00,000
Additional paid-in capital	2,85,00,000
Retained earnings	4,40,00,000

Kirk has decided to issue a 5% stock dividend simultaneously with a ₹10 per share cash dividend. The date of declaration is November 12, and the payment date is November 29.

Required

Prepare all journal entries necessary to record the declaration and payment of dividends. Assume that the stock was trading for ₹100 on the date of declaration and ₹120 on the date of payment. Also, assume the cash dividends were not paid on the additional shares of stock from the stock dividend.

23. Effect of Dividends

Elam Enterprises is considering the following three actions regarding its equity:

Action 1: Declaring a 30% stock dividend.
Action 2: Declaring a ₹12,00,000 cash dividend.
Action 3: Declaring a 2-for-1 stock split.

Required

Describe whether each action would *increase, decrease,* or *not affect* the following: (1) Total Stockholders' Equity, (2) Retained Earnings, (3) Contributed Capital, (4) Par Value per Share, and (5) Price per Share.

24. Stock Dividends versus Stock Splits

Morgan Incorporated is looking to increase its number of shares of outstanding common stock to bring down its stock price. The board of directors is trying to decide if a 2-for-1 stock split or a 100% stock dividend is more appropriate. Morgan's stockholders' equity follows:

Common stock, ₹2 par, 100,000 shares issued and outstanding	₹ 2,00,000
Additional paid-in capital	6,60,000
Retained earnings	7,75,000
Total stockholders' equity	₹16,35,000

Required

a. Assess the pros and cons of the stock split versus the stock dividend.
b. Create a new stockholders' equity section if Morgan chooses (1) a stock dividend or (2) a stock split.

25. Cash Dividends

Cope Company declares a ₹9,00,000 dividend. Cope's common stock has a ₹5 par value and 80,000 shares outstanding. Cope's preferred stock is 5%, ₹12 par, and there are 20,000 shares outstanding. Cope has not paid dividends in the past three years. Cope's preferred stock is cumulative.

Required

a. Determine how the ₹9,00,000 in dividends should be allocated to preferred and common stockholders.
b. Prepare the journal entry that would be recorded on the date of declaration.
c. Determine how the ₹9,00,000 in dividends should be allocated to preferred and common stockholders, assuming that the preferred stock is noncumulative.

26. Preferred Stock Cash Dividends

The equity section of Jeans Incorporated is as follows:

Preferred stock, 5% cumulative, 6,000 shares issued and outstanding	₹1,20,000
Common stock, ₹1 par value, 36,000 shares issued	1,80,000
Retained earnings	2,50,000
Treasury stock, 6,000 shares, at cost	(30,000)
Total stockholders' equity	₹5,20,000

Required

Calculate the amount of dividends allocated to common and preferred stockholders under the following situations: (a) ₹18,000 of total dividends and no preferred dividends in arrears and (b) ₹24,000 of total dividends and two years of preferred dividends in arrears. How much did each common stockholder receive per share under each scenario?

27. Treasury Stock

On January 15, Capital Corporation purchased 2,000 shares of its own common stock when the stock was trading at ₹45. On June 15, Capital Corporation reissued 500 of these same shares for ₹50 per share.

Required

Prepare the journal entries to record the purchase and reissuance of the treasury stock both under Indian and U.S. GAAP. Use the cost method.

28. Treasury Stock

The equity section of Wilkins Homes' (U.S.A.) balance sheet at the beginning of the year is as follows:

Common stock, $1 par value, 100,000 shares issued	$ 1,00,000
Additional paid-in capital	7,00,000
Retained earnings	8,25,000
Treasury stock (2,000 shares)	(20,000)
Total stockholders' equity	$16,05,000

During the year, Wilkins reissues 1,000 shares of treasury stock for $15 per share and then purchases an additional 1,600 shares of treasury stock at $16 per share.

Required

a. Prepare the journal entries to record the treasury stock transactions.
b. Prepare the equity section of Wilkins' balance sheet after the treasury stock transactions.

29. Reporting Stockholders' Equity

A portion of the balance sheet of Amanda Airlines appears below:

Common stock, ₹5 par, 50,000 shares issued, 40,000 outstanding	₹ (a)
Additional paid-in capital	(b)
Total contributed capital	17,00,000
Retained earnings	7,50,000
(d)	(80,000)
Total stockholders' equity	₹ (c)

Required

Fill in missing values a–d and determine the cost per share of the treasury stock.

30. Evaluate Equity

The following is selected financial information for Lee Incorporated:

(in millions)	2013	2012
Average common stockholders' equity	₹3,430.5	₹2,921.6
Dividends declared on common stock	125.5	104.3
Net income	775.9	691.4

Required

a. Calculate the return on equity for Lee Incorporated for 2013 and 2012. Round percentages to one decimal point (i.e., 9.4%).
b. Calculate the dividend payout ratio for 2013 and 2012. Round percentages to one decimal point (i.e., 9.4%).
c. Compare the financial performance for the two years and comment on which year was more successful, based on these measures, and possible reasons why.

31. Evaluate Equity

Laura's Boutique is trying to calculate different financial measures to analyze its performance. Net income for the year was ₹80 million. There are 150 million shares issued and 125 million shares outstanding.

Required

a. Calculate earnings per share for the year.
b. Interpret the results of this calculation. What could the company possibly do to improve this financial measure?

32. Evaluate Equity

Kristi's Kites provided the following information from its financial statements:

Net income	₹1,64,500
Average number of common shares outstanding	2,35,000
Average stockholders' equity	₹5,76,000

Required:

Calculate the earnings per share and return on equity for Kristi's Kites. Round percentages to one decimal point (i.e., 9.4%). How are the two profitability ratios different?

33. Evaluate Equity

Kay Company's stock on the last day of the year was ₹39. Kay reported dividends per share of ₹0.49 and total dividends of ₹6,37,000 on its statement of stockholders' equity. Net income for the year was ₹40,00,000. The average number of common shares outstanding is 13,00,000.

Required:

a. Calculate the dividend payout ratio and the dividend yield for Kay Company. Round percentages to one decimal point (i.e., 9.4%).
b. Where do you find dividends paid in the statement of cash flows?

34. Accounting Terms

The following is a list of terms and definitions associated with equity:

1. Preemptive right
2. Sole proprietorship
3. Right to dividends
4. Public corporation
5. Right to residual assets
6. Par value
7. Right to vote
8. Contributed capital

a. Ensures that stockholders receive a proper portion of assets upon liquidation.
b. Ensures that stockholders can participate in the company they own.
c. Ensures that stockholders can maintain their ownership percentage when new shares are issued.
d. Ensures that stockholders receive a proper portion of dividends paid.
e. An arbitrary value that determines an entity's legal capital.
f. A corporation whose stock is available to the public at large.
g. A form of business with one owner.
h. The equity generated through the sale of capital stock.

Required

Match each term with the appropriate definition.

35. Accounting Terms

The following is a list of terms and definitions associated with equity:

1. Treasury stock
2. Cumulative
3. Stock split
4. Dividend
5. Stock dividend
6. Non-cumulative
7. Authorized shares
8. Preferred stock

a. The number of shares the corporate charter allows a company to issue.
b. A form of capital stock that receives certain priorities over common stock.
c. A company's own common stock that has been issued to an investor, repurchased by the company, and is being held by the company for future use.
d. A distribution to owners.
e. A type of preferred stock that grants to stockholders preference for current-year dividends only.
f. A type of preferred stock that grants to stockholders preference to current-year dividends as well as all unpaid dividends from prior years.
g. A distribution of a company's own common stock to existing stockholders.
h. This increases a company's shares of stock according to some specified ratio.

Required
Match each term with the appropriate definition.

PROBLEMS

36. Recording and Reporting Equity

Camp Corporation had the following balances in its stockholders' equity at January 1:

Common stock, ₹2 par value, 450,000 shares issued	₹ 9,00,000
Additional paid-in capital	12,00,000
Retained earnings	22,25,000
Treasury stock, at cost, 8,000 shares	(48,000)

During the year, Camp Corporation had the following transactions related to stockholders' equity:

Mar. 1 Issued 2,00,000 shares of common stock for cash at ₹8 per share.

July 1 Declared a 10% stock dividend, payable August 1. The stock was trading at ₹7 per share on July 1.

Aug. 15 Declared a ₹0.50 per share cash dividend to stockholders of record on September 1, payable September 15.

Oct. 1 Bought back 6,000 shares of common stock for ₹45,000.

In addition to the above transactions, assume that during the year Camp generated net income of ₹5,20,000.

Required

a. Prepare the journal entries to record the four transactions.
b. Post all necessary items to a Retained Earnings T-account to update the account. Hint: Do not forget the effect of net income.
c. Prepare Camp's December 31 stockholders' equity section.
d. Using end-of-year outstanding shares, calculate earnings per share for the year.

37. Errors in Equity Transactions

McLelland Industries had the following stockholders' equity balances:

	December 31	January 1
Preferred stock, ₹5 par value, 6,400 shares issued and outstanding	₹ 38,400	₹ 32,000
Common stock, ₹1 par value, 28,200 and 28,000 shares issued, respectively	35,000	28,000
Additional paid-in capital	6,78,000	7,00,000
Retained earnings	80,600	77,000
Treasury stock, at cost, 1,720 and 2,000 shares, respectively	(39,600)	(48,000)

When asked why the company's equity balances changed during the year, McLelland provided the following explanations:

Preferred stock—The market value of the shares rose during the year from ₹5 to ₹6. The increase was placed in an Investment in Preferred Stock account.

Common stock—The issuance of 200 shares for cash was recorded entirely in the account.

Additional paid-in capital—Cash dividends paid during the year were subtracted from this account.

Retained earnings—Net income of ₹12,000 was added to the account during the closing process. Also, the stock dividend taken from treasury stock (see below) was subtracted from the account.

Treasury stock—A 1% common stock dividend (280 shares when the market price was ₹30) was recorded using only the retained earnings and treasury stock accounts. The dividend was declared and distributed on the same day, so one entry was made.

Required

a. Identify all errors in McLelland's treatment and prepare the incorrect entries that McLelland most likely made.
b. Prepare, if necessary, the correct entries that McLelland should have made.
c. Prepare a corrected stockholders' equity section as of December 31.

38. Evaluating Equity

The following are financial measures from the financial statements of Brown Buildings for the past two years:

	2013	2012
Total assets	₹42,55,350	₹38,95,700
Total liabilities	20,50,150	19,80,300
Total stockholders' equity	22,05,200	19,15,400

Required

a. Conduct a horizontal analysis of Brown Buildings. Comment on your findings and possible reasons for these findings.
b. Conduct a vertical analysis for both years for Brown Buildings. Compare and briefly interpret the results of the two years.

39. Evaluating Equity

Olson Outlet Malls is trying to determine if its equity is comparable to other malls in the area.

	2013	2012
Total assets	₹13,74,000	₹15,06,000
Total liabilities	₹ 5,88,000	₹ 7,32,000
Total stockholders' equity	₹ 7,86,000	₹ 7,74,000
Net income	₹ 1,98,500	
Average number of common shares outstanding	2,66,000	
Average stockholders' equity	₹ 7,80,000	
Market price of stock	₹ 21	
Total dividends	₹ 59,000	
Dividends per share	₹ 0.223	

Required

a. Conduct horizontal and vertical analyses for Olson. Round percentages to one decimal point (i.e., 9.4%).
b. Calculate the earnings per share and return on equity. Round percentages to one decimal point (i.e., 9.4%).
c. Calculate the dividend payout ratio and the dividend yield. Round percentages to one decimal point (i.e., 9.4%).
d. Interpret the results of your calculations.

CASES

40. Research and Analysis

Access the 2012–13 annual report for **Emami Limited** by clicking on the *Company Information* and *Financial Information* links at www.emamiltd.in.

Required

1. Examine the company's balance sheet and conduct horizontal and vertical analyses of the company's total shareholders' equity. Round percentages to one decimal point (i.e., 9.4%).
2. Calculate the company's 2012–13 return on equity ratio. Using the dividend and price data, calculate the company's 2012–13 dividend yield from cash dividends assuming that an investor purchased the stock at the low price during the first quarter of 2012–13. Round percentages to one decimal point (i.e., 9.4%).
3. Examine the company's statement of retained earnings and determine the value of bonus dividends, if any, declared during 2010.
4. Examine the financing activities section of the company's statement of cash flows. How would you characterize the company's activity over the past three years?
5. Based on your answers above, write a paragraph explaining your opinion of Emami Ltd 2012–13 equity position. Use your answers as supporting facts.

41. Research and Analysis

Access the 2012–13 annual report for **Sun Pharma** by clicking on the *INVESTOR INFORMATION, SEC FILINGS,* and *ANNUAL REPORTS* links at www.sunpharma.com.

Required

a. Conduct horizontal and vertical analyses of the equity accounts of the company. Round percentages to one decimal point (i.e., 9.4%).
b. Calculate the following ratios for the company: return on equity; earnings per share; dividend payout ratio; and dividend yield. Use dividends paid for dividend ratios. Also, use the 2011–12 year ending stock price for the dividend yield calculation. Round percentages to one decimal point (i.e., 9.4%).
c. Evaluate the information in (a) and (b). Would this be a company in which you would want to invest?

42. Entrepreneurial Decision Making

Jeff Blake is an entrepreneur and owner of Wood Creations, a sole proprietorship. The business, which manufactures tables, chairs, cabinets, and other furniture, is growing, and Jeff is exploring the idea of purchasing a brand new manufacturing facility. Because he does not have the money to do so, he believes his options are to borrow the money or to convert the business to a corporation and sell stock.

Required

Describe the decision that you think Jeff should make. Make sure to explain the advantages and disadvantages of the course of action that you choose.

43. Written Communication

A friend of yours has e-mailed you to ask for some investing advice. He is considering buying stock in a certain company and is trying to determine whether he wants to invest in the company's common or preferred stock.

Required

Draft an e-mail to your friend explaining to him the similarities and differences between common and preferred stock. Include reasons why you feel one might be more preferable over the other.

reviewcard CHAPTER 10 Stockholders' Equity

Learning Objectives		Key Concepts
LO1	Describe the characteristics of the corporate form of business.	The corporation is a separate legal entity formed under state law. Advantages include the limited liability of the owners, the ability to raise capital by the sale of stock to investors, and the ease of transferring ownership by selling one's stock. Disadvantages include double taxation and increased regulation.
LO2	Describe the characteristics of common stock and how it is recorded and reported.	Common stock is the basic form of capital stock that is issued for ownership in a corporation. Shares held by entities other than the corporation are called outstanding shares. Most common stock has a par value, which is an arbitrary value that determines an entity's legal capital. When recording common stock, the common stock account is increased for the par value of the stock, while the additional paid-in capital account or share premium is increased by the excess paid over par value. The balances associated with common stock are reported in the stockholders' equity section of the balance sheet.
LO3	Understand cash dividends, stock dividends, and stock splits.	A cash dividend is a distribution of earnings to the owners in the form of cash. A stock dividend is a distribution of a company's own common stock to existing shareholders. Small stock dividends are recorded at market value, while large stock dividends are recorded at par value. A stock split is the decrease or increase in the number of shares authorized, issued, and outstanding through some specified ratio, such as 2-for-1.
LO4	Describe the characteristics of preferred stock and how it receives preference in dividends.	Preferred stock is a form of capital stock that receives priorities over common stock. Most preferred stock relinquishes the right to vote in exchange for preference to dividends and residual assets. Preferred stock is recorded in a similar manner as common stock and is reported in the stockholders' equity section of the balance sheet.

Key Definitions

Authorized shares The number of shares of stock that a company can legally issue.

Cash dividend A distribution of cash to stockholders.

Common stock The most common type of capital stock.

Contributed capital The amount of capital raised by issuing stock to investors in exchange for an ownership claim on company assets.

Cost method A method of recording the purchase of treasury stock at its cost of acquisition.

Cumulative preferred stock Stock that carries the right to receive current-year dividends and all unpaid dividends from prior years before dividends are paid to common stockholders.

Date of declaration The date on which a corporation's board of directors declares a dividend.

Date of record The date that determines who receives a dividend; the stock's owner on the date of record receives the dividend.

Dividend A distribution of profits to a corporation's owners.

Dividend payout ratio A comparison of a company's dividends to its earnings that measures the percentage of current earnings distributed to owners.

Dividend yield ratio A comparison of dividends per share to the market price per share of stock that measures the percentage return from dividends.

Dividends in arrears The accumulated value of unpaid prior-year dividends.

Earnings per share A comparison of a company's net income to the number of shares of common stock outstanding that measures the ability to generate equity through profitable operations.

Issued shares The number of shares a company has distributed to owners to date.

Noncumulative preferred stock Stock that carries the right to receive current-year dividends only.

Learning Objectives		Key Concepts
LO5	Describe the characteristics of treasury stock and how it is recorded and reported.	Treasury stock is common stock that has been repurchased by the company. Treasury stock is recorded at cost. Because the treasury stock account represents the amount of capital returned to shareholders, it is reported in the stockholders' equity section of the balance sheet as a negative number.
LO6	Evaluate equity through the calculation and interpretation of horizontal, vertical, and ratio analyses.	Earnings per share shows a company's profitability per share of stock outstanding and is easily comparable across different companies. Return on equity shows the ability of a company to effectively use capital provided by stockholders to generate income. The dividend payout ratio shows what percentage of earnings is distributed to owners. The dividend yield shows the percentage return dividends provide on an investment in the company's stock.

Key Definitions (continued)

Outstanding shares The number of shares that have been issued and are still held by someone other than the issuing company.

Par value An arbitrary value that determines an entity's legal capital.

Payment date The date on which a dividend will be distributed.

Preferred stock A form of capital stock that receives one or more priorities over common stock.

Return on equity A comparison of a company's net income to total stockholders' equity that measures the ability to use existing equity to generate additional equity.

Stock dividend A distribution of a company's common stock to existing stockholders.

Stock split An increase in a company's shares of stock according to some specified ratio.

Treasury stock Common stock that a company reacquires from its stockholders.

Key Formulas

Earnings per Share	$\dfrac{\text{Net Income}}{\text{Average Number of Common Shares Outstanding}}$
Average Common Shares Outstanding	$\dfrac{\text{Beginning shares outstanding} + \text{Ending shares outstanding}}{2}$
Return on Equity	$\dfrac{\text{Net Income}}{\text{Average Stockholders' Equity}}$
Average Equity	$\dfrac{\text{Beginning equity} + \text{Ending equity}}{2}$
Dividend Payout Ratio	$\dfrac{\text{Dividends}}{\text{Net Income}}$ or $\dfrac{\text{Dividends per Share}}{\text{Earnings per Share}}$
Dividend Yield	$\dfrac{\text{Dividends per share}}{\text{Market Price per share}}$
Horizontal Analysis	$\text{Percentage change in account balance} = \dfrac{\text{Rupee change}}{\text{Prior-year balance}}$
Vertical Analysis	*For the Balance Sheet*: $\text{Percentage} = \dfrac{\text{Account Balance}}{\text{Total Assets}}$ or *For the Income Statement*: $\dfrac{\text{Account Balance}}{\text{Net Sales or Revenue}}$
Stock Dividend	If Small: Outstanding Shares × Percentage × Market Value If Large: Outstanding Shares × Percentage × Par Value

Statement of Cash Flows

Learning Objectives

After studying the material in this chapter, you should be able to:

LO1 Describe the purpose and format of the statement of cash flows.

LO2 Describe the process of preparing the statement of cash flows.

LO3 Prepare the operating activities section of the statement of cash flows using the direct method.

LO4 Prepare the operating activities section of the statement of cash flows using the indirect method.

LO5 Prepare the investing activities section of the statement of cash flows.

LO6 Prepare the financing activities section of the statement of cash flows.

LO7 Evaluate the statement of cash flows through the calculation and interpretation of ratio analyses.

Introduction

As discussed in Chapter 1, the statement of cash flows provides information on how a company generates and distributes cash over a period of time. This chapter examines the purpose and format of the statement of cash flows and also demonstrates how the statement is prepared. The chapter concludes with an analysis of how to use the statement to generate useful information about a company and its cash.

LO1 The Statement of Cash Flows

One of the most important resources of any company is cash. If a company cannot generate sufficient cash, its ability to continue operations is significantly limited. As a result, management, investors, and creditors want to know how a company is managing its cash. How did the company use its cash? How did it generate cash? What are the prospects of the company paying a cash dividend? Will the company be able to satisfy its upcoming interest and loan obligations? Does the company have enough cash to expand its manufacturing facilities? Answers to these and other questions can be found through an examination of the statement of cash flows.

The **statement of cash flows** is a financial statement that summarizes a company's inflows and outflows of cash over a period of time. Its purpose is to inform users on how and why a company's cash changed during the period. So that it is as informative as possible, the statement groups and reports cash flows in three major categories: operating, investing, and financing. Cash flows from each of the three categories are then combined to determine the company's net change in cash and cash equivalents. This net change will be equal to the difference between the beginning and ending cash and cash equivalents balances from the balance sheet. Note that from this point forward, the term *cash* will be used to represent cash and cash equivalents.

Statement of cash flows A financial statement that summarizes a company's inflows and outflows of cash over a period of time with a purpose to inform users on how and why a company's cash changed during the period.

CHAPTER 11

One of the keys to success for a company like Under Armour is to convert its merchandise into cash.

The basic structure of the statement is as follows:

Cash Flows Provided (Used) by Operating Activities
+/− Cash Flows Provided (Used) by Investing Activities
+/− Cash Flows Provided (Used) by Financing Activities
Net Increase (Decrease) in Cash
+ Cash, Beginning of Year
Cash, End of Year

The following sections discuss the three groupings of cash flows. For illustration purposes, Exhibit 11-1 contains Tata Steel's statement of cash flows for the year ending March 31, 2013. All rupee amounts are in crores.

Exhibit 11-1 Tata Steel Hundred and sixth annual report 2012–13

Cash Flow Statement for the year ended March 31, 2013

			₹ **crores**
		Year ended 31.03.2013	Year ended 31.03.2012
A. Cash Flow from Operating Activities:			
Profit before tax		7,836.60	9,857.35
Adjustments for:			
Depreciation and amortization expense	1,640.38		1,151.44
Impairment of fixed assets	4.01		6.90
(Profit)/Loss on assets sold/discarded	3.00		52.98
Provision for diminution in the value of investments	90.13		—
Provision for doubtful advances in the nature of loans	610.63		—
Profit on sale of noncurrent investments	(12.33)		(511.01)
(Gain)/Loss on cancellation of forwards, swaps and options	127.93		41.92
Interest and income from current investments	(330.62)		(863.83)
Income from noncurrent investments	(702.35)		(117.50)
Finance costs	1,876.77		1,925.42
Provision for wealth tax	2.00		1.70
Exchange (gain)/loss on revaluation of foreign currency loans and swaps	440.75		283.59
		3,750.30	1,971.61
Operating Profit before Working Capital Changes		**11,586.90**	11,828.96
Adjustments for:			
Trade and other receivables	873.33		1,512.79
Inventories	(398.95)		(905.23)
Trade payables and other liabilities	987.33		1,106.58
		1,461.71	1,714.14
Cash Generated from Operations		**13,048.61**	13,543.10
Direct tax paid		**(1,979.94)**	(3,119.25)
Net Cash Flow from/(used in) Operating Activities		**11,068.67**	10,423.85
B. Cash Flow from Investing Activities:			
Purchase of fixed assets[2]	(7,508.55)		(7,059.20)
Sale of fixed assets	14.51		9.19
Purchase of investments in Subsidiaries[3]	(2,123.81)		(2,541.97)
Purchase of other noncurrent investments	(255.41)		(55.36)
Sale of non-current investments	0.87		—
Sale/Redemption of investments in subsidiaries	231.32		576.10
(Purchase)/Sale of current investments (net)	991.70		2,226.19
Inter-corporate deposits/Shareholders' loan given	(127.30)		(585.93)
Repayment of inter-corporate deposits/shareholders' loan	50.00		4,006.87
Interest received	59.09		447.50
Dividend received	145.18		117.50
Net Cash Flow from/(used in) Investing Activities		**(8,522.40)**	(2,859.11)
			Year ended 31.03.2012
C. Cash Flow from Financing Activities:			
Issue of Equity Shares	0.02		534.60
Capital contributions received	5.58		13.02
Proceeds from Hybrid Perpetual Securities	—		775.00
Proceeds from borrowings	6,087.61		2,317.43
Repayment of borrowings	(7,181.00)		(8,212.56)
Amount received/(paid) on cancellation of forwards, swaps and options	(122.81)		(31.82)
Expenses (incurred)/reimbursed on issue of equity instruments	2.40		(16.79)
Distribution on Hybrid Perpetual Securities	(265.76)		(222.47)
Interest paid[2]	(1,456.42)		(1,592.85)
Dividend paid	(1,165.46)		(1,151.06)
Tax on dividend paid	(185.75)		(179.23)
Net Cash Flow from/(used in) Financing Activities		**(4,281.59)**	(7,766.73)
Net increase/(decrease) in cash and cash Equivalents		**(1,735.32)**	(201.99)
Opening Cash and Cash Equivalents		**3,900.53**	4,102.52
		2,165.21	3,900.53

One of the most important resources of any company is cash. If a company cannot generate sufficient cash, its ability to continue operations is significantly limited.

Cash Flows from Operating Activities

Cash flows provided (used) by operating activities are those cash inflows and outflows arising from the company's operations. These inflows and outflows are sometimes called operating cash flows and would include the following:

- Cash inflows from sales or services
- Cash outflows for operating items such as inventory purchases, salaries, insurance, and supplies

Basically, any cash flow associated with a company's revenues or expenses should be considered an operating cash flow. Because of this, the net cash flow from operating activities can be thought of as net income on a cash basis.

Operating cash flows are reported first on the statement of cash flows. Like most companies, Tata Steel reports operating cash flows using the indirect method. The indirect method calculates operating cash flows by adjusting net income from an accrual basis to a cash basis. This calculation will be demonstrated in a later section. For now, you should simply note that many of the adjustments in Exhibit 11-1 involve accounts associated with operations—depreciation expense, accounts receivable, inventory, accounts payable, and income taxes. Tata Steel generated ₹11,068.67 crore of cash from operations in 2012–13.

Cash Flows from Investing Activities

Cash flows provided (used) by investing activities are those cash inflows and outflows arising from the acquisition and disposal of non-current assets. They are often called investing cash flows and would include the following:

- Cash inflows from the sale of property, facilities, equipment, or investments
- Cash outflows for the purchase of property, facilities, equipment, or investments

Investing cash flows are reported after operating activities. Exhibit 11-1 reveals that Tata Steel experienced net cash outflows from investing activities of over ₹(8,522.40) crore. The main reason for the negative cash flow was purchase of ₹7,508.55 crore of fixed assets and ₹7,508.55 crore of investments in subsidiary. In fact, in each of the years presented, the bulk of Tata Steel's net investing cash outflows resulted from these purchases. This makes sense for a company that is growing.

Cash Flows from Financing Activities

Cash flows provided (used) by financing activities are those cash inflows and outflows associated with the generation and return of capital. These are often called financing cash flows and would include the following:

- Cash inflows from borrowings or stock issuances
- Cash outflows to satisfy debt obligations or to repurchase treasury stock
- Cash outflows for dividends to stockholders

Basically, any cash flows associated with debt or equity (other than interest and dividend received) are considered to be financing cash flows.

Financing cash flows are reported after investing cash flows. Exhibit 11-1 reveals that Tata Steel had ₹(4,281.59) crore cash flow in 2012–13 from financing activities. The majority of that net outflow was due to repayment of borrowings. According to the statement, Tata Steel repaid borrowings of ₹(7,181.00) crore during the year.

Cash flows provided (used) by operating activities Cash inflows and outflows arising from the company's operations; sometimes called operating cash flows.

Cash flows provided (used) by investing activities Cash inflows and outflows arising from the acquisition and disposal of non-current assets; often called investing cash flows.

Cash flows provided (used) by financing activities Cash inflows and outflows associated with the generation and return of capital; often called financing cash flows.

Net Increase (Decrease) in Cash

After a company reports its operating, investing, and financing cash flows, it sums the three and reconciles the company's beginning and ending cash balances. The following is a condensed version of Tata Steel's statement of cash flows, showing only the major subtotals:

Tata Steel's 2012–13 Condensed Statement of Cash Flows

(in crores)	March 31, 2013	March 31, 2012	March 31, 2011
Net Cash from Operating Activities	₹ 11,068.67	₹10,423.85	₹8,542.72
Net Cash used in Investing Activities	(13,288.13)	(2,859.11)	(13,288.13)
Net Cash from Financing Activities	(4,281.59)	(7,766.73)	5,652.81
Net increase (decrease) in Cash and Cash equivalents	(1,735.32)	(201.99)	907.4
Opening Cash and Cash equivalents	3,900.53	4,102.52	3,234.14
Closing Cash and Cash equivalents	₹ 2,165.21	₹ 3,900.53	₹4,141.54

Tata Steel's net decrease in cash during 2012–13 was over ₹1,735.32 crore. This decrease is due to cash outflow on account of investing, and financing activities. Adding to the 2012–13 balance of ₹ (1,735.32) crore to the beginning balance of cash of ₹3,900.53 crore yields the 2012–13 year-end balance in cash of ₹2,165.21 crore. Both the ₹3,900.53 crore and ₹2,165.21 crore can be found in the Tata Steel 2012 and 2013 balance sheet.

Additional Disclosures

All publicly traded companies prepare the statement of cash flows using a format similar to what has been described. In some cases, companies must also make one or both of the following two disclosures.

- Significant non-cash investing or financing activities
- Cash paid for interest and taxes

The first disclosure relates to significant investing or financing transactions in which no cash is exchanged. Examples would include the purchase of property through the issuance of mortgage debt, the conversion of long-term debt into common stock, or in some countries payment of dividends by the issuance of stock. Even though such transactions do not involve cash, they are important for properly understanding a company's cash flows. Therefore, they are disclosed either on the face of the statement or in the notes to the financial statements. Armour USA makes the following disclosures on its statement of cash flows.

The only significant non-cash activity reported in by Armour, USA in 2010 is the purchase of property and equipment through certain obligations. While the schedule does not provide further explanation on the nature of the obligations, it does reveal that the company acquired over $3 million in fixed assets by creating future obligations rather than paying cash.

Under Armour's 2010 Disclosures of Non-Cash Financing and Investing Activities

(in thousands)	2010	2009	2008
Purchase of property and equipment through certain obligations	$2,922	$4,784	$2,486
Purchase of intangible assets through certain obligations	—	2,105	—

The second disclosure relates to interest and taxes. When a company uses the indirect method to report operating cash flows, in some countries the amount of interest and taxes paid are not shown on the statement. However, accounting standards require that companies disclose the amount of interest and taxes paid. Companies like Under Armour often disclose this information at the bottom of their statements of cash flows. The final two rows of Under Armour's statement are as follows.

Under Armour's 2010 Disclosure of Interest and Taxes Paid

	2010	2009	2008
Cash paid for income taxes	$38,773	$40,834	$29,561
Cash paid for interest	992	1,273	1,444

In India interest and taxes paid are shown in the cash flow statement as one can see in Exhibit 11-1.

LO2 Preparing the Statement of Cash Flows

Chapter 4 discussed the preparation of the income statement, the statement of retained earnings, and the balance sheet. Each of these statements is prepared with numbers from an adjusted trial balance. That is, they are prepared by rearranging numbers already provided by the accounting system.

The preparation of the statement of cash flows is different. First, information is collected from a variety

MAKING IT REAL

Having positive cash flows gives companies flexibility to do many different things. For one company, it recently resulted in a "first" in its history.

Cisco Systems Inc. was founded in 1984. Over the 25+ years of its existence, it had never paid a cash dividend to its stockholders, choosing instead to use its cash to grow its business. However, due in part to its solid cash position and healthy cash flows, that all changed in 2011. On March 18, 2011, Cisco's Board of Directors approved the initiation of quarterly cash dividends to its shareholders. The company further stated that the dividend would be the first to be paid to stockholders in the company's history. The dividend was set at $.06 per share.

Eimantas Buzas/Shutterstock

Source: http://newsroom.cisco.com/press-release-content?type=webcontent&articleId=5967558.

MARUTI SUZUKI ANALYSIS

Look at Maruti Suzuki's Statement of Cash Flows in Appendix C. In the most recent year, what were the company's net cash flows from operating, investing, and financing activities? Also, what amount of cash was paid for capital expenditures and dividends in the most recent year? Finally, how much did the company pay in income taxes in the most recent year?

In the most recent year, Maruti Suzuki generated net cash flows of ₹43,842 million from operating activities and net cash flows of ₹(35,741) from investing activities and (9,663) million from financing activities. During the most recent year, the company paid ₹38,549 million for capital expenditures, ₹2,167 million for dividends, and ₹5,333 million for income taxes.

of sources. Second, preparing the statement requires an examination of the changes in all non-cash accounts. To understand why, consider the fundamental accounting equation:

$$\text{Assets} = \text{Liabilities} + \text{Equity}$$

Cash can be isolated by breaking it out from other assets to yield the following:

$$\text{Cash} + \text{Non-Cash Assets} = \text{Liabilities} + \text{Equity}$$

Moving non-cash assets from the left side of the equation to the right side then results in the following:

$$\text{Cash} = \text{Liabilities} + \text{Equity} - \text{Non-Cash Assets}$$

Using Δ to denote a change, this equation can also be rewritten to show that the change in cash for a given period is equal to the changes in all other non-cash accounts (liabilities, equity, and non-cash assets):

$$\Delta\,\text{Cash} = \Delta\,\text{Liabilities} + \Delta\,\text{Equity} - \Delta\,\text{Non-cash Assets}$$

As a result, to explain a company's change in cash, you must explain the changes in the company's non-cash accounts. And to do that, you need the following three items:

- A comparative balance sheet
- An income statement
- Additional information on changes in account balances

A comparative balance sheet provides the beginning and ending balances of all non-cash accounts, from which changes for the period are calculated. An income statement provides a company's revenue and expense balances for the period. These balances are used to prepare the operating activities section of the statement of cash flows. Additional information on changes in account balances is needed to determine if a balance changed because of non-cash activity. For example, the issuance of stock to satisfy a debt obligation changes both equity and liability balances, but cash is not affected. Knowledge of such significant non-cash transactions keeps one from erroneously concluding that the company received cash for the issuance of stock and paid cash for the retirement of the debt.

Direct method Method of reporting cash flows from operating activities in which cash inflows and outflows from operations are reported separately on the statement of cash flows.

Indirect method Method of reporting cash flows from operating activities in which net income is adjusted from an accrual basis to a cash basis.

To explain a company's change in cash, you must explain the changes in the company's non-cash accounts.

Direct and Indirect Methods for Operating Cash Flows

When preparing the statement of cash flows, all companies report cash flows from operating, investing, and financing activities. The manner in which cash flows from investing and financing activities are reported is the same for all companies. However, companies can report their cash flows from operating activities using one of two methods:

- Direct Method
- Indirect Method

Under the **direct method**, a company calculates and reports its cash inflows from operations followed by its cash outflows for operations. Typically, cash outflows are broken out into a few categories including cash payments for inventory, operating expenses, interest, and taxes. The difference between inflows and outflows is the company's net cash flow from operating activities. The method is called "direct" because both inflows and outflows are shown directly on the statement.

Under the **indirect method**, a company reports its cash flows from operating activities by adjusting its net income from an accrual basis to a cash basis. The method is called "indirect" because it does not directly report cash inflows and cash outflows from operations. Rather, it reports the adjustments necessary to convert net income to the net cash flow from operating activities. Adjustments typically arise from non-cash revenues and expenses and/or changes in current assets and current liabilities.

Both the indirect and direct methods will yield the same net cash flows from operating activities. The only difference between the methods is the manner in which cash flows are reported. Because in some countries accounting standards require that companies using the direct method must also disclose their cash flows under the indirect method, the vast majority of companies choose the indirect method.

The vast majority of publicly traded companies use the **indirect method** to report cash flows from operating activities.

Exhibit 11-2 Hardin Supply Company Financial Statements

Hardin Supply Company
Income Statement
For the Year Ending December 31, 2012
(in thousands)

Sales		$432
Cost of goods sold		281
Gross profit		$151
Operating expenses:		
Depreciation expense	$25	
Insurance expense	14	
Salaries expense	63	
Utilities expense	28	130
Operating income		$ 21
Gain on sale of equipment		1
Income before taxes		$ 22
Income tax expense		8
Net income		$ 14

Hardin Supply Company
Comparative Balance Sheet
December 31, 2012

	2012	2011
Cash and cash equivalents	$ 18	$ 45
Accounts receivable	45	41
Inventory	101	92
Prepaid insurance	11	15
Total current assets	175	193
Long-term investments	22	0
Equipment, at cost	232	166
Less: Accumulated depreciation	(57)	(37)
Total assets	$372	$322
Accounts payable	$ 37	$ 29
Salaries payable	21	21
Utilities payable	27	22
Taxes payable	0	7
Total current liabilities	85	79
Long-term debt	45	0
Total liabilities	130	79
Common stock	165	165
Retained earnings	87	78
Treasury stock	(10)	0
Total stockholders' equity	242	243
Total liabilities and stockholders' equity	$372	$322

Example Data

To demonstrate how to prepare a statement of cash flows, the information for Hardin Supply Company, USA in Exhibit 11-2 will be used. Note that Hardin provides both an income statement and a comparative balance sheet and that all numbers are in thousands. For simplicity, references to thousands will be omitted in the discussions. Additional information will be provided as needed.

LO3 Reporting Cash Flows from Operating Activities—Direct Method

This section demonstrates the calculation of cash flows from operating activities under the direct method.

When reporting operating cash flows under the direct method, companies calculate and report cash receipts from operating activities and cash payments for operating activities. Cash receipts are calculated by converting revenues from the income statement to cash collections. Cash payments are calculated by converting expenses from the income statement to cash payments.

The following sections demonstrate this conversion process. The first section considers cash receipts from customers. The next sections consider cash payments in three main groups: cash paid for inventory, for operating expenses, and for income taxes. For each calculation, two approaches are demonstrated—one focusing on the changes in account balances and another using a debit/credit approach.

Cash Received from Customers

Hardin's income statement shows that the company generated $432 in sales during the year. To determine cash receipts from those sales, the balance sheet account related to sales—accounts receivable—must be examined.

Hardin's balance sheet shows that accounts receivable increased $4 during the year. The accounts receivable account increases when sales are made but no cash is collected. Therefore, a $4 increase means that $4 of Hardin's $432 of sales were not collected during the year. Therefore, cash collections were $428.

Sales for the period	$432
Less: Increase in accounts receivable	4
Cash collected from sales	$428

Note that had Hardin's accounts receivable decreased during the year, the decrease would have been added to sales.

The conversion of sales to cash collections can be summarized as follows:

Balance from Income Statement	Adjustment	Balance for Statement of Cash Flows
Sales	− Increase in accounts receivable or + Decrease in accounts receivable	= Cash collected from sales

A second approach for calculating cash receipts from sales is to prepare the journal entry that Hardin would hypothetically make if it recorded its annual sales and the change in receivables in only one entry.

Given sales of $432, Hardin would credit Sales for $432. Hardin would also debit Accounts Receivable for $4 to reflect the increase in the account. To balance the entry, Hardin would debit Cash for $428. Thus, cash collections from sales are $428.

Hypothetical Entry	Accounts Receivable	4	
	Cash	428	
	Sales		432

Cash Paid for Inventory

Hardin's income statement shows that the company had $281 of cost of goods sold during the year. To convert this expense to cash paid for inventory, Hardin must first calculate total purchases for the period and then calculate the cash paid for those purchases.

To calculate purchases, Hardin must examine the inventory account. Inventory increased by $9 during the year. An increase in inventory means that Hardin bought more inventory than it sold. Therefore, Hardin must have purchased $290 of inventory during the year.

Inventory sold during the period	$281
Plus: Increase in inventory	9
Inventory purchased during the period	$290

Note that had Hardin's inventory decreased during the year, the decrease would have been subtracted from inventory to calculate purchases.

To calculate cash paid for these purchases, Hardin must examine accounts payable. Accounts payable increased $8 during the year. The accounts payable account increases when purchases are made but no cash is paid. Therefore, Hardin must have paid for only $282 of its $290 in purchases.

Inventory purchased during the period	$290
Less: Increase in accounts payable	8
Cash paid to suppliers for the period	$282

Note that had Hardin's accounts payable decreased during the year, the decrease would have been added to purchases to calculate cash paid.

The conversion of cost of goods sold to cash paid for inventory can be summarized as shown on the next page.

Cash paid for inventory can also be determined by preparing the entry that Hardin would hypothetically make to record the activity in the cost of goods sold, inventory, and accounts payable accounts.

Given cost of goods sold of $281, Hardin would debit Cost of Goods Sold for $281. Hardin would also debit Inventory $9 for its increase during the year and credit Accounts Payable $8 for its increase during the year. To balance the entry, Hardin would credit Cash for $282. Thus, cash paid for inventory is $282.

Balance from Income Statement	Adjustment		Adjustment	Balance for Statement of Cash Flows
Cost of goods sold	+ Increase in inventory or − Decrease in inventory	= Purchases	− Increase in accounts payable or + Decrease in accounts payable	= Cash paid for inventory

Hypothetical Entry			
	Cost of Goods Sold	281	
	Inventory	9	
	Accounts Payable		8
	Cash		282

Cash Paid for Operating Expenses

Hardin's income statement shows several operating expenses. The following sections demonstrate how operating expenses are converted to cash paid. The first section illustrates an expense related to a current asset. The second section illustrates two expenses relating to current liabilities.

Insurance Expense Hardin's income statement shows $14 of insurance expense during the year. To determine the cash paid for insurance, the related balance sheet account—prepaid insurance—must be examined.

Prepaid insurance decreased $4, meaning that Hardin used $4 of insurance it had purchased in a previous period. As a result, cash paid for insurance in the current period was only $10.

Insurance expense for the period	$14
Less: Decrease in prepaid insurance	4
Cash paid for insurance	$10

Note that had Hardin's prepaid insurance increased during the year, the increase would have been added to insurance expense.

The conversion of insurance expense to cash paid for insurance is summarized at the bottom of this page.

Using the entry approach to calculate cash payments for insurance, Hardin would debit Insurance Expense for $14 and credit Prepaid Insurance for $4. Cash would then be credited to balance the entry, showing cash payments for insurance to be $10.

Hypothetical Entry			
	Insurance Expense	14	
	Prepaid Insurance		4
	Cash		10

Salaries Expense and Utilities Expense Hardin's income statement shows $63 of salaries expense and $28 of utilities expense during the year. To determine the cash paid for these operating expenses, the related balance sheet accounts—salaries payable and utilities payable—must be examined.

Salaries payable did not change during the year, so Hardin must have paid exactly $63 to employees.

Salaries expense for the period	$63
Change in salaries payable	0
Cash paid to employees	$63

Balance from Income Statement	Adjustment	Balance for Statement of Cash Flows
Insurance expense	+ Increase in prepaid insurance or − Decrease in prepaid insurance	= Cash paid for insurance

Utilities payable increased $5 during the year, meaning that Hardin incurred utilities during the year for which it did not pay. Therefore, Hardin paid only $23 for utilities during the year.

Utilities expense for the period	$28
Less: Increase in utilities payable	5
Cash paid for utilities	$23

Note that had Hardin's utilities payable decreased during the year, the decrease would have been added to utilities expense.

The conversion of these operating expenses to cash paid for salaries and utilities can be summarized as follows:

Balance from Income Statement	Adjustment	Balance for Statement of Cash Flows
Salaries expense	− Increase in salaries payable or + Decrease in salaries payable	= Cash paid for salaries
Utilities expense	− Increase in utilities payable or + Decrease in utilities payable	= Cash paid for utilities

Using the entry approach to calculate the cash payments for salaries, Hardin would debit Salaries Expense for $63. Nothing is recorded for Salaries Payable because the account balance was unchanged. Cash is then credited to balance the entry, showing cash payments to be $63.

Hypothetical Entry			
	Salaries Expense	63	
	Cash		63

For utilities, Hardin would debit Utilities Expense for $28 and credit Utilities Payable for $5. Cash would be credited to balance the entry, showing cash payments to be $23.

Hypothetical Entry			
	Utilities Expense	28	
	Utilities Payable		5
	Cash		23

Cash Paid for Taxes

Hardin's income statement shows $8 of income tax expense during the year. To determine the cash paid for taxes, the related balance sheet account—taxes payable—must be examined.

IFRS

Under GAAP, cash flows associated with taxes are classified as operating activities. Under IFRS, they are also classified as operating activities unless they can be specially identified with investing or financing activities.

Taxes payable decreased $7 during the year, meaning that Hardin paid not only current-year taxes of $8, but also $7 of prior-year taxes. Thus, taxes paid in this period were $15.

Income tax expense for the period	$ 8
Plus: Decrease in taxes payable	7
Cash paid for taxes	$15

Note that had Hardin's taxes payable increased during the year, the increase would have been subtracted from income tax expense.

The conversion of income tax expense to cash paid for taxes is summarized at the bottom of this page.

To calculate cash payments using the entry method, Hardin would debit Income Tax Expense for $8 and debit Taxes Payable for $7. Cash would be credited to balance the entry, showing cash payments to be $15.

Hypothetical Entry			
	Income Tax Expense	8	
	Taxes Payable	7	
	Cash		15

Balance from Income Statement	Adjustment	Balance for Statement of Cash Flows
Income tax expense	- Increase in taxes payable or + Decrease in taxes payable	= Cash paid for taxes

Other Revenues and Expenses

Hardin's income statement contains two additional items: depreciation expense and gain on sale of equipment. For the following reasons, these items are ignored under the direct method.

Recall from Chapter 8 that depreciation expense is a non-cash charge, meaning that cash is not affected when depreciation is recorded. As a result, depreciation expense is not included when preparing the operating activities section under the direct method. This is always the case.

Recall also from Chapter 8 that a gain on the sale of equipment occurs when cash received from the sale exceeds the equipment's book value. Because the sale of equipment is an investing activity, all cash received from the sale will be reported as a cash inflow from investing activities. As a result, the gain on the sale is not included when preparing the operating activities section under the direct method. The same would be true for a loss on the sale of equipment or any other gain or loss from investing or financing activity.

Net Operating Cash Flows

Based on the previous calculations, Hardin's operating activities section of its statement of cash flows is shown in Exhibit 11-3. A summary of adjustments used to generate the numbers is found in Exhibit 11-4.

Exhibit 11-3 Hardin's Operating Cash Flows Using the Direct Method

Cash flows from operating activities		
Cash receipts from customers		$428
Less cash payments:		
To suppliers	$282	
To employees	63	
For insurance	10	
For utilities	23	
For taxes	15	393
Net cash provided by operating activities		$ 35

The indirect method calculates and reports net cash flows from operating activities by adjusting net income from an accrual basis to a cash basis.

LO4 Reporting Cash Flows from Operating Activities—Indirect Method

This section demonstrates the calculation of cash flows from operating activities under the indirect method.

When reporting operating cash flows under the indirect method, companies calculate and report net cash flows from operating activities by adjusting net income from an accrual basis to a cash basis. This requires many adjustments, but they can be grouped into three main types:

- Non-cash effects on net income
- Gains and losses from investing and/or financing activities
- Changes in current assets and liabilities

The following sections demonstrate these adjustments using the Hardin Supply Company information in Exhibit 11-2.

Exhibit 11-4 Summary of Adjustments Used in the Direct Method

Balance from Income Statement	Adjustment			Balance for Statement of Cash Flows
Sales	− Increase in accounts receivable	OR	+ Decrease in accounts receivable	= Cash collected from sales
Cost of goods sold	+ Increase in inventory	OR	− Decrease in inventory	= Cash paid for inventory
		and		
	− Increase in accounts payable	OR	+ Decrease in accounts payable	
Operating expenses	+ Increase in current asset	OR	− Decrease in current asset	= Cash paid for operations
		or		
	− Increase in current liability	OR	+ Decrease in current liability	
Income tax expense	− Increase in taxes payable	OR	+ Decrease in taxes payable	= Cash paid for taxes

Adjustments for Non-Cash Items

Accrual-based net income often includes expenses that have no related cash consequences. The most common example is depreciation expense, which is an allocation of the historical cost of a fixed asset. While depreciation reduces accrual-based net income, it does not result in any cash payment. Therefore, to adjust net income to a cash basis, the effect of depreciation must be removed from net income. This is accomplished by adding depreciation expense back to net income. Other examples of non-cash expenses are amortization expense, bad debt expense, and impairment losses.

The general adjustment for all non-cash expenses is therefore as follows:

> **Adjustment rule for non-cash expenses**
> Add back to net income all non-cash expenses

Hardin Supply Company's income statement in Exhibit 11-2 shows only one non-cash expense: depreciation expense of $25. Therefore, the $25 would be added back to net income.

Adjustments for Gains and Losses from Investing and Financing Activities

Sometimes, a company's net income will include a gain or loss arising from an investing or financing activity. For example, a company might generate a gain from the sale of equipment or a loss from the sale of an intangible asset. Another company might generate a gain from the early retirement of debt or a loss from a bond redemption.

When such activity occurs, the entire cash inflow associated with the transaction will be reported as either an investing or financing cash flow. As a result, the effect of the gain or loss must be removed from net income so that operating cash flows are not affected by the transaction. Gains must be subtracted from income, and losses must be added back to income.

> **Adjustment rules for gains and losses from investing and financing activities**
> Subtract from net income any gains arising from investing or financing activities
> Add back to net income any losses arising from investing or financing activities

Hardin's income statement shows only one gain or loss from an investing or financing activity: a $1 gain on the sale of equipment. Because the cash received from the sale will be reported as an investing cash flow, the effect of the gain must be removed from income. Therefore, income is reduced by $1.

Adjustments for Current Assets and Current Liabilities

The third type of adjustment involves the changes in a company's current assets and current liabilities. Current assets and current liabilities change during a period because a company's revenues do not equal cash received and its expenses do not equal cash paid.

For example, a change in accounts receivable means that a company's cash collections do not equal its sales revenue. If accounts receivable increases, sales revenue is greater than cash collections. If accounts receivable decreases, cash collections are greater than sales revenue. Likewise, a change in salaries payable means that a company's cash payments do not equal its salaries expense. If salaries payable increases, salaries expense is greater than cash payments. If salaries payable decreases, cash payments are greater than salaries expense.

Because the indirect method adjusts accrual-based income to cash-based income, these differences must be removed from accrual-based net income. That is, the revenues and expenses of net income must be adjusted so that they reflect cash receipts and cash payments. This is accomplished with the following adjustments:

> **Adjustment rules for current assets and current liabilities**
> Add a decrease in current assets to net income
> Subtract an increase in current assets from net income
> Add an increase in current liabilities to net income
> Subtract a decrease in current liabilities from net income

Hardin's balance sheet shows changes in several current assets and current liabilities. The following sections describe the adjustment that each change requires.

Change in Accounts Receivable Hardin's balance sheet shows a $4 increase in accounts receivable. Accounts receivable increases when sales are made without receiving cash. Therefore, $4 of Hardin's reported sales revenue was not collected in cash and must be removed from revenues. Removing $4 from revenue is accomplished by subtracting $4 from net income.

Change in Inventory Hardin's balance sheet shows that inventory increased by $9 during the year.

Inventory increases when a company purchases more inventory that it sells. Therefore, Hardin must have purchased $9 more in inventory than it sold during the year. So that net income reflects all payments for purchases, the $9 must be added to cost of goods sold. This results in a reduction to net income of $9.

Change in Prepaid Insurance Hardin's balance sheet shows a decrease in prepaid insurance of $4. Prepaid insurance decreases when a company uses insurance that it has already purchased. Thus, a decrease of $4 means that Hardin used $4 of insurance that it purchased in a previous period. As a result, insurance expense is $4 greater than the cash paid for insurance and should be reduced to reflect the cash paid for insurance. Reducing expenses by $4 is accomplished by adding $4 to net income.

Change in Accounts Payable Hardin's balance sheet shows that accounts payable increased by $8 during the year. Accounts payable increases when inventory is purchased without paying cash, so an $8 increase means that Hardin did not pay for $8 of its purchases calculated previously. Therefore, the $8 must be removed from expenses. This is accomplished by adding $8 to net income.

Change in Utilities Payable Hardin's balance sheet shows an increase of $5 in utilities payable. Utilities payable increases when a company incurs utilities expense but does not pay cash. Thus, the $5 increase means that Hardin's expenses are $5 greater than the cash paid. As a result, the $5 of expenses must be removed from net income. This is accomplished by adding $5 to net income.

Change in Taxes Payable Hardin's balance sheet shows that taxes payable decreased $7 during the period to end at a zero balance. Taxes payable decreases when a company pays not only for current-period taxes but also prior-period taxes. The $7 decrease therefore means that Hardin paid $7 more than it expensed. As a result, the $7 should be added to expenses. This is accomplished by subtracting $7 from net income. In India, instead of reporting change in taxes payable, actual tax paid is subtracted as can be seen in Exhibit 11.1.

Net Operating Cash Flows

The six adjustments from changes in current assets and current liabilities, along with the two adjustments for non-cash items, are shown in Exhibit 11-5. The adjustments result in $35 in net cash provided by operating activities. If you are learning both the direct and indirect methods, you should note that the $35 is the same as calculated under the direct method.

Exhibit 11-5 Hardin's Operating Cash Flows Using the Indirect Method

Cash flows from operating activities		
Net income		$14
Adjustments to reconcile net income to net cash provided by operating activities		
Depreciation expense	$25	
Gain on sale of equipment	(1)	
Increase in accounts receivable	(4)	
Increase in inventory	(9)	
Decrease in prepaid insurance	4	
Increase in accounts payable	8	
Increase in utilities payable	5	
Decrease in taxes payable	(7)	21
Net cash provided by operating activities		$35

LO5 Computing Cash Flows from Investing Activities

This section demonstrates the calculation of cash flows from investing activities. Recall that investing activities include the purchase and sale of non-current assets such as fixed assets, intangible assets, and long-term investments.

To calculate cash flows from investing activities, all changes in non-current assets must be examined. In general, an increase in a non-current asset suggests a purchase and therefore a cash outflow. A decrease suggests a sale and therefore a cash inflow. However, to be sure, any available information on the changes must be examined to determine whether the change resulted from a non-cash transaction or whether the change was the net effect of both increases and decreases to the account.

To illustrate, consider again Hardin's balance sheet in Exhibit 11-2. It shows three non-current asset accounts: "Investments, Fixed Assets, and Accumulated Depreciation." In the following sections, each account balance is examined to determine Hardin's cash flows from investing activities.

© KRISTIAN SEKULIC /SHUTTERSTOCK.COM

Investing activities include the purchase and sale of non-current assets such as fixed assets, intangible assets, and long-term investments.

Investments

According to Hardin's balance sheet, investments increased $22. Without any information to the contrary, it is assumed that Hardin bought investments for $22 cash. Thus, a cash outflow of $22 from the purchase of investments is reported in investing activities.

Equipment

Hardin's balance sheet shows a $66 increase in equipment during the year. Thus, Hardin must have purchased equipment during the year. Hardin's income statement shows a $1 gain on the sale of equipment. Thus, Hardin must have sold equipment during the year. As a result, there are both cash inflows and outflows related to equipment. Each will be considered separately.

Cash Inflows Hardin discloses that the $1 gain on the sale of equipment arose from selling equipment with a cost of $10 and accumulated depreciation of $5 for $6. Thus, a $6 inflow from the sale of equipment should be included in investing activities. Note here that the gain from the sale is ignored. Only the cash flow from the sale is of interest at this point. The gain is accounted for in operating activities.

Cash Outflows Hardin's equipment account increased $66 during the year. Absent any additional information, it would be assumed that Hardin purchased $66 in equipment for cash. However, Hardin's additional information discloses that equipment with a cost of $10 was sold during the year. Therefore, Hardin must have purchased $76 in equipment during the year. The calculation of purchases is shown as follows.

Beginning balance	$166		
Plus: Purchases	??	⟶	?? = $76
Less: Sales	10		
Ending balance	$232		

Accumulated Depreciation

Recall from Chapter 8 that accumulated depreciation is the account that collects depreciation expense. Therefore it changes when either depreciation expense is recorded or fixed assets are sold. Depreciation expense does not affect cash, and any sale of equipment is already considered when examining the equipment account. Therefore, the change in the accumulated depreciation account can be ignored.

Summary of Investing Cash Flows

The three cash flows from investing activities are shown in Exhibit 11-6. The three items resulted in a net cash outflow from investing activities of $(92). Hardin was using its cash to invest in additional non-current assets.

Exhibit 11-6 Hardin's Investing Cash Flows

Cash flows from investing activities	
Purchase of equipment	$(76)
Sale of equipment	6
Purchase of investments	(22)
Net cash used in investing activities	$(92)

LO6 Computing Cash Flows from Financing Activities

This section demonstrates the calculation of cash flows from financing activities. Recall that financing activities include generating and repaying capital to investors and creditors. Common financing activities include the issuance of stock or debt and the repurchase of stock, the payment of dividends, and the repayment of debt. Note that although payments of dividends to stockholders are considered a financing activity, payments of interest to creditors are not. Because interest is an expense that is reported on the income statement, payments for interest are reported as operating activities rather than financing activities. In India, however, interest paid is shown as a financing activity and not as operating activity. Thus, interest paid is added to profit while calculating profit from operating activity and shown as outflow while calculating cash flow from financing activity. Interest received on investment is considered while calculating cash flow from investment activity.

To calculate cash flows from financing activities, the balances for long-term liabilities, equity accounts, and dividends must be examined. In general, an increase in a liability or an equity account such as common stock suggests a cash inflow from either borrowing or selling stock. A decrease in a liability or an increase in treasury stock or dividends suggests a cash outflow from payments to creditors or investors. However, to be sure, any available information on the changes must be examined to determine whether the change resulted from a non-cash transaction or whether the change was the net effect of both increases and decreases to the account.

To illustrate, consider again Hardin's balance sheet in Exhibit 11-2. It shows one long-term liability and three equity accounts. Hardin provides no additional information regarding the accounts. In the following sections, each account balance is examined to determine Hardin's cash flows from financing activities.

Long-Term Debt

According to Hardin's balance sheet, long-term debt increased $45 during the year. Absent any information to the contrary, it is assumed that Hardin borrowed $45 in cash. Thus, a cash inflow of $45 from the issuance of debt is reported in financing activities.

Common Stock

Hardin's balance sheet shows no change in the common stock account. Thus, absent any additional information, it is assumed there was no effect on cash from the common stock account.

Treasury Stock

Hardin's balance sheet shows a $10 increase in treasury stock. Recall from Chapter 10 that the treasury stock account records the cost of a company's own stock that has been repurchased. Absent any additional information telling us otherwise, it is assumed that Hardin purchased the stock for $10 cash. Thus, a cash outflow of $10 from the purchase of treasury stock is reported in financing activities.

Common financing activities include the issuance of stock or debt and the repurchase of stock, the payment of dividends, and the repayment of debt.

Retained Earnings

The fourth and final account is retained earnings. Recall from earlier chapters that the retained earnings balance is affected by two things—net income and dividends declared. Net income increases the balance while dividends decrease the balance. Hardin's balance sheet shows that retained earnings increased $9 during the year, from $78 to $87. Hardin's income statement shows that net income was $14. Therefore dividends declared can be calculated as follows:

Retained earnings, beginning balance	$78	
Plus: Net income	14	
Less: Dividends declared	??	→ ?? = $5
Retained earnings, ending balance	$87	

Now that dividends declared are known, the amount paid can be calculated. If dividends were not paid, the balance sheet would show a balance in dividends payable in current liabilities. Neither year shows a balance, so all $5 of the dividends must have been paid. Thus, a cash outflow of $5 from the payment of dividends is reported in financing activities.

Net Financing Cash Flows

The three cash flows from financing activities are shown in Exhibit 11-7. The three items resulted in a net cash inflow from financing activities of $30. Hardin generated $30 more from financing activities than it paid.

Exhibit 11-7 Hardin's Financing Cash Flows

Cash flows from financing activities	
Issuance of long-term debt	$45
Payment of dividends	(5)
Purchase of treasury stock	(10)
Net cash provided by financing activities	$30

The statement of cash flows reports how a company generated and used its cash during the year.

Complete Statement of Cash Flows—Indirect Method

Hardin's final statement of cash flows, using the indirect method, is shown in Exhibit 11-8. The net decrease in cash of $27 corresponds to the change in the cash account from Hardin's balance sheet.

Exhibit 11-8 Hardin Supply Company Statement of Cash Flows

Hardin Supply Company
Statement of Cash Flows
For the Year Ending December 31, 2012

Cash flows from operating activities		
Net income		$ 14
Adjustments to reconcile net income to net cash provided by operating activities		
Depreciation expense	$ 25	
Gain on sale of equipment	(1)	
Increase in accounts receivable	(4)	
Increase in inventory	(9)	
Decrease in prepaid insurance	4	
Increase in accounts payable	8	
Increase in utilities payable	5	
Decrease in taxes payable	(7)	21
Net cash provided by operating activities		$ 35
Cash flows from investing activities		
Purchases of equipment	$(76)	
Sale of equipment	6	
Purchases of investments	(22)	
Net cash used in investing activities		(92)
Cash flows from financing activities		
Issuance of long-term debt	$ 45	
Payment of dividends	(5)	
Purchase of treasury stock	(10)	
Net cash provided by financing activities		30
Net decrease in cash		$(27)
Cash, beginning of the year		45
Cash, end of the year		$ 18

Free cash flow The excess cash a company generates beyond what it needs to invest in productive capacity and pay dividends to stockholders.

LO7 Analyzing a Company's Statement of Cash Flows

The statement of cash flows reports how a company generated and used its cash during the year. As a result, the statement can be used to answer many question about a company's cash. Two of the broader questions that can be addressed are as follows:

1. Is the company able to generate enough cash to grow?
2. Is the company able to generate enough cash to satisfy its obligations?

The following sections examine these questions for Tata Steel. The examination will require the information from the company's statement of cash flows and notes to the financial statements. The required information is found in Exhibit 11-9, which is excerpted from Tata Steel's 2012–13 Annual Report.

Exhibit 11-9 Account Balances from Tata Steel's 2012–13 Annual Report

Source	Accounts	March 31, 2013	March 31, 2012
Statement of Cash Flows	Cash flows from operating activities	₹11,068.67	₹10,423.85
	Capital expenditures	(7,508.55)	(7,059.20)
	Dividends	(1,165.46)	(1,151.06)

Free Cash Flow

When assessing a company's cash flows, a commonly used calculation is free cash flow. **Free cash flow** is the cash a company generates in excess of its investments in productive capacity and payments to stockholders in the form of dividends. Free cash flow is a measure of a company's ability to generate cash for expansion, for other forms of improved operations, for the repayment of debt, or for increased returns to stockholders. While free cash flow can be defined in many ways, the most straightforward definition is as follows:

MARUTI SUZUKI ANALYSIS

Look at Maruti Suzuki's Statement of Cash Flows and the last paragraph in Note 6 in Appendix C. Calculate and interpret (1) free cash flow and (2) cash flow adequacy ratio.

(1) Free cash flow:

₹43,842– ₹38,549 – ₹2,167 = ₹3,126

Maruti Suzuki generated ₹3126 million in free cash flow in the most recent year. This cash could be used for further expansion, to pay down debt balances, or for other purposes determined by company management.

(2) Cash flow adequacy ratio:

₹3,126/₹8,463 = 0.37

The 0.37 cash flow adequacy ratio indicates that Maruti Suzuki can pay less than half the average debt coming due in the coming years. Thus, the company currently has cash flow to service its maturing debt.

Cash flows from operating activities
Less: Capital expenditures
Less: Dividends
Free cash flow

The calculation starts with cash flows from operating activities, which is a measure of a company's ability to generate cash from its current operations. It then subtracts capital expenditures, which refers to the cash that a company spends on fixed assets during the year, and dividends, which are payments to stockholders during the year. The cash that remains is "free" to be used as the company chooses.

Tata Steel's 2013 free cash flow is calculated as follows from the information in Exhibit 11-1:

	March **31,** **2013**	March **31,** **2012**
Cash flows from operating activities	₹11,068.67	₹10,423.85
– Capital expenditures	(7,508.55)	(7,059.20)
– Dividends	(1,165.46)	(1,151.06)
Free cash flow	₹2,394.66	₹2,213.59

In 2011–12, Tata Steel generated positive free cash flow. That is, it generated more cash from operations than it paid for fixed assets and dividends. As a result, the company spent less cash than it generated for operation. Again, Tata Steel generated positive free cash flow in 2012–13. As a result, the company generated cash that was free to be used for other purposes.

Cash Flow Adequacy Ratio

An important ratio that is commonly used to assess a company's cash is the cash flow adequacy ratio. The **cash flow adequacy ratio** compares free cash flow to the average amount of debt maturing in the next five years or long-term debt outstanding on the balance sheet date. It is calculated as follows:

Cash flow adequacy ratio Compares free cash flow to the average amount of debt maturing in the next five years and measures the ability to pay maturing debt.

$$\text{Cash flow adequacy ratio} = \frac{\text{Free cash flow}}{\text{Long-term outstanding loan}}$$

Because this ratio compares free cash flow to maturing debt, it represents a company's ability to generate enough cash to pay its debt. In general, companies would like this ratio to be higher rather than lower. All other things equal, a higher ratio indicates a greater ability to generate sufficient cash from operations to pay upcoming debt.

Tata Steel's 2012–13 cash flow adequacy ratio is calculated as follows.

$$\frac{2{,}394.66}{23{,}565.57} = 0.10$$

The 0.10 ratio indicates that Tata Steel generated over ₹0.10 paise in free cash flow for every ₹1 of debt outstanding as on March 31, 2010. Thus, it appears that Tata Steel is not generating sufficient cash to service its upcoming debt payments.

CONCEPT QUESTIONS

1. What are the three sections found on the statement of cash flows?
2. Give an example of a transaction that would be classified under each of the three sections on the statement of cash flows.
3. What two additional disclosures are made on the statement of cash flows?
4. What three pieces of information are needed to prepare a statement of cash flows?
5. Describe the two methods for reporting operating cash flows. Do they result in the same amount? Which one is used by most companies?
6. Computing operating cash flows under the direct method requires the conversion of certain balances into cash receipts and cash payments. What are those balances?
7. Describe the following conversions under the direct method: sales to cash receipts; cost of goods sold to cash paid for inventory; and salaries expense to cash payments for salaries.
8. What are the three main types of adjustments used when computing operating cash flows under the indirect method?
9. Under the indirect method, what adjustments to net income are required for the following: non-cash expenses; gains and losses from non-operating activities; and changes in current assets and current liabilities?
10. Changes in what accounts must be examined to calculate investing cash flows? What does an increase in those accounts suggest? What does a decrease suggest?
11. Changes in what accounts must be examined to calculate financing cash flows? What does an increase in those accounts suggest? What does a decrease suggest?
12. Are interest payments to creditors considered a financing activity? What about dividend payments to stockholders?
13. What is free cash flow and how is it calculated?
14. What does the cash flow adequacy ratio show and how is it calculated?

MULTIPLE CHOICE

1. Which of the following regarding the statement of cash flows is *incorrect*?
   a. It is one of the four basic financial statements.
   b. Information about a company's cash payments and receipts is provided.
   c. It is a reconciliation of the cash in the company's bank accounts to the balance sheet.
   d. It is divided into three main sections.
2. Which of the following is an example of a cash flow resulting from an operating activity?
   a. Cash received from the sale of inventory.
   b. Cash received from the sale of common stock.
   c. A cash dividend payment.
   d. Cash paid for equipment
3. The statement of cash flows presents a company's cash flows for a period of time divided into what three sections?
   a. Operating, Investing, and Non-Operating.
   b. Operating, Financing, and Non-Operating.
   c. Operating, Investing, and Financing.
   d. Investing, Financing, and Non-Operating.
4. Which of the following cash flows is an example of a financing activity?
   a. Cash payments for inventory.
   b. Cash paid to acquire new manufacturing equipment.
   c. Cash received from the issuance of common stock.
   d. A stock dividend issued to the stockholders of a company.
5. Which of the following is an example of an investing cash flow?
   a. Cash received from sale of long-term investment.
   b. Cash paid for equipment.
   c. Cash received from sale of building.
   d. All of the above.
6. Which of the following is an additional disclosure often included on the statement of cash flows?
   a. Significant non-cash investing and financing activities.
   b. Cash paid for interest and taxes.
   c. Neither a nor b.
   d. Both a and b.
7. A company recently purchased new land by issuing bonds payable. Under which section of the statement of cash flows would this transaction appear?
   a. Operating activities
   b. Investing activities
   c. Financing activities
   d. Additional disclosure of non-cash transactions
8. Which of the following is *correct* about the statement of cash flows?
   a. Operating cash flows can be calculated with either the direct method or the income method.
   b. Financing cash flows are normally shown as the last section on the statement.
   c. The statement shows the cash subtotals associated with four types of activities.
   d. Investing cash flows only relate to stocks and bonds.
9. A company shows sales of ₹1,00,000 during the year. The company's balance in accounts receivable decreased ₹6,000 during the year. How much cash was received from customers during the year?
   a. ₹98,000 b. ₹94,000
   c. ₹1,00,000 d. ₹1,06,000

10. A company's balance in inventory is ₹53,000 at the beginning and end of the year. Its beginning balance in accounts payable is ₹30,000, and its ending balance is ₹35,000. Cost of goods sold for the year is ₹78,000. How much cash was paid for inventory during the current year?
    a. ₹73,000   b. ₹83,000
    c. ₹78,000   d. ₹88,000
11. A company's income statement shows insurance expense of ₹6,000 for the current period. The balance sheet shows that the balance in prepaid insurance increased from ₹9,000 to ₹11,000 during the year. How much cash was paid for insurance during the year?
    a. ₹8,000   b. ₹11,000
    c. ₹9,000   d. ₹6,000
12. A company's income statement shows salaries expense of ₹2,20,000 for the current year. The balance in salaries payable increased ₹30,000 during the year. How much cash was paid for salaries during the year?
    a. ₹2,20,000   b. ₹1,90,000
    c. ₹2,50,000   d. ₹30,000
13. Which of the following would not be reported on a statement of cash flows prepared under the direct method?
    a. Cash receipts from customers.
    b. Gain on sale of equipment.
    c. Cash paid to suppliers.
    d. Cash paid for taxes.
14. A company generates net income of ₹75,000 during the year. In that same year, accounts payable decreased ₹5,000, inventory decreased by ₹2,000, and accounts receivable increased by ₹4,000. Using the indirect method, calculate operating cash flows.
    a. ₹66,000   b. ₹76,000
    c. ₹68,000   d. ₹74,000
15. Which of the following would not be an adjustment to net income under the indirect method of calculating operating cash flows?
    a. Gain on the sale of equipment
    b. An increase in prepaid insurance
    c. Depreciation expense
    d. Each of the above would be an adjustment under the indirect method
16. When calculating operating cash flows under the indirect method, an increase in a current asset should be ______ to net income and a decrease in a current liability should be ______ to net income?
    a. subtracted, added
    b. added, subtracted
    c. subtracted, subtracted
    d. added, added
17. Under the indirect method of calculating operating cash flows, which of the following would be added to net income?
    a. Increase in current assets
    b. Non-cash expenses
    c. Gain on sale of equipment
    d. Decrease in current liabilities
18. Which of the following activities would *not* be classified under the investing activities section on the statement of cash flows?
    a. Cash paid for the stock of another company
    b. The purchase of new equipment
    c. Cash paid to purchase treasury stock
    d. Buying a patent from a competitor
19. A review of Smith Inc.'s balance sheet shows that the balance in long-term investments increased ₹1,20,000 during the year while the balance in the equipment account increased ₹55,00,000. Additional information shows that the company sold for ₹5,00,000 cash some equipment with a cost of ₹15,00,000. What is the net cash used in investing activities for the prior year?
    a. ₹77,00,000   b. ₹67,00,000
    c. ₹72,00,000   d. None of the above
20. Which of the following activities would *not* be classified under the financing activities section of the statement of cash flows?
    a. Issuance of common stock for cash.
    b. Payment of principal on bonds.
    c. Cash received from a note issued to a creditor.
    d. Dividends declared but not yet paid.
21. If a company issues long-term debt for ₹5,00,000 in cash, declares and pays dividends of ₹1,50,000, and announces plans to repurchase ₹2,50,000 worth of treasury stock, what is the net cash provided (used) by financing activities?
    a. ₹1,00,000 provided
    b. ₹1,00,000 used
    c. ₹4,00,000 provided
    d. ₹3,50,000 provided
22. The cash flow adequacy ratio:
    a. Compares free cash flow to the average amount of debt maturing in five years.
    b. Provides an indication of a company's ability to generate enough cash to pay its debts.
    c. Both a and b
    d. Neither a nor b
23. Free cash flow is calculated as:
    a. Net income less capital expenditures and dividends
    b. Cash from operating activities less capital expenditures
    c. Cash from operating activities less net income
    d. Cash from operating activities less capital expenditures and dividends

BRIEF EXERCISES

1. Classify Cash Flows

A company has the following cash transactions during the year:

a. Purchases inventory
b. Issues long-term debt
c. Purchases a building
d. Sells common stock to investors
e. Pays an account payable

Required
Identify whether each item a) is a cash inflow or outflow and b) should be reported as an operating, investing, or financing cash flow.

2. Calculate Cash Paid for Salaries

A company has salaries expense of ₹2,50,000 for the year. During the year salaries payable increased ₹25,000. Cash also decreased ₹40,000.

Required
Determine the amount of cash paid for salaries during the year.

3. Calculate Cash Collections

McDoogle Company's balance sheet showed an accounts receivable balance of ₹7,50,000 at the beginning of the year and ₹9,70,000 at the end of the year. McDoogle reported sales of ₹1,15,00,000 on its income statement.

Required
Using the direct method, determine the amount that McDoogle will report as cash collections in the operating activities section of the statement of cash flows.

4. Calculate Cash Paid for Taxes

Brandon Manufacturing uses the direct method for its statement of cash flows and provides the following account balances:

Taxes payable, beginning of year	₹1,40,000
Taxes payable, end of year	80,000
Tax expense during the year	3,20,000

Required
Calculate cash paid for taxes.

5. Identify Indirect Method Adjustments

A company experiences the following items during the year:

a. Depreciation expense
b. Increase in income taxes payable
c. Decrease in accounts receivable
d. Increase in prepaid expenses
e. Gain on sale of investments

Required
Identify whether each item would be an addition to or subtraction from net income when calculating operating cash flows using the indirect method.

6. Calculate Operating Cash Flows Using the Indirect Method

A company generated ₹12,42,000 in net income during the year. Also during the year, the company recorded ₹1,28,000 in depreciation expense and experienced a ₹23,000 decrease in accounts receivable and a ₹47,600 increase in accounts payable.

Required
Calculate the company's operating cash flows using the indirect method.

7. Reporting Cash Flows from Sale of Equipment

A company sells equipment with a book value of ₹2,30,000 for ₹2,50,000 cash.

Required
How would the sale of equipment be reported on the statement of cash flows under the a) indirect method and b) the direct method?

8. Calculate Investing and Financing Cash Flows

Scott Inc. had the following activities during the year:

- Purchased a building by paying ₹4,00,000 down and financing the remaining ₹10,00,000 on a 5-year note.
- Reissued 1,000 shares of treasury stock with a cost of ₹50 per share for ₹80 per share.
- Issued a ₹2,00,000 dividend to stockholders, half of which was paid in common stock.
- Sold equipment for cash. The equipment had a book value of ₹2,85,000, and Scott recognized a gain of ₹20,000 on the sale.
- Sold investments for ₹3,72,000 cash, recognizing a loss of ₹11,000.

Required
For each item, calculate Scott's net cash flow and identify whether the cash flow is an investing activity or a financing activity. Ignore any effects on operating cash flows.

9. Calculate Free Cash Flow and Cash Flow Adequacy Ratio

During the year, Lewis Jewellers generated net income of ₹3,03,000 and cash flow from operations of ₹3,40,000. Lewis also bought a building for ₹2,65,000 to open a new store and paid ₹22,000 in dividends. Lewis calculates that over the next five years, the company will have ₹10,000 of debt maturing annually.

Required
Calculate Lewis' free cash flow and cash flow adequacy ratio.

EXERCISES

10. Classify Cash Flows

A company enters into the following transactions:

a. Issued ₹2,50,000 of common stock for cash.
b. Issued a long-term note in exchange for a machine worth ₹50,000.
c. Received ₹2,10,000 in cash from collecting accounts receivable.
d. Paid ₹75,000 on accounts payable.
e. Issued ₹5,00,000 of common stock to satisfy a ₹5,00,000 note payable.
f. Declared and paid a cash dividend of ₹7,80,000.
g. Sold an investment costing ₹1,00,000 for ₹1,00,000 in cash.

Required
Classify each transaction as a cash inflow or a cash outflow from operating activities, investing activities, or financing activities, or as a non-cash transaction.

11. Classify Cash Flows

A company enters into the following transactions:

a. Interest is paid on a note payable.
b. Salaries are paid to the company's employees.
c. Bonds are issued in exchange for cash.
d. Income taxes are paid by the company.
e. New heavy machinery is purchased with cash.
f. Convertible bonds are issued in exchange for land.
g. Cash dividends are paid to stockholders.
h. The common stock of another company is purchased as an investment.
i. The company purchases its own common stock.
j. Common stock is given to the bank in return for cancellation of a note.
k. An amount due from a customer is collected.
l. Intangible assets are purchased from another company for cash.

Required
Indicate whether each transaction would appear under operating activities, investing activities, or financing activities. Also note if a transaction is a significant non-cash transaction that would require additional disclosure.

12. Classify Cash Flows

A company entered into the following transactions:

a. Purchased new machinery for ₹2,40,000 cash.
b. Paid a ₹2,500 account payable relating to inventory.
c. Recorded cash sales of ₹52,000.
d. Purchased a new warehouse for ₹275,000. The seller of the building accepted 10,000 shares of common stock as payment.
e. Issued bonds at face value for ₹25,000.
f. Purchased 200 shares of treasury stock for ₹7,000.
g. Purchased a new light truck for ₹18,000 by signing a 180-day note payable.
h. Collected a ₹3,000 receivable from a customer.
i. Sold 250 shares of Microsoft stock for its book value of ₹25,000.
j. Paid ₹2,000 for renewal of an insurance policy.
k. Paid dividends of ₹5,000 in cash.

Required
Classify each transaction as a cash inflow or outflow from operating activities, investing activities, or financing activities, or as an item reported in a supplemental schedule of the statement of cash flows.

13. Calculate Cash Received from Sales

Mueller Industries uses the direct method for its statement of cash flows and provides the following account balances:

Accounts receivable, beginning of year	₹ 1,25,000
Accounts receivable, end of year	85,000
Credit sales during the year	2,25,000
Cash sales during the year	35,000

Required
Calculate cash received from customers.

14. Calculate Cash Paid for Inventory

Key Locks Group uses the direct method for its statement of cash flows and provides the following account balances:

Inventory, beginning of year	₹ 55,000
Inventory, end of year	40,000
Accounts payable, beginning of year	15,000
Accounts payable, end of year	10,000
Cost of goods sold during the year	1,75,000

Required
Calculate cash paid to suppliers for inventory.

15. Calculate Cash Paid for Operating Expenses

The following information is available for a company's rent and income taxes:

Prepaid rent, beginning of year	₹25,000
Prepaid rent, end of year	31,000
Rent expense	40,000
Cash paid for rent during the year	??

Income taxes payable, beginning of year	₹25,000
Income taxes payable, end of year	31,000
Income tax expense	40,000
Cash payments for income taxes during the year	??

Required
Calculate the missing information.

16. Prepare Operating Cash Flows Under the Direct Method

Searcy Enterprises provides the following information at year end:

Sales	₹ 3,20,000
Cost of goods sold	1,80,000
Salaries expense	45,000
Income tax expense	12,000
Increase in accounts receivable	2,000
Decrease in inventory	4,000
Increase in accounts payable	6,000
Increase in salaries payable	5,000
Decrease in taxes payable	1,000

Required
Prepare the operating activities section of the statement of cash flows using the direct method.

17. Classify Adjustments Under the Indirect Method

A company that uses the indirect method to report operating activities experiences the following events:

a. Decrease in accounts payable.
b. Increase in accounts receivable.
c. Purchase of a new conveyer belt system.
d. Purchase of company's own common stock.
e. Gain on the sale of old conveyer belt system.

f. Depreciation expense.
g. Increase in inventory.
h. Increase in bonds payable.
i. Bad debt expense.

Required
Indicate whether each item should be added to net income, deducted from net income, or not reported in the operating activities section of the statement of cash flows.

18. Prepare Operating Cash Flows Under the Indirect Method

The following information was reported by Shady Imports Company:

	2013	2012
Accounts receivable	₹55,000	₹47,000
Inventory	35,000	45,000
Prepaid insurance	12,000	10,000
Accounts payable	22,000	15,000
Income taxes payable	10,000	14,000
Interest payable	12,000	9,000
Net income	45,000	
Depreciation expense	25,000	

Required
Prepare the operating activities section of the statement of cash flows using the indirect method and explain why cash flows from operating activities is more or less than net income.

19. Calculating Operating Cash Flows Using the Indirect Method

Cornett Systems provides the following information from the most recent year:

Net income	₹74,40,000
Increase in net current assets	2,70,000
Increase in net current liabilities	3,10,000
Gain on sale of investments	35,000
Depreciation expense	8,60,000
Loss on bond redemption	56,000
Purchase of equipment	6,23,000

Required
Prepare the operating activities section of Cornett's statement of cash flows using the indirect method.

20. Adjustments to Net Income Under the Indirect Method

A company reports the following operating cash flows on its statement of cash flows (in millions):

Net income		₹98
Adjustments to reconcile net income to net cash		
provided by operating activities		
Accounts receivable	₹(32)	
Inventory	12	
Prepaid insurance	(5)	
Accounts payable	(13)	
Salaries payable	0	
Taxes payable	2	(36)
Net cash provided by operating activities		₹62

Required
Identify whether the following account balances increased or decreased during the year: (a) accounts receivable, (b) inventory, (c) prepaid insurance, (d) accounts payable, (e) salaries payable, and (f) taxes payable.

21. Interpreting Operating Cash Flows

The CEO of Cassette Tape Manufacturers is pleased because the company's cash flows from operations exceed net income. He considers this a sign of success. Cassette Tape's statement of cash flows shows the following operating cash flows:

Net income		₹ 94,350
Adjustments to reconcile net income to net		
cash provided by operating activities		
Increase in accounts receivable	₹(3,22,840)	
Increase in inventory	(8,590)	
Increase in accounts payable	4,83,000	74,260
Net cash provided by operating activities		₹10,17,760

Required
Discuss whether the CEO should be pleased with the operating cash flows. Specifically, what items may indicate that Cassette Tape has a potential problem?

22. Understanding Adjustments Under the Indirect Method

A company reports the following adjustments to net income under the indirect method of calculating operating cash flows:

Increases to net income	Decreases to net income
Decrease in accounts receivable	Decrease in accounts payable
Decrease in prepaid insurance	Decrease in salaries payable
Increase in taxes payable	Gain on sale of equipment
Depreciation expense	

Required
For each item, explain the circumstances that would require the adjustment. For example, a *decrease in accounts receivable* means that cash collections for the year are greater than sales. Therefore, a decrease in accounts receivable is added to net income.

23. Compare Direct and Indirect Methods

The following items may or may not appear on the statement of cash flows:
a. Net income
b. Cash paid for equipment
c. Cash received from customers
d. Increase in accounts receivable
e. Gain on sale of investment
f. Cash received from issuing bonds
g. Decrease in prepaid insurance
h. Cash paid for insurance

i. Convert bonds into common stock
j. Dividends paid
k. Depreciation expense
l. Cash paid for salaries

Required
Identify whether each item (1) would not appear on the statement of cash flows, (2) would appear on the statement if the direct method is used, (3) would appear on the statement if the indirect method is used, or (4) would appear on a statement if either the direct or indirect method is used.

24. Classifying Transactions Under the Indirect Method

The following is a list of transactions and changes in account balances that occurred during the year:
a. Income taxes payable decreased.
b. Paid cash in satisfaction of a matured bond payable.
c. Paid a cash dividend.
d. Accounts payable increased.
e. Accounts receivable doubled before returning to the beginning balance by year end.
f. Sold equipment for cash at a gain.
g. Purchased a new warehouse by issuing bonds.
h. Purchased inventory for cash.
i. Purchased treasury stock.

Required
Assuming the indirect method for operating activities, indicate whether each transaction would be included in operating activities, investing activities, financing activities, non-cash disclosures, or not reported. Note that some transactions may impact multiple sections.

25. Calculate Cash Flows from Investing Activities

The following information is taken from the balance sheet of Cheese Wheel Company:

	2013	2012
Equipment	₹85,000	₹1,20,000
Accumulated depreciation	50,000	55,000

Depreciation expense of ₹15,000 was reported on the 2013 income statement. Equipment with an original cost of ₹35,000 was sold for its book value.

Required
Compute the amount of cash received from the sale of the equipment.

26. Calculate Cash Flows from Investing Activities

The following transactions occurred during the year:
a. A new warehouse was purchased for ₹11,00,000 cash.
b. The company's own common stock was purchased for ₹2,20,000.
c. An old warehouse costing ₹8,00,000 was sold for ₹4,50,000, resulting in a gain of ₹50,000.
d. The company purchased stock in Boston Beer Inc. for ₹75,000 cash.
e. Stock of Tazer Inc. was sold for ₹1,25,000, resulting in a gain of ₹7,500.

Required
Use this information to compute cash flows from investing activities.

27. Calculate Cash Flows from Financing Activities

The following transactions occurred during the year:
a. Common stock was issued in exchange for a new heavy truck.
b. A cash dividend of ₹2,00,000 was paid.
c. A 90-day note payable was issued for ₹50,000 cash.
d. ₹2,50,000 was paid to acquire the company's own common stock.
e. Depreciation expense for the year was ₹3,00,000.
f. Bonds with a face value of ₹2,50,000 were issued at par.

Required
Use this information to compute cash flows from financing activities.

28. Interpreting Investing and Financing Cash Flows

Jones Corp. reports the following cash flows from investing and financing activities over the past three years (in thousands):

	2013	2012	2011
Cash flows from investing activities (in lakhs)			
Capital expenditures	₹(803)	₹(2,768)	₹ (752)
Sale of investments	—	1,204	—
Purchase of investments	—	(1,204)	—
Net cash used by investing activities	₹(803)	₹(2,768)	₹ (752)
Cash flows from financing activities			
Issuance of long-term debt	—	—	₹3,200
Payment of dividends	₹(50)	₹ (50)	(66)
Purchase of treasury stock	—	(1,200)	—
Net cash used/provided by financing activities	₹(50)	₹(1,250)	₹3,134

Required
From the information above, describe the major ways in which Jones used investing and financing cash flows over the last three years.

29. Errors in Statement of Cash Flows

Waggoner Company prepares the following statement of cash flows under the direct method:

Waggoner Company Statement of Cash Flows December 31, 2013		
Cash flows from operating activities (in millions)		
Cash receipts from customers		₹423
Less cash payments		
To suppliers	₹ 91	
For equipment	44	

To employees	58	
For taxes	12	205
Net cash used by operating activities		₹218
Cash flows from investing activities		
Depreciation expense	₹ 14	
Purchase of short-term investments	(28)	
Net cash used by investing activities		(14)
Cash flows from financing activities		
Payment of dividends	₹ 7	
Repayment of bonds	(105)	
Net cash used by financing activities		(98)
Net increase in cash		₹106
Cash, beginning of the year		10
Cash, end of the year		₹ 88

Required

Identify the errors Waggoner has made in its statement and prepare a corrected statement. Assume that the beginning and ending cash balances are correct.

30. Analyzing Cash Flows

Lowball Ltd. and Cheapskate Inc. are both no-frills, discount distribution companies. The following financial information regarding each company is available:

	Lowball	Cheapskate
Cash flows from operating activities	₹2,25,000	₹2,25,000
Net income	1,25,000	1,25,000
Capital expenditures	50,000	65,000
Dividends declared and paid	30,000	10,000
Average amount of debt maturing in 5 years	20,000	30,000

Required

a. Indicate which company generated more free cash flow.
b. Indicate which company has the better cash flow adequacy ratio.
c. Does one company have a better cash position? If so, explain why.

31. Evaluate Cash Flows

Newberry Company provides the following information from the past three years: (in '000)

	2013	2012	2011
Capital expenditures	₹ 72,185	₹ 47,246	₹ 32,180
Dividends	5,800	5,350	5,015
Operating cash flows	1,11,408	1,30,230	1,27,560
Average debt maturing in five years	64,257	50,937	45,780

Required

For each year, calculate Newberry's free cash flow and cash flow adequacy ratio. What can you conclude about Newberry's financial condition?

PROBLEMS

32. Prepare Operating Cash Flows

The following information is provided for HMG Company: (in '000)

Balances at 31/3	2013	2012
Accounts receivable	₹ 2,500	₹ 1,500
Inventory	26,000	32,000
Supplies	2,000	1,000
Accounts payable	4,000	3,000
Taxes payable	2,000	3,500
Interest payable	1,500	2,500
2013 Income Statement		
Sales		₹80,000
Cost of goods sold		55,000
Gross profit		₹25,000
Supplies expense		6,000
Depreciation expense		2,000
Total operating expenses		₹ 2,000
Income before interest and taxes		₹17,000
Interest expense		4,000
Income before taxes		₹13,000
Income tax expense		4,000
Net Income		₹ 9,000

Required

Prepare the operating activities section of the statement of cash flows using the a) direct method and b) indirect method.

33. Comparing Net Income and Cash Flows

The following events occurred at Clark Corp. during its first year of business ending on December 31:

- Clark sold ₹7,80,000 of common stock for cash.
- Clark paid ₹75,000 at the beginning of the year to rent office space for the year.
- Computer equipment was purchased for ₹2,50,000 cash at the beginning of the year. The equipment is expected to be useful for 5 years with no salvage value. Clark uses straight-line depreciation.
- Service revenue in the first year amounted to ₹12,00,000, ₹2,50,000 of which was on account.
- Accounts receivable from customers at the end of the year totaled ₹50,000.
- Salaries expense amounted to ₹6,25,000 for the year. Salaries payable at the end of the year was ₹30,000.
- Clark declared and paid a ₹50,000 cash dividend to stockholders at the end of the first year.

Required

a. Prepare Clark's income statement for the year.
b. Prepare Clark's complete statement of cash flows for the year using the direct method.
c. Explain why Clark generated more or less operating cash flows than net income.

34. Prepare a Statement of Cash Flows Using the Indirect Method

The comparative balance sheet for Two Kicks Company is as follows:

Comparative Balance Sheets at 12/31		
	2013	2012
Cash and cash equivalents	₹ 65,000	₹ 45,000
Accounts receivable	50,000	55,000
Inventory	1,25,000	1,75,000
Property and equipment	9,30,000	7,45,000
Accumulated depreciation	(2,70,000)	(2,00,000)
Total assets	₹ 9,00,000	₹ 8,20,000
Accounts payable	₹ 1,10,000	₹ 1,05,000
Bonds payable (long-term)	1,80,000	2,00,000
Total liabilities	2,90,000	3,05,000
Common stock	3,50,000	2,80,000
Retained earnings	2,60,000	2,35,000
Total stockholders' equity	6,10,000	5,15,000
Total liabilities and stockholders' equity	₹ 9,00,000	₹ 8,20,000

The following additional information is available:

a. Net income for 2013 was ₹50,000.
b. Cash dividends of ₹25,000 were paid during the year.
c. A portion of outstanding bonds matured and were redeemed for cash by the bondholders. No new bonds were issued during the year.
d. Common stock was issued for cash.
e. Property and equipment were purchased for cash. No long-term assets were sold during the year.
f. The change in accumulated depreciation is a result of depreciation expense.

Required

Prepare a complete statement of cash flows for the year using the indirect method for the operating activities section.

35. Prepare a Statement of Cash Flows

Available financial information for Blue Bomber Company is as follows:

Comparative Balance Sheets at 12/31		
	2013	2012
Cash and cash equivalents	₹ 75,000	₹ 45,000
Accounts receivable	45,000	55,000
Inventory	2,00,000	1,75,000
Prepaid insurance	30,000	35,000
Total current assets	3,50,000	3,10,000
Equipment	8,00,000	7,20,000
Accumulated depreciation	(2,40,000)	(1,70,000)
Total equipment	5,60,000	5,50,000
Total assets	₹ 9,10,000	₹8,60,000
Accounts payable	₹1,10,000	₹1,15,000
Accrued salaries	10,000	35,000
Total current liabilities	1,20,000	1,50,000
Bonds payable	1,80,000	2,30,000
Total liabilities	3,00,000	3,80,000
Common stock	3,50,000	2,50,000
Retained earnings	2,60,000	2,30,000
Total stockholders' equity	6,10,000	4,80,000
Total liabilities and stockholders' equity	₹9,10,000	₹8,60,000

Income Statement For the Year Ending 12/31/13	
Sales	₹4,50,000
Cost of goods sold	2,25,000
Gross profit	₹2,25,000
Depreciation expense	70,000
Other operating expenses	30,000
Income before interest and taxes	₹1,25,000
Interest expense	20,000
Income before taxes	₹1,05,000
Income tax expense	30,000
Net Income	₹ 75,000

The following additional information is available:

a. Cash dividends of ₹45,000 were declared and paid during the year.
b. Equipment was purchased for cash.
c. A portion of bonds payable matured and was paid with cash.
d. Common stock was issued for cash.

Required

Prepare a complete statement of cash flows for Blue Bomber for 2013 using the direct method for the operating activities section. In a separate schedule, show the operating activities section using the indirect method.

36. Prepare a Statement of Cash Flows

The following is Folex Company's income statement and balance sheet (in millions):

Income Statement For the Year Ending 12.31.13	
Sales	₹750
Cost of goods sold	450
Gross profit	₹300
Operating expenses	100
Income before interest and taxes	₹200
Interest expense	15
Income before taxes	₹185
Income tax expense	75
Net income	₹110

Balance Sheet December 31		
	2013	2012
Cash	₹ 45	₹ 80
Accounts receivable	155	115
Inventory	225	190
Prepaid insurance	22	32
Total current assets	447	417

Property and equipment	1,250	1,050
Accumulated depreciation	(175)	(140)
Total property and equipment	1,075	910
Total assets	₹1,522	₹1,327
Accounts payable	₹ 120	₹ 135
Income taxes payable	155	175
Total current liabilities	275	310
Bonds payable	400	325
Total liabilities	675	635
Common stock	525	475
Retained earnings	322	217
Total stockholders' equity	847	692
Total liabilities and stockholders' equity	₹1,522	₹1,327

The following additional information is available:

i) Operating expenses include ₹35 million of depreciation.
ii) Property and equipment were acquired for cash.
iii) Additional common stock was issued for cash.
iv) Additional cash was obtained by issuing bonds.
v) Dividends were paid.

The CEO has posed some questions regarding this year's results. She is pleased that the profit margin is approaching 15 percent. However, the decrease in the cash balance during such a profitable year troubles her.

Required

a. Prepare a complete statement of cash flows for Folex using the direct method for operating cash flows. Prepare a separate schedule showing operating cash flows using the indirect method.
b. Based on the statement you prepare, explain to the CEO why cash decreased during a profitable year.

CASE

37. Research and Analysis

Access the 2012–13 annual report for **Tata Consultancy Services Limited (TCS)** by clicking on the *Investor Relations* and *Annual Reports* links at www.tcs.com.

a. Examine the company's statement of cash flows and calculate the company's free cash flows in each of the last three years.
b. Identify the year in which the change in cash was positive and identify the company action that enabled it to increase its cash position.
c. Based on your answers above, write a paragraph describing Callaway's cash position over the past three years.

38. Ethics in Accounting

You are the accountant of a small company that wants to expand. The CEO is negotiating a loan with the bank, and the bank requires a statement of cash flows. The CEO is concerned because operating cash flows are down compared to prior years. The main reason is deteriorating collections from accounts receivables. The CEO presents three options to address the situation prior to year end and the preparation of the statement of cash flows:

Option 1: Convert some of the oldest receivables to long-term notes receivable

Option 2: Sell some receivables to a collector for ₹0.65 per ₹1 of receivables

Option 3: Delay payment of all outstanding accounts payable until the next year

Required

a. Comment on the appropriateness of each option.
b. Is there an ethical dilemma involved?
c. How would you respond to the CEO?

39. Research and Analysis

Access the 2013 annual report of **Waste Management**, USA, by clicking on the *Investor Relations, Financial Reporting*, and *Annual Reports* links at www.wm.com.

Required

a. Review the company's statement of cash flows and calculate free cash flow for each of the three years presented.
b. According to the statement, in what major way did the company use its free cash flow over the three-year period?
c. What is the major difference between net income and operating cash flows? Does that make sense for a company like Waste Management?
d. What is your overall impression of the company's statement of cash flows?

40. Entrepreneurial Decision Making

James M. Jones Jr. is an entrepreneur and the founder of Tasty Cakes Bakery. During the last year, Tasty Cakes generated ₹4,00,000 in operating cash flows, paid ₹1,00,000 in capital expenditures (as he does almost every year), and paid ₹50,000 in dividends. Jones is interested in significantly expanding this year. To do so, he needs to spend ₹10,00,000 on equipment in addition to his normal capital expenditures. He believes that if he buys the equipment, his operating cash flows will surely increase by 25% and possibly could double. He has spoken with the bank, which has offered the following two installment note options where an equal amount of principal is due each year:

Option 1: Two-year, 5%, ₹10,00,000 installment note

Option 2: Six-year, 10%, ₹10,00,000 installment note

Required

a. Calculate Tasty Cake's free cash flow.
b. Identify the advantages and disadvantages of each option the bank provides.
c. Which option should Jones choose and why?

reviewcard CHAPTER 11 Statement of Cash Flows

Learning Objectives		Key Concepts
LO1	Describe the purpose and format of the statement of cash flows.	The statement of cash flows summarizes a company's inflows and outflows of cash over a period of time. It reports cash flows in three major categories: operating, investing, and financing activities. The net cash flows from these three activities is equal to the change in cash from the balance sheet.
LO2	Describe the process of preparing the statement of cash flows.	The process of preparing the statement of cash flows involves the collection of information from a company's comparative balance sheet and income statement and the explanation of the changes in the account balances.
LO3	Prepare the operating activities section of the statement of cash flows using the direct method.	The direct method of reporting net cash flows from operating activities calculates cash inflows from customers and subtracts cash outflows from operations, interest, and taxes.
LO4	Prepare the operating activities section of the statement of cash flows using the indirect method.	The indirect method of reporting net cash flows from operating activities adjusts net income from an accrual basis to a cash basis. Required adjustments include non-cash expenses, gains and losses from investing and financing activities, and changes in current assets and current liabilities.
LO5	Prepare the investing activities section of the statement of cash flows.	Net cash flows from investing activities are calculated by examining all changes in non-current assets. Those changes involving an exchange of cash are included as investing cash flows.
LO6	Prepare the financing activities section of the statement of cash flows.	Net cash flows from financing activities are calculated by examining all changes in long-term liabilities, equity accounts, and dividends. Those changes involving an exchange of cash are included as financing cash flows.
LO7	Evaluate the statement of cash flows through the calculation and interpretation of ratio analyses.	Free cash flow is a measure of a company's ability to generate cash for expansion, improvements, repayment of debt, and/or increased returns to stockholders. The cash flow adequacy ratio measures a company's ability to generate enough cash to pay the long-term outstanding loan.

Key Definitions

Cash flow adequacy ratio Compares free cash flow to the average amount of debt maturing in the next five years and measures the ability to pay maturing debt.

Cash flows provided (used) by financing activities Cash inflows and outflows associated with the generation and return of capital; often called financing cash flows.

Cash flows provided (used) by investing activities Cash inflows and outflows arising from the acquisition and disposal of non-current assets; often called investing cash flows.

Cash flows provided (used) by operating activities Cash inflows and outflows arising from the company's operations; sometimes called operating cash flows.

Direct method Method of reporting cash flows from operating activities in which cash inflows and outflows from operations are reported separately on the statement of cash flows.

Free cash flow The excess cash a company generates beyond what it needs to invest in productive capacity and pay dividends to stockholders.

Indirect method Method of reporting cash flows from operating activities in which net income is adjusted from an accrual basis to a cash basis.

Statement of cash flows A financial statement that summarizes a company's inflows and outflows of cash over a period of time with a purpose to inform users on how and why a company's cash changed during the period.

Key Formula

Cash flow adequacy ratio $= \frac{\text{Free cash flow}}{\text{Long-term outstanding loan}}$

Demonstration Problem

A company provides the following comparative balance sheets and income statement. Prepare the company's statement of cash flows for the year using the direct method for operating cash flows. In a supplemental schedule, show operating cash flows under the indirect method. Assume that the change in equipment was caused by a purchase of equipment for cash.

Income Statement
For the Year Ended December 31, 2013

Service revenue	₹ 40,000
Depreciation expense	(20,000)
Salaries expense	(13,000)
Income before taxes	₹ 7,000
Income tax expense	(2,000)
Net income	₹ 5,000

Balance Sheet
December 31, 2013

	2013	2012
Cash and cash equivalents	₹ 1,000	₹ 2,000
Accounts receivable	7,000	8,000
Equipment	100,000	73,000
Accumulated depreciation	(55,000)	(35,000)
Total assets	₹ 53,000	₹ 48,000
Salaries payable	₹ 5,000	₹ 1,000
Common stock	22,000	22,000
Retained earnings	26,000	25,000
Total liabilities and stockholders' equity	₹ 53,000	₹ 48,000

Demonstration Problem Solution

Cash received from customers:

Service revenue + decrease in accounts receivable
= ₹40,000 + ₹1,000 = ₹41,000

Cash paid to employees:

Salaries expense – increase in salaries payable
= ₹13,000 – ₹4,000 = ₹9,000

Cash paid for income taxes:

Income tax expense +/– change in income tax payable
= ₹2,000 + ₹0 = ₹2,000

Cash paid for equipment:

Change in equipment balance is attributable to equipment bought for cash = ₹27,000

Cash paid for dividends:

Beginning retained earnings + net income – dividends
= ending retained earnings
₹25,000 + ₹5,000 – ?? = ₹26,000 ?? = ₹4,000

Statement of Cash Flows
For the Year Ended December 31, 2013

Cash flows from operating activities		
Cash receipts from customers		₹ 41,000
Less cash payments:		
to employees	₹ (9,000)	
for taxes	(2,000)	(11,000)
Net cash provided by operating activities		₹ 30,000
Cash flows from investing activities		
Cash paid for equipment	₹ (27,000)	
Net cash used in investing activities		(27,000)
Cash flows from financing activities		
Cash paid for dividends	₹ (4,000)	
Net cash used in financing activities		(4,000)
Net decrease in cash and cash equivalents		₹ (1,000)
Cash, beginning of year		2,000
Cash, end of year		₹ 1,000

Supplemental schedule:
Operating cash flows using the indirect method

Net income		₹ 5,000
Adjustments to reconcile net income to cash provided by operating activities:		
Depreciation expense	₹ 20,000	
Decrease in accounts receivable	1,000	
Increase to salaries payable	4,000	25,000
Net cash provided by operating activities		₹ 30,000

Financial Statement Analysis

Learning Objectives

After studying the material in this chapter, you should be able to:

LO1 Understand the nature of financial statement analysis.

LO2 Calculate and interpret horizontal and vertical analyses.

LO3 Assess profitability through the calculation and interpretation of ratios.

LO4 Assess liquidity through the calculation and interpretation of ratios.

LO5 Assess solvency through the calculation and interpretation of ratios.

LO6 Calculate and interpret a DuPont analysis.

Introduction

The first eleven chapters of this book examined the various aspects of financial accounting, which is the process of identifying, measuring, and communicating economic information to permit informed decisions. This chapter demonstrates how to analyze the products of this process—the income statement, the balance sheet, the statement of stockholders' equity, and the statement of cash flows—to make informed decisions about a company. That is, the chapter focuses on financial statement analysis. It will use the financial statements of JSL Stainless Ltd as an example.

LO1 Financial Statement Analysis

Financial statement analysis is the process of applying analytical tools to a company's financial statements to understand the company's financial health. The goal of such an analysis is to provide some context for understanding the accounting numbers on the financial statements. Ultimately, financial analysis should help an investor, creditor, or any other interested party better understand a company's financial position and therefore make better decisions about the company. Enabling good decisions is one goal of financial accounting, and it should be the product of financial statement analysis.

Financial analysis requires the following:

- Financial information
- Standards of comparison
- Analysis tools

Financial statement analysis The process of applying analytical tools to a company's financial statements to understand the company's financial health.

Financial Information

All publicly traded companies must prepare audited financial statements each year and file them with the Securities and Exchange Board of India (SEBI). These statements include the income statement, the balance sheet, the statement of stockhold-

Financial statement analysis can help investors understand how effectively and efficiently a company like JSL Stainless Ltd. is profiting from its customers.

ers' equity, and the statement of cash flows. Financial statements contain multiple years of data for comparative purposes and are the starting point for any analysis.

In addition to financial statements, companies provide other information that should be consulted to augment a financial analysis. For example, a company's notes to its financial statements will provide further explanation of items on the financial statements and additional disclosures not included on the statements. A company's Management's Discussion and Analysis (MD&A) will contain management's commentary on many aspects of company operations and future plans. Even company press releases, earnings reports, and notifications of stockholder meetings can contain helpful information. Finally, it is always a good idea to consult independent, third-party analysis.

In this chapter, the financial information provided by JSL Stainless Ltd. will be used to illustrate the process of financial analysis. Our focus will be predominantly on information from the income statement and the balance sheet. As a result, only those two statements are shown in the text. However,

Enabling good decisions is one goal of financial accounting, and it should be the product of financial statement analysis.

when information beyond those statements is required, it will be provided in the text.

Standards of Comparison

When conducting a financial analysis, there should be some benchmarks for comparison. The most common benchmark is the prior year(s) of the same company. This is often called an intracompany comparison because it is a comparison within a company. Horizontal analysis is an excellent example of an intracompany analysis.

Another common benchmark is competitors. Comparisons among competitors are often called intercompany comparisons because they are between companies. Vertical analysis is an excellent tool for intercompany analysis because it removes the effect of company size.

A final benchmark is industry standards. Often, industry benchmarks can be obtained from financial websites.

The analysis in this text will use both intracompany and intercompany comparisons. For intercompany comparisons, the text will use JSL Stainless Ltd. and Tata Steel.

Analysis Tools

There are many analysis tools used to conduct a financial analysis. Three of the more common are the following: horizontal analysis, vertical analysis, and ratio analysis. Horizontal analysis is a comparison of a company's financial results across time. Vertical analysis is a comparison of financial balances to a base account from the same company. Ratio analysis is a comparison of different balances from the financial statements to provide the context to understand the financial results. Typically, multiple individual ratios are grouped together to assess a company's profitability, its ability to satisfy its debts, and its ability to survive in the long term.

The remainder of this text demonstrates and discusses horizontal, vertical, and ratio analyses of JSL's financial statements.

Horizontal analysis An analysis technique that calculates the change in an account balance from one period to the next and expresses that change in both dollar and percentage terms.

LO2 Horizontal and Vertical Analyses

Horizontal Analysis

Horizontal analysis was first introduced in Chapter 2. Recall that horizontal analysis is a technique that compares account balances over time. Formally, **horizontal analysis** is an analysis technique that calculates the change in an account balance from one period to the next and expresses that change in both rupee and percentage terms. The actual calculations are as follows.

$$\text{Rupee change in account balance} = \text{Current year balance} - \text{Prior year balance}$$

$$\text{Percentage change in account balance} = \frac{\text{Rupee change}}{\text{Prior year balance}}$$

Horizontal analysis is a simple but powerful analysis tool. It reveals significant changes in account balances and therefore identifies items for further investigation. For example, an unusually large increase in operating expenses focuses attention on why those expenses increased so much. That is the nature of horizontal analysis—it often provides the right questions to ask.

Horizontal analysis is calculated for both the balance sheet and the income statement. Changes in critical account balances—such as inventory for a retailer or liabilities for a company in financial trouble—are usually examined first. Also examined are any significant changes in other account balances. Insignificant changes are often ignored because they would not affect decision making.

As you consider the results of a horizontal analysis, keep in mind a large percentage change may not be as significant as it seems. For example, an account that grows from ₹1 million to ₹3 million experiences a 200% increase, but such an increase is immaterial to a ₹50 billion company. Therefore, a review of horizontal analysis should consider both the rupee and percentage changes.

Balance Sheet Analysis Exhibit 12-1 contains a horizontal analysis of JSL Stainless Ltd's Balance Sheet as on March 31, 2013, and March 31, 2012.

The analysis shows positive changes in all asset accounts except investments and cash and bank balance. Overall, JSL Stainless Ltd. added ₹83,752.04 lakh in total assets, which represents a 5.34% growth rate. JSL's total noncurrent assets decreased by ₹30,785.65 lakh that is by around 2.9%. Though one can see an increase of ₹5,304.17 lakh in tangible assets, intangible assets decreased by more than ₹136 lakh. The company experienced the largest rupee and

Horizontal analysis is a simple but powerful analysis tool. It often provides the right question to ask.

percentage changes in Inventory (38.10%). Receivables represent uncollected sales, so an increase of more than 26% can be a troubling sign and should be investigated further. The cash and bank balance also decreased by over 46%. Goodwill is an intangible asset that is created when a company purchases another company at a premium. JSL did not experience any such acquisition.

The analysis also shows changes in all noncurrent liability accounts. Both long- and short-term borrowings have increased. Overall, noncurrent liabilities increased by 9.6%. In effect, JSL Stainless Ltd. grew its assets by growing its liabilities. Whether the company can pay off these liabilities is a question to consider further when conducting ratio analysis.

An examination of equity shows a large decrease in the company's largest equity account, retained earnings, 33%. Such a decrease is the result of loss from operations and is a sign of weak financial performance. There is also a very small increase in the company's additional paid-in capital account.

Overall, the horizontal analysis shows the growth in total asset by over 5% of the company is financed through increases in borrowings. Of potential concern is the large growth in inventory and receivable and decrease in cash and bank balance.

Income Statement Analysis Exhibit 12-2 contains a horizontal analysis of income statement for the financial year ending March 31, 2013, and March 31, 2012.

The analysis shows that revenue increased by over 30% while cost of material, manufacturing, and others going up by over 53% and personnel cost going up by 45%.

Further JSL Stainless Ltd. witnessed an increase of over 91% in finance cost, all other expenses increased

Exhibit 12-1 Horizontal Analysis of JSL Stainless Ltd. March 31, 2013 Condensed Balance Sheet

Description	*As at 31.03.2013*	*(₹ In lakhs)* *As at 31.03.2012*	*₹ Change*	*% Change*
Equity and Liabilities				
Shareholders Funds				
Share Capital	4,081.55	3,790.11	291.44	7.69
Reserves and Surplus	1,43,503.37	2,14,423.20	−70,919.83	−33.07
	1,47,584.92	2,18,213.31	−70,628.39	−32.37
Noncurrent Liabilities				
Long-term borrowings	8,76,435.33	7,71,257.61	1,05,177.72	13.64
Deffered tax liabilities (net)	1,592.61	39,456.81	−37,864.20	−95.96
Other Long-term liabilities	12,124.05	1,265.03	10,859.02	858.40
Long-term provisions	952.64	868.55	84.09	9.68
	8,91,104.63	8,12,848.00	78,256.63	9.63
Current Liabilities				
Short-term borrowings	2,02,312.22	1,53,145.13	49,167.09	32.10
Trade payables	2,97,534.06	2,03,394.68	94,139.38	46.28
Other current liabilities	1,13,809.93	1,81,074.75	−67,264.82	−37.15
Short-term provisions	283.59	201.44	82.15	40.78
	6,13,939.80	5,37,816.00	76,123.8	14.15
Total	16,52,629.35	15,68,877.31	83,752.04	5.34
Assets				
Noncurrent Assets				
Fixed Assets				
Tangible assets	9,80,416.08	9,75,111.91	5,304.17	0.54
Intangible assets	292.03	428.95	−136.92	−31.92
Capital work-in-progress	14,590.34	45,663.86	−31,073.52	−68.05
Intangible assets under development	846.76	483.2	363.56	75.24
Noncurrent investments	17,111.20	16,886.20	225	1.33
Long-term loans and advances	15,576.14	20,603.13	−5,026.99	−24.40
Other noncurrent assets	1,772.89	2,213.84	−440.95	−19.92
	10,30,605.44	10,61,391.09	−30,785.65	−2.90
Current Assets				
Current investments	219.54	104.00	115.54	111.10
Inventories	3,27,642.11	2,70,275.89	57,366.22	21.23
Trade receivables	1,90,901.73	1,50,566.46	40,335.27	26.79
Cash and Bank Balances	8,778.94	16,419.81	−7,640.87	−46.53
Short-term loans and advances	94,032.44	69,652.12	24,380.32	35.00
Other current assets	449.15	467.94	−18.79	−4.02
	6,22,023.91	5,07,486.22	1,14,537.69	22.57
Total	16,52,629.35	15,68,877.31	83,752.04	5.34

Exhibit 12-2 Horizontal Analysis of JSL Stainless Ltd. March 31, 2013 Condensed Income Statement

Description	For the year ended 31.03.2013	For the year ended 31.03.2012	₹ Change	% Change
	(₹ In lakhs)			
Income				
Revenue from operations (Gross)	11,12,188.27	8,49,833.01	2,62,355.26	30.87138966
Less: Excise Duty on sales	83,567.33	60,728.17	22,839.16	37.61
Revenue from operstions (Net)	10,28,620.94	7,89,104.84	2,39,516.10	30.35
Other Income	4,413.15	7,530.62	−3,117.47	−41.40
Total	10,33,034.09	7,96,635.46	2,36,398.63	29.67
Expenses				
Cost of materials consumed	7,29,398.63	5,48,442.31	1,80,956.32	32.99
Purchase of Trading Goods	2,629.51	9,689.84	−7,060.33	−72.86
Changes in inventories of finished goods, work in progress and Trading goods	(36,382.97)	(43,533.62)	7,150.65	−16.43
Employee benefits expenses	24,632.61	16,983.32	7,649.29	45.04
Finance costs	99,029.31	51,680.03	47,349.28	91.62
Depreciation and amortization expense	70,130.96	40,860.75	29,270.21	71.63
Other Expenses				
Manufacturing Expenses	1,96,825.69	1,37,646.27	59,179.42	42.99
Administrative Expenses	12,943.88	7,821.98	5,121.90	65.48
Selling expenses	37,076.41	21,650.52	15,425.89	71.25
Total	11,36,284.03	7,91,241.40	3,45,042.63	43.61
Profit/ (Loss) before exceptional and extraordinary items and tax	(1,03,249.94)	5,394.06	−1,08,644.00	−2,014.14
Exceptional items–Gain/(Loss)	(16,696.06)	(20,775.93)	4,079.87	−19.64
Profit/(Loss) before tax	(1,19,946.00)	(15,381.87)	−1,04,564.13	679.79
Tax Expense				
Provision for Deferred Tax	(37,864.20)	(4,989.86)	−32,874.34	658.82
Previous Year Taxation Adjustment	—	(0.86)		
Profit/(Loss) for the year	(82,081.80)	(10,391.15)	−71,690.65	689.92
Earnings per share (in ₹)				
Basic	(43.15)	(5.52)	−37.63	681.70
Diluted	(43.15)	(5.52)	−37.63	681.70

during the year. With total cost going up by 43.60%, the net loss before tax registered an increase of around 680%.

Overall, JSL Stainless steel financial performance has been very poor. Its operation cost, employee benefit cost, and finance cost have all gone up. its loss has increased by around 680%.

Vertical Analysis

Vertical analysis was also introduced in Chapter 2. Recall that vertical analysis is a technique that compares account balances within one year. Formally, **vertical analysis** is an analysis technique that states each account balance on a financial statement as a percentage of a base amount on the statement. The base account is total assets

MAKING IT REAL

A retailer can grow sales by adding new stores and/or increasing sales in existing stores. A horizontal analysis does not distinguish between those two sources of sales growth. It only shows total sales growth. Because investors want to know how much of the growth is attributable to each source, some companies disclose "same-store" or "comparable-store" sales in their Management's Discussion and Analysis (MD&A). Same-store sales represent the growth in sales for stores that were open all year in both years presented. In its 2010 MD&A,

© AP IMAGES/JIM MONE

Best Buy, a US company, reports that the 1.2% increase in sales revenue " resulted primarily from the net addition of 147 new stores ... and the positive impact of foreign currency exchange rate fluctuations ..." but was " partially offset by a (1.8%) comparable stores sales decline." This shows that had Best Buy not opened stores during the year, it likely would have seen a decline in overall sales revenue. The company acknowledged its discussion that "customers appetite for certain product categories was below industry expectations."

for the balance sheet and either sales or revenues for the income statement. The actual calculation is as follows.

	For the Balance Sheet		For the Income Statement
Percentage =	$\frac{\text{Account balance}}{\text{Total Assets}}$	or	$\frac{\text{Account balance}}{\text{Net Sales or Revenue}}$

Like horizontal analysis, vertical analysis is a simple but powerful tool. The dividing of each account balance by either assets or revenues accomplishes two purposes. First, it shows the relative importance of each account to the company. Second, it standardizes the account balances by firm size so that companies of different sizes can be compared.

To illustrate, suppose a company with ₹10 million in total assets has ₹1 million in cash while another company with ₹100 billion in assets has ₹10 billion in cash. The ₹100 billion company has more cash, but it is also a much bigger company. A vertical analysis would show that each company has 10% of its assets in cash (₹1/₹10 = ₹10/₹100 = 10%). By dividing by total assets, the analysis makes possible a meaningful comparison of two companies of vastly different sizes. Because vertical analysis removes the effect of size, an analysis prepared on a financial statement is appropriately called a common-size financial statement.

Balance Sheet Analysis Exhibit 12-3 contains a vertical analysis of JSL Stainless Ltd. Balance Sheet as on March 31, 2013.

Exhibit 12-3 Vertical Analysis of JSL Stainless Ltd. March 31, 2013, Condensed Balance Sheet

Description	*As at 31.03.2013*		*(₹ In lakhs) As at 31.03.2012*	
Equity and Liabilities				
Shareholders Funds				
Share Capital	4,081.55	0.25	3,790.11	0.24
Reserves and Surplus	1,43,503.37	8.68	2,14,423.20	13.67
	1,47,584.92	8.93	2,18,213.31	13.91
Noon-Current Liabilities				
Long-term borrowings	8,76,435.33	53.03	7,71,257.61	49.16
Deffered tax liabilities (net)	1,592.61	0.10	39,456.81	2.51
Other Long-term liabilities	12,124.05	0.73	1,265.03	0.08
Long-term provisions	952.64	0.06	868.55	0.06
	8,91,104.63	53.92	8,12,848.00	51.81
Current Liabilities				
Short-term borrowings	2,02,312.22	12.24	1,53,145.13	9.76
Trade payables	2,97,534.06	18.00	2,03,394.68	12.96
Other current liabilities	1,13,809.93	6.89	1,81,074.75	11.54
Short-term provisions	283.59	0.02	201.44	0.01
	6,13,939.80	37.15	5,37,816.00	34.28
Total	16,52,629.35	100.00	15,68,877.31	100.00
Assets				
Non-Current Assets				
Fixed Assets				
Tangible assets	9,80,416.08	59.32	9,75,111.91	62.15
Intangible assets	292.03	0.02	428.95	0.03
Capital work-in-progress	14,590.34	0.88	45,663.86	2.91
Intangible assets under development	846.76	0.05	483.2	0.03
Non-current investments	17,111.20	1.04	16,886.20	1.08
Long-term loans and advances	15,576.14	0.94	20,603.13	1.31
Other non-current assets	1,772.89	0.11	2,213.84	0.14
	10,30,605.44	62.36	10,61,391.09	67.65
Current Assets				
Current investments	219.54	0.01	104.00	0.01
Inventories	3,27,642.11	19.83	2,70,275.89	17.23
Trade receivables	1,90,901.73	11.55	1,50,566.46	9.60
Cash and Bank Balances	8,778.94	0.53	16,419.81	1.05
Short-term loans and advances	94,032.44	5.69	69,652.12	4.44
Other current assets	449.15	0.03	467.94	0.03
	6,22,023.91	37.64	5,07,486.22	32.35
Total	16,52,629.35	100.00	15,68,877.31	100.00

The analysis shows large percentages of assets in both inventory and fixed assets. Such percentages are not surprising given that JSL Stainless Ltd. is a steel manufacturer. Of some concern is the high percentage

Vertical analysis An analysis technique that states each account balance on a financial statement as a percentage of a base amount on the statement.

associated with receivables 12.23%% in March 2012 and 19.8% in March 2013) and the decreased percentage associated with cash (1% in March 2012 versus 0.5% in March 2013). The ability of JSL Stainless Ltd. to collect cash from its receivables should be monitored.

The analysis of liabilities and equity shows that about 53% of the company's assets are generated by long-term borrowings. In total, 65% of JSL Stainless Ltd. assets are generated by liabilities. This is a slight more from March 2012, when 58.9% of assets were generated by liabilities.

The vertical analysis also discloses that noncurrent investment of the company remained at 1% in March 2012 and in March 2013.

Income Statement Analysis Exhibit 12-4 contains a vertical analysis of JSL Stainless Ltd, 2012–13 income statement.

The analysis shows that cost of goods sold is approximately 68% of sales revenue, leaving only about 22% for generating profit after making go all other expenses. There is an increase in cost of goods sold as compared to 2011–12 when it was around 65%. There has also been substantial increase in employee benefits, finance, deprecation and amortization cost. Overall, the total cost as percentage of net revenue has gone up from around 100% to more than 110%. Thus the company has experienced more loss in 2012–13 as compared to 2011–12.

Now that horizontal and vertical analyses have been conducted on both the income statement and the balance sheet, attention can be shifted to ratio analyses, starting with an analysis of JSL Stainless' profitability.

Everyone associated with a company—stockholders, creditors, employees, suppliers—wants the company to generate profits.

LO3 Profitability Analysis

One of the most important aspects of any financial analysis is profitability. Everyone associated

Exhibit 12-4 Vertical Analysis of JSL Stainless Ltd. March 31, 2013, Condensed Income Statement

(₹ In lakhs)

Description	*For the year ended 31.03.2013*		*For the year ended 31.03.2012*	
Income				
Revenue from operations (Gross)	11,12,188.27	108.12	8,49,833.01	107.6958304
Less: Excise Duty on sales	83,567.33	8.12	60,728.17	7.695830379
Revenue from operstions (Net)	10,28,620.94	100.00	7,89,104.84	100
Other Income	4,413.15	0.43	7,530.62	0.954324396
Total	10,33,034.09	100.43	7,96,635.46	100.9543244
Expenses				
Cost of materials consumed	7,29,398.63	70.91	5,48,442.31	69.50183071
Purchase of Trading Goods	2,629.51	0.26	9,689.84	1.227953436
Changes in inventories of finished goods, work in progress and Trading goods	(36,382.97)	-3.54	(43,533.62)	-5.516836014
Employee benefits expenses	24,632.61	2.39	16,983.32	2.152226059
Finance costs	99,029.31	9.63	51,680.03	6.549196936
Depreciation and amortization expense	70,130.96	6.82	40,860.75	5.178114229
Other Expenses				
Manufacturing Expenses	1,96,825.69	19.13	1,37,646.27	17.44334378
Administrative Expenses	12,943.88	1.26	7,821.98	0.991247247
Selling expenses	37,076.41	3.60	21,650.52	2.743681055
Total	11,36,284.03		7,91,241.40	100.2707574
Profit/ (Loss) before exceptional and extraordinary items and tax	(1,03,249.94)	−10.04	5,394.06	0.683566964
Exceptional items - Gain/(Loss)	(16,696.06)	−1.62	(20,775.93)	−2.632847874
Profit/(Loss) before tax	(1,19,946.00)	−11.66	(15,381.87)	−1.949280909
Tax Expense				
Provision for Deferred Tax	(37,864.20)	-3.68	(4,989.86)	−0.632344366
Previous Year Taxation Adjustment	-		(0.86)	−0.000108984
Profit/(Loss) for the year	(82,081.80)	-7.98	(10,391.15)	−1.316827559
Earnings per share (in ₹)				

with a company—stockholders, creditors, employees, suppliers—wants the company to generate profits. To determine a company's profitability, one can look at net income, but that tells only a portion of the story. It does not reveal how efficiently and effectively those profits were generated. To find out, one must compare net income to other company values such as sales, assets, equity, outstanding shares, and market prices.

The following ratios are commonly used to analyze profitability. Note that each ratio compares net income to some other financial aspect of the company. Because each ratio reveals something different about a company's income, they are best used in tandem so that a broad understanding of a company's profitability can be obtained.

Profitability Ratio	Relationship
Profit Margin	Income to Sales
Return on Equity	Income to Stockholders' Equity
Return on Assets	Income to Total Assets
Earnings per Share	Income to Shares Outstanding
Price to Earnings	Income to Stock Price

In the following sections, the text will explain each ratio and show the calculation for JSL's most recent year. Unless otherwise noted, data for each calculation is obtained from Exhibits 12-1 or 12-2. Immediately after the calculation, JSL Stainless Ltd's ratios for the current and prior two years and Tata Steel's current and prior year ratios will be provided for comparison purposes. After all ratios are presented, a summary of what was learned from the ratios about JSL's profitability will be provided.

Profit Margin

The **profit margin ratio** compares net income to net sales and measures the ability of a company to generate profits from sales. A higher ratio indicates a greater ability to generate profits from sales.

$$\text{Profit Margin} = \frac{\text{Net Income}}{\text{Net Sales}}$$

$$\frac{₹(82{,}081.80)}{₹10{,}28{,}620.94} = (9.98)\%$$

	2012–13	2011–12	2010–11
JSL	(9.98)%	(1.32)%	4.67%
Tata Steel	13.25%	19.73%	23.36%

JSL's 2012–13 profit margin is (9.98)%, meaning that the company made a loss of around 10 paise for every rupee of sales in 2012–13. While JSL was profitable in 2010–11, it was making loss in 2011–12 and 2012–13. Tata Steel was profitable in 2012–13 though its net income as a percentage of net revenue has gone down from 19.73% in 2011–12 to 13.25% in 2012–13.

Return on Equity

The **return on equity ratio** compares net income to the average balance in stockholders' equity during the year. The ratio represents how effectively a company uses the equity provided by stockholders during the year to generate additional equity for its owners. Stockholders naturally want this ratio to be as high as possible.

$$\text{Return on Equity} = \frac{\text{Net Income}}{\text{Average Stockholders' Equity}}$$

where average equity is as follows:

$$\frac{\text{Beginning equity} + \text{Ending equity}}{2}$$

$$\frac{₹(82{,}081.80)}{(₹1{,}47{,}584.92 + ₹2{,}18{,}213.31)/2} = (44.88)\%$$

	2012–13	2011–12	2010–11
JSL	(44.88)%	(4.68)%	15.27%
Tata Steel	9.43%	15.51%	16.37%

The 2012–13 ratio of (44.88)% shows that JSL Stainless Ltd. has made a loss of 44.88 paise for every rupee of resources provided by stockholders. This loss is higher than the ratios in the prior year. Notice in 2010–11 JSL had a positive return on equity. Notice also that Tata Steel's return on equity exceeds JSL in 2012–13.

Return on Assets

The **return on assets ratio** compares net income to average total assets during the year. It represents a company's ability to generate profits from its entire resource base, not just those resources provided by owners. Like

Profit margin ratio Compares net income to net sales and measures the ability to generate profits from sales.

Return on equity ratio Compares net income to average stockholders' equity and measures the ability to generate profits from equity.

Return on assets ratio Compares net income to average total assets and measures the ability to generate profits from assets.

©PHOTOS.COM/THINKSTOCK

the return on equity, investors would like the ratio as high as possible.

$$\text{Return on Assets} = \frac{\text{Net Income}}{\text{Average Total Assets}}$$

where average assets is as follows:

$$\frac{\text{Beginning total assets} + \text{Ending total assets}}{2}$$

$$\frac{₹(82{,}081.80)}{(₹16{,}52{,}629.35 + ₹15{,}68{,}877.31)/2} = (5.00)\%$$

	2012–13	2011–12	2010–11
JSL	(5.00)%	(0.69)%	(2.41)%
Tata Steel	5.12%	7.68%	8.44%

The 2012–13 ratio of (5.00)% shows that JSL made a loss of 5 paise for every rupee of assets it possessed during the year. This loss was higher than 2011–12 and profitability much lower than Tata Steel ratio. JSL's was not effective in the current year at using its existing resources to generate profits.

Earnings per Share

Earnings per share compares a company's net income to the average number of shares of common stock outstanding during the year. The ratio represents the return on each share of stock owned by an investor. Although companies normally disclose earnings per share on their income statements, the calculation will be demonstrated nonetheless.

Earnings per share Compares net income to common stock outstanding and represents profits generated per share of stock.

Price to earnings ratio Compares net income to a company's stock price and provides an indication of investor perceptions of the company.

The price to earnings ratio provides an indication of current investor perceptions of the company.

$$\text{Earnings per Share} = \frac{\text{Net Income}}{\text{Average Number of Common Shares Outstanding}}$$

where average outstanding shares is as follows:

$$\frac{\text{Beginning outstanding shares} + \text{Ending outstanding shares}}{2}$$

The beginning and ending outstanding shares are collected from the textual information given in the Schedule to the Balance Sheet and are rounded to lakh as follows: 18,73,15,792 = 1,873.16 lakh and 18,55,82,172 = 1,855.82 lakh.

$$\frac{₹(82{,}081.80)}{(₹20{,}40{,}77{,}547 + 18{,}95{,}05{,}625)/2} = (0.04)\%$$

	2011–12	2011–12	2010–11
JSL	₹(0.04)	₹(0.01)	₹ 17.07
Tata Steel	₹ 52.13	₹ 72.53	74.37

The ₹(0.04) value shows that JSL made a loss of ₹0.04 for every share of common stock outstanding during the year. This loss is higher than 2011–12. Note that in 2010–11 JSL made profit of ₹17.07 for ever share of common stock outstanding. Tata Steel's earning per share of ₹52.13 is lower than 2011–12 and 2010–11.

Price to Earnings Ratio

The **price to earnings ratio** compares net income to the current market price of the company's common stock. Because a company's stock price represents the value of the company per share of stock, the ratio uses earnings per share rather than net income. It is also the first ratio in which income is in the denominator rather than the numerator. That is why the ratio is called price to earnings rather than earnings to price.

$$\text{Price to Earnings Ratio} = \frac{\text{Current Stock Price per Share}}{\text{Earnings per Share}}$$

Because the price to earnings ratio uses stock prices, it provides an indication of current investor perceptions of the company. For example, a price to earnings ratio of 10 means that investors are willing to pay ten times current earnings per share to buy one share of stock. A ratio of 15 means that investors will pay fifteen times current earnings. A higher price to earnings ratio generally indicates that investors are more optimistic about the future prospects of a company. A lower ratio generally indicates that investors are less optimistic about the company's future.

The following calculation of JSL's March 2013 price to earnings ratio uses the ₹82.75 stock price at the close of business on March 31, 2013, the end of the company's fiscal year.

$$\frac{₹47.55}{₹(0.04)} = \text{NA}$$

	March 31, 2013	March 31, 2012	March 31, 2011
JSL	NA	NA	4.85
Tata Steel	6.00	6.50	8.34

JSL has a negative EPS. Negative EPS numbers are usually reported as "not applicable." Shareholders of company with a negative P/E should be aware that they are buying a share of a company that has been losing money per share of its stock. Tata Steel has a positive price to earnings ratio.

A company must maintain the ability to pay its liabilities as they come due.

Summary of Profitability

Based on the five ratios examined, it is clear that JSL is not a profitable company. This is a trend to watch closely, especially in an industry that depends on industrial spending.

LO4 Liquidity Analysis

A major concern in any financial analysis is an assessment of a company's liquidity. **Liquidity** refers to the ability of a company to satisfy its short-term obligations. A company must maintain the ability to pay its liabilities as they come due. Failing to do so can result in additional expenses and, ultimately, bankruptcy. As a result, everyone associated with a company—stockholders, creditors, employees, suppliers—wants to see adequate liquidity.

The following ratios are commonly used to assess a company's liquidity. While each ratio reveals information on its own, using the ratios in tandem provides a much

Liquidity The ability of a company to satisfy its short-term obligations.

MARUTI SUZUKI ANALYSIS

Using Maruti Suzuki's information in Appendix C, calculate Maruti Suzuki's profitability ratios and make a general assessment about the company's profitability. Maruti Suzuki's stock price on March 31, 2013, was ₹1,280.

Profit Margin: **Net Income/Sales = ₹23,921 ÷ ₹4,26,126 = 5.61%**

Return on Equity: **Net Income/Average Stockholders' Equity = ₹23,921 ÷ [(₹1,85,789 + ₹1,51,874) ÷ 2] = 14.12%**

Return on Assets: **Net Income/Average Total Assets = ₹23,921 ÷ [(₹2,66,880 + ₹2,23,022) ÷ 2] = 9.77%**

Earnings per Share: **Net Income/Average Outstanding Shares = ₹23,921 ÷ [(302.08 + 288.91) ÷ 2] = ₹80.95**

Price to Earnings Ratio: **Stock Price/Earnings per Share = ₹1,280 ÷ ₹80.95 = 15.81**

Maruti Suzuki shows many positive signs of profitability. It earns over 5.5 paise for every rupee of sales, over 14 paise for every rupee provided by stockholders, and ₹80.95 for every outstanding share of common stock. With a 15.81 price to earnings ratio, stockholders appear optimistic about Maruti Suzuki's future prospects.

richer understanding of liquidity. Note that each ratio focuses on some aspect of either current liabilities or current assets.

Liquidity Ratios	Relationship
Current Ratio	Current Assets to Current Liabilities
Quick Ratio	Cash-like Assets to Current Liabilities
Receivables Turnover Ratio	Sales to Accounts Receivable
Inventory Turnover Ratio	Cost of Goods Sold to Inventory

As in the previous section on profitability, the following sections will explain and calculate each ratio for JSL Stainless Ltd using data from Exhibits 12-1 and 12-2. A comparison of JSL Stainless Ltd and Tata Steel ratios will follow each calculation. After all ratios are presented, a summary of what was learned about JSL Stainless Ltd liquidity will be provided.

Current Ratio

The **current ratio** is one of the most frequently used ratios in financial analysis. It compares current assets to current liabilities. It therefore compares assets that should be turned into cash within one year to liabilities that should be paid within one year. A higher ratio indicates more assets available to satisfy current obligations and therefore greater liquidity.

$$\text{Current Ratio} = \frac{\text{Current Assets}}{\text{Current Liabilities}}$$

$$\frac{₹6,22,023.91}{₹16,52,629.35} = 0.38$$

	March 31, 2013	March 31, 2012	March 31, 2011
JSL	0.38	0.32	1.61
Tata Steel	0.70	0.76	2.20

JSL's ratio of 0.38 shows that it had ₹0.38 in current assets for every rupee of current liabilities. This is more or less the same as that of previous year, meaning that JSL has more or less same assets available to satisfy current obligations like that of previous year. Tata Steel's liquidity is better than JSL, but Tata Steel's liquidity has reduced compared to previous year.

While the trend in JSL's liquidity should be monitored, a ratio less than one is a cause for alarm. In fact, many investors would be critical of maintaining a current ratio too less or too high. They would rather the company keep only an adequate amount of assets in current assets and invest the rest in more productive and higher-yielding assets such as property, equipment, or investments.

Current ratio Compares current assets to current liabilities and measures the ability to pay current obligations.

Quick ratio Compares cash and near-cash assets to current liabilities and measures the ability to pay current liabilities immediately.

Receivables turnover ratio Compares credit sales to average accounts receivable and measures the ability to make and collect sales.

Quick Ratio

While the current ratio is an excellent measure of liquidity, it does have some limitations. In particular, current assets often include inventory that must be sold before cash can be generated to pay off current liabilities. Because of this, several additional ratios are used to provide more detail regarding a company's liquidity. One is the quick ratio.

The **quick ratio** compares a company's cash and near-cash assets, called *quick assets,* to its current liabilities. Quick assets include cash, short-term investments, and accounts receivable. Sometimes called the *acid-test ratio,* the quick ratio measures the degree to which a company could pay off its current liabilities immediately. Like the current ratio, a higher quick ratio indicates greater liquidity.

$$\text{Quick Ratio} = \frac{\text{Cash} + \text{Short-term Investments} + \text{Accounts Receivable}}{\text{Current Liabilities}}$$

$$\frac{₹8,778.94 + 1,90,901.73 + 94,032.44}{₹\ 6,13,939} = 0.48$$

	March 31, 2013	March 31, 2012	March 31, 2011
JSL	0.48	0.44	0.63
Tata Steel	0.32	0.40	1.84

JSL's ratio of 0.48 shows that at the end of its fiscal year, the company had ₹0.48 in cash and near-cash assets for every rupee of current liabilities. This indicates that JSL could pay nearly 50% of its current liabilities if they came due immediately. Although current liabilities will not likely come due immediately, the ratio is high compared to the ratio from 2012, but less compared to 2011. This is an issue to continue to monitor.

Receivables Turnover Ratio

The **receivables turnover ratio** compares a company's credit sales during a period to its average accounts receivable balance during that period. It measures a company's ability to make and collect sales. A higher turnover ratio means that the company is better able to generate and collect sales. Therefore, a higher ratio generally leads to better liquidity. Because credit sales are not usually reported by companies, the ratio uses net sales as a substitute.

$$\text{Receivables Turnover Ratio} = \frac{\text{Net Sales}}{\text{Average Accounts Receivables}}$$

where average accounts receivable is as follows:

$$\frac{\text{Beginning accounts receivable + Ending accounts receivable}}{2}$$

$$\frac{₹10,28,620.94}{(₹1,90,901.73 + ₹1,50,566.46)/2} = 6.02$$

	March 31, 2013	March 31, 2012	March 31, 2011
JSL	6.02	5.79	5.89
Tata Steel	44.91	50.95	68.13

JSL's ratio of 6.02 is though higher than its previous two ratios, but much lower than Tata Steel's current-year ratio. This is a cause for some concern. Why has JSL's ability to collect its receivables is so low compared to Tata Steel? One clue is the substantial increase in receivables—from ₹1,50,566.46 lakh in 2012 to ₹1,90,901.73. The horizontal analysis in Exhibit 12-1 shows this to be a 26.79% increase. The vertical analysis in Exhibit 12-2 shows that receivables as a percentage of assets went up from 9.60% to 11.55%. Such a change in receivables should be investigated further to determine whether there is a significant problem with collections.

Inventory Turnover Ratio

The **inventory turnover ratio** compares a company's sales during a period to its average inventory balance during that period. It reveals how many times a company is able to sell its inventory balance in a period. In general, companies want this ratio to be higher because it indicates that the company sold more inventory while maintaining less inventory on hand. This means that the company generated more sales revenue while reducing the costs of stocking inventory on the shelves.

$$\text{Inventory Turnover Ratio} = \frac{\text{Net Sales}}{\text{Average Inventory}}$$

where average inventory is as follows:

$$\frac{\text{Beginning inventory + Ending inventory}}{2}$$

$$\frac{₹10,28,620.94}{(3,27,642.11 + 2,70,275.89)/2} = 3.44$$

	March 31, 2013	March 31, 2012	March 31, 2011
JSL	3.44	3.28	3.64
Tata Steel	7.55	8.38	10.33

A 3.44 ratio shows that during 2012–13 JSL sold ₹3.44 of inventory for every rupee of inventory it had on its shelves. Notice that this has improved compared to 2011–12, but less than 2010–11 and it is also less than Tata Steel. It appears that JSL's ability to sell inventory is stable.

Inventory turnover ratio Compares cost of goods sold to average inventory and measures the ability to sell inventory.

MARUTI SUZUKI ANALYSIS

Using Maruti Suzuki's information in Appendix C, calculate Maruti Suzuki's liquidity ratios and make a general assessment about the company's liquidity.

Current Ratio: Current Assets/Current Liabilities = ₹1,09,248 ÷ ₹68,280 = 1.6

Quick Ratio: (Cash + Short-term Investments + Accounts Receivable + Other Current Assets)/Current Liabilities = (₹7,750 + ₹63,451 + ₹14,237 + ₹5,403) ÷ ₹68,280 = 1.33

Receivables Turnover: Net Sales/Average Accounts Receivable = ₹4,26,126 ÷ [(₹14,237 + ₹9,376) ÷ 2] = 36.10

Inventory Turnover: Net Sales/Average Inventory = ₹4,26,126 ÷ [(₹18,407 + ₹17,965) ÷ 2] = 23.43

While Maruti Suzuki carries more in current assets than current liabilities, the quick ratio shows that the company also maintain very high levels of quick assets given current liabilities. However, the inventory turnover ratio indicates that the company is successful in selling its inventory. Therefore, Maruti Suzuki appears to have adequate liquidity.

If a company cannot satisfy its obligations and becomes insolvent, it can fall into bankruptcy, which can result in significant losses to investors and creditors.

Summary of Liquidity Analysis

Based on the four ratios examined, it appears that JSL Stainless Ltd has just sufficient liquidity. The majority of its current assets are tied up in inventory, but it appears that the company is selling through its inventory just adequately. Of potential concern is the increase in accounts receivable. While not yet a threat to liquidity, it is a trend to watch closely. Tata Steel's liquidity is much better than JSL.

LO5 Solvency Analysis

A third component of any financial analysis is an examination of solvency. **Solvency** refers to a company's ability to satisfy its long-term obligations. If a company cannot satisfy its obligations and becomes *insolvent*, it can fall into bankruptcy, which can result in significant losses to investors and creditors. Therefore, both investors and creditors are interested in assessing solvency.

A company's solvency is related to its use of financial leverage. **Financial leverage** refers to the degree to which a company obtains capital through debt rather than equity in an attempt to increase returns to stockholders. Leverage is beneficial to stockholders when the return on borrowed funds exceeds the cost of borrowing those funds. In that case, leverage is positive. It is harmful, or negative, when the cost of borrowing the funds exceeds the return on those borrowed funds. As a company uses more financial leverage, it creates an opportunity for greater returns to stockholders, but it also creates greater solvency risk.

Although it is impossible to know whether a company will or will not be able to pay future obligations and remain solvent, the following three ratios can provide some indication of a company's general solvency.

Financial leverage The degree to which a company obtains capital through debt rather than equity in an attempt to increase returns to stockholders.

Debt to assets ratio Compares total liabilities to total assets and measures the percentage of assets provided by creditors.

© AP IMAGES/PRNEWSFOTO/MITSUBISHI DIGITAL ELECTRONICS AMERICA, INC.

Solvency Ratios	Relationship
Debt to Assets	Total Liabilities to Total Assets
Debt to Equity	Total Liabilities to Total Equity
Times Interest Earned	Net Income to Interest Expense

As in the previous sections, the following sections will explain and calculate each ratio for JSL Stainless Ltd using data from Exhibits 12-1 and 12-2. A comparison of JSL Stainless Ltd's and Tata Steel's ratios will follow each calculation. After all ratios are presented, a summary of what was learned about JSL's solvency will be provided.

Debt to Assets Ratio

The **debt to assets ratio** compares a company's total liabilities to its total assets and yields the percentage of assets provided by creditors. As such, the ratio provides a measure of a company's capital structure. Capital structure refers to the manner in which a company has financed its assets—either through debt or equity—and is also an indication of how much financial leverage a company is using. Since debt and any related interest must be repaid, companies with a higher percentage of assets provided by creditors have a riskier capital structure. In other words, they are using more financial leverage, and they therefore have a greater risk of insolvency.

$$\text{Debt to Assets Ratio} = \frac{\text{Total Liabilities}}{\text{Total Assets}}$$

$$\frac{₹15,05,044.43}{₹16,52,629.35} = 0.91$$

	March 31, 2013	March 31, 2012	March 31, 2011
JSL	0.91	0.86	0.84
Tata Steel	0.46	0.45	0.48

JSL's ratio of 0.91 shows that around 91 paise of liability is required to generate every rupee of assets. This ratio is higher than the previous year's. It indicates an increasingly risky capital structure and greater use of financial leverage. The ratio for Tata Steel is 0.46. Notice that Tata Steel is moving in the exact opposite direction. Its ratio is around 0.45 over the three years showing that it is taking on a less risky capital structure over time compared to JSL.

Debt to Equity Ratio

The **debt to equity ratio** compares a company's total liabilities to its total equity. Like the debt to assets ratio, this ratio provides a measure of a company's capital structure and financial leverage by directly comparing the two aspects of capital structure—liabilities and equity. Higher debt to equity ratios indicate a riskier capital structure and therefore greater risk of insolvency. Companies with higher debt to equity ratios are also said to be highly leveraged.

$$\text{Debt to Equity Ratio} = \frac{\text{Total Liabilities}}{\text{Total Equity}}$$

$$\frac{₹15{,}05{,}044.43}{₹1{,}47{,}584.92} = 10.19$$

	March 31, 2013	March 31, 2012	March 31, 2011
JSL	10.19	6.36	5.25
Tata Steel	0.84	0.83	0.91

JSL's ratio of 10.19 shows that it had ₹10 of liabilities for every rupee of equity at the end of the most recent year. This is higher than in the previous two years, indicating that its capital structure is becoming more dependent on liabilities and therefore riskier. Tata Steel's ratio is just above 0.80 indicating a lower reliance on liabilities and therefore lower risk. As you can see, the interpretation of the debt to equity ratio is the same as the debt to assets ratio.

Times Interest Earned

In addition to examining a company's capital structure, it is wise to assess whether a company can pay the interest on its debt. To answer this question, many use the times interest earned ratio.

The **times interest earned ratio** compares a company's net income to its interest expense. It shows how well a company can pay interest out of current-year earnings. As such, it helps creditors and investors determine whether a company can service its current debt by making its required interest payments.

Times Interest Earned Ratio =

$$\frac{\text{Net Income} + \text{Interest Expense} + \text{Income Tax Expense}}{\text{Interest Expense}}$$

Debt to equity ratio Compares total liabilities to total equity and measures a company's capital structure and financial leverage.

Times interest earned ratio Compares net income to interest expense and measures the ability to pay interest out of current earnings.

MARUTI SUZUKI ANALYSIS

Using Maruti Suzuki's information in Appendix C, calculate Maruti Suzuki's solvency ratios and make a general assessment about the company's solvency.

Debt to Assets Ratio: **Total Liabilities/Total Assets = ₹81,091 ÷ ₹2,66,880 = 0.30**

Debt to Equity Ratio: **Total Liabilities/Total Equity = ₹81,091 ÷ ₹1,85,789 = 0.44**

Times Interest Earned: **Net Income + Interest Expense + Income Tax Expense/Interest Expense = (₹23,921 + ₹1,898 + ₹5,989) ÷ ₹1,898 = 16.76**

According to these ratios, Maruti Suzuki finances its assets with more equity than liabilities. The times interest earned ratio shows that the company can comfortably pay interest expense with current year earnings. Thus, Maruti Suzuki's solvency appears secure.

Note that the ratio adjusts net income by adding back interest expense and income tax expense. These are added back to "gross up" income to the amount of earnings that were available to make interest payments. Once this adjustment is made, the ratio yields the number of times that current interest payments could be made out of current earnings. A higher ratio indicates a greater ability to make payments, and therefore less risk of insolvency.

$$\frac{₹(4,220.63)}{₹99,029.31} = (0.04)$$

	March 31, 2013	March 31, 2012	March 31, 2011
JSL	(0.04)	1.10	2.01
Tata Steel	5.53	5.85	8.52

JSL's ratio of (0.04) indicates that the company aren't earning enough to pay off its creditors. Note Tata Steel's 5.53 ratio indicates that the company earned 5.5 times more than its interest expense.

Summary of Solvency

Based on the three ratios examined, it appears that JSL's capital structure is trending toward more debt. Thus, its solvency risk has increased, and it is a trend to watch. However, it appears that JSL Stainless Ltd. is increasingly finding it difficult to handle the increased borrowing risk.

LO6 DuPont Analysis

All investors want to maximize the returns on their investments in a company. An investor's return is measured by the return on equity. To better understanding how the return was generated, investors often conduct a DuPont analysis.

A **DuPont analysis** provides insight into how a company's return on equity was generated by decomposing the return into three components: operating efficiency, asset effectiveness, and capital structure. The actual calculations of the analysis are as follows.

DuPont analysis Decomposes a company's return on equity into measures of operating efficiency, asset effectiveness, and capital structure.

DuPont Analysis

Operating Efficiency		*Asset Effectiveness*		*Capital Structure*		*Return on Equity*
$\frac{\text{Net Income}}{\text{Sales}}$	×	$\frac{\text{Sales}}{\text{Assets}}$	×	$\frac{\text{Assets}}{\text{Equity}}$	=	$\frac{\text{Net Income}}{\text{Equity}}$

The first component is a company's operating efficiency. It is calculated as net income divided by sales, which is also known as the profit margin ratio. This component reveals a company's ability to turn sales into profits. The higher the ratio, the more efficient a company is in turning sales into profits.

The second component is a company's effectiveness at using its assets. It is calculated as sales divided by assets. This ratio is commonly known as the asset turnover ratio. It measures the ability of a company to generate sales from its asset base. The higher the ratio, the more effective a company is in generating sales given its assets.

The third component is a company's capital structure. For this analysis, it is calculated as assets divided by equity. This ratio is similar to the debt to assets and debt to equity ratios in that it measures how a company has generated its assets. The higher the ratio, the more a company is financing its assets with debt rather than equity. So, a higher ratio means more financial leverage and a riskier capital structure. Sometimes, this ratio is called the leverage multiplier.

JSL Stainless Ltd's most recent DuPont analysis is shown as follows. Also shown are the results of the same analysis for the prior year. Note that the return on equity numbers are slightly different than those calculated previously in the text because a DuPont analysis does not use average equity in the calculation of return on equity.

JSL Stainless Ltd
DuPont Analysis
March 31, 2013

$\frac{\text{Net Income}}{\text{Sales}}$	×	$\frac{\text{Sales}}{\text{Assets}}$	×	$\frac{\text{Assets}}{\text{Equity}}$	=	$\frac{\text{Net Income}}{\text{Equity}}$
$\frac{₹(82,081.80)}{₹10,28,620.94}$	×	$\frac{₹10,28,620.94}{₹16,52,629.35}$	×	$\frac{₹16,52,629.35}{₹1,47,584.92}$	=	$\frac{₹(82,081.80)}{₹1,47,584.92}$
(0.08)	×	0.62	×	11.20	=	(0.56)
March 31, 2012						
(0.01)	×	0.50	×	7.18	=	(0.04)

The analysis shows clearly why JSL's return to its owners decreased from 2012 to 2013. The sales to assets multiplier went up from 0.50 to over 0.6. and its assets to equity multiplier also has gone up from 7.18 to 11.20. Though sales went up in 2013 as compared to 2012, loss went up from ₹(10,391.15) lakh to ₹(82,081.80) lakh. Quite simply, profits from sales were down in 2013, resulting in a negative return on equity.

One of the main benefits of a DuPont analysis is the ability to ask what-if questions. For example, what if JSL was able to obtain profit on each rupee of sales like in the previous year? How would that affect the return to owners? The analysis shows that the 2013 return would be 0.07 (.01 × 0.62 × 11.20 = 0.07).

Alternatively, what if JSL took a riskier leverage position by increasing its assets to equity ratio from 11.20 to 12.0? Is that in the best interests of owners? Assuming nothing else changes, the answer is "No." The return on equity would rise to 0.59 (0.08) × 0.62 × 12.0 = (0.59).

Finally, what if the market for steel took a significant downturn and JSL was only able to generate sales of 0.40 times assets on hand? Would that significantly affect the return to investors? The analysis shows that it would. The return would fall almost in half to 0.36 (0.08) × 0.40 × 11.20 = (0.36).

Like all ratio analyses, the DuPont analysis is a helpful tool for providing feedback on past performance and expectations for future performance. As such, it is relevant information that can affect the decision making of managers, investors, and creditors.

MARUTI SUZUKI ANALYSIS

Using Maruti Suzuki's information in Appendix C, conduct a DuPont analysis. What would happen to Maruti Suzuki's return on equity if it could generate 10 per cent more profit from sales?

$$\frac{\text{Net Income}}{\text{Sales}} \times \frac{\text{Sales}}{\text{Assets}} \times \frac{\text{Assets}}{\text{Equity}} = \frac{\text{Net Income}}{\text{Equity}}$$

$$\frac{₹23{,}921}{₹4{,}26{,}126} \times \frac{₹4{,}26{,}126}{₹2{,}66{,}880} \times \frac{₹2{,}66{,}880}{₹1{,}85{,}789} = \frac{₹23{,}921}{₹1{,}85{,}789}$$

$$0.06 \times 1.60 \times 1.44 = 0.13$$

If Maruti Suzuki's could increase its profit margin by 10%, it would increase the return to its owners from 13% to 16% (0.07 × 1.60 × 1.44). A small change in profits can create large changes in stockholder returns.

CONCEPT QUESTIONS

1. What three items does a financial analysis require?
2. What are some common standards of comparison in a financial analysis?
3. Which type of analysis compares account balances over time?
4. Describe the calculations associated with a horizontal analysis.
5. What type of analysis compares each account on a statement to a base amount?
6. What base amounts are used in vertical analyses of the income statement and the balance sheet?
7. Identify five ratios commonly used to analyze a company's profitability.
8. Show the calculation of each of the five profitability ratios and describe what each ratio reveals.
9. What does liquidity refer to?
10. Identify four ratios commonly used to analyze a company's liquidity.
11. Show the calculation of each of the four liquidity ratios and describe what each ratio reveals.
12. What does solvency refer to?
13. Identify three ratios commonly used to analyze a company's solvency.
14. Show the calculation of each of the three solvency ratios and describe what each ratio reveals.
15. A DuPont analysis breaks a company's return on equity into three components. Describe those components.
16. Why is a DuPont analysis valuable?

MULTIPLE CHOICE

1. In a horizontal analysis, the change in an account balance is expressed as a percentage change compared to:
   a. net income.
   b. total assets.
   c. prior-year account balance.
   d. both A and B.
2. Pauley Corp.'s balance in inventory increased from ₹50,000 to ₹60,000. A horizontal analysis of inventory would show:
   a. a 20.0% increase in inventory.
   b. a 12.5% decrease in inventory.
   c. a 12.5% increase in inventory.
   d. none of the above.
3. A horizontal analysis of sales and cost of goods sold yields the following:

Sales	15.8%
Cost of Goods Sold	18.9%

   Which of the following best describes these results?
   a. The company's cost of sales grew faster than its sales
   b. The company's cost of sales fell faster than its sales
   c. The company's sales fell slower than its cost of sales
   d. None of the above
4. When performing a vertical analysis, which of the following is usually the base amount for accounts payable?
   a. Net income
   b. Total liabilities
   c. Total assets
   d. Common stock
5. The following example shows what type of analysis?

	Account Balance	Percentage
Cash	₹ 1,50,000	15%
Equipment	3,50,000	35%
Property	5,00,000	50%
Total Assets	₹10,00,000	100%

   a. Horizontal analysis
   b. Ratio analysis
   c. Vertical analysis
   d. Fundamental analysis
6. A financial statement on which a vertical analysis is conducted is often called:
   a. a standardized statement.
   b. a common-size statement.
   c. a same-size statement.
   d. none of the above.
7. A vertical analysis can be used to compare different companies because it removes the effects of:
   a. accounting techniques.
   b. company profitability.
   c. company size.
   d. none of the above.
8. Profitability ratios usually compare some financial aspect of a company to:
   a. current assets.
   b. total assets.
   c. net income.
   d. stock price.
9. Which of the following is not a profitability ratio?
   a. Inventory turnover
   b. Earnings per share
   c. Profit margin
   d. Price to earnings
10. Dividing net income by average total assets yields:
    a. return on equity.
    b. return on assets.
    c. profit margin.
    d. price to earnings.
11. Which of the following would be considered good news for a company?
    a. Its return on assets decreases
    b. Its return on equity stays the same
    c. Its profit margin increases
    d. Its earnings per share decreases

12. A company reports net income of ₹45,00,000 when the balance in stockholder's equity increased from ₹2,00,00,000 to ₹3,00,00,000. What is the company's return on equity?
    a. 22.5%
    b. 15.0%
    c. 18.0%
    d. 9.6%
13. Which of the following ratios assists in evaluating a company's ability to pay its short-term obligations?
    a. Current ratio
    b. Debt to equity ratio
    c. Debt to assets ratio
    d. Return on assets
14. Liquidity refers to:
    a. the ability to be profitable.
    b. the ability to pay short-term obligations.
    c. the ability to generate cash from receivables.
    d. the ability to profit from sales.
15. Which of the following would likely be considered bad news for a company?
    a. Its inventory turnover ratio decreased dramatically
    b. Its quick ratio increased significantly
    c. Its receivables turnover ratio increased slightly
    d. Its current ratio was unchanged
16. A company has a current ratio of 1.5. This means that:
    a. the company has ₹1.50 in current assets for every ₹1.00 in current liabilities.
    b. the company earned ₹1.50 per share of stock.
    c. the company has more current liabilities than current assets.
    d. none of the above.
17. A company reports ₹4,56,000 in cost of goods sold in a year when its inventory increased from ₹60,000 to ₹86,000. What was the company's inventory turnover ratio?
    a. 5.3
    b. 7.6
    c. 6.2
    d. 8.1
18. Solvency refers to:
    a. the ability to sell inventory.
    b. the ability to pay short-term obligations.
    c. the ability to generate cash from receivables.
    d. the ability to pay long-term obligations.
19. Which of the following ratios is not a solvency ratio?
    a. Debt to assets ratio
    b. Debt to equity ratio
    c. Times interest earned ratio
    d. Inventory turnover ratio
20. The debt to assets ratio can be viewed as a good indicator of a company's:
    a. stock price.
    b. capital structure.
    c. liquidity.
    d. profitability.
21. Which of the following is not one of the three components in a DuPont analysis?
    a. Operating efficiency
    b. Asset effectiveness
    c. Capital structure
    d. All of the above are components of a DuPont analysis

BRIEF EXERCISES

1. Financial Statement Analysis

Financial statement analysis is defined as the process of applying analytical tools to a company's financial statements to understand the company's financial health.

Required

Identify and briefly describe the three items required to conduct successful financial statement analysis.

2. Calculate Horizontal Analysis

At the end of 2013, a company has a balance of ₹17,55,000 in cash and cash equivalents. At the beginning of the year, the company had a ₹15,60,000 balance.

Required

Perform a horizontal analysis of cash and briefly explain the result. Round percentages to one decimal point (i.e., 12.8%).

3. Calculate Vertical Analysis

Alyssa's Sporting Goods generated gross profit of ₹25,50,000 and net sales of ₹40,90,000 during the year. Operating expenses were ₹6,55,000.

Required

Perform a vertical analysis of operating expenses and briefly explain the result. Round percentages to one decimal point (i.e., 12.8%).

4. Calculate Profit Margin

Jim's Computer Warehouse produced net income of ₹1,50,000 and cost of goods sold of ₹4,00,000 for the year. Net sales were ₹9,80,000.

Required

Calculate Jim's profit margin for the year and briefly explain the result. Round percentages to one decimal point (i.e., 12.8%).

5. Calculate Return on Assets

During 2012–13, a company generated net income of ₹15,80,000. Total assets at the beginning of the year were ₹1,48,00,000 while they were ₹1,51,50,000 at the end of the year.

Required
Calculate the company's return on assets and briefly explain the result. Round percentages to one decimal point (i.e., 12.8%).

6. Calculate Earnings Per Share

During 2013, Blue Corporation produced net income of ₹15,50,000. The average number of shares of common stock outstanding for the year was 4,98,000.

Required
Calculate Blue's earnings per share for the year and briefly explain the result.

7. Calculate Current Ratio

A company has current assets of ₹1,55,900 and total assets of ₹3,78,000. Current liabilities are ₹1,21,500, and total liabilities are ₹2,65,350.

Required
Calculate the company's current ratio and briefly explain the result.

8. Calculate Inventory Turnover Ratio

In 2013, Ralph's Rug Outlet generated net sales of ₹12,50,000 and cost of goods sold of ₹7,23,000. Ralph's average inventory of rugs during the year was ₹95,300.

Required
Calculate Ralph's inventory turnover ratio for the year and briefly explain the result.

9. Calculate Debt to Assets Ratio

A company has current assets of ₹155,900 and total assets of ₹3,78,000. Current liabilities are ₹1,21,500 and total liabilities are ₹2,65,350.

Required
Calculate the company's debt to assets ratio and briefly explain the result.

10. Calculate Times Interest Earned Ratio

Stinky Carpet Cleaning Service produced net income of ₹12,56,000 in 2013. Interest expense was ₹1,25,500 during the year, and income tax expense was ₹4,20,000.

Required
Calculate Stinky's times interest earned ratio and briefly explain the result.

11. DuPont Analysis

After conducting a DuPont analysis, it is determined that a company's operating efficiency is 0.035. Asset effectiveness is 3.08, and capital structure is 2.65.

Required
Calculate the company's return on equity.

EXERCISES

12. Horizontal Analysis

The following asset information is available for BSI Inc.:

	2013	2012
Cash	₹ 35,000	₹ 60,000
Accounts receivable	60,000	55,000
Inventory	1,25,000	1,75,000
Total current assets	2,20,000	2,90,000
Property and equipment	1,75,000	1,50,000
Total assets	₹3,95,000	₹4,40,000

Required
Prepare a horizontal analysis of BSI's assets. Round percentages to one decimal point (i.e., 12.8%).

13. Horizontal Analysis

The income statements of Crisp Corp. for the past two years are as follows:

Income Statements For the Years Ending December 31	2013	2012
Sales	₹3,00,000	₹2,50,000
Cost of goods sold	1,25,000	1,00,000
Gross profit	₹1,75,000	₹1,50,000
Operating expenses	75,000	50,000
Operating income	₹1,00,000	₹1,00,000
Interest expense	35,000	15,000
Income before taxes	₹ 65,000	₹ 85,000
Income tax expense	25,000	30,000
Net income	₹ 40,000	₹ 55,000

Required
Prepare and interpret a horizontal analysis of Crisp's income statements. Round percentages to one decimal point (i.e., 12.8%).

14. Vertical Analysis

The following asset information is available for LOC Inc.:

	2013
Cash	₹ 1,50,000
Accounts receivable	3,00,000
Inventory	7,50,000
Total current assets	12,00,000
Property and equipment	20,50,000
Total assets	₹32,50,000

Required
Prepare a vertical analysis of assets. Round percentages to one decimal point (i.e., 12.8%).

15. Vertical Analysis

The income statements of High Noon Corp. for the past two years are as follows:

Income Statements For the Years Ending December 31		
	2013	2012
Sales	₹7,25,000	₹7,00,000
Cost of goods sold	3,45,000	3,85,000
Gross profit	₹3,80,000	₹3,15,000
Operating expenses	1,75,000	1,80,000
Operating income	₹2,05,000	₹1,35,000
Interest expense	45,000	40,000
Income before taxes	₹1,60,000	₹ 95,000
Income tax expense	55,000	30,000
Net income	₹1,05,000	₹ 65,000

Required

Prepare and interpret a vertical analysis of High Noon's income statements. Round percentages to one decimal point (i.e., 12.8%). What was the most significant reason for the change in profitability?

16. Interpret Horizontal Analysis

Three companies report the following horizontal analyses:

	Company A	Company B	Company C
Accounts receivable	1.1%	14.1%	2.1%
Inventory	10.4	(1.7)	6.4
Sales	(3.2)	1.6	8.6
Total assets	1.4	(2.5)	7.0

Required

For each company, describe what the percentages reveal about the company. Which of the companies would you be most concerned about?

17. Interpret Vertical Analysis

A grocery store and a jewelry store provide the following vertical analyses of certain accounts:

	Company A	Company B
Gross profit	26.0%	55.2%
Operating expenses	22.2	48.0
Net income	3.8	7.2
Inventory	30.4	68.2
Property and equipment	57.8	32.5

Required

Identify which company is likely the grocer and which is likely the jewelry store. Explain the reasons for your conclusions.

18. Identify Ratios

The following ratios are often used in financial statement analysis:

_________ Return on equity
_________ Debt to assets ratio
_________ Times interest earned
_________ Quick ratio
_________ Inventory turnover ratio
_________ Price to earnings ratio
_________ Profit margin
_________ Current ratio
_________ Debt to equity ratio

Required

Identify each ratio as a profitability, liquidity, or solvency ratio.

19. Interpret Ratios

The following information is available for Warmouth Enterprises:

	2013	2012
Profit margin	8.7	8.3
Return on assets	10.2	10.4
Price to earnings ratio	13.5	12.0
Quick ratio	0.8	0.9
Inventory turnover ratio	5.5	7.2
Receivables turnover ratio	11.3	15.5
Times interest earned	7.2	6.4

Required

For each ratio, indicate whether the change in the ratio is favorable or unfavorable and why.

20. Define Ratios

The following statements describe various financial statement analysis ratios:

a. Shows the return to each share of stock owned by an investor
b. Measures the difference between quick assets and current liabilities
c. Measures the ability of a company to generate profits from sales
d. Provides a measure of a company's capital structure
e. Shows a company's ability to generate profits from its entire resource base
f. Gives information as to how a company manages its inventory
g. Measures a company's capital structure using liabilities and equity
h. Shows how effectively a company uses its current equity to generate additional equity
i. Gives a less strict measure of a company's ability to meet its short-term obligations
j. Shows how well a company can pay interest on debt out of current-year earnings
k. Measures a company's ability to make and collect sales
l. Provides an indication of current investor perceptions of the company

Required

Identify the appropriate ratio for each of the descriptions.

21. Profitability Ratios

The following financial information about Cloudburst Co. is available:

Sales	₹60,00,000
Net income	13,00,000
Average total assets	90,00,000
Average stockholders' equity	44,00,000

The following additional information is available:

- 5,00,000 shares of common stock were outstanding during the year.
- The stock was recently trading for ₹5.00 per share.

Required

Compute the following ratios: profit margin, return on equity, return on assets, earnings per share, and price to earnings. Round percentages to one decimal point (i.e., 12.8%).

22. Profitability Ratios

The following financial information about NGC Company is available:

Net income	₹ 15,00,000
Common shares outstanding, January 1	4,00,000
Common shares outstanding, December 31	5,00,000
Market price at December 31	₹ 100.00
Sales	₹ 94,50,000
Total assets, January 1	₹ 80,00,000
Total assets, December 31	₹1,00,00,000
Stockholders' equity, January 1	₹ 45,00,000
Stockholders' equity, December 31	₹ 47,50,000

Required

Compute and interpret the following ratios: profit margin, return on equity, return on assets, earnings per share, and price to earnings. Round percentages to one decimal point (i.e., 12.8%).

23. Profitability Ratios and Leverage

The following financial information about Stephens Company is available:

Net income	₹ 45,00,000
Sales	₹4,80,50,000
Average assets	₹2,93,00,000
Average equity	₹ 73,00,000
Common shares outstanding January 1	5,00,000
Common shares outstanding December 31	7,50,000
Market price at December 31	₹ 90.35

Required

Calculate all profitability ratios for Stephens. Round percentages to one decimal point (i.e., 12.8%).

Does it appear that the company is using financial leverage effectively or ineffectively? Why?

24. Liquidity Ratios

The following information was taken from the financial statements of Connor Cookers and Olson Ovens:

(in millions)	2013	2012
Total current assets		
Connor Cookers	₹ 46,448	₹2,49,664
Olson Ovens	1,55,117	1,53,188
Cash		
Connor Cookers	24,311	48,936
Olson Ovens	28,894	28,406
Accounts receivable		
Connor Cookers	8,216	1,86,766
Olson Ovens	1,14,645	1,14,511
Inventory		
Connor Cookers	13,921	13,962
Olson Ovens	11,578	10,271
Current liabilities		
Connor Cookers	69,036	74,457
Olson Ovens	80,220	85,037
Sales		
Connor Cookers	2,07,349	1,94,655
Olson Ovens	1,60,123	1,76,896
Cost of goods sold		
Connor Cookers	80,153	79,411
Olson Ovens	76,740	71,561

Required

For each company, compute the following 2013 ratios: receivables turnover ratio, inventory turnover ratio, current ratio, and quick ratio. Based in your calculations, discuss the liquidity of each company.

25. Transactions Affecting Liquidity Ratios

Robinson Tools has ₹50,000 of quick assets, ₹1,35,000 of total current assets, and ₹1,00,000 of total current liabilities prior to the following transactions.

1. Made sales on account of ₹10,000
2. Paid cash for accounts due to suppliers, ₹15,000
3. Received cash for accounts receivable of ₹15,000
4. Prepaid expenses of ₹7,500 with cash
5. Purchased inventory of ₹20,000 on account
6. Paid a ₹5,000 cash dividend
7. Repaid short-term loans of ₹10,000 with cash
8. Purchased short-term investments of ₹15,000 with cash
9. Borrowed ₹25,000 from the bank by signing a 90-day note
10. Sold inventory of ₹30,000 for cash

Required

Indicate whether each transaction would increase, decrease, or have no effect on Robinson's current and quick ratios. Treat each transaction independently.

26. Solvency Ratios

The following information was taken from the financial statements of TKO Company:

	2013	2012
Total assets	₹20,00,000	₹12,50,000
Total liabilities	7,50,000	7,50,000
Total equity	12,50,000	5,00,000
Operating income	3,50,000	3,00,000
Interest expense	70,000	75,000

Required

Compute the debt to assets ratio, the debt to equity ratio, and times interest earned for both years.

27. Solvency Ratios

The following financial information regarding Foshee Flapjacks is available:

2013 Balance Sheet	
Total assets	₹53,00,000
Total liabilities	14,00,000
Total stockholders' equity	39,00,000

2012 Income Statement	
Sales	₹25,00,000
Cost of goods sold	12,50,000
Gross profit	₹12,50,000
Operating expenses	4,00,000
Operating income	₹ 8,50,000
Interest expense	1,00,000
Income before taxes	₹ 7,50,000
Income tax expense	2,50,000
Net income	₹ 5,00,000

Required

Compute the following ratios: debt to assets, debt to equity, and times interest earned. Discuss the solvency of Foshee Flapjacks. Does the company rely more on equity or debt to finance its operations?

28. Sensitivity of Solvency Ratios

The following financial information regarding Wick Industries is available:

Total liabilities	₹1,50,000
Total equity	4,00,000
Total assets	5,50,000
Income tax expense	20,000
Net income	35,000
Operating cash flows	1,25,000
Interest expense	15,000

Wick would like to increase its return to stockholders. To do so, it wants to increase its debt to assets ratio to 0.70 by issuing debt and buying back common stock.

Required

a. Calculate Wick's current debt to equity, debt to assets, and times interest earned ratios.
b. How much debt would Wick have to issue to buy enough common stock to raise its debt to assets ratio to 0.70?
c. What would concern you about Wick's plan?

29. DuPont Analysis

The following financial information about Carbon Company is available:

	2013
Total average assets	₹2,00,000
Total average equity	1,25,000
Sales	35,000
Net income	7,000

Required

Prepare a DuPont analysis for Carbon Company.

30. DuPont Analysis

The following financial information about Cole's Colas, Inc., is available:

	2013
Total average assets	₹3,50,000
Total average equity	1,90,000
Sales	55,000
Net income	9,000

Required

Prepare a DuPont analysis for Cole's Colas and interpret each component of the analysis.

31. DuPont Analysis

During the year, Shields Corp. generated net income of ₹1,23,547 on sales of ₹15,40,005. At the end of the year, Shields had total assets of ₹9,20,558 and total equity of ₹4,03,346.

Required

a. Conduct a DuPont analysis to identify Shields' return on equity and the return's three components.
b. Shields is considering plans that would either (1) double its operating efficiency or (2) increase its capital structure by half of its current value. Which plan would provide the greatest increase to return on equity?

32. Financial Analysis Terms

The following is a list of terms and definitions associated with financial statement analysis tools:

1. Horizontal analysis
2. Current ratio
3. Vertical analysis
4. Quick ratio
5. Profit margin
6. Inventory turnover ratio
7. Return on equity
8. Price to earnings ratio
9. Capital structure
10. Dividend payout ratio

a. A comparison of net income to sales that measures a company's ability to generate profits
b. A liquidity ratio that compares cash and near cash assets to current liabilities
c. The mix of debt and equity that a company uses to generate its assets
d. Compares the income of a company in terms of earnings per share with the price of one share of stock
e. A technique that calculates both the dollar and percentage change in account balances from one term to the next
f. A measure of how many times a company is able to sell its inventory balance in a period
g. A technique that compares account balances within one year
h. A measure of the percentage of earnings that a company pays out as dividends
i. A ratio comparing a company's current liabilities to current assets
j. A comparison of net income to the average balance in stockholders' equity during the year

Required
Match each term with the appropriate definition.

33. Financial Analysis Terms

The following is a list of terms and definitions associated with financial statement analysis tools:

1. Return on assets
2. Debt to equity ratio
3. Earnings per share
4. Times interest earned
5. Financial leverage
6. Receivables turnover ratio
7. Debt to assets ratio
8. Solvency
9. Liquidity
10. DuPont analysis

a. A company's ability to continue in business in the long term by satisfying long-term obligations
b. A technique that breaks return on equity into three components
c. A comparison of net income to average total assets during the period
d. Refers to a company's ability to meet its short-term obligations
e. The practice of obtaining capital through debt rather than equity to increase returns for the stockholders
f. A comparison of total liabilities to total stockholders' equity
g. A measure of how often a company turns over its receivables balance during the year
h. A comparison of net income before interest and taxes to interest expense
i. Net income presented on a per share basis
j. A comparison of total liabilities to total assets

Required
Match each term with the appropriate definition.

PROBLEMS

34. Analyzing Financial Statements

The following financial information is available for Last Chance Repossessions Company as of December 31, 2013 (in millions):

Comparative Balance Sheet	2013	2012
Cash	₹ 15	₹ 10
Accounts receivable	30	25
Inventory	75	75
Prepaid insurance	10	15
Total current assets	130	125
Property and equipment	500	400
Accumulated depreciation	100	85
Total property and equipment	400	315
Total assets	₹530	₹440
Accounts payable	₹ 40	₹ 50
Other current liabilities	25	40
Total current liabilities	65	90
Bonds payable	75	150
Total liabilities	140	240
Common stock	290	150
Retained earnings	100	50
Total stockholders' equity	390	200
Total liabilities and stockholders' equity	₹530	₹440

Income Statement	2013
Sales	₹400
Cost of goods sold	210
Gross profit	₹190
Operating expenses	55
Operating income	₹135
Interest expense	15
Income before taxes	₹120
Income tax expense	50
Net income	₹ 70

Required

Calculate all profitability, liquidity, and solvency ratios (except earnings per share, price to earnings, and debt to equity) and comment on Last Chance's overall profitability, liquidity, and solvency. Round percentages to one decimal point (i.e., 12.8%).

35. Analyzing Financial Statements

Amanda's Anchors has applied for a loan from a local bank. The bank is basing its decision on the following information:

Ratio	Industry Average
Current ratio	1.50
Quick ratio	0.80
Receivables turnover ratio	18.00
Inventory turnover ratio	20.00
Debt to assets ratio	0.56
Times interest earned	6.52
Profit margin	10.25%
Return on assets	11.50%
Return on equity	20.30%

Amanda's Anchors
Income Statement
For the Year Ending December 31, 2013 (in millions)

Sales	₹60
Cost of goods sold	35
Gross profit	₹25
Operating expenses	10
Operating income	₹15
Interest expense	2.5
Income before taxes	₹12.5
Income tax expense	6.5
Net income	₹ 6

Amanda's Anchors
Balance Sheet

	December 31, 2013	December 31, 2012
Cash	₹ 7.5	₹ 6.0
Accounts receivable	0.3	2
Inventory	3	2
Prepaid insurance	0.5	0.5
Total current assets	14	10.5
Property and equipment	60	55
Accumulated depreciation	14	11
Total property and equipment	46	44
Total assets	₹60	₹54.5
Accounts payable	₹ 6	₹ 6
Other current liabilities	4	4.5
Total current liabilities	10	10.5
Bonds payable	15	15
Total liabilities	25	25.5
Common stock	25	25
Retained earnings	10	40
Total stockholders' equity	35	29
Total liabilities and stockholders' equity	₹60	₹54.5

Required

For Amanda's Anchors, calculate the ratios for which the bank has an industry average. After comparing Amanda's ratios to the industry averages, should the bank approve the loan? Why or why not?

36. Using Ratios to Evaluate a Business Purchase

Overtake Financial Group is a large corporation whose sole activity is the acquisition of quality subsidiary companies. You are a senior analyst for Overtake, and your manager has just come to you with the following financial statements for Burning Corn Company, an ethanol producing firm based in Nebraska, which is currently trading at ₹500 per share. He wants you to analyze the company and give a recommendation on whether or not to submit a bid for Burning Corn.

Burning Corn Company Comparative Balance Sheet at December 31		
	2013	2012
Cash	₹ 10,000	₹ 20,000
Accounts receivable	30,000	45,000
Inventory	1,05,000	75,000
Prepaid insurance	5,000	15,000
Total current assets	1,50,000	1,55,000
Property and equipment	3,75,000	3,25,000
Accumulated depreciation	55,000	40,000
Total property and equipment	3,20,000	2,85,000
Total assets	₹4,70,000	₹4,40,000
Accounts payable	₹ 60,000	₹ 50,000
Notes payable	25,000	25,000
Total current liabilities	85,000	5,000
Bonds payable	2,80,000	2,80,000
Total liabilities	3,65,000	3,55,000
Common stock (Avg. 100,000 shares outstanding)	75,000	75,000
Retained earnings	30,000	10,000
Total stockholders' equity	1,05,000	85,000
Total liabilities and stockholders' equity	₹4,70,000	₹4,40,000

Burning Corn Company 2013 Income Statement	
Sales	₹2,50,000
Cost of goods sold	1,50,000
Gross profit	₹1,00,000
Administrative expenses	25,000
Depreciation expense	15,000
Total operating expenses	40,000
Operating income	₹ 60,000
Interest expense	10,000
Income before taxes	₹ 50,000
Income tax expense	25,000
Net income	₹ 25,000

Required

Prepare a brief written analysis of Burning Corn's profitability, liquidity, and solvency. Include a table of calculated ratios and your recommendation on whether Overtake should bid on the company. Round percentages to one decimal point (i.e., 12.8%).

CASES

37. Research and Analysis

Access the 2012–13 annual report for **Raymond Limited** by clicking on the *About Us, Investor Relations,* and *Annual Reports* links at www.raymond.in/inv.

Required

a. Examine the company's income statement and balance sheet and calculate all profitability, liquidity, and solvency ratios for 2012–13. To calculate the price to earnings ratio, use the high stock price for the fiscal quarter ended March 31, 2013.

b. Based on your answers above, write a paragraph explaining your opinion of the financial health of Raymond Limited.

c. Calculate a DuPont analysis and explain what would happen to the company's return on equity if it was able to improve its operating efficiency by one paise.

38. Research and Analysis

Access the 2011 annual report of **American Eagle Outfitters** by clicking on the *About AEO Inc., AE Investment Info,* and *Historical Annual Reports* links at www.ae.com. Also, access the 2010 annual report of **Gap Inc.** by clicking on the *Investors, Financials,* and *Annual Reports & Proxy* links at www.gapinc.com.

Required

a. Conduct horizontal and vertical analyses on each company's income statement.

b. Compute all profitability ratios (except price to earnings) for each company for the most recent year.

c. Compare the profitability of each company.

d. Conduct a DuPont analysis.

e. Which company's stockholders would benefit the most from a $0.01 increase in profits per dollar of sales?

39. Ethics in Accounting

Retraction Company currently has a line of credit with HSC Bank. The interest rate on the line of credit increases from 7.25% to 10.25% if the following terms of the credit agreement are not met:

a) Retraction's current ratio must remain above 1.2 at all times.

b) Retraction's times interest earned must be 3.0 or greater at all times.

The following preliminary financial information has been prepared by the accountants of Retraction Company:

Current assets	$1,00,000
Current liabilities	75,000
Income before interest and taxes	25,000
Interest expense	7,000

Your senior accounting manager calls to your attention that current assets include $10,000 worth of an investment in callable bonds, which do not mature for 5 years but will be callable if the company so desires in 10 months. He also notes $12,000 worth of revenue, which is attributed to a service contract for which Retraction has received payment but has not yet performed the services. There should be no reasonable reason why the contract will not be fulfilled.

Required

a. Based on the financial information presented above, is Retraction within the guidelines set forth in its credit agreement?
b. Would you change the treatment of the two items your senior manager brought to your attention? Do you see any problem with the way these items are classified? Explain your answer.
c. Based on your response to part (b), prepare revised financial information if it is necessary. If you revised the information, is Retraction still compliant with its loan agreement?

40. Written Communication

The following financial ratios have been provided to you by your company:

	2013	2012	2011
Horizontal analysis of sales	47.0%	26.0%	15.0%
Profit margin	8.2%	7.5%	6.8%
Return on equity	13.1%	12.3%	11.1%
Current ratio	2.4	2.1	1.8
Quick ratio	0.9	1.1	1.2
Inventory turnover ratio	4.4	4.6	4.7
Debt to assets ratio	0.8	0.7	0.6

Your boss has asked you to prepare a press release to highlight the company's financial results. Analysts have been predicting a strong year, and the CEO wants these highlights to reflect that.

Required

Prepare a brief press release describing the general performance of the company. Use the ratios as supporting evidence.

reviewcard CHAPTER 12 Financial Statement Analysis

Learning Objectives		Key Concepts
LO1	Understand the nature of financial statement analysis.	Financial analysis is the process of applying analytical tools to a company's financial statements to understand the company's financial health. The goal of financial analysis is to provide the context necessary to understand a company's financial information and to make good decisions. Financial analysis requires financial information, standards of comparison, and analysis tools such as horizontal analysis, vertical analysis, and ratio analysis.
LO2	Calculate and interpret horizontal and vertical analyses.	Horizontal analysis is used to compare both the dollar change and the percent change of an account balance from one period to the next. Vertical analysis is used to compare account balances within one year by expressing them as a percentage of a base amount on the financial statement.
LO3	Assess profitability through the calculation and interpretation of ratios.	Profitability refers to the ability of a company to generate profits effectively and efficiently. The following five ratios are commonly used to assess a company's profitability: profit margin, return on equity, return on assets, earnings per share, and price to earnings. Each of these ratios compares net income to some other financial aspect of the company in question.
LO4	Assess liquidity through the calculation and interpretation of ratios.	Liquidity refers to the ability of a company to satisfy its short-term obligations. The following four ratios are commonly used to assess a company's liquidity: current ratio, quick ratio, receivable turnover ratio, and inventory turnover ratio. Each of these ratios focuses on some aspect of either current assets or current liabilities.
LO5	Assess solvency through the calculation and interpretation of ratios.	Solvency refers to the ability of a company to satisfy its long-term obligations and therefore to continue in business over the long term. The following three ratios are commonly used to assess a company's solvency: debt to assets ratio, debt to equity ratio, times interest earned.
LO6	Calculate and interpret a DuPont analysis.	A DuPont analysis decomposes a company's return on equity into three parts: operational efficiency, asset effectiveness, and leverage. The analysis reveals how a company generated its return to stockholders and allows a stockholder to determine how the return would be affected by changes in operations, asset use, or capital structure.

Key Definitions

Current ratio Compares current assets to current liabilities and measures the ability to pay current obligations.

Debt to assets ratio Compares total liabilities to total assets and measures the percentage of assets provided by creditors.

Debt to equity ratio Compares total liabilities to total equity and measures a company's capital structure and financial leverage.

DuPont analysis Decomposes a company's return on equity into measures of operating efficiency, asset effectiveness, and capital structure.

Earnings per share Compares net income to common stock outstanding and represents profits generated per share of stock.

Financial leverage The degree to which a company obtains capital through debt rather than equity in an attempt to increase returns to stockholders.

Financial statement analysis The process of applying analytical tools to a company's financial statements to understand the company's financial health.

Horizontal analysis An analysis technique that calculates the change in an account balance from one period to the next and expresses that change in both dollar and percentage terms.

Inventory turnover ratio Compares cost of goods sold to average inventory and measures the ability to sell inventory.

Liquidity The ability of a company to satisfy its short-term obligations.

Price to earnings ratio Compares net income to a company's stock price and provides an indication of investor perceptions of the company.

Profit margin ratio Compares net income to net sales and measures the ability to generate profits from sales.

Quick ratio Compares cash and near-cash assets to current liabilities and measures a company's ability to pay current liabilities immediately.

Receivables turnover ratio Compares credit sales to average accounts receivable and measures the ability to make and collect sales.

Key Definitions (continued)

Return on assets ratio Compares net income to average total assets and measures the ability to generate profits from assets.

Return on equity ratio Compares net income to average stockholders' equity and measures the ability to generate profits from equity.

Times interest earned ratio Compares net income to interest expense and measures the ability to pay interest out of current earnings.

Vertical analysis An analysis technique that states each account balance on a financial statement as a percentage of a base amount on the statement.

Demonstration Problem

The following information was taken from past financial statements of The Great Company.

	Current Year	Prior Year
Current assets	₹3,650	₹3,797
Quick assets	1,952	2,314
Total assets	9,955	9,863
Current liabilities	3,658	3,488
Total liabilities	7,731	7,603
Total stockholders' equity	2,224	2,260
Net sales	9,252	
Cost of sales	3,708	
Income before interest and taxes	2,028	
Interest expense	54	
Net income	1,385	
Other information:		
Common stock shares outstanding	1,007	1,044
Stock price at year end	₹23.55	

Calculate all profitability, liquidity, and solvency ratios for the current year.

Demonstration Problem Solution

Profitability ratios:		
Profit margin	₹1,385 ÷ ₹9,252	15.0%
Return on equity	₹1,385 ÷ [(₹2,224 + ₹2,260) ÷ 2]	61.8%
Return on assets	₹1,385 ÷ [(₹9,955 + ₹9,863) ÷ 2]	14.0%
Earnings per share	₹1,385 ÷ [(1,007 + 1,044) ÷ 2]	₹1.35
Price to earnings	₹23.55 ÷ ₹1.35*	17.4

* EPS is taken from the above calculation

Liquidity ratios:		
Current ratio	₹3,650 ÷ ₹3,658	1.00
Quick ratio	₹1,952 ÷ ₹3,658	0.53
Receivables turnover ratio	₹9,252 ÷ [(₹920 + ₹1,202) ÷ 2]	8.72
Inventory turnover ratio	₹3,708 ÷ [(₹1,094 + ₹928) ÷ 2]	3.67
Solvency ratios:		
Debt to assets	₹7,731 ÷ ₹9,955	0.78
Debt to equity	₹7,731 ÷ ₹2,224	3.48
Time interest earned	₹2,028 ÷ ₹54	37.56

Key Formulas

Profitability Ratios

$$\text{Profit Margin} = \frac{\text{Net Income}}{\text{Net Sales}}$$

$$\text{Return on Equity} = \frac{\text{Net Income}}{\text{Average Stockholders' Equity}}$$

$$\text{Return on Assets} = \frac{\text{Net Income}}{\text{Average Total Assets}}$$

$$\text{Earnings per Share} = \frac{\text{Net Income}}{\text{Average Number of Common Shares Outstanding}}$$

$$\text{Price to Earnings Ratio} = \frac{\text{Current Stock Price per Share}}{\text{Earnings per Share}}$$

Liquidity Ratios

$$\text{Current Ratio} = \frac{\text{Current Assets}}{\text{Current Liabilities}}$$

$$\text{Quick Ratio} = \frac{\text{Cash} + \text{Short-term Investments} + \text{Accounts Receivable}}{\text{Current Liabilities}}$$

$$\text{Receivables Turnover Ratio} = \frac{\text{Net Sales}}{\text{Average Accounts Receivables}}$$

$$\text{Inventory Turnover Ratio} = \frac{\text{Cost of Goods Sold}}{\text{Average Inventory}}$$

Solvency Ratios

$$\text{Debt to Assets Ratio} = \frac{\text{Total Liabilities}}{\text{Total Assets}}$$

$$\text{Debt to Equity Ratio} = \frac{\text{Total Liabilities}}{\text{Total Equity}}$$

$$\text{Times Interest Earned Ratio} = \frac{\text{Net Income} + \text{Interest Expense} + \text{Income Tax Expense}}{\text{Interest Expense}}$$

DuPont Analysis

Operating Efficiency × *Asset Effectiveness* × *Capital Structure* = *Return on Equity*

$$\frac{\text{Net Income}}{\text{Sales}} \times \frac{\text{Sales}}{\text{Assets}} \times \frac{\text{Assets}}{\text{Equity}} = \frac{\text{Net Income}}{\text{Equity}}$$

ACCT

Appendix A
Investments

Learning Objectives

After studying the material in this chapter, you should be able to:

LO1 Identify and understand the accounting for different types and classifications of investments.

Investments

Companies commonly invest in other entities by purchasing debt securities or equity securities issued by those entities.

A *debt security* is a financial instrument issued by an entity (such as a corporation or a municipality) to borrow cash from another entity. A common example of a debt security is a bond. When a company invests in a debt security, it is in effect loaning cash to the borrowing entity. In return, the investing company usually receives periodic interest payments from the borrowing entity. In most cases, the investing company can sell the debt security at any time or hold it until it matures.

An *equity security* is a financial instrument issued by an entity to raise capital in exchange for an ownership interest in the entity. A common example of an equity security is common stock issued by a corporation. When a company invests in an equity security, it is entitled to any dividends paid by the issuing entity. Most equity securities can be sold at almost any time.

This appendix focuses on how to account for investments in debt securities and investments in equity securities in which the investor does not have a significant influence over the target company. Usually, investments of less than 20% of the target company's common stock meet this criteria. The accounting for investments that are greater than 20% is left to more advanced textbooks.

To illustrate the accounting for investments, the following four events associated with investments will be considered.

- Purchasing the investment
- Recording periodic investment income
- Reporting the investment on the balance sheet
- Selling the investment

Recording the Purchase of Investments

Like other assets, investments are recorded at the cost of acquisition. To illustrate, suppose that on January 1, 2013, Abernathy Inc. purchases the following investments: a ₹100,000 20-year bond issued by the Infrastructure Company, 6,000 shares of Eagle Company common stock for ₹60,000, and 500 shares of C & L Ltd. common stock for ₹10,000. Abernathy would record the purchases as follows.

Jan. 1 2013	Investment in Infrastructure Bonds	100,000	
	Investment in Eagle Company	60,000	
	Investment in C & L Ltd.	10,000	
	Cash		170,000
	(To record purchase of investments)		

Assets	=	Liabilities	+	Equity
+100,000				
+60,000				
+10,000				
−170,000				

The entry increases each investment account for the cost of each security and reduces Abernathy's Cash account for the total cost of the purchase. Because Abernathy has simply exchanged cash for other assets, total assets remain unchanged.

Recording Investment Income

Investment income from debt or equity securities is recorded when earned. Because debt securities pay interest and equity securities distribute dividends, periodic investment income will be recorded as either interest revenue or dividend revenue. Both interest revenue and dividend revenue are reported on the income statement, usually as part of other revenues and expenses.

To illustrate, suppose that Abernathy receives ₹5,000 of interest on the Infrastructure bonds on June 30 and ₹3,000 of cash dividends from Eagle Company on September 15. Abernathy would record the receipts as follows.

June 30	Cash	5,000	
	Interest Revenue		5,000
	(To record receipt of interest)		

Assets	=	Liabilities	+	Equity
+5,000				+5,000

Sept. 15	Cash	3,000	
	Dividend Revenue		3,000
	(To record receipt of dividends)		

Assets	=	Liabilities	+	Equity
+3,000				+3,000

In both entries, Abernathy increases Cash to reflect the cash that is flowing into the company from its investments. The first entry increases Interest Revenue while the second increases Dividend Revenue. In both entries, assets and equity increase. Similar entries would be made each time interest or dividends are received.

Reporting Investments on the Balance Sheet

Like other assets, investments are reported on the balance sheet. However, the manner in which they are reported depends on how they are classified. Accounting rules require that investments in debt securities and equity securities without significant influence be classified into one of the following three categories. Each category is based on what management intends to do with the investments.

- Held-to-Maturity Securities
- Trading Securities
- Available-for-Sale Securities

Held-to-maturity securities are those securities that an investor has the positive intent and ability to hold until they mature. Since equity securities such as common stock do not mature, only debt securities can be classified as held-to-maturity securities. Investments in held-to-maturity securities are reported on the balance sheet at their historical costs. They are reported as non-current assets.

Trading securities are those securities that an investor intends to sell in the near term. Either debt or equity securities can be classified as trading securities. However, common stock is the most common type of trading security. Trading securities are reported on the balance sheet at their market values. This is an exception to the cost principle, but it is allowed because market values of most equity securities are objectively measured and easily known. Trading securities are included in current assets.

Available-for-sale securities are those securities that a company does not intend to hold to maturity but also does not intend to sell in the near term. In other words, an available-for-sale security is any security that is neither a held-to-maturity security nor a trading security. Either debt or equity securities can be classified as available-for-sale securities. Like trading securities, available-for-sale securities are reported on the balance sheet at their market values. Available-for-sale securities are usually reported as non-current assets.

Because trading and available-for-sale securities are reported at their market values, adjustments may be necessary at the balance sheet date. For example, if the market value of a trading security is greater than its cost, the investment account must be increased. If the market value of an available-for-sale security is less than its cost, the investment account must be decreased.

To illustrate, suppose that Abernathy is preparing its balance sheet on December 31, 2013. It has decided to hold the Infrastructure bonds for the full 20 years, to sell the Eagle investment within 90 days, and to hold the C & L investment indefinitely. The following table contains each investment, its classification, its cost and market values as of December 31, and any resulting unrealized gain or loss.

Investment	Classification	Original Cost	Dec. 31 Market Value	Unrealized gain or (loss)
Infrastructure Bonds	Held-to-maturity	₹100,000	₹99,000	₹ (1,000)
Eagle	Trading	60,000	64,300	4,300
C & L	Available-for-sale	10,000	9,800	(200)

The unrealized gain or loss is the difference between an investment's cost and its market value. When the market value exceeds the cost, Abernathy has an unrealized gain. When the cost exceeds the market value, Abernathy has an unrealized loss. The term *unrealized* is used because Abernathy still owns the investments. A gain or loss is *realized* only when an investment is sold and cash is received.

Because the Infrastructure bonds are classified as held-to-maturity, they are reported at their cost of ₹100,000. The market value and the unrealized loss are ignored, and no adjustment is needed.

Because the Eagle investment is classified as trading, it must be reported at its market value of ₹64,300. Therefore, Abernathy must adjust the investment account with the following entry.

Dec. 31 2013	Investment in Eagle Company	4,300	
	Unrealized Gain on Trading Securities		4,300
	(To adjust investment to market value)		

Assets	=	Liabilities	+	Equity
+4,300				+4,300

In this entry, Abernathy first increases the investment account by ₹4,300 so that the balance in the account rises from ₹60,000 to ₹64,300. Abernathy then increases Unrealized Gain on Trading Securities to reflect the increase in the value of Abernathy's investment. Unrealized gains or losses on trading securities are treated like any other revenue or expense—they are included in the calculation of net income. In this case, the gain would be reported in other revenues on the income statement, which results in an increase to equity.

Because the C & L investment is classified as available-for-sale, it too must be reported at its market value. However, the adjustment is a little different than the Eagle example.

Dec. 31	Unrealized Gain/Loss on Available-for-Sale Securities	200	
	Investment in C & L Ltd.		200
	(To adjust investment to market value)		

Assets	=	Liabilities	+	Equity
−200				−200

In this entry, Abernathy decreases the investment account by ₹200 so that the balance in the account decreases from ₹10,000 to ₹9,800, the market value. Abernathy then debits Unrealized Gain/Loss on Available-for-Sale Securities to reflect the decrease in the value of Abernathy's investment. Unlike the unrealized gain account used for the trading security, this unrealized gain/loss account for available-for-sale securities is not included in the calculation of net income. Rather, it is reported on the balance sheet as an increase or decrease to equity. Specifically, it is reported as a component of Accumulated Other Comprehensive Income, a line item within the stockholders' equity section of the balance sheet. Note that the account can have either a debit or credit balance. A debit balance represents unrealized losses to date while a credit balance represents unrealized gains to date. According to AS 13 of India, any reduction in the carrying amount and any reversals of such reduction should be charged or credited to the profit and loss statement.

After both adjustments are made, the investment balances on the December 31 balance sheet would appear as follows.

Investments on December 31 Balance Sheet	
Current assets	
Trading securities	₹ 64,300
Noncurrent assets	
Held-to-maturity securities	100,000
Available-for-sale securities	9,800

Recording the Sale or Maturity

The recording of the maturity or sale of an investment also depends on how the investment is classified. The following sections demonstrate how each classification is handled.

Held-to-Maturity Securities When a held-to-maturity security matures, a company must record the cash that is received at maturity and eliminate the investment account. When a held-to-maturity security is sold, a company must record the cash from the sale, eliminate the investment account, and record any difference as a gain or loss from the sale.

To illustrate a maturity, suppose that Abernathy holds the Infrastructure bonds until they mature. Abernathy will record the receipt of ₹100,000 as follows.

At maturity	Cash	100,000	
	Investment in Infrastructure Bonds		100,000
	(To record maturity of bonds)		

Assets	=	Liabilities	+	Equity
+100,000				
−100,000				

In this entry, Abernathy is simply increasing Cash and decreasing the investment account. Because Abernathy is exchanging one asset for another, total assets remain unchanged.

To illustrate a sale, suppose that Abernathy sells the Infrastructure bonds for ₹101,000 immediately after an interest payment. Abernathy will record the sale as follows.

		Debit	Credit
	Cash	101,000	
	Gain on Sale of Investment		1,000
	Investment in Infrastructure Bonds		100,000
	(To record sale of bonds)		

Assets	=	Liabilities	+	Equity
+101,000				+1,000
−100,000				

In this entry, Abernathy increases Cash for the amount received, eliminates the investment account, and increases Gain on Sale of Investment for the difference of ₹1,000.

Trading Securities When a trading security is sold, any cash received is recorded, the investment account is eliminated, and any gain or loss on the sale is recorded.

To illustrate, suppose that on February 15, 2013, Abernathy sells its investment in Eagle Company when the market value of the investment is ₹65,200. Abernathy would make the following entry to record the sale.

Date	Account	Debit	Credit
Feb. 15 2013	Cash	65,200	
	Investment in Eagle Company		64,300
	Gain on Sale of Investment		900
	(To record sale of investment at a gain)		

Assets	=	Liabilities	+	Equity
+65,200				+900
−64,300				

In this entry, Abernathy first increases Cash for the amount received from the sale. It then decreases Investment in Eagle Company by ₹64,300 since that was its balance on December 31. The difference between the cash received and the current account balance is the amount of gain realized on the sale. Therefore, Gain on Sale of Investment is increased by ₹900. As a result of this sale, both assets and equity increased ₹900.

Note in this example that Abernathy's total gain on the value of the investment was ₹5,200 (sales price − cost = ₹65,200 − ₹60,000 = ₹5,200). A portion of that gain (₹4,300) was included in net income in the prior period when the investment was adjusted to its market value. The remainder of the gain (₹900) was included in net income when the investment was sold. So, the ₹5,200 total gain was spread across two accounting periods.

Available-for-Sale Securities When an available for-sale security is sold, any cash received is recorded, the investment and any existing unrealized gain or loss are eliminated, and any realized gain or loss on the sale is recorded.

To illustrate, suppose that Abernathy sells its investment in C & L Ltd. for ₹9,700 on March 8, 2013. At the time of the sale, Abernathy would make the following entry.

Date	Account	Debit	Credit
Mar. 8 2013	Cash	9,700	
	Loss on Sale of Investment	300	
	Unrealized Gain/Loss on Available-for-Sale Securities		200
	Investment in C & L Ltd.		9,800
	(To record sale of investment at a gain)		

Assets	=	Liabilities	+	Equity
+9,700				−300
−9,800				+200

In this entry, Abernathy increases Cash for the amount of cash received. Because the Investment in C & L Ltd. account was adjusted to ₹9,800 on December 31, Abernathy decreases the account by ₹9,800 to eliminate it. Furthermore, the Unrealized Gain/Loss balance of ₹200 that was created on December 31 is also eliminated since Abernathy no longer has that unrealized loss. Finally, Abernathy records .a realized loss on the investment of ₹300. This is the difference between the amount received from the sale and the original cost of the investment. This ₹300 loss is included in the calculation of net income along with other expenses and revenues.

MARUTI SUZUKI ANALYSIS

Look at the Short-Term Investments paragraph in Maruti Suzuki's first note in Appendix C. How does Maruti Suzuki classify and report its investments?

Note 1.8 to the Financial Statements of Maruti Suzuki's Annual Accounts states "Current investments are valued at the lower of cost and fair value. Long-term investments are valued at cost except in the case of other than temporary decline in value, in which case the necessary provision is made".

EXERCISES

1. Investment Classifications

Below is a list of the various investments of Baldy Corporation:

1. Shares of GM stock to be held indefinitely
2. State bonds that will be held until they mature
3. Corporate bonds that the company might or might not sell
4. 15-year Nike bonds that the company plans to sell quickly
5. Target common stock which the company is actively trying to sell

Required

Identify each of the investments as held-to-maturity, available-for-sale, or trading securities.

2. Debt Security Investment

On January 1, 2013, the Hackman Company purchases ₹300,000 of 8% bonds for face value. Hackman plans to hold the bonds until they mature on January 1, 2020. Interest is paid semiannually on June 30 and December 31. Hackman's year-end is December 31.

Required

a. How should Hackman classify its investment? Explain your answer.
b. Prepare all appropriate journal entries for 2013. Be sure to include any necessary adjusting entry at year-end.

3. Equity Security Investment

On December 1, 2013, Wallace, Inc., purchases 500 shares of King Corporation common stock at ₹30 per share. Wallace plans to sell it at a profit as soon as it rises in value. On December 22, King declares a dividend of ₹1 per share to be paid on January 5, 2014. At December 31, 2013, King's stock was trading at ₹35 per share. Wallace sells the stock at ₹34 per share on January 15, 2014.

Required

a. How should Wallace classify its investment? Explain your answer.
b. Prepare all necessary journal entries from the purchase of the stock to its sale.
c. What is the effect of these transactions on the 2013 and 2014 income statements?

4. Equity Security Investment

On January 31, 2013, the Coburn Company purchases 10,000 shares of Hughes Corporation common stock at ₹10 per share. Coburn plans to hold the stock for an extended period of time rather than place it in its active trading portfolio. At December 31, 2013, Hughes common stock is trading at ₹8 per share. On March 31, 2014, Coburn sells the stock for ₹90,000.

Required

a. How should Coburn classify its investment? Explain your answer.
b. Prepare all necessary journal entries from the purchase of the stock through to its sale.
c. What is the effect of these transactions on the 2013 and 2014 income statements?

5. Effect on Net Income

The following is a list of possible events:

1. Trading securities appreciate in value over the course of the year.
2. Held-to-maturity securities are redeemed at maturity.
3. Available-for-sale securities are sold for less than their market value.
4. Available-for-sale securities appreciate in value during the current period.
5. Interest payments are received in the current year.
6. Trading securities are sold at a value greater than market value.

Required

Identify whether each item increases, decreases, or has no effect on net income for the current period.

PROBLEMS

6. Investment Entries

Huang Ltd, enters into the following transactions during 2013:

Jan. 1	Purchased ₹100,000, 6%, 10-year corporate bonds at face value. The bonds pay interest annually on December 31. Huang plans to hold the bonds to maturity.
Mar. 31	Purchased 500 shares of Bubbles Ltd., common stock at ₹30 per share. Huang plans to hold the shares indefinitely.
Nov. 15	Purchased 300 shares of Lib, Ltd., common stock at ₹45 per share. Huang plans to sell these shares in January.
Dec. 8	Received a dividend of ₹1 per share on the Lib Ltd., stock.
Dec. 31	Received interest payment on the corporate bonds purchased on January 1.
Dec. 31	Noted the following market values: Bubbles stock—₹40 per share; Lib stock—₹44 per share; corporate bonds—₹98,000.

Required

a. Prepare all appropriate journal entries associated with Huang's investments during 2013, including any necessary adjustments at year-end.
b. Determine the net effect on 2013 net income of all investment activity.

Appendix B
Time Value of Money

Introduction

When decisions are affected by cash flows that are paid or received in different time periods, it is necessary to adjust those cash flows for the time value of money (TVM). Because of our ability to earn interest on money invested, we would prefer to receive ₹1 today rather than a year from now. Likewise, we would prefer to pay ₹1 a year from now rather than today. A common technique used to adjust cash flows received or paid in different time periods is to discount those cash flows by finding their present value. The **present value (PV)** of cash flows is the amount of future cash flows discounted to their equivalent worth today. To fully understand the calculations involved in finding the present value of future cash flows, it is necessary to step back and examine the nature of interest and the calculation of interest received and paid. Interest is simply a payment made to use someone else's money. When you invest money in a bank account, the bank pays you interest for the use of your money for a period of time. If you invest ₹100 and the bank pays you ₹106 at the end of the year, it is clear that you earned ₹6 of interest on your money (and 6 percent interest for the year).

Future Value

Mathematically, the relationship between your initial investment (present value), the amount in the bank at the end of the year (future value), and the interest rate (r) is as follows:

$$FV_{(\text{Year 1})} = PV(1 + r)$$

In our example, $FV_{(\text{Year 1})} = 100(1 + 0.06) =$ ₹106. If you leave your money in the bank for a second year, what happens? Will you earn an additional ₹6 of interest? It depends on whether the bank pays you simple interest or compound interest. **Simple interest** is interest on the invested amount only, whereas **compound interest** is interest on the invested amount plus interest on previous interest earned but not withdrawn. Simple interest is sometimes computed on short-term investments and debts (that is, those that are shorter than six months to a year). Compound interest is typically computed for financial arrangements longer than one year. We will assume that interest is compounded in all examples in this book. Extending the future-value formula to find the amount we have in the bank in two years gives us the following formula:

$$FV_{(\text{Year 2})} = PV(1 + r)(1 + r)$$

or

$$FV_{(\text{Year 2})} = PV(1 + r)^2$$

In our example, $FV_{(\text{Year 2})} = 100(1 + 0.06)^2$, or ₹112.36. We earned ₹6.36 of interest in Year 2—₹6 on our original ₹100 investment and ₹0.36 on the ₹6 of interest earned but not withdrawn in Year 1 (₹6 × 0.06).

In this example, we have assumed that compounding is on an annual basis. Compounding can also be calculated semiannually, quarterly, monthly, daily, or even continually. Go back to our original ₹100 investment in the bank. If the bank pays 6 percent interest compounded semiannually instead of annually, we would have ₹106.09 after one year. Note that the interest rate is typically expressed as a percentage rate per year. We are

Present value (PV) The amount of future cash flows discounted to their equivalent worth today.

Simple interest Interest on the invested amount only.

Compound interest Interest on the invested amount plus interest on previous interest earned but not withdrawn.

Exhibit B-1 The Impact of More Frequent Compounding on the Future Value of ₹100

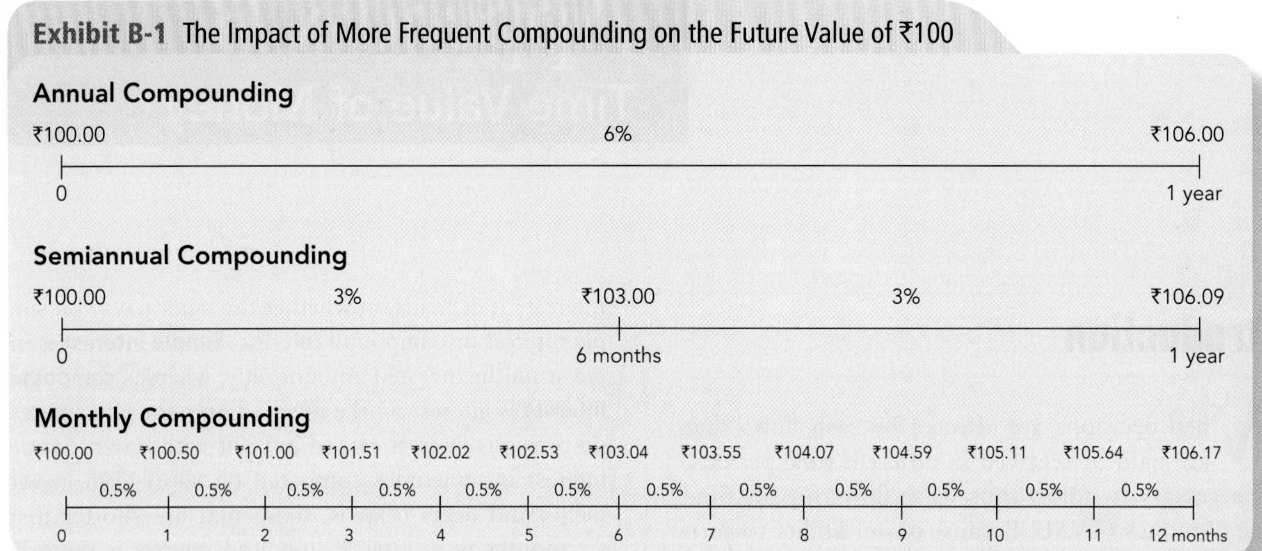

really earning 3 percent for each semiannual period, not 6 percent. It is usually easier to visualize the concept of interest rate compounding graphically, with the help of time lines. Exhibit B-1 graphically demonstrates the impact of annual, semiannual, and monthly compounding of the 6 percent annual rate on our original ₹100 investment.

Mathematically, our formula for future value can once again be modified slightly to account for interest rates compounded at different intervals. $FV_{(n \text{ periods in the future})} = PV(1 + r)^n$, where n is the number of compounding periods per year multiplied by the number of years, and r is the annual interest rate divided by the number of compounding periods per year. Before the advent of handheld calculators and computers, tables were developed to simplify the calculation of FV by providing values for $(1 + r)^n$ for several combinations of n and r. These tables are still commonly used, and an example is provided in Exhibit B-2. The factors in Exhibit B-2 are commonly referred to as cumulative factors (CF) and are simply calculations of $(1 + r)^n$ for various values of n and r.

Using this new terminology, the future value formula is simply

$$FV_{(n \text{ periods in the future})} = PV(CF_{n,r})$$

Exhibit B-2 Future Value of ₹1

n/r	0.5%	1%	2%	3%	4%	5%	6%	7%	8%	10%	12%
1	1.0050	1.0100	1.0200	1.0300	1.0400	1.0500	1.0600	1.0700	1.0800	1.1000	1.1200
2	1.0100	1.0201	1.0404	1.0609	1.0816	1.1025	1.1236	1.1449	1.1664	1.2100	1.2544
3	1.0151	1.0303	1.0612	1.0927	1.1249	1.1576	1.1910	1.2250	1.2597	1.3310	1.4049
4	1.0202	1.0406	1.0824	1.1255	1.1699	1.2155	1.2625	1.3108	1.3605	1.4641	1.5735
5	1.0253	1.0510	1.1041	1.1593	1.2167	1.2763	1.3382	1.4026	1.4693	1.6105	1.7623
6	1.0304	1.0615	1.1262	1.1941	1.2653	1.3401	1.4185	1.5007	1.5869	1.7716	1.9738
7	1.0355	1.0721	1.1487	1.2299	1.3159	1.4071	1.5036	1.6058	1.7138	1.9487	2.2107
8	1.0407	1.0829	1.1717	1.2668	1.3686	1.4775	1.5938	1.7182	1.8509	2.1436	2.4760
9	1.0459	1.0937	1.1951	1.3048	1.4233	1.5513	1.6895	1.8385	1.9990	2.3579	2.7731
10	1.0511	1.1046	1.2190	1.3439	1.4802	1.6289	1.7908	1.9672	2.1589	2.5937	3.1058
11	1.0564	1.1157	1.2434	1.3842	1.5395	1.7103	1.8983	2.1049	2.3316	2.8531	3.4785
12	1.0617	1.1268	1.2682	1.4258	1.6010	1.7959	2.0122	2.2522	2.5182	3.1384	3.8960
24	1.1272	1.2697	1.6084	2.0328	2.5633	3.2251	4.0489	5.0724	6.3412	9.8497	15.1786
36	1.1967	1.4308	2.0399	2.8983	4.1039	5.7918	8.1473	11.4239	15.9682	30.9127	59.1356
48	1.2705	1.6122	2.5871	4.1323	6.5705	10.4013	16.3939	25.7289	40.2106	97.0172	230.3908

With 6 percent annual compounding, our ₹100 investment grows to

$$₹100(CF_{1,6\%}) = ₹100(1.060) = ₹106.00$$

With 6 percent semiannual compounding,

$$₹100(CF_{2,3\%}) = ₹100(1.0609) = ₹106.09$$

With 6 percent monthly compounding,

$$₹100(CF_{12,.5\%}) = ₹100(1.0617) = ₹106.17$$

Most financial calculators will compute future value after the user inputs data for present value, the annual interest rate, the number of compounding periods per year, and the number of years. For example, using a business calculator to compute the future value of ₹100.00 with 6 percent annual compounding requires the following steps:

Keys	Display	Description
1 [P/YR]	1.00	Sets compounding periods per year to 1 because interest is compounded annually
100 [±] [PV]	−100.00	Stores the present value as a negative number
6.0 [I/YR]	6.0	Stores the annual interest rate
1 [N]	1	Sets the number of years or compounding periods to 1
[FV]	106.00	Calculates the future value

Calculating the future value of ₹100 with 6 percent monthly compounding simply requires changing both the compounding periods per year (*P/YR*) and number of compounding periods (*N*) to 12.

Keys	Display	Description
12 [P/YR]	12	Sets compounding periods per year to 12
12 [N]	12	Sets the number of compounding periods to 12
[FV]	106.17	Calculates the future value

Exhibit B-3 Finding the Future Value Using the FV Function in Excel

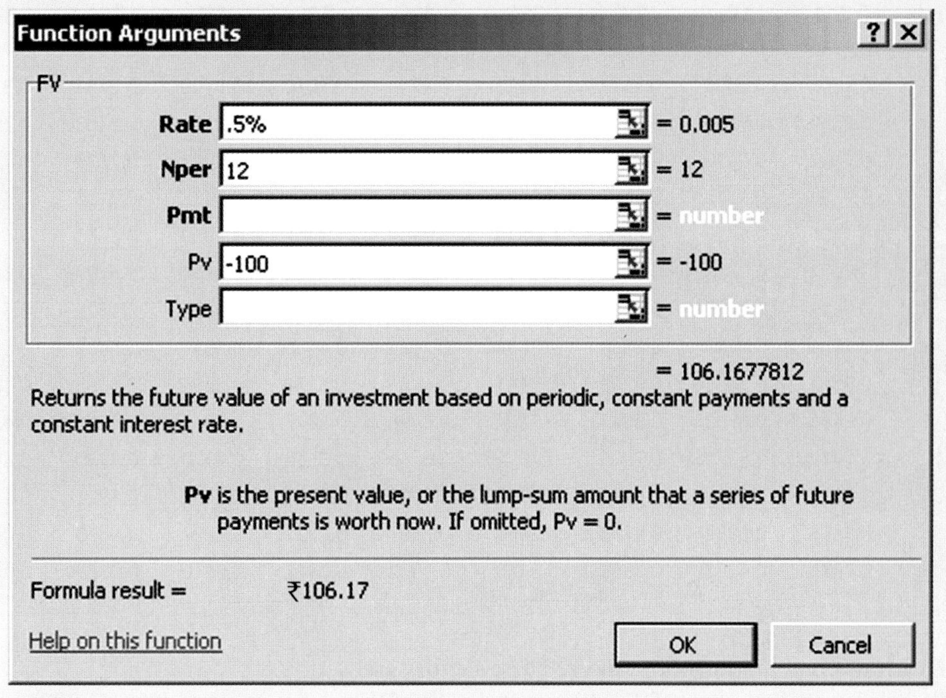

Likewise, many spreadsheet programs have built-in functions (formulas) that calculate future value. The Excel function called FV simply requires input of an interest rate (Rate), number of compounding periods (Nper), and present value (Pv) in the following format: =FV(Rate, Nper, Pmt, Pv, Type).[1] Entries for Pmt and Type are not applicable to simple future-value problems. To calculate the future value of ₹100 in one year at 6 percent interest compounded monthly, enter =FV(.5%,12,−100). Excel returns a value of ₹106.17 (see Exhibit B-3).

Present Value

A present value formula can be derived directly from the future value formula. If

$$FV_{(n \text{ periods in the future})} = PV(1 + r)^n$$

then

$$PV = \frac{FV}{(1 + r)^n} \quad \text{or} \quad PV = FV\left(\frac{1}{(1 + r)^n}\right)$$

Just as a cumulative factor table was developed to calculate $(1 + r)^n$, present value tables calculate $1 \div (1 + r)^n$

[1]Built-in functions can be accessed in Microsoft Excel by clicking on the Paste function icon, clicking on *financial,* and then scrolling down to the desired function.

Exhibit B-4 Present Value of ₹1

n/r	0.5%	1%	2%	3%	4%	5%	6%	7%	8%	10%	12%
1	0.9950	0.9901	0.9804	0.9709	0.9615	0.9524	0.9434	0.9346	0.9259	0.9091	0.8929
2	0.9901	0.9803	0.9612	0.9426	0.9246	0.9070	0.8900	0.8734	0.8573	0.8264	0.7972
3	0.9851	0.9706	0.9423	0.9151	0.8890	0.8638	0.8396	0.8163	0.7938	0.7513	0.7118
4	0.9802	0.9610	0.9238	0.8885	0.8548	0.8227	0.7921	0.7629	0.7350	0.6830	0.6355
5	0.9754	0.9515	0.9057	0.8626	0.8219	0.7835	0.7473	0.7130	0.6806	0.6209	0.5674
6	0.9705	0.9420	0.8880	0.8375	0.7903	0.7462	0.7050	0.6663	0.6302	0.5645	0.5066
7	0.9657	0.9327	0.8706	0.8131	0.7599	0.7107	0.6651	0.6227	0.5835	0.5132	0.4523
8	0.9609	0.9235	0.8535	0.7894	0.7307	0.6768	0.6274	0.5820	0.5403	0.4665	0.4039
9	0.9561	0.9143	0.8368	0.7664	0.7026	0.6446	0.5919	0.5439	0.5002	0.4241	0.3606
10	0.9513	0.9053	0.8203	0.7441	0.6756	0.6139	0.5584	0.5083	0.4632	0.3855	0.3220
11	0.9466	0.8963	0.8043	0.7224	0.6496	0.5847	0.5268	0.4751	0.4289	0.3505	0.2875
12	0.9419	0.8874	0.7885	0.7014	0.6246	0.5568	0.4970	0.4440	0.3971	0.3186	0.2567
24	0.8872	0.7876	0.6217	0.4919	0.3901	0.3101	0.2470	0.1971	0.1577	0.1015	0.0659
36	0.8356	0.6989	0.4902	0.3450	0.2437	0.1727	0.1227	0.0875	0.0626	0.0323	0.0169
48	0.7871	0.6203	0.3865	0.2420	0.1522	0.0961	0.0610	0.0389	0.0249	0.0103	0.0043

for various combinations of *n* and *r*. These factors are called discount factors, or DFs. An example of a DF table is provided in Exhibit B-4. Our PV formula can now be rewritten as follows:

$$PV = FV(DF_{n,r})$$

Now we are ready to calculate the present value of a future cash flow. For example, how much must be invested today at 8 percent compounded annually to have ₹1,000 in two years? Mathematically,

$$PV = ₹1{,}000\left(\frac{1}{(1 \times 0.08)^2}\right) = ₹857.34$$

or using the DF table,

$$PV = ₹1{,}000(DF_{2,.08}) = ₹1{,}000(0.8573) = ₹857.30 \text{ (rounded)}$$

Once again, the frequency of compounding affects our calculation. Just as more frequent compounding *increases* future values, increasing the frequency of compounding decreases present values. This is demonstrated in Exhibit B-5 for annual, semiannual, and quarterly compounding.

Exhibit B-5 The Impact of More Frequent Compounding on the Present Value of ₹1,000

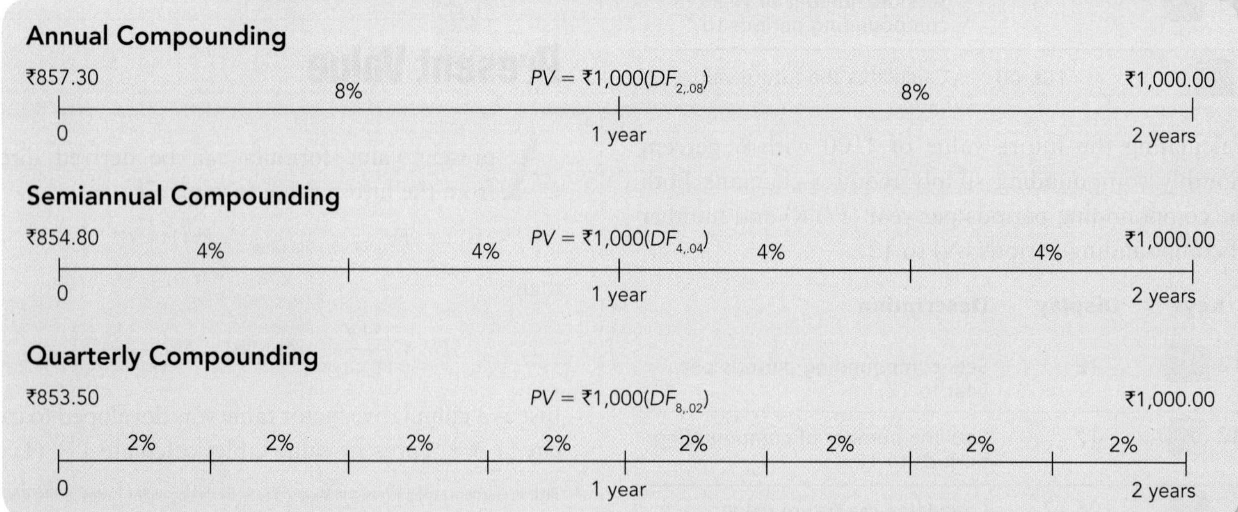

Using a business calculator to compute present value is similar to computing future value. For example, the present value of ₹1,000 received or paid in two years at 8 percent compounded quarterly requires the following steps:

Keys	Display	Description
4 [P/YR]	4.00	Sets the compounding periods per year to 4
1,000 [FV]	1000.00	Stores the future value as a positive number
8.0 [I/YR]	8.0	Stores the annual interest rate
8 [N]	8.0	Sets the number of compounding periods to 8
[PV]	-853.49	Calculates the present value

In Microsoft Excel, the built-in function is called PV and requires input of the applicable interest rate (Rate), number of compounding periods (Nper), and future value (Fv) in the following format: =PV(Rate, Nper, Pmt, Fv, Type). In the previous example, entering =PV(2%,8,−1000) returns a value of ₹853.49. Note once again that Pmt and Type are left blank in simple present value problems, as they were in future value calculations (see Exhibit B-6).

When *FV* and *PV* are known, either formula can be used to calculate one of the other variables in the equations (*n* or *r*). For example, if you know that your ₹100 bank deposit is worth ₹200 in six years, what rate of interest compounded annually did you earn? Using the mathematical present value formula,

$$PV = FV\left(\frac{1}{(1+r)^n}\right) \quad \text{or} \quad ₹100 = ₹200\left(\frac{1}{(1+r)^6}\right)$$

Simplifying by dividing each side by ₹100, $1 = 2 \div (1 + r)^6$, and multiplying each side by $(1 + r)^6$, the equation is simplified to $(1 + r)^6 = 2$. The value of r can be calculated by using a financial calculator or mathematically by using logarithmic functions.[2] When using a business calculator, the following steps are typical:

Keys	Display	Description
1 [P/YR]	1.00	Sets compounding periods per year to 1
200 [FV]	200	Stores the future value
100 [±] [PV]	-100	Stores the present value as a negative number
2 [N]	2.0	Sets the number of compounding periods to 2
[I/YR]	0.122462	Calculates the annual interest rate

The tables can also be used to solve for n and r. Using our table formula, $PV = FV(DF_{n,r})$, if $PV = 100$ and $FV = 200$, DF must be equal to 0.5. If we know that n is equal to 6, we can simply move across the table until we find a factor close to 0.5. The factor at 12 percent is 0.5066. If we examine the factors at both 10 percent (0.5645) and 14 percent (0.456), we can infer that the actual interest rate will be slightly higher than 12 percent. Our logarithmic calculation is 12.2462 percent. In Microsoft Excel, the RATE function requires input of Nper, Pv, and Fv in the following format:

Exhibit B-6 Finding the Present Value Using the PV Function in Excel

Function Arguments

PV

Rate	2%	= 0.02
Nper	8	= 8
Pmt		= number
Fv	-1000	= -1000
Type		= number

= 853.4903712

Returns the present value of an investment: the total amount that a series of future payments is worth now.

Fv is the future value, or a cash balance you want to attain after the last payment is made.

Formula result = ₹853.49

Help on this function

OK Cancel

[2]In logarithmic form, $(1 + r)^6 = 2$ can be rewritten as $\log(1 + r)^6 = \log 2$, or $6 \log(1 + r) = \log 2$. Therefore, $\log(1 + r) = \log 2 \div 6$, which simplifies to $\log(1 + r) = 0.1155245$. Switching back to the equivalent exponential form, $e0.1155245 = (1 + r)$, $(1 + r) = 1.122462$, and $r = 0.122462$ (12.2462%).

Exhibit B-7 Finding the Interest Rate Using the RATE Function in Excel

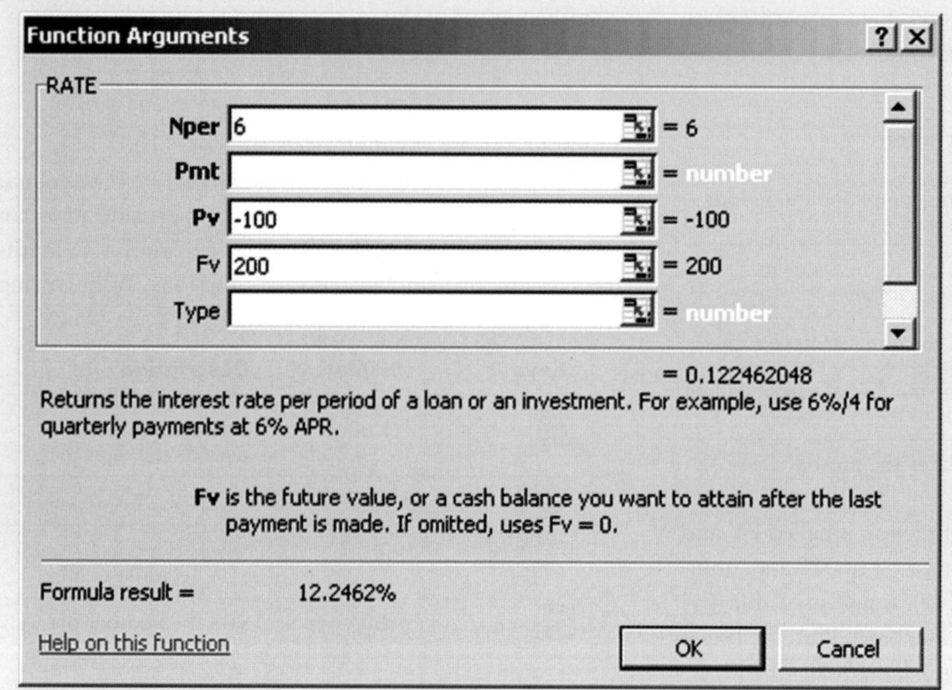

=RATE(Nper, Pmt, Pv, Fv, Type, Guess). Because Excel uses an iterative trial-and-error method to calculate the interest rate, Guess provides a starting point. It is generally not necessary but may be required in complicated problems. Entering =RATE(6,−100,200) returns an interest rate of 12.2462 percent (see Exhibit B-7).

The calculation of n is done in a similar fashion. If we know that our investment earns 12 percent but do not know how long it will take for our ₹100 to grow to ₹200, mathematically, we have the following:

$$PV = FV\left(\frac{1}{(1 + r)^n}\right)$$

or

$$₹100 = ₹200\left(\frac{1}{(1 + 0.12)^n}\right)$$

Solving the equation by using logarithms or a financial calculator gives us an n of 6.116 years.[3] Using the DF formula, DF must again be equal to 0.5. If r is known to be 12 percent, we simply move down the 12 percent column until we find a DF close to 0.5. Not surprisingly, we find a factor of 0.5066 for an n of 6. Examining the factors for an n of 5(0.5674) and 7(0.4523), we can infer that the actual time will be something slightly greater than 6 years. The NPER function in Microsoft Excel requires input of Rate, Pmt, Pv, Fv, and Type in the following format: =NPER(12%,−100, 200), and returns a value of 6.116 years. Note that Pv is entered as a negative amount and that Pmt and Type are not necessary, as this is essentially a present value problem (see Exhibit B-8).

Exhibit B-8 Finding the Number of Periods Using the NPER Function in Excel

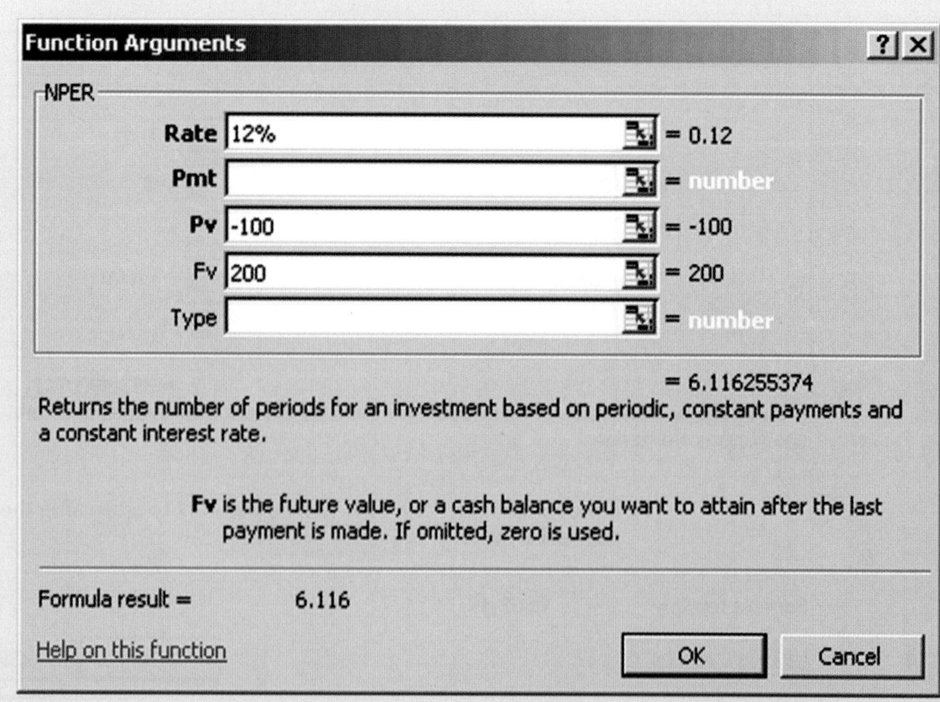

[3]Using a business calculator, simply input 1 P/YR, 200 FV, 100 PV, and 12 I/YR and solve for n. In logarithmic form, $(1 + 0.12)^n = 2$ can be rewritten as $\log(1 + 0.12)^n = \log 2$, or $n \log 1.12 = \log 2$. Therefore, $n = (\log 2) \div (\log 1.12) = 6.116$.

Annuities

An **annuity** is a series of cash flows of equal amount paid or received at regular intervals.[4] Common examples include mortgage and loan payments. The present value of an ordinary annuity (PVA) is the amount invested or borrowed today that will provide for a series of withdrawals or payments of equal amount for a set number of periods. Conceptually, the present value of an annuity is simply the sum of the present values of each withdrawal or payment. For example, the present value of an annuity of ₹100 paid at the end of each of the next four years at an interest rate of 10 percent looks like this:

PVA — 10% — ₹100 — 10% — ₹100 — 10% — ₹100 — 10% — ₹100

0 — 1 year — 2 years — 3 years — 4 years

Although cumbersome, the present value of an annuity can be calculated by finding the present value of each ₹100 payment, using the present value table on page B-4 (see Exhibit B-4).

$$PVA = ₹100(DF_{1,.10}) + ₹100(DF_{2,.10}) + ₹100(DF_{3,.10}) + ₹100(DF_{4,.10})$$

$$= ₹100(0.9091) + ₹100(0.8264) + ₹100(0.7513) + ₹100(0.6830)$$

$$= ₹316.98$$

[4]An ordinary annuity is paid or received at the end of each period, whereas an annuity due is paid or received at the beginning of each period. In examples throughout this book, we will assume the annuity is ordinary.

The mathematical formula for PVA can be derived from the formula for PV and is equal to:

$$PVA_{n,r} = R\left(\frac{1 - \frac{1}{(1+r)^n}}{r}\right)$$

where R refers to the periodic payment or withdrawal (commonly called a rent). Calculated values for various combinations of n and r are provided in Exhibit B-9.

Exhibit B-9 Present Value of an Ordinary Annuity

n/r	0.50%	1%	2%	3%	4%	5%	6%	7%	8%	10%	12%
1	0.9950	0.9901	0.9804	0.9709	0.9615	0.9524	0.9434	0.9346	0.9259	0.9091	0.8929
2	1.9851	1.9704	1.9416	1.9135	1.8861	1.8594	1.8334	1.8080	1.7833	1.7355	1.6901
3	2.9702	2.9410	2.8839	2.8286	2.7751	2.7232	2.6730	2.6243	2.5771	2.4869	2.4018
4	3.9505	3.9020	3.8077	3.7171	3.6299	3.5460	3.4651	3.3872	3.3121	3.1699	3.0373
5	4.9259	4.8534	4.7135	4.5797	4.4518	4.3295	4.2124	4.1002	3.9927	3.7908	3.6048
6	5.8964	5.7955	5.6014	5.4172	5.2421	5.0757	4.9173	4.7665	4.6229	4.3553	4.1114
7	6.8621	6.7282	6.4720	6.2303	6.0021	5.7864	5.5824	5.3893	5.2064	4.8684	4.5638
8	7.8230	7.6517	7.3255	7.0197	6.7327	6.4632	6.2098	5.9713	5.7466	5.3349	4.9676
9	8.7791	8.5660	8.1622	7.7861	7.4353	7.1078	6.8017	6.5152	6.2469	5.7590	5.3282
10	9.7304	9.4713	8.9826	8.5302	8.1109	7.7217	7.3601	7.0236	6.7101	6.1446	5.6502
11	10.6770	10.3676	9.7868	9.2526	8.7605	8.3064	7.8869	7.4987	7.1390	6.4951	5.9377
12	11.6189	11.2551	10.5753	9.9540	9.3851	8.8633	8.3838	7.9427	7.5361	6.8137	6.1944
24	22.5629	21.2434	18.9139	16.9355	15.2470	13.7986	12.5504	11.4693	10.5288	8.9847	7.7843
36	32.8710	30.1075	25.4888	21.8323	18.9083	16.5469	14.6210	13.0352	11.7172	9.6765	8.1924
48	42.5803	37.9740	30.6731	25.2667	21.1951	18.0772	15.6500	13.7305	12.1891	9.8969	8.2972

The PVA formula can therefore be rewritten as follows:

$$PVA = R(DFA_{n,r})$$

As previously discussed, common examples of annuities are mortgages and loans. For example, say you are thinking about buying a new car. Your bank offers to loan you money at a special 6 percent rate compounded monthly for a 24-month term. If the maximum monthly payment you can afford is ₹399, how large a car loan can you get? In other words, what is the present value of a ₹399 annuity paid at the end of each of the next 24 months, assuming an interest rate of 6 percent compounded monthly?

Annuity A series of cash flows of equal amount paid or received at regular intervals.

Using a time line, the problem looks like this:

PVA	₹399	₹399	₹399	₹399	₹399	₹399	₹399	₹399	₹399	₹399	₹399	₹399	₹399	₹399	₹399	₹399	₹399	₹399	₹399	₹399	₹399	₹399	₹399	₹399
	0.5%	0.5%	0.5%	0.5%	0.5%	0.5%	0.5%	0.5%	0.5%	0.5%	0.5%	0.5%	0.5%	0.5%	0.5%	0.5%	0.5%	0.5%	0.5%	0.5%	0.5%	0.5%	0.5%	0.5%
0																								24 months

Mathematically,

$$PVA_{24,.005} = 399\left(\frac{1 - \dfrac{1}{(1 + 0.5)^{24}}}{0.005}\right)$$

Using the DFA table,

$$PVA_{24,.005} = ₹399(DFA_{24,.005}) = ₹399(22.5629) = ₹9,002.60 \text{ (rounded)}$$

The following steps are common when using a business calculator:

Keys	Display	Description
12 [P/YR]	12.00	Set periods per year
2×12 [N]	24.00	Stores number of periods in loan
0 [FV]	0	Stores the amount left to pay after 2 years
6 [I/YR]	6	Stores interest rate
399 [±] [PMT]	-399.00	Stores desired payment as a negative number
[PV]	9,002.58	Calculates the loan you can afford with a ₹399 per month payment

In Microsoft Excel, the PV function is used to calculate the present value of an annuity, with additional entries for the payment amount (Pmt) and type of annuity (Type). The payment is entered as a negative number, and the annuity type is 0 for ordinary and 1 for an annuity due. The format is therefore PV(Rate, Nper, Pmt, Fv, Type). Entering =PV(.5%,24,−399,0,0) returns a value of ₹9,002.58 (see Exhibit B-10).

The PVA formula can also be used to calculate R, r, and n if the other variables are known. This is most easily accomplished using the DFA table or using a financial calculator. If you are in USA and the car you want to buy costs \$20,000 and you can afford a \$3,000 down payment (your loan balance is \$17,000), how much will your 36 monthly payments be, assuming that the bank charges you 6 percent interest compounded monthly?

Using the DFA table,

$$PVA_{36,.005} = R(DFA_{36,.005})$$
$$\$17,000 = R(32.871)$$
$$R = \$517.17$$

The following steps are common when using a business calculator:

Keys	Display	Description
12 [P/YR]	12.00	Set periods per year
3×12 [N]	36.00	Stores number of periods in loan
0 [FV]	0	Stores the amount left to pay after 3 years
6 [I/YR]	6	Stores interest rate
17,000 [PV]	17,000	Stores amount borrowed
[PMT]	-517.17	Calculates the monthly payment

In Microsoft Excel, the calculation is simply =PMT (.005,36,−17000,0,0) (see Exhibit B-11).

In a similar fashion, assume that a used-car dealer offers you a "special deal" in which you can borrow \$12,000 with low monthly payments of \$350 per month for 48 months. What rate of interest are you being charged in this case? Using the DFA table,

$$PVA_{48,.??} = \$350(DFA_{48,.??})$$
$$\$12,000 = 350(DFA_{48,.??})$$
$$DFA_{48,.??} = 34.2857$$

Looking at the row for an n of 48, we see that a DFA of 34.2857 is about halfway between an r of 1 percent and r of 2 percent (closer to 1 percent), which means that you are being charged an annual rate of almost 18 percent (1.5% × 12)—not such a good deal after all! Using a business calculator, observe the following:

Keys	Display	Description
12 [P/YR]	12.00	Set periods per year
4×12 [N]	48.00	Stores number of periods in loan
0 [FV]	0	Stores the amount left to pay after 4 years
12,000 [PV]	12,000	Stores amount borrowed
350 [±] [PMT]	-350	Stores the monthly payment
[I/YR]	17.60	Calculates the annual interest rate

Exhibit B-10 Finding the Present Value of an Annuity Using the PV Function in Excel

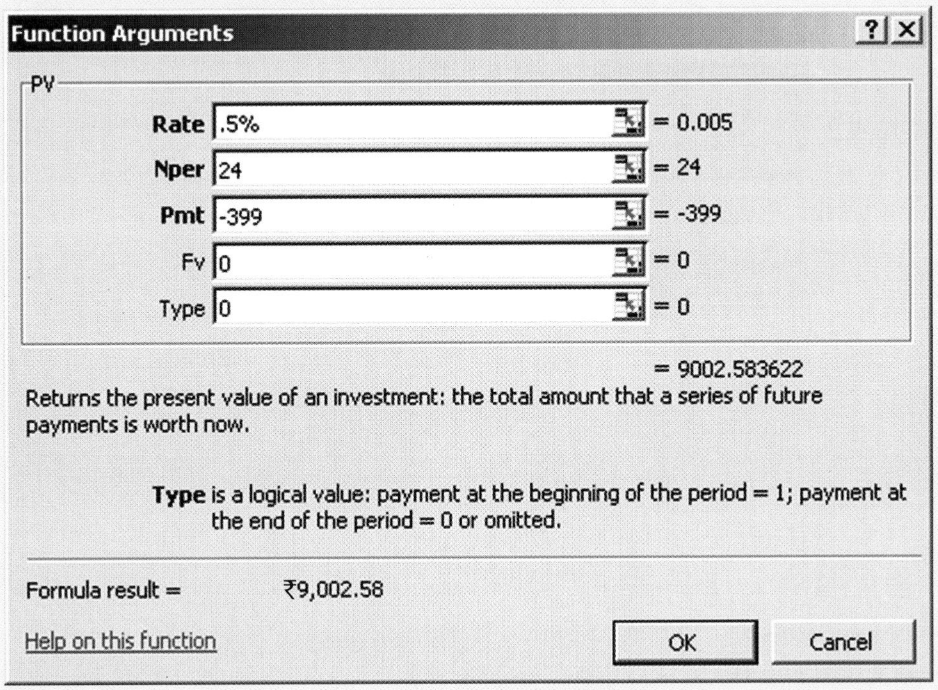

Function Arguments
PV
Rate .5% = 0.005
Nper 24 = 24
Pmt -399 = -399
Fv 0 = 0
Type 0 = 0
= 9002.583622
Returns the present value of an investment: the total amount that a series of future payments is worth now.
Type is a logical value: payment at the beginning of the period = 1; payment at the end of the period = 0 or omitted.
Formula result = ₹9,002.58
Help on this function
OK
Cancel

Exhibit B-11 Finding the Payment Using the PMT Function in Excel

Function Arguments
PMT
Rate .5% = 0.005
Nper 36 = 36
Pv -17000 = -17000
Fv 0 = 0
Type 0 = 0
= 517.1729367
Calculates the payment for a loan based on constant payments and a constant interest rate.
Type is a logical value: payment at the beginning of the period = 1; payment at the end of the period = 0 or omitted.
Formula result = $517.17
Help on this function
OK
Cancel

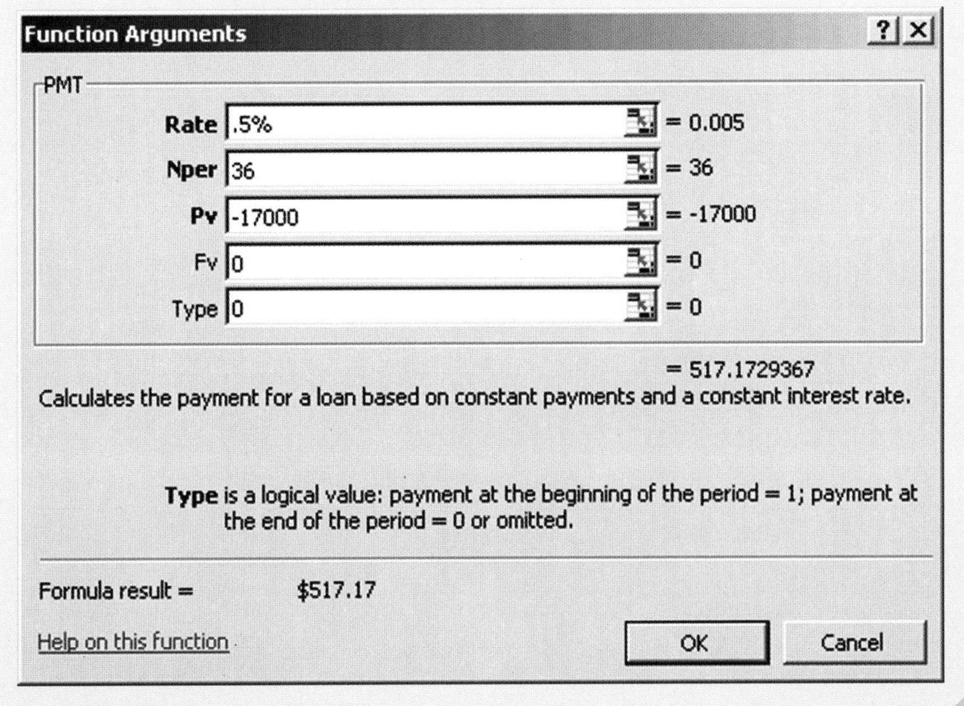

In Excel, =RATE(48, −350,12,000,0) generates a monthly rate of 1.4667 percent and an annual rate of 17.60 percent. The use of the RATE function requires that the payments are the same each period. Excel's IRR function is more flexible, allowing different payments. However, each payment has to be entered separately. For example, if the car is purchased for $17,000 with annual payments of $4,000, $5,000, $6,000, and $7,000 at the end of each of the next four years, the interest rate charged on the car loan can be calculated by using the IRR function (see Exhibit B-12).

Exhibit B-12 Finding the Interest Rate Using the IRR

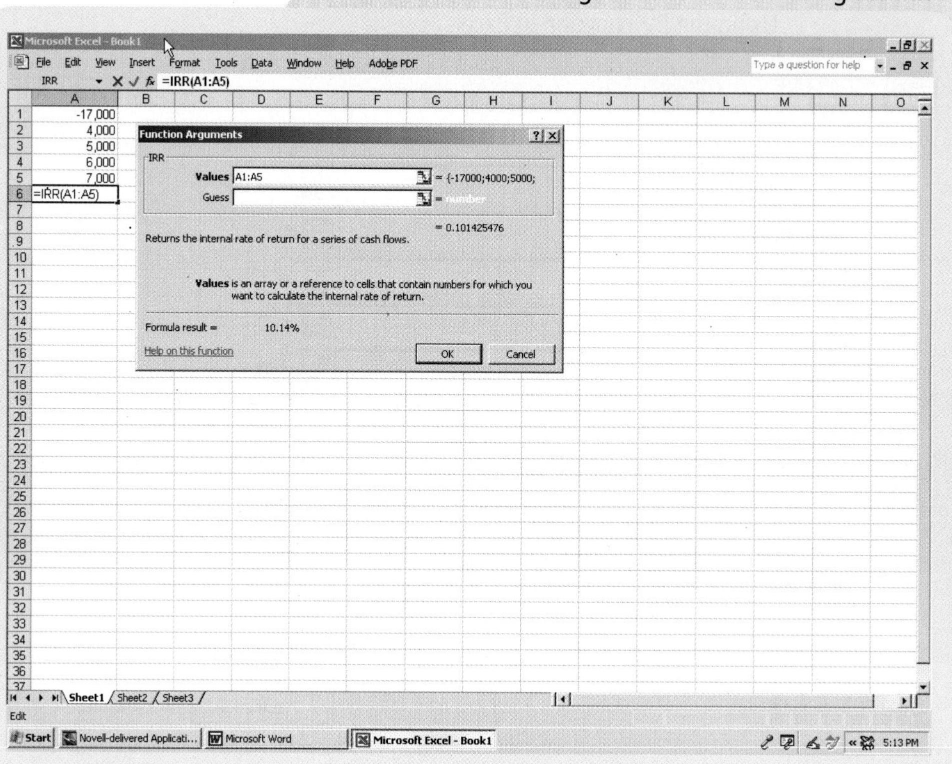

Appendix C

Maruti Suzuki India Limited*
(Excerpted)

MARUTI SUZUKI

Way of Life!

Maruti Suzuki India Limited

Annual Report 2012–13

*Source: www.marutisuzuki.com

Independent Auditors' Report

To the Members of Maruti Suzuki India Limited

REPORT ON THE FINANCIAL STATEMENTS

1. We have audited the accompanying financial statements of Maruti Suzuki India Limited (the "Company"), which comprise the Balance Sheet as at 31st March 2013, and the Statement of Profit and Loss and Cash Flow Statement for the year then ended, and a summary of significant accounting policies and other explanatory information, which we have signed under reference to this report.

MANAGEMENT'S RESPONSIBILITY FOR THE FINANCIAL STATEMENTS

2. The Company's Management is responsible for the preparation of these financial statements that give a true and fair view of the financial position, financial performance and cash flows of the Company in accordance with the Accounting Standards referred to in sub-section (3C) of section 211 of 'the Companies Act, 1956' of India (the "Act") and Accounting Standard 30, Financial Instruments: Recognition and Measurement issued by the Institute of Chartered Accountants of India to the extent it does not contradict any other accounting standard referred to in sub-section (3C) of Section 211 of the Act. This responsibility includes the design, implementation and maintenance of internal control relevant to the preparation and presentation of the financial statements that give a true and fair view and are free from material misstatement, whether due to fraud or error.

AUDITORS' RESPONSIBILITY

3. Our responsibility is to express an opinion on these financial statements based on our audit. We conducted our audit in accordance with the Standards on Auditing issued by the Institute of Chartered Accountants of India. Those Standards require that we comply with ethical requirements and plan and perform the audit to obtain reasonable assurance about whether the financial statements are free from material misstatement.

4. An audit involves performing procedures to obtain audit evidence, about the amounts and disclosures in the financial statements. The procedures selected depend on the auditors' judgment, including the assessment of the risks of material misstatement of the financial statements, whether due to fraud or error. In making those risk assessments, the auditors consider internal control relevant to the Company's preparation and fair presentation of the financial statements in order to design audit procedures that are appropriate in the circumstances. An audit also includes evaluating the appropriateness of accounting policies used and the reasonableness of the accounting estimates made by Management, as well as evaluating the overall presentation of the financial statements.

5. We believe that the audit evidence we have obtained is sufficient and appropriate to provide a basis for our audit opinion.

OPINION

6. In our opinion, and to the best of our information and according to the explanations given to us, the accompanying financial statements give the information required by the Act in the manner so required and give a true and fair view in conformity with the accounting principles generally accepted in India:

   (a) in the case of the Balance Sheet, of the state of affairs of the Company as at 31st March 2013;

   (b) in the case of the Statement of Profit and Loss, of the profit for the year ended on that date; and

   (c) in the case of the Cash Flow Statement, of the cash flows for the year ended on that date.

EMPHASIS OF MATTER

7. We draw attention to Note 32(a)(vii) of the financial statements regarding demands received from Haryana State Industrial & Infrastructure Development Corporation Limited towards enhanced compensation for Company's freehold land at Manesar amounting to ₹ 5,012 million, ₹ 1,376 million and ₹ 86 million; against the demand of ₹ 5,012 million the Company's impleadment application has been heard and the order has been reserved by the Hon'ble Supreme Court of India; against the demand of ₹ 1,376 million, the Company has filed an appeal with the Hon'ble High Court of Punjab and Haryana; and against the demand of ₹ 86 million, the Company is in the process of obtaining more information. Accordingly, no provision is considered necessary towards enhanced compensation for the aforesaid freehold land. Our opinion is not qualified in respect of this matter.

REPORT ON OTHER LEGAL AND REGULATORY REQUIREMENTS

8. As required by 'the Companies (Auditor's Report) Order, 2003', as amended by 'the Companies (Auditor's Report) (Amendment) Order, 2004', issued by the Central Government of India in terms of sub-section (4A) of section 227 of the Act (hereinafter referred to as the "Order"), and on the basis of such checks of the books and records of the Company as we considered appropriate and according to the information and explanations given to us, we give in the Annexure a statement on the matters specified in paragraphs 4 and 5 of the Order.

9. As required by section 227(3) of the Act, we report that:

   (a) We have obtained all the information and explanations which, to the best of our knowledge and belief, were necessary for the purpose of our audit;

(b) In our opinion, proper books of account as required by law have been kept by the Company so far as appears from our examination of those books;

(c) The Balance Sheet, Statement of Profit and Loss, and Cash Flow Statement dealt with by this Report are in agreement with the books of account;

(d) In our opinion, the Balance Sheet, Statement of Profit and Loss, and Cash Flow Statement dealt with by this report comply with the Accounting Standards referred to in sub-section (3C) of section 211 of the Act and Accounting Standard 30, Financial Instruments: Recognition and Measurement issued by the Institute of Chartered Accountants of India to the extent it does not contradict any other accounting standard referred to in sub-section (3C) of Section 211 of the Act;

(e) On the basis of written representations received from the Directors as on 31st March 2013, and taken on record by the Board of Directors, none of the Directors is disqualified as on 31st March 2013, from being appointed as a Director in terms of clause (g) of sub-section (1) of section 274 of the Act.

For **Price Waterhouse**

Firm Registration Number: 301112E
Chartered Accountants

ABHISHEK RARA
Partner
Membership Number : 077779

Place : New Delhi
Date : 26th April 2013

Annexure to Auditors' Report

Referred to in paragraph 8 of the Auditors' Report of even date to the members of Maruti Suzuki India Limited on the financial statements as of and for the year ended 31st March 2013

i. (a) The Company is maintaining proper records showing full particulars, including quantitative details and situation, of fixed assets.

(b) The fixed assets are physically verified by the Management according to a phased programme designed to cover all the items, except furniture and fixtures, office appliances and certain other assets having an aggregate net book value of ₹ 1,299 million, over a period of three years which, in our opinion, is reasonable having regard to the size of the Company and the nature of its assets. Pursuant to the programme, a portion of the fixed assets has been physically verified by the Management during the year and no material discrepancies have been noticed on such verification.

(c) In our opinion, and according to the information and explanations given to us, a substantial part of fixed assets has not been disposed off by the Company during the year.

ii. (a) The inventory (excluding stocks with third parties) has been physically verified by the Management during the year. In respect of inventory lying with third parties, these have substantially been confirmed by them. In our opinion, the frequency of verification is reasonable.

(b) In our opinion, the procedures of physical verification of inventory followed by the Management are reasonable and adequate in relation to the size of the Company and the nature of its business.

(c) On the basis of our examination of the inventory records, in our opinion, the Company is maintaining proper records of inventory. The discrepancies noticed on physical verification of inventory as compared to book records were not material.

iii. The Company has not taken/ granted any loans, secured or unsecured, from/ to companies, firms or other parties covered in the register maintained under Section 301 of the Act. Therefore, the provisions of Clause 4(iii)[(b),(c) and (d) /(f) and (g)] of the said Order are not applicable to the Company.

iv. In our opinion, and according to the information and explanations given to us, having regard to the explanation that for certain items of inventory purchased which are of special nature for which suitable alternative sources do not exist for obtaining comparative quotations, there is an adequate internal control system commensurate with the size of the Company and the nature of its business for the purchase of inventory, fixed assets and for the sale of goods and services. Further, on the basis of our examination of the books and records of the Company, and according to the information and explanations given to us, we have neither come across, nor have we been informed of any continuing failure to correct major weaknesses in the aforesaid internal control system.

v. (a) According to the information and explanations given to us, we are of the opinion that the particulars of all contracts or arrangements that need to be entered into the register maintained under Section 301 of the Act have been so entered.

(b) In our opinion and according to the information and explanations given to us, the transactions made in pursuance of such contracts or arrangements and exceeding the value of Rupees Five lakhs amounting to ₹ 49,485 million in respect of purchase of goods including components and services from the holding company where we are unable to comment as there are no comparable market prices available being goods including components and services of specialised nature.

vi. The Company has not accepted any deposits from the public within the meaning of Sections 58A and 58AA of the Act and the rules framed there under.

vii. In our opinion, the Company has an internal audit system commensurate with its size and the nature of its business.

viii. We have broadly reviewed the books of account maintained by the Company in respect of products where, pursuant to the rules made by the Central Government of India, the maintenance of cost records has been prescribed under clause (d) of sub-section (1) of Section 209 of the Act, and are of the opinion that, prima facie, the prescribed accounts and records have been made and maintained. We have not, however, made a detailed examination of the records with a view to determine whether they are accurate or complete.

ix. (a) According to the information and explanations given to us and the records of the Company examined by us, in our opinion, the Company is regular in depositing the undisputed statutory dues, including provident fund, investor education and protection fund, employees' state insurance, income tax, sales tax, wealth tax, service tax, customs duty, excise duty and other material statutory dues, as applicable, with the appropriate authorities.

(b) According to the information and explanations given to us and the records of the Company examined by us, the particulars of dues of income tax, sales tax, wealth tax, service tax, customs duty and excise duty as at 31st March 2013 which have not been deposited on account of a dispute, are as follows:

(₹ in million)

Name of the statute (Nature of dues)	Amount under dispute	Amount deposited under dispute	Period to which the amount relates	Forum where the dispute is pending
Income Tax Act, 1961 (Tax & Interest)	13,795	6,766	1991 to 2012	Income Tax Appellate Tribunal/ High Court/AO (Tax Deducted at Source)
Wealth Tax Act, 1957 (Tax)	1	1	1997 to 1998	High Court
Haryana General Sales Tax Act (Tax & Interest)	3	-	1983 to 1988	Assessing Authority
Delhi Sales Tax Act (Tax)	47	2	1987 to 1991	Additional Commissioner
The Central Excise Act, 1944 (Duty, Interest & Penalty)	10,680	377	May 1989 to August 2012	Customs Excise & Service Tax Appellate Tribunal/ High Court/ Supreme Court
The Finance Act, 1994 (Service Tax, Interest & Penalty)	2,782	14	September 2004 to December 2012	Customs Excise & Service Tax Appellate Tribunal/Commissioner (Appeals)
Customs Act, 1962 (Duty & Interest)	27	22	February 2003 to August 2003	Customs Excise & Service Tax Appellate Tribunal

For detailed listing refer Note 55 annexed to the financial statements

x. The Company has no accumulated losses as at the end of the financial year and it has not incurred any cash losses in the financial year end on that date or in the immediately preceding financial year.

xi. According to the records of the Company examined by us and the information and explanation given to us, the Company has not defaulted in repayment of dues to any financial institution or bank or debenture holders as at the balance sheet date.

xii. The Company has not granted any loans and advances on the basis of security by way of pledge of shares, debentures and other securities. Therefore the provisions of Clause 4(xii) of the Order are not applicable to the Company.

xiii. As the provisions of any special statute applicable to chit fund/ nidhi/ mutual benefit fund/ societies are not applicable to the Company, the provisions of Clause 4(xiii) of the Order are not applicable to the Company.

xiv. In our opinion, the Company is not dealing in or trading in shares, securities, debentures and other investments. Accordingly, the provisions of Clause 4(xiv) of the Order are not applicable to the Company.

xv. In our opinion, and according to the information and explanations given to us, the Company has not given any guarantee for loans taken by others from banks or financial institutions during the year. Accordingly, the provisions of Clause 4(xv) of the Order are not applicable to the Company.

xvi. In our opinion, and according to the information and explanations given to us, the term loans have been applied, on an overall basis, for the purposes for which they were obtained.

xvii. According to the information and explanations given to us and on an overall examination of the balance sheet of the Company, we report that, no funds raised on short-term basis have been used for long-term investment.

xviii. The Company has not made any preferential allotment of shares to parties and companies covered in the register maintained under Section 301 of the Act during the year. Accordingly, the provisions of Clause 4(xviii) of the Order are not applicable to the Company.

xix. The Company has not issued any debentures during the year and does not have any debentures outstanding as at the beginning of the year and at the year end. Accordingly, the provisions of Clause 4(xix) of the Order are not applicable to the Company.

xx. The Company has not raised any money by public issues during the year. Accordingly, the provisions of Clause 4(xx) of the Order are not applicable to the Company.

xxi. During the course of our examination of the books and records of the Company, carried out in accordance with the generally accepted auditing practices in India, and according to the information and explanations given to us, we have neither come across any instance of fraud on or by the Company, noticed or reported during the year, nor have we been informed of any such case by the Management.

For **Price Waterhouse**

Firm Registration Number: 301112E

Chartered Accountants

ABHISHEK RARA

Partner

Membership Number : 077779

Place : New Delhi

Date : 26th April 2013

Balance Sheet
As at 31st March 2013

(All amounts in ₹ million, unless otherwise stated)

	Notes to Accounts	As at 31.03.2013	As at 31.03.2012
EQUITY AND LIABILITIES			
SHAREHOLDERS' FUNDS			
Share Capital	2	1,510	1,445
Reserves and Surplus	3	184,279	150,429
		185,789	**151,874**
NON-CURRENT LIABILITIES			
Long Term Borrowings	4	5,429	-
Deferred Tax Liabilities (Net)	5	4,087	3,023
Other Long Term Liabilities	6	1,036	966
Long Term Provisions	7	2,259	1,693
		12,811	**5,682**
CURRENT LIABILITIES			
Short Term Borrowings	8	8,463	10,783
Trade Payables	9	41,674	33,499
Other Current Liabilities	10	11,661	15,892
Short Term Provisions	11	6,482	5,292
		68,280	**65,466**
TOTAL		**266,880**	**223,022**
ASSETS			
NON-CURRENT ASSETS			
Fixed Assets			
Tangible Assets	12	95,765	73,108
Intangible Assets	13	2,227	2,099
Capital Work in Progress	14	19,422	9,419
		117,414	**84,626**
Non-Current Investments	15	18,485	13,933
Long Term Loans and Advances	16	12,787	13,410
Other Non-Current Assets	17	8,946	263
		157,632	**112,232**
CURRENT ASSETS			
Current Investments	18	52,298	47,541
Inventories	19	18,407	17,965
Trade Receivables	20	14,237	9,376
Cash and Bank Balances	21	7,750	24,361
Short Term Loans and Advances	22	11,153	7,783
Other Current Assets	23	5,403	3,764
		109,248	**110,790**
TOTAL		**266,880**	**223,022**

The notes are an integral part of these financial statements

This is the Balance Sheet referred to in our report of even date.

For **Price Waterhouse**
Firm Registration Number: 301112E
Chartered Accountants

ABHISHEK RARA
Partner
Membership Number - 077779

Place: New Delhi
Date: 26th April 2013

KENICHI AYUKAWA
Managing Director & CEO

SHINZO NAKANISHI
Director

AJAY SETH
Chief Financial Officer

S. RAVI AIYAR
Executive Director (Legal)
& Company Secretary

Statement of Profit and Loss
For the year ended 31st March 2013

(All amounts in ₹ million, unless otherwise stated)

	Notes to Accounts	For the year ended 31.03.2013	For the year ended 31.03.2012
REVENUE FROM OPERATIONS			
Gross Sale of Products	24	481,147	386,141
Less: Excise Duty		55,021	39,082
Net Sale of Products		426,126	347,059
Other Operating Revenue	25	9,753	8,812
		435,879	355,871
Other Income	26	8,124	8,268
Total Revenue		**444,003**	**364,139**
EXPENSES			
Cost of Material Consumed	45(i)	305,741	267,055
Purchase of Stock-in-Trade	49	19,613	15,325
Change in Inventories of Finished Goods, Work-in-Progress and Stock-in-Trade	27	234	(1,297)
Employees Benefit Expenses	28	10,696	8,013
Finance Costs	29	1,898	552
Depreciation and Amortisation Expense	30	18,612	11,384
Other Expenses	31	57,737	42,072
Vehicles / Dies for Own Use		(438)	(427)
Total Expenses		**414,093**	**342,677**
Profit before Tax		**29,910**	**21,462**
Less : Tax Expense - Current Tax		7,228	4,138
- MAT Credit Availed		(904)	-
- Deferred Tax	5	(335)	972
Profit for the Year		**23,921**	**16,352**
Basic / Diluted Earnings Per Share of ₹ 5 each (in ₹)	50	**79.19**	**56.60**

The notes are an integral part of these financial statements

This is the Statement of Profit and Loss referred to in our report of even date.

For **Price Waterhouse**
Firm Registration Number: 301112E
Chartered Accountants

ABHISHEK RARA
Partner
Membership Number - 077779

Place: New Delhi
Date: 26th April 2013

KENICHI AYUKAWA
Managing Director & CEO

SHINZO NAKANISHI
Director

AJAY SETH
Chief Financial Officer

S. RAVI AIYAR
Executive Director (Legal)
& Company Secretary

Cash Flow Statement

For the year ended 31st March 2013

(All amounts in ₹ million, unless otherwise stated)

		For the year ended 31.03.2013	For the year ended 31.03.2012
A.	**CASH FLOW FROM OPERATING ACTIVITIES:**		
	Net Profit before Tax	29,910	21,462
	Adjustments for:		
	Depreciation and amortisation	18,612	11,384
	Finance cost	1,898	552
	Interest income	(3,134)	(4,036)
	Dividend income	(417)	(699)
	Net loss on sale / discarding of fixed assets	331	157
	Profit on sale of investments (Net)	(4,101)	(2,442)
	Provisions no longer required written back	(472)	(1,091)
	Unrealised foreign exchange (gain)/ loss	1,425	556
	Operating Profit before Working Capital changes	**44,052**	**25,843**
	Adjustments for changes in Working Capital :		
	- Increase/(Decrease) in Trade Payables	6,400	7,416
	- Increase/(Decrease) in Short Term Provisions	268	254
	- Increase/(Decrease) in Long Term Provisions	996	1,195
	- Increase/(Decrease) in Other Current Liabilities	(477)	2,000
	- Increase/(Decrease) in Other Long Term Liabilities	70	7
	- (Increase)/Decrease in Trade Receivables	(3,693)	(1,131)
	- (Increase)/Decrease in Inventories	3,485	(3,815)
	- (Increase)/Decrease in Long Term Loans and Advances	2,358	(863)
	- (Increase)/Decrease in Short Term Loans and Advances	(2,215)	(947)
	- (Increase)/Decrease in Other Current Assets	(1,930)	(1,970)
	- (Increase)/Decrease in Other Non Current Assets	(139)	119
	Cash generated from Operating Activities	**49,175**	**28,108**
	- Taxes (Paid) (Net of Tax Deducted at Source)	(5,333)	(2,509)
	Net Cash from Operating Activities	**43,842**	**25,599**
B.	**CASH FLOW FROM INVESTING ACTIVITIES:**		
	Purchase of Fixed Assets	(38,549)	(29,697)
	Sale of Fixed Assets	449	67
	Sale of Investments	118,332	159,780
	Purchase of Investments	(127,492)	(167,598)
	Investments in Deposits with Banks	(15,000)	(22,600)
	Maturities of Deposits with Banks	22,600	24,130
	Interest Received	3,502	4,261
	Dividend Received	417	699
	Net Cash from Investing Activities	**(35,741)**	**(30,958)**

Cash Flow Statement

For the year ended 31st March 2013

(All amounts in ₹ million, unless otherwise stated)

	For the year ended 31.03.2013	For the year ended 31.03.2012
C. CASH FLOW FROM FINANCING ACTIVITIES:		
Proceeds from Short Term borrowings	8,463	10,783
Repayment of Short Term borrowings	(10,783)	(312)
Proceeds from Long Term borrowings	1,688	-
Repayment of Long Term borrowings	(4,510)	(1,362)
Interest Paid	(2,003)	(426)
Dividend Paid	(2,167)	(2,167)
Corporate Dividend Tax Paid	(351)	(351)
Net Cash from Financing Activities	**(9,663)**	**6,165**
Net Increase/(Decrease) in Cash & Cash Equivalents	**(1,562)**	**806**
Cash and Cash Equivalents as at 1st April (Opening Balance)	**1,761**	**955**
Cash and cash equivalents as at 1st April 2012 [acquired pursuant to a scheme of amalgamation (refer note 37)]	1,051	-
Cash and Cash Equivalents as at 31st March (Closing Balance)	**1,250**	**1,761**
Cash and Cash Equivalents comprise	**1,250**	**1,761**
Cash & Cheques in Hand	1,031	696
Balance with Banks	219	65
Balance with Scheduled Banks in Deposit Accounts	-	1,000

Notes:

1 The above Cash Flow Statement has been prepared under the indirect method as set out in Accounting Standard -3 on "Cash Flow Statement" notified under Section 211 (3C) of the Companies Act, 1956.

2 Cash and Cash Equivalents include ₹ 6 million (Previous Year ₹ 5 million) in respect of unclaimed dividend, the balance of which is not available to the Company.

3 Figures in brackets represents cash outflow.

This is the Cash Flow Statement referred to in our report of even date

For **Price Waterhouse**
Firm Registration Number: 301112E
Chartered Accountants

ABHISHEK RARA
Partner
Membership Number - 077779

Place: New Delhi
Date: 26th April 2013

KENICHI AYUKAWA
Managing Director & CEO

AJAY SETH
Chief Financial Officer

SHINZO NAKANISHI
Director

S. RAVI AIYAR
Executive Director (Legal)
& Company Secretary

Notes
To The Financial Statements

(All amounts in ₹ million, unless otherwise stated)

1. **SUMMARY OF SIGNIFICANT ACCOUNTING POLICIES**

1.1 GENERAL INFORMATION

The Company is primarily in the business of manufacturing, purchase and sale of motor vehicles, components and spare parts ("automobiles"). The other activities of the Company comprise facilitation of Pre-Owned Car sales, Fleet Management and Car Financing. The Company is a public company listed on the Bombay Stock Exchange (BSE) and the National Stock Exchange (NSE).

1.2 BASIS FOR PREPARATION OF FINANCIAL STATEMENTS

These financial statements have been prepared in accordance with the generally accepted accounting principles in India under the historical cost convention on an accrual basis. These financial statements have been prepared to comply in all material respects with the applicable accounting principles in India, the applicable accounting standards notified under Section 211(3C) [Companies (Accounting Standards) Rules, 2006 as amended] of the Companies Act, 1956, Accounting Standard 30, Financial Instruments: Recognition and Measurement issued by the Institute of Chartered Accountants of India to the extent it does not contradict any other accounting standard referred to Section 211 (3C) [Companies (Accounting Standards) Rules, 2006 as amended] of the Act, other recognised accounting practices and policies and the relevant provisions of the Companies Act, 1956.

All assets and liabilities have been classified as current or non-current as per the Company's operating cycle and other criteria set out in the Revised Schedule VI to the Companies Act, 1956. Based on the nature of products and the time between the acquisition of assets for processing and their realisation in cash and cash equivalents, the Company has ascertained its operating cycle as 12 months for the purpose of current – non current classification of assets and liabilities.

1.3 REVENUE RECOGNITION

Domestic and export sales are recognised on transfer of significant risks and rewards to the customer which takes place on dispatch of goods from the factory and port respectively.

The Company recognises income from services on rendering of services.

1.4 FIXED ASSETS

Tangible Assets

a) Fixed assets (except freehold land which is carried at cost) are carried at cost of acquisition or construction or at manufacturing cost (in case of own manufactured assets) in the year of capitalisation less accumulated depreciation.

b) Assets acquired under finance leases are capitalised at the lower of their fair value and the present value of minimum lease payments.

Intangible Assets

Lumpsum royalty is stated at cost incurred as per the relevant licence agreements with the technical know-how providers less accumulated amortisation.

1.5 BORROWING COSTS

Borrowing costs that are directly attributable to the acquisition, construction or production of qualifying assets are capitalised till the month in which each asset is put to use as part of the cost of that asset.

1.6 DEPRECIATION / AMORTISATION

a) Tangible fixed assets except leasehold land are depreciated on the straight line method on a pro-rata basis from the month in which each asset is put to use.

Depreciation has been provided at the rates prescribed in Schedule XIV to the Companies Act, 1956 except for certain fixed assets where, based on the management's estimate of the useful lives of the assets, higher depreciation has been provided on the straight line method over the following useful lives:

Plant and Machinery	8 – 11 Years
Dies and Jigs	4 Years
Electronic Data Processing Equipment	3 Years

In respect of assets whose useful life has been revised, the unamortised depreciable amount is charged over the revised remaining useful lives of the assets.

b) Leasehold land is amortised over the period of lease.

c) All assets, the individual written down value of which at the beginning of the year is ₹ 5,000 or less, are depreciated at the rate of 100 per cent. Assets purchased during the year costing ₹ 5,000 or less are depreciated at the rate of 100 per cent.

Notes
To The Financial Statements

(All amounts in ₹ million, unless otherwise stated)

d) Lump sum royalty is amortised on a straight line basis over 4 years from the start of production of the related model.

1.7 INVENTORIES

a) Inventories are valued at the lower of cost, determined on the weighted average basis and net realisable value.

b) Tools are written off over a period of three years except for tools valued at ₹ 5,000 or less individually which are charged to revenue in the year of purchase.

c) Machinery spares (other than those supplied along with main plant and machinery, which are capitalised and depreciated accordingly) are charged to revenue on consumption except those valued at ₹ 5,000 or less individually, which are charged to revenue in the year of purchase.

1.8 INVESTMENTS

Current investments are valued at the lower of cost and fair value. Long-term investments are valued at cost except in the case of other than temporary decline in value, in which case the necessary provision is made.

1.9 RESEARCH AND DEVELOPMENT

Revenue expenditure on research and development is charged against the profit for the year in which it is incurred. Capital expenditure on research and development is shown as an addition to fixed assets and depreciated accordingly.

1.10 FOREIGN CURRENCY TRANSLATIONS AND DERIVATIVE INSTRUMENTS

a) Foreign currency transactions are recorded at the exchange rates prevailing at the date of the transactions. Exchange differences arising on settlement of transactions are recognised as income or expense in the year in which they arise.

b) At the balance sheet date, all monetary assets and liabilities denominated in foreign currency are reported at the exchange rates prevailing at the balance sheet date by recognising the exchange difference in the statement of profit and loss. However, the exchange difference arising on foreign currency monetary items that qualify and are designated as hedge instruments in a cash flow hedge is initially recognised in 'hedge reserve' and subsequently transferred to the statement of profit and loss on occurrence of the underlying hedged transaction.

c) Effective 1st April 2008, the Company adopted Accounting Standard-30,"Financial Instruments: Recognition and Measurement" issued by The Institute of Chartered Accountants of India to the extent the adoption does not contradict with the accounting standards notified under Section 211(3C) of the Companies Act, 1956 and other regulatory requirements. All derivative contracts (except for forward foreign exchange contracts where underlying assets or liabilities exist) are fair valued at each reporting date. For derivative contracts designated in a hedging relationship, the Company records the gain or loss on effective hedges, if any, in a hedge reserve, until the transaction is complete. On completion, the gain or loss is transferred to the statement of profit and loss of that period. Changes in fair value relating to the ineffective portion of the hedges and derivatives not qualifying or not designated as hedges are recognised in the statement of profit and loss in the accounting period in which they arise.

d) In the case of forward foreign exchange contracts where an underlying asset or liability exists, the difference between the forward rate and the exchange rate at the inception of the contract is recognised as income or expense over the life of the contract. Profit or loss arising on cancellation or renewal of a forward contract is recognised as income or expense in the year in which such cancellation or renewal is made.

1.11 EMPLOYEE BENEFIT COSTS

Short - Term Employee Benefits:

Recognised as an expense at the undiscounted amount in the statement of profit and loss for the year in which the related service is rendered.

Post Employment and Other Long Term Employee Benefits:

(i) The Company has Defined Contribution Plans for post employment benefit namely the Superannuation Fund which is recognised by the income tax authorities. This Fund is administered through a Trust set up by the Company and the Company's contribution thereto is charged to statement of profit and loss every year. The Company also maintains an insurance policy to fund a post-

(All amounts in ₹ million, unless otherwise stated)

employment medical assistance scheme, which is a Defined Contribution Plan administered by The New India Insurance Company Limited. The Company's contribution to State Plans namely Employees' State Insurance Fund and Employees' Pension Scheme are charged to the statement of profit and loss every year.

(ii) The Company has Defined Benefit Plans namely Gratuity, Provident Fund and Retirement Allowance for employees and Other Long Term Employee Benefits i.e. Leave Encashment / Compensated Absences, the liability for which is determined on the basis of an actuarial valuation at the end of the year based on the Projected Unit Credit Method and any shortfall in the size of the fund maintained by the Trust is additionally provided for in the statement of profit and loss. The Gratuity Fund and Provident Fund are recognised by the income tax authorities and is administered through Trusts set up by the Company.

Termination benefits are immediately recognised as an expense.

Gains and losses arising out of actuarial valuations are recognised immediately in the statement of profit and loss as income or expense.

1.12 CUSTOMS DUTY

Custom duty available as drawback is initially recognised as purchase cost and is credited to consumption of materials on exported vehicles.

1.13 GOVERNMENT GRANTS

Government grants are recognised in the statement of profit and loss in accordance with the related schemes and in the period in which these accrue.

1.14 TAXES

Tax expense for the year, comprising current tax and deferred tax, is included in determining the net profit/ (loss) for the year.

Current tax is recognised based on assessable profit computed in accordance with the Income Tax Act and at the prevailing tax rate.

Deferred tax is recognised for all timing differences. Deferred tax assets are carried forward to the extent it is reasonably / virtually certain (as the case may be) that future taxable profit will be available against which such deferred tax assets can be realised. Such assets are reviewed at each balance sheet date and written down to reflect the amount that is reasonably/ virtually certain (as the case may be) to be realised.

Minimum Alternative Tax credit is recognised as an asset only when and to the extent there is convincing evidence that the Company will pay normal income tax during the specified period. Such asset is reviewed at each balance sheet date and the carrying amount is written down to the extent there is no longer convincing evidence to the effect that the Company will pay normal tax during the specified period.

Deferred tax assets and liabilities are measured at the tax rates that have been enacted or substantively enacted at the balance sheet date.

1.15 DIVIDEND INCOME

Dividend from investments is recognised when the right to receive the payment is established and when no significant uncertainty as to measurability or collectability exits.

1.16 INTEREST INCOME

Interest income is recognised on the time basis determined by the amount outstanding and the rate applicable and where no significant uncertainty as to measurability or collectability exists.

1.17 IMPAIRMENT OF ASSETS

At each balance sheet date, the Company assesses whether there is any indication that an asset may be impaired. If any such indication exists, the Company estimates the recoverable amount. If the carrying amount of the asset exceeds its recoverable amount, an impairment loss is recognised in the statement of profit and loss to the extent the carrying amount exceeds the recoverable amount.

1.18 ROYALTY

a) The Company pays / accrues for royalty in accordance with the relevant licence agreements with the technical know-how provider.

b) The lump sum royalty incurred towards obtaining technical assistance / technical know-how to manufacture a new model/ car, ownership of which rests with the technical know how provider, is recognised as an intangible asset in accordance with the requirements of Accounting Standard-26 "Intangible Assets". Royalty payable on sale of products i.e. running royalty is charged to the statement of profit and loss as and when incurred.

Notes
To The Financial Statements

(All amounts in ₹ million, unless otherwise stated)

1.19 PROVISIONS AND CONTINGENCIES

Provisions: Provisions are recognised when there is a present obligation as a result of a past event, it is probable that an outflow of resources embodying economic benefits will be required to settle the obligation and there is a reliable estimate of the amount of the obligation. Provisions are measured at the best estimate of the expenditure required to settle the present obligation at the balance sheet date and are not discounted to their present value.

Contingent Liabilities: Contingent liabilities are disclosed when there is a possible obligation arising from past events, the existence of which will be confirmed only by the occurrence or non occurrence of one or more uncertain future events not wholly within the control of the Company or a present obligation that arises from past events where it is either not probable that an outflow of resources will be required to settle or a reliable estimate of the amount cannot be made.

1.20 LEASES

As a lessee

Leases in which a significant portion of the risks and rewards of ownership are retained by the lessor are classified as operating leases. Payments made under operating leases are charged to the statement of profit and loss on a straight-line basis over the period of the lease or the terms of underlying agreement/s as the case may be.

As a lessor

The Company has leased certain tangible assets and such leases where the Company has substantially retained all the risks and rewards of ownership are classified as operating leases. Lease income on such operating leases are recognised in the statement of profit and loss on a straight line basis over the lease term which is representative of the time pattern in which benefit derived from the use of the leased asset is diminished.

1.21 CASH AND CASH EQUIVALENTS

In the cash flow statement, cash and cash equivalents include cash in hand, demand deposits with banks, other short-term highly liquid investments with original maturities of three months or less.

Notes
To The Financial Statements

(All amounts in ₹ million, unless otherwise stated)

2. SHARE CAPITAL

	As at 31.03.2013	As at 31.03.2012
Authorised Capital		
3,744,000,000 equity shares of ₹ 5 each (Previous year 744,000,000 equity shares of ₹ 5 each)	**18,720**	**3,720**
Issued, Subscribed and Paid up		
302,080,060 equity shares of ₹ 5 each (Previous year 288,910,060 equity shares of ₹ 5 each) fully paid up	1,510	1,445
	1,510	**1,445**

Reconciliation of the number of shares outstanding

	As at 31.03.2013		As at 31.03.2012	
	Numbers of Shares	Amount	Numbers of Shares	Amount
Balance as at the beginning of the year	288,910,060	1,445	288,910,060	1,445
Share issued in the ratio of 1:70 to the shareholders of erstwhile Suzuki Powertrain India Limited pursuant to a scheme of amalgamation (Refer Note 37)	13,170,000	65	-	-
Balance as at the end of the year	**302,080,060**	**1,510**	**288,910,060**	**1,445**

Equity shares held by the holding company

	As at 31.03.2013		As at 31.03.2012	
	Numbers of Shares	Amount	Numbers of Shares	Amount
Suzuki Motor Corporation, the holding company	169,788,440	848	156,618,440	783
	169,788,440	**848**	**156,618,440**	**783**

Rights, preferences and restriction attached to shares

The Company has one class of equity shares with a par value of ₹ 5 per share. Each shareholder is eligible for one vote per share held. The dividend proposed by the Board of Directors is subject to the approval of the shareholders in the ensuing Annual General Meeting, except in case of interim dividend. In the event of liquidation, the equity shareholders are eligible to receive the remaining assets of the Company, after distribution of all preferential amounts, in proportion to their shareholding.

Notes
To The Financial Statements

(All amounts in ₹ million, unless otherwise stated)

Shares held by each shareholder holding more than 5 per cent of the aggregate shares in the Company

	%	Number of Shares	%	Number of Shares
Suzuki Motor Corporation (the holding company)	56.21	169,788,440	54.21	156,618,440
Life Insurance Corporation of India	6.29	18,993,815	8.45	24,399,405

Shares allotted as fully paid up pursuant to contract(s) without payment being received in cash (during 5 years immediately preceding 31st March 2013)

13,170,000 Equity Shares have been allotted as fully paid up during the current year to Suzuki Motor Corporation pursuant to the scheme of amalgamation with Suzuki Powertrain India Limited (refer note 37).

3. RESERVES AND SURPLUS

		As at 31.03.2013		As at 31.03.2012
Reserve created on Amalgamation (Refer Note 37)		**9,153**		**-**
Securities Premium Account		**4,241**		**4,241**
General Reserve				
Balance as at the beginning of the year	15,852		14,217	
Add : Transferred from Surplus in Statement of Profit and Loss	2,392		1,635	
Balance as at the end of the year		**18,244**		**15,852**
Hedge Reserve				
Balance as at the beginning of the year	(441)		194	
Less : Release / adjustments during the year	(39)		635	
Balance as at the end of the year		**(402)**		**(441)**
Surplus in Statement of Profit and Loss				
Balance as at the beginning of the year	130,777		118,578	
Addition on Amalgamation (Refer Note 37)	3,565		-	
Add : Profit for the year	23,921		16,352	
Less : Appropriations:				
Transferred to General Reserve	2,392		1,635	
Proposed dividend	2,417		2,167	
Dividend distribution tax	411		351	
Balance as at the end of the year		**153,043**		**130,777**
		184,279		**150,429**

(All amounts in ₹ million, unless otherwise stated)

4. LONG TERM BORROWINGS

(Refer Note 37)

	As at 31.03.2013	As at 31.03.2012
Unsecured		
Foreign currency loans from banks	3,920	-
Loans from holding company	1,509	-
	5,429	-

1. Foreign currency loans from banks include:
   - loan amounting to ₹ 2,264 million (USD 41 million) taken from Japan Bank of International Cooperation (JBIC) at an interest rate of LIBOR + 0.125, repayable in 6 half yearly instalments starting September 2014 (acquired pursuant to a scheme of amalgamation, refer note 37). The repayment of the loan is guaranteed by Suzuki Motor Corporation, Japan (the holding company).
   - other long term foreign currency loans amounting to ₹ 1,656 million (USD 30 million) taken from banks during the year at an average interest rate of Libor + 1.375 and repayable in July 2015.
2. A loan amounting to ₹ 1,509 million (USD 27 million) taken from the holding company at an interest rate of LIBOR + 0.48, repayable in 6 half yearly instalments starting September 2014 (acquired pursuant to a scheme of amalgamation, refer note 37).

5. DEFERRED TAX LIABILITIES (NET)

Major components of deferred tax arising on account of timing differences along with their movement as at 31st March 2013 are :

		Movement		
	As at 31.03.2012	Pursuant to amalgamation (refer note 37)	during the year*	As at 31.03.2013
Deferred Tax Assets				
Provision for doubtful debts / advances	176	-	(45)	131
Contingent provisions	152	-	30	182
Others	497	17	(44)	470
TOTAL (A)	**825**	**17**	**(59)**	**783**
Deferred Tax Liabilities				
Depreciation on fixed assets	3,450	1,083	(1,021)	3,512
Exchange gain on capital accounts	(259)	-	(227)	(486)
Allowances under Income Tax Act, 1961	657	-	1,187	1,844
TOTAL (B)	**3,848**	**1,083**	**(61)**	**4,870**
Net Deferred Tax Liability (B) - (A)	**3,023**	**1,066**	**(2)**	**4,087**
Previous Year	1,644	-	1,379	3,023

* Includes adjustment of ₹ 333 million (Previous year ₹ 407 million) on account of reclassification to "Deferred Tax Liabilities" from "Provision for Taxation".

Note: Deferred Tax Assets and Deferred Tax Liabilities have been offset as they relate to the same governing taxation laws.

Notes
To The Financial Statements

(All amounts in ₹ million, unless otherwise stated)

6. OTHER LONG TERM LIABILITIES

	As at 31.03.2013	As at 31.03.2012
Deposits from dealers, contractors and others	1,036	966
	1,036	**966**

7. LONG TERM PROVISIONS

	As at 31.03.2013		As at 31.03.2012	
Provisions for Employee Benefits				
Provision for retirement allowance (Refer Note 28)		42		35
Other Provisions				
Provision for litigation / disputes	992		909	
Provision for warranty & product recall	1,216		739	
Others	9	2,217	10	1,658
		2,259		**1,693**

Details of Other Provisions:

	Litigation / Disputes		Warranty/ Product Recall		Others	
	2012-2013	2011-2012	2012-2013	2011-2012	2012-2013	2011-2012
Balance at the beginning of the year	909	897	1,331	929	10	16
Additions during the year	111	102	544	581	-	1
Utilised/ reversed during the year	28	90	210	179	1	7
Balance as at the end of the year	**992**	**909**	**1,665**	**1,331**	**9**	**10**
Classified as Long Term	992	909	1,216	739	9	10
Classified as Short Term	-	-	449	592	-	-
TOTAL	**992**	**909**	**1,665**	**1,331**	**9**	**10**

a) Provision for litigation / disputes represents the estimated outflow in respect of disputes with various government authorities.

b) Provision for warranty and product recall represents the estimated outflow in respect of warranty and recall cost for products sold.

c) Provision for others represents the estimated outflow in respect of disputes or other obligations on account of excise duty, export obligation, etc.

d) Due to the nature of the above costs, it is not possible to estimate the timing / uncertainties relating to their outflows as well as the expected reimbursements from such estimates.

Notes
To The Financial Statements

(All amounts in ₹ million, unless otherwise stated)

8. SHORT TERM BORROWINGS

	As at 31.03.2013	As at 31.03.2012
Unsecured		
From banks - cash credit	725	80
From banks - buyers credit and packing credit loans	7,738	10,703
	8,463	**10,783**

9. TRADE PAYABLES

	As at 31.03.2013	As at 31.03.2012
Due to Micro and Small enterprises	273	288
Others	41,401	33,211
	41,674	**33,499**

The Company pays its vendors within 30 days and no interest during the year has been paid or is payable under the terms of the Micro, Small and Medium Enterprises Development Act, 2006.

96 - 97

10. OTHER CURRENT LIABILITIES

		As at 31.03.2013		As at 31.03.2012
Current maturities of long term debts		-		1,586
Interest accrued but not due on:				
- Borrowings	205		126	
- Deposits from dealers, contractors and others	23	228	43	169
Unclaimed dividend *		6		5
Creditors for capital goods	4,035		5,223	
Other payables	2,071		1,746	
Book overdraft	594		1,366	
Advances from customers/dealers	1,590		2,449	
Statutory dues	2,704		2,163	
Deposits from dealers, contractors and others	433	11,427	1,185	14,132
		11,661		**15,892**

* Unclaimed dividend do not include any amount due to be deposited to the Investor Education and Protection Fund under Section 205C of the Companies Act, 1956.

Notes
To The Financial Statements

(All amounts in ₹ million, unless otherwise stated)

11. SHORT TERM PROVISIONS

	As at 31.03.2013		As at 31.03.2012	
Provisions for Employee Benefits				
(Refer Note 7 and 28)				
Provision for retirement allowances	2		2	
Provision for compensated absences	1,274	1,276	850	852
Other provisions				
(Refer Note 7)				
Provision for warranty & product recall	449		592	
Provision for proposed dividend*	2,417		2,167	
Provision for corporate dividend tax	411		351	
Provision for taxation [Net of tax paid ₹ 69,884 million (Previous year ₹ 63,730 million) and Minimum Alternate Tax credit availed ₹ 904 million (previous year Nil)]	1,929	5,206	1,330	4,440
		6,482		**5,292**

* The final dividend proposed for the year is as follows:

	As at 31.03.2013	As at 31.03.2012
On equity shares of ₹ 5 each:		
Amount of dividend proposed	2,417	2,167
Dividend per equity share	₹ 8.00	₹ 7.50

Notes
To The Financial Statements

12. TANGIBLE ASSETS

(All amounts in ₹ million, unless otherwise stated)

Particulars	Gross Block					Depreciation / Amortisation					Net Block	
	As at 01.04.2012	Acquired pursuant to a scheme of amalgamation*	Addition	Deductions/ Adjustments	As at 31.03.2013	Upto 01.04.2012	Acquired pursuant to a scheme of amalgamation	For the year	Deductions/ Adjustments	As at 31.03.2013	As at 31.03.2013	As at 31.03.2012
Freehold Land (Note 1,3 & 4)	12,304	105	3,097	(2,363)	13,143	-	-	-	-	-	13,143	12,304
Leasehold Land	1,864	-	133	-	1,997	22	-	15	-	37	1,960	1,842
Building	10,929	1,106	3,346	(1)	15,380	1,816	142	390	(1)	2,347	13,033	9,113
Plant and Machinery	116,587	29,780	18,205	(4,463)	160,109	68,112	13,055	16,979	(4,049)	94,097	66,012	48,475
Electronic Data Processing Equipment	1,412	82	213	(142)	1,565	1,143	64	192	(131)	1,268	297	269
Furniture, Fixtures and Office Appliances	911	27	158	(10)	1,086	326	8	58	(5)	387	699	585
Vehicles	677	13	245	(180)	755	157	3	67	(45)	182	573	520
TOTAL (A)	**144,684**	**31,113**	**25,397**	**(7,159)**	**194,035**	**71,576**	**13,272**	**17,701**	**(4,231)**	**98,318**	**95,717**	**73,108**
Assets given on operating lease:												
Plant and Machinery	-	353	-	(276)	77		89	10	(70)	29	48	-
TOTAL (B)	**-**	**353**	**-**	**(276)**	**77**	**-**	**89**	**10**	**(70)**	**29**	**48**	**-**
TOTAL [(A) + (B)]	**144,684**	**31,466**	**25,397**	**(7,435)**	**194,112**	**71,576**	**13,361**	**17,711**	**(4,301)**	**98,347**	**95,765**	**73,108**
Previous Year Figures	116,729	-	29,506	(1,551)	144,684	61,892	-	11,011	(1,327)	71,576	73,108	

(1) Freehold land costing ₹ 8,129 million (Previous year ₹ 5,268 million) is not yet registered in the name of the Company.

(2) Plant and Machinery (gross block) includes pro-rata cost amounting to ₹ 374 million (Previous year ₹ 374 million) of a Gas Turbine jointly owned by the Company with its group companies and other companies.

(3) A part of freehold land of the Company at Gurgaon and Manesar has been made available to its group companies.

(4) Adjustments to free hold land include ₹ 2,354 million accrued in the previous year as price adjustment claimed by the authority which allotted the land in an earlier year reversed in the current year [Refer Note 32(vii)].

13. INTANGIBLE ASSETS

Particulars	Gross Block					Depreciation / Amortisation					Net Block	
	As at 01.04.2012	Acquired pursuant to a scheme of amalgamation*	Addition	Deductions/ Adjustments	As at 31.03.2013	Upto 01.04.2012	Acquired pursuant to a scheme of amalgamation	For the year	Deductions/ Adjustments	As at 31.03.2013	As at 31.03.2013	As at 31.03.2012
Own Assets (Acquired):												
Lump sum royalty	2,663	574	658	-	3,895	564	203	901	-	1,668	2,227	2,099
TOTAL	**2,663**	**574**	**658**	**-**	**3,895**	**564**	**203**	**901**	**-**	**1,668**	**2,227**	**2,099**
Previous Year Figures	648	-	2,015	-	2,663	191	-	373	-	564	2,099	

* Refer note 37

Notes
To The Financial Statements

(All amounts in ₹ million, unless otherwise stated)

14. CAPITAL WORK IN PROGRESS

	As at 31.03.2013	As at 31.03.2012
Plant and Machinery	18,019	7,101
Civil Work in Progress	1,403	2,318
	19,422	**9,419**

15. NON-CURRENT INVESTMENTS
(Refer Note 54)

		As at 31.03.2013		As at 31.03.2012
Trade Investment (valued at cost, unless otherwise stated)				
Investment in subsidiaries (unquoted equity instruments)	91		15	
Investment in joint ventures (unquoted equity instruments)	999		1,071	
Investment in associates:				
- quoted equity instruments	111		111	
- unquoted equity instruments	220		4,171	
		1,421		5,368
Other Investment (valued at cost unless otherwise stated)				
Investment in mutual funds - unquoted	17,064		8,565	
Investment in preference shares - unquoted	50		50	
	17,114		8,615	
Less: Provision for diminution, other than temporary, in value of investments in preference shares	50	17,064	50	8,565
		18,485		**13,933**
Aggregate value of unquoted investments		18,424		13,872
Aggregate value of quoted investments		111		111
Market value of quoted investments		1,474		1,723
Aggregate value of provision for diminution other than temporary in value of investments		50		50

(All amounts in ₹ million, unless otherwise stated)

16. LONG TERM LOANS AND ADVANCES

		As at 31.03.2013		As at 31.03.2012
Capital Advances				
Unsecured - considered good	4,937		4,644	
- considered doubtful	76		13	
	5,013		4,657	
Less: Provision for doubtful capital advances	76	4,937	13	4,644
Security Deposits				
Unsecured - considered good		103		98
Loans and Advances to Related Parties				
Unsecured - considered good (Refer Note 37)		-		1,800
Taxes Paid Under Dispute				
Unsecured - considered good		7,497		6,481
Inter corporate deposits - considered doubtful	125		125	
Less: Provision for doubtful deposits	125	-	125	-
Other Loans and Advances				
Secured - considered good	10		12	
Unsecured - considered good	240		375	
- considered doubtful	63		73	
	313		460	
Less: Provision for doubtful other loans and advances	63	250	73	387
		12,787		**13,410**

Notes
To The Financial Statements

(All amounts in ₹ million, unless otherwise stated)

17. OTHER NON-CURRENT ASSETS

	As at 31.03.2013		As at 31.03.2012	
Interest Accrued on Deposits, Loans and Advances				
Secured - considered good		6		11
Unsecured - considered good	49		-	
- considered doubtful	-		1	
	49		1	
Less Provision for doubtful interest	-	49	1	-
Long term deposits with banks with maturity period more than 12 months		8,500		-
Claims				
Unsecured - considered good	385		246	
- considered doubtful	27		27	
	412		273	
Less Provision for doubtful claims	27	385	27	246
Others		6		6
		8,946		**263**

18. CURRENT INVESTMENTS
(Refer Note 54)

	As at 31.03.2013	As at 31.03.2012
Investment in mutual funds - unquoted	52,298	47,541
	52,298	**47,541**

(All amounts in ₹ million, unless otherwise stated)

19. INVENTORIES
(Refer Note 47)

		As at 31.03.2013		As at 31.03.2012
Components and Raw Materials		9,831		9,913
Work in Progress		1,127		593
Finished Goods Manufactured				
Vehicles	4,807		5,334	
Vehicle spares and components	311		173	
		5,118		5,507
Traded Goods				
Vehicle	5		297	
Vehicle spares and components	1,343	1,348	1,189	1,486
Stores and Spares		546		275
Tools		437		191
		18,407		**17,965**
Inventory includes in transit inventory of:				
Components and Raw Materials		3,247		4,165
Traded Goods - vehicle spares		26		43

20. TRADE RECEIVABLES

Unsecured - considered good				
Outstanding for a period exceeding six months from the date they are due for payment	34		18	
Others	14,203	14,237	9,358	9,376
Unsecured - considered doubtful				
Outstanding for a period exceeding six months from the date they are due for payment	35		35	
Less Provision for doubtful debts	35	-	35	-
		14,237		**9,376**

Notes
To The Financial Statements

(All amounts in ₹ million, unless otherwise stated)

21. CASH AND BANK BALANCES

		As at 31.03.2013		As at 31.03.2012
Cash and Cash Equivalents				
Cash on hand	6		5	
Cheques and drafts on hand	1,025		691	
Bank balances in current accounts	213		60	
Deposits (less than 3 months original maturity period)	-	1,244	1,000	1,756
Other Bank Balances				
Deposits (more than 3 months and upto 12 months original maturity period)	3,000		5,600	
Deposits (more than 12 months original maturity period)	3,500		17,000	
Unclaimed dividend accounts	6	6,506	5	22,605
		7,750		**24,361**

22. SHORT TERM LOANS AND ADVANCES

(considered good, unless otherwise stated)

Loans and Advances to Related Parties				
Unsecured		1,073		867
Balance with Customs, Port Trust and Other Government Authorities				
Unsecured		6,770		5,044
Other Loans and Advances				
Secured	4		5	
Unsecured	3,306	3,310	1,867	1,872
		11,153		**7,783**

23. OTHER CURRENT ASSETS

(considered good, unless otherwise stated)

Interest Accrued on Deposits, Loans and Advances				
Secured	6		6	
Unsecured	89	95	530	536
Claims				
Unsecured		1,593		788
Other receivable - steel coils				
Unsecured		3,710		2,431
Others				
Unsecured		5		9
		5,403		**3,764**

Notes
To The Financial Statements

(All amounts in ₹ million, unless otherwise stated)

24. GROSS SALE OF PRODUCTS
(Refer Note 47)

	For the year ended 31.03.2013	For the year ended 31.03.2012
Vehicles	441,163	362,111
Spare parts / dies and moulds / components	39,984	24,030
	481,147	**386,141**

25. OTHER OPERATING REVENUE

Income from services [Net of expenses of ₹ 1,083 million (Previous Year ₹ 689 million)]	2,252	1,719
Sale of scrap	3,597	2,950
Cash discount received	1,810	2,018
Others	2,094	2,125
	9,753	**8,812**

26. OTHER INCOME

	For the year ended 31.03.2013		For the year ended 31.03.2012	
Interest Income (gross) on:				
a) Fixed deposits	2,220		2,330	
b) Corporate bonds	-		528	
c) Receivables from dealers	699		665	
d) Advances to vendors	69		210	
e) Income tax refund	141		295	
f) Others	5	3,134	8	4,036
Dividend Income from:				
a) Long term investments	74		60	
b) Others	343	417	639	699
Net gain on sale of investments				
a) Long term	4,087		2,434	
b) Short term	14	4,101	8	2,442
Provisions no longer required written back		472		1,091
		8,124		**8,268**

Notes
To The Financial Statements

(All amounts in ₹ million, unless otherwise stated)

27. CHANGE IN INVENTORIES OF FINISHED GOODS, WORK-IN-PROGRESS AND STOCK-IN-TRADE

(Refer Note 37)

	For the year ended 31.03.2013		For the year ended 31.03.2012	
Work in Progress				
Opening stock	593		457	
Add: Acquired pursuant to a scheme of amalgamation	199		-	
Less: Closing stock	1,127	(335)	593	(136)
Vehicles - Manufactured and Traded				
Opening stock	5,631		4,220	
Add: Acquired pursuant to a scheme of amalgamation	51		-	
Less: Closing stock	4,812		5,631	
	870		(1,411)	
Less: Excise duty on increase / (decrease) of finished goods	9	861	(289)	(1,122)
Vehicle Spares and Components - Manufactured and Traded				
Opening stock	1,362		1,323	
Less: Closing stock	1,654	(292)	1,362	(39)
		234		**(1,297)**

28. EMPLOYEE BENEFIT EXPENSES

	For the year ended 31.03.2013	For the year ended 31.03.2012
Salaries, wages, allowances and other benefits [Net of staff cost recovered ₹ 38 million (Previous year ₹ 120 million)]	9,152	6,660
Contribution to provident and other funds	669	853
Staff welfare expenses	875	500
	10,696	**8,013**

The Company has calculated the various benefits provided to employees as under:

A. Defined Contribution Plans

a) Superannuation Fund

b) Post Employment Medical Assistance Scheme.

During the year the Company has recognised the following amounts in the statement of profit and loss :-

	31.03.2013	31.03.2012
Employers Contribution to Superannuation Fund*	51	44
Employers Contribution to Post Employment Medical Assistance Scheme.*	3	2

(All amounts in ₹ million, unless otherwise stated)

B. State Plans

a) Employers contribution to Employee State Insurance

b) Employers contribution to Employee's Pension Scheme 1995

During the year the Company has recognised the following amounts in the statement of profit and loss :-

	31.03.2013	31.03.2012
Employers contribution to Employee State Insurance*	13	2
Employers contribution to Employee's Pension Scheme 1995*	90	80

* Included in 'Contribution to Provident and Other Funds' above

C. Defined Benefit Plans and Other Long Term Benefits

a) Contribution to Gratuity Funds - Employee's Gratuity Fund.

b) Leave Encashment/Compensated Absence.

c) Retirement Allowance

d) Provident Fund

In accordance with Accounting Standard 15 (revised 2005), an actuarial valuation was carried out in respect of the aforesaid defined benefit plans and other long term benefits based on the following assumptions.

	31.03.2013				31.03.2012			
	Provident Fund	Leave Encashment/ Compensated Absence	Employees Gratuity Fund	Retirement Allowance	Provident Fund	Leave Encashment/ Compensated Absence	Employees Gratuity Fund	Retirement Allowance
Discount rate (per annum)	8.50%	8.00%	8.00%	8.00%	8.25%	9.00%	9.00%	9.00%
Rate of increase in compensation levels	Not Applicable	6.00%	6.00%	Not Applicable	Not Applicable	6.00%	6.00%	Not Applicable
Rate of return on plan assets.	8.60%	Not Applicable	8.00%	Not Applicable	8.55%	Not Applicable	9.00%	Not Applicable
Expected average remaining working lives of employees (years)	21	21	21	21	25	22	22	22

Estimates of future salary increases considered in actuarial valuation take account of inflation, seniority, promotion and other relevant factors such as supply and demand in the employment market.

Notes
To The Financial Statements

(All amounts in ₹ million, unless otherwise stated)

Changes in present value of obligations

	31.03.2013				31.03.2012			
	Provident Fund	Leave Encashment/ Compensated Absence	Employees Gratuity Fund	Retirement Allowance	Provident Fund	Leave Encashment/ Compensated Absence	Employees Gratuity Fund	Retirement Allowance
Present value of obligation as at beginning of the year	5,459	850	848	37	4,539	753	827	37
Add: Acquisition on amalgamation (Refer Note 37)	-	20	23	-	-	-	-	-
Interest cost	454	56	68	3	396	57	73	3
Current service cost	801	97	80	6	615	56	51	-
Benefits paid	294	171	55	-	101	141	28	-
Actuarial (gain) / loss on obligations	(411)	422	162	(2)	10	125	(75)	(3)
Present value of obligation as at the year end	6,009	1,274	1,126	44	5,459	850	848	37

Changes in the fair value of plan assets

	31.03.2013		31.03.2012	
	Provident Fund	Employees Gratuity Fund	Provident Fund	Employees Gratuity Fund
Fair value of Plan Assets as at beginning of the year	5,480	907	4,670	827
Expected return on Plan Assets	456	73	399	74
Contribution	839	115	615	28
Benefits paid	294	55	101	28
Actuarial (gain)/ loss on obligations	(27)	(86)	(103)	6
Fair value of plan assets as at the year end	6,508	1,126	5,480	907

(All amounts in ₹ million, unless otherwise stated)

Reconciliation of present value of defined benefit obligation and fair value of assets

	31.03.2013				31.03.2012			
	Provident Fund	Leave Encashment/ Compensated Absence	Employees Gratuity Fund	Retirement Allowance	Provident Fund	Leave Encashment/ Compensated Absence	Employees Gratuity Fund	Retirement Allowance
Present value of obligation as at the year end	6,009	1,274	1,126	44	5,459	850	848	37
Fair value of plan assets as at the year end	6,508	-	1,126	-	5,480	-	907	-
Surplus/ (Deficit)	499	(1,274)	-	(44)	21	(850)	60	(37)
Unfunded net asset/ (liability) recognised in balance sheet.	**-**	**(1,274)**	**-**	**(44)**	**-**	**(850)**	**-**	**(37)**
Classified as Long Term	**-**	**-**	**-**	**42**	**-**	**-**	**-**	**35**
Classified as Short Term	**-**	**1,274**	**-**	**2**	**-**	**850**	**-**	**2**
TOTAL	**-**	**1,274**	**-**	**44**	**-**	**850**	**-**	**37**

	31.03.2011			31.03.2010		
	Leave Encashment/ Compensated Absence	Employees Gratuity Fund	Retirement Allowance	Leave Encashment/ Compensated Absence	Employees Gratuity Fund	Retirement Allowance
Present value of obligation as at the year end	753	827	37	659	734	29
Fair value of plan assets as at the year end	-	827	-	-	734	-
Surplus/ (deficit)	(753)	-	(37)	(659)	-	(29)
Unfunded net asset/ (liability) recognised in balance sheet.	(753)	-	(37)	(659)	-	(29)

Notes
To The Financial Statements

(All amounts in ₹ million, unless otherwise stated)

	31.03.2009		
	Leave Encashment/ Compensated Absence	Employees Gratuity Fund	Retirement Allowance
Present value of obligation as at the year end	550	621	27
Fair value of plan assets as at the year end	-	621	-
Surplus/ (deficit)	(550)	-	(27)
Unfunded net asset/ (liability) recognised in balance sheet.	(550)	-	(27)

Expenses recognised in the statement of profit & loss

	31.03.2013				31.03.2012			
	Provident Fund*	Leave Encashment/ Compensated Absence**	Employees Gratuity Fund*	Retirement Allowance**	Provident Fund*	Leave Encashment/ Compensated Absence**	Employees Gratuity Fund*	Retirement Allowance**
Current service cost	801	97	80	6	615	56	51	-
Interest cost	454	56	68	3	396	57	73	3
Expected return on plan assets	(456)	-	(73)	-	(399)	-	(74)	-
Settlement cost	-	-	-	-	-	-	-	-
Net actuarial (gain)/ loss recognised during the year	(438)	422	76	(2)	113	125	(81)	(3)
Total expense recognised in statement of profit & loss	361	575	151	7	725	238	-	-

* Included in "Contribution to provident and other funds" above

** Included in "Salaries, wages, allowances and other benefits" above

(All amounts in ₹ million, unless otherwise stated)

Constitution of Plan Assets	Provident Fund				Gratuity			
	31.03.2013	%	31.03.2012	%	31.03.2013	%	31.03.2012	%
(a) Debt Funds	6,222	96%	5,196	95%	394	35%	324	36%
(b) Others	286	4%	284	5%	732	65%	583	64%
TOTAL	**6,508**	**100%**	**5,480**	**100%**	**1,126**	**100%**	**907**	**100%**

a) The return on the investment is the nominal yield available on the format of investment as applicable to Approved Gratuity Fund under Rule 101 of Income Tax Act 1961.

b) Expected contribution on account of Gratuity and Provident Fund for the year ending 31st March 2014 can not be ascertained at this stage.

c) The contribution towards provident fund for employees of erstwhile Suzuki Powertrain India Limited (SPIL) have been deposited with the office of Regional Provident Fund Commissioner (RPFC) till 17th March 2013 i.e. upto the effective date of amalgamation (refer note 37). The Company and the employees of SPIL are in the process of filing application/s with the RPFC for transfer of accumulated provident fund contribution till 17th March 2013 to the provident fund trust of the Company. The employees of SPIL have become members of Maruti Provident Fund Trust with effect from 17th March 2013 and their provident fund contribution post that date has been deposited with the above mentioned trust. Accordingly, the present value of the obligation of the employees' share of SPIL has been computed from 17th March 2013.

29. FINANCE COSTS

	For the year ended 31.03.2013		For the year ended 31.03.2012	
Interest on :				
- Foreign currency loans from banks	323		15	
- Buyers' credit and export credit	908		273	
- Deposits from dealers, contractors and others	656	1,887	259	547
Other borrowing costs		11		5
		1,898		**552**

30. DEPRECIATION & AMORTISATION EXPENSE

(Refer Note 12 & 13)

	For the year ended 31.03.2013	For the year ended 31.03.2012
Depreciation / amortisation on tangible assets	17,711	11,011
Amortisation on intangible assets	901	373
	18,612	**11,384**

Notes
To The Financial Statements

(All amounts in ₹ million, unless otherwise stated)

31. OTHER EXPENSES

		For the year ended 31.03.2013		For the year ended 31.03.2012
Consumption of stores		1,864		911
Power and fuel [Net of amount recovered ₹ 1,101 million (Previous year ₹ 1,716 million)]		4,937		2,295
Rent (Refer Note 51)		184		156
Repairs and maintenance :				
- Plant and machinery	1,026		531	
- Building	188		163	
- Others	277	1,491	210	904
Insurance		136		91
Rates, taxes and fees		1,149		826
Royalty		24,538		18,031
Tools / machinery spares charged off		2,547		1,548
Net loss on foreign currency transactions and translation		1,519		1,810
Advertisement		3,536		2,781
Sales promotion		2,179		1,965
Warranty and product recall		544		581
Transportation and distribution expenses		5,501		4,631
Net loss on sale / discarding of fixed assets		331		157
Provision for doubtful advances		63		-
Provision for doubtful debt		-		21
Other miscellaneous expenses		7,218		5,364
		57,737		**42,072**

(All amounts in ₹ million, unless otherwise stated)

32. CONTINGENT LIABILITIES

a) Claims against the Company disputed and not acknowledged as debts:

Particulars			As at 31.03.2013	As at 31.03.2012
(i)	**Excise Duty**			
	(a)	Cases decided in the Company's favour by Appellate authorities and for which the department has filed further appeal and show cause notices / orders on the same issues for other periods	2,990	2,717
	(b)	Cases pending before Appellate authorities in respect of which the Company has filed appeals and show cause notices for other periods	10,484	2,167
	(c)	Show cause notices on issues yet to be adjudicated	8,581	12,675
		TOTAL	**22,055**	**17,559**
		Amount deposited under protest	361	3
(ii)	**Service Tax**			
	(a)	Cases decided in the Company's favour by Appellate authorities and for which the department has filed further appeal and show cause notices / orders on the same issues for other periods	3,767	3,701
	(b)	Cases pending before Appellate authorities in respect of which the Company has filed appeals and show cause notices for other periods	2,857	309
	(c)	Show cause notices on issues yet to be adjudicated	1,358	1420
		TOTAL	**7,982**	**5,430**
		Amount deposited under protest	3	3
(iii)		**Income Tax**		
	(a)	Cases decided in the Company's favor by Appellate authorities and for which the department has filed further appeals	5,918	6,230
	(b)	Cases pending before Appellate authorities / Dispute Resolution Panel in respect of which the Company has filed appeals	12,058	9,699
		TOTAL	**17,976**	**15,929**
		Amount deposited under protest	6,770	6,135
(iv)		**Customs Duty**		
		Cases pending before Appellate authorities in respect of which the Company has filed appeals	118	118
		Amount deposited under protest	22	22
(v)		**Sales Tax**		
		Cases pending before Appellate authorities in respect of which the Company has filed appeals	50	50
		Amount deposited under protest	2	2

Notes
To The Financial Statements

(All amounts in ₹ million, unless otherwise stated)

(vi) Claims against the Company for recovery of ₹ 604 million (Previous year ₹ 576 million) lodged by various parties

(vii) The Company's impleadment application in the pending appeal by Haryana State Industrial & Infrastructure Development Corporation Limited ("HSIIDC"), relating to the demand raised for additional compensation by landowners for land acquired from them at Manesar for industrial purposes, has been heard and the order has been reserved by the Supreme Court against the demand of ₹ 5,012 million. The demand for ₹ 1,376 million for remaining part of land of the Company at Manesar was received from HSIIDC in the current year consequent to the order of the Punjab and Haryana High Court ("Court") and the Company has filed an appeal in the Court.

The Company is in the process of gathering more details for a demand of ₹ 86 million from HSIIDC, raised on erstwhile Suzuki Powertrain India Limited (merged with the Company with effect from 1st April 2012, refer note 37), consequent to the order of the Supreme Court, towards enhanced compensation relating to the demand raised for additional compensation by landowners for land acquired from them for industrial purposes at Manesar.

As the amounts, if any, of final price adjustment(s) is not determinable at this stage, the amount of ₹ 2,354 million provided in the previous year based on an earlier demand of HSIIDC has been reversed and the Company considers that no provision is required to be made at present. Any additional compensation, if payable, will have the effect of enhancing the asset value of the freehold land.

(viii) In respect of disputed Local Area Development Tax (LADT) (upto 15th April 2008) / Entry Tax, the Sales tax department has filed an appeal in the Supreme Court of India against the order of the Punjab & Haryana High Court. The amounts under dispute are ₹ 21 million (previous year ₹ 21 million) for LADT and ₹ 15 million (previous year ₹ 13 million) for Entry Tax. The State Government of Haryana has repealed the LADT effective from 16th April 2008 and introduced the Haryana Tax on Entry of Goods into Local Area Act, 2008 with effect from the same date.

b) The amounts shown in the item (a) represent the best possible estimates arrived at on the basis of available information. The uncertainties and possible reimbursements are dependent on the outcome of the different legal processes which have been invoked by the Company or the claimants as the case may be and therefore cannot be predicted accurately. The Company engages reputed professional advisors to protect its interests and has been advised that it has strong legal positions against such disputes.

33. Outstanding commitments under Letters of Credit established by the Company aggregate ₹ 6,488 million (Previous year ₹ 1,773 million).

34. Estimated value of contracts on capital account, excluding capital advances, remaining to be executed and not provided for, amount to ₹ 28,760 million (Previous year ₹ 26,338 million).

35. Consumption of raw materials and components has been computed by adding purchases to the opening stock and deducting closing stock physically verified by the management.

36. The Company was granted sales tax benefit in accordance with the provisions of Rule 28C of Haryana General Sales Tax Rules, 1975 for the period from 1st August 2001 to 31st July 2015. The ceiling amount of concession to be availed of during the entitlement period is ₹ 5,644 million. Till 31st March 2013, the Company has availed of / claimed sales tax benefit amounting to ₹ 2,483 million (Previous year ₹ 2,331 million).

37. The scheme of amalgamation of Suzuki Powertrain India Limited (SPIL) with the Company as approved by the High Court of Delhi has become effective on 1st April 2012 on completion of all the required formalities on 17th March 2013. The scheme envisages transfer of all properties, rights and powers and liabilities and duties of the amalgamating company to the amalgamated company.

SPIL was primarily engaged in the business of engineering, manufacturing, assembling and selling all kinds of powertrain parts and components for automobiles, which includes engines and transmissions for such engines and their components like transmission cases, gears, shafts and yorks.

(All amounts in ₹ million, unless otherwise stated)

The amalgamation was accounted for under the "Pooling of Interest Method" as prescribed by the Accounting Standard 14 "Accounting for Amalgamations" notified under Companies (Accounting Standards) Rules.

The assets and liabilities of the amalgamating company have been accounted for in the books of account of the Company in accordance with the approved scheme.

i) The assets and liabilities as at 1st April 2012 were incorporated at book value of SPIL, subject to adjustments made to ensure uniformity of accounting policies.

ii) The authorised capital of SPIL after splitting each share into 2 shares of face value of ₹ 5 each has became part of authorised share capital of the Company.

iii) The balance of 'Surplus of Statement of Profit and Loss' of SPIL amounting to ₹ 3,565 million (net of adjustments on account of policy differences of ₹ 275 million) as at 1st April 2012 have been included in the balance of 'Surplus of Statement of Profit and Loss' of the Company.

iv) 395,100,000 equity shares of ₹ 10 each fully paid in SPIL held as investment by the Company have been cancelled and extinguished.

v) The equity shareholders of SPIL have, for every 70 fully paid equity shares of ₹ 10 each held as on the record date, been issued 1 fully paid equity share of ₹ 5 each of the Company. Accordingly, the Company has issued 13,170,000 equity shares on 29th March 2013 thereby increasing its equity capital to ₹ 1,510 million.

vi) The surplus amounting to ₹ 9,153 million, arising as a result of the amalgamation, i.e. excess of the value of net assets of SPIL transferred to the Company over the paid-up value of shares issued to equity shareholders of SPIL, has been added to the reserves of the Company.

vii) The amounts relating to SPIL as at 1st April 2012 included in the terms of the scheme in the financial statements of the Company are as below:

	Net Amount
Assets	
Fixed assets (net) (including capital work-in-progress ₹ 2,949 million)	21,425
Cash and Bank balances	1,051
Current Assets and Loans and Advances	9,080
TOTAL	**31,556**
Liabilities	
Long Term Borrowings	5,337
Long Term Liabilities and Provisions	1,108
Current Liabilities and Provisions	8,376
TOTAL	**14,821**
Net assets acquired on Amalgamation (a)	16,735
Transfer of balances of Amalgamated Company	
Reserves & Surplus (b)	3,565
Less:-	
Adjustment for cancellation of Company's investment in Transferor Company (c)	3,951
Shares issued in the ratio of 1:70 to the shareholders of erstwhile Suzuki Powertrain India Limited, pursuant to the scheme on amalgamation (d)	66
Credited to Reserve on Amalgamation (a) – (b) – (c) – (d)	**9,153**

Notes
To The Financial Statements

(All amounts in ₹ million, unless otherwise stated)

38. The Company has considered "business segment" as its primary segment. The Company is primarily in the business of manufacture, purchase and sale of motor vehicles, components and spare parts ("automobiles"). The other activities of the Company comprise facilitation of pre-owned car sales, fleet management and car financing. The income from these activities, which are incidental to the Company's business, is not material in financial terms but such activities contribute significantly in generating the demand for the products of the Company. Accordingly, the Company operates in one business segment and thus no business segment information is required to be disclosed.

The "Geographical Segments" have been considered for disclosure as the secondary segment, under which the domestic segment includes sales to customers located in India and the overseas segment includes sales to customers located outside India.

Financial information of geographical segments is as follows:-

	2012-2013				2011-2012			
Particulars	Domestic	Overseas	Unallocated	Total	Domestic	Overseas	Unallocated	Total
Revenue from external customers	441,803	49,097	8,124	499,024	354,651	40,302	8,268	403,221
Segment assets	187,212	8,777	70,891	266,880	152,070	7,577	63,375	223,022
Capital expenditure during the year	36,058	-	-	36,058	32,315	-	-	32,315

Notes:-

a) Domestic segment includes sales and services to customers located in India

b) Overseas segment includes sales and services rendered to customers located outside India.

c) Unallocated assets include other deposits, dividend bank account and investments.

d) Segment assets includes fixed assets, inventories, sundry debtors, cash and bank balances (except dividend bank account), other current assets, loans and advances (except other deposits).

e) Capital expenditure during the year includes fixed assets (tangible and intangible assets) other than acquired pursuant to scheme of amalgamation (refer Note 37) and net addition to capital work in progress.

39. THE FOLLOWING EXPENSES INCURRED ON RESEARCH AND DEVELOPMENT ARE INCLUDED UNDER RESPECTIVE ACCOUNT HEADS:

	2012-2013	2011-2012
Revenue Expenditure		
Employees remuneration and benefits	1,530	1,416
Other expenses of manufacturing and administration	1,003	810
Capital Expenditure	2,613	1,491
	5,146	**3,717**

CORPORATE OVERVIEW MANAGEMENT REVIEW STATUTORY REPORTS FINANCIAL STATEMENTS

(All amounts in ₹ million, unless otherwise stated)

40. AUDITORS' REMUNERATION*

	2012-2013	2011-2012
Statutory audit	12.40	10.00
Other audit services / certification	1.03	1.48
Reimbursement of expenses	0.71	0.37

*Excluding service tax

41. CIF VALUE OF IMPORTS

	2012-2013	2011-2012
Raw materials and components	42,344	30,451
Capital goods	14,762	11,625
Stores and spares	663	667
Dies and moulds	8	15
Other items	120	465

42. EXPENDITURE IN FOREIGN CURRENCY (ACCRUAL BASIS)

	2012-2013	2011-2012
Fees for technical services	1,164	753
Travelling expenses	443	89
Running royalty	24,538	18,031
Lumpsum royalty	629	2,015
Supervision charges capitalised	1,070	1,086
Interest	1,130	274
Others	2,046	1,432

43. EARNINGS IN FOREIGN CURRENCY

	2012-2013	2011-2012
Export of goods (FOB basis)	45,514	36,918

44. DIVIDEND REMITTED IN FOREIGN CURRENCY (CASH BASIS)

	2012-2013	2011-2012
Dividend for the year 2011-12 (Previous year 2010-11)	1,175	1,175
No. of non-resident shareholders	1	1
No. of shares for which dividend remitted	156,618,440	156,618,440

Notes
To The Financial Statements

(All amounts in ₹ million, unless otherwise stated)

45. VALUE OF IMPORTED AND INDIGENOUS MATERIALS CONSUMED

		2012-2013	2011-2012
i)	**Raw Materials and Components**		
	Imported	36,801	28,324
	Indigenous	268,940	238,731
		305,741	**267,055**
	Percentage of Total Consumption		
	Imported	12%	11%
	Indigenous	88%	89%
ii)	**Machinery Spares**		
	Imported	514	460
	Indigenous	1,201	751
		1,715	**1,211**
	Percentage of Total Consumption		
	Imported	30%	38%
	Indigenous	70%	62%
iii)	**Consumption of Stores**		
	Imported	193	91
	Indigenous	1,671	820
		1,864	**911**
	Percentage of Total Consumption		
	Imported	10%	10%
	Indigenous	90%	90%

46. LICENSED CAPACITY, INSTALLED CAPACITY AND ACTUAL PRODUCTION

Product	Unit	Licensed Capacity	Installed Capacity**	Actual Production
Passenger Cars and				
Light Duty Utility Vehicles	Nos.	-*	1,260,000	1,168,917
		(-)*	(1,260,000)	(1,134,607)

Notes:

* Licensed Capacity is not applicable from 1993-94.

**Installed Capacity is as certified by the management and relied upon by the auditors, being a technical matter.

Previous Year figures are in brackets.

(All amounts in ₹ million, unless otherwise stated)

47. SALES, OPENING STOCK AND CLOSING STOCK

Product	Sales		Opening Stock		Closing Stock	
	Qty.(Nos.)	Value	Qty.(Nos.)	Value	Qty.(Nos.)	Value
Passenger vehicles	**1,171,434**	**441,163**	**16,485**	**5,631**	**13,065**	**4,812**
	(1,133,695)	(362,111)	(16,222)	(4,220)	(16,485)	(5,631)
Spare parts and Components	*	**39,950**	*	**1,362**	*	**1,654**
	*	(24,001)	*	(1,323)	*	(1,362)
Dies and moulds	*	34	*	-	*	-
	*	(29)	*	-	*	-
Work in progress		**NA**		**593**		**1,127**
	*	(NA)	*	(457)	*	(593)

Notes :

1. Traded goods comprise vehicles, spares, components and dies and moulds. During the year 13 vehicles (previous year 561 vehicles) were purchased
2. Closing Stock of vehicles is after adjustment of 29 vehicles (previous year - 61) totally damaged.
3. Sales quantity excludes own use vehicles 834 Nos. (previous year - 961 Nos.)
4. Sales quantity excludes sample vehicles 53 Nos. (previous year - 188 Nos.)
5. Previous year figures are in brackets.

   * In view of the innumerable sizes/numbers (individually less than 10 per cent) of the components, spare parts and dies and moulds it is not possible to give quantitative details.

118 - 119

48. STATEMENT OF RAW MATERIALS AND COMPONENTS CONSUMED

		2012-13		2011-2012	
Group Of Material	Unit	Qty.	Amount	Qty.	Amount
Steel coils	MT	210,595	11,448	200,256	10,568
Ferrous castings	MT	27,765	3,329	16,831	1,874
Non-ferrous castings	MT	28,673	4,727	15,507	2,302
Other components		*	284,419	*	250,636
Paints	K.LTR	6,811		5,795	
	MT	6,381	1,818	6,043	1,675
			305,741		**267,055**

* In view of the innumerable sizes/numbers (individually less than 10 per cent) of the components, spare parts and dies and moulds it is not possible to give quantitative details.

49. PURCHASE OF STOCK IN TRADE

	2012-2013	2011-2012
Traded spares	19,525	14,431
Traded vehicles	25	862
Others	63	32
	19,613	**15,325**

Notes
To The Financial Statements

(All amounts in ₹ million, unless otherwise stated)

50. STATEMENT OF EARNING PER SHARE

	2012-2013	2011-2012
Net Profit after tax attributable to shareholders (in million ₹)	23,921	16,352
Weighted average number of equity shares outstanding during the year (Nos)	302,080,060	288,910,060
Nominal value per share (In ₹)	5.00	5.00
Basic/diluted earning per share (In ₹)	**79.19**	**56.60**

51. MINIMUM LEASE PAYMENTS OUTSTANDING AS ON 31ST MARCH 2013 IN RESPECT OF ASSETS TAKEN ON NON-CANCELLABLE OPERATING LEASES ARE AS FOLLOWS

a) As a lessee

	31.03.2013			31.03.2012
Due	**Total Minimum Lease Payments Outstanding as on 31st March 2013**			**Total Minimum Lease Payments Outstanding as on 31st March 2012**
	Premises	**Cars**	**Total**	**Premises**
Within one year	50	4	54	49
Later than one year but less than five years	222	5	227	212
Later than five years	682	-	682	741

	31.03.2013			31.03.2012
	Minimum Lease Payment			**Minimum Lease Payment**
Charged to rent expense	60	6	66	57

The Company has taken certain premises on cancellable operating lease. The rent expense amounting to ₹ 118 million (Previous year ₹ 99 million) has been charged to the statement of profit and loss.

b) As a lessor

The Company has given certain plant and machineries on cancellable operating lease. The rental income arising of the same amounting to ₹ 10 million has been credited to statement of profit and loss.

52. DERIVATIVE INSTRUMENTS OUTSTANDING AT THE BALANCE SHEET DATE:

1(a) Forward Contracts against imports and royalty:

- Forward contracts to buy JPY 45,200 million (Previous year JPY 48,477 million) against USD amounting to ₹ 26,053 million (Previous year ₹ 29,794 million).
- Forward contracts to buy USD 20 million (Previous year USD 90 million) against INR amounting to ₹ 1,086 million (Previous year ₹ 4,579 million).

The above contracts have been undertaken to hedge against the foreign exchange exposures arising from transactions like royalty and import of goods.

(All amounts in ₹ million, unless otherwise stated)

(b) Forward Contracts / Range Forward contract against Exports:

- Forward contracts to sell USD 150 million (Previous year USD 25 million) against INR amounting to ₹ 8,144 million (Previous year ₹ 1,272 million).
- Forward contracts to sell EURO NIL (Previous year EURO 28 million) against INR amounting to NIL (Previous year ₹ 1,901 million)
- Range Forward Contracts to sell USD NIL (Previous year USD 30 million) against INR amounting NIL (Previous year ₹ 1,526 million)

The above contracts have been undertaken to hedge against the foreign exchange exposures arising from export of goods.

(c) USD Floating rate/INR Floating rate cross-currency swap:

Outstanding USD/INR Floating rate cross-currency swap is USD 69.51 million (Previous year USD 31.175 million) amounting to ₹ 3,773 million (Previous year ₹ 1,586 million)

(d) Forward Contracts against Buyers Credit :

Forward Contracts to buy JPY 798 million (Previous year JPY 3,961 million) against INR amounting to ₹ 460 million (Previous year ₹ 2,434 million).

Forward Contracts to buy USD 165 million (Previous year USD 108 million) against INR amounting to ₹ 8,933 million (Previous year ₹ 5,495 million).

The above contracts have been undertaken to hedge against the foreign exchange exposure arising from foreign currency loan.

2 The foreign currency exposures that are not hedged by a derivative instrument or otherwise are as follows:

(In million)

As at 31.03.2013

	YEN	INR Equivalent	USD	INR Equivalent	EURO	INR Equivalent	GBP	INR Equivalent
Receivables	177	101	54	2,919	4	257	5	394
Payables	7,192	4,105	17	944	18	1,270	0.6	49

As at 31.03.2012

(In million)

	YEN	INR Equivalent	USD	INR Equivalent	EURO	INR Equivalent
Receivables	32	20	4	182	10	715
Payables	2,709	1,691	22	1,118	2	133

Note: The above details include the derivative instruments and foreign currency exposure unhedged, as acquired pursuant to scheme of amalgamation (refer note 37)

(All amounts in ₹ million, unless otherwise stated)

53. STATEMENT OF TRANSACTIONS WITH RELATED PARTIES

Holding Company

Suzuki Motor Corporation

Joint Ventures

Mark Exhaust Systems Limited
Bellsonica Auto Component India Private Limited
FMI Automotive Components Limited
Krishna Auto Mirrors Limited
Inergy India Automotive Components Limited
Maruti Insurance Broking Private Limited
Manesar Steel Processing India Private Limited

Subsidiaries

Maruti Insurance Agency Services Limited
Maruti Insurance Agency Logistics Limited
Maruti Insurance Distribution Services Limited
Maruti Insurance Agency Network Limited
Maruti Insurance Agency Solutions Limited
True Value Solutions Limited
Maruti Insurance Business Agency India Limited
Maruti Insurance Broker Limited
J.J. Impex (Delhi) Private Limited **

Key Management Personnel

Mr Shinzo Nakanishi
Mr.Shuji Oishi (upto 28th April 2012)
Mr Tsuneo Ohashi
Mr Keiichi Asai
Mr.Kazuhiko Ayabe (w.e.f 28th April 2012)

Associates

Asahi India Glass Limited
Bharat Seats Limited
Caparo Maruti Limited
Climate Systems India Limited
Denso India Limited
Jay Bharat Maruti Limited
Krishna Maruti Limited
Machino Plastics Limited
SKH Metals Limited
Nippon Thermostat (India) Limited
Sona Koyo Steering Systems Limited
Magneti Marelli Powertrain India Private Limited
Suzuki Powertrain India Limited*

Fellow Subsidiaries (Only with whom the Company had transactions during the current year)

Jinan Qingqi Suzuki Motorcycle Co., Limited
Magyar Suzuki Corporation Limited
PT Suzuki Indomobil Motor (Former PT Indomobil Suzuki International)
Suzuki Australia Pty. Limited
Suzuki Austria Automobile Handels G.m.b.H.
Suzuki Auto South Africa (Pty) Limited
Suzuki Cars (Ireland) Limited
Suzuki France S.A.S.
Suzuki GB PLC
Suzuki International Europe G.m.b.H.
Suzuki Italia S.P.A.
Suzuki Motor (Thailand) Co., Limited
Suzuki Motor Iberica, S.A.U.
SUZUKI MOTOR POLAND SP. Z.O.O. (Former Suzuki Motor Poland Limited)
Suzuki Motorcycle India Private Limited
Suzuki New Zealand Limited
Suzuki Philippines Inc.
Taiwan Suzuki Automobile Corporation

	2012-2013							2011-2012						
	Joint Ventures	Subsidiaries	Associates	Holding Company	Fellow subsidiaries	Key Management Personnel	Total	Joint Ventures	Subsidiaries	Associates	Holding Company	Fellow subsidiaries	Key Management Personnel	Total
Outstanding at Year End														
Loans and advances recoverable														
Asahi India Glass Limited	-	-	342	-	-	-	342	-	-	303	-	-	-	303
Others	144	10	247	301	29	-	731	104	9	2,183	45	23	-	2,363
TOTAL	**144**	**10**	**589**	**301**	**29**	**-**	**1,073**	**104**	**9**	**2,486**	**45**	**23**	**-**	**2,667**
Amount Recoverable														
SKH Metals Limited	-	-	762	-	-	-	762	-	-	563	-	-	-	563
Jay Bharat Maruti Limited	-	-	620	-	-	-	620	-	-	-	-	-	-	-
Bellsonica Auto Component India Pvt Ltd	856	-	-	-	-	-	856	987	-	-	-	-	-	987
PT Suzuki Indomobil Motor	-	-	-	-	1,063	-	1,063	-	-	-	-	692	-	692
Others	441	7	493	85	1,088	-	2,114	10	-	686	22	515	-	1,233
TOTAL	**1,297**	**7**	**1,875**	**85**	**2,151**	**-**	**5,415**	**997**	**-**	**1,249**	**22**	**1,207**	**-**	**3,475**

Index

A

E

F

G

H

I

J

L

N

Q

R

S

T

U

comprehensivereview

ACCOUNTING ASSUMPTIONS AND PRINCIPLES

A. Economic entity: Financial activities of a business can be separated from the financial activities of the business's owner(s).

B. Time period assumption: Economic information can be meaningfully captured and communicated over short periods of time, such as one month or one quarter.

C. Going concern assumption: A company will continue to operate into the foreseeable future.

D. Monetary unit assumption: The dollar is the most effective means to communicate economic activity.

E. Revenue recognition principle: Revenue should be recorded when a resource has been earned. A resource is earned when either the sale of the good or the provision of the service is substantially complete and collection is reasonably assured.

Example: Lawn Service, Inc., mowed 10 lawns at $20 each in June. Total revenue that would be recognized is $200.

F. Matching principle: Expenses should be recorded in the period resources are used to generate revenues.

G. Cost principle: Assets should be recorded and reported at the cost paid to acquire them.

H. Cash basis of accounting: Records revenue when cash is received and records expenses when cash is paid.

I. Accrual basis of accounting: Records revenue when they are earned and records expenses when they are incurred. This is the application of revenue recognition and matching principle.

FINANCIAL STATEMENTS

A. Income Statement

1. The financial statement that shows a company's assets, liabilities, and equity at a specific point of time.
2. A financial statement that shows a company's revenues and expenses over a specific period of time.
3. Its purpose is to demonstrate the financial success or failure of the company over a specific period of time.
4. **Basic Structure of the Statement:**
   Revenues > Expenses = Net Income or
   Revenues < Expenses = Net Loss.
   Example: Net Sales = ₹2,000M, Cost of Sales = ₹1,000M, Interest = ₹500M, and Depreciation = ₹200M. Net Income would equal ₹300M or (₹2,000 – ₹1,000 – ₹500 – ₹200).

Exhibit 1-1 Income Statement for Garment Business, Inc.

Garment Business, Inc
Income Statement
For the Two Months Period Ending June 30

Revenues		₹16,000
Expenses:		
Material	₹6,500	
Interest	500	
Depreciation	1,750	
Total expenses		8,750
Net income		₹7,250

B. Statement of Retained Earnings

1. The financial statement that shows a company's assets, liabilities, and equity at a specific point of time.
2. Shows the change in a company's retained earnings over a specific period of time.
3. Reports how equity is growing as a result of profitable operations and is distributed in the form of dividends.
4. The statement of retained earnings links the income statement and the balance sheet.
5. **Basic Structure of Statement:**
   Retained Earnings, Beginning Balance
   +/– Net Income/Loss
   – Dividends
   = Retained Earnings, Ending Balance

   Example: In 2011, Lawn Service, Inc. reported ₹50 million of net income and paid ₹20 million of dividends to shareholders during the year. The previous retained earnings were ₹800 million. How much is 2011 Retained Earnings?

Retained Earnings, Beginning Balance	₹800
+/– Net Income/Loss	₹50
– Dividends	(₹20)
= Retained Earnings, Ending Balance	₹830

Exhibit 1-3 Statement of Retained Earnings for Garment Business, Inc.

Garment Business, Inc.
Statement of Retained Earnings
For the Two Months Period Ending June 30

Retained earnings, May 1	₹0
+ Net income	7,250
– Dividends	0
Retained earnings, June 30	₹7,250

C. Balance Sheet:

1. Its purpose is to show, at a given point in time, a company's resources and its claims against those resources.
2. Referred to as a snapshot in time.
3. **Asset:** An economic resource that is objectively measurable, that results from a prior transaction, and that will provide future economic benefit. Examples are Cash, Inventory, and Supplies.
4. **Liability:** An obligation of a business that results from a past transaction and will require the sacrifice of economic resources at some future date. Examples are Accounts Payable, Notes Payable, and Taxes Payable.
5. **Equity:** The difference between a company's assets and liabilities and represents the share of assets that are claimed by the company's owners. Examples are Contributed Capital (resources that investors contribute to a business in exchange for ownership interest) and Retained Earnings (equity generated and retained from profitable operations).
6. **Basic Structure of Statement:**
   Assets = Liabilities + Equity

D. Relationship Among Financial Statements: When preparing financial statements, the income statement must be prepared first, followed by statement of retained earnings and then the balance sheet.

Exhibit 2-1 Asian Paints Classified Balance Sheet

ASIAN PAINTS LIMITED

Balance Sheet as at March 31, 2013

	As at 31.03.2013 Current Year	As at 31.03.2012 Previous Year
		(₹ in crores)
EQUITY AND LIABILITIES		
Share holder's Funds		
Share Capital	95.92	95.92
Reserves and Surplus	2,926.34	2,391.86
	3,022.26	2,487.78
NONCURRENT LIABILITIES		
Long-Term Borrowings	46.76	52.11
Deferred Tax Liability (Net)	143.33	80.75
Other Long-Term Liabilities	0.50	3.62
Long-Term Provisions	76.77	65.16
	267.36	201.64
CURRENT LIABILITIES		
Short-Term Borrowings	—	110.51
Trade Payables	1,214.12	1,034.68
Other Current Liabilities	720.99	606.33
Short-Term Provisions	423.55	355.07
	2,358.66	2,106.59
Total	5,648.28	4,796.01
ASSETS		
NONCURRENT ASSETS		
Fixed Assets		
Tangible Assets	2,074.91	987.79
Intangible Assets	26.98	21.25
Capital work-in-progress	52.55	602.84
	2,154.44	1,611.88
Non-Current Investments	359.70	279.22
Long Term Loans and Advances	92.88	180.52
CURRENT ASSETS		
Current Investments	90	263
Inventories	1,480.79	1,264.42
Trade Receivables	633.88	500.24
Cash and Bank Balances	566.86	500.97
Short-Term Loans and Advances	164.08	100.5
Other Current Assets	105.65	95.26
	3,041.26	2,724.39
Total	5,648.28	4,796.01

Exhibit 1-4 Relationship Among Financial Statements

Income Statement

Revenues	₹16,000
– Expenses	8,750
Net income	₹7,250

Statement of Retained Earnings

Retained earnings, May 1	₹0
+ Net income	7,250
– Dividends	0
Retained earnings, June 30	₹7,250

Balance Sheet

Total assets	₹36,750
Liabilities	₹20,500
Contributed capital	9,000
Retained earnings	7,250
Total liabilities and equity	₹36,750

E. Statement of Cash Flows

1. A financial statement that reports a company's sources and uses of cash over a specific period of time.
2. Its main purpose is to inform users about how and why a company's cash changed during the period.
3. Reports a company's cash inflows and outflows from its operating, investing, and financing activities.
   a. **Financing activities:** Generating and repaying cash from creditors and investors.
   Example: Owner contributed ₹100 to Lawn Service, Inc. The ₹100 is considered a cash inflow from financing activities.
   b. **Investing activities:** The buying and selling of revenue-generating assets.
   Example: A lawn mower is purchased for ₹300. The ₹300 is considered a cash outflow from investing activities.
   c. **Operating activities:** The operation of a business such as the purchase of supplies, payment of employees, and the sale of products.
   Example: An employee spent ₹100 gas to operate lawn mower. The ₹100 is considered a cash outflow from operating activities.
   d. **Basic Structure of the Statement:**
   Cash Inflows Provided (Used) by Operating Activities
   +/− Cash Flows Provided (Used) by Investing Activities
   +/− Cash Flows Provided (Used) by Financing Activities
   = Net Increase (Decrease) in Cash
   e. **Direct Method:** A company calculates and reports its cash inflows from operations followed by its cash outflows for operations.

Exhibit 11-3 Hardin's Operating Cash Flows Using the Direct Method

Cash flows from operating activities		
Cash receipts from customers		$428
Less cash payments:		
To suppliers	$282	
To employees	63	
For insurance	10	
For utilities	23	
For taxes	15	393
Net cash provided by operating activities		$ 35

f. **Indirect Method:** A company reports cash flows from operating activities by adjusting its net income from an accrual basis to the cash basis.

Exhibit 11-5 Hardin's Operating Cash Flows Using the Indirect Method

Cash flows from operating activities		
Net income		$14
Adjustments to reconcile net income to net cash provided by operating activities		
Depreciation expense	$25	
Gain on sale of equipment	(1)	
Increase in accounts receivable	(4)	
Increase in inventory	(9)	
Decrease in prepaid insurance	4	
Increase in accounts payable	8	
Increase in utilities payable	5	
Decrease in taxes payable	(7)	21
Net cash provided by operating activities		$35

QUALITATIVE CHARACTERISTICS OF ACCOUNTING INFORMATION

A. **Understandability:** Accounting information should be comprehensible by those willing to spend a reasonable amount of time studying it.
B. **Relevance:** Accounting information should have the capacity to affect decisions.
C. **Reliability:** Accounting information should be dependable to represent what it purports to represent.
D. **Comparability:** Accounting information should be comparable across different companies.
E. **Consistency:** Accounting information should be comparable across different times periods within a company.
F. **Materiality:** The threshold over which an item could begin to affect decisions.
G. **Conservatism:** When uncertainty exists, accounting information should present the least optimistic alternative.

FIXED ASSETS

A. **Recording Fixed Asset:** Includes all costs incurred to get the asset delivered, installed, and ready to use. Examples of expenditures are purchase price and delivery costs.

Journal Entry:

Delivery Truck	XXX	
Cash		XXX
(To record the purchase of the truck)		

B. **Depreciation:** The process of allocating the cost of a fixed asset over its useful life.

Journal Entry:

Depreciation Expense	XXX	
Accumulated Depreciation		XXX
(To record depreciation expense)		

C. **Net book value:** The unexpired cost of a fixed asset, calculated by subtracting accumulated depreciation from the cost of the fixed asset.

SHOW CONDENSED DATA on top, left hand side of page 173 (2008 note)

Property and equipment, at cost	₹1,977,253
Accumulated depreciation and amortization	(206,881)
Net property and equipment	₹1,770,372

D. **Calculating Depreciation Expense**

1. **Straight-line method:**

$$\text{Depreciation Expense} = \frac{\text{Cost} - \text{Salvage Value}}{\text{Useful Life}}$$

2. **Double-Declining-Balance:**

Depreciation Expense =
(Straight-Line Rate × 2) × (Cost − Accumulated Depreciation)

3. **Units-of-activity method:**

Depreciation Expense = Depreciation Expense per unit × Units of Activity

$$\text{Depreciation Expense per unit} = \frac{\text{Cost} - \text{Salvage Value}}{\text{Useful Life in Units}}$$

BONDS

A. **Bond:** A financial instrument in which a borrower promises to pay future interest and principal to a creditor in exchange for the creditor's cash today.

B. **Bond Issuance**

1. **Par Value:** When a bond pays interest at a rate that is equal to what creditors demand in the market, the creditors will buy at its face value (Stated Interest Rate = Market Interest Rate).

Journal Entry:

Cash	XXX	
Bonds Payable		XXX

2. **Discount:** Bonds that are issued for less than face value are issued at a *discount (Stated Rate < Market Rate).*

Journal Entry:

Cash	XXX	
Discount on Bonds Payable	XXX	
Bonds Payable		XXX

3. **Premium:** Bonds issued for more than face value are issued at a *premium (Stated Rate > Market Rate)*

Journal Entry:

Cash	XXX	
Premium on Bonds Payable		XXX
Bonds Payable		XXX

comprehensivereview

STOCKHOLDERS' EQUITY

A. Common Stock: The most common type of capital stock.

Journal Entry:

Cash	XXX	
Common Stock		XXX
(To record sale of stock at par value)		

Suppose a company issues 100 shares of $1 par value stock for $5 per share on April 5.

Cash	500	
Common Stock		100
Additional Paid-In Capital		400

B. Treasury Stock: Common stock that a company reacquires from it stockholders.

Journal Entry:

Treasury Stock	XXX	
Cash		XXX
(To record purchase of treasury stock)		

C. Dividend: A distribution of profits to owners.

Journal Entries:

Retained Earnings	XXX	
Dividends Payable		XXX
(To record declaration of dividend)		
Dividends Payable	XXX	
Cash		XXX
(To record payment of dividend)		

BUSINESS FORMS

A. Sole proprietorship: A business owned by one person and is the most common type of business in the United States.

B. Partnership: A business that is formed when two or more proprietors join together to own a business.

C. Corporation: A separate legal entity that is established by filing articles of incorporation in a state.

SINGLE-STEP VERSUS MULTI-STEP INCOME STATEMENT

A. Single-step income statement: Calculates total revenues and total expenses and then determines net income in one step by subtracting total expenses from total revenues (or Revenues − Expenses = Net Income or Net Loss).

B. Multi-step income statement: Calculates income by grouping certain revenues and expenses together and calculating several subtotals of income: gross profit, operating profit, income before taxes, and net income.

HORIZONTAL AND VERTICAL ANALYSES

A. Horizontal Analysis: Method of analyzing a company's account balances over time.

Formulas:

Rupee Change in Account Balance: Current Year Balance − Prior Year Balance

Percentage Change in Account Balance: $\frac{\text{Rupee Change}}{\text{Prior Year Balance}}$

Example

	March 31, 2011	March 31, 2010	%
Merchandise Inventories	₹1,071.76	₹743.14	40.44%*

*₹1,071.76 − ₹763.14 = ₹308.14; ₹308.62/₹763.14 = 40.44%

B. Vertical Analysis: Method of comparing a company's account balances within one year.

Formulas:

$$\text{Percentage} = \frac{\text{Balance Sheet Account Balance}}{\text{Total Assets}} \quad \text{or} \quad \frac{\text{Income Statement Account Balance}}{\text{Net Sales or Revenue}}$$

Example

	March 31, 2011	%
Merchandise inventories	₹1,071.76	27.75%*
Total Assets	₹3,861.66	100.0%

*₹1,071.76 / ₹3,861.66 = 27.75%

TRANSACTION ANALYSIS AND RECORDING TRANSACTIONS

A. An **accounting transaction** is any economic event that affects a company's assets, liabilities, and equity at the time of the event. Every accounting transaction must affect at least two accounts (also known as dual nature of accounting).

KEY INFORMATION

1. Circle Films issues 3,000 shares of common stock to investors for ₹15,000 cash.
2. Circle Films purchases a video camera for ₹9,000.
3. Circle Films receives a ₹1,500 payment immediately after filming a customer's wedding.
4. Circle Films receives a ₹2,000 deposit from a customer to film her parents' fiftieth wedding anniversary.
5. Circle Films paid ₹250 cash to run an ad in the local paper.

TRANSACTION SUMMARY:

	ASSETS	=	LIABILITIES	+	EQUITY
#1	+ ₹15,000 cash				+ ₹15,000 common stock
#2	− ₹9,000 cash + ₹9,000 equipment				
#3	+ ₹1,500 cash				+ ₹1,500 retained earnings
#4	+ ₹2,000 cash		+ ₹2,000 unearned revenue		
#5	− ₹250 cash				− ₹250 retained earnings

B. A **journal** is a chronological record of transactions. Entries recorded in the journal are called journal entries.

GENERAL JOURNAL (Using key information above)

Transaction	Account Names and Explanation	Debit	Credit
#1	Cash	15,000	
	Common Stock		15,000
#2	Equipment	9,000	
	Cash		9,000
#3	Cash	1,500	
	Service Revenue		1,500
#4	Cash	2,000	
	Unearned Revenue		2,000
#5	Advertising Expense	250	
	Cash		250

Exhibit 2-2 Asian Paints Limited Multi-step Income Statement

Statement of Profit and Loss
for the year ended March 31, 2013
Asian Paints Limited

(₹ in crores)

	Year 2012–13	Year 2011–12
(I) INCOME		
Revenue from sales of goods and services (Net of discounts)	9,990.04	8,708.30
Less: Excise Duty	1,068.91	783.60
Revenue from sales of goods and services (Net of discounts and excise duty)	8,921.13	7,924.70
Other Operating Revenue	50.57	39.46
Other Income	126.15	141.49
Total Revenue (I)	**9,097.85**	**8,105.65**
(II) Expenses		
Cost of Materials Consumed	5,125.48	4,722.74
Purchases of Stock-in-Trade	199.56	138.67
Changes in inventories of finished goods, work in progress and stock-in-trade	(136.17)	(115.07)
Employee Benefits Expense	404.59	341.63
Other Expenses	1,830.97	1,524.44
Total (II)	**7,424.43**	**6,612.41**
EARNINGS BEFORE INTEREST, TAX, DEPRECIATION AND AMORTISATION (EBITDA) (I) - (II)	1,673.42	1,493.24
Depreciation and Amortisation Expense	126.98	99.49
Finance Costs	30.56	30.82
PROFIT BEFORE TAX	**1,515.88**	**1,362.93**
less: **Tax Expenses**		
Current Tax	406.03	402.76
Deferred Tax	62.59	4.16
(Excess) Tax provision for earlier years	(2.74)	(2.38)
Total Tax Expenses	465.88	404.54
PROFIT AFTER TAX	**1,050.00**	**958.39**
Earnings per share (₹) Basic and diluted (Face value of ₹10 each)	109.47	99.92

Significant Accounting Policies

Notes are an integral part of the financial statements

C. A **trial balance** is a listing of accounts and their balances at a specific point in time.

Circle Films Trial Balance XXX	Debit	Credit
Cash	9,250	
Equipment	9,000	
Unearned Revenue		2,000
Common Stock		15,000
Service Revenue		1,500
Advertising Expense	250	0
Total	18,500	18,500

THE T-ACCOUNT

A. All accounts can be characterized or represented in the following form known as a T account due to its resemblance to a capital T.

B. The left side of an account is the debit side. The right side of an account is the credit side.

Examples of T-Account Mechanics

Asset		Liability		Equity	
1,000	5,000	2,000	6,000	7,000	2,000
4,000	3,000	1,000	4,000		3,000
8,000		3,000			3,000
5,000			4,000		1,000

C. To increase an account balance, record on the same side as the normal balance. To decrease an account balance, record on the opposite side as the normal balance.

Exhibit 3-3 Summary of Debit and Credit Rules

Type of Account	Normal Balance	Increase with a	Decrease with a
Asset	Debit	Debit	Credit
Liability	Credit	Credit	Debit
Equity	Credit	Credit	Debit
Revenue	Credit	Credit	Debit
Expense	Debit	Debit	Credit
Dividend	Debit	Debit	Credit

UNCOLLECTIBLE RECEIVABLES

A. **Bad Debt Expense:** The expense resulting from the inability to collect accounts receivable.

B. **Direct write-off method:** Bad debt expense is recorded when a company determines that a receivable is uncollectible and removes it from its records. GAAP prohibits the use of direct method because it violates the matching principle.

Recording Bad Debt Expense & Write Off Receivable: On April 2, 2011, Thompson Inc. determines that Brandon LLC will be unable to pay its receivable amounting to ₹4,000.

April 2011	Bad Debt Expense	4,000	
	Accounts Receivable—Brandon LLC		4,000

C. **Allowance method:** Method in which companies use two entries to account for bad debt expense—one to estimate the expense and a second to write off receivables.

1. **Recording Bad Debt:** Based on past experience, Duncan Sports estimates that ₹8,000 of 2011 sales will not be collected.

End of 2009	Bad Debt Expense	8,000	
	Allowance for Bad Debts		8,000
	(To record bad debt expense)		

2. **Recording a Write-Off:** Suppose that Duncan Sports determines in 2010 that a ₹2,500 receivable from William Johnson is uncollectible and decides to write it off the books.

2010	Allowance for Bad Debts	2,500	
	Accounts Receivable—William Johnson		2,500
	(To record write-off)		

3. **Recording the Recovery of a Write-Off:** Suppose William Johnson pays his bill in full later during 2010.

2010	Accounts Receivable—William Johnson	2,500	
	Allowance For Bad Debts		2,500
	(To reverse the original write-off)		
	Cash	2,500	
	Accounts Receivable—William Johnson		2,500
	(To collect the receivable)		

RATIOS

A. **Allowance Ratio:** Allowance for Bad Debts/Gross Accounts Receivable.

B. **Fixed Asset Turnover Ratio** = Total Revenues/Average Net Book Value of Fixed Assets

C. **Cash Flow Adequacy Ratio:** Free cash flow/Average amount of debt maturing in five years

D. **Free Cash Flow:** Cash flows from operating activities − Capital expenditures − Dividends

Profitability

E. **Profit Margin:** Net Income/Net Sales

F. **Return on Equity:** Net Income/Average Stockholders' Equity

G. **Return on Assets:** Net Income/Average Total Assets

H. **Earnings per Share:** Net Income/Average Number of Common Shares Outstanding.

I. **Price to Earnings Ratio:** Current Market Price per Share/Earnings per Share

Liquidity

J. **Current Ratio:** Current Assets/Current Liabilities

K. **Quick Ratio:** (Cash + Short-term Investments + Accounts Receivable)/Current Liabilities

L. **Receivables Turnover Ratio:** Net Sales/Average Accounts Receivables

M. **Days-in-Receivables Ratio:** 365/Receivables Turnover Ratio

N. **Inventory Turnover Ratio:** Cost of Goods Sold/Average Inventory

O. **Days-in-Inventory Ratio:** 365/Inventory Turnover Ratio

Solvency

P. **Debt to Assets** = Total Liabilities/Total Assets

Q. **Debt to Equity** = Total Liabilities/Total Equity

R. **Times Interest Earned** = (Net Income + Interest Expense + Income Tax Expense)/Interest Expense

DuPont Analysis

S. **Return on Equity** = Operating Efficiency × Asset Effectiveness × Capital Structure

RECORDING INVENTORY

A. Perpetual inventory system: Updates the inventory account each time inventory is bought or sold.

Entries:

Suppose that Devon Gifts purchases ₹20,000 of inventory on account on Oct. 10.

Oct. 10	Inventory	20,000	
	Accounts Payable		20,000
	(To record purchase of inventory)		

Suppose that Devon pays a third-party carrier ₹300 to transport the inventory to its warehouse on Oct. 10.

Oct. 10	Inventory	300	
	Cash		300
	(To record transportation-in)		

Suppose that on Oct. 12 Devon is granted a ₹1,000 reduction in the cost of the merchandise due to blemishes on the inventory.

Oct. 12	Accounts Payable	1,000	
	Inventory		1,000
	(To record purchase allowance granted by vendor).		

Suppose Devon pays its remaining ₹19,000 bill to the vendor on Oct. 15, which qualifies Devon for a 1% discount.

Oct. 15	Accounts Payable	19,000	
	Inventory		190*
	Cash		18,810
	(To record payment)		

*19,000 × .01

On Nov. 2, Devon sells inventory costing ₹400 for ₹600 cash.

Nov. 2	Cash	600	
	Sales		600
	Cost of Goods Sold	400	
	Inventory		400
	(Record the sale of inventory)		

B. Periodic inventory system: Updates the inventory account only at the end of an accounting period.

INVENTORY COSTING METHODS

A. Specific identification: Determines cost of goods sold based on the actual cost of each inventory item.

B. First-in, first-out (FIFO) method: Calculates cost of goods sold based on the assumption that the first unit of inventory available for sale is the first unit sold.

C. Last-in, first-out (LIFO) method: Calculates cost of goods sold based on the assumption that the last unit of inventory available for sale is the first unit sold.

D. Moving average method: Calculates cost of goods sold based on the average unit cost of all inventory available for sale.

$$\text{Average Unit Cost} = \frac{\text{Cost of Goods Available for Sale}}{\text{Units Available for Sale}}$$

In a period of rising inventory prices	Ending Inventory	Cost of Goods Sold
FIFO yields:	Highest	Lowest
Moving average yields:	Middle	Middle
LIFO yields:	Lowest	Highest